THE VOLCANI

TOM SIMKIN AND RICHARD S. FISKE

KRAKATAU 1883

ERUPTION AND ITS EFFECTS

with the collaboration of **SARAH MELCHER** and **ELIZABETH NIELSEN**

SMITHSONIAN INSTITUTION PRESS

Washington, D.C. 1983

Library of Congress Cataloging in Publication Data

Simkin, Tom
  Krakatau, 1883—the volcanic eruption and its effects.

  Bibliography: p.
  Includes index.
  1. Krakatoa (Indonesia)—Eruption, 1883.
  I. Fiske, Richard S.   II. Title.
QE523.K73S55   1983   551.2'1'09598   83–14818
ISBN 0–87474–841–0

Contents

We dedicate this book to the many careful observers
whose words we reproduce here, and to
our families for persevering through these and other
Krakatau words during the last 9 months.

Preface

The Smithsonian Institution has long had a special interest in volcanology. Founder James Smithson, a Fellow of the Royal Society of London, wrote in the Society's Philosophical Transactions for 1813: "a high interest attaches itself to volcanoes, and their ejections. They cease to be local phenomena; they become principal elements in the history of our globe; they connect its present with its former condition; and we have good grounds for supposing, that in their flames are to be read its future destinies." C.G. Abbot, fifth Secretary of the Institution, was an early investigator of volcanic influences on climate (see p. 420-422), and William Foshag, who documented the growth and development of the Mexican volcano Parícutin in the 1940s, is an example of the many Smithsonian curators who have had active research programs in volcanology. Inspired by the multi-disciplinary interest in the 1963 birth of Surtsey, a new volcanic island off the south coast of Iceland, the Institution founded the Center for Short-Lived Phenomena in late 1967, to act as a communication hub for natural events needing prompt scientific attention. This involvement in gathering data on contemporary volcanism around the world has grown, and in 1975 the Center was replaced in this museum by the Scientific Event Alert Network, or SEAN. Reports from this global network of correspondents are regularly disseminated through the geological and geophysical communities to stimulate work on active volcanoes. We also compile records of older eruptions in a computer data bank that is easily updated and manipulated for studies of recent volcanism.

From these programs, as well as from our own research in volcanology, we have developed two biases that have led directly to this book. First, our involvement with SEAN, and the monitoring of contemporary eruptions, has heightened our appreciation for the value of eyewitness accounts—the first-hand descriptions of dynamic processes that are essential to understanding many eruptions. Second, our work with the volcano data file has pushed us towards the Catastrophists' viewpoint that, while the ordinary eruptions should be carefully documented, it is the extraordinary events that must be milked for all the information they can be made to yield. The classic dictum of Uniformitarianism—"the present is the key to the past"—does not strictly hold for volcanology, because the eruptions that leave substantial deposits and create widespread effects simply do not take place very often. The once-a-decade eruptions are different, in more than the matter of scale, from the eruptions

y physiological means. Hence
students who think that, if any
it were that of Spinoza, and
work of Mr. Spencer and Prof.
heritance which Spinoza left

one his difficult work well. The
ith great care, and the style of
reproduced with some success.
f Spinoza have entertained very
l teaching has been due in no
y inaccurate translation which
it. The present volume should
popular conception of Spinoza's

n of what has already been in-
nns, it is right to contrast the
s who accept Spinoza's applica-
ds to metaphysical questions, with
nt and those who are currently
ians. It is the more desirable to
use, although there is much comans do little (if anything) more
m of the naturalist (or, as he
gmatic) doctrine, there is but
ism has been considered, much
soning upon the old lines about
and of God to the world as
ase from another branch of
ed a rule calling upon them to
ld not be a new trial of all
ot be sufficiently borne in mind
here are only two courses open
scientious thinkers. Either they
er from the discussion of an in-
problems which are suggested by
hey must be at the pains, however
he nature of the sceptical doubts
bear upon the possibility of these
be added that to single them out
easy a task as might be supposed.
on why the study of Spinoza's
so much difficulty is that the
hich guides men of the highest
ew and unknown regions raised
the investigations of Kant sub-
the consequences of a more pro-
t of view. That difficulties arise
the nature of God was for Spinoza,
impossibility of reasoning on such
dinary facts of experience. In
l method culminated in the
t of this kind, just as in Hume
paralysis of speculation. Had
action between different kinds of
ystem must have become in a
cal in its tendencies—sceptical

the difficulties raised by himself, and made the inquiry
the preliminary to a radically different discussion of the
issues raised in philosophy and science alike. It were
well if the fact were less left out of account that the rule
obtained by Kant for a new trial of these issues has never
yet been discharged. R. B. HALDANE

LETTERS TO THE EDITOR

[*The Editor does not hold himself responsible for opinions expressed
by his correspondents. Neither can he undertake to return,
or to correspond with the writers of, rejected manuscripts.
No notice is taken of anonymous communications.*
[*The Editor urgently requests correspondents to keep their letters
as short as possible. The pressure on his space is so great
that it is impossible otherwise to insure the appearance even
of communications containing interesting and novel facts.*]

The Krakatoa Eruption

THE Council of the Royal Society has appointed a Committee
for the purpose of collecting the various accounts of the volcanic
eruption at Krakatoa, and attendant phenomena in such form as
shall best provide for their preservation and promote their usefulness.

The Committee invite the communication of authenticated
facts respecting the fall of pumice and of dust, the position and
extent of floating pumice, the date of exceptional quantities of
pumice reaching various shores, observations of unusual disturbances of barometric pressure and of sea-level, the presence of
sulphurous vapours, the distances at which the explosions were
heard, and exceptional effects of light and colour in the
atmosphere.

The Committee will be glad to receive also copies of published
papers, articles, and letters bearing upon the subject.

Correspondents are requested to be very particular in giving
the date, exact time (stating whether Greenwich or local), and
position whence all recorded facts were observed. The greatest
practicable precision in all these respects is essential.

All communications are to be addressed to
G. J. SYMONS,
Chairman Krakatoa Committee
Royal Society, Burlington House, W., February 12

The Remarkable Sunsets

THE following facts in reference to the unusual sunsets, as
witnessed in the United States, will I hope be of sufficient
value to your readers to justify an insertion in the pages of
NATURE.

The place from which I write is 1063 feet above sea-level,
40° 48′ 47″ N. lat. and 81° 53′ 37″ W. long. from Greenwich.
The main features of the exhibition here have been the crimson
glow—the first and after-glow, with other accompanying colours,
closely corresponding with those in England and Europe.
Hence I need not occupy your pages with a special description.

I have on record seven cases, nearly all the weather would
permit one to see. These occurred on November 27, December
9, 10, 25, and 28, and on January 13 and 17.

The first and second glow have extended in two or three
instances, though faintly, to the zenith, and the first has occasionally been reflected on the eastern sky. On December 28, the
most brilliant exhibition in the series, an arch was formed in the
east, the colours red and yellowish green, very soft, and much
blended. The crimson glow on the sky flooded the western
sides of buildings with an unearthly light, and cast faint shadows
across the snow. The appearance of the after-glow, when the
sun had reached a certain angle in its decline, favours the view
that it is a reflection of the first. If this be true, it is not neces-

Figure 1. This letter, shown here in the February
14, 1884, issue of *Nature*, also appeared in *The
Times* and other periodicals. It resulted in a wealth
of reports to the Royal Society, many of which were
used in the Society's 1888 report and others which
appear in Part II of this volume.

that can be observed with relative ease. Even the common types of volcanism are sufficiently unpredictable, infrequent, and geographically scattered that they normally can only be witnessed with good planning, logistic skill, a healthy travel budget, and a certain amount of luck.

Therefore, we undertook, in the centennial year of Krakatau's 1883 eruption, a harder look at this classic benchmark event in the history of volcanology. Like most linguistically crippled, English-speaking geologists, our knowledge of Krakatau came from the obligatory descriptions in textbooks, supplemented by a few scattered papers and the famous Royal Society report of 1888. The latter, while containing many marvelous eyewitness accounts of distant effects, carried no first-person reports of the eruption. However, the report's introduction described the Society's widespread appeal for accounts (see Figure 1). In hopes of finding more information, we visited the Royal Society and, with their generous permission and help, photographed many hundreds of newspaper clippings, letters, and reports from their archives. Some of this material appears in Part II of this book, but it has been supplemented by library research here, particularly at the Library of Congress, National Archives, U.S. Geological Survey, and our own Smithsonian Library.

As we learned more about the eruption, we soon recognized the importance of the monograph published by Verbeek in 1885. This impressively scholarly and timely work is filled with valuable information, but only Verbeek's short preliminary report, translated in *Nature* in mid-1884, seems to have been read by most English-speaking writers. We therefore set about obtaining the translations from this important monograph that appear as Part III of this book.

Finally, we recognized that most readers interested in the eyewitness accounts and Verbeek's second-person synthesis (of these and more accounts) would be interested in subsequent attempts to explain the various phenomena observed. Many of these accounts are out of print, or otherwise difficult to obtain, so we have selected several interpretive accounts and reprinted them as Part IV of this book.

An essential element in this project has been our support from the Seidell Fund, a bequest to the Smithsonian from Atherton Seidell upon his death in 1961. Dr. Seidell was an eminent chemist, and author of the standard reference *Seidell's Solubility Tables*, an exhaustive work that required enormous efforts in ferreting out data from obscure and hard-to-find documents. This experience prompted his bequest to promote science by making such documents more widely available. Furthermore, he made sure that the will benefited the buyers of books such as this, by underwriting the cost of publication, rather than the *preparation* of the book (a cost here borne by this museum). This book comes to you with the compliments of Atherton Seidell.

For permission to publish copyrighted materials (all acknowledged in the text) we thank: Academic Press; *Bulletin Volcanologique*; Cambridge University Press; Elsevier Scientific Publishing Company; *Nature*; Prentice Hall Publishing Company; Royal Society of London; *Science*; University of California Press; Volcanological Survey of Indonesia; and *Weatherwise*.

Illustrations of a 100-year-old event have not been easily found, but we have had excellent help from many people. Valuable 1886 photographs were supplied by the Royal Institute for the Tropics, in Amsterdam, and we particularly thank Henk van der Flier, Curator of Ecology. David Bryden, of the Science Museum, London, was especially helpful with the Ascroft sunset sketches, and Valentine Abdy performed exceptional detective work in Paris, tracking down photographs from the Archives Nationales and the family collections of R. Bréon. Miss Mary Baker and Mrs. Malcolm Williams generously supplied photographs accompanying the tape recording of their father's eyewitness account from the ship *W.H. Besse*. A.R. Woolley, of the British Museum (Natural History), kindly shared helpful information gained in his research for their Krakatau Centennial exhibit, and we also thank the David David Gallery, Philadelphia, and the Mary Evans Picture Library, London, for illustration assistance. The 1979 scientific expeditions to Krakatau by Maurice and Katia Krafft, and Steve Self, returned excellent color photographs, and the evening sky photographs of A.B. and M.P. Meinel provide modern counterparts for the atmospheric effects of the Krakatau eruption. Here at the Smithsonian we thank the Office of Photographic Services for many processing jobs, and both Chip Clark and Walt Brown for documentation and scanning electron microscope photography, respectively. Our main reference map, Figure 8, benefits from the topographic separates generously supplied by the Defense Mapping Agency, for which we especially thank Mr. Lee Strum.

This book has been typeset directly from magnetic discs encoded in this department and at the University of Illinois. Converting from one word processor system to another was difficult, and we are grateful to Joe Russo, Gary Gautier, and Lindsay McClelland for help with the electronic data processing involved in the project.

Libraries and archives have made enormous contributions to this book. First we thank C.R. Argent and archivist L. Townsend who facilitated access to our most important source, the Royal Society of London archives. Smithsonian Librarians—particularly Jack Marquardt, Carolyn Hahn, Gloria Atkinson, and Janette Saquet—located references from the flimsiest citations (often wrong), and work at the Library of Congress was aided by James Flatness, of the Geographic and Map Division. At the National Archives, we were greatly helped by Ron Swirczek, and at the New York Public Library by R. Lombardo. We also give special thanks to Mary Desautels, whose thorough searching of microfilmed newspapers and journals of 1883–4 uncovered some of our most valuable (and entertaining) accounts.

Translation from the Dutch has been an important part of this book, and Joseph A. Nelen, of this museum, has been our constant consultant on his native language. As with the English-language accounts, many translated accounts were not selected for publication, but the translations nevertheless had to be made before they could be evaluated for inclusion in the book. Thus Joe has translated far more than is shown here and we have pestered him unmercifully with questions about interpretation and meaning. We are most grateful to him for his swift, competent, and ever-cheerful help. Much of Verbeek's monograph was translated on a contractual basis by E.M. Koster van Groos and we particularly thank her husband Gus who translated the more specialized geology sections and reviewed the remainder amidst a busy teaching and research program at the University of Illinois. We are also grateful to Professor H.-U. Schmincke, of Ruhr-Universität Bochum, who fitted the translation of several long German accounts into an equally busy schedule.

The interdisciplinary aspects of this project have strained our limited backgrounds and we are grateful to many people for assistance. We particularly thank the Meinels (University of Arizona) and Alan Robock (University of Maryland) for meteorological guidance, and Ir.C. Blotwyck (Mineralogical Geological Museum, Delft University of Technology) for his biography of R.D.M. Verbeek (p. 279). Here at the Smithsonian, we thank Don Fisher and Steve Kraft (Smithsonian Institution Press) for careful editorial scrutiny and book design, respectively, and Paul Taylor (Curator of Anthropology) for information about Indonesia. Many others in this museum have helped, including nearly everyone in our Department of Mineral Sciences, and we are ever grateful.

Our two principal collaborators have been Sarah Melcher and Elizabeth Nielsen. Sarah organized the Royal Society materials, managed most of the reference (and illustration) searches, and was responsible for the bibliography. Elizabeth handled the large number of complex data processing tasks involved in transforming old letters, journal articles, and our scribbles direct to disk for typesetting. She organized the illustrations, drafted 3 maps, compiled the index, and, with Sarah, contributed substantially to the Chronology. Both made good use of their training in geology and contributed to the project in a multitude of ways. Our debt to them is large.

While it is both customary and pleasurable to acknowledge many friends for their contributions to this project, the acknowledgment of an enemy is neither. Our unrelenting enemy has been time, and the book falls short of what, with more time, we would like it to be. What began nine months ago as a seemingly simple task—gathering some interesting accounts of a famous eruption for publication on its centennial anniversary—has grown enormously, and it is only now, as we struggle towards an outrageously stretched deadline, that we recognize the number and wealth of accounts that we have not yet seen. This important eruption touched many lives, and in a time when people seemed to pay more attention both to the natural world around them and to their own written observations of that world. We encourage readers who know of Krakatau accounts not mentioned here to send them to us at the museum. They will be archived with the materials assembled for this book and, who knows, they might become part of a more comprehensive book honoring Krakatau's bicentennial!

I. Introduction

The Eruption and Its Importance

On August 27th and 28th, 1883, the following telegrams reached Singapore from Batavia (now Jakarta), the capital of the Dutch East Indies and 160 km E of Krakatau:

Batavia, August 27: During night terrific detonations from Krakatau (volcanic island, Straits Sunda) audible as far as Soerakarta,—ashes falling as far as Cheribon—flashes plainly visible from here.

Noon.—Serang in total darkness all morning—stones falling. Village near Anjer washed away.

Batavia now almost quite dark—gas lights extinguished during the night—unable communicate with Anjer—fear calamity there—several bridges destroyed, river having overflowed through rush sea inland.

Batavia noon 28th August.—All quiet again. Sky clear. Temperature went down ten degrees yesterday, quite chilly towards evening. Bamboo houses along beach washed away by tidal wave, which however was not very high. Birds roosted during darkness and cocks crowed hard as ashes cleared way. Fish dizzy and caught with glee by natives. Town now covered with thin layer of ashes, giving roads a quaint, bright look. All through drizzly ash rain distinctly heard falling. Vibrations of atmosphere very strong during eruption, but earth did not quake.

Later:—Telegraph Inspector of Java Government lines reports: "Yesterday morning early while trying to repair lines between Serang and Anjer saw high column sea approaching with roaring noise. Fled inland, knows nothing more of fate of Anjer but believes all lost."

At Anjer *Sunday evening* strong detonations heard and felt. Sea rising and falling three feet at intervals of 10 and 15 minutes, smashing all boats. Six shocks earthquake during night.

Batavia 11 a.m. Today. Anjer, Tjeringin and Telok Betong destroyed.

11:30 a.m.—Light-houses, Straits Sunda disappeared.

12 noon.—Where once Mount Krakatau stood the sea now plays.

These telegrams, in terse eloquence, capture the principal elements of the disaster:

• The explosions were heard on Rodriguez Island, 4653 km distant across the Indian Ocean, and over 1/13th of the earth's surface.

• Ash fell on Singapore 840 km to the N, Cocos (Keeling) Island 1155 km to the SW, and ships as far as 6076 km WNW. Darkness covered the Sunda Straits from 10 a.m. on the 27th until dawn the next day.

• Giant waves reached heights of 40 m above sea level, devastating everything in their path and hurling ashore coral blocks weighing as much as 600 tons.

• At least 36,417 people were killed, most by the giant sea waves, and 165 coastal villages were destroyed.

• When the eruption ended only 1/3 of Krakatau, formerly 5 × 9 km, remained above sea level, and new islands of steaming pumice and ash lay to the north where the sea had been 36 m deep.

The eruption came at a time of rapid changes in communications technology. Successful experiments had been made with both telephone and radio, but neither was to become effective for international communication until the 20th century. The telegraph system, however, had been in existence for 40 years and Europe had been linked by cable to both India and North America since the 1860's. Telegrams bearing news of the Krakatau eruption spread quickly and accounts soon appeared in newspapers around the world. Furthermore, the eruption took place not in some remote corner of the globe, but in the middle of the Sunda Straits, the narrow passage through which much of the world's maritime traffic was funneled. For centuries, the volcano had been a familiar nautical landmark, and sailors passing through the Straits after the eruption soon spread news of the devastation throughout the maritime nations.

Much of the importance of the Krakatau eruption stems from the fact that its news traveled so fast, because the eruption's effects also traveled far beyond the Sunda Straits and observations made at great distances from the volcano could be connected to the eruption.

• Every recording barograph in the world documented the passage of the airwave, some as many as 7 times as the wave bounced back and forth between the eruption site and its antipodes for 5 days after the explosion.

• Tide gauges also recorded the sea wave's passage far from Krakatau. The wave "reached Aden in 12 hours, a distance of 3800 nautical miles, usually traversed by a good steamer in 12 days."[1]

• Blue and green suns were observed as fine ash and aerosol, erupted perhaps 50 km into the stratosphere, circled the equator in 13 days.

• Three months after the eruption these products had spread to higher latitudes causing such vivid red sunset afterglows that fire engines were called out in New York, Poughkeepsie, and New Haven to quench the apparent conflagration. Unusual sunsets continued for 3 years.

• Rafts of floating pumice—locally thick enough to support men, trees, and no doubt other biological passengers—crossed the Indian Ocean in 10 months. Others reached Melanesia, and were still afloat two years after the eruption.

• The volcanic dust veil that created such spectacular atmospheric effects also acted as a solar radiation filter, lowering global temperatures as much as 1/2°C in the year after the eruption. Temperatures did not return to normal until 1888.

These distant observations combined with widespread reports about the eruption itself to stimulate multidisciplinary interest in Krakatau, with intellectual feedback, cross-fertilization, and the realization that geologists, hydrologists, meteorologists, and artist/observers of the evening sky all contribute to an understanding of such a catastrophic event. No doubt the disastrous loss of so many lives helped capture the attention of the public, but we believe that Krakatau's fame comes mainly from the fact that its distant effects

Figure 2. Photograph of Krakatau eruption, May 27, 1883. Taken one week after the eruption's start during the Schuurman expedition described on p. 63. Three months later, during the darkness and chaos of the culminating eruption, no photographs were taken, and we know of no photographs on other days (but see Figure 9). Engravings from this photograph were used in *The Graphic* (August 11, 1883), in the Royal Society report of 1888 (as plate I), and elsewhere. The photograph is from NW of the erupting vent Perboewatan. It was obtained from the grandson of R. Bréon, leader of the French expedition to Krakatau in 1884.

Figure 4. Multidisciplinary interest in Krakatau is exemplified by the revegetation of devastated oceanic islands. Here a coconut sprouts on the barren, ash-covered beach of Anak Krakatau in May, 1932. Revegetation of Krakatau after its 1883 burial under tens of meters of hot pumice, is discussed on p. 424. Photograph by C.C. Reijnvaan and published by Docters van Leeuwen (1936, photo 56).

Figure 3. Giant sea wave, or tsunami, as sketched in March, 1900 *St. Nicholas* magazine (p. 890). The steamer *Berouw*, apparently shown here, was carried 2½ km inland and stranded at Telok Betong (see p. 91) where the wave reached 24 m above sea level (see p. 87).

were observed by such a large part of the world's population–at a time when rapid communication and news publication made them aware of the connection between the eruption and their own observation of its effects.

Thus Krakatau can lay claim to the title of history's most famous eruption. Tambora, in 1815, was larger by most measures (including death toll) but global communications at the time could not bring it the widespread attention it deserved. The A.D. 79 eruption of Vesuvius has certainly caught the fascination of the public, but more for the historical glimpse of Pompeii and Herculaneum than for the eruption that destroyed them. Large eruptions such as Alaska's Katmai, in 1912, may be so remote as to have little historic record,[2] or that record may be wholly in the form of native legends, as in the ca. A.D. 1700 eruption of Long Island, Papua New Guinea.[3] For North America, at least, it seems likely that the much smaller 1980 eruption of Mount St. Helens may soon replace Krakatau as history's most famous eruption, partly because of the exceptional media coverage of that event, and partly because of its extraordinarily thorough investigations.[4] This eruption is already becoming the "eruption example of choice" in textbooks and lectures just as Krakatau has been for several generations.

The fame of the Krakatau eruption, however, rests on firm foundations and its importance to science has been undeniably great. First there is the geologic understanding of calderas. These large, circular, depressions (such as Crater Lake, Oregon) are well known in volcanic regions but in 1883 they were only just being named.[5] Verbeek, the Dutch Mining engineer studying Krakatau immediately after the eruption, correctly deduced that the missing portion of the island had collapsed into the circular void left by the eruption of huge volumes of pumice. Alternative explanations, such as the forceful blasting out of the missing portion of Krakatau, have not been supported, and Krakatau remains a type example of caldera collapse. The eruption was called "a turning point in history for the science of meteorology" by Kiessling,[6] for its contribution to understanding of stratospheric circulation patterns, optical effects (and climatic impact) of fine particles at high altitudes, and propagation of explosive waves through the atmosphere. Oceanographers have learned from the giant sea waves and biologists have extensively studied the return of life to these islands covered, in 1883, with tens of meters of hot pumice and ash.

The principal importance of Krakatau, however, is that it was a large natural event with extraordinary impact on the atmosphere and oceans. This impact came at a time of great growth in science, technology, and communication, resulting in swift attention to this great natural event. The world quickly learned that the impacts of such a large geophysical event are global and that they demonstrate the interdependence of land, sea, and air.

Therefore, the aim of this book, on the occasion of this important eruption's 100th anniversary, is to gather together:

(1) Eyewitness accounts of the eruption and its effects. These accounts carry information, and commonly a sense of immediacy, too often lost in derivative accounts. Furthermore, we have been impressed with the quality of expression, as well as observation, in these accounts. One hundred years ago, without television, people seem to have paid more attention to the natural world around them, and without the telephone they certainly paid more attention to their written words.

(2) The official report, completed in Java 1½ years after the eruption by R.D.M. Verbeek, and here translated into English for the first time. This impressive monograph combined field investigations (before as well as after the eruption), access to eyewitnesses and newspaper accounts, plus all other government reports from the archipelago. No other publication on the eruption had any of these advantages.

(3) Subsequent interpretations of the eruption and its effects. During the hundred years since the eruption, ideas have changed with advances in other areas, increased perspective, new data, and developments at the volcano itself (such as the growth of the new volcano Anak Krakatau since 1927, erosion of the short-lived islands north of Krakatau, and continued revegetation of the main islands). We have attempted to extract current explanations of most features plus, in many areas, some feeling for the development of these explanations during the last 100 years.

In gathering this information, however, we have had considerable difficulty with local names, customs, geography, and a plethora of interconnected accounts. Therefore, before beginning the eyewitness accounts, we attempt to arm the reader with some background information on how the 1883 eruption compares with others in the historic record; what the East Indies, and the world, were like in 1883; some basic reference maps for spatial orientation; and a chronology that serves as a time index relating the various accounts and events covered in the remainder of the book. First, however, a few words on our editorial conventions.

Editorial Conventions

In parts II, III, and IV the words of other authors appear in this (roman, upright) typeface. Where we have omitted authors' words, we have inserted ellipsis points (. . .). A centered line of five ellipsis points indicates a paragraph or more has been omitted. Where we have inserted our own words—either to condense or to illuminate the author's words—we have used brackets [like this] and the same typeface. *Where our words occur as introductory or bridging paragraphs, however, they are recognizable by the typeface of this sentence (oblique, sloping) and irregular right margins.*

Krakatau was the accepted spelling for the volcano in 1883 and remains the accepted spelling in modern Indonesia. In the original manuscript copy submitted to the printers of the 1888 Royal Society Report, now in the archives of the Royal Society, this spelling has been systematically changed by a neat red line through the final *au* and the replacement *oa* entered above; a late policy change that, from some of the archived correspondence, saddened several contributors to the volume. While *Krakatoa* is well established in the English language literature, we have used *Krakatau* ourselves, but made no effort to standardize spelling throughout the book. We have counted 16 spellings of *Krakatau*, some discussed with the name's origin by Verbeek (p. 190) and van den Berg (p. 291), but all of them—by phonetics or context—have obviously referred to the main subject of this book and we have not changed the original spelling.

A few Dutch names, such as Calmeijer and Beijerinck, have appeared alternately as Calmeyer and Beyerinck, and we have changed these to the latter form for ease in pronunciation. Names such as Pulo Soengan, the island squarely in the middle of the

Sunda Straits known as Dwars-in-den-weg by the Dutch and translated to "Thwart-the-way" or "Right-in-the-Fairway" by the English, have normally been changed or referred (in brackets) to the usage most common in our reading (in this case Dwars-in-den-weg). This causes problems in the many cases where Dutch names widely used in 1883 have been changed in modern Indonesia, but we have placed modern names in parentheses on our main map (p. 24–25) where they differ significantly from those used in the text. In general, we have interfered with the original text locations as little as possible, adding information in brackets only where the places mentioned do not appear on our main map.

We have used metric units of measurement, converting obscure units to metric (in brackets) but normally not converting English units. W.J. Humphreys, in the preface to his classic textbook *Physics of the Air*,[7] wrote that he had not converted original data to metric because it was awkward ". . . and also unnecessary, since every scientist who, musically speaking, has begun to play tunes and quit just running scales, is quite familiar with both systems." Those words were written in 1928, and metrification has come a long way since. "Miles" and "inches" are taken to be English unless otherwise stated (e.g., "geographical miles," "German inches") and such non-English units are converted to metric in brackets. See also Verbeek's discussion of units in his foreword (p. 187). We have abbreviated metric units as follows:

km	= *kilometer*	=	*0.621 miles*
m	= *meter*	=	*3.281 feet*
cm	= *centimeter*	=	*0.394 inches*
mm	= *millimeter*	=	*0.039 inches*
μm	= *micrometer*	=	*0.00004 inches*
kg	= *kilogram*	=	*0.454 pounds*
g	= *gram*	=	*0.035 ounces*

We have used standard compass notation for giving directions throughout the text as explained in the accompanying figure. When more detailed compass directions are given in a ship's log (e.g. SW × ½W) we have converted this to bearings (000° = N) in brackets. We have abbreviated directions using the same convention and substituted numerals for numbers written out by original authors (thus "twenty five kilometers northwest" becomes "25 km NW"). Distances between points located by their coordinates have been computed by the formula: distance (km) $= 111.195 \cos^{-1}[(\sin \text{Lat}_A)(\sin \text{Lat}_B) + (\cos \text{Lat}_A)(\cos \text{Lat}_B)(\cos \text{Long}_{A-B})]$.

Geologic terminology has been unavoidable, but we have tried to introduce the more important concepts in general terms and to define the more esoteric words in brackets. The interested reader, though, may want to consult a volcanological textbook such as Decker and Decker (1981), Macdonald (1972), or Williams and McBirney (1979) (cited fully in our Bibliography and listed here in order of increasing technical detail). A general geologic textbook might also be helpful, such as Arthur Holmes' classic *Principles of Physical Geology* (his 4-page treatment of Krakatau, for example, is characteristically lucid and accurate).

Finally, we should mention the system by which we reference sources and notes. Rather than encumber the text with academic referencing (authors' names and year of publication in parentheses), we have used superscript numbers that unobtrusively capture this, and footnote information, for scholarly readers. These numbers refer to the end of each text section. There authors are listed alphabetically, so that readers can quickly see what work has (or has not) been cited, but the full title and citation is given only in the Bibliography to avoid unnecessary repetition.

Krakatau in 1883: Historical and Volcanological Context

In the year before the eruption, the world had lost Charles Darwin, Ralph Waldo Emerson, Karl Marx, and Jesse James. However, the world had also gained new citizens: at the time of the eruption, Stravinsky, Picasso, and FDR were 1 year old; Bartok, Fleming, and Mencken were 2; and Einstein was 4. In that year Twain was writing *Huckleberry Finn*, and Brahms his Third Symphony, the Impressionists were painting in Europe, and Gilbert and Sullivan were the toasts of London. The concepts of evolution, germ theory of disease, and heredity were still in their first generation; while words such as "chromosome," "electron," and "radioactivity" were not yet known. The first gasoline-powered automobile was 2 years (and airplane 20 years)

in the future. Trains and steamships, however, were rapidly interconnecting the world. The opening of the Suez Canal in 1869 had greatly stimulated commerce between Europe and Asia, and the transcontinental railroad system in the United States, also established in 1869, was expanding rapidly. With such expansion in trade and transport came the great European rush to colonize Africa. In the United States, subjugation of the native Americans was midway between Custer's defeat at the Little Bighorn (1876) and the massacre at Wounded Knee Creek (1890).[8]

European influence in the East Indies had been largely Portuguese in the 16th century, followed by two centuries of the Dutch East India Company. In 1799 the Netherlands Government revoked the bankrupt Company's charter and assumed both its assets and its debts. But Islam had come to the Indies by the 13th century, and several Muslim states were not yet under Dutch rule. The Sultanate of Bantam, in westernmost Java, remained independent until 1813, and Atjeh, in NW Sumatra, was locked in bitter warfare with the Dutch from 1873 to 1904. At the time of the eruption, however, Dutch colonial policy was in what was known as the Liberal Period, a time of great economic expansion and increased humanitarian consideration for the people of the archipelago.[9]

The islands were administratively divided into Residencies (see Figure 7) which were again divided into Departments, or *Afdeelingen*. A dual system of administration was headed, on the Dutch side, by a Resident in charge of each Residency, and a Controller (*Controleur*) in each Department. The highest native official in each Residency was the Regent, assisted by a *Patih*, or Vice-Regent, and in each Department a *Wedana*, or district officer. This system remained in effect until the end of colonial rule after Japanese occupation in World War II.

Indonesia is a nation of volcanoes. The earth's crust below the Indian Ocean, moving northeastward at speeds of perhaps 6 cm per year, is pulled below the thicker crust of the Asian continent, and this great zone of collision (subduction) has produced a mighty chain of volcanoes running over 3000 km along the length of Sumatra, Java, and the Lesser Sunda Islands. More volcanoes mark the Banda arc, and the tectonically complex regions of Halmahara, Sulawesi, and Sangihe, running northward toward the Philippines.[10]

No nation has more volcanoes than Indonesia. In Holocene time—the last 10,000 years—at least 132 volcanoes have been active and 76 of these have had historic eruptions.[11] Ranking next are Japan, the United

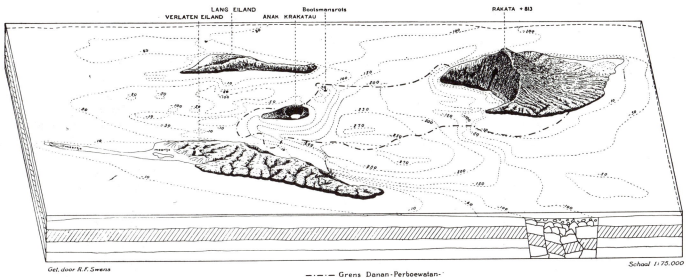

Get. door R.F. Swens

—·—·— Grens Danan-Perboewatan-
Rakala voór 1883.

Schaal 1:75.000

Figure 6. Block diagram of Krakatau group in 1933, after the birth of Anak Krakatau. View looking east shows original shoreline of Krakatau (dashed line), and lines of equal depth (in fathoms) are shown superimposed on the sea surface. Drawn by R.F. Swens and published by Ch.E. Stehn (1933c, figure 4).

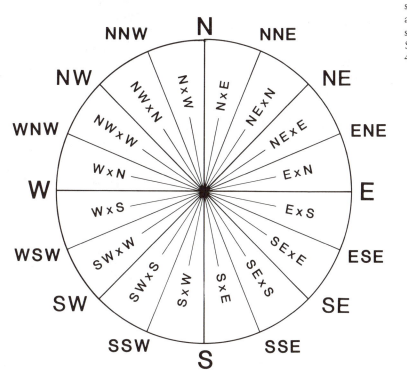

Figure 5. The 32 points of the compass. Used for directional bearings throughout text.

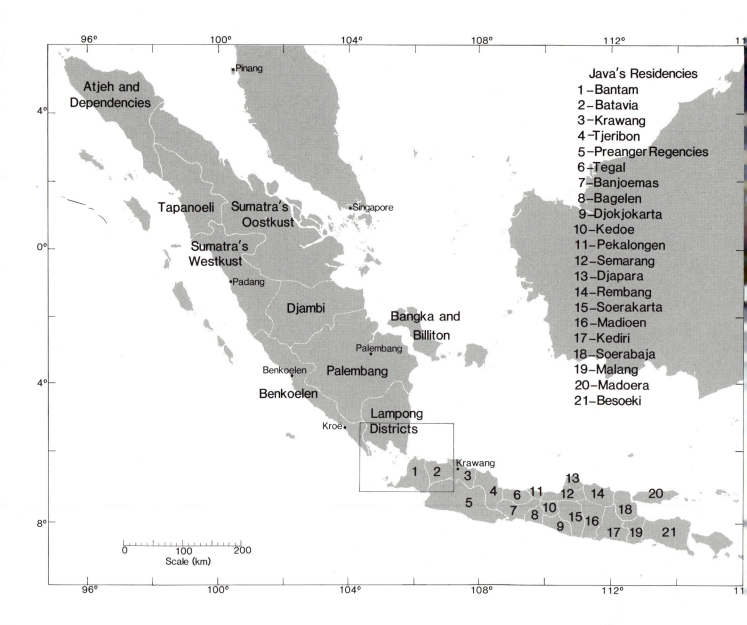

Figure 7. Administrative divisions (Residencies) of Java and Sumatra. Boundaries shown by white lines, and area of detailed map (Figure 8) by dark rectangle. Distant cities mentioned frequently in the text are also identified. Map compiled from *Java en Modoera* (Indonesia (Oceania), Java, 1875, Dornseiffen) and *Sumatra Islands Administrative Map* (1941, Topo. Dienst).

22

States, and Russia, with 55, 53, and 50 historically active volcanoes, respectively. Known eruptions from Indonesian volcanoes number 972, or 17% of the world's total. This high number of eruptions, however, combines with a high population density, resulting in 83 eruptions that have caused fatalities: 33% of the world's total. But despite this toll of Indonesian volcanoes, population density remains strongly correlated with volcanic activity because new ash revitalizes and fertilizes old soil in regions where nutrients are swiftly leached by heavy rainfall.[12] Volcanism in densely populated Java, for example, is far more vigorous than in more sparsely settled Sumatra,[13] and Mohr has pointed out[14] that Krakatau's 1883 ash greatly improved agricultural yields of the badly leached soils in southern Sumatra.

Volcanology has no instrumentally determined scale of eruption "bigness" comparable to seismology's magnitude scale for earthquakes. A common question at the time of any large eruption, however, is "how does it compare with Krakatau?" Four common measures, together with likely values for Krakatau, are: (1) volume of erupted products (18 km^3 as estimated by Verbeek from field measurements),[15] (2) energy coupled into the airwave, as calculated from distant barograph measurements (1–5 × 10^{24} ergs, or 100–150 megatons),[16] (3) eruptive cloud height (estimates range from 37 km to 100 miles, but 50 km seems the most commonly used),[17] and (4) duration of main explosive phase (approximately 23 hours from 1 p.m. on the 26th to noon on the 27th). Comparing these values to others in the historic record[18] suggests that eruptions of this size take place somewhere on earth once or twice per century.

Much larger eruptions, however, are not far away in either space or time. The above-mentioned 1815 Tambora eruption, 1400 km E of Krakatau, produced 5 times as much tephra,[19] and 75,000 years ago the eruption that resulted in Lake Toba, 1200 km NW of Krakatau, produced an estimated 1000 km^3 of tephra.[20] It is hard to overemphasize the fact that volcano lifetimes are vastly longer than human memories, and many volcanoes remain capable of devastating eruptions for as much as 10 million years (or vastly longer than the lifetime of all mankind!). Periods of surficial quiet at volcanoes often mask a slow build-up to an eruption proportional in size to its length of repose, and quiet periods may span tens of thousands of years.[21] The 1883 eruption of Krakatau was large in the historic record, and we can learn much from its study, but perhaps its most important lesson is that

it happened at a volcano widely regarded as extinct. We now know that it had erupted 200 years earlier, but the lush re-vegetation less than 50 years[22] after 1883 shows how quickly nature masks the evidence of past eruptions in the tropics. Our data bank shows 710 volcanoes with probable Holocene eruptions that have, like Krakatau in 1883, been apparently quiet for 200 years. These, together with more that may have been quiet throughout the Holocene, are likely to be the Krakataus of the future.

Maps

Many accounts of the Krakatau eruption assumed a familiarity with local geography that is simply not shared by most of us reading them 100 years later at substantial distances from the scene. Verbeek's account alone contains nearly 300 place names in the East Indies, and many of these occur in different forms in different texts. Most of these names fortunately occur only once or twice, and we have been able to reduce the place names that the reader *must* know to the 23 shown in large letters on the accompanying map, plus another 22 (shown in smaller letters) that *should* be learned. For all others, with the exception of the few that we have not been able to find ourselves, we have attempted to insert location information (in brackets) with each significant text occurence. We have not, however, attempted to standardize place name spelling or to cross-reference variants throughout the text. Readers should know that the prefix *Tji* ("river") is sometimes spelled *Chi*; the letters *oe, o,* and *u,* are often substituted for each other (e.g., *Telok, Teloek,* and *Teluk,* meaning "bay,") as are *k* and *c* (e.g., *kampong,* and *campong,* meaning "village"); and words phonetically similar to their English equivalents (e.g., *Eiland, Baii*) are left alone.

We have attempted to include an English translation in brackets after the first use of important names, as well as location information, but the book was not assembled in either a strictly sequential or a leisurely way, and reference to the index may help solve location problems that remain.

Some of the original authors' maps have been reduced; therefore, the ratio scales on these maps are now incorrect. See figure legends for proper scales.

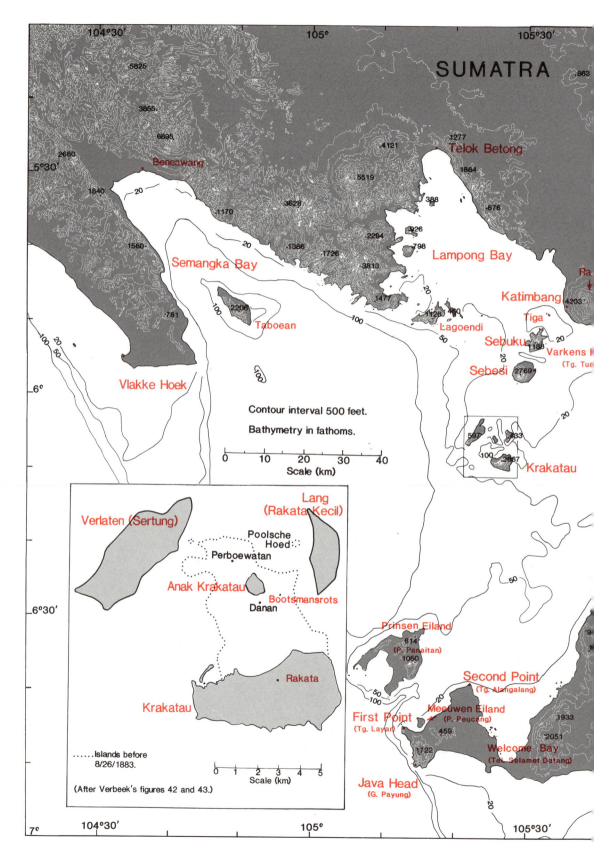

SUMATRA

104°30'
105°
105°30'

·5825

·3855

·6895

·2660
Beneawang

5°30'
1840
·20

·1170
·3628

·1560
Semangka Bay
·1386
·1726

·2206
Taboean
·781

·4121
·1277
Telok Betong
·1864

·5519
·388
·676

·926
·2294
·798
Lampong Bay
·3813

Katimbang
·147
4203

1126
Tiga
·160
Lagoendi
188
Sebuku
·20

Sebesi
Varkens
(Tg. Tua

·2769

Contour interval 500 feet.
Bathymetry in fathoms.

6°
Vlakke Hoek

0   10   20   30   40
Scale (km)

597
·833

·100
·2667
Krakatau

50

Verlaten (Sertung)
Lang
(Rakata Kecil)

Poolsche
Hoed

Perboewatan

Anak Krakatau
Bootsmansrots
Danan

Prinsen Eiland
614
(P. Panaitan)
1050

6°30'

Second Point
(Tg. Alangalang)

Meeuwen Eiland
First Point
(P. Peucang)
(Tg. Layar)
459

1722

Rakata

Krakatau

Welcome Bay
(Tel. Selamet Datang)

Java Head
(G. Payung)

1933
2051

·20

······Islands before
8/26/1883.

0 1 2 3 4 5
Scale (km)

(After Verbeek's figures 42 and 43.)

7°
104°30'
105°
105°30'

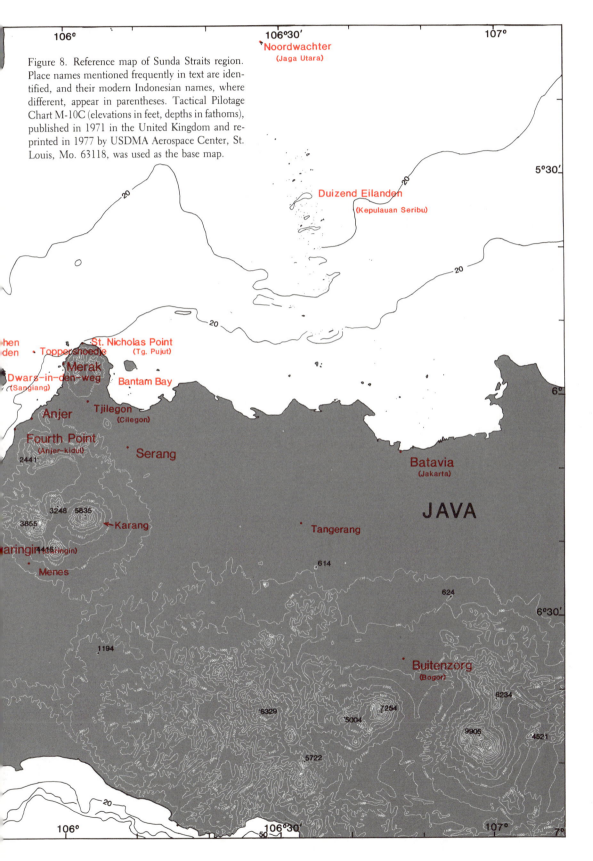

Figure 8. Reference map of Sunda Straits region. Place names mentioned frequently in text are identified, and their modern Indonesian names, where different, appear in parentheses. Tactical Pilotage Chart M-10C (elevations in feet, depths in fathoms), published in 1971 in the United Kingdom and reprinted in 1977 by USDMA Aerospace Center, St. Louis, Mo. 63118, was used as the base map.

Chronology

The Chronology that follows began as an informal way of reducing our own confusion with a multitude of overlapping reports. It became a useful way of identifying gaps and conflicts in the record, and we include it here as a time frame of reference for the reader just as the map provides a spatial frame of reference.

Our source for each piece of information is shown either by a superscript number keyed to "Notes and References," following this section, or by the page in our book (in parentheses) where we quote the original source. The Chronology becomes, then, a time/date index to the book.

We have also used a subject code, shown at the start of the Chronology, enabling readers interested in a specific type of information to find relevant dated observations by scanning the "code" column.

The times shown are generally those given in the original account, with some distant times being converted to Krakatau time (but identified with original times in the remarks). The use of original times introduces some ambiguity that is difficult to avoid. Standard time zones were not yet in effect; ships did not adjust all log entries to local civil time; the mechanical clocks of 1883 were no doubt subject to inaccuracies; and in the days before radio there was no convenient way to synchronize timepieces. Although the times given below are nominally "Krakatau time," we have made no effort to convert times from Batavia (5.7 minutes ahead of local civil time at Krakatau) or other nearby places. The uncertainty of the time observations themselves greatly exceeds the local time correction in most cases.

During the paroxysmal eruption, in particular, conflicting times may seem to add to the confusion, rather than reduce it. These conflicting times, though, help to illustrate the uncertainty involved in the reconstruction of these events. The reader should keep in mind Verbeek's understated words (p. 204 in our text).

If one also takes into consideration that complete darkness very quickly reigned, and that everybody was extremely tense under the circumstances, then it is quite understandable that the few time computations we received about the arrival of the waves on the coast of Bantam are not too accurate.

Code

A = Airwaves and acoustics
B = Biology
C = Casualties
D = Darkness
E = Electrical effects
I = Investigations and surveys
O = Optical effects
P = Pumice (floating)
S = Seismicity
T = Tephra (mostly ashfall)
V = Volcanism
W = Wave (tsunami)

Distances and directions from Krakatau unless otherwise note

Year	M/Day	Code	Remarks
416		V	Javanese legend describes violent eruption of a volcano "Kapi" in the Sunda Straits. "At last the mountain Kapi with a tremendous roar burst into pieces and sank into the deepest of the earth. The water of the sea rose and inundated the land." (308)
1511			Portuguese conquer Malacca.
1602			Dutch East India Company founded.
1611		I	Name "Karkata" (Sanskrit for "crab") appears on a small map of Sunda Strait. "Rakata" is also "crab" in old Javan language. (291)
1658			First use of name "Krakatau," by Wouter Shouten. (284)
1679	07		Vogel passes through Sunda Straits in July and September 1679. Krakatau does not show "anything unusual." (189)
1680	05	VP	Eruption begins, according to a ship's captain who (as related by Vogel) "experienced an earthquake" and a "tremendous thundering," smelled sulphur, and observed floating pumice in the vicinity of Krakatau. (286)
	11		Christopher Frike travels through Strait, but is unaware of any activity at Krakatau. (189)
1681	02/01	V	Eruption witnessed by Vogel. However, no logbooks of passing ships mention eruption during these months. Hesse saw "trees sticking out high on the mountain, which looked completely burned, but we could not see the fire itself" when passing 11/19/1681. (286) Both van den Berg and Verbeek conclude that Vogel exaggerated size of eruption. (189, 287)
1748	07	I	Sketch of Krakatau shows form essentially equal that of 1596 sketch (and that of early 1883 surveys).[23] See Figure 62, p. 289.
1780	02	I	Homeward-bound ships of James Cook (killed in Hawaii 1 year earlier) find thermal spring and some inhabitants on Krakatau. Subsequently used as a penal colony. (290)
1799	12/31		Dutch East India Company dissolved.
1849		I	Buyskes sketches Krakatau from WSW (see Figure 50). (194)
1854		I	Richard maps Krakatau islands. Slight modifications in 1874. (190)
1877		I	Verbeek visits Sebesi and Seboekoe, islands just N of Krakatau. (191)
1880	07	I	Verbeek visits young (presumably 1680) lava flows of Perboewatan (NNW Krakatau); also Lang and Poolsche Hoed. (190) He sketches Krakatau from NNW (see Figure 50). (194)
	09/01	S	Earthquakes are felt as far as northern Australia; the lighthouse on Java's First Point (74 km SSE) is damaged. Verbeek[24] describes this as greatest of many earthquakes in Sunda Straits. (Intensity I, on I-to-III scale, of Milne.)[25] Milne places epicenter of earthquake at 4:35 p.m. on 9/01 in Bantam.
1882	03/10	S	Earthquake at 4:57 p.m., again intensity I and felt in Bantam, but with epicenter in Pekalongen, 485 km E of Krakatau.[25]

27

1883	M/Day	Hr-Mn	Code	Remarks
	04/13		VT	Eruption of Lamongan (900 km E) around midnight. Ashfall until 4/15. [26]
	05/09		S	Earthquakes felt at Java's First Point (through 5/10). (197)
	05/15 +		S	Earthquakes felt at Ketimbang (40 km NNE), repeated through 5/20. (197)
	05/17	1025	S	Light tremor felt at Anjer (55 km E). (197)
	05		V	Before 5/20, "some passing vessels reported having seen smoke and steam [at Krakatau], but the inhabitants of Anjer took them for clouds." (59)
	05/20	0600	VT	"From 6 to 10 o'clock there was a tremendous eruption, with continual shaking and heavy rain of ashes," telegraphed from Lloyd's agent in Anjer. (61) Helmsman at anchor close to Krakatau sees activity in northern crater from 6 to 10 o'clock. (196)
		0900	V	*Elisabeth* (31 km N) describes vapor cloud rising quickly to 11 km altitude within ½ hr. Hollmann gives 10:30 a.m. for time. (59)
		1000	A	Explosions are heard clearly in Batavia (Djakarta, 160 km E) on 5/20 from 10 a.m. to 1 p.m., 6:45 to 8 p.m., 11:30 p.m. to 1 a.m. on 5/21. (196)
			W	*Samarang* experiences heavy swell from 10 to 12 in the morning from NNE and NW while enroute from Batavia to Merak. (199)
		AM	OV	*Actaea* (145 ± 28 km W) observes "peculiar light green colour" in the ESE sky, while "from E to ENE there was a dark blue cloud, which reached from the horizon to a zenith." (60) A column of smoke in direction of Krakatau is observed from Ketimbang in morning. (196)
		1055	A	Batavia Observatory Director van der Stok notes time of first explosions heard by him. (58)
		1100	A	Explosions first heard in Buitenzorg (162 km ESE) and continue intermittently until 5/22. Rumblings first heard at same time in Tangerang, last until 3:30 p.m., and are heard again from 6:30 to 7:30 p.m. (196)
		1115	A	Muted rumblings are heard on Noordwachter Island (145 km NE) at 11:15 a.m., and between noon and 12:30 p.m.; they are also heard on 5/21. (199)
		PM	T	*A.R. Thomas*, within 8 km, reports ashfall. [27] Ashfall begins in early afternoon at Vlakken Hoek lighthouse (75 km SSW) and continues until 5/23. (199)
		1400	DT	*Actaea* (193 km W), notes it is "quite dark." "Fine dust commenced to fall," continuing all night until about 9 a.m. on 5/21 (375 km WSW) and small quantities of ash again fell that night. (60)
		1600	TO	Ashfall begins on *Elisabeth*, continues for 2 days of sailing to SW. The sun, when visible through ash, is azure blue color. (59)
		1800	EVT	*Zeeland* passes between Krakatau and Sebesi and sees black cloud above island with continuous lightning and crackling, followed by heavy ashfall. (197)
		1830	A	Rumblings are heard at Ketimbang from 6:30 to 9 p.m., on 5/21 from midnight to 1:30 a.m., and 8 to 9:30 a.m. (196)

M/Day	Hr-Mn	Code	Remarks
05/21	0750	A	"Rather loud" explosions heard at Batavia, continue to 9 a.m. Earlier explosions heard 4–5 a.m. (196)
	0900	TO	Ashfall ends on *Actaea* when 375 km WSW. Sun "like dull silver." (60)
	1000	T	Ashfall at Ketimbang until noon. (196)
	AM	TO	Sprinkling of ash at Telok Betong (80 km NNW), Semangka (125 km NNW) and Buitenzorg (162 km ESE).[28]
	1200	A	More explosions heard in Batavia at noon, 4 p.m., and midnight. (196)
	PM	V	Sebesi residents report to Ketimbang that they were on Krakatau when it erupted from coast. (61)
05/22		P	Floating pumice reaches Vlakke Hoek. (200)
	0300	A	Explosions heard in Batavia to 4 a.m.; also 5:30 to 6:30 a.m. (196)
	0630	T	Ashfall on *Archer* (269 km W) continues until 1:30 p.m. (138 km W). Black cloud observed above Krakatau. (197)
	1735	P	*Archer* encounters floating pumice 63 km W. (197)
	2000	TEP	*Sunda* passes Krakatau between 8 and 10 o'clock in the evening. Dr. Sulzer observes numerous lightning flashes and strong explosions. Dense ashfalls 7 miles past Krakatau; encounter floating pumice 10 miles from Krakatau. (197)
	PM	TV	"Fire" on Krakatau seen as far as Anjer. (61) Detonations and ashfall continue at Telok Betong (but not on 5/23).[29]
05/23	PM	TP	*Conrad*, passing Krakatau to north, reports ash rain (1.5 inches on deck) and 1.5 m of pumice on the water. (61) Ship encountering floating pumice off Vlakke Hoek (95 km W) finds it increases toward Krakatau.[28]
05/24		T	Ashfall on Timor (2170 km E). Source probably closer than Krakatau.[61]
05/27	0200	S	Two shocks are felt at Tjiringin at 2 and 3:55 a.m.; last is also felt in Pandeglang (74 km E × N). (198)
	0330	S	Earthquake ("horizontal shock") at Telok Betong lasts 15 sec. (198) Three "heavy jolts" are felt at 3:30 and 4:20 a.m. at lighthouse on Java's First Point. (198)
	0400	S	Two shocks are noticed at Vlakke Hoek lighthouse at 4 and 4:30 a.m. (198)
	AM	VI	An investigating party from Batavia, with mining engineer Schuurman, reaches Krakatau. Explosions are heard every 5–10 min from Perboewatan; the vapor column rises 2–3 km; the active vent is described (see Figure 10). Trees on northern Krakatau are leafless and 2 ft of ash overlies 1 ft of pumice at the beach. Hamburg photographs the volcano in action (see Figures 2 and 9). (63)
		V	Apparent decline in volcanic activity begins (though no actual interruption).[27]

M/Day	Hr-Mn	Code	Remarks
	AM (cont.)	I	Dutch *Sumatra* takes soundings near Krakatau.[27]
05/31		S	During night of 5/31–6/1 (around midnight), hopper *Bintaing* is "suddenly rocked" in water at anchorage of Blinjoe (500 km N). (199)
06		V	Seaman Dalby of *Hope* (anchored off Anjer) notices "long straight column of black smoke" rising from Krakatau. (66)
		I	Commander of Navy reports no rise in sea floor because of May activity. (198)
06/05		V	Eruption of Marapi (Sumatra's west coast, 841 km NW). About 6:30 a.m. ashfall at Padang Pandjang (833 km NW).[26] No records of activity at Krakatau during first half of June. (318)
06/19		VA	Smoke from Krakatau is seen from Anjer and explosions are heard. (199) According to Tenison-Woods this was seen on 6/16. (66)
06/24		T	A second column of steam recognized.[28] First view of volcano from Anjer in 5 days as the east wind displaces "thick bank of smoke and ash" over island. Two separate vapor columns are seen, the larger being to the north; very slight earthquake felt. (66) Observations from Ketimbang suggest conspicuous summit of Perboewatan had disappeared.[28]
06/28		V	Violent explosions and smoke in the night reported from Anjer.[29]
		VA	Controller of Ketimbang reported that Krakatau continuously expelled smoke in June, sometimes accompanied by heavy noises, being the loudest during the nights of 6/28 and 6/30. (199)
07		VS	Continued eruptions from 2 locations; continued earthquakes; occasional violent explosions.[27] *Cheyebassa* passes Krakatau "sending up volumes of smoke, but nothing more."[30]
07/03	0300	V	Verbeek, returning from Netherlands on board *Princes Marie*, sees vague red glimmer from Krakatau through dense hazy sky; no ash. (199)
07/09		P	RMS *Quetta* passes through Straits of Sunda ("sailed close under the then active Krakatau") then sails west through continuous field of pumice for 3 days and 1380 km (left pumice on evening of 7/12). Barnacles noted on pumice. (67)
07/17	1230	O	Brilliant solar halo seen by *Belfast* (2883 km NW) and another blue moon at sunset.[29]
07/25		V	Eruption of Merapi (Java, 577 km E). Formation of a new eruption cone in the old crater.[26]
08/01		P	*Siam* sails for 4 hrs through floating pumice 1816 km W of Krakatau. (201)
08/11		IVT	H.J.G. Ferzenaar visits and maps Krakatau (Figure 11). Now 3 major vapor columns (the newer one from Danan) as well as 11 other visible steam vents; all vegetation is destroyed; a dust mantle on the shore is 0.5 m thick. (67)
		P	*Idomene* encounters floating pumice on 8/11 and 8/12 1930 km W. (201)

M/Day	Hr-Mn	Code	Remarks
08/12		V	McLeod sails near north Krakatau, describing (new?) vent "only a few meters above sea level." Cloud height 3400 m. (68)
08/14	1100	TA	*Madura* travels in ash from 11 a.m. to 3 p.m. Passes Krakatau under pitch black sky. Dull explosions are heard. (200)
08/16	PM	T	*Loudon* encounters heavy ashfall passing Krakatau in the afternoon. (200)
08/18	0200	T	Steamship *Europa* passes Krakatau. Dark clouds over volcano but no rain, only fine ash, on ship. At noon 251 km W of Krakatau.[68]
08/21		O	Remarkable sunsets from South Africa on 21st and 22nd.[29]
08/22	1900	O	Capt. Watson, of *Charles Bal*, notes "the sea suddenly assumed a milky-white appearance" with strong white haze or silvery glare in E to NE (from 1046 km S). This occurs again between 9 and 10 p.m. (102)
	PM	ET	*Medea* records vivid lightning around vast eruptive column during the evening; showers of sand and gravel on 23rd. (97)
08/23	AM	T	Passengers on *Princes Wilhelmina* see thick column of smoke rising from crater; dense ashfall. (68)
08/25		V	Eruption of Goengeong Api at Groot Sangi, Menado (probably Awu, 2447 km ENE) during night until 8/26.[26]
			Mail steamer *Prins Frederik* passes near Krakatau on way to the Netherlands. (215)
	PM	A	*Princes Wilhelmina* (then near Batavia) records "in the afternoon about 7 shakes and heavy blows in the distance were heard (as if from thunder)." (68)
			New Telegraph Master, Schruit, arrives in Anjer. (72)
		A	Explosions are heard on the night of 8/25–26 on board the *Bay of Naples* 120 miles S of Java's First Point. (215)
	1900	T	Ash and pumice are reported falling on Telok Betong, 80 km NNW.[27] Russell[29] says "fall of ashes in evening."
08/26	0600		*Besse* starts westward from Batavia anchorage. (98)
	0900		Beginning of long account by Tenison-Woods[33] states "daylight began to fade" at 9 and "like night" at 11 a.m. in Batavia. He apparently mistakes these observations from following day (no other account of darkness in Batavia Sunday morning).
	1000	T	Very fine ashfall recorded on *Princess Wilhelmina* in Batavia harbor until 3 p.m. (112)
		TC	Lampong Bay residents flee to high ground by noon. Later they are badly burned by tephra flows/falls, including "hot ashes [that] came up through crevices of the floor." (84)

M/Day	Hr-Mn	Code	Remarks
08/26 (cont.)	1200+		Beginning of personal account by Sidney Baker, son of Captain of *Besse*. (99)
	PM	A	Batavia hears "distant rumbling noise like thunder" in afternoon. (105)
	1300	WV	Anjer telegraph master (Schruit) goes to lunch; notes sea level oscillations. "Krakatau was already in eruption." (72)
	1306	A	Explosion arrival in Batavia timed by Observatory Director (originated at 12:53 according to Latter (390)). No gas works recording available. Explosions heard at Buitenzorg and Batavia "about 1 p.m."[28]
	1400	AD	Tremendous explosion. Captain of *Medea* (122 km E × N) first hears eruption, notes a black cloud and measures it to be 26 km high; detonations occur every 10 min. (96) The telegraph operator at Anjer informs Batavia of Krakatau and of darkness and smoke there.[39]
			Berbice (37 km S of Vlakke Hoek) reports sky dark.[31]
	1400+	D	Sky darkening on both sides of the Strait.[28,31]
	1430	VT	*Charles Bal*, from 25 km SW, notes "agitation" and expulsion of tephra. (103)
		D	First Point lighthouse (74 km SSE) notes "in the north very cloudy" at 2:30 p.m. (207)
	1445	V	*Loudon*, after boarding 111 passengers, leaves Anjer for Telok Betong. Soon notes Krakatau "casting forth enormous columns of smoke." (90)
	1500	A	Detonations increase in loudness.[28] Like cannon shots alternating with a thundering rumble at Kroë, 194 km NW, accompanying shocks rattle doors. (213) *Airlie* (670 km N) reports continual detonations, and "whole ship shook" at 3 p.m.[29] Sounds heard in Serang and Bandoeng (82 and 258 km E); explosions increase in severity toward 5 o'clock. (203)
	1534	AW	Origin time of first explosion recorded at Batavia Gas Works. (Corresponds with origin of first wave at 3:37 p.m. which was recorded at Batavia at 6:10 p.m., see Latter's table, p. 390.)
	1600	A	The first explosions are heard in Tangerang (140 km E) (203), a loud bang is heard in Telok Betong (209), and sounds reported louder in Batavia at 4 or 4:30. (108)
	1630	A	Explosions are heard on Boompjes Eiland (330 km E) at 4:30 p.m. and during the night of the 26–27th. (215)
	1700	AT	Detonations even louder ("heard all over the island of Java"); warm pumice and ash rain begin to fall in the near areas.[28] Hail of pumice (bigger pieces "quite warm") begins on *Charles Bal* (15 km S). Larger pumice stopped after 1 hr but smaller ash continued. (103) *Medea* anchors 149 km E of Krakatau and measures 40° vertical angle to approaching cloud top. (96)
		WT	The first wave floods part of the campong Beneawang on Semangka Bay between 5 and 6 in the evening; no serious damage is done; a rain of coarse ash follows. (211)
		V	Eruptions of Krakatau beginning in the afternoon, especially increase in severity around 5 o'clock. (218)

32

M/Day	Hr-Mn	Code	Remarks
08/26 (cont.)	1707	A	First major explosion (of 9) recorded (at 5:20 p.m.) at Batavia Gas Works.[32] Latter puts origin time at 5:05 p.m. and notes its amplitude (17 mm) near those of earlier 3:34 p.m. (16 mm) and 4:54 p.m.(18 mm) explosions recorded at Batavia. No record at Batavia from 5:52 to 11:40 p.m. (390)
	1730	WA	First of many small tsunami mentioned by Judd (described by Tenison-Woods,[33] but without times); others continue at irregular intervals throughout the night. (300) "A particularly heavy detonation" is heard.[32]
		W	First significant rise in water, 1–2 m, is noticed at Anjer; no flooding occurs, but several vessels break loose and damage the drawbridge. (205)
	1800	D	Anjer telegraph master (Schruit) notes unusual darkness, answers Weltevreden that Krakatau is still erupting, then telegraph line goes dead. (72)
		ET	*Berbice* reports "thunder and lightning" and sudden ashfall. (102)
		T	"Rain of ashes and small bits of stone" begins in Lampong Bay. Stiff breeze from NW and WNW. (90)
		W	Beach south of Tjaringin (50 km ESE) is already flooded 2 m above normal level.[27] First wave floods pier at Telok Betong, forcing people to flee. (209) The sea becomes quite turbulent around 6 o'clock, and again at 6:30 and 10:30 a.m. Monday. (218)
	1801	OE	Sunset, local civil time, at Krakatau. Civil twilight (artificial light needed outside) 6:22 p.m. and nautical twilight (horizon indistinct) 6:47 p.m.
	1800+	OE	*Sir Robert Sale* (about 70 km NE) describes sunset sky presenting "a most terrible appearance, the dense mass of clouds being covered with a murky tinge, with fierce flashes of lightning."[28]
		D	"Pitch dark" reported at Anjer in one account,[34] but "sky is unusually dark" in another. (72)
	1810	TD	First Point lighthouse reports dry ashfall with some coarse pumice. Sky dark at 6 p.m. Wind changes to N'ly at 7 p.m. At 7:30, pumice no longer falling (but ashfall continues). (207)
	1830	W	In Telok Betong, "by 6:30 sea quite calm, level of the sea 1 m lower than pier, a moment afterwards 1 m above it." (86)
		T	Ashfall at Telok Betong intensifies and is mixed with pumice pieces the size of beans. (210) McLeod[35] gives 7 p.m. as "first reported ashfall" at Telok Betong.
		TD	Ash starts to fall at Vlakke Hoek and continues until 10:30 Monday evening the 27th; it remains dark all day Monday; no mud falls. (212)
	1900	W	Controller Beyerinck, at Ketimbang, notes several boats being thrown on beach. (83)
		W	Several houses are destroyed in Tjaringin between 7 and 9 o'clock; fires are started 3 times (by lamps tipped over) and fought until 2 a.m. (206)

M/Day	Hr-Mn	Code	Remarks
08/26 (cont.)	1900+	W	Brief account by survivor from Telok Betong who is thrown down by 8 waves while awaiting *Loudon*. (86) Schruit sees severe water oscillation at Anjer, but "we felt no alarm." (72)
	1930	WCS	The Chinese camp and the quarry facilities at Merak, 53 km ESE, are washed away. (77) Metzger[31] says 7 or 7:30 for "heavy detonations" and end of Chinese camp; Wharton[32] says the same, adding that the wave at Anjer "was only about 5 ft high." Anjer telegrams describe "sea rising and falling 3 ft at intervals of 10 and 15 min, smashing all boats. Six earthquake shocks during the night."[36] Tenison-Woods[33] also reports 6 earthquakes during evening. (See 08/27 0200 entry.)
		W	*Loudon* anchors off Telok Betong (90).
	1950	S	Severe earthquakes reported at Java's First Point. (227)
	PM	A	"Distant rumbling noise like thunder" heard in Batavia. (105)
	2000	A	Eight o'clock gun at Batavia is likened to a child's pistol compared with Krakatau. (105)
		W	Batavia tide gauge begins to show small oscillations. (377)
	2030	VS	Anjer telegraph master (Schruit) starts dinner. Soon violent eruptions occur. "Ground shook as if Judgement Day." (72)
		W	Beyerinck family leaves home for their mountain hut after large wave at Ketimbang. (83)
	2100	A	*Graaf van Bylandt* hears explosions "in very short succession after 9 o'clock" from 800 km NW. (130)
	2130	T	Shower of ashes begins to fall at Anjer; sea calm. (72) Verbeek reports some ashfall at 9 p.m. (205).
	2200	AE	Heavy weather, with thunder and lightning, until Monday morning (the 27th) at First Point lighthouse. (207)
		W	Sirik (9 km S of Anjer) is partially submerged.[37] Wharton[32] and Metzger[31] give the time as 1:00 a.m. on the 27th. At Katimbang, "a noise was heard of a far-off wave" and people fled to higher ground.[27]
	2210	A	Residents of Daly Springs, Australia (3252 km ESE), awakened at midnight (local time) by "an explosion resembling the blasting of a rock." (146)
	2300	TV	"Balls of white fire" and "chains of fire" are viewed above Krakatau from *Charles Bal* (20 km ESE), as are "hot, choking, sulphurous" wind and warm seawater. "The [sounding] lead came up from the bottom at 30 fathoms [55 m] quite warm." (103)
		AE	"Heavy blows" at short intervals heard clearly in Batavia Harbor on *Princes Wilhelmina*, particularly strong until 4 a.m., with "strong and nearly uninterrupted lightning in the direction of Krakatau." (112)
	2332	A	At 11:32 and 18 seconds central time Batavia, the astronomical clock stops at the time-ball because of the continuous vibration. (202)

34

M/Day	Hr-Mn	Code	Remarks
08/27	0000+	W	Sea calm "towards midnight" at Telok Betong. [31]
		TE	*Berbice* (96 km SW) notes ash showers becoming heavier, electrical phenomena, lightning and thunder are becoming worse. Several men struck by electrical discharge; crew sent below. (102)
	0100	W	Sirik (9 km S of Anjer) is partially submerged, [31,32] but Anjer telegraph master Schruit, visiting canal, notes only small sea level oscillation. (72) See also entry for 08/26 2200.
		W	Boat from *Loudon* returns from Telok Betong pier reporting it partly under water and surf too strong to land. (90)
		W	Water is high at the Vlakke Hoek lighthouse, but not a flood. (212)
	0130	W	A great tsunami damages Telok Betong. [28] "One account mentions a wave at Telok Betong." [32] Verbeek says water still high in coastal campong at Telok Betong. (210)
	0155	A	Several gas lanterns in the street and house gaslights suddenly dim in Batavia at 1:30 a.m. (probably 1:55 a.m. according to Verbeek). Several glass windows are broken in stores in downtown Batavia. (202) Explosions are heard in Singapore and Penang (1400 km NNW). (79) Gas lamps and lanterns dim suddenly again before 3 a.m. (probably during explosion of 2:38 according to Verbeek). Bulb of an unlit lamp is broken. (202)
	0200	T	*Berbice* has accumulated 3 ft of tephra on deck in 8 hrs. Tephra burned holes in clothing. (102)
		W	Beyerinck's house at Ketimbang is ripped from its base by a wave. (208)
		SA	Two earthquakes reported at Anjer at 2 and 3 a.m., and at Java's First Point at 1:30, 3, and 4 a.m., but Verbeek suspects all are air wave effects. (227)
	0225	A	Origin of air wave arriving at Batavia at 2:38 a.m. [32]
	0300	T	Ashfall begins at Kroë, 194 km WNW. (213)
		W	*Berbice* notes a 20 ft (6 m) wave, "heavy seas rushing on." [33] [Probably erroneous reference to 3 p.m. wave; see 08/27 1500 entry below.]
	0400	AE	*Charles Bal* (40 km E) notes roaring is less continuous but more explosive. "The sky one second intense blackness and the next a blaze of fire" with strong electrical effects. Wind, between SSW and WSW, "strong but very unsteady." (103)
		O	A reddish light is seen over a large area from northern Semangka Bay between 4 and 5 a.m. (211)
	0430	T	Wet ashfall accompanied by rain and SW wind, at First Point lighthouse. (207)
	0443	A	Origin of air wave arriving at Batavia at 4:56 a.m. [32]
	0530	A	First of 4 culminating explosions occurs. (304) "Heavy" air wave recorded at Batavia Gas Works at 5:43. [32] Latter (390) gives origin of 5:28 a.m. for this,

35

M/Day	Hr-Mn	Code	Remarks
08/27 (cont.)	0530 (cont.)		and 40 mm amplitude. Notes no sea wave at Tjaringin (according to Verbeek).
	DAWN	W	*Berouw* is seen stranded on shore at Telok Betong. (90) (See entry for 0630 below.)
		D	At daybreak, a dark black cloud is seen from the *Besse* rising slowly in the west, obscuring the sun, and blackening the sky. (98)
	0600	W	At Semangka Bay "sunken cliffs were visible; a little while afterwards a wave came and returned, but another followed, which did much damage; soon after this it became quite dark, mud and ashes poured down; several waves followed."[31]
		T	Very fine ash layer covers the ground in Batavia (no exact time for the ashfall). (202)
		D	There is some daylight at the Vlakke Hoek lighthouse and the light is extinguished for a short while, but it is soon relit when it turns dark again. (212)
			Residents of Telok Betong begin to evacuate to higher places at 6 a.m.; but some return to the valley to save what they can. Several Europeans are still in the valley at 9 or 9:30. (210)
		D	It fails to become light at First Point lighthouse; light stays lit. (207)
		W	Dutch pilot sees wave approaching Anjer "about six a.m." (73) Latter (390) correlates this wave with explosion originating at 5:34 a.m. which was recorded at Batavia Gas Works (26 mm), giving 6:15 for arrival of wave at Anjer. Metzger[31] says 6:00 for wave at Anjer, and Wharton[32] says about 0630. See also 0630 entries. *Charles Bal* makes no mention of wave but was roughly between Krakatau and Anjer at the time.[31]
	0603	D	Official sunrise time for Krakatau (civil twilight 5:42 a.m. and nautical twilight 5:17 a.m.) but darkness remains after dawn.
	AM	T	*Sir Robert Sale* (about 64 km E) reports falling pumice the size of pumpkins. Wet ash had begun falling 10–11 a.m. the previous day.[28]
		W	Account of a young man from Anjer (Lloyd's subagent Schuit) begins. (74)
		T	In Muntok (450 km N), a very fine layer of dust is discovered on the furniture and on leaves of trees on the morning of the 27th. (214)
	0630	WA	Latter (390) gives time of tsunami hitting Telok Betong (and stranding of *Berouw* and *Marie*) as 6:30 and correlates with major wave which reaches Batavia at 8:19 a.m. and originated at 5:46 a.m. This corresponds to 30 mm amplitude explosion recorded at Batavia, which originated at Krakatau at 5:43 a.m. Latter gives subsequent explosions (and amplitudes) as 5:53 (26 mm), 6:34 (24 mm), 6:36 (41 mm), 6:50 (26 mm), 7:13 (28 mm), 8:07 (24 mm), 8:31 (14 mm), 8:41 (18 mm), 8:59 (18 mm), 9:08 (9 mm), 9:16 (29 mm), 9:27 (12 mm), 9:39 (15 mm), 9:58+ (>67 mm), 10:44 (13 mm), and 10:45 (41 mm). Verbeek's time for big wave almost completely destroying Anjer. (205) Verbeek also gives 6:30 as time for Telok Betong wave: Big flood wave destroys harbor light, coal storage, and warehouse on pier; moves

M/Day	Hr-Mn	Code	Remarks
08/27 (cont.)	0630 (cont.)		*Berouw* into Chinese camp; damages salt warehouse; and washes away Kankoen and all other campongs along the sea. (210) This destruction described by eyewitness as shortly after 6:20 a.m. (88)
	0644	A	Second of the four culminating explosions occurs. (304) Batavia gauge records air wave at 6:57 a.m.[32] (Latter's 6:36 a.m. explosion. See 08/27 0630 entry.)
	0700	T	Ashfall begins at Batavia. (108) U.S. Consulate reports ashfall beginning "about 9 o'clock."[62]
			Salt ship *Marie* leaves Telok Betong. (210)
		WC	Some time after 7 a.m. (correct time not available) the water swells in Beneawang on Semangka Bay and then falls without causing a noticeable flood. A much bigger wave soon follows washing away Controller's house and 300 natives who had fled there. (211) Described by Le Sueur. (89)
		W	*Loudon* observes 4 successive high waves at Telok Betong; harbor light disappears; and *Berouw*, a cross-boat, and a few proas are thrown ashore. However, inhabitants of Telok Betong and van Sandick (engineer on *Loudon*) report wave at 6:30, not 7. (217) *Loudon* starts steaming toward Anjer at 7:30 a.m. (91)
	0730	W	Engineer Abell leaves Merak for Batavia. "Looking back from the mountain road, he saw a 'colossal wave' . . . ." (77)
	0745	W	Wave is 1 m high in a stone sentry box at Telok Betong (20 m elevation?). Verbeek notes that other accounts do not mention the second wave. (210)
	0800	TD	Sky completely overcast at First Point lighthouse. Severe thunder and moist ashfall. Completely dark by 9 a.m. (207) Ash showers becoming heavier on *Berbice*. (102) Ashfall begins on *Charlotte*, 226 km S (236), and continues through the evening.[29]
		W	Time used by Latter (390) for destruction of Tjaringin and 9 other villages, from Verbeek. (206)
		W	Sea relatively quiet at Telok Betong after 8 o'clock. (211)
		DT	Daylight again seen on *Berbice*. Weather calm and clear, but ship covered by at least 8 inches of tephra. (271)
	0807	A	Origin time of large (24 mm) explosion timed by Director of Batavia Observatory (used by Latter in calibrating times). (390)
	0820	A	Heaviest explosion occurs in Batavia (according to others it was a little later at 8:25 or 8:30), during which strong tremors were felt and many buildings made crackling noises. (202)
	0830		*Charles Bal* passes Anjer "close enough in to make out the houses, but could see no movement of any kind." (103)
		VT	Eruption of Marapi (Sumatra).[26] "At once a heavy explosion [and] a thick cloud of smoke arose." More activity, including ashfall, at 10:50–11 a.m. This and other distant activity discussed by Metzger.[31]
		A	After this time, no sounds are heard in Buitenzorg. (201)

M/Day	Hr-Mn	Code	Remarks
08/27 (cont.)	0900	TD	Sky begins to darken at Batavia.[34] Ash begins falling very heavily near Krakatau, as reported by three ships within 64 km: *Charles Bal*, *Sir Robert Sale*, and *Norham Castle*.[27] Ashfall begins again on *Princes Wilhelmina* in Batavia Bay. (112)
		W	Second and larger wave left no survivors at Anjer. (74) McColl also says 9 a.m.
		W	Immense wave at Merak. Only one European (Pechler) escapes by climbing hill. However, Verbeek attributes Merak destruction to great wave after 10 o'clock. (204)
		D	South of Tjaringin, it is somewhat lighter Monday morning until 9 o'clock; then it is completely dark until Tuesday morning (the 28th). (206)
	0906	WA	Apparent origin of major wave reaching Batavia at 11:39 a.m. and correlated, by Latter, with explosion at 9:16 a.m. (29 mm). May also be wave described by survivor at Vlakke Hoek (see 1030 entry below). (390)
	0929	A	Airwave origin arriving at Batavia 9:42.[32]
	0930	T	"Downpour of ashes, later stones and mud" at Telok Betong barracks. (88)
			Pilot leaves the *Besse* near Bantam Bay. (98)
	0958+	A	Origin time of paroxysmal explosion according to Latter (390) and Strachey. (370) Details listed below from previously accepted times of 10 and 10:02 a.m. Gas Works amplitude >67 mm!
	1000	DE	"Sky is completely darkened at Kroë" accompanied by lightning and constant thunder. (213)
		TD	*Loudon* forced by heavy ashfall (with "pieces several inches thick") and darkness to anchor in Lampong Bay in 15 fathoms of water. "In total darkness" by 10:30. W'ly winds to "hurricane force." (91)
		WV	*Marie*, also in Lampong Bay, notes "three heavy seas came after each other; quite dark; at once a fearful detonation. Sky in fire, damp." (88)
		DT	*Annerley* lit all lights because of darkness. "It commenced raining ashes and pumice stone and our barometer was rising and falling 5-10ths of an inch within a minute." Ship turned back to weather in lee of North Watcher Island, 145 km NE. (98)
		TD	It grows increasingly dark in Batavia between 10 and 11 o'clock. At 11 a.m., ashfall begins; it is almost completely dark until noon, then becomes slowly lighter until 2 p.m. when ashfall stops. Temperature begins falling at 10 a.m. At noon and 1 p.m., temperature is 7°C below that of previous or following days. (106, 202)
		TDW	Ashfall begins after 10 a.m. at Tangerang (140 km E) and increases at 11 a.m. Lamps must be lit at noon. Ashfall stops at 4:30 p.m. A strange noise is heard from the north between 11 a.m. and noon, caused by incoming tide. (203)

M/Day	Hr-Mn	Code	Remarks
08/27 (cont.)	1000 (cont.)	AE	An explosion as if from a battery of nearby guns startles everyone in Telok Betong. Verbeek cites other reports that give time as 9:45, 9, 8:45, and even 8:30 a.m. A ray of light and continuous lightning accompany it from the direction of Krakatau. (211)
		D	Darkness sets in between 10 and 11 o'clock over the entire Residency of Lampong. (212)
		EA	Lightning hits the lighthouse tower at Vlakke Hoek and thunder is heard from 8 a.m. to noon. (212)
		DT	After 10 o'clock it becomes darker in Benkoelen; it is completely dark at 11 o'clock; ash starts to fall at noon and continues until 11 a.m. on the 28th. (213)
		D	It becomes dark in Moeara Doea (225 km NW) at 10 o'clock, in Batoe Radja at 11, and in Palembang (350 km N × W) around 1 p.m. (214)
		V	Eruptions of Krakatau reach their maximum intensity at 10 o'clock, after which they decrease greatly in strength, and end completely on the morning of Tuesday, the 28th. (218)
		W	Controller Abell and the Wedana left Tjilegon for Merak because of a report that part of Merak had been destroyed on Sunday evening. At 10 o'clock they reach the village of Sangkanila (close to Merak and very near the sea). After about 5 min, Abell sees a wave as high as a "coconut tree" approaching, and narrowly escapes by climbing nearby hills. Looking back, they see the entire coastline under water. Soon afterwards, it becomes dark and ashfall begins. It becomes lighter at 2:15 p.m. and they begin their return trip to Tjilegon, where they arrive at 1:00 a.m. on the 28th. (204)
		W	Lighthouse on Java's Fourth Point is destroyed after 10 o'clock. (205)
		T	Greatest wave leaves Krakatau, reaches Batavia tide gauge at 12:36. (264, 380)
		WC·	"An immense wave inundated the whole of the foreshores of Java and Sumatra, bordering the Strait of Sunda, and carried away the remaining portions of the towns of Tjiringin, Merak, and Telok Betong, as well as many other hamlets and villages near the shore" at "sometime after 10 o'clock."[32]
	1002	A	Third and greatest explosion occurs which is clearly heard in Singapore (146), Ceylon, and over 4700 km away.[36,38] Strachey gives 10:03 Batavia time (9:58 Krakatau time) from air wave data. Gasometer shows 10:15 arrival at Batavia. (370)
	1002+	ATE	Schruit in Anjer describes "frightful sound" followed by heavy ashfall and lightning, and decreasing noise. "Then commenced a heavy mud rain which was terrific in the extreme." (80) No sounds are heard in the immediate area after 10 a.m. (374), though explosions on a minor scale continue, with a lull in the afternoon.[28]
		A	Tydemann feels air pressure changes shortly after 9:30 in Batavia Bay. Repeated perhaps 15 min later. (111)

M/Day	Hr-Mn	Code	Remarks
08/27 (cont.)	1002+(cont.)	TW	*Besse* (83 km ENE) describes cloud "darker than darkest night," "hurricane" winds, currents to 12 knots, and barometer jumping "an inch at a time." (98) Captain's son describes strong currents ("it took the sounding lead astern like a chip and we never were able to get to the bottom"), 6–7 inches ash on deck, and wind "not blowing at great speed." (100)
		W	Water recorded only 1–2 m below top of hill at Telok Betong barracks. (88)
	1015	DA	Lamps must be lit in Buitenzorg. At 10:30 Verbeek sees a dense yellowish-gray cloud descend to the ground at his home in Buitenzorg. At 11:20 "real" ashfall begins and ends at 2 p.m. After 3 a wet, cold fog hangs everywhere in Buitenzorg, with a weak smell of sulphuric acid. There are no sounds heard in the afternoon, but rumblings are heard from 7 p.m. until 2:30 a.m. on the 28th. They are stronger between 10 and 11 p.m. but weaker than those in the morning. (201)
		ATD	An explosion is heard in Serang, and darkness sets in at 10:30 a.m. At 11:10 a.m. a telegram from Serang reports the hail of pumice stones, followed by a mud rain, which attaches itself to tree leaves and branches and breaks them under its weight. At 11:30 a.m., the telegraphic connection between Serang and Batavia is interrupted until noon on the 28th. At noon (on the 27th) the mud rain stops and only drier ashfall continues until 11 p.m. At 2 p.m. some light is seen in the east; rumbling is heard again; and sulphur smell is very strong and unpleasant. At 4 p.m. the lights are still on in Serang, but a glimmer of light is filtering in. (203)
	1018	W	*Berouw* is lifted from the beach and stranded 1.8 miles (2.8 km) inland, 30 ft (9 m) above sea level; crew of 28 is killed. (376)
	1030	W	Big wave rolls in at Vlakke Hoek, taking everything except the lighthouse tower. (212) (See Plate 5A.)
		DTE	Becomes totally dark on *Loudon*; heavy ash and mud rain starts to fall, accompanied by thunder, lightning, and a very strong wind from west. At peak of storm, *Loudon* lets go anchor. Lightning strikes on mast conductor 6–7 times, and pumice rain turns to mud rain. ("In the space of 10 minutes the mud lay half a foot deep.") (91)
	1032	WC	A wave destroys Tjiringin and the remains of Merak, killing over 10,000 people.[27] Wharton[32] says 10:30. (See also 0800 entry.)
	1045	A	Origin time of last major explosion (41 mm) recorded at Batavia. (390) Royal Society gives 10:52. (304)
	1100	DT	"Darker than at night" at Kroë, with "dense coarse ashfall." (213) *Berbice* reports strong wind from SE. (102)
		TD	Batavia learns of Merak disaster in telegram from Serang. Lines farther west had been destroyed. "Pitch dark" in Batavia. (109) "By 11:30 a.m. Batavia was in utter darkness as night, which continued until about 1:30 p.m."[62]
		W	Seawater at Benkoelen (437 km NW) first withdraws, exposing the beach for a distance of 50 m. (213)
	1110	E	Lightning hits First Point Lighthouse, burning convict workers through

M/Day	Hr-Mn	Code	Remarks
08/27 (cont.)	1110 (cont.)		chains. Tsunami not noticed until effects visible at dawn the next morning. (207)
	1115	AT	"A fearful explosion" is observed on *Charles Bal* (75 km NE). Three successive waves cover much of Topperhoedje and seem to run right onto Java shore. The sky rapidly darkens, with strong wind from SW to S. At 11:30 a.m., *Charles Bal* is "enclosed in a darkness that might almost be felt, and then commenced a downpour of mud, sand, and I know not what." At noon, "the darkness was so intense that we had to grope our way about the decks, . . . the roaring of the volcano and lightning being something fearful." (103) Verbeek believes these times are 1 hr late.
	1120	T	"Real" ashfall begins at Buitenzorg, to 2 p.m. (202)
	1130	WC	A great tsunami damages the Benkoelen lighthouse (440 km NW), Pajoeng, and many places at the head of Semangka Bay: 2,500 people killed at Beneawang, 327 killed at Tandjoengan and Tanot Bringen, and 244 killed at Betong (all around 125 km NW).[27]
		W	Water reaches its highest level at Noordwachter (145 km NNE) at 11:30 according to lighthouse keeper, but it could be later, probably noon, according to Verbeek. (215)
	1130+	T	Katimbang reports rain of stones as large as fists; at noon darkness, heavy rain of hot ash for ¼ hr, then cold ash.[31]
	1200	TD	*Loudon* notes "wind dropped away entirely" but darkness and mud rain "remained as before." Ship anchors again. (91)
		W	Batavia records 14 sea waves with a steady period in the next 36 hr.[32]
		A	Barometric pressure changes observed by Tydemann over past 2 hours decrease and end "by 12 o'clock." (111)
		TD	Hopper barge *Tegal*—having encountered tephra, increasing darkness, and rough seas after leaving Batavia—is forced to anchor east of St. Nicholas Point.[31] Besse, in same area, reports "midnight at noon." (99)
		W	Wave height of 1.5 m at Laboean-Maringai, on Sumatra's east coast. (209)
		W	Witness describes his boat being washed into street at Batavia. (109)
		TP	*Berbice* under full sail for Java head makes slow progress through pumice. Sees Java Head light at midnight. (271)
	1210	W	The sea reaches its highest level, ~2 m above Batavia Level (B.L.), in the Havenkanaal at Batavia. Water rises again at 2 and 4 p.m., but not as high as at 12:10. (202) Verbeek gives these data for Batavia's Tjiliwong River water gauge separate from nearby Tandjong Priok gauge (see 1230 entry below).
	1230	TD	Ashfall stops almost completely at Kroë. Less chilly, but darkness still intense. (213) Pumice fall sometime during the day on *Ardgowan*, 2203 km W.[29]
		W	The first and biggest wave reaches its highest level, 2.35 m above Batavia

41

M/Day	Hr-Mn	Code	Remarks
08/27 (cont.)	1230 (cont.)		Level (B.L.), at the self-registering water gauge in Tandjong Priok (Figure 112). Water then recedes and reaches lowest level of − 3.15 m (below B.L.) at 1:30 p.m. Maximum of second wave is + 1.95 m at 2:30 p.m., minimum of − 1.5 at 3:30 p.m. Third wave had maximum of + 1.24 m at 4:30 p.m., with a minimum of − 0.40 at 5:30 p.m. (202)
	1236	W	Time given by Wharton as peak of wave at Batavia (377) but see previous entry. Latter's table (390) lists 12:16 as arrival (but Krakatau airwave arrived at 10:08 a.m.).
		T	Neale describes Batavia's damage. "Worst was over" with sky clearing and noise weaker. 3–4 inches of ash left at Batavia. (107)
	PM +	C	*Bay of Naples* (222 km S of Java's First Point) "encountering carcasses of animals including even those of tigers, and about 150 human corpses of which 40 were Europeans, besides enormous trunks of trees borne along by the current." (133)
	1300	D	Activity calms down on board the *Loudon*, but it remains dark all day. (218)
	1315	W	First wave at Painan (755 km NW) reaches its highest level, 3 m above high tide, at 1:15 or 1:30. At 2 o'clock a second wave reaches a level of 4 m above high tide mark. Rise and fall is noticed until 7 p.m. on 27th. (214)
	1325	W	First wave at Padang (800 km NW) reaches its highest level at 1:25, the second at 2:20, the third at 3:12. Total of 13 waves are seen until 7:30 a.m. on 28th. (214)
	1330	D	Weather "slightly better" at First Point lighthouse. Wind light, but darkness continues. (207)
	1348	A	Approximate end (Krakatau time) of sounds "like the distant roar of heavy guns" heard several times during the previous night and morning, at intervals of 3–4 hours, on Rodriguez Island, 4653 km WSW. (146)
	1400	D	Mudfall ceases on *Charles Bal*, 90 km NE. "We could see some of the yards aloft." (103)
		TD	"Mud rain changed into a light ash rain" in Lampong Bay. "The darkness remained the same until the following morning."[27]
		T	"Real" ashfall ends in Buitenzorg. (202)
	1445	W	Water rose again in Batavia harbor stranding *Princes Wilhelmina*. (113)
	1500	DT	It becomes a little lighter on the *Besse*, but ashfall continues. (98)
		W	Sky clears and *Tegal* continues west.[31] (98) *Marie* reports "three seas again, after this the sea quite calm." (88)
		W	*Berbice* reports wave 20 ft high striking the ship "so hard that the chronometers were arrested." Thunder continued and barometers violently agitated between 28 and 30 inches. Darkness and storm continue until 6 p.m., lightning shows surrounding pumice and ash. (81)

M/Day	Hr-Mn	Code	Remarks
08/27 (cont.)	1500 (cont.)	W	Eleven waves are observed between 3 p.m. on 27th and 6 a.m. on 28th in Tjabang (144 km N), with an average height of 0.75 m. (209)
	1600	T	Ashfall begins on Cocos Island, 1155 km SW × W, and continues until midnight on the 29th.[29]
		ATW	*Besse's* first officer reports wind and ashfall moderating, explosions nearly ceased. Current toward volcano had been at rate of 12 miles per hour. (99)
		W	The wave reaches the Rambattan (335 km E) at 4 o'clock; second wave arrives between 5:30 and 6:30 p.m. (203)
		W	Wave at Ondiepwater Eiland (365 km NW × N) reaches its highest level. (214)
	1615	W	Water in Toboali (364 km NNW) reaches its highest point. (214)
	1630	DA	Tremendous explosion heard at Kroë; darkness still intense. (213) Detonations gradually diminishing from this hour to 6 a.m. on the 28th.[32]
	1700	DA	*Charles Bal* notes horizon visible in NE, but sky dark and heavy until midnight, with occasional ashfall. Though 65–70 miles from North Watcher (Noordwachter), roaring of the volcano still audible. (103)
		W	Sea rises 2 m above normal high water in Tjilatjap in the Residency of Banjoemas, cutting loose all loading proas and flooding part of the village to height of ⅓–⅔ m. (208)
		T	Ashfall stops, leaving *Princes Wilhelmina* covered with 5 mm of dust in Batavia harbor. (113)
	PM+	TD	*Annerley*, at North Watcher Island, notes "towards night the wind had died out and the ashes stopped, but it was black as night." (98)
	1730	W	Big wave reaches its highest mark at Billiton Island (450 km NNE). (214)
	1800	W	Water floods Japara (580 km E) to a height of 0.5 m. (203)
	1900	W	Wave is observed in Teladas. (209)
	1930	W	Large tsunami recorded by Batavia tide gauge, according to Nature.[50] No such record mentioned by Verbeek or shown in Latter's table (390). (6:58 p.m. wave measured 1.5 ft and 8:25 p.m. wave 0.16 ft.)
	2000?		Steamer *Batavia* sails from Padang (800 km NW) to Vlakke Hoek during evening.[28]
	2000	A	Rumbling is heard again in Batavia until late in the evening. (202) Also strong in Buitenzorg 10–11 p.m. (201) (See 1015 entry above.)
			Controller Le Sueur and natives arrive at Penanggoengan from Beneawang. After an hour of rest they leave for Pajoeng (2 hr from Beneawang). (212)
	2100	W	Sea level drops near Bombay (4500 km and 11 hr from Krakatau wave origin) and "the fish, not having sufficient time to retire with the waves, remained

M/Day	Hr-Mn	Code	Remarks
08/27 (cont.)	2100 (cont.)		scattered on the seashore" where they were picked up by grateful bystanders before the large wave returned. (147)
		T	Ashfall begins on *Graaf van Bylandt* between 9 and 10 o'clock. One inch accumulation by morning (437 km NW). (130)
	2230	T	Ashfall ends at Vlakke Hoek. (212)
	2300	VEW	Last violent explosion.[28] *Tegal* sees bright light in direction of Krakatau during the night. Also notes lightning, fireballs, and sea-quakes.[31]
08/28	0000	T	Ashfall begins on *Brani*, and continues until 11 a.m. on the 28th (1541 km WNW to 1509 km W × N). Ashfall again on night of 8/28–29. (236)
	0112	W	Wave measures 26 inches high on tide gauge at Port Elizabeth, South Africa (381), having traveled 7546 km in 15 hr and 12 min (496 km/hr).
	0130	T	Ashfall ends at First Point lighthouse. (207)
	0200	T	After rain shower, "air became loaded with a fine dust, which fell in great quantities on deck" of *Castledon* (1318 km W). Still falling at 2 p.m.[40]
	0230		Noises cease to be heard.[28] (6:00 for end of detonations according to Wharton[32]).
	0300	P	*Annerley* leaves North Watcher for Sunda Straits "steaming through a sea of pumice stone and debris of all sorts." (98) Stayed close to Java shore and reported no eruptions at Krakatau.[28]
		D	Moon shines on destruction at Telok Betong. (211)
	0500	A	Air wave reaches antipodes, near Bogota, Colombia, 19 hr after origin. Bounces back toward Krakatau, starting second of seven recorded passages over earth's surface.[27]
		T	Schruit starts "fatiguing walk under heavy showers of mud" toward Anjer. (80)
	0600	T	Ashfall continues at Kroë. Ash accumulation 5 cm thick. At 8 a.m. ash is cleared from all roofs; faint sun is visible. Ashfall begins again at 9 a.m. (213)
	0630	P	*Loudon* under way again, but unable to go directly to Anjer because of thick pumice (7–8 ft measured) on water north of Krakatau. (91)
	AM	V	*Batavia* sailing on from Vlakke Hoek, recognizes that northern part of Krakatau has disappeared. (215)
	0800	D	*Berbice* reports daylight at last; ship is covered with ash 8 inches thick, 40 tons having been swept overboard during eruption. (271)
	1100?	V	*Sir Robert Sale* and *Norham Castle* pass within 16 km, report no activity from Krakatau.[27]
	1100 +	C	Telegrams from Batavia: "Anjer, Tjeringin, and Telok Betong destroyed [11:00]. Lighthouses, Straits Sunda disappeared [11:30]. Where once Mount Krakatau stood the sea now plays [12:00]." (14)

M/Day	Hr-Mn	Code	Remarks
08/28 (cont.)	1200	T	Ashfall on *County of Flint* (1494 km W × S). (236) "Great quantity of dust falling at noon."[29]
	1200?		*Loudon*, steaming south of Krakatau, notices "that the middle of the island had disappeared and that no smoke was to be seen in any direction." Later notices "reef" running 10 km N of Krakatau with "various craters now and then sending columns of smoke on high." (91)
	1400	T	"Fine white powder" falling on *Simla*, 1895 km W,. Continues for 6 hr.[29]
	1600	V	*Loudon* reaches Anjer. Finds Resident of Bantam ashore and leaves at 4:50 p.m. to transport him to Bantam Bay. Returns to Straits at 7:30. (92) Passing Krakatau during night enroute to Kroë, note some continuing ashfall, but "the volcanoes were quiet." (96)
	2135	W	Wave (12 mm) reaches Le Havre, France, tide gauge 32½ hours and 17,960 km from culminating explosion at Krakatau.[27]
08/29	0000	P	*Berbice*, after sailing through pumice for 12 hrs, sights First Point Light. Later passed Princes Island, noting 18–24 inch thick banks of pumice. (271)
	0600	TP	*Castledon* (see entry for 08/28 0200) collects dust from deck and sees pumice on ocean, (1373 km W, and 119 km S of 8/28 position). "Dust still falling at 2 p.m." on *Castledon*.[40] Dust falling on Ardgowan, 2263 km W, from 7 a.m.[29]
	1500	PV	*Loudon* meets *Bylandt* in Kroë. (130) *Bylandt* leaves at 5:00 p.m.; describes pumice and newly formed reef north of Krakatau steaming like "the blowing of a whale." (130)
	PM	PCT	*Berbice* sees pumice and corpses covering sea between Krakatau and Java. (271) Ashfall on *British Empire*, 2859 km W × N, continues until evening of 30th. (236)
	2000		*Besse* passes Anjer on way home to Boston. (130)
08/30			*San Francisco Chronicle* reports disappearance of "Kandang range of mountains" on Java, death of 20,000 Chinese in Batavia, and sundry other misinformation. (160)
	0000	TV	Ashfall (½ inch) ends at Cocos Island, 1155 km SW × W.[29] Ashfall on *Meda* during night of 8/30–31 off coast of Australia, 1000 miles SSE. (236)
	1200	W	Last tidal oscillation at Batavia, "after that the condition became normal."[24]
08/31			Siamese barque *Thoon Kramoom* (370 km N during 27–28th) sails south through Straits for Falmouth.[28]
09/01		T	Ashfall ends on *Lennox Castle*, 1973 km W × S.[29]
		I	Verbeek, in Buitenzorg, completes preface to his 674-page monograph on Sumatra's West Coast.[51]

M/Day	Hr-Mn	Code	Remarks
09/01 (cont.)	AM		*Kedirie* arrives at Kalianda on Ketimbang rescue. (209)
	0345	S	Earthquake felt in Menes (56 km SSE); again at 4:30 a.m.[26]
	0400	S	Earthquake felt in Tjimanoek (72 km ESE), 2 tremors.[26]
	1500	A	Air wave recorded on 7th passage at Washington, D.C., 125 hours after main explosion.[38]
			Bylandt arrives in Batavia.[43]
09/02		I	USS *Juniata* sails from Singapore. Ordered by U.S. Navy on 8/31 to survey Straits with USS *Enterprise*.[44]
	0700	PV	*Cheyebassa* passes through debris-filled Strait. Notes Krakatau "still smoking in places where it had not been smoking previously." (132)
	1700	O	At Trinidad, the 5 o'clock sun "looked like a blue globe . . . and after dark we thought that there was a fire in the town, from the bright redness in the heavens." (155)
09/03	0700		*Kedirie* arrives in Batavia with Beyerincks. (127)
	1100	A	*Cheyebassa* (when 260 km WNW) hears loud explosions from Straits. (132)
		PC	*Prins Hendrik* fails to reach Vlakke Hoek light because of pumice, but another ship learns that 10 of 19 lighthouse staff died.[31]
		PC	*Enterprise*, off Vlakke Hoek at 8:00 a.m., finds "sea covered with floating pumice and drift wood . . . trees of large size stripped bare." By 4:00 p.m. passed eleven corpses, and at 4:45 stopped by *Prins Hendrik* and learned of eruption.[63]
09/04		I	*Kedirie* returns to Straits. Describes floating debris and devastation between Dwars-in-den-weg, Sebesi, and Radja Bassa. (131)
09/05		I	The Prince of Orange organizes collections for aid and relief.[45]
09/06	0800	T	Fine ash falls on *Scotia*, 5321 km W × N, 10 days after paroxysm. Continues until 9/08, when 6076 km WNW.[29]
09/07		T	McLeod lands on Verlaten, measures 120°F surface temperature and >155°F below mud surface. (134)
09/08		W	Dwars-in-den-weg found (by *Juniata*) unchanged except for irregular stripping of vegetation that had led to reports of island having been split into 5 parts. (135)
		IC	Dr. Gelpke, dispatched by Dutch Government, describes burial, looting, and crop effects on Bantam (particularly Tjiringin). Observations made 8 days after eruption (9/4). (117)
09/09		I	*Juniata* finds no bottom with 20 fathom line inside Rakata caldera wall. Description of changes and 2 reefs not charted by Dutch. (136) HMS *Hydrograaf* later finds no bottom with 200-fathom (365 m) line. (138)

M/Day	Hr-Mn	Code	Remarks
09/09 (cont.)		O	*Charles Bal*'s Captain Watson, now 1285 km NNE of Krakatau in the South China Sea, notes "the sun rose perfectly green, and so continued for forty-eight hours; and that the moon and the stars have a green light as well."[53]
	0600	P	*Airlie* passes through large quantities of pumice 293 km W, to 2 p.m.,[40] 13 days after 8/27 (22.5 km/day). Meanwhile, *Gipsy* is passing through May pumice 2584 km W.[40]
09/10	1600	V	*Juniata* notes "north end of Lang Island emitting smoke and sulphurous vapors from crevices and fissures in the surface deposit. The same was noticed on the reefs between Lang and Verlaten Islands." Harrington lands on Lang. (136)
	1743	O	Sunsets "coloured a bright pea green," seen from Madras, India (3500 km WNW).[52]
09/11		IW	Wave heights of 40 ft estimated by *Juniata* from inspection of west Java coast, but over 100 ft at Telok Betong. (136)
09/12	0035	O	Moon, near the horizon, appears pale green from Madras.[52]
	DAWN	O	Sun rises pale green, turning to bright green 40 min later, as seen from Madras.[52]
09/13		I	British consul Kennedy's report from Batavia.[46]
09/13+		O	Sunrises and sunsets remarkably colored.[52]
09/14		C	*Straits Times* reports "at Katimbang, where hot ashes and pumice fell, 7000–8000 corpses still remained unburied 18 days after the calamity." Graphic description of Telok Betong. (127)
		S	Four earthquakes felt in Padang during night of 9/14–15.[64]
09/16		P	*Prins Hendrik* (Dutch man-of-war sent to assist traffic in Straits) tries to enter Semangka Bay. Finds pumice to 5 ft thick "and one could stand on it." Much difficulty landing and maneuvering out of Bay.[31]
09/17		P	Pumice collected by *Amy Turner* 272 km SW × W of Krakatau, later given to J.P. Iddings for petrographic study. (292)
	1030	A	Loud explosions too irregular to be a salute are heard at Antjol (east of Batavia) and at Tanjong Priok between 10:30 and 11:30. (219)
09/18		P	HMS *Magpie* reaches Krakatau (ordered to Straits but found "Dutch authorities were not in need of assistance"). Floating pumice (fragments to 3 ft diameter) covered sea, and volcanic mud covered the rest: "giving an appearance of desolation and ruin hardly possible to describe." Fumaroles on Verlaten. Sketches.[65]
	1245	S	Earthquake felt in Ranjkas Betong (Bantam). Recorded at 1300 at Malimping (Bantam) and Java's First Point.[26]
09/19		C	Corpses still unburied on Telok Betong beaches. (128)

M/Day	Hr-Mn	Code	Remarks
09/19 (cont.)		S	Earthquake recorded at Java's First Point.[26] *Enterprise* visits Anjer ruins. Next day sounding around Krakatau. "Smoke constantly rising from the island."[63]
09/20		O	"First indisputable series" of volcanic sunsets sketched by Ascroft, from London. (158)
	0600	P	*Marie Alfred* passes through banks of 8/27 pumice 472 km W (19.7 km/day).[27]
09/22			"Fancy Fair" fundraiser for relief efforts. (Figure 43)
09/26 +		AS	"Detonations [from Krakatau] were distinctly heard, and tremors of the ground noticed in this city [Penang?]."[47]
10/04		I	Government orders, and appoints Verbeek to lead, investigation of the results of the Krakatau eruption. (171)
10/08 +		I	Mr. McColl (Lloyd's agent at Batavia), Rev. Neale (British Chaplain at Batavia), and Mr. Schuit (Lloyd's agent at Anjer) survey the wreck of Java's NW coast. Coral blocks up to 100 tons lie on coast at Merak; no buildings remain; largest tsunami must have been over 135 ft (40 m) high; 2700 reported dead in the district. Tjilegon and Tjiadieng totally destroyed; people already rebuilding. At Anjer no buildings remain, only stones of old fort and lagoons. (119)
10/08	2325	O	A strange light is seen in Serang on the night of 10/8–9. It remains light even after the moon had set at 11:25 p.m., although it is foggy and cloudy, as if the moon continues to shine through a haze. The phenomena continues until daybreak. (219)
10/10	2200	WA	A big wave floods the beach 75 m beyond its normal flood mark in Tjikawoeng on Welkomst Baai (65 km S). A rumbling sound from the direction of Krakatau is heard there and farther north at Soemoer. (219)
		V	The *Hydrograaf* is anchored 8 km N of Rakata Peak and 2 km from north end of Lang Island on 10/10. The steamship *Koningin Emma* is moored that night at the "searock." Neither ship (nor other ship in the Straits) notices an eruption on 10/10, or any other day between 8/28 and 10/10. The mud on Calmeyer, which is completely dry on 10/17, was not erupted on 10/10 because *Hydrograaf* was anchored between Calmeyer and Krakatau that evening. (219)
10/11		I	Verbeek and his staff depart on *Kedirie* for field investigation and return on 10/28. (171)
10/13	1600	P	*Hottenburn* stopped by "tremendous fields of pumice" in passage through Sunda Straits.[40]
10/15		IT	Verbeek arrives on new island of Calmeyer. Finds temperature 42°C (108°F) and pumice covered by 20 cm of darker ash.[24]
10/16		IT	Verbeek lands on Krakatau for 2 days. Finds mudflows from 600 m (200 m below summit) post-dating erosion of pumice. Believes 10/10 eruption product (??). Notes carbonate spheres to 6 cm on top of pumice.[24]
10/17		P	Resident of Bantam reports Lampong Bay again open for navigation and Telok Betong is once more accessible.[48] (See 12/15 entry.)

M/Day	Hr-Mn	Code	Remarks
10/19		A	Rumbling sounds from the west, attributed to Krakatau, are sporadically heard from Friday the 19th to Sunday evening the 21st in Tangerang and Mauk (20–30 km W of Batavia). (219)
		I	Verbeek arrives at Vlakken Hoek on the 19th and at Java's First Point on the 20th during bad weather, rain and wind. He does not hear any rumbling sounds during his entire trip. (220)
	DUSK	O	"Sun glows" are first reported in the U.S. at Yuma, Arizona.[41]
10/20		EA	Air vibrations and lightning in the direction of Krakatau are observed in Tjilegon (70 km E) on Saturday and Sunday nights, the 20th and 21st. (219)
10/22		B	McLeod records renewal of vegetation in Straits: "Everything had become green again" 8 weeks after the eruption. (134)
10/30	DUSK	O	"Sun glows" are first reported in eastern U.S.[41]
11		I	Verbeek visits the devastated coastal region west of Batavia, making a survey there and in the coastal areas in Bantam to determine the width of destroyed areas and heights of waves. (171)
11/01		C	32,635 counted fatalities.[31]
11/05		V	McLeod notes "some light seen on mountain," attributed to smoldering trees. (134)
11/08		O	First strong afterglow observed from London. Possibly some indication of afterglow on 9/8, and certain effects visible 9/20. (158)
11/09		P	Semangka Bay, blocked since the eruption by floating pumice, is free. (130)
11/12		V	Krakatau supposedly active during the night of 11/12–13, according to a report from Merak. (220)
11/17	1200	P	May pumice floating 2200 km to W (avg. speed since 5/20 = 23.4 km/day).[27]
11/26	1640	O	Ascroft paints famous sunset sequence at Chelsea. (Plates 10 and 11).
11/27	1200	O	Sun cast "ruby light over the landscape" of SE Maine at *noon*. (158)
	DUSK	O	Fire engines are summoned at New York City, Poughkeepsie, and New Haven because of brilliant sunset afterglows. (157) First of "remarkable sunsets" observed by Stoddard in Ohio.[49]
12		V	Marapi active (Sumatra, 841 km NW).[26]
12/06		P	*Bothwell Castle* enters pumice 2800 km W of Krakatau. Report "seamen walked about on the patches." (153)
		O	*Nature* correspondence large enough that a special section is devoted to "The Remarkable Sunsets." Ended after 1/10/1884 issue. (159)
	1930	S	An earthquake is felt over a large part of Bantam. (227)
12/15		P	Lampong Bay, which had been blocked by fields of pumice, is free. (130) (See 10/17 entry.)
12/28		O	Frederic Church paints sunset over Lake Ontario. (Plate 14A)

Year	M/Day	Code	Remarks
1884	01	S	Earthquakes are felt at the Vlakke Hoek lighthouse in January and February 1884. (227)
	0101?	I	French "Commission des Voyages et Missions" directs Bréon and Korthals to visit Krakatau and report.[28]
	0105	P	Reeves first encounters floating pumice 4232 km WSW of Krakatau, lost sight of it 3320 km W of Krakatau. (152)
	01/06	V	"Increased action [at] Lamongan" (900 km E × S). Noises heard and fire ejected.[26]
	01/10	I	Papers read before Royal Society result (1 week later) in a resolution founding the Krakatoa Committee.[27]
	02/11	I	Ramsey starts work as Secretary to the Royal Society Krakatoa Committee. Leaves 11/29.[27]
	02/14	I	Royal Society's request for information is published in Nature. (Figure 1)
	02/19	I	Verbeek completes preliminary "short report." Published in official *Javasche Courant* 3/7 and translated in Nature 5/1.[24]
	02/20+	A	Well-known eruption sounds are heard again in Batavia on 2/20 and following days, and in the evening one can periodically see a flickering light in the west. (220).
	02/23	SA	Near Batavia ground tremors, rattling of doors and windows, and a red glow in the west are observed in the evening. Between 8 and 8:30 p.m., a villager notices flickers of light and rumbling as from thunder, with an occasional dull bang, but no tremors or red glow. (220)
	04/14	V	Eruption of Lamongan until 4/16 (900 km E × S).[26]
	05/10	O	Ascroft sketches Bishop's Ring and afterglow from Chelsea. (Plate 9A).
	05/26	IB	French Commission finds Steers and Calmeyer Islands gone (eroded to 4 m below sea level, but see 09/1884 entry), and describes rockfalls on Rakata caldera wall. First biological observations. (142)
	06/23	V	"Again somewhat higher activity at Lamongan."[26]
	07	PC	Pumice (with skeletons) land on Zanzibar beaches, 6170 km W of Krakatau about the third week in July. (153)
	08	I	Verbeek visits Krakatau for second time with steamship *Argus*, in order to determine changes during the first year since the eruption; also visits Verlaten and Bootsmanrots, which could not be reached during first visit because of heavy surf. (171)
	09	I	Verbeek visits Krakatau for third time with citizens from Batavia on board *Billiton*, and takes photographs of the pumice field on NW part of Krakatau. (171) In August and September, Steers is still clearly visible as sandbank above water during low tide; therefore report of French Commision, that it had disappeared totally in May 1884, is not correct. (142)

Year	M/Day	Code	Remarks
	09/08	V	"Volcano Rendjani on Lombok (1245 km E × S) emitted smoke and ash for several days."[26]
	09/14	P	Pumice lands at Durban, S Africa (Reeves' letters say 9/27–28). Average speed over 8170 km is 21.3 or 20.6 km/day, depending on which date of arrival is used.
	12/06	S	Earthquake felt over most of Bantam at 7:03 p.m.[26]
	12/10	T	"Ash fell at Oro-oro-Poelee [eastern Java], . . . ash fall in the evening at 10:00 [source is Semeru, 857 km E × S of Krakatau]."[26]
1885	04	V	"Towards the end of April subterranean sounds were heard in the neighbourhood day after day, and flames arose from the crater. The rocks which emerged from the sea during the last eruption suddenly disappeared."[54]
	05/01	I	Verbeek signs the preface to his book.
	09/03	O	Ascroft sketches crepuscular rays from Chelsea. (Plate 12A)
1886	early	O	Optical effects no longer reported. (159)
	06/20	IB	First botanist, Treub, visits Krakatau. Finds 26 species of plants. (426) With Verbeek on his fifth visit. (Figures 40 and 131)
	06/21	I	Photographs of Rakata (Figure 39), Merak and Anjer devastation photos earlier.
	09/13	O	Ascroft's last Krakatau sunset sketch. (Plate 12B)
1887	05/17	I	Kratatau Exhibit at Royal Society. Report manuscript submitted to Council in spring.
1888	09	I	Publication of Royal Society of London Report (delayed last 6 months by color frontispiece); 1100 copies.
1896	09	IB	Boerlage and Burok make first botanical visit to Lang Island, finding rich vegetation (and resident topographic survey crew).[66]
1897	03	IB	Treub returns to Krakatau with Penzig and other botanists.[55]
1899	03/31	A	Great noise, accompanied by booming sound, heard twice from Krakatau.[55]
1908	08/07		Cool recognizes reported "eruptions" are actually rockfalls on steep Rakata cliff. (310)
1915	11?	IB	Händl starts two-year residence on SE Krakatau with "4 European families and about 30 coolies."[66]
1919	04/24	IB	Docters van Leeuwen first lands on SE Krakatau. (424)
	10/06	I	Scientific party burns Händl's fields (and much of island) as an experiment (?). End of occupancy by Händl's followers.[66]

Year	M/Day	Code	Remarks
1927	06/29	V	Stehn mentions that gas bubbles were observed by fishermen at future site of Anak Krakatau in June. (324) Furneaux[27] gives date as 6/29 and adds a "red glow" seen at night. Sudradjat (361) later (1981) suggests morphologic evidence of earlier submarine activity in 1919 bathymetric survey.
	12/29	V	Columns of smoke shoot 60–1200 m high.[42] Anak Krakatau begins in earnest. (324)
1928	01/03	V	Stehn's first visit: notes 6 vents on NNW line ~500 m long. (326)
	01/24	S	Seismograph 150 km away (Weltevreden) records first of 5 events in 3 days at 1048Z. None recorded in 1927. (338)
	01/26+	V	Anak Krakatau I: crater rim first emerges above sea level, 3 m high × 175 m long; destroyed by surf 9 days later (2/4).[42]
1929	01/07	S	Seismic tremors increase.[42]
	01/25	VW	Stehn's study of wave propagation from Anak Krakatau submarine explosions. (334)
	01/28	V	Anak Krakatau II: above sea level 156 days (to 7/3).[42]
	02/03	V	11,791 explosions within 24 hours.[42]
	05/20	IB	Fourth Pacific Science Conference, Batavia. (436)
1930	06/13	V	Anak Krakatau III: above sea level 57 days (to 08/09).[42]
	06/25	V	14,269 explosions in five hours.[42]
	08/12	V	Anak Krakatau IV.[42] Main, 3-year, island-building eruption ends 8/15, but intermittently active ever since. Only years without reported activity are: '48, '51, '54, '56–7, '64, '66–8, '70–1, '74, '76–7, '82, and (so far) '83.
1933	08/27		Fiftieth aniversary issue of *Java Bode*
1938	10/18	I	Howel Williams submits caldera paper to press. Published 1941. (341–350)
1929	06/17	I	Surveyor on Anak Krakatau notices unusal compass needle oscillations; leaves just before eruption. (341)
1942	01/10		First Japanese landing on Netherlands-Indian soil.
1945	08/17		Declaration of Indonesia's independence, 3 days after end of world War II.
1949	12/27		Sovereignty transferred from Dutch to Indonesians. Republic of Indonesia announced 8/1950.
1950		VB	New volcanic cone appears (363) with main vent to south of former center. By 10/1952 the new rim was 72 m high and vegetation growing since the late 1940's was covered by 3 m of tephra.[56]
	12	I	Neumann van Padang completes catalog of Indonesian volcanoes; Part I of Catalog of Active Volcanoes of the World (published 1951)

Year	M/Day	Code	Remarks
1951	10/05	B	Biological expedition (Hoogerwerf, Borssum Waalkes) starts 10 days on islands. Finds unburnt wood remains from 1883 on W Rakata. (437)
1955		W	Ewing and Press suggest anomalous 1883 disturbances by distant tide gauges result from air-to-sea coupling. (382)
1960	01/12	I	Decker-Hadikusumo visit to Anak Krakatau notes new cinder cone in crater—first subaerial vent—and documents new growth phase. Decker and Hadikusumo calculate 0.3 km³ total addition since birth of Anak Krakatau, a growth rate that would require 600 more years to produce volume "missing" in 1883 collapse.[58]
1961		V	Vigorous year at Anak Krakatau (Figure 107). De Nève believes first lava flow probably 1961.
1963	03/15	I	Zen and Hadikusumo on Anak Krakatau, note dramatic changes including first lava flow.[59]
1968	09/27	I	Indonesian-Japanese expedition starts 5-day study.[60]
1969			"Krakatoa, East of Java": epic novel and ABC-Cinerama motion picture. The title tells all.
1979	09/12	V	Anak Krakatau photographed by Maurice Krafft (Plate 16A) shortly after end of most recent lava flow.
1981	10/20	V	Anak Krakatau's most recent reported eruption. Ash columns to 1 km high. (359)

F. Notes and References

[1]*Nature*, October 22, 1885, p. 603. (Anonymous review of Verbeek's book.)

[2]Griggs (1922).

[3]Blong (1982).

[4]Lipman and Mullineaux (1981).

[5]Dutton (1884) (and see p. 309).

[6]Kiessling (1887, p. 37).

[7]Humphreys (1940, p. vi.).

[8]Williams (1975).

[9]Van Niel (1963).

[10]See the paper by Toksöz and other *Scientific American* reprints brought together in one volume by Wilson (1976). A more general treatment of plate tectonics can be found in Sullivan (1974) and more specific discussion of Indonesian tectonics in papers by Hutchison (1982), Ninkovich (1976), and Hamilton (1981).

[11]These, and following data, from Simkin et al. (1981) with updated information from our volcano data file. The earliest "historic" eruption in Indonesia was A.D. 1006 and we have records of only 12 historic eruptions, from 3 volcanoes, before A.D. 1500.

[12]Pelzer (1963).

[13]Simkin and Siebert (1983).

[14]Mohr (1944, p. 528–533).

[15]See p. 235. Later workers (e.g., Self and Rampino, see p. 351) have generally accepted this value.

[16]First calculated by Pekeris (1939) as 8.6×10^{23} ergs, Harkrider and Press (1967) obtained 5×10^{24} ergs from resonant coupling to sea waves, and Yokoyama (1981) obtained 1.4×10^{24} ergs by applying the method of Hunt et al. (1960) to the Tokyo barogram. Press and Harkrider (see p. 382) estimated 100–150 megatons.

[17]Because of widely distributed ash from earlier eruptions, nobody saw the culminating eruption cloud. The initial cloud height was 26 km at 2 p.m. Sunday (see p. 96), and several estimates of the main cloud have been based on proportions between this and the 10 a.m. paroxysm the next day. Among those favoring a 50 km height are Verbeek (see p. 230), Archibald ("some of the material was projected to a height of 160,000 ft or more," Royal Society Report, p. 380), and Lamb (1970). Williams (1941, see our p. 344) used 50 *miles*, or 80 km, and that figure has been repeated by some workers (e.g., Macdonald, Decker and Decker), but in his 1979 textbook (p. 138) with A.R. McBirney, Williams used 50 km. Reverend Bishop's (1886) estimate of 100 miles is probably high (see Archibald, Royal Society Report, p. 334), and "about 40 km" has been estimated by Rampino and Self (1982) on the basis of eruption dynamics.

[18]These 4 measurements, plus more qualitative descriptions, have been combined by Newhall and Self (1982) in a Volcanic Explosivity Index (VEI) and this is incorporated in our Smithsonian compilation of global Holocene volcanism (Simkin et al., 1981). Krakatau's 1883 eruption is assigned a VEI of 6, and this is matched or exceeded by 4 other eruptions since 1700 (Tambora 1815, Santa Maria 1902, Katmai 1912, and Quizapu 1932). Another 17 eruptions this large are in our data bank, but on the basis of recently measured tephra volumes rather than historic observations.

[19]Rampino and Self (1982).

[20]Ninkovich et al. (1978).

[21]See Smith and Luedke (1983) for a thoughtful discussion of these points, with particular emphasis on the western U.S. Smith's 1979 paper expands upon the correlation of eruption size with repose interval, and this correlation is documented from the Holocene record by figure 6 in our *Volcanoes of the World*.

[22]See photographs in the last chapter of this book (p. 424).

[23]Neumann van Padang (1955).

[24]Verbeek (1884).

[25]Milne (1911).

[26]Verbeek (1885, note 423, p. 533–543).

[27]Furneaux (1964).

[28]Judd (1888a).

[29]Russell (1888, p. 264–312).

[30]*London Times*, October 9, 1883.

[31]Metzger (1884).

[32]Wharton (1888).

[33]Tenison-Woods (1884).

[34]Archibald (1888).

[35]McLeod (1884).

[36]*Ceylon Observer*, September 6, 1883.

[37]*Ceylon Observer*, November 15, 1883.

[38]Strachey (1888).

[39]Neale (1885).

[40]Meldrum (1885).

[41]Hazen (1884).

[42]Neumann van Padang (1951).

[43]*Penang Times*, September 4, 1883.

[44]*New York Times*, September 1, 1883.

[45]*New York Times*, September 6, 1883.

[46]Kennedy (1884).

[47]Reprinted from *Straits Times* in *Times of Ceylon* of October 3, 1883.

[48]*London and China Telegraph*, December 20, 1883.

[49]*Nature* (29:355–358).

[50]*Nature* (32:603).

[51]Verbeek (1883a).

[52]Smith (1884).

[53]Sturdy (1884, p. 391).

[54]Anonymous note in *Nature*, June 18, 1885, p. 161, and not mentioned in any other reports known to us.

[55]Kusumadinata (1979, p. 103) cites *Natuurk Tijdschr. Nederl. Ind.*, p. 101.

[56]Kusumadinata (1979).

[57]Hoogerwerf (1953).

[58]Decker and Hadikusumo (1960).

[59]Zen and Hadikusumo (1964).

[60]Zen (1970).

[61]Forbes (1884, p. 148).

[62]Letter to John Davis, Assistant Secretary of State, Washington, D.C., from Oscar Hatfield, Consul of United States at Batavia, in Consular Dispatches from Batavia, General Records of the Department of State (Record Group 59), U.S. National Archives, Washington, D.C.

[63]Log Book of USS *Enterprise*, Commander A.S. Barker, U.S. Navy, in Records of the Bureau of Naval Personnel (Record Group 24), U.S. National Archives, Washington, D.C.

[64]Van Sandick (1884c, p. 153).

[65]HMS *Magpie* (1883?).

[66]Backer (1929).

[67]Ernst (1908).

[68]Verbeek (1885, addenda, p. 479).

PART
401

PRICE
6D.

THE
LEISURE HOUR

MAY, 1885.

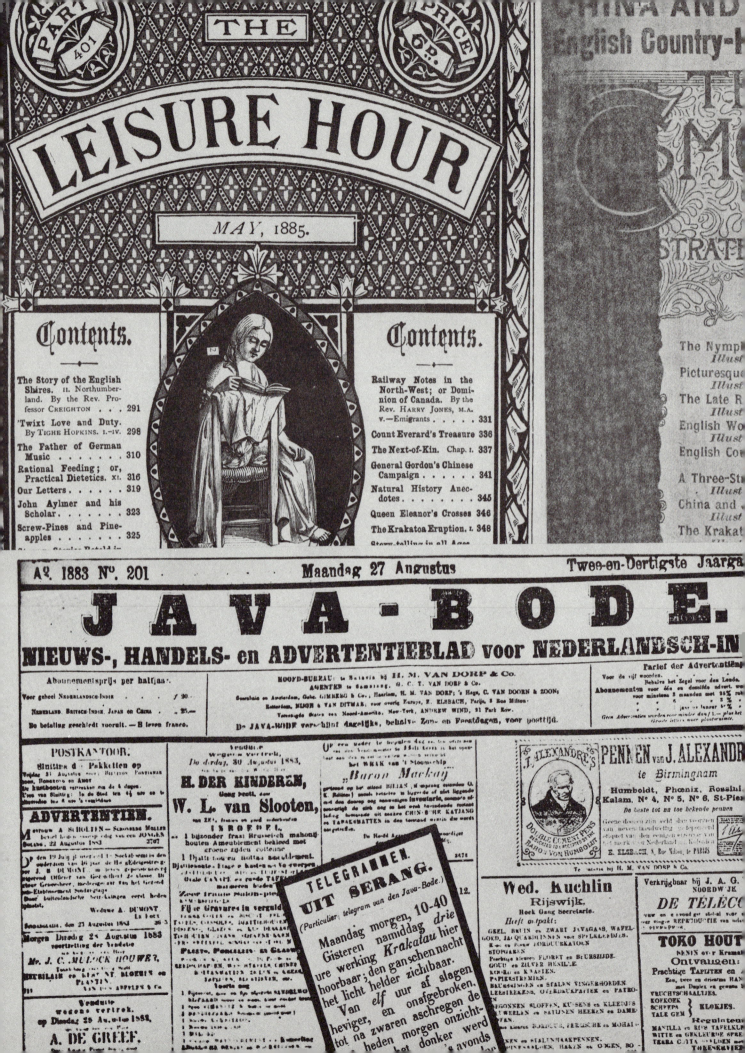

Contents.

Contents.

CHINA AND
English Country-

THE

STRATI

A°. 1883 N°. 201   Maandag 27 Augustus   Twee-en-Dertigste Jaarga

JAVA-BODE.

NIEUWS-, HANDELS- en ADVERTENTIEBLAD voor NEDERLANDSCH-IN

Abonnementsprijs per halfjaar:

Voor geheel NEDERLANDSCH-INDIE . . . . f 20.—

NEDERLAND, BRITSCH-INDIE, JAPAN en CHINA . . 25.—

De betaling geschiedt vooruit.— B leven franco.

HOOFD-BUREAU: te Batavia bij H. M. VAN DORP & Co.
AGENTEN te Samarang, G. C. T. VAN DORP & Co.
Correlaie en Amsterdam, Gebr. GIMBERG & Co., Haarlem, H. M. VAN DORP; 's Hage, C. VAN DOORN & ZOON;
Rotterdam, NIJGH & VAN DITMAR, voor overig Europa, E. ELSBACH, Parijs, 8 Rue Milton;
Vereenigde Staten van Noord-Amerika, New-York, ANDREW WIND, 91 Park Row.
De JAVA-BODE verschijnt dagelijks, behalve Zon- en Feestdagen, voor posttijd.

Tarief der Advertentie

Voor de vijf woorden.
    Behalve het Zegel voor den Lande
Abonnements voor dien en dezelfde advert. en
    voor minstens 3 maanden met 33⅓ pct.
Advertentien en langer v
    jaar en langer 25 p
Geen Advertentien worden voor minder dan f 1.— plus het
    Grootste letters naar plaatsruimte.

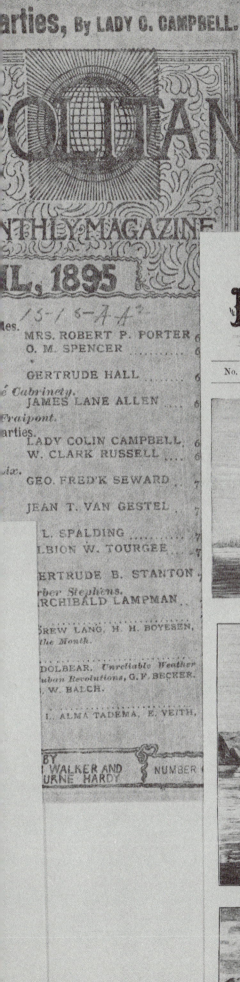

II. Narrative Descriptions:
The Eyewitness Accounts

THE ILLUSTRATED LONDON NEWS

No. 2316.—VOL. LXXXIII.   SATURDAY, SEPTEMBER 8, 1883.   WITH TWO SUPPLEMENTS   SIXPENCE. By Post, 6½d.

ISLAND OF KRAKATOA, IN THE STRAITS OF SUNDA, THE CENTRE OF THE LATE VOLCANIC ERUPTION, SAID TO HAVE DISAPPEARED.

EAST COAST AND ISLANDS OF THE STRAITS OF SUNDA, WITH ANJER, A PORT OF JAVA.

In 1883 many of the techniques now used to document volcanic eruptions were not available. Although seismographs had been developed, no world-wide network had been attempted and we know of no operating seismograph within 5000 km of Krakatau. Satellites, of course, were far in the future. Sound recording, like telephone and radio, had been invented but was not yet in use in the eastern hemisphere. Flexible film had also been invented, but the motion pictures and conveniently portable cameras that it made possible were not yet known. Half-tone reproductions of photographs had been run in a few newspapers, but printing was largely limited to engravings. The written word, however, flourished. Distant friends and relations maintained vigorous correspondence, and personal journals were common. Newspapers were the primary providers of information on events, and widespread interest in the Krakatau eruption assured that newspapers in the English colonies such as Ceylon (Sri Lanka) and the Malay Peninsula (Singapore, Pinang, and settlements along the Malacca Straits east of Sumatra) quickly ran translations of the eyewitness accounts appearing originally in Dutch and other languages. We reprint below the accounts of 87 eyewitnesses, together with a few second-person narratives written at the time. The sequence is roughly chronologic, but we have subdivided the accounts geographically from August 26th onward._

May-to-August, 1883

The events of 1883 began in May. Earthquakes were felt at Java's First Point (70 km SSW of Krakatau) on May 9–10, and at Katimbang (40 km NNE) on May 15–20.[1] The first record of explosions at Krakatau came on May 20th at 10:55 a.m. when the Director of the Observatory at Batavia noticed vibrations and banging of loose windows in his house.[2] Some minor volcanic activity may have preceded this, however, as mentioned by the Reverend Tenison-Woods in his account:[3]

In May last some passing vessels reported having seen smoke and steam, but the inhabitants of Anjer took them for clouds. On the 20th of May, however, there could be no doubt that the crater had broken out afresh. On that day and the next loud reports of distant explosions were heard at Anjer. These were followed by concussions which startled the inhabitants. They caused the doors and windows to rattle and brought down lighter articles from their shelves. Some faint echoes were heard as far as Batavia, a distance of nearly 100 miles [160 km] as the crow flies. Telegrams from Anjer of that date report that Krakatoa was seen to cast forth fire, smoke, and ashes, accompanied by explosions and continuous rumbling sounds, which were apparently preparatory to an extensive eruption.

The best view of the eruption's start, however, was from the German warship Elisabeth in the Sunda Straits. First a brief report by the ship's Captain Hollmann:[4]

On May 20 at 10:30 in the morning, a volcanic eruption was observed on the Island of Krakatau from the ship. At first we saw from the island a white cumulus cloud rising fast. It rose almost vertically until, after about half an hour, it had reached a height of about 11,000 m. Here it started to spread like an umbrella, probably because it had reached the height of the anti-trade [westerly] winds, so that soon, only a small part of blue sky was seen above the horizon. When, at about 4:00 in the afternoon, a light SSE breeze started, it brought fine ash dust which increased strongly on the 21st of May and fell at a uniform intensity until the 22nd so that the entire ship was covered in all its parts with the uniform fine gray dust layer. The thickness of the ash rain that had fallen within 24 hours on the ship was about 2–4 cm. When the strong ashfall started, the ship was about 100 nautical miles away and when the ash rain started to decrease on May 22 about 300 nautical miles away from the island of Krakatau in the direction SW½W [bearing 230°] whereas the wind was always from the SE. The sun, as far as visible through the light dust, was always of an azure blue color. The ashfall decreased on the 22nd without a change in wind, but we noticed some dust in the air during the next few days.

The Elisabeth's Marine Chaplain Heims provides a second, more descriptive, account of the eruption's first two days:[5]

The warship had steamed away from the quay of Anjer at 9 o'clock in the morning, with the proud home flag flying in the wind, taking a course towards WSW. . . . The crew had assembled on the upper deck in clean Sunday clothes to be mustered in divisions. The commander had just looked at the parading crew and started to inspect his pretty clean ship, when a certain motion was noticed among the officers which were assembled on the upper deck and the bridge in their Sunday clothes. Glasses and heads all turned towards the lonely countryside in which the shores of Sumatra and Java coincided with the small island of Krakatau: There, at least 17 nautical miles [31 km] distant, an enormous shining wide vapor column rose extremely rapidly to half the horizon, and reached within very short time the colossal height (measured) not below 11,000 m, contrasting in its light-colored snow-like appearance with a clear blue sky. It was convoluted like a giant wide coral stock, resembling a club or, for that matter, a giant cauliflower head, except that here everything was in imposing gigantic internal motion; driven by the enormous pressure from beneath, new turbulent masses were generated in majestic convolutions out of the single closely packed and layered three dimensional steam balls. Nevertheless, the outline of the continuously growing gigantic phenomenon remained clear and sharply bordered, only the top of which started to lean towards us. It appeared as if the wind at that height had started to blow it across until new clouds were pushed forward with irresistible force, resembling the convoluting steam column from the smoke stack of a gigantic standing locomotive engine. With time, darker colors were mixed in with the wide shining glaring color of the water vapors; dark streaks rose from below, especially on one side, whereas on the other side at the base a weak red glow was visible. Finally, a white blue-gray wall resembling a mighty, dark, fan-shaped thundercloud, wide at the top and narrower at the base, covered everything and extended widely over the sky. We had just been witnesses of a powerful volcanic eruption, which had taken place on the island of Krakatau which is 2,600 ft [790 m] high. We did not hear any detonations. In any case we were happy with the attention shown to us and the splendor of the farewell signal. The last view of

Asia and the stations were imposing enough.

The service was finished after three quarters of an hour and after that the clear sky was largely covered. It was thick and heavy in the east. Early in the afternoon, the SE trade wind, which we had hoped for, started mightily, and we hoped that we could turn off the fire in the engine as soon as possible. However, the sky darkened continuously until a homogeneous gray cloud covered the entire horizon. We should not remain in doubt for long about the nature of these clouds. The fresh wind came from the sea and not from land, and brought along very fine ash rain, which laid a light-gray, slightly yellowish, extremely fine, pulverized mass on the entire ship. It penetrated everything; a thin white fluffy material, which was laid down like a real frost over the deck and the masts during the afternoon. On the other side towards the land it had become pitch-dark. At the time of the eruption we were about 12 German miles [89 km] from the coast. We noticed here the strange phenomenon that the ejected lava dust had been transported over the sea by a higher air current, the anti-trade winds from the land, while the slowly sinking particles were taken up by the lower SE trade wind and were driven towards us. The veil over the sky was so dense and uniform that the almost full moon was only barely visible during the night.

On the next morning, May 21, the ship, which was so clean 24 hours ago, looked very strange: It looked like a mill ship or, more precisely, like a floating cement factory. On the outside, everything—ship's wall, torpedo pipes, the entire masts, etc.—was covered very uniformly with a gray sticky dust; the map house on the bridge seemed to have been colored light during the night; all windows and deck lights were covered; on deck the fine mass was spread more than 1 cm thick; it had accumulated thick and heavy on the sails; the steps of the crew sounded muffled on the soft dust, and they themselves looked like honorable miller's apprentices, everything looked so very much covered with powder. Early in the morning the officers on deck were allowed to wear white jackets, which was not normally allowed during duty, because dark garments were just about impossible in the fine intense ash fall which continued to unload above us, penetrating all rooms and every nook and cranny. It was as effective in the battery as on top of the ship and covered the old flowers in the officers' mess with a white flour even though the windows were completely shut. It was deposited as a thick slime on all greasy iron parts; it filled the folds in the covers of the

cannons; when the ship moved, it went up in big clouds and it was very annoying for the eyes and also increasingly for the lungs. A first look at this metamorphosed ship generated a wintery impression. The people enjoyed collecting the lava dust as polishing material and it was not very heavy work to collect the stuff in sacks and boxes. However, to remove the dust in the cabin had to be given up soon as an impossible task.

The sky above this ash rain disaster appeared like a large bell made of rather dull milky glass in which the sun hung like a light blue lamp, a very strange phenomenon as a consequence of the abnormal absorption of the light rays. There was a plentiful supply of lava dust up there in the form of thick massive snow clouds and it snowed with few interruptions happily into the night. For another 75 German miles [560 km] we had to sit in the evening with our faces looking backwards when we sat together trying to get some air. The distribution of the ashfall would be over an area at least as large as Germany. The light in the morning looked very similar to that during an eclipse, and above the blue sea it lay, like a strange matte brownish shine while the wind was blowing strongly.

On May 22, the sky was still uniformly gray but no more ash fell.

Another ship, sailing west from Krakatau in the Indian Ocean, added more information on unusual optical effects and distant ashfall from the eruption.[6]

At noon on May 20 the Actaea was in 6°50′S and 104°2′E [145 km W of Krakatau], and on the morning of that day a "peculiar light green colour" was observed in the sky to the ESE, while "from E to ENE there was a dark blue cloud, which reached from the horizon to the zenith.[7] At about 2 p.m. it was quite dark. What appeared to be a rain squall rose up from the east, but, instead of rain, a kind of very fine dust commenced to fall, and very soon everything was covered; ships, sails, rigging and men were all dust colour; nothing could be seen 100 yards off. The fall continued steadily all night, and stopped about 9 a.m. on Monday the 21st [375 km SSW]. When we saw the sun it looked like dull silver. At noon we were in lat. 8°15′S and long. 102°28′E, distant from Java Head about 170 miles. The sky all round remained a dusty hue, and small quantities of dust again fell during the night. The sky did not assume a natural appearance till the 23rd."

The mainland village nearest to Krakatau was Katimbang, 40 km NNE, on the SE end of Sumatra. In his book on Krakatau,[8] Rupert Furneaux has gathered the account of Mrs. Beyerinck, wife of the Dutch Controller at Katimbang.

"We were much bothered by the sounds and tremors that Sunday morning," she wrote later. They lasted all day, and the tremors were best observed in the bathroom where the surfaces of the water barrels were continuously in motion. The rumbling noise appeared to come from the south, from the Java shore, but nothing unusual could be seen. A number of ships were navigating the Straits, their white sails glinting in the sun, their smoke hanging lazily in the brilliant sky.

• • • • •

On that Monday afternoon, eight fishermen from Sebesi, another island in the Straits, came to report to the Controller of Katimbang that they had been over to Krakatoa in their proa to get wood for building. They told Mr. and Mrs. Beyerinck that as they walked into the forest rising from the beach they had heard cannon fire and had remarked that "there must be a warship in the neighbourhood." They went on felling trees until they heard another bang. This made them curious and they ran to the beach. Hardly had they reached it when the earth burst open at their feet, throwing up stones and ash. They fled as fast as they could and swam to a small island, one to which they could normally have waded. Now the tide was high and they had great difficulty in getting back to their proa.

Mrs. Beyerinck told her husband not to let the men fool him. An eruption, she pointed out, could not begin on the beach. The Controller replied he had thought of that too, but no amount of questioning would shake the men's story. An hour later Mr. Beyerinck had an opportunity to test it for himself. The Resident of the Lampong district arrived by boat with orders from the Governor-General at Batavia to go to Beyerinck's department, the two officials saw with their own eyes that the fishermen's story was true. Near the

beach, the earth was belching fire and smoke. The Resident telegraphed Batavia that Perboewatan, the northernmost of Krakatoa's three cones, was active, a report which was confirmed by the Resident of Bantam who quoted his native assistant as saying that the sounds were similar to the noise of an anchor chain being raised.

A May 23 telegram from Lloyd's agent in Batavia,[9] reported the eruption continuing, but that shocks were no longer felt in Batavia. Included in this account is the following telegraphed report from Anjer, the main port of call on Java's west coast, dated May 23, 3:47 a.m.

"On Sunday morning last, from 6 to 10 o'clock, there was a tremendous eruption, with continual shaking and heavy rain of ashes. On Sunday evening and Monday morning it was continued. Last night the eruption was distinctly visible here. Smoke was seen until 12 o'clock; afterwards it cleared up a little. At this moment the air is clouded again." Captain Ross [of the *Haag*] reports from Anjer that on May 22 he was sailing near Java's First Point and tried to get Prinsen Island in sight, but found that it was surrounded by clouds. Then steered for Krakatau, but found it to be the same there. The captain observed that the lower island or mountain situated on the north side of Krakatau was totally surrounded by smoke, and from time to time flames arose with loud report. Fire had broken out in several places, and it was very likely that the trees in the neighbourhood had caught fire. The mountain of Krakatau had been covered all over on the north side with ashes. The captain could not make out the condition of the mountain, as he kept away as far as possible, being afraid of the wind falling and vessel being drifted on to the island. The strongest fire was on the evening of May 22, with heavy explosions and detonations. The fire was also seen at that time at Anjer, but on account of the heavy smoke nothing could be perceived, as all the islands remained clouded. The captain did not experience any shower of ashes. The master of the steamer *Conrad*, which arrived at Batavia on May 24, reports having passed Krakatau on the north side the previous night, and met with heavy rains of ashes, covering the decks, &c., with about 1½ inches of ashes. He

Figure 9. Upper: Ash and steam boil upward from Krakatau on May 27, 1883, one week after the eruption began and 3 months before its culmination. Only the vent Perboewatan was active at that time. Like Figure 2, this was taken by the photographer Hamburg, during the Schuurman expedition to Krakatau. It was obtained by us from the grandson of R. Bréon, leader of the French expedition to Krakatau in 1884. Lower: Island portion of another Hamburg photograph obtained from Phot. Bibl. Nat. Paris. These and other photographs all show some retouching, but the same shoreline elements appear (from different vantage points) in all. Here the irregular ridge of Danan is visible behind the active vent Perboewatan.

also had to cut his way through about 1½ m of pumice-stone, which occasioned a delay of about five hours.

This eruption stimulated much interest,[10] and the Netherlands-Indies Steamship Company filled the Governor General Loudon, a ship that was to play a major role in the August paroxysmal eruption, with 86 passengers for an excursion to Krakatau. The group landed on the island on 27 May and returned to Batavia the next day. The mining engineer J. Schuurman was in the group, and provided the following detailed report to Verbeek:[11]

Toward midnight, steaming off Anjer, a fiery radiance, occasionally seen in the direction of the island of Rakata at the horizon, attested to the activity of the volcano. It was a purple fiery glow, appearing for a short while every five to ten minutes, from which a fire rain fell.

At daybreak, Sunday May 27, the steamer was several miles north of its destination. The island of Rakata consists of the peak, a mountain which rises on the south side straight up to a height of 822 m, in the middle a much less high mountain range, and the northern part which is relatively flat with an approximately 100 m high top, which consists of the mountain Perboewatan, the presently active volcano. The view of the island was fantastic; it was bare and dry, instead of rich with tropical forests, and smoke rose from it like smoke coming from ovens. Only the high peak had some green left, but the flat northern slope was covered with a dark gray ash layer, here and there showing a few bare tree stumps as meager relics of the impenetrable forests which not too long ago covered the island. Horrible was the view of that somber and empty landscape, which portrayed itself as a picture of total destruction rising from the sea, and from which, with an incredible beauty and thundering power, rose a column of smoke. The cloud was only several dozens of meters wide at its foot, wheeling to a height of 1000 to 1200 m while widening, then rising from there to 2000 to 3000 m in height and in the meantime fading in color, delivering its ash to the eastern wind, which, falling as a dark fog, formed the background of the tableau.

Overpowering was the impression of this proud natural scene, which reminded me in all seriousness of the angry, driven play of the elements, to which the rising, black, changing to a silver-white column of smoke, was attesting. It took a long time to get over the amazement of this immense spectacle and for the attention, tired of its attempt to comprehend everything, to focus on a single point of observation. But then the column of smoke made the most fantastic impression, with its constantly changing, never returning, phases. Although rising continuously, it increased significantly in size from its foot, through extremely powerful exhalations of smoke clouds every 5 to 10 minutes, which announced themselves with a frightful rumbling, and it was during these periodic eruptions that the dark-colored smoke which was belched out rose with much higher speed than normal and caused a hail of stones to fall from a height of approximately 200 m, which on board looked like black dots flying through the air. And then, it seemed that once in a while these dark-colored smoke clouds even glowed during the day, while at night they appeared to transform into red flames, with the hail of stones, which was hardly noticeable during the day, changing to a hail of fire at night; this undoubtedly can be explained by the the glowing content of the crater being reflected on the smoke clouds and by the stones which glowed when they were ejected.

A single lightning bolt in the column of smoke was the only sign of electrical activity.

In addition to the island of Rakata, the nearby Verlaten Island had also suffered from the eruption. Its forests, although leafless, were intact. The island reminded me of a forest view in winter, with its heavy gray ash layer. The ashfall also had reached Lang Island and the small island of Poolsche Hoed, although much less so; at least on these islands the greenery was not destroyed.

Of our visit to the island of Krakatau itself, for which Captain Lindeman of the *Loudon* was nice enough to make a small boat available, the following can be reported. Taking course along the north coast of the island, which is rocky and rises steeply from the sea, we landed in a place where the coast flattened to a wide beach. The beach itself offered nothing exceptional, but it was covered to the high water line with fine gray ash. The low and high tide cut a profile of the eruption—the only thing found on the island—which showed that, although the island seemed covered only with ash, the volcano did not only eject that material; on the white sand, which was the real beach, a one-foot-thick layer of pumice was present and dumped on top of it was a layer of ash two feet thick.

Only sporadically did we find rocks of a different nature in this three-foot-thick volcanic layer, about which more follows.

The ash, seemingly spread loosely, in reality was packed enough to carry us, and when we discovered that our feet only sank in it to our ankles, there were no more objections to a trip inland. Following in the footsteps of the bravest, or perhaps the most foolhardy, we climbed the bare hills, which did not offer any other obstacles than the loose ash. First the journey led us over a hill, where some trees showed through the ash as bare stumps several meters high, and from which the branches seemed to have been torn off by force. The wood was dry, without signs of burning or charring; no leaf or branch could be found in the ash, and it is therefore likely that the deforestation must be attributed to a whirlwind, as it often develops in turbulent air during volcanic eruptions as a result of local heating of the atmosphere.

Soon every sign of vegetation disappeared and, surrounded by the bare somber ash hills, which prevented the sight of the sea, but not of the roaring column of smoke, we continued the journey up the mountain. At last we climbed the last hill and we were standing at the steep east edge of the crater wall.

There we found in the ash a nice dish-shaped basin about 1000 m in diameter (*AB*, Figure 10). Located about 40 m deep in the basin was a circular bottom which had sagged several meters (*CD*). The bottom was estimated to be 150 to 250 m in diameter and was covered with a dull shiny crust. Through this crust, the powerful column of smoke escaped with a frightening noise, from a circular area of approximately 50 m in diameter (*FG*) on the west edge away from us.

The sketch, Figure 10, shows a vertical section, taken in the E-W direction over the middle of the crater, and also a map of this place. From point *A*, the part *GHBI* was invisible because of falling ash, while the part *IK* of the crater wall had been cut through. Whether at that place a lava flow made its way through, I only dare to suggest because of the darkness which obscured that area.

Although the ashfall, driven by the wind, fell in a westerly direction and obscured the whole view, the hail of stone fell around the column of smoke on the crust of the crater mouth and on the crater wall where many pieces of pumice were found on the ash, while the more massive and heavier rocks had sunk into the ash.

We did not find any signs of glowing liquid lava at the point of eruption, because the smoke clouds released from the crater pool were completely opaque; only a rosy glow occasionally showed a fiery reflection of the crater contents.

The clouds of smoke appeared to break through as with difficulty but with unmatched force, and they seemed to flee in numerous closely linked, tremendous bubbles whose internal friction caused the turning and convoluting movement of the clouds in the lower part of the column of smoke, reaching a height of 1200 m. Only at the edges of the point of eruption could the exhalation of steam from a number of gaps and cracks be observed.

The crust at the mouth of the crater, as is mentioned earlier, had a black somewhat shiny color, standing out sharply against the gray ash which covered the crater wall, reminiscent of the crust of blast furnace slags.

Finally, the products of this volcanic eruption require further explanation. In addition to the steam from the column of smoke, which is the main ingredient and which changed into white clouds as it freed itself from its ash content, one also recognized among the gaseous products sulphuric acid, which made itself known by its smell, and among the sublimated matter sulphur, which formed deposits with the exception of two small solfataras, on the ash, covering some hills, and giving it a greenish yellow color.

Among the solid material ejected by the volcano, the ash deserves first mention. It is gray in color, fine-grained, and under the microscope it consists mainly of colorless and brown glass, mixed with small fragments of augite, plagioclase and magnetite. [Verbeek describes the ash starting on p. 255.]

After the ash, pumice must be mentioned as a product, which was ejected in considerable quantities.

The beach profile shows a pumice layer 1 ft thick, with 2 ft of ash on top. One could possibly see in the pumice the product of the eruption in its most violent period. That it was not only ejected during that time, but continues to come from the crater, was proven by the widely distributed pieces of pumice, in size almost never larger than 0.1 m³.

Finally we come to the rocks, which, although rarely ejected, possibly deserve the most attention, as the non- or least modified representatives of the crater contents.

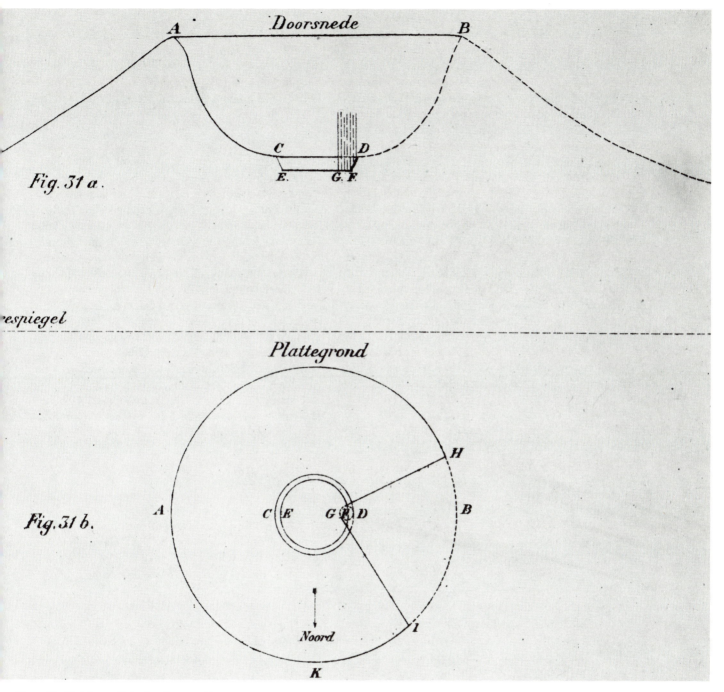

Figure 10. Sketch map (below) and cross-section (above) of Perboewatan crater, by J.A. Schuurman on May 27, 1883. Diameter AB is 980 m, and elevations above sea level of crater floor CD and rim AB are 58 m and 100 m, respectively (vertical exaggeration of section is 10:1). The dashed line represents the destroyed western crater rim largely obscured by fumes. North is toward the bottom of the map and other letters are explained in Schuurman's text. This illustration is figure 31 in Verbeek's Atlas.

Here and there in the crater bowl, holes were seen in the ash which contained a green-black, glassy volcanic rock the size of a head at a depth of 1 to 1½ ft. These were very brittle, splitting when touched lightly and thus proved to be in a state of high tension. Under the microscope, the rock appeared to be composed mainly of an uncolored glassy material, in which were found, in addition to some colorless plagioclase, green augite, and black magnetite crystals, and numerous microliths which show a clear flow structure. Small and large pieces of these augite andesite pitchstones or obsidians were also found on the beach. One side was completely changed into pumice, while the other side retained its massive glassy structure.

Besides these pitchstones, a black, rather porous piece of lava was found on the beach, which turned out to be a very clean augite andesite with olivine, a basalt, if you wish, which under the microscope appeared to be composed of a dark glassy material.

And this ends my story. We started our return trip to Batavia at 8 o'clock in the evening, thankful for the beauty and for a spectacle which made a deep impression on all and an unforgettable one on most.

Following the reports of this important expedition, widely publicized in the Java newspapers, H.O. Forbes added this cautionary note:[12]

After the 28th [of May], curiosity in these volcanic phenomena seems to have abated, and during the next eight or nine weeks, though the eruption continued with great vigour, little is recorded of its progress; indeed so completely did it seem to have been forgotten, that visitors to Batavia, unless they had made inquiries, might have failed to hear of its existence at all. During this period no local disturbances to attract attention or to cause the least alarm are recorded. From the logs of ships in the neighbourhood of the Straits, about the middle of August, numerous extracts have been published; but many of them show that they have been written either with the mind bewildered and confused by the terrifying incidents amid which the officers found themselves, or from the after-recollection of the events, of which under such conditions the important dry facts of time, place, and succession, are liable to be unconsciously misstated. Much is therefore lost which might have been known; but a few are of the utmost value.

In June, Seaman Dalby, 21 years old and 6 months away from England on the Liverpool barque Hope, *first saw Krakatau. He recorded his recollections in 1937, at age 75, for radio, and the first of two excerpts from that account*[13] *follows:*

We were lying off Anjer, a town of 25,000 inhabitants, at the western end of Java, on the Straits of Sunda, which lie between Java and Sumatra. We were awaiting orders, Anjer being a calling station for this purpose. It was a real paradise, a profusion of vegetation rising from the seashore to the summit of hills several thousand feet high. I well remember one particular evening, just at the time when the land and sea breezes were at rest, the very atmosphere impressed one with a mystical awe. It was enhanced by the subtle scent of the spice trees, so plentiful on the island, and, to crown it all, the sweet yet weird and melancholy chant of some natives, paddling their canoe close in to the dark shore. There were three of us in the boat, and we rested a long time trying to take in the strange grandeur of our surroundings; it was at this time that we noticed a long straight column of black smoke, going up from the peak of Krakatoa Island. . . .

In late June a second column of vapor and ash was recognized, with a new vent on Danan joining the earlier vent on the lower flank of Perboewatan to the NW. Tenison-Woods reports:[3]

There was a kind of lull at Krakatoa until the 16th of June, when another outburst was heard at Anjer, but a thick bank of smoke and ash remained over the island for five days. When this was dispelled by an east wind on Sunday, the 24th, the inhabitants of Anjer could see two dense columns of smoke ascending, the larger being on the north side of the island. Very slight shocks of earthquakes began to be felt, and then for a time all was quiet again, except an occasional booming like a distant gun.

Explosions increased at the end of the month,[14] *however, and additional evidence of vigorous pre-*

August volcanism comes from pumice masses floating in the Indian Ocean.[15]

. . . after passing, in the R.M.S. *Quetta*, the Straits of Sunda on July 9 last (having sailed close under the then active Krakatoa), we traversed a continuous field, unbroken as far as the eye could reach, of pumice, every day till the evening of the 12th, when our position must have been six hours (60 miles) to the west of our noon position, 93°54′E long. and 5°53′S lat. Capt. Templeton assured me that there was, singularly enough, a current against us all the way from the Straits of one-third of a mile per hour. There can be no doubt that this pumice came from Krakatoa. . . . The pumice knobs were all water worn, and a few had barnacles of about one inch in length growing on them.

The last person known to walk on northern Krakatau before its destruction was Captain H.J.G. Ferzenaar, Chief of the Surveying Brigade in Bantam. He visited the island on August 11 to assess the feasibility of a detailed survey. The sketch map that he made on that brief visit (Figure 11) remains the most detailed topographic description of the island before its collapse on August 26–27. Ferzenaar's private report to the Chief of the Topographic Service, as reprinted by Verbeek,[16] *begins:*

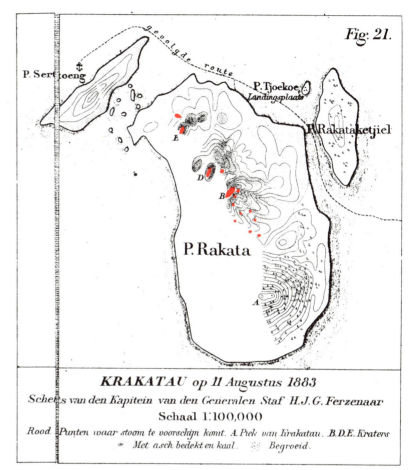

KRAKATAU op 11 Augustus 1883

Schets van den Kapitein van den Generalen Staf H.J.G. Ferzenaar

Schaal 1:100,000

Rood Punten waar stoom te voorschijn komt. A. Piek van Krakatau. B.D.E. Kraters
Met asch bedekt en kaal. *Begroeid.*

Figure 11. Sketch map prepared by Captain H.J.G. Ferzenaar on August 11, 1883. Captain Ferzenaar was the last person to set foot on the island prior to the paroxysmal eruptions of August 26 and 27, 1883. "A" is Rakata Peak; "B," "D," and "E" are craters; and red indicates active vents. Stipple pattern indicates areas covered with ash, and heavier stipple pattern indicates destruction of vegetation as well. Dashed line shows route followed by Ferzenaar. Long dimension of main island is 8.5 km. This map is figure 21 in Verbeek's Atlas.

On the evening of the 10th, I went by proah majang (inland vessel) to Po. Rakata, returning to Tjaringin on the evening of the 12th. The Governor of Tjaringin was unable to keep his promise to accompany me, so I made the trip alone.

A survey of the island has to wait until later, because measuring there is still too dangerous; at least I would not like to accept the responsibility of sending a surveyor. I made a sketch of the island on a scale of 1:100,000 with branches at 50 m distance, which is herewith offered. The outline of the islands is reproduced from the marine map of Sunda Strait; the heights are estimates, while the shape of the terrain was sketched as I travelled around. I did not sail around the west and south sides—the west side because we would then be downwind and heavy smoke would obscure every-

thing anyway. The route we followed is indicated by a dotted line.

The part represented by fine dots is completely devastated; some tree stumps are left, but the area is completely bare of branches and leaves. The ground at the beach is covered with a layer of ash, approximately 0.5 m thick. The tops, from which most smoke rose, are marked B, D, and E. Colossal, dirty grayish white- and pink-colored columns of smoke still appeared continuously. In the other places which are marked in red, smoke was also rising, but to a lesser extent. At the tops *C* and *E* the earlier eruption (of 1680) must have taken place; these parts are also totally bare without any sign of earlier trees. According to a local, who was my guide and who had been there several times before, there were only rocks, no vegetation; those rocks are now all covered with ash. The NW portion of top *B* burst apart (or collapsed) during the recent eruption.

Poeloe Sertoeng (Verlaten Island) is covered with a layer of ash; the trees are still there, but all are bare. Po. Rakata Ketjiel (Lang Island) and Tjoekoe (Poolsche Hoed) suffered the least; there, the leaves on the trees were charred only on the west side. The direction of the eruption, therefore, must have been to the NW.

I did some digging on the beach and found the top layer to consist of gray ash, ash mixed with sulphur underneath, and at last pumice; these stones thus seemed to have been ejected first. [Verbeek describes these specimens starting on p. 255.]

A large portion of Po. Rakata could be mapped from the other islands, but I consider a survey on the island itself inadvisable.

Ferzenaar's caution was well advised. During the following two weeks, several ships in the Straits reported vigorous ashfall (see Chronology), and more distant observations of stratospheric effects indicate that these eruptions were not trivial.[17] The day after Ferzenaar's visit, the Dutch man-of-war Prins Hendrik passed close to Krakatau and Mr. McLeod's account[18] of the vent locations is puzzlingly different from Ferzenaar's. In describing the vents as near sea level, he supports the Beyerinck account reprinted near the start of this section but conflicts with Ferzenaar. McLeod's account, which follows, is not mentioned by Verbeek, the Royal Society report, or Furneaux, and we are unable to resolve this difference.

My ship closely approached the island on August 12 of this year, thus 14 days before the large eruption. I passed the island on the north side and could see clearly where the new opening of the crater was. It appeared to be a small hole, maybe 100 ft in diameter, only a few meters above sea level. From the opening hot water vapor rose with great velocity. It probably was steam mixed with other fine divided material and the color was grayish. It shot out in a straight column and started condensing a few hundred feet above the opening, slowly forming larger and larger clouds, which rose higher and higher. Measured from a suitable distance later the column height was 3400 m. . . . Besides rising, part of the column also turned downwards creating a thick fog on the other side of the island, which spread as far as the eye could see. The irritating smell of sulfurous acid could be clearly sensed in the cloud. A continuous rumbling could be heard apparently coming from high up in the cloud; toward evening there were continuous small flashes of lightning. During the time I spent cruising in the Sunda Strait, I also noticed in the evening that neutralization of electricity appeared to occur between the volcanic cloud and the atmosphere. Krakatau and nearby islands, except for Verlaten Island, seemed to have suffered little thus far. Only this island and the part of Krakatau NW of the crater (that is, downwind of the dominating monsoon) appeared covered with a thick layer of yellow grayish ash originating from the May 20 eruption site. A few places a fine light-blue smoke rose, making one think of wood smoldering under the ash.

The last of the ship reports was from the mail steamer Princes Wilhelmina, and excerpts from the log of Captain Visman read:[19]

Thursday, August 23th at the entrance of Sunda Straits coming from the west, passed between the islands of Krakatau and Sebesie; had during about an hour to pass through a rain of very fine dust of light brown colour; to the east of Krakatau the sky clear again, wind ESE, light breezes.

Heavy clouds of smoke arising from the crater on the NW side of the island. Verlaten Island and Krakatau covered with a gray dust and trees quite leafless. Barometer 763.5. Therm. 28.5°C.

Saturday August 25th. In the afternoon about 7 shakes and heavy blows in the distance were heard (as from thunder) in the W and WSW. Wind variable. Bar: 762. Therm. 29°C.

August 26–27: The Paroxysm

Volcanic activity at Krakatau was vigorous in August, but increased dramatically on Sunday, August 26th, and culminated the next day. For close descriptions of activity at the volcano itself, we must again rely on the ships that happened to be in the Sunda Straits at the time, but the coastal areas on either side were heavily populated, and the paroxysmal events of August 26–27—the sounds, the ashfall, the darkness, and particularly the devastating sea waves—brought the volcano to these coastal residents. We start our selection of August 26–27 eyewitness acounts with descriptions by survivors from these coastal areas, then move to shipboard accounts from the Straits, and finally to more distant areas affected by the eruption (but only after much of the drama had been played out unknown to them).

Java Coast

The most heavily populated and prosperous area near Krakatau was Java's west coast. This meant that it had the largest number of victims, but also the largest number of survivors, and a ready market for the written descriptions of their harrowing experiences. We have selected 5 eyewitness accounts from the Java coast, but first give a pre-eruption description of Anjer, the west coast's main city.

The Illustrated London News[20] mentions

. . .the well-known commercial port of Anjer, where all homeward bound ships of every nation were accustomed to call in passing the Straits, to obtain needful supplies for the voyage across the Indian Ocean. Java sparrows were usually purchased at Anjer, for presents to friends at home; but they would often die on the first cold night.

The following description of Anjer is by Tenison-Woods in the Sydney Morning Herald:[3]

All those who have come to Australia by the Queensland mail line must remember both Krakatau

and Anjer. The latter was the first township met in the Straits after passing the lighthouse. European vessels generally stopped there to take a pilot, and newcomers were always delighted with the beautiful aspect of the bay. The shore was fringed by a close growth of cocoa-nut palms, backed by a dense shade of tropical fruit trees, such as jack fruit, mango and plantain. Amidst this foliage, solid white buildings with red-tiled roofs peeped out here and there. In the distance were two high volcanic ranges, lying NE and SE. The town was exceedingly pretty. Buried in shade, it was in a wide picturesque valley, while the Resident's house fronted a magnificent green esplanade beautifully shaded by the drooping branches of the warignen trees. The European residents were hardly more than 50, living, as in most Javanese towns, in picturesque tropical villas, enclosed with the usual Dutch gardens. But there was a large population otherwise. The town had a Chinese quarter, full of shops; an Arab quarter, somewhat like it, though smaller; and a very large campong of Javanese or Sundanese. The district was the ancient kingdom of Bantam, from which the kings or sultans were only finally deposed about 40 years ago. It has long had a place in history. The Dutch and English contended for its possession for some years ere the former prevailed, and near Anjer there are the ruins of an old fort built 250 years since, and built so solidly that even the tidal wave which destroyed almost everything broke over that and left it standing [see Figure 14, p. 75]. Anjer was connected with Batavia by a magnificent post road, well metalled and shaded by a perfect avenue of tamarind trees. There were post houses and stables built every six miles. The teeming population of the rich surrounding district kept this road a scene of ceaseless activity. Within a radius of five miles round Anjer some 20 populous campongs might be counted. Thus morning, noon, and even night, the picturesque throng of market women, native officials, and the characteristic thatched carts with their pairs of bramin bulls or single buffaloes made the road a varied panorama of life and industry such as can only be seen in Java.

To this thriving city, on the evening of August 25, came the newly appointed Telegraph-master. Mr. Schruit's story [21] begins:

Not knowing Anjer, I had left my wife and children at Batavia, with the intention to bring them to my

Figure 12. Anjer, as seen from the sea. Upper engraving, from The Graphic of September 8, 1883 (p. 244) was titled "View of Anjer, showing the [Fourth Point] lighthouse," and was from a sketch by C.H. Rosher of London. The lower engraving, from the Illustrated London News of September 8, 1883 (p. 225) was titled "East coast and islands of the Straits of Sunda, with Anjer, a port of Java."

Figure 13. Anjer scenes before the tsunami of August 27. Photographs from the 1895 account of J.T. van Gestel (see p. 162). Residence was van Gestel's, and street scene showed large "warignen" (banyan) tree later uprooted and washed away by the tsunami.

new station as soon as I had got a house ready to receive them. It is hardly necessary to say that on my arrival I took up my quarters in the hotel, and sought acquaintances first amongst the members of my department with whom I passed the Saturday evening very agreeably.

The next day I went direct to the office to ascertain its condition, and found the dwelling-house most agreeable and commodious, it lay close to the beach, and the view from it was extensive and fine; so that I much regretted not having at once brought my family with me. How thankful was I, however, a few hours later that Providence had thus guided me. I remained at the office the whole morning up to l o'clock p.m., and then went for a meal, intending to return at 2 o'clock. In the meantime, I met another telegraphist near the beach, and we remained there for a few minutes. Krakatau was already in eruption, and we plainly heard the rumbling of an earthquake in the distance. Looking seaward, I observed an alternate rising and falling of the surface, and asked my companion whether the tide was ebbing or flowing? We thought it was ebb-tide, but a sudden rising of the water showed that such was not the case. Even after observing this appearance, I was far from doubting that the dreadful sea-quaking which had such calamitous consequences had already begun.

At about 6 o'clock, we remarked that it was unusually dark. Weltevreden [9 km S of Batavia] then signalled to us that the trembling of the earth was very severe, and asked if Krakatau was still in eruption. I replied that it was, and at once received a request to remain on the line till 7 o'clock. With this command, I charged one of my confrères, and signalled assent, when suddenly the line broke, and I obtained contact with the line that goes to Merak.

As soon a possible, I went with one of the telegraphists along the line, and ran through the fort, where I was told that a schooner had broken her cable. I proceeded to the landing place, which is a canal near the fort, and reached the draw-bridge the rails of which had already been knocked away. There, a fearful sight met my eyes; a schooner and twenty-five or thirty praws were being carried up and down between the draw-bridge and the ordinary bridge as the water rose and fell and nothing remained unbroken.

But we felt no alarm as the water did not overflow its banks. Not entertaining any idea of danger, I sat down to table at about half past 8.

Of course, I had made the necessary arrangements for beginning the repair of the broken line the first thing in the morning.

In the course of the evening, I had frequent occasion to exert my powers of persuasion in the endeavour to reassure several ladies who were greatly alarmed and excited by the surrounding phenomena, and indeed not without reason. Krakatau began, a little later in the evening, an active eruption; a violent thunder-storm broke over us, and the ground shook and trembled as if "the day of judgement" had come.

At half-past 9, the elements had apparently calmed down, and a gentle shower of ashes began to fall; the sea was very still, so that everyone recovered his usual frame of mind.

For precaution I went out during the night, or about l o'clock in the morning, to the canal to take another look at the damage done, accompanied by the harbour-master and two neighbours, but we could discover nothing more than the appearance already observed the previous afternoon, viz., the rising and falling of the surface of the sea. [This is the exact time, by other accounts,[22] that the village of Sirik, only 10 km S of Anjer, was partially submerged by a large wave.]

After my nocturnal visit, I went to bed and fell asleep. Suspecting no danger I rested till early in the morning of Monday, the 27th August, that unhappy day which will be written in history with such sanguinary letters. At about a quarter after 5, I was dressed and out near the bridge, where the line-watcher and telegraphist were already busy with the repair of the line.

I there met some of the towns-people; amongst others Nevianus Schmit, who, after hearing my account of what had happened, kindly offered to fetch me a cup of tea. Whilst I was expecting this friendly mark of attention, I happened to look up and perceived an enormous wave in the distance looking like a mountain rushing onwards, followed by two others that seemed still greater. I stood for an instant on the bridge horrified at the sight, but had sufficient presence of mind to warn the telegraphist and line-watcher of the danger, and then ran as fast as my legs could carry me. The roaring wave followed as fast, knocking to atoms everything that came in its way.

Never have I run so fast in my life, for, in the most literal sense of the word, death was at my heels; and it was the thought of my wife and our children, who would be left destitute by my losing my life, that gave me superhuman strength. The flood-wave was hardly thirty paces from me. It had destroyed the draw-bridge, the hotel, the house of the Assistant Resident, in short everything that it struck.

At last, I fell utterly exhausted with my race against death, on a rising ground, and saw to my amazement the wave retreating. I gasped for breath, but a hearty offering of thanks to Heaven rose through my choking throat, for my deliverance and for the Providential care by which my family had been left in Batavia. Had they been at Anjer, there would bave been no chance of safety, for I should at the first sight of the danger have hastened to their assistance, in which case we must all have been drowned.

An elderly Dutch pilot, employed in guiding ships through the Straits, gave this account[23] of his experience:

I have lived in Anjer all my life, and little thought the old town would have been destroyed in the way it has. I am getting on in years, and quite expected to have laid my bones in the little cemetery near the shore, but not even that has escaped, and some of the bodies have actually been washed out of the graves and carried out to sea. The whole town has been swept away, and I have lost everything except my life. The wonder is that I escaped at all. I can never be too thankful for such a miraculous escape as I had.

The eruption began on the Sunday afternoon. We did not take much notice at first, until the reports grew very loud. Then we noticed that Krakatoa was completely enveloped in smoke. Afterwards came on the thick darkness, so black and intense that I could not see my hand before my eyes. It was about this time that a message came from Batavia inquiring as to the explosive shocks, and the last telegram sent off from us was telling you about the darkness and smoke. Towards night everything became worse. The reports became deafening, the natives cowered down panic-stricken, and a red fiery glare was visible in the sky above the burning mountain. Although Krakatoa was twenty-five miles away, the concussion and vibration from the constantly repeated shocks was most terrifying. Many of the houses shook so much that we feared every minute would bring them down. There was little sleep for any of us that dreadful night. Before daybreak on Monday, on going out of doors, I found

the shower of ashes had commenced, and this gradually increased in force until at length large pieces of pumice-stone kept falling around. About six a.m. I was walking along the beach. There was no sign of the sun, as usual, and the sky had a dull, depresssing look. Some of the darkness of the previous day had cleared off, but it was not very light even then. Looking out to sea I noticed a dark black object through the gloom, travelling towards the shore.

At first sight it seemed like a low range of hills rising out of the water, but I knew there was nothing of the kind in that part of the Soenda Strait. A second glance—and a very hurried one it was—convinced me that it was a lofty ridge of water many feet high, and worse still, that it would soon break upon the coast near the town. There was no time to give any warning, and so I turned and ran for my life. My running days have long gone by, but you may be sure that I did my best. In a few minutes I heard the water with a loud roar break upon the shore. Everything was engulfed. Another glance around showed the houses being swept away and the trees thrown down on every side. Breathless and exhausted I still pressed on. As I heard the rushing waters behind me, I knew that it was a race for life. Struggling on, a few yards more brought me to some rising ground, and here the torrent of water overtook me. I gave up all for lost, as I saw with dismay how high the wave still was. I was soon taken off my feet and borne inland by the force of the resistless mass. I remember nothing more until a violent blow aroused me. Some hard firm substance seemed within my reach, and clutching it I found I had gained a place of safety. The waters swept past, and I found myself clinging to a cocoanut palm-tree. Most of the trees near the town were uprooted and thrown down for miles, but this one fortunately had escaped and myself with it.

The huge wave rolled on, gradually decreasing in height and strength until the mountain slopes at the back of Anjer were reached, and then, its fury spent, the waters gradually receded and flowed back into the sea. The sight of those receding waters haunts me still. As I clung to the palm-tree, wet and exhausted, there floated past the dead bodies of many a friend and neighbour. Only a mere handful of the population escaped. Houses and streets were completely destroyed, and scarcely a trace remains of where the once busy, thriving town originally stood. Unless you go yourself to see the ruin you will never believe how completely the place has been swept away. Dead bodies, fallen trees, wrecked houses, an immense muddy morass and great pools of water, are all that is left of the town where my life has been spent. My home and all my belongings of course perished—even the clothes I am wearing are borrowed—but I am thankful enough to have escaped with my life, and to be none the worse for all that I have passed through.

A younger Anjer resident, whose running days were not yet behind him, also escaped the wave, and later gave the following account [24] to Reverend Neale (see p. 120).

I had heard the deafening reports from Krakatoa on Sunday afternoon, and had seen later on the dense black smoke and the glare of fiery light resting upon the summit of the volcano. Still we all hoped for the best. But on the following morning, when the darkness remained instead of light, and the shower of ashes increased, I grew more alarmed. It seemed to me that if matters got worse we should be completely buried by falling lava, like some of the places in olden times were, and that a dreadful death awaited us if we remained in the town. I therefore thought it best to get as far away from Krakatoa as possible. It was still quite early when I decided upon making for the neighbouring hills, several miles distant. I had a number of relations living in the town, but they seemed to fancy themselves safe enough at home, and they accordingly remained behind. I never saw any of them again alive. Five of them perished, and, worst of all, only two of their bodies were recovered. These were found buried beneath the ruined house in which they met their end, and were scarcely recognisable. The others must have been carried out to sea, and probably formed part of the many hundreds seen later on floating in the Straits of Soenda by the captains of passing vessels. I had not proceeded a great distance from Anjer when the first volcanic wave broke upon the coast. Of course, even that one was terrible enough, but it was nothing to be compared with the second one, which followed a little later. I could see that the town had been seriously injured by the inundation, and no doubt some lives were lost even in that first overflow. Alarmed by what I had already noticed, I quickened my pace inland. The farther from the coast, I thought, the safer I should be, and so it proved. The site of Anjer is, for the most part, very level ground;

but four of five miles away are some hills, densely covered with cocoa-nut palm-trees. These formed a pretty background to the town. I decided to make to this rising ground as fast as I possibly could. As I proceeded I found some of my neighbours from Anjer making for the same spot. Some of them were fortunate enough to reach this place of safety before the final destruction came. Others whom I passed on the way were overtaken by the second wave, or rushing torrent, and at once found a watery grave.

Breathless with running, I came as fast as possible up the densely wooded slopes, and was only just in time. The great wave, sweeping all before it, was close on my heels as the rising ground brought me safely out of its reach. Its fury was much spent as it broke upon the hills, but it was very powerful even then. But the higher ground soon checked its force, and sent it back again towards the sea. Of the actual destruction I saw but little. I was too much frightened to stop and watch the ruin it caused. My one idea was to get as high up as I was able, and of course I thought of nothing else at the time.

There were some terrible scenes afterwards on the roads leading into the interior of the island. All the natives in the neighbouring *kampongs* turned against us, and refused those of us who had escaped the least help or food. Many of the Europeans—especially the women—exhausted with fatigue, and almost frightened out of their lives, were sinking down in a helpless state by the wayside. Although the worst was over as regards the volcanic wave, many sank down and died on the road from exhaustion and neglect. Not only did many of the natives refuse to help us in the least, but they actually drove us fiercely from their houses. The reason of this was that . . . the Javanese are exceedingly superstitious, and attributed their misfortunes to us.

The first wave described in these accounts was not the largest to hit Anjer that morning, but the accounts vividly explain why there were few witnesses to the later waves. Tenison-Woods[3] discusses a second wave:

At 9 o'clock another tidal wave struck the coast. It was far higher than the first. From the mischief done at the Government quarry at the Island of Merak the water must have reached the almost incredible height

Figure 14. Destruction at Anjer. Photographs, probably taken in early 1886, by the Batavia firm of Woodbury and Page. The top scene, near the Fort, shows the setting of Anjer; the middle scene shows remains of the Anjer Hotel, where the young telegraph operator stayed just before the town was destroyed (see his account on p. 72); and the bottom scene shows all that was left of the massive fort walls. Photographs from the archives of the Royal Institute for the Tropics, Amsterdam.

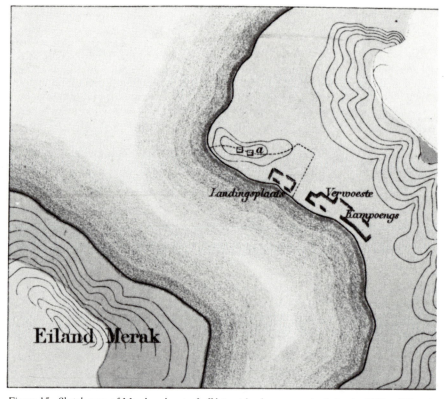

Figure 15. Sketch map of Merak and part of off-lying island (lower left) on the NW coast of Java. Shaded pattern paralleling coastline indicates areas destroyed by tsunami. The letter "a" indicates the destroyed hilltop house of Engineer Nieuwenhuijs (and site, in 1885, of New Anjer telegraph). The locations of the wharf ("landingsplaats") and destroyed villages ("verwoeste kampoengs") are also shown. Distance from wharf to island is 370 m. This map is figure 24 in Verbeek's Atlas.

of 180 ft [later estimates were 135 ft and less]. Anjer, and every trace of animal and vegetable life along the coast, was completely washed away. Nothing is known of the details. A telegraph operator sent to repair the line towards Anjer reported that as he approached the coast, at about 9 a.m., he had seen the ocean advancing like an enormous rampart of water, and that he had fled to the high ground. He knew nothing more except that he had heard an awful roaring noise as the sea struck the land, but he believed that Anjer and all the coast towns and villages were destroyed. Nothing more than this was known until the scene of the disaster was visited. Not one survivor remained to tell the tale of the how the second tidal wave overwhelmed Anjer.

The Fourth Point lighthouse, just south of Anjer, did survive the first wave, however. It was seen standing by a ship that passed at 8:30 that morning (see p. 103) although there were no signs of life at Anjer. Captain van Doorn, an early visitor to the devastated area, reports:[25]

It was a dreadful narrative which was related to us by a native, a lighthouse-keeper of Fourth Point, one of the few men at the lighthouse, who by a wonder was saved.

When the wave approached, all fled to the tower (the light was 46 m above the sea), which, though shaking, resisted the violent waves for a long time. It was a terrible moment, when at last an enormous rock, which was swept away by the stream, crushed the base of the tower, which then fell down. The man who was saved saw his wife and his children drowned before his eyes. He related this fact in the very resigned way of a Javanese, and considered it the most natural thing in the world that he was now obliged to light the interim light, which was erected as soon as possible.

The shape of a giant sea wave, as it hits the shoreline, depends greatly on the configuration of the ocean bottom approaching that shoreline, and the same wave may affect neighboring shorelines in very different ways. At Merak, 12 km N of Anjer, the Straits are both narrow and shallow. The waves were highest here—causing the above-mentioned "mischief" at Merak—and a Javanese survivor gave the following account when Neale visited Merak 6 weeks later:[26]

I was working a long way from the sea—four or five paalen [5–6 km] from the coast. A lot of other natives were with me in the *paddee* field. We were cultivating rice. We had gone to work as usual, in spite of the volcano. We did not think it would hurt us. And all of a sudden there came a great noise. We looked round at once and saw a great black thing, a long way off, coming towards us. It was very high and strong, and we soon saw that it was water. Trees and houses were washed away as it came along. The people near began to cry out and run for their lives. Not far off was some steep sloping ground. We all ran towards it and tried to climb up out of the way of the water. It was too quick for most of them, and many were drowned almost at my side. I managed to get a long way up, and then the water came very near to me. When I thought I was safe I looked back and saw the wave wash the people down one after the other as they tried to scramble out of its way. There was a general rush to climb up in one particular place. This caused a great block, and many of them got wedged together and could not move. Then they struggled and fought, screaming and crying out all the time. Those below tried to make those above them move on again by biting their heels. A great struggle took place for a few moments, but all was soon over. One after another they were washed down and carried far away by the rushing waters. You can see the marks on the side of the hill where this fight for life took place. Some of those who were washed off dragged others down with them. They would not let go their hold, nor could those above them release themselves from this death-grip. Many were high enough up to have altogether escaped if they had not thus been dragged down by their unfortunate companions.

Furneaux[27] adds more information about Merak:

One European and one native only survived at Merak. Twenty-seven hundred of its inhabitants died, including thirteen Europeans, among whom were K.A. Naumann and his wife, Overseer H.B. van Diest and his wife, Overseer J. Kaal, Machinist S.C. van Essen, his wife and four children, Storekeeper T.S. Townsend and his child.

The story of their deaths is one of the strangest of the whole disaster, for they were sheltered on top of the hill behind the town. It was 130 ft high, yet the great wave roared up its slopes and destroyed all the stone-built European houses on its top, leaving only the foundation of Naumann's house. [Another account[65] gives the hill height as 115 ft and the wave as 135 ft, or 41 m, above sea level.] Works Accountant E. Peckler saw the wave coming. He ran further up the hill, the wave gaining upon him. He fell exhausted, expecting to be engulfed. Looking back he saw the wave rushing towards him. Heaving himself up, he ran further, falling on his knees and losing consciousness. When he regained his senses, he saw the wave receding. All the houses were gone. Engineer Abell also saw the wave. He left Merak at 7:30 that morning to report to his chief in Batavia. Looking back from the mountain road, he saw "a colossal wave" roaring up the shore. It was higher that the highest coconut palm, he recalled later. No one in its path could have survived, he told his chief. The wall of water rushed over the land, looking like something he could not have "dreamed in a nightmare."

Other accounts from the coast between Merak and Anjer were gathered by Tenison-Woods:[3]

A survivor on the coast north of Anjer related to me some of what followed. The ashes fell more thickly and the detonations were every moment more continuous and violent until it began a sustained and

Figure 16. "Before and after" scenes at Merak. Etching at top shows dwellings of Europeans employed at the Merak stone quarries (from Illustrated London News, 8 September, 1883). Photograph at bottom, apparently of the same general area as seen above, shows destruction of railroad tracks, scattering of industrial debris, and the total absence of any structures on the level surface in the middle background (from archives of the Royal Institute for the Tropics, Amsterdam).

awful roar, which seemed to crush out every other sound. The inhabitants showed the utmost alarm. The Chinese, collecting what valuables they could gather, made their way down to the sea beach, and tried to secure boats. In the villages there was much confusion. Even the lamps they carried gave scarcely a glimmer through the falling ash. The roads or streets could not be made out. Only at intervals could voices be heard. The crowd on the beach increased, but here a new phenomenon was manifested—the sea was violently agitated. Those who were trying to get into boats found the waters advancing and receding to an alarming extent; at one moment the boats would be left high and dry, and next the crowd would be swept back by a swelling tide. Many no doubt were drowned in this manner. The sea was evidently feeling the effect of those explosions which move from the flooding of the crater. Soon the water began to rise and fall as much as 10 ft at intervals of quarter of an hour, smashing all the craft and strewing the beach with wreckage. Those who would reach the villages again did so where the way was strewn with prostrate forms, uttering loud cries and prayers. The ash aggregating in the steam began to fall in large lumps, crushing through the branches and causing loss of life. An Englishman at Chikaudie Ndie [100 km E of Krakatau], writes:—"Every one was afoot. The reports sounded louder and louder, until the ground shook sensibly. . . . Evening set in. The detonations far from diminishing increased in violence, startling the people with new cries every two or three minutes."

No doubt many would have escaped to the hills that night, but the question was whither were they to go. The darkness made every road impassable. The only safe place was the hills, but few would think so. Once past the cultivated grounds, the jungle of the hillside is pathless, and swarms with wild beasts. No doubt some did try and escape towards Batavia, but the road lies along the coast, and here, in due time, the waters swept them away.

Imagination may try to picture the last night in the history of these places, the last of the earthly existence of so many. In pitchy darkness and sulphurous fumes that were stifling, those who had the shelter of houses remained under cover. Mothers gathered their children around them awaiting the return of light to find some way of escape. During the lingering hours six very severe shocks of earthquake were felt, so that the houses were abandoned. The roaring of the sea became fearful. At 2 o'clock in the morning a frightful explosion and concussion was heard at Batavia, and such was its force that the gaslights in the streets and houses were extinguished. All fled to the streets. The sound and the cause of it must have been of appalling magnitude. It was heard not only at Batavia but at Singapore, and even at Penang, some 900 miles away. What it was to the poor inhabitants of the coast can scarcely be told. In the confusion and fears of this night of horrors even the few who survived have little to tell. Morning brought no light, but it brought an end to the sufferings of all save a few. About six in the morning the great roar of the first tidal wave was heard. A rushing wind was driven before it as it came on like an immense dark wall. Its height has been variously computed at from 50 to 100 ft. Need it be said that it bore down all before it? One of the survivors records "I suddenly heard a cry 'Bunjir datant,'—a flood is coming, and turning round I saw in the distance, an enormous, black-looking mass of water, appearing at first sight mountains high, rush on with a fearful roar and lightning-like rapidity. At the next moment I was swept off my feet, and found myself struggling amidst the waters thinking that my hour was come." This man was caught in a cocoanut palm, and from thence got on to the floating wreckage of a house roof. He adds—"I looked around and a fearful sight met my eyes. Where Anjer stood I saw nothing but a foaming and furiously rushing flood above the surface of which only a couple of trees and tops of houses were visible. Presently the water fell with great rapidity and flowed back into the sea. I saw it ebb away from under my feet. I again stood on firm ground. But what a sight met my half stupefied gaze. It was a scene of the utmost confusion. Immense quantities of broken furniture, beams, broken earthenware, amid human corpses formed heaps and masses on every side; I crept on my knees over the ruins and the dead, often entangled amid corpses, their garments, and house spoil. At last I reached higher ground in the neighbourhood of the Chinese quarter, where I met one sole Chinese survivor who gave me some brandy."

This survivor escaped along the high road to Serang. Some natives and Europeans who were on the hill at the Residency also escaped. The waters just swept the summit and threw the inmates of the houses off their feet, but was not deep enough to drown many. When the waves retired, all who could do so fled to the hills or along the road, but the number was but a handful compared to those who had perished. At this time many houses were left standing and the place was not utterly ruined. This is all we know.

This survivor's escape to the interior[28] takes us back to the Telegraph-master whose account started this chapter (p. 69). His continued report describes conditions inland on that fateful morning.[21]

As soon as I recovered my breath, I ran on to Kares [4 km SSE of Anjer], where I was out of danger, and where I obtained writing materials from the Assistant Wedono and wrote a service-report to the Chief Inspector and to the Resident of Bantam, which I sent by a messenger. As soon as this service was performed, I thought it my duty to return to Anjer, to endeavour to save anything that could be saved. But I had hardly got outside the house, when I perceived a lady rushing towards me with frightful anxiety and almost without clothes. This was Madam S———, the poor lady who had had the misfortune to lose her two children, and who had been obliged to leave her husband in the next village, with his spine injured, to hasten for assistance. We offered all the help we could, and borrowed for the sorely tried woman a sarong and kabaya (articles of native clothing). And we requested the Assistant Wedono to have a litter prepared so that we might go in search of Mr. S———. In the meantime it was half-past 9, when we were ready to turn our steps towards Anjer. Kares is about 2½ miles from Anjer; and after having walked about a mile through a slight shower of ashes, all of a sudden we heard a frightful sound in the direction of Krakatau, followed by a heavy fall of ashes and flashes of lightning. We continued our march, and heard in quick succession four more claps of thunder, after which the noise calmed by degrees. Then commenced a heavy mud-rain which was terrific in the extreme. Many escaped natives from Anjer came to meet us, making loud lamentations and calling out *"Ayer datang, tuan, tuan ada di blakan."* "Water coming, the gentlemen are behind."

Immediately on this warning we took a cross cut and ran till we reached the village of Jahat. The occupants of this village, which consisted of four or five houses, dragged us in, as it were; and as it had become pitch dark notwithstanding the mud rain, they came out to meet us with torches. It was evident that these poor people were glad to see Europeans amongst them, and that their presence diminished their dread and anxiety.

At that moment the weather was most dreadful; the cracking of the trees, the snapping off of bamboos,

the heavy rain and the thick darkness combined to make me think it an image of hell. In the place where I found myself there were about 150 people who had fled from the surrounding dangers, Chinese and natives together; and as I observed some of them drinking water in a reckless manner, I made inquiries as to the supply, and at once took possession of all there was at hand. The number of refugees continued to increase, and as their first cry was for water, I began to fear that necessary of life would run short. So I sat upon the water vat, and quenched the thirst of the crowd by means of small draughts.

But the little crowd was by no means so quiet and still as natives and Chinese usually are in the presence of Europeans. They began to lament their hard lot and to complain more or less against the "Company"* who, by the war against Atjeh [NW Sumatra], was the cause of all disasters. Towards me and the other Europeans they were however very obliging, and they seemed to derive consolation from our assurances. They followed our movements, and declared that they would go wherever we went.

At first going any further was out of the question, for each and all had need of rest. There was no help for it. We formed a kind of circle, those that could not sleep remained sitting, and thus we passed full 17 hours. At 3 o'clock in the morning the moon appeared, and I took the opportunity of reconnoitering the neighbourhood. Whilst thus engaged, I met a Sundanese woman, who asked me if I wanted biscuits, and on my affirmative answer I got about twenty water-crackers, which I shared fraternally with my companions—we had had no food since 9 o'clock the previous morning. When it became light, about 5 o'clock, we started on our way towards Anjer. We took a supply of torches with us and advised the natives and Chinese to go to Mantjah [9 km SE of Anjer], where they would soon receive succour from the authorities, as I had already reported its need to the Resident. After a fatiguing walk under heavy showers of mud, through which we came to places where we sank a foot in mud, we at length reached Kares. The house of the Assistant Wedono had fallen in, and Madame Schuit, together with the family of the Wedono, was in the

*The Government is still spoken of by the natives of Java generally as the "Company," although the existence of the old Company ceased on the annexation of Holland to France. [The editor of the Ceylon Observer here adds "that 'Company Jau' is still believed by the mass of Hindus to rule India. All public gardens in India are termed 'Company Bagh.' "]

mesijit (a small mosque), into which we entered. We did not hear a word of reproach on account of this desecration. Indeed one obliging native brought us cigarettes which were by many gladly lighted. The ladies received us with great joy; they had passed a wretched night like ourselves, and escaping from the ruined house, they had stood in the showers of mud until they held up.

After the Wedono had had food cooked for us, my messenger returned from Anjer, and declared that there was no longer any such place, and that its site was not approachable. The Wedono advised us not to attempt to reach it, but considered it best to climb up a hill for the purpose of trying ourselves to ascertain what had become of Anjer. We then started, Madame S. accompanied us, and we soon reached the hill. The site where Anjer had once stood was before us, but every vestige of it was level with the ground; not a tree, not a house, nothing was there left. The sight was fearful, and the impression it made on the refugees was most sad.

We therefore decided to turn our backs on the site of Anjer, and took our way along a road all but impassable, from fallen trees, broken branches, and the showers of mud. This road led to Geintoen. We got there about 10 o'clock, and were again supplied with food, there was not much, but it was a great relief to us. At 11 o'clock the doctor with his family arrived, and as the ladies were too much fatigued to go any further, it was decided that only the men would undertake the journey to Mantjah.

About half-a-mile from that place we met the horses which the Resident had sent for our use, and close to Mantjah we found the Resident himself and his suite. At Mantjah, there were come some other refugees and among them Madame B., and after being refreshed with a draught of wine we went on to Tjelegon [15 km E of Anjer], and remained there till 8 o'clock the following morning, when we began the journey to Serang. After a few more mischances and great fatigue we arrived there. I was kindly entertained by the Controller, and began slowly to recover from the fatigues I had undergone, thankful indeed to the Almighty that my life had been spared.

Sumatra Coast

Although less populated than the Java coast, part of the Sumatra coast is significantly closer to Krakatau and directly in the path of the main volcanic blasts. Many residents who escaped the giant sea waves perished from burns. Furthermore, the bays of Sumatra were completely blocked by floating pumice from the eruption, and news of this region was slow to reach Java and the world. Tenison-Woods[3] describes this most devastated region, immediately north of Krakatau, as seen by the first rescuers:

The district of Katimbang is a series of villages which lie along the seashore, at the foot of a lofty and perfectly conical volcanic mountain, called Rajah Bassa. It is near the eastern entrance of Lampong Bay, and hardly 15 miles from Krakatoa. All along the coast the country was devastated, and the ground covered with a layer of ashes. It was a search party from Batavia that made their way through this, and ascended the hills with great difficulty. They found that the inhabitants had fled to a place called Kali Antoe [Kalianda?, 8 km N of Katimbang]. This village was wholly destroyed. The houses had nearly all fallen in, owing to the weight of ash on the roof. In fact, only one was standing where the Controller and his family and a European clerk were found. They were in a deplorable condition, and covered with burns. They were all removed on litters. The account they gave of the night of the eruption was fearful. In the expressive language of one of them, "No human tongue could tell what happened. I think hell is the only word applicable to what we saw and went through. I am sure I was burnt mainly by fire that spurted out of the ground as we went along. At first, thinking only of the glowing ash showers, we endeavoured to shelter ourselves under beds, taking the risk of the house falling in, which no doubt it did on a great many, but the hot ashes came up through the crevices of the floor, and burned us still more."

The rescued Controller and family were the Beyerincks, whose description of the eruption's beginning in May is reprinted above (p. 61). The

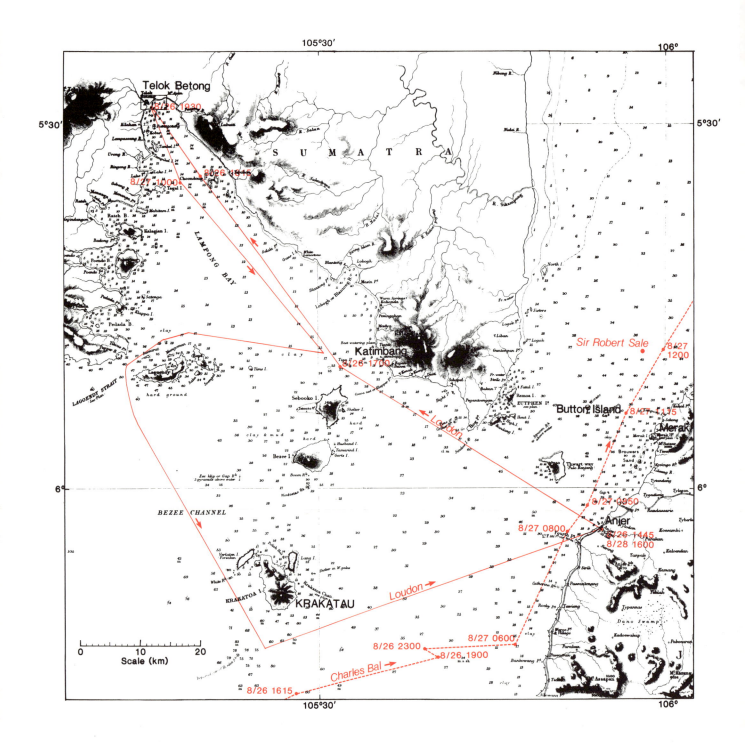

Beyerincks' story, as assembled by Rupert Furneaux,[29] continues with the beginning of the paroxysmal phase on Sunday afternoon, August 26.

It is difficult to discern from Mrs. Beyerinck's long and agonised story what she and her husband saw and heard at that time. They were less than twenty-four miles from the point of eruption, closer than any [surviving narrators] except Captain Watson of the *Charles Bal.* Mrs. Beyerinck says she heard a distinct noise and noticed that Krakatoa was no longer visible, being surrounded by pitch-black clouds through which the sun looked blood red and its rays reddish. She does not remark on the size or shape of the cloud or the intensity of the explosions which others observed so accurately. Between 1 p.m. on August 26th and September 1st when she and her husband were rescued, Mrs. Beyerinck underwent an experience that almost unhinged her mind. Her actions on reaching home that day bespeak her fears; what she saw and heard must have frightened her nearly out of her wits.

· · · · ·

Controller Beyerinck went to the beach, where he saw the *Loudon* steaming up the coast on her voyage to Telok Betong, and he watched heavy waves throwing native proas on shore, where they were dashed to pieces. The highest waves reached the outbuildings of his own house. By 8 p.m. Mr. Beyerinck's mind was made up. He sent his clerk, Mr. Tojaka, to his wife with the message to prepare herself and the children for immediate flight. The children were to be warmly dressed, and she was to give them a good meal. Mrs. Beyerinck had got the children dressed sometime before the message came, but she herself was still wearing a sarong. In her story, which was published in several Javanese newspapers, Mrs. Beyerinck de-

Figure 17. British Admirality Chart of 1875, showing relationship of Krakatau to Katimbang, 40 km NNE on the flank of Mt. Raja Bassa. Locations of detailed maps shown for Merak (Figure 15) and Telok Betong (Figure 19). Also superimposed are the tracks of the Loudon and the Charles Bal. From the collections of the Library of Congress, Geography and Map Division.

scribed the last wretched evening she spent at her home, surrounded by her faithful servants.

If I shut my eyes, I see it all before me, the pieces of chicken, the rice and my faithful young Radjah exhorting me to eat. "You must eat, Madam, for you don't know what is going to happen. Come now, take a little rice." He served some up but I could not get it down. It was as if my throat was sealed. I went to the front balcony. The pumice had been falling for hours but in pieces no bigger than peas. Then I saw someone coming up the garden with a lantern. It was Jeroemoeidi (one of her servants), who said to me in a very worried manner "The *Antoe Laoet* (the Sea Ghost) is close by. The sea has gone. Far, far away I hear the waves." "How can it have gone? Perhaps it is at low ebb?" I asked. "Come and see. It should now be high tide. It is a worrying sight, for all the coral reefs along the coast, which at the lowest ebb lie a fathom below the surface and which I can sail over in my sloop, are now dried out." A whole lot of natives now came up to the house and corroborated Jeroemoeidi's story.

My eldest boy was playing with the *ayah* on the sofa. My eldest girl was standing in the bedroom. I was lying on the bed and the maid was standing near me. I was feeding my youngest son. Then I heard, above the noise of the pumice falling on the roof, above the thunder from the mountain, a frightful roaring which approached at lightning speed. My hair stood on end. I leapt up clutching my youngest child and shouted, "Come here, come here, everyone together." The wave reached the house but it didn't go further than the back yard. It destroyed the office and surrounding outhouses, and my husband and Mr. Tojaka were only just able to escape with their lives by climbing up a cocoa-nut tree after they had fled from the office. As soon as the wave receded my husband dashed to the house, but he could not get upstairs as the stairs had been washed away. He shouted, "Wife, wife, come downstairs quickly, just jump and I'll catch you," and to the servant he called, "Turn the horses and animals loose."

It must have been about 8:30 p.m. when the Beyerinck family began their flight into the interior, an experience Mrs. Beyerinck hoped she would never have to go through again. They did not dare take the coastal road and they were forced to walk through an extensive paddy field full of water, and then through a wood in which there was no path. They sank into mud at every step. Sometimes it reached Mrs. Beyerinck's knees. Behind came a terrible roaring, as if the sea was trying to catch them. When Mrs. Beyerinck tried to say something to Mr. Tojaka, who was helping her along, she found she could not speak. She tried to make a noise. It felt as though her throat was dried out and someone was trying to cut her tonsils with a knife. She felt her neck. To her horror it was covered with leeches. When they reached the wood, the party lost their way. A crowd of natives came fleeing in their direction. One of them led the way, the Beyerincks following, holding on to one another. They reached their hut [at 400 ft elevation on the slopes of Radjah Bassa] at midnight. Mrs. Beyerinck laid the exhausted children on the bed and opened the box of provisions which yielded some seltzer water and a bottle of orange syrup. The family settled down in the tiny room which had two windows covered by bamboo slats. Mrs. Beyerinck thanked God they had at last reached safety. No one could sleep, for the noises coming from Krakatoa were quite ghastly. Around the hut lay thousands of terrified natives, moaning and crying and praying to Allah for deliverance.

· · · · ·

At about 5:00 a.m. my husband said to one of the servants, who had faithfully stood by us, "Kill a chicken and cook some soup quickly, maybe we shall have to flee still further." I wanted to go out and see what it was like. My husband said, "I shouldn't. It will only worry you." Naturally I went in spite of what he said. But what I saw then! Thousands of tongues of fire lit up the surroundings, some only small tongues, some longer. As they disappeared they left a greenish light. Others quickly filled their place. On tops of the trees I saw flames. I heard a crack and noticed a sheet of fire right by me. The sea was not to be seen. Everything was smothered in ash. I could not see my hand before me. I went into the house again. The soup was served. We started to eat and as far as I remember there were sixteen of us in the room.

· · · · ·

Natives sent on reconnaissance by Controller Beyerinck at 6 a.m. returned to the hut on the slopes of Mount Radjah Bassa to report that Katimbang had disappeared. The great wave which came at 10:30 a.m. swept in unobserved, but Mrs. Beyerinck seems to be describing the aftereffects of the Big Bang:

Someone burst in shouting "shut the doors, shut the doors." Suddenly it was pitch dark. The last thing I saw was the ash being pushed up through the cracks in the floorboards, like a fountain.

I turned to my husband and heard him say in despair "Where is the knife? The knife on the table. I will cut all our wrists, then we shall be sooner released from our suffering." The knife could not be found.

I felt a heavy pressure, throwing me to the ground. Then it seemed as if all the air was being sucked away and I could not breathe. Large lumps clattered down on my head, my back and my arms. Each lump was larger than the others. I could not stand.

I don't think I lost consciousness for I heard the natives praying and crying "Allah il Allah."

I felt people rolling over me. I was kicked and I felt a foot on part of my body.

No sound came from my husband or children. Only part of my brain could have been working for I didn't realise I had been burnt and everything which came in contact with me was hot ash, mixed with moisture. I remember thinking, I want to get up and go outside. But I could not. My back was powerless.

After much effort I did finally manage to get to my feet but I could not straighten my back or neck. I felt as if a heavy iron chain was fastened around my neck and was pulling me downwards.

Propping my hands on my knees, I tottered, doubled-up, to the door. I knew it was in the corner. It was stuck fast. I fell to my knees in the ash.

Later I noticed that the door was ajar and I forced myself through the opening. I looked for the stairs. I tripped and fell. I realised the ash was hot and I tried to protect my face with my hands. The hot bite of the pumice pricked like needles.

My long hair, which reached to my knees, usually knotted in a tight bun, was loose.

Without thinking I walked hopefully forward. Had I been in my right mind I would have understood what a dangerous thing it was to do, to leave the vicinity of that house and plunge into the hellish darkness.

Then came sudden, terrifying stillness.

When I had walked about 15 paces, still in my doubled-up position, I stubbed my toe on something very peculiar. I ran up against large and small branches and did not even think of avoiding them. I entangled myself more and more in that nightmare of branches, all entirely stripped of leaves.

My hair got caught up, and each time with a twist of the head I managed to free myself. Then something got hooked into my finger and hurt. I noticed for the first time that the skin was hanging off everywhere, thick and moist from the ash stuck to it. Thinking it must be dirty, I wanted to pull bits of skin off, but that was still more painful. My tired brain could not make out what it was. I did not know I had been burned.

Worn out, I leaned against a tree.

· · · · ·

Controller Beyerinck carried his wife to the hut. "Let us stay here and die together," he cried. "No, we shall be rescued and taken to hospital in Batavia," she answered, hearing the sound of her own voice as if another person spoke. "Who knows whether Batavia still exists," Mr. Beyerinck told her.

Of the three thousand natives who clustered around the hut, one thousand died of burns, and the skins of those who survived were blistered and burned. The body of one man was found weeks later sprawled in a sheet of pumice, his arms spread, his legs askew, just as he fell in panic-stricken flight. Only in SE Sumatra did Krakatoa itself claim victims, by its burning ash and red-hot pumice; elsewhere it was the waves that killed.

Mrs. Beyerinck sat on the ground by the hut. The

ayah gave her the youngest child. From the way his mouth was working, she could see he must be terribly thirsty. She tried to give him her breast, but suddenly the child lay still in her arms. She felt him all over and laid her ear to his heart. She could hear nothing. "Thank God this child is at least put out of his agony," she told the *ayah*, who cried bitterly; but Mrs. Beyerinck could not shed a tear. It would have been a great relief to cry, but she could not. "Wrap the child in a blanket and lay it on the bed," she tried to say, but the frightful thirst caused by the hot ash dried the words in her throat. Let Mrs. Beyerinck tell her own story:

There was still deep darkness. We couldn't light a fire, as matches went out immediately. At last the head boy, the only remaining male servant, managed to start a small fire, and we began to hear signs of life from the people in the village, some of whom came to the light, asking for water. They were crazy from thirst and anxiety, so that it began to be dangerous for us. My husband said, "I have no weapons, but there is an axe behind the bed." The house-boy fetched it. When my husband held it he said, "I cannot do anything with it. I have lost the use of my hand." "Then give it to me," I said and clutched the axe. I was suddenly furious that my children's lives depended on it. I would have cut down the first person to stand in my way. When three men came towards the hut, the house-boy advised us to put out the fire, as one of them was carrying a kris. We quickly threw ash on the fire and again we were in darkness. I don't know how long we had been sitting when we saw people approaching, carrying torches. There must have been thirty of them. They shouted, "Sir, if you are still alive, come with us. We must leave because soon there will be more fire." "From whence?" asked my husband. "From Radjah Bassa, look," they cried. We looked up and saw a ray of greenish light on the mountain. "Wait for us; we'll get ready," my husband answered.

Once again the Beyerincks turned to flee, in the mistaken belief that the old volcano on the slopes of which they were sheltering was about to join Krakatoa in eruption. . . . The refugees descended the mountain and set off across the paddy fields below. It took them fifteen minutes to reach the woods. The path had vanished. . . .

. . . Some people came up. They had survived the ash rain by bathing in a river. All their houses had collapsed, and most of the inhabitants of the district had been killed, they told the Controller. It started to rain again, no longer ash, but hot, heavy mud. The Beyerincks did not dare return to their hut, because so many dead lay there. She sent a servant back instead, to bring down a large table, under which she placed the children. She and her husband lay on either side to protect them. All this was done, she says, by the light from a tiny flame made by the house boy from a piece of felt-roofing. She sent him to fetch water from the river. He returned to report it was not fit to drink. It was all muddy. "Perhaps it may be better in a couple of hours," he said, when the water from the well on the mountain cleared it. So it proved, but the water was still covered with ash. It quenched their thirsts, but the "more we drank, the thirstier we got," found Mrs. Beyerinck.

· · · · ·

On standing up, which was very difficult, I noticed that my limbs were swollen to three times their normal size. No one spoke. We all held our breath for, after such a long darkness, we yearned for God's heavenly sun or moonlight. The circle of light gradually became blood-red. The strong wind tore apart the mass of ash, and we saw the wonderful, glittering sunlight.

· · · · ·

She and Mr. Tojaka caught up with Mr. Beyerinck. It was light enough to see for some distance. She could see across the Straits. "Where was Krakatoa?" she wondered. She could see only half of the large cone; the smaller cones were gone. Where six days before they had risen into the sky, eight little islands had sprung up, and from each smoke arose. Near at hand she saw that all the villages by the beach had gone. On the sea floated a wide belt of pumice. On it lay roofs of houses, fallen trees, their branches snapped, and dark shapes which she could not at first identify, and which she learned later were the bodies of men and animals.

· · · · ·

. . .At last, on Saturday, September 1st, a current forced a gap in the pumice and he [Captain 't Hoen, the commander of the *Kedirie*] was able to send a boat ashore near the village of Kali Antoe. In the only house still standing he found the Controller of Katimbang and his family.

They were in a deplorable condition, Captain 't Hoen saw at once, all covered with burns. "How can I get them to hospital alive," he wondered.

He did manage to transport them to the Batavia hospital, however, and they recovered fully. Others were not so fortunate.

The principal port on Sumatra's east coast is Telok Betong, at the back of Lampong Bay where the Koeripan River enters the sea. A European survivor writes[30] *on 1 September:*

Figure 18. General view of Telok Betong, at the head of Lampong Bay, Sumatra, before it was destroyed in August 1883. All lowland areas were swept totally clean by the tsunami. Engraving from Illustrated London News, 8 September, 1883. For 1979 view from this same general location, see color Plate 14C.

When on the night of the 26th August, I was awaiting at the pier the arrival of the mail steamer Governor General Loudon, I was nearly swept away by the sea suddenly rising high. The furious waves struck me down among the large boulders 8 times, but thanks to Providence I had strength enough to save myself and struggle out of the water. On this occasion an immense number of persons were killed. The Government offices no longer exist. Nothing has been spared, not even a single tree, and this devastation extends half way up the highest hill here called the Kunjit. When total darkness set in here at about 9 o'clock in the forenoon, all the Europeans had betimes taken refuge in the house of the Resident. The remaining property is gone. The Residency was, however, spared from its being on ground 37 m high. The tidal wave rose to 35 m [subsequent calculations[31] place the wave height at 26.5 m]. We had thus a very narrow escape from destruction. We have been six days with the Resident. There is, however, great want of provisions, and no steamer has yet arrived. The sea is full of pumice.

Metzger[32] gives the following account from ships near Telok Betong (but the more detailed accounts from the Loudon appear in the next section).

The Loudon came to anchor off Telok Betong at 7 p.m. Rough sea, boats could not communicate. They observed that there was something wrong, but could not make out what it was. The Dutch bark Marie, which was there also (there are two vessels of the same name, Marie and Maria, in the list, the one, Marie, of 570, the other, Maria, of 790 tons) reported: At 7:30 currents observed in different directions, some small vessels lost their anchors, ten persons saved from being drowned. From Telok Betong is reported: By 6:30 sea quite calm, level of the sea 1 m lower than pier, a moment afterwards 1 m above it; people who were at the end of the pier, about 1000 m distant from the shore, had to walk back through the water, which was done without accidents.

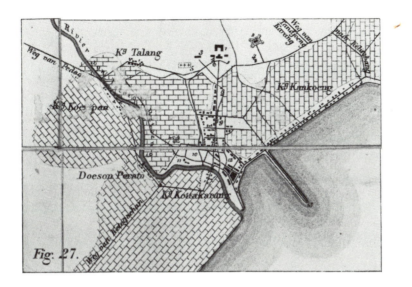

Fig. 27.

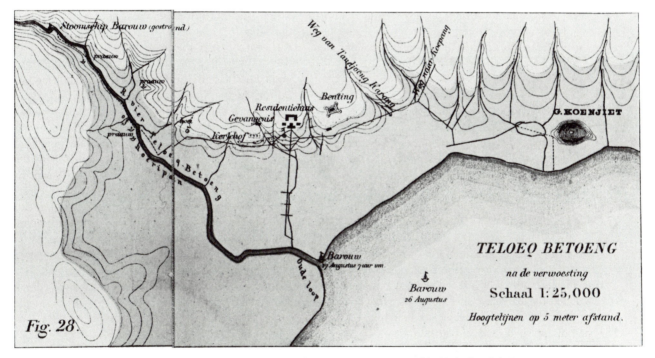

Fig. 28.

TELOEQ BETOENG

na de verwoesting

Schaal 1:25,000

Hoogtelijnen op 5 meter afstand.

Figure 19. "Before and after" maps of Telok Betong. These maps, figures 27 and 28 in Verbeek's Atlas, are both at the same scale and the width represented by the upper (1877) map is 2.9 km. In the upper map, made by J.F. de Corte and published in the 1881 Yearbook of the Mines, main buildings are shown in black and the brick-like patterns show individual districts (Kampong Koitakerang, for instance, is bounded by the major road to ("weg van") Ketegoehan, the River Koeripan to the north, and the sea). Numbers identify: (1) Resident's house; (2) fort; (3) prison; (4) canteen (dining hall); (5) cemetery; (6) Resident's office; (7) old fort; (8) school; (9) telegraph; (10) esplanade; (11) hotel; (12) Chinese quarter; (13) signal beacon.

On the lower map, prepared by Verbeek and de Corte in October after the catastrophic waves, only a few of these numbered features remain. The shaded area is that destroyed by the tsunami, and the contour interval represents 5 m. The Resident's house (see Verbeek's chromolithograph, Plate 2D) survived, as did the cemetery, prison, and fort, but all buildings at lower elevations were destroyed. Successive positions of the Berouw (see p. 90) are shown, and "praauw" marks the final resting place of several smaller boats. "Oude loop" indicates the former course of the river near its mouth. "Boei" marks the position of the Berouw's large mooring buoy, now a monument in Teluk Betung and the place from which color Plate 14C was taken, overlooking the modern city.

During the night the waves were heard causing an awful devastation. At Telok Betong, by 10 o'clock, several vessels were thrown on the beach (among which the steamer *Berouw*, draft 1.75 m., 4 guns, 30 h.p., 4 Europeans, 24 natives), houses swept away, people drowned, &c.; towards midnight calm.

. . . . .

The mate of the *Marie* reports: August 27, in the morning the sea was calmer, but queer weather, sky threatening, prepared the third anchor. At once we saw an immense wave at the horizon making rapidly its way on to us; we spiked up the hatches, and after having done it the first wave struck the vessel, and threw it on the beach; after the wave had flowed off, the *Marie* was literally on dry sand; one could have walked around the vessel. Part of the crew left the ship. . . . By 10 a.m. three heavy seas came after each other; quite dark; at once a fearful detonation. Sky in fire, damp. By 3 p.m. three seas again, after this the sea quite calm. Dark till next morning, then (28th) *Marie* was found afloat again.

The first wave that destroyed Anjer on the morning of the 27th was widespread. A Dutch soldier stationed at the Telok Betong barracks reported:[33]

At 6:20 I went to Kampong Kankong, about 1400 m distant from the barracks, to see the destruction which the wave had caused the night before. After I was there I saw a wave rushing on to us; we hastened to the hills, the villagers following us. When I had reached the barracks [on the Talang Hill, about 25 m above the level of the sea], I saw Kampong Kankong had disappeared, and so had the other villages near the beach. Before the darkness began the water rose. At Katimbang they perceived in the morning what damage had been done—by little and little it became dark.

. . . . .

By 9:30 a.m. a downpour of ashes, later stones and mud; about half an hour afterwards the level of the water was only 1 or 2 m below the top of the hill. Now it was taken into consideration to give up the barracks and retire to a higher point. In the night the rain of mud ceased by little and little, the sky cleared

up, stars appeared. When, at Katimbang, it had become quite dark, fearful detonations, like thunder and reports of guns, were heard. By 11:30 pouring down of stones began (the biggest as large as a fist). Half an hour after, 12 o'clock, it became quite dark; heavy rain of ashes soon afterwards, hot ashes (during a quarter of an hour), then cold ashes; darkness continued (it is not said when it dawned).[34]

Two further accounts describe the conditions in Telok Betong just after the wave devastation. The first is from a man who, after escaping to a nearby village on the 27th, returned to Telok Betong the next day.[35]

The sun did not show itself again until Tuesday morning. What a scene was then beheld. Everything was covered with a layer of ashes and mud one foot deep. When I again found myself at Telok Betong and came near the Residency, I was overpowered by horror. At the foot of the hill on which that house stands lay a plain bare and laid waste. Nothing is left of Telok Betong and the surrounding villages. A few natives only could be seen on the plain, trying to salvage some of their furniture. But it was in vain; the sea had carried everything away save corpses and the Government iron cash boxes. Amongst the corpses were those of four Europeans, namely two sailors and two soldiers. One sailing vessel [the *Marie*] laden with salt held to her anchors and now rides securely in deep water. The misery is great. Our buffaloes, cattle, and horses have nothing to eat. Deer and wild pigs even come into the villages in search of food. Rice is short, and there is a lack of drinking water. All the available water tastes of sulphur and is muddy.

The second account, written from Telok Betong two weeks after the paroxysm, also begins on the 28th.[36]

In tense anxiety of what to expect, we sat awaiting morning, when the terrible news came that the water had previously risen as high as the floor of the Government buildings, so everyone realised they had lost everything. But nobody could believe that. It was simply unbelievable. So, with torches, people went to the scene of the disaster to investigate. The terrible news proved only too true. The floating wood, which had been carried as high as the Residency, was the surest sign that it was no use to hope for the impossible. So it was decided to wait till the daylight, which should prove that everything was lost and one would have to start life all over again.

At last morning came. In front of us was what was once a town, but there was no destruction. There was simply. . . nothing. Everything seemed to have vanished into the sea, except, as by pure magic, all the corpses, just as if to show us how many casualties the disaster had caused. Under those circumstances, however, there wasn't much time to moan. The corpses had to be buried to prevent epidemics, which would have caused an even greater disaster. The damage and the total number of casualties was impossible to guess. There we stood, having lost everything, not knowing where aid would come from. Luckily we could rely on the Resident and his wife, who gave us all shelter in their house, and the meals looked like the food of kings under our circumstances.

At this moment we are already their guests for a fortnight, and how many more days are there to come?

The other major indentation in Sumatra's SE coast, Semangka Bay, was also affected by the eruption and sea waves. The destruction of Beneawang, the capital of Semangka Department and located at the north end of the Bay, is described by Controller P.L.C. Le Sueur.[37]

At 6 o'clock I went to the beach. The sea was so low that many cliffs were visible. It looked queer and I did not feel at ease. I called for van Zuylen, my assistant, so that we could draw up a report to the Resident about what had happened.

It was just past 7 and the lights were on. A moment later van Zuylen said "I am sorry, but I would like to stop for a moment. I don't feel at ease."

Scarcely were these words uttered when we heard a terrible noise. Then, women and children fled from their houses shouting "The water is coming. The water is coming."

Van Zuylen, the servant and I left the house in a hurry and invited everyone to take shelter in my house,

which they accepted. I did so because my house was built on piles and situated on a hill.

The water once again returned to the sea. Everybody calmed down. But only for a short while because, almost at once, we heard the water approaching again with a terrible noise. 200–300 people were sheltering in my house.

I walked from one side to another to maintain peace and quiet. Suddenly I heard the front portion of the house collapse, and the water rushed in. I advised everyone to go to the rear.

But, my God, scarcely was I standing then the house collapsed completely and all of us were dragged along by the current.

I got hold of a shelf, with which I floated along until I was pulled by the legs and let go of the shelf.

After that I got hold of a few pieces of thin wood and managed to stay afloat until the water returned to the sea and I felt solid ground under my feet.

However, I stayed where I was and covered my head with my coat to protect myself against the mud rain.

I heard men, women and children call for help, but any help was impossible.

I could not raise myself out of weakness and fear and could not see a thing.

Suddenly the water returned with the same force. I said a quick prayer, asking for help for myself and everybody and prepared myself for death. The water took hold of me, turned me around and threw me away with a terrible force.

Then I got stuck between two floating houses. I couldn't breathe any more and I thought that the end was come.

But suddenly they parted and I got hold of a banana trunk and stuck to it with all my strength. I don't know how long I floated around, but again the water returned to the sea and once again I stood on solid ground.

Again I sat there for at least an hour without moving and it was dark everywhere and the mud rain was still going on. I did hear people shout, but that was all.

A moment later I heard a native talking to a few women. I called out to them and proposed we walk along together, which was accepted. I left my place with closed eyes and touched the ground all around, leaving the sea behind me. I did not have any clothes on any more, except a vest which was badly torn anyway, so I walked stark naked in the cold and mud rain.

Soon I discovered that the three persons had departed, as I did not hear them any more.

I would have given a thousand guilders if I could only have refound my previous place, as where I was walking now the ground was covered with thorns and nasty bushes, and all the time I fell over trees and the debris of houses.

Walking along for some time, I at last heard voices again. I opened my eyes and saw a native with some women. I told them I was the Controller, and together we reached Penanggoenga [15 km NW of Beneawang] that evening at 8 o'clock. My ordeal had lasted from 8 in the morning until 8 in the evening.

Straits of Sunda (Ships' Accounts)

Observations at sea provided the best descriptions of the activity at the volcano itself. The giant sea waves that so dominated the reports from coastal areas were, in open water, long and gentle swells that excited no notice at all from most moving ships, and the seamen, with no homes and families threatened on shore, gave more attention to the natural phenomena around them. These natural phenomena were spectacular, and different ships emphasized different aspects. A ship captain with a cargo of inflammable petroleum products was understandably sensitive to the lightning and other remarkable electrical effects of the eruption, whereas a ship at anchor quickly recognized the strong currents of the tsunami. At least a dozen ships were in or near the Straits during the eruption's paroxysmal phase, and we have selected eyewitness accounts from seven, ending with that of the ship that passed within 20 km of the volcano at the eruption's peak. Locations of these ships are shown on the reference map (p. 82).

The first accounts carry on the reports from the Sumatra coast, as the Governor General Loudon passed much of the eruption in Lampong Bay near Telok Betong. This ship, a 1239 ton government mail steamer based at Batavia, was the largest of the group recorded here, and the only one permanently based in the area. The first of three accounts from the Loudon is by her Captain, T.H. Lindemann, and begins after the ship docked at Anjer at 2:00 o'clock on August 26. She had left Batavia roadstead at 8:10 that morning, but no notice was taken of activity at Krakatau.[38]

At Anjer we took on board 111 passengers, coolies and women bound for Sibogha, and left Anjer roadstead again at 2:45 p.m. [see Figure 12], and taking our bearings from the land we ran past Pulo Soengjan, or "Right in the Fairway" Island, past Hog Point and Lampong Bay, and then discovered that the island of Krakatau was casting forth enormous columns of smoke. At 5 p.m. Pulo Tiga Island lay about half a mile to the west of us. Were steering then NW¼N (time bearing). At 6:15 p.m. the southernmost of the Chandon Islands was bearing NE.

Laid the course next for the roadstead of Telok Betong, which we reached at 7:30 p.m., and where we anchored in six fathoms of water with thirty fathoms shackle outside the hawse-pipe.

From 6 o'clock we had rain of ashes and small bits of stone, and there was a stiff breeze from the NW and WNW.

Monday, August 27th.—Finding that at midnight on the evening of our arrival there was still no boat come off to us from the shore, and as the weather was now much calmer, I sent the first mate in the gig with a crew of six men to find out what was the reason of this. About 1 a.m. he returned, and stated that it had been impossible to land on account of the heavy current and surf; also that the harbour pier-head stood partly under water.

The Government steamer *Berouw*, which lay anchored near the pier-head, hailed the mate as he was returning on board, and the people on board her then stated to him that it was impossible to land anywhere, and that a boat which had put off from the shore had already been wrecked. That by 6 p.m. on Sunday evening it had already begun to be stormy, and that the stormy weather had been accompanied by a current which swept round and round (apparently a sort of whirlpool). When the mate had come on board, we resolved to await daylight before taking any further steps; however, for the sake of security, we steamed several ships' lengths outwards, because the sound of a ship's bell which seemed to be approaching us made us suspect that the ship must be adrift, and wishing therefore to avoid a collision we re-anchored in nine fathoms with thirty fathoms shackle outside the hawse-pipe. We kept the ordinary sea-watch, and afterwards heard nothing more of the bell. When day broke, it appeared to us to be still a matter of danger to send a boat ashore; and we also discovered that a revenue cutter was foul of a sailing-vessel which lay in the roadstead, and that the *Berouw* was stranded. However, owing to the violent winds and currents, we did not dare to send a boat to her assistance.

About 7 a.m. we saw some very high seas, presumably an upheaval of the sea, approaching us up the roadstead. These seas poured themselves out upon the shore and flowed inland, so that we presumed that the inhabitants who dwelt near the shore must be drowned. The signal beacon was altogether carried away, and the *Berouw* then lay high upon the shore among the cocoanut trees. [And as far as ascertained since, every soul on board was killed. The steamer now lies two miles inland.[39] See Figure 30, p. 129.] Also the revenue cutter lay aground, and some native boats which had been lying in the neighbourhood at anchor were no more to be seen.

Since it was very dangerous to stay where we were, and since if we stayed we could render no assistance, we concluded to proceed to Anjer under steam, and there to give information of what had taken place, weighed anchor at 7:30 a.m., and following the direction of the bay steered thereupon southwards. At 10 a.m. we were obliged to come to anchor in the bay in 15 fathoms of water because the ash rain kept continually growing thicker and thicker, and pumice-stone also began to be rained, of which some pieces were several inches thick. The air grew steadily darker and darker, and at 10:30 a.m. we were in total darkness, just the same as on a very dark night. The wind was from the westward, and began to increase till it reached the force of a hurricane. So we let down both anchors and kept the screw turning slowly at half speed in order to ride over the terribly high seas [Or, as he says elsewhere, "Squalls, storms, and seas as high as the heavens."[39]] which kept suddenly striking us presumably in consequence of a "sea quake," and made us dread being buried under them.

Awnings and curtains from forward right up the mainmast, three boat covers, and the uppermost awning of the quarter deck were blown away in a moment. Some objects on deck which had been lashed got loose and were carried overboard; the upper deck hatchways and those on the main deck were closed tightly, and the passengers for the most part were sent below. Heavy storms. The lightning struck the mainmast conductor six or seven times, but did no damage. The rain of pumice-stones changed to a violent mud rain, and this mud rain was so heavy that in the space of ten minutes the mud lay half a foot deep.

Kept steaming with the head of the ship as far as possible seawards for half an hour when the sea began to abate, and at noon the wind dropped away entirely.

Then we stopped the engine. The darkness however remained as before, as did also the mud rain. The barometer at that time stood again at 763.25 mm. Sounded the pumps. No water. Let the crew and also such passengers as were on deck work at throwing the mud overboard. At 2 p.m. the barometer was 763.30. The mud rain changed into a light ash rain.

Tuesday, August 28th.[40]—The darkness remained the same until the following morning at 4 a.m. At daybreak began to get the chain clear and weigh the anchor; got under steam at 6.30 a.m.; made out then Tims Island, bearing S by W [191°], and Pulo Soengal Island, bearing SW½W [230°]. Held on our course for Pulo Tiga Island and fell in with much ash and drift-wood.

When we got about two miles off Pulo Tiga, it appeared that a connection had been formed between the islands just mentioned stretching to Seboekoe Island, and thence to the mainland. Whether this connection was formed out of solid ground or only out of pumice-stone and trunks of trees is not known. What is certain is, that at the distance at which we then lay, it looked exceedingly like solid ground, and so we thereupon turned back in order to look for another passage. The very same phenomenon as had revealed itself near Pulo Tiga was discovered also between Tims Island, Seboekoe, and Pulo Soenchal, and we, therefore, resolved to make our way out through the Strait of Lagoendie. This channel we found relatively clear, that is, in comparison with the other part of the bay. Having got outside we discovered that here also we were entirely shut in; so steamed very slowly, stopping every now and then close by the so-called layer, and made it out at last to be floating pumice-stone, through noticing that the layer was heaved up and down by the motion of the surf.

Now steamed somewhat faster, and when we got into the middle of the layer before referred to found it to be 7 or 8 ft thick. It took us ten minutes to get clear of it, and then we held our course south of Krakatau, the serang [a sort of boatswain[39]] being in the fore-yard, a man on the look out forward, and the captain and first mate on the bridge.

As we steamed past Krakatau we noticed that the middle of the island had disappeared, and that no smoke was to be seen in any direction. However, when we got east of Krakatau, we discovered that between that island and Sebesie a reef had formed, and that various craters planted on that reef were now and then sending columns of smoke on high. [In another place he says also that, "Also half of the island 'Right in the Fairway' had disappeared, and what is left of it has been broken into fragments with open spaces between them."[39] As we neared the coast of Java we observed that here, too, everything had been laid desolate.

We also perceived that the lighthouse on Java's Fourth Point was entirely washed away; nothing remaining except a stump some feet high.

At 4 o'clock reached Anjer roadstead, and although there was nothing more to be seen of the place itself the captain and the first engineer went ashore to learn what information was to be obtained.

Ashore we met the Resident of Bantam, and concluded to return straight on board in order to convey his Honour to the roadstead of Bantam, and this because the Resident assured us that it was of very great importance in the public interest that such should be done.

We left Anjer Roads at 10 minutes to 5 o'clock, steamed round St. Nicholas' Point, and went on taking our bearings for the Island of Pulo Pundjang, and steering into Bantam Bay.

We arrived at our destination at 6:50 p.m.; by request of the Resident, put him on board a ship which lay in the roads there, and after having done this at 7:30 we got under steam again and made for Kroë [on Sumatra's west coast].

A brief account by the Loudon's second engineer, recorded several years later,[41] adds more detail, plus an appreciation of the seamanship involved in bringing the ship safely through those extraordinary days.

We were anchored off Telok Betong, in Sumatra, when the chief officer and myself observed a dark line out at sea which bore the appearance of a tidal wave. While we were remarking this, the Captain (who was just then taking his bath) rushed on to the bridge, and telegraphed to the engine-room to steam slow ahead up to the anchors. I was engaged in carrying out this order when the wave came up to the ship. First she dropped; then heaved up and down for some five minutes. There were three waves. When I came on deck again, the long pier, which had been crowded with Europeans who had come out of the town (they had experienced a shock of earthquake during the night),—this pier, the houses and offices, had dis-

appeared, in fact, the whole town was gone. A government steamboat lying at anchor (with steam up) in the bay was landed high on the tops of the palm trees in company with some native boats. That was the first intimation we received that Krakatoa was in eruption, and from that time, eight o'clock, onwards through the day the rumbling thunders never ceased, while the darkness increased to a thick impenetrable covering of smoky vapour. Shortly after this we got under way, and proceeded until the darkness made it impossible to go on further. It was while we were thus enveloped in darkness that the stones and cinders discharged by the mountain began to fall upon the ship. In a short time the canvas awning and the deck were covered with ashes and stones, to the depth of two feet, and all our available men were employed in removing the falling mass, which would otherwise have sunk the ship. We had a large number of natives on board, and 160 European soldiers. The latter worked with the energy of despair at their task of clearing the deck, in spite of the twofold danger of being burnt and stunned by the hot falling stones. While we were engaged in this struggle, and enveloped in the sheer blackness of a veritable hell, a new and terrible danger came upon us. This was the approach of the tidal wave caused by the final eruption, which occurred about 12:30 to 1 p.m. The wave reached us at 2 p.m. or thereabouts, and made the ship tumble like a seesaw. Sometimes she was almost straight on end, at other times she heaved over almost on her beam-ends. We were anchored and steaming up to our anchors as before, and as before we managed to escape destruction. All the passengers and the crew gave themselves up for lost, but there was no panic, and the Captain handled the ship splendidly throughout. He received a gold medal from the Government in recognition of his indomitable courage in saving the ship and passengers. Well, you can fancy what it was like when I tell you that the Captain was lashed with three ropes along the engine-room companionway, while I was lashed down below to work the engines. The men were dashed from one side of the engine-room to the other.

However, it remains for a passenger aboard the Loudon, the Public Works Engineer N.H. van Sandick, to give the most graphic account of that ship's remarkable adventure.[42]

When one looks at a Dutch Indies newspaper, the possibility exists that there is little in it which interests you. However, if you have already been stationed there for some time, you will probably look over the passenger lists of the departing and arriving ships of the Dutch Indies Steamship Company, which you find in every newspaper. Suppose, for instance, that you are a government official and as such have several transfers already behind you. With a certain *Schadenfreude* [malicious pleasure] you observe that you are not the only one in the army of officialdom, who, from time to time in the interest of your country, has been suddenly transferred into totally strange surroundings, under new circumstances and in a new job, thus describing a colossal parabola through the meandering emerald belt.

But whomever you look for among your acquaintances in the passenger list, you will always find, after the first class travellers have been named, the following sentence: "Further passengers: His Majesty's troops, exiles, Arabs, Chinese and natives."

Such a ship offers a remarkable scene. On the fore part of the ship swarm a colorful mixture of races. His Majesty's troops are accompanied by loving wives or housekeepers; and, as in the passenger list the military are mentioned in one breath with exiles and natives, so it is also on board, concerning their bedding down, etc. But, enough. Some newspapers these days place a semicolon between "troops" and "exiles" which really ought to be considered necessary.

On Aug. 26, 1883, the steamer *Governor General Loudon*, Captain Lindemann, left in the morning from Batavia, destination Kroë, Benkoelen, Padang, and Atjeh [Sumatra]. Among the passengers all categories were represented. The majority however consisted of 300 exiles. For the uninformed, be it remarked that with this term are meant persons who have been condemned to forced labor in or outside the chain. Locally they are called "chain boys"; and, especially in the outer colonies, they perform valuable services in the execution of public works, military expeditions, etc.

In the afternoon at 3 o'clock the *Loudon* dropped anchor in the roadstead of Anjer. There 100 Bantammers, which were hired as coolies for the building of a lighthouse on the island of Bodjo [off the west coast of central Sumatra], came aboard. The weather then was beautiful. The white plastered houses of Anjer glittered in the sunshine near the seashore, in the background the mountains, and in front of it the deep blue sea. Clearly the lighthouse of Java's Fourth Point

silhouetted itself against the sky. The Dutch flag on the grounds of the Assistant Resident flapped happily; every house could be distinguished and subconsciously the thoughts wander back to the first arrival in the Indies from Europe. Anjer is then the first place which brings welcome greetings from a distance.

If we, who were aboard the *Loudon* in the roads of Anjer, would have declared that the last day of Anjer's existence had already begun, we definitely would have been considered deranged.

When our coolies were aboard, the *Loudon* set course past Dwars-in-den-Weg and Varkenshoek into the Bay of Lampong toward Telok Betong. To portside we saw in the distance the island of Krakatau, known for its first volcanic eruption several months ago. Krakatau is an old acquaintance of the *Loudon*. When, after the first eruption, a pleasure trip was made to see the volcano, the *Loudon* brought passengers to the island for 25 guilders each. Many landed that time and climbed the volcano; and all experienced a festive and pleasant day.

The volcano on Krakatau gave us a free performance. Although we were far away from the island, we saw a high column of black smoke rise above the island; the column widened toward the top to a cloud. Also there was a continual ash fall. Toward evening, at 7 o'clock, we were in the Bay of Lampong, in the roads of Telok Betong, where anchor was dropped and it soon became night.

The ashfall increased steadily, while the sea was stormy. The *Loudon* telegraphed to shore for a sloop to land the passengers, but neither sloop nor load proa arrived. The *Loudon* itself lowered a boat to make connection with shore. However it was impossible to land, since there was a high surf at the coast, so the boat returned without accomplishing its purpose.

The harbor light on the light tower continued to burn, although something unusual seemed to occur: now and then alarm signals were observed from the proas laying in the roadstead. Instead of the ash, we received meanwhile a rain of pumice. Fortunately, the night had passed and it became light, so that we could see Telok Betong. While all of Anjer is located near the seashore, at Telok Betong the military encampment and the house of the Resident are built on a hill farther away from the coast. The largest part of Telok Betong, however, is located near the seashore. The European houses, some covered with tiles, some with *atap* [palm thatch], could be distinguished from the native houses, which on Sumatra completely differ in building style from the Javanese houses seen at

Anjer.

Telok Betong is the capital of the Residency Lampongsche Districten, and seen from aboard it looked very picturesque against the strongly overgrown green background of the Lampong Mountains.

However the last hour of Telok Betong had already sounded. The government steamer *Berouw* and the cruise boat had already been beached by the sea during the night and the harbor light continued to burn, although the sun already had risen above the houses.

Suddenly, at about 7 a.m., a tremendous wave came moving in from the sea, which literally blocked the view and moved with tremendous speed. The *Loudon* steamed forward in such a way that she headed right into the wave. One moment . . . and the wave had reached us. The ship made a tremendous tumbling; however, the wave was passed and the *Loudon* was saved. The wave now reached Telok Betong and raced inland. Three more similar colossal waves followed, which destroyed all of Telok Betong right before our eyes. The light tower could be seen to tumble; the houses disappeared; the steamer *Berouw* was lifted and got stuck, apparently at the height of the cocoanut trees; and everything had become sea in front of our eyes, where a few minutes ago Telok Betong beach had been. The impressiveness of this spectacle is difficult to describe. The unexpectedness of what is seen and the tremendous dimensions of destruction, in front of one's eyes make it difficult to describe what has been viewed. The best comparison is a sudden change of scenery, which in fairy tales occurs by a fairy's magic wand, but on a colossal scale and with the conscious knowledge that it is reality, and that thousands of people have perished in an indivisible moment, that destruction without its equal has been wrought, and that the observer is in threatening danger of life. Taking all these things together the impression caused by such a natural scene can possibly be described, but it stops short of reality.

Thus the *Loudon* had survived a sea tremor which had destroyed Telok Betong. Since the telegraph office there also had disappeared, it probably would take a long time before Java received tidings of the Telok Betong disaster, more so since it could be assumed that the telegraph cable from Anjer to Telok Betong had been broken. The Captain therefore decided to steam back to Anjer to make his report there.

If any present on the *Loudon* had been exposed to mortal danger, certainly they were the passengers destined for Telok Betong, who had not been landed because it had been impossible to establish connections with shore. Usually Anjer is not a regular stop, but since the coolies were supposed to board ship there, Anjer had been included. To this event, the passengers for Telok Betong give thanks for their lives. Otherwise the *Loudon* would have arrived several hours earlier at the roads of Telok Betong, and, since there certainly still would have been communication with the shore, the passengers would have been landed and gone to a certain death.

Meanwhile, we steamed forward and soon the roads of Telok Betong were lost from view, and we hoped soon to be out of the Bay of Lampong. But we would not get away that easily. It became darker and darker, so that already at 10 a.m. there was the most Egyptian darkness. This darkness was complete. Usually even on a dark night one can still distinguish some outlines of, for instance, white objects. However, here a complete absence of light prevailed. The sun climbed higher and higher, but none of her rays reached us. Even on the horizon not the faintest light could be seen and not a star appeared in the sky.

This darkness continued for 18 hours. It is self-evident that the *Loudon* during this pole-night had to "winter over" in the bay. Meanwhile a dense mud rain fell, covering the deck more than half a meter thick and penetrating everywhere, which was especially bothersome to the crew, whose eyes, ears, and noses were liberally filled with a material which made breathing difficult. Off and on again, ash and pumice fell. The compass showed the strangest deviations. Fierce sea currents were observed in diverging directions. The barometer meanwhile read very high, which certainly was difficult to explain. Breathing, however, was not only made difficult by ash, mud, and pumice particles, but the atmosphere itself had also changed. A devilish smell of sulfurous acid spread. Some felt buzzing in the ears, others a feeling of pressing on the chest and sleepiness. In short, the circumstances left something to be desired, since it would have been quite natural if we all had choked to death.

However, the *Loudon* was exposed to entirely different dangers. After the darkness had fallen for some time the sea became stormy. The wind increased and became a flying hurricane. Following, there were a series of sea tremors. These evidenced themselves by very high waves, which formed suddenly. A few of these hit the *Loudon* sideways, so that she was lifted up and leaned sideways to the extent that danger of capsizing threatened. The ship then made motions, so that everything rolled over and resembled being in the Gulf of Biscay. Also during these tremors lightning hit the mast up to seven times, moving first along the lightning rod and then after that, still above the ship, jumping over to the water with a demonical, snapping noise. At such a moment, everything was suddenly clearly lit, showing how everything had been tinted ash gray by the mud rain, making one impulsively think of a ghost ship.

The fire hoses stood ready on the deck, since there was every chance that the ship might catch fire. It is most amazing that this did not happen, and it amazes me that the *Loudon* was able to survive such seas. Always there was steam and she steamed slowly forward behind both anchors.

Besides lightning and thunder, another electrical phenomenon could be observed. At the protruding tips of mast and spars little flames went back and forth. The natives entertain the superstition that this St. Elmo's fire is the harbinger of the ship being wrecked. Thus, as soon as a little flame appeared, no matter how high in the rigging, the native sailors climbed the ropes to extinguish it and thus drive off this messenger of bad tidings. Although the muddy rain had made the ropes slippery, and in spite of the heavy rolls made by the ship, they raced to the top and pounded the flames, which to their despair were not extinguished, but darted off.

These were hours which were not lightly forgotten. After each sea tremor, an amazing stillness and calmness of the sea existed, and also the muddy rain stopped temporarily. This calm was even more disquieting than the hurricane. The cries for help of the chain boys and coolies in the foreship could then be heard continually, as well as their "*La Illah ill' Allah*", their prayer to the God of the Islam.

Honor to the cook, who in spite of all sea tremors, had managed to prepare food. Of course everything had the *couleur locale*, which means that the food was not completely free of ash, mud and pumice: But, a dinner there was.

Seldom has the daybreak been greeted with more joy than aboard the *Loudon* on August 28. At about 4 a.m., after we had spent a full 18 hours in the darkness, a faint light was observed at the horizon, a faint moon broke through and the air became less oppressive. It became still lighter and the sea could be seen again: So there was a chance to get out of the bay. There was still some pumice and ashfall, but at least there was light. The Sumatra coastline was close. The shore here looked terribly pitiful, everything bare, the trees toppled over by the weight of ash and mud, or carried off by the waves of the sea tremor. Every-

where the sea was covered with pumice and driftwood, and farther away in the direction of Poeloe Tiga, the entrance to the bay had been closed off by complete islands of pumice, which stuck out in the sea as reefs and which formed a connection between Poeloe Tiga, Seboekoe and the solid shore.

Since the ship route in the Lagoendie Straits [the SW entrance to Lampong Bay] was relatively open, course was set in that direction. Soon a pumice island, which was about 3 m thick and which blocked the way, could be seen to rise there also. However the *Loudon* had to get out of the Bay of Lampong at any price and thus bravely steamed toward the pumice island; and the island opened up and let the *Loudon* pass, while the pumice closed itself again behind the ship—thus we steamed straight through the island. The *vangpijp* [seawater (coolant) intake] of the engine did became clogged, but luckily we were already through the island in open sea and saved!

The *Loudon* looked terrible! No dredger could look as dirty and messy. Everything was covered with foul, stinking mud. Zola could have described it well. If the ship would have been sunk for about 10 years and then raised, this is what she probably would have looked like. All tents and loose objects on deck were lost.

The Captain decided to return to Anjer to report. The course taken was through the Sunda Strait, east and later south of Krakatau. When we saw the island on the port side, it was evident that there was a connection between the phenomena to which we almost had fallen victim and the volcano on Krakatau, which up to now had been viewed as a novelty, useful as a target for a picnic.

The island had spit itself out (please forgive the indelicate expression, but I cannot find a better one) and had largely disappeared. A steep crater wall could still be seen, while the other half of the mountain had completely disappeared and had become sea. In the vertical crater wall large fissures and cracks, filled with vapor, could be seen. In the sea itself, between Krakatau and Sebesie, where yesterday there was a passage, all kinds of volcanic reefs could be seen rising up out of the sea. The activity here was in full swing. At eight locations, columns could be seen forming, originating from a black speck. The black speck became larger and developed a white rim; the column then rose to great height and disappeared, to soon make room for a renewed phenomenon. Were these water spouts or volcanic eruptions? It is difficult to decide.

Meanwhile, we approached the Java coastline and

the Bantam shore. The influence of Krakatoa had not just stretched itself to the Bay of Lampong. The Bantam shore was a terrible scene. From Tjeringen to old Bantam everything resembled a desert.

Again we anchored in the roads of Anjer, not even two days after our departure on the 26th. But Anjer is no more—it had been wiped away, no trace, no stone can be seen anymore. Only one stump, the stone foundation of the earlier existing lighthouse on Java's Fourth Point, remains. It is the only cemetery monument contrasting with the gray color of the tremendous burial ground, which appeared before our eyes from the deck of the *Loudon*. The spot, which earlier showed thriving *kampongs* (villages) and a European settlement, had become an even, gray plain. The river of Anjer was completely filled with mud; not even a ruin remained; everything was wiped away and leveled to the ground. A more complete destruction is unthinkable. A few leafless trees, also ash gray in color, stuck out above the plain.

The islands in the Sunda Straits have also shared in the destruction. They are bare and all plant growth has disappeared. The wave here must have run inland several tens of meters high, judging from the expanse which apparently has been directly destroyed by the water. Dwars-in-den-weg has been split in pieces, many other small islands have had to give up a share to the destructive elements. Everywhere the sea is covered with driftwood and pumice.

. . . . .

From the deck of the *Loudon* we observed that a few Europeans were moving around on the rubble of Anjer. The Captain then went ashore and met there, where Anjer once stood, the Resident of Bantam, Spaan, who was accompanied by van der Ploeg, the first engineer of the Department of Public Works to arrive, and the Controller, Ten Cate, who had come from Serang with exceptional effort, to assess the situation of the destroyed regions and to be able to offer immediate aid. These gentlemen came aboard and were transported by the *Loudon* to the roadstead of Bantam. The tidings we received from them were terrible. Numerous fellow countrymen had been killed, and the impact was greater when one has known many of them. Although Resident Spaan had been able to help out significantly when Bantam had been hit by cattle pestilence, famine and fever epidemics in 1880 and 1881, now a large area, namely the coastal area, Tjeringen, Anjer, and Merak had been hit by a disaster that did not have its equal, and so suddenly that rescue was impossible.

After dropping off Resident Spaan in Bantam, the *Loudon* set course toward the west trying once more to reach her initial destination. Steaming through the Sunda Strait, she passed Krakatau for the third time. The volcanoes were quiet now. *For good measure*, there was still some ashfall during the night from August 28–29, after which the Indian Ocean was finally reached with stops at Kroë and Benkoelen. The farther north the less damage was seen. All they met, however, agreed that repeatedly during one 24 hour period noises were heard as of tremendously loud cannon shots.

It is strange that aboard the *Loudon* this noise was not heard in spite of the fact that the ship was in the center of the action during the eruption.

The writer will not discuss further aspects of the disaster. These aspects have been made sufficiently known from land-based observation posts. We believed however that it was of interest to look at it from a sea-based post, especially since they had been so close to Krakatau during the eruption.

While the Loudon was boarding her passengers in Anjer that Sunday afternoon, the Medea had passed the Straits and was approaching Batavia Bay when they witnessed the early development of the eruptive cloud. The Medea's Captain, who later provided specimens of volcanic ash to Professor Joly (see p. 296), made the only known measurements of the cloud's height. As is already clear from the foregoing accounts, darkness caused by the volcanic ash soon prevented any observations of the later, and no doubt larger, eruptive clouds. The Captain's important account, as related by Joly, follows.[43]

Captain W. Thomson heard the first explosion of Krakatoa at two o'clock on August the 26th. He was then in Lat. 5°56'S, Long. 106°31'E. Immediately after, and before the second explosion, which succeeded in ten minutes, a "black mass, rolling up, like smoke, in clouds was observed to the westward." It attained an altitude of about 12°; and, as the *Medea* will be found to have been just seventy-six miles, as the crow flies, from Krakatoa, a height of about seventeen miles [26 km] is obtained for the cloud.

At five o'clock the *Medea* came to anchor in Lat. 5°58'S, Long. 106°46'E, 89.3 miles direct from Krakatoa. The dust cloud had meanwhile been going up suddenly with each explosion; and now, as Captain

Figure 20. "Watching the eruption," a drawing by F.H. Schell, from van Gestel's 1895 account. The ship is not identified, and the scene may have been like that witnessed by the Medea on August 26, but during most of the eruption's culminating activity on August 27 near-total darkness precluded any "watching the eruption."

Thomson cast anchor, he read the angle of elevation of the cloud, it was 40°. Obviously the column had advanced towards him; but some idea of its approach may be gathered from his subsequent statement that "the wind during the whole of the eruption was WSW, force between 3 and 4." Taking its velocity as twenty-one miles per hour, its advance in the three hours since the first explosion would be sixty-three miles. On this assumption the altitude of the cloud would be twenty-one miles. Other observations from other points of view would be of interest.

Captain Thomson's narrative is one of much interest from the intelligence and care displayed in his observations, although made under trying circumstances.

He records "electrical displays" round the vast column of smoke (steam) ascending from Krakatoa on the evening of the 22nd of August. These took the form of vivid lightning, flashes darting from and around

the column. Showers of sand and gravel on the 23rd. The terrific explosions of the 26th and 27th are described as "shaking the ship." He was then some eighty miles off, with an intervening screen of mountainous country.

On the paroxysmal day after Captain Thompson's cloud measurements, and from a similar position north of the Straits, Captain Sampson of the Norham Castle made the following entry in his log.[44]

We are under a continual rain of pumice-stone and dust. So violent are the explosions that the ear-drums of over half my crew have been shattered. My last thoughts are with my dear wife. I am convinced that the Day of Judgment has come.

Further north, the Annerly was approaching the Straits, and Captain Strachan later reported to the ship's owners:[45]

The *Annerley* arrived at [the Straits[46]] from Singapore on the 27th August. For some 24 hours previous we had been having some queer looking weather, but at 10 a.m. that morning it was so dark that we had to light all the lights. It commenced raining ashes and pumice stone, and our barometer was rising and falling 5-10ths of an inch, within a minute. I bore up and ran back for the North Watcher Island [145 km NE of Krakatau], and came to under the lee of it. Towards night the wind had died out and the ashes stopped, but it was as black as night. At 3 a.m. on the 28th we proceeded, and as we neared Sunda Straits we were steaming through a sea of pumice stone and *débris* of all sorts. A storm of tidal wave had swept the coast, carrying everything before it. Anjer and its lighthouse were gone, a small portion of the foundation only standing. The whole coast right to Java Head had been swept, and it was hard to distinguish the points as we came along, and harder to believe it was the coast of Java—such a change from what it used to be. The lighthouse keeper asked for news, which we gave him. He said he had had fearful weather, and promised to report us as early as possible. We had some of the ashes as far as 100 miles clear of Java Head.

Nearer to the volcano, the American barque W.H. Besse was on her way home from Batavia, by way of the Indian Ocean, and spent much of that fateful Monday 83 km ENE of Krakatau. We present three separate accounts from that vantage point as all contribute to a joint description of the events.[47] The first is an excerpt from the ship's log.[48]

Aug. 26.—This day commences with light airs and calms. Light airs throughout the day. At 5:30 p.m., wind hauling ahead, let go starboard anchor with thirty fathoms chain, clewed up and furled all sail. Adam Light [likely the light on Kombuis Island[49]] bore W 1-4 S and E by S [bearing 264°(?)[49] and 101°]. Throughout the afternoon and night, heard heavy reports, like the discharge of heavy artillery, sounding in the direction of Java Island. Very dark and cloudy throughout the night, with continual flashes of lightning. Barometer 30.15.

Aug. 27.—Commences with strong breezes, and thick, cloudy weather. Barometer 30.12. At 9:30 a.m.,

pilot left ship. Hove the lead every fifteen minutes. At daylight noticed a heavy bank to the westward, which continued to rise; and, the sun becoming obscured, it commenced to grow dark. The barometer fell suddenly to 29.50, and suddenly rose to 30.60. Called all hands, furled everything securely, and let go the port anchor with all the chain in the locker. By this time the squall struck us with terrific force, and we let go starboard anchor with eighty fathoms chain. With the squall came a heavy shower of sand and ashes, and it had become by this time darker than the darkest night. *The barometer continued to rise and fall an inch at a time.* The wind was blowing a hurricane, but the water kept very smooth. A heavy rumbling, with reports like thunder, was heard continually; and the sky was lit up with fork lightning running in all directions, while a strong smell of sulphur pervaded the air, making it difficult to breathe. Altogether, it formed one of the wildest and most awful scenes imaginable.

The tide was setting strong to the westward throughout the gale, at the rate of ten knots per hour. At 3 p.m. the sky commenced to grow lighter, although the ashes continued to fall. The barometer rose to 30.30, and dropped gradually to 30.14, when it became stationary. The whole ship, rigging and masts, were covered with sand and ashes to the depth of several inches.

The second report from the W.H. Besse is taken from the logbook of the First Officer:[50]

Sunday, August 26, 1883.—The day commenced with strong breezes and thick cloudy weather; at 4 a.m. hove short; at 6 a.m. got under weigh, wind SW; at 4 p.m. wind hauling ahead, came to anchor; the sky at this time having a threatening appearance; atmosphere very close and smoky, at 5 p.m. heard a quick succession of heavy reports sounding like the broadside of a man-of-war only far louder and heavier; heard these reports at intervals throughout the night; the sky was intensely dark, the wind having a dull moaning; through the rigging also noticed a light fall of ashes. The sun when it rose next morning (*Monday, August 27*) had the appearance of a ball of fire, the air so smoky, could see but a short distance; at 6 a.m. thinking the worst of the eruption was over as the reports were not so frequent or heavy as during the night, got under weigh, having a fair wind, was

Figure 21. Painting of the American barque W.H. Besse, by R.B. Spencer. The Besse was anchored NE of Krakatau during the paroxysmal phase of the eruption and its crew had a spectacular encounter with the volcano (see 3 eyewitness accounts starting on p. 98). The thirty stars on the American flag flying from the stern of the Besse indicates that the flag was made sometime in the period 1848–1850. This photograph courtesy of Mary Baker of Newton Center, Massachusetts, granddaughter of the Besse's Captain Benjamin C. Baker.

in hopes to get out clear of the straits before night; *at 10 a.m. were within 6 miles of St. Nicholas Point,*[51] *when we heard some terrific reports* also observed a heavy black bank rising up from the direction of Krakatoa Island, the barometer fell an inch at one jump, suddenly rising and falling an inch at a time, called all hands, furled all sails securely, which was scarcely done before the squall struck the ship with terrific force; let go port anchor and all the chain in the locker, wind increasing to a hurricane; let go starboard anchor, it had gradually been growing dark since 9 a.m. and by the time the squall struck us, it was darker than any night I ever saw; this was midnight at noon,[52] a heavy shower of ashes came with the squall, the air being so thick it was difficult to breathe, also noticed a strong smell of sulphur, all hands expecting to be suffocated; the terrible noises from the volcano, the sky filled with forked lightning, running in all directions and making the darkness more intense than ever; the howling of the wind through the rigging formed one of the wildest and most awful scenes imaginable, one that will never be forgotten by any one on board, all expecting that the last days of the earth had come; the water was running by us in the direction of the volcano at the rate of 12 miles an hour, at 4 p.m.

wind moderating, the explosions had nearly ceased, the shower of ashes was not so heavy; so was enabled to see our way around the decks; the ship was covered with tons of fine ashes resembling pumice stone, it stuck to the sails, rigging and masts, like glue; so it was weeks before it was all removed, some of it still remaining on the wire backstays; one seaman was severely injured by walking off the forward house [in the darkness], so that he died the day after the ships arrival in Boston.

All day—*Tuesday, August 28*—crew were employed in shovelling the ashes off the decks and clearing the cables and heaving up one anchor.

The third eyewitness account comes from the young son of the Besse's Captain Baker. It is transcribed from a recording made with his family about 1946, only a few years before the speaker's death.[53]

I'll tell you about Krakatau. It was when I was a small boy, as you well know, on my father's ship with my mother, comprising his family which sailed around

Figure 22. Sidney Tucker Baker, age 11, son of the Besse's Captain B.C. Baker. This photograph was taken in Hong Kong, just months before the Besse sailed toward the Sunda Straits in late August 1883. Sidney Baker's reminiscences were recorded in 1946, when he was 74 years old, and a transcript of this remarkable account appears on p. 99. Photograph courtesy of Mary Baker, daughter of Sidney Baker.

the world with him. We were on our way home from Manila, where we had stopped to load sugar, and then we had a very eventful passage on the way in; struck on a reef, got off of the reef, went to Batavia where we went into dry dock, and my mother and I stayed up in the mountains until the vessel was repaired. This took some 3 or 4 months. When we left, the ship was on the island of New Amsterdam in Batavia Harbor.

We started on our way towards home, down the Straits of Sunda, and it was a clear day as I recall it, and perhaps toward the afternoon we noticed the cloudiness in the atmosphere seemed to be filled with a haze and with dust, or with sort of a mist. A little later, the atmosphere commenced to cloud up and there was evidence of a disturbance in the atmosphere. We put the pilot ashore; he had his own boat with him and, incidentally, we discovered that he never reached the shore. We started on our way, and the cloudiness increased. The air seemed to be filled with dust, so much so that we feared suffocation. It became black, so black that you couldn't see your hand before your face. I've never imagined that the atmosphere could be so dense.

While the wind was not blowing at a great speed, we noticed there was an increasing current in the water and we felt from the rumblings in the distance that there might be an earthquake nearby, or some other upheaval, and that the indications showed that a tidal wave was possible. We took in all our sails, let go both anchors, and incidentally, the old craft that we were in, the W.H. Besse which was then modern in its equipment, had wonderful ground tackle and a great deal of chain. If it had not been for this we would never have survived.

The tidal wave did come. The current was so severe that we were unable to get a sounding with a 16 foot lead. It took the lead astern like a chip and we never were able to get to the bottom until after the tidal wave had subsided. Our ground tackle held; that's why we are here. Ashes commenced to fall about the ship, and on the ship, and in the water. And there were perhaps 6 or 7 inches of ashes all over the vessel. I recall my father's taking me up into the bow of the vessel where we had a gauge, which was very much like a car spring only much larger, on each anchor chain. And the gauge was pulled way beyond anything that we had ever seen it. We were afraid that the pull on the vessel from the current would pull the nose out of the vessel, and then of course we would be lost.

At about this time there were tremendous rumblings, and crashings, and flashes off in the distance, which were unlike and greater than anything you could imagine. This was due, we learned afterwards, to the eruption of Krakatau when it blew its head off and practically the whole island went up in the air.

My mother and I were in the cabin; we did not have electric lights in those days but we had pretty good lights. And our mate, now afterwards master of his own ship, was going on deck and he looked into the cabin, saw my mother and me. I will read you a letter which he wrote us many years after that, on the anniversary of the eruption. It registered in his mind, as it did in the minds of us all, as a mark in our lifetime. And he always, on the anniversary, took note of the recurrence of the event. I will read you now the letter.

Tomorrow is the anniversary of the eruption of Krakatau. Every year on this date, the incidents in connection with this earthquake are vividly impressed on my memory, and I think of your father and mother and yourself on this eventful date. I shall never forget looking into the cabin during the height of the eruption and seeing you and your mother sitting there, and I can say that at that time I never expected to see you again. I felt like going in and bidding you both good-bye before the finish. But I caught myself in time, thinking it was useless to frighten your mother unnecessarily. It has been two years since I had the pleasure of visiting you at your home in Newark, and will say I enjoyed my brief call very much and was sorry I could not have spent more time with you.

It was a terrible experience. The air was filled with dust and ashes. The reverberations of the explosions were something that are unbelievable. Adjectives fail to describe the racket and turmoil. But after a while the current subsided, or the tidal wave, rather, subsided. The atmosphere cleared, if I remember correctly, way late in the afternoon. We finally got up anchor and started for Anjer, which was at the entrance of the Strait. This city had gone under water completely. I have heard my father say that the hotel in which he had stopped was underwater to such an extent that he could sail over it and drop his anchor down the chimney. We passed over all kinds of debris, refuse, villages that had been swept from their locations by the tidal wave, dead bodies galore (really, we had a job dodging them), animals and all kinds of evidences of the upheaval. The water was of a, not a slate, but sort of dullish yellow color from the ashes which had not settled. They floated on the water until we were 500 miles out at sea before we struck anything like blue water. The air there at night was filled with

ashes, or not filled with ashes I should say, but sunsets and the sunrises were tinged by the effects of dust in the air. And after we got home, we found that the condition had existed all around the world, such as was described in the book Mrs. Baker just read an excerpt from. . . .

We had gone a long ways and we had a still further eventful voyage before us. . . . We landed in Boston and when we arrived we were supposed to come from the depths of the sea. Everyone thought that we were lost. Our craft was the nearest surviving ship to the island. Others that were nearer were lost. The dry dock which we had left the day before in Batavia Harbor was carried some 100 miles by the tidal current down the coast and wrecked. We only had one day there between us and a fatality.

I don't remember the exact date. . . . The letter which I read to you from Captain Gibbs was dated August 26, 1927, and he refers to the anniversary as the 44th anniversary of the eruption of Krakatau.

I don't remember my age. I refuse to answer such a question. I was a small boy but I was able to have a perfectly good recollection, and I was an embryo sailor at that time. I can't tell you my exact age at that time. I think possibly between 11 or 12 years old.

You don't look at a tidal wave; a tidal wave looks at you! It sweeps over from the submersion of the descent of the earth in an earthquake. The waters come rush over the ground and it creates a current beyond anything you can imagine, takes everything before it. High, yes, comes in high, rolling in; it may be like a big wave, I can't tell you. But this tidal wave, the evidence that we had of it was in a current like a millrace running by the ship, to such an extent, as I told you before, that we thought that the vessel would either drag its anchors or pull its bow out of the ship.

To the south of the volcano, was the Berbice, on her way from New York to Batavia. In addition to the cargo of petroleum we mentioned above, she was also carrying a small package of great historical significance. In New York, Captain Logan had been given 5 seedling rubber trees from Brazil with the request that they be delivered swiftly to the Botanical Gardens at Buitenzorg. Despite the problems related below, they were delivered and successfully began a flourishing industry.[54] *As the Berbice entered the Straits on the 26th, however, the darkness and lightning ahead caused Captain*

Logan to shorten all sail. At 6 o'clock they entered a heavy shower of volcanic ash and, realizing it was no mere storm, remained south of the Straits. The ship's log at midnight begins:[3]

The ash-shower is becoming heavier, and is intermixed with fragments of pumice-stone. The lightning and thunder became worse and worse; the lightning flashes shot past around the ship; fire-balls continually fell on the deck, and burst into sparks. We saw flashes of lightning falling quite close to us on the ship; heard fearful rumblings and explosions, sometimes upon the deck and sometimes among the rigging. The man at the wheel felt strong electric shocks on one arm. The copper sheathing of the rudder became glowing from the electric discharges. Fiery phenomena on board the ship manifested themselves at every moment. Now and then, when any sailor complained that he had been struck, I did my best to set his mind at ease, and endeavoured to talk the idea out of his head, until I myself, holding fast at the time to some part of the rigging with one hand, and bending my head out of reach of the blinding ash shower which swept past my face, had to let go my hold, owing to a severe electric shock in the arm. I was unable to move the limb for several minutes afterwards. I now had sails nailed over the hatches lest the fire falling around should set my inflammable cargo in a blaze. I also directed the rudder to be securely fastened, ordered all the men below, and remained on deck with only my chief officer. At 2 a.m. on Monday, the 27th, the ashes, three feet thick, were lying on the ship. I had continually to pull my legs out of the ashy layers to prevent them from being buried therein. I now called all hands on deck with lanterns to clear away the ashes, though the weather was unchanged, and the fearful electric phenomena, explosions, and rumbles still continued. The ashes were hot, though not perceived to be so at the moment of their falling on the skin. They burned large holes in our clothing and in the sails. At 8 in the morning there was no change. At that hour it was still quite dark, and the ash showers were becoming heavier. Clearing away the ashes was continually proceeded with until 11 a.m. A high continuous wind set in from the SE, which varying afterwards made the ship list considerably from the weight of ash on our masts and rigging. A heavy sea came rushing on about 3 in the afternoon. It rose to a height of 20 ft, swept over the ship, making her quiver from stem to stern with the shock. Meanwhile the storm continued.

The mercurial barometer did not stand still from 28 to 30 inches. When I went to examine my chronometers I found that they had all stopped, probably owing to the shaking of the ship from the concussions. Up to 6 p.m., the darkness and the storm still continued, but the sea had become calmer. The flashes of light showed it to be covered with pumice and ash on all sides. After this the weather moderated and the sky cleared. [A short continuation of this account appears in Verbeek's note number 133 on p. 271.]

Our final, and perhaps most dramatic, eyewitness account from the Straits is by Captain Watson of the Charles Bal. This ship, out of Belfast and bound for Hong Kong, sailed northward past the volcano at the peak of the eruption, and no other survivors had a closer view at that critical time. Captain Watson's account begins on August 22, when first encountering evidence of earlier Krakatau volcanism some 1050 km S of the volcano.[55]

About 7 p.m. on the 22nd of August, in latitude 15°30'S and longitude 105°E, the sea suddenly assumed a milky-white appearance, beginning to the eastward , but soon spreading all around, and lasting until about 8 p.m. There were some cumulus clouds in the sky, but many stars were shining, and from E to NE a strong, white haze or silvery glare; this occurred again between 9 and 10 p.m., but disappeared when the moon rose. The clouds appeared to be edged with a pinkish coloured light, the sky also seeming to have extra light in it, as when the aurora is showing faintly.

On the 24th, in 9°30'S 105°E [380 km S of Krakatau], this was repeated, showing when the sky was overcast, but disappearing when the moon rose.

On the night of the 25th, standing in for Java Head, the land was covered with thick dark clouds and heavy lightning was frequent. On the morning of the 26th made Java Head light, about 9 a.m. passed Prince's Island, and had a sharp squall from WSW, with torrents of rain.

At noon, [wind WSW, weather fine,] Krakatoa was NE of us, but only the lower portion of the east point was to be seen, the rest of the island being enveloped in heavy blackness.

At 2:30 p.m. we noticed some agitation about the point of Krakatoa, clouds or something being propelled from the NE point with great velocity. At 3:30 we heard above us and about the island a strange sound as of a mighty crackling fire, or the discharge of heavy artillery at one or two seconds' interval. At 4:15 p.m., Krakatoa bore N½E [bearing 006°], ten miles distant. We observed a repetition of the noise noted at 3:30, only much more furious and alarming; the matter, whatever it was, being propelled with amazing velocity to the NE. To us it looked like blinding rain, and had the appearance of a furious squall, of ashen hue. At once shortened sail, to topsails and foresail. At five the roaring noise continued and was increasing [wind moderate from SSW;] darkness spread over the sky, and a hail of pumice-stone fell on us, of which many pieces were of considerable size and quite warm. We were obliged to cover up the skylights to save the glass, while our feet and heads had to be protected with boots and sou-westers. About 6 the fall of larger stones ceased, but there continued a steady downpour of a smaller kind, most blinding to the eyes, and covering the decks to 3 or 4 inches very speedily. While an intense blackness covered the sky and land and sea, we sailed on our course, until at 7 p.m. we got what we thought was a sight of Fourth Point light; then brought ship to the wind, SW, as we could not see any distance, and knew not what might be in the strait.

The night was a fearful one: the blinding fall of sand and stones, the intense blackness above and around us, broken only by the incessant glare of varied kinds of lightning, and the continued explosive roars of Krakatoa, made our situation a truly awful one.

At 11 p.m., having stood off from the Java shore, wind strong from the SW, the island, being distant WNW eleven miles, became visible. Chains of fire appeared to ascend and descend between it and the sky, while on the SW end there seemed to be a continued roll of balls of white fire. The wind, though strong, was hot and choking, sulphurous, with a smell as of burning cinders, some of the pieces falling on us being like iron cinders. The lead came up from the bottom at thirty fathoms quite warm.

From midnight to 4 a.m. of the 27th, the wind was strong, but unsteady, between SSW and WSW. The same impenetrable darkness continued, while the roaring of Krakatoa less continuous, but more explosive in sound; the sky one second intensely black, the next a blaze of light. The mast-heads and yard-arms were studded with corposants and a peculiar pink flame came from fleecy clouds which seemed to touch the mast-heads and yard-arms.

At 6 a.m., being able to make out the Java shore, set sail, and passed Fourth Point lighthouse. At 8 hoisted our signal letter, but got no answer. At 8:30 passed Anjer with our name still hoisted, and close enough in to make out the houses, but could see no movement of any kind; in fact, through the whole strait we did not see a single moving thing of any kind on sea or land.

At 10:15 a.m. [Verbeek (see p. 217) notes that this and the following times appear to be one hour later than the actual times.] passed the Button Island [Toppershoedje] one-half to three-quarters of a mile off; the sea being like glass all around it, and the weather much finer looking, with no ash or cinders falling; wind light at SE.

At 11:15 there was a fearful explosion in the direction of Krakatoa, then over 30 miles distant. We saw a wave rush right on to the Button Island, apparently sweeping entirely over the southern part, and rising half-way up the north and east sides, 50 or 60 feet, and then continuing on to the Java shore. This was evidently a wave of translation and not of progression, for it was not felt at the ship. This we saw repeated twice, but the helmsman said he saw it once before we looked. At the same time the sky rapidly covered in; the wind came strong from SW to S; and by 11:30 a.m. we were enclosed in a darkness that might almost be felt, and then commenced a downpour of mud, sand, and I know not what, the ship going NE by N, 7 knots per hour under three lower topsails. We set the side-lights, placed two men on the look-out forward, the mate and second mate on either quarter, and one man washing the mud from the binnacle glass. We had seen two vessels to the N and NW of us before the sky closed in, adding not a little to the anxiety of our position.

At noon the darkness was so intense that we had to grope our way about the decks, and although speaking to each other on the poop, yet we could not see each other. This horrible state and downpour of mud, and débris, continued until 1:30, the roaring of the volcano and lightning from the volcano being something fearful. By 2 p.m. we could see some of the yards aloft, and the fall of mud ceased; by 5 p.m., the horizon showed out to the northward and eastward, and we saw West Island [130 km NE of Krakatau] bearing E by N, just visible. Up to midnight the sky hung dark and heavy, a little sand falling at times, and the roaring of the volcano very distinct, although

we were fully 75 miles from Krakatoa. Such darkness and such a time in general, few would conceive, and many, I dare say, would disbelieve. The ship, from truck to water-line, was as if cemented; spars, sails, blocks, and ropes were in a terrible mess; but thank God, nobody hurt nor was the ship damaged. But think of Anjer, Merak, and other little villages on the Java coast!

Batavia and Inland Java

Areas distant from Krakatau did not receive the weaker signals of the eruption, and many were unaware of the activity until hearing the culminating explosion of 10 o'clock Monday morning. Ships in the Indian Ocean learned of the eruption days later, when volcanic ash fell on them, and newspaper accounts of the disaster did not appear in Europe and North America until the last days of August. In Batavia, however, 160 km from the volcano and with intense citizen interest in the Sunda Straits region, the impact of the eruption was delayed but nonetheless strong. We reprint two detailed accounts from Batavia, plus excerpts from a few of the many others that were written. The first is from the Reverend Philip Neale, British Chaplain at Batavia.[56]

On the day in question [August 26] everything was much as usual in Batavia. The fierce rays of a tropical sun were beating down upon the busy streets of the city, which always bear an Oriental appearance. It was near the close of the period of the year known as the dry monsoon, and the parched ground and dusty streets told how much rain was needed. For six months at a time, that is from April to October, scarcely any rain ever falls, and in a country such as Java, notorious for its unhealthy climate and damp unwholesome heat,

Figure 23. Lightning in eruptive cloud like that seen by ships near Krakatau. No photographs were taken of that lightning, but this was taken 50 years later at the same location, during a May 1, 1933, eruption of Anak Krakatau. The 15 minute time exposure was taken by Charles Stehn from Lang Island about 9 p.m. and appears in his 1933 Umschau paper (figure 5).

the commencement of the wet monsoon is always a welcome period. On this Sunday afternoon, therefore, when a distant rumbling noise like thunder was heard in the city, it was generally thought that the first tropical storm of the season was coming earlier than usual. But on examining the sky, strangely enough, all was bright and cloudless, with no sign of an approaching storm. But soon the rumbling noise increased, distant reports were heard as of heavy guns being fired at a distance, and the people in Batavia quickly became aware of the unwelcome fact that something more startling was taking place around them than a mere thunderstorm. "What can it be?" was the oft-repeated question as the Europeans, that evening, took their usual stroll at sunset under the lovely tamarind avenues which encircle the Konings Plein, the favourite promenade of Batavian citizens, and on all sides was heard the unanimous opinion "that it was another of our volcanoes at work."

When the sun went down and darkness came on, the reports became more loud and distinct, and anxiety increased as to what might happen.

So far no one had for a moment dreamt of distant Krakatoa being the culprit. It was too far away even to be suspected, and the general impression was that one of the adjacent mountains, such as Gedeh or Salak, the nearest volcanoes to Batavia, must be the scene of the disturbance.

As the evening passed by matters grew worse. Louder and more threatening became the distant thundering reports, and at times distinct shocks of explosions could be heard shaking the houses to their very foundations. At eight p.m., when the night gun is always fired from one of the Government forts, the report was so faint as scarcely to be heard, being drowned in the din of the atmospheric disturbances. Throughout the night matters continued much the same. Sleep was out of the question, and the long weary hours of night were spent by many a resident in anxiously watching the course events might take. At one time it was fancied that an earthquake—a by no means uncommon event in Java—was imminent, and many a cautious householder retired from the precincts of a house which he feared at any moment might fall and crush him. An English lady told me afterwards how she had carried her little children into the open air and had kept them outside the house all night. In some parts of the city the walls of the houses shook and quivered so ominously, as shock succeeded shock, that a general rush was made outside.

The streets and houses presented a strange appearance. Many a portly Dutchman could be seen strolling about the streets, in the hope of finding greater safety than in his own dwelling. Whole families of women and children again were huddled together beneath the tropical trees and shrubs in their gardens, whilst others paced with anxious steps the wide marble verandahs surrounding their houses, ready to rush forth at the slightest sign of coming destruction.

Wearily the hours of night dragged on. About 2 a.m., after an explosive shock more severe that the rest, the alarming discovery was made that the gas in Batavia had been affected. In some quarters of the city the street lamps for a considerable distance were suddenly quenched, and in many private houses the gas was also extinguished. The anxiety was naturally increased by the darkness, and it may easily be imagined how eagerly the first ray of morning light was looked for. At last it came—the day which was to bring death and destruction to many thousand homes in Java. But how unlike the usual tropical day it was. There was no bright dazzling sunshine to scatter away the dark shadows and gloomy forebodings of the previous night. A dull heavy leaden sky, completely obscuring the sun, was all that could be seen. The morning also was comparatively cold—a noticeable fact in a trying climate, which seldom varies day or night throughout the whole year more that 10 or 12 degrees. The average temperature in Batavia is about 75 degrees at night, and 85 degrees by day, but then it must be remembered that the Java heat is moist and damp, and consequently much more unhealthy and injurious than an increased range of the thermometer in a drier climate. On this occasion the glass fell to 65 degrees in the shade, a fact unknown before in the meteorological annals of the city.

It was a cold dull morning then as the work of the busy Batavian day commenced. The shocks which had caused so much dismay and terror in the night were now less frequent and more indistinct. Business was beginning as usual. Crowds of natives were wending their way citywards on foot. Steam trams filled with clerks and officials bore their living freight from the various suburbs. Merchants in private carriages, or *dos à dos* (as the public two-wheeled conveyances are called), were rapidly driving to their handsome offices in the Kali-Besar or chief business centre in Batavia. All were eagerly discussing the previous night's events, and all sanguine that the worst was over. Nothing, all this time, was definitely known as to which volcano had been the cause of so much alarm. Of course vague surmises were common enough, but still no one thought of looking as much as ninety miles away for the scene of the disturbance.

But in the course of the morning, when all were congratulating themselves that matters were no worse, a marked change began in the aspect of affairs. The sky became darker and more threatening, and after a time a peculiar rain of ashes began to fall. This was of a grey colour, and soon the ground and streets were covered with it. For several hours there was a gentle fall—at one time coarse and large as a pin's head, at another as thin and fine as dust. Some of each kind I have now in my possession, taken up from one of the suburbs of Batavia shortly after it fell. Both kinds were submitted to a Dutch analyst for examination, and to him I am indebted for the names of the component parts. He tells me that the two showers were identical except that the second fall of ash was much finer than the first. It consisted principally of siliceous sand, with sulphuret of iron, phosphates and silicates of lime and magnesium, while the whole had a strong sulphuric smell.

While this rain of ash continued, thick darkness enveloped the city. Traffic and business were suspended. Gas was lighted everywhere in the hope that the darkness would soon pass off, but still it continued for several hours.

· · · · ·

The Europeans also thought it wiser to suspend business on account of the darkness and to leave the city for their suburban homes. The buildings which they use in Batavia for offices are very old, and though roomy and convenient for their purpose they would easily be overthrown in the event of an earthquake. About noon, therefore, on that eventful Monday (August 27) there was a steady outpour of merchants from Batavia, and the city was soon wearing a deserted appearance. It was well that it did so, for a more startling event had yet to come.

Suddenly, without any warning, a tidal wave . . . made itself felt in the city. The Dutch capital has no harbour, and the only approach to it is by a long canal nearly two miles in length, lined on either side by massive brick walls. In this channel, leading from the roadstead to the city wharves, the water rose at an alarming rate and burst over the adjoining land. This was the first intimation at Batavia of the terrible wave which (as we discovered later on) was the messenger of death to so many thousand inhabitants on the western shores of Java. Its effects in the city were quite bad enough. Although this great torrent of water had

travelled nearly ninety miles it dashed up the Batavian canal with great power. In spite of distance, its fury was not then fully spent. In the streets of the capital, adjoining the canals and wharves, the water rose to a depth of several feet, and the people had to run for their lives. Not long afterwards I steamed down the canal in a launch, and saw the destruction which had been caused. In several places the massive brickwork lining the sides had been swept away, leaving huge gaps in the masonry of many feet. The surrounding country also had been seriously inundated, great pools of water being visible everywhere. Fortunately the loss of life in Batavia was very small, and must have been confined to the natives who are always to be found along the banks of the canal. A little village on the coast, a short drive from the capital, was less fortunate, however. There was nothing there to break the force of the rushing waters as they dashed in all their fury on the northern shore of the island, and the country round being very flat, a serious loss of life occurred. The huge tidal wave broke over the native *kampong* (or village), and several hundred bodies were subsequently reported by the Government Resident of the district to be lying dead in the market-place.

Such were the events in the city of Batavia and its suburbs on that memorable Monday. As soon as the wave had spent its fury on the coast, the worst was over. The shower of ashes ceased, and the darkness cleared off. Weaker and weaker grew the distant shocks, and at last they died away altogether. Traffic was once more resumed along the ash-strewn streets, which now had a grey coating some three or four inches in depth. On all sides trees were to be seen with broken branches, weighed down and snapped off, by the great pressure of the ashes which had rested upon them. The fowls which had gone to roost at midday, when the darkness was at its worst, again came forth to begin their day a second time.

Additional information, extracted from Tenison-Woods' long account, follows:[3]

In the afternoon of Sunday the 26th of August, a rumbling sound was continually heard throughout the old and new city of Batavia. The old city is at the end of the mole or canal entrance from the sea. It is a crowded mass of Dutch houses, some 200 years old or more, and is principally inhabited by Chinese,

Figure 24. Batavia scenes. Sketches in the September 15, 1883 Graphic made from photographs by Woodbury and Page. Top shows a private home, typically single-story (to avoid earthquake damage) and with large verandah. Middle shows the Kali Bessar, or Great River: much of the city being connected by a system of canals with the main canal, or mole, running south through the city center. Bottom shows the Pasar Bahru, or new market, near the landing place in the native quarter.

besides forming the business part of the city for merchants, banks, consuls, &c. The new part of the city is an open and spacious area of fine villas and public buildings, principally built along or near the canal. The sounds coming from the west were like distant thunder, varied by violent detonations and concussions. Doors and windows rattled so that some uneasiness was felt. When night came on a dull red glow in the western sky showed that the outbreak wherever it occurred was at no great distance. The inhabitants had heard about Krakatau, and knowing that it was nearly 100 miles away were not much disturbed. But the explosions were so very loud and distinct as night went on that many began to have misgivings, especially as the rumbling was often ominously like an earthquake, and seemed to shake the ground. Few could sleep tranquilly. Crowds began to gather in the streets, and at 2 a.m. there was such an awful explosion that most persons rushed out of their houses. . . . Sleep was impossible for the rest of night. . . .

When morning broke the light was found to be obscured. The sun did not shine, and the whole sky seemed overcast in a very strange manner. At about 7 o'clock a shower of ashes commenced to fall, and then a general feeling of alarm began to be felt as to the appalling nature of the outburst, and those places nearer to it than Batavia. The fall was intermittent until the business day began in the old town. Then the sky became pale yellow and more obscure. The ash shower was very dense, giving a deadness to the sounds of life, and leading to a kind of suffocating feeling. The gloom rapidly deepened, and by midday it was quite dark, so that lamps had to be lit in the offices and houses. A silent feeling of dread took possession of every one. Little business was done, and most persons in the city went home to their families to be ready for any catastrophe which might terminate these fearful appearances.

Notwithstanding the excitement generally prevailing (says one correspondent), and, though everyone was prepared for something dreadful, no one had the slightest idea what was to be the issue, or of what nature was the phenomenon then occurring a few leagues off, whereby so many people met with a miserable death. From the lack of sunshine, the temperature fell several degrees, people shivered with cold, or perhaps partly from anxiety and fear, especially when lamps had to be used at midday. Business of all kinds ceased. Those who could left off work and hastened home. In the lower city all the labourers from Bantam struck work, and made off in crowds. Soon half the city was forsaken. The ash shower became heavier. Meanwhile there was a great uproar, confusion, and tumult in the Chinese quarter. Every

Chinaman who could get hold of a boat brought his family, valuables, and available supplies of food into it, not knowing that the water to which he was entrusting them was just the quarter from which danger was most to be feared. Shortly before noon, the water in the mole canal rose suddenly to an alarming extent. A great sea wave came rushing up it, like a mountain, and made itself felt along all the W and NW coast of Java. It forced its way into the rivers, causing them to rise several yards and overflow their banks. Indescribable was the confusion into which prahus, sampans, kongtongs, junks, and steam launches were thrown in the lower city, and equally beyond description was the confusion in old Batavia, not only from the flooding of the streets, but from the natives and Chinese seeking safety in flight. To give some idea of the tidal wave and its force, it may be mentioned that the most strong stone coping of the wall of the mole was dismantled, and the wall itself ruined. At Tanjong Priok, the water rose 10 ft in a few minutes [tide gauge (Figure 112, p. 378) shows 7½ ft rise], and not only wholly overflowed a portion of Lower Batavia quite suddenly, but also bore fully laden prahus 30 or 40 yards ashore. This tidal wave was repeated again in the afternoon, but not so violently. However great was the force exerted by this heavy flow, there came a moment when it ceased, and the water, in masses of immense height, suddenly ebbed away, and left the canal beds and sea shore high and dry. An ebb and flow of some few minutes succeeded, and all became calm and fine again. The thick, heavy, and oppressive atmosphere, charged with sulphurous fumes, begain to clear up somewhat, despite the cold. It became lighter, and by the increasing light the inhabitants beheld a sight seldom witnessed. The streets and roads, the houses and the trees, were everywhere covered with a thick coating of white ash, giving just the appearance of a country in Europe after a heavy snowstorm.

The following excerpts are translated from the newspaper Java Bode.[57] They supplement the two foregoing accounts, but there are some minor discrepancies among the three that we cannot resolve.

When at about 2 p.m. [the 26th], a message was signalled to Anjer asking for information about the sounds heard, the reply from there was: "It is so dark here that one's hand cannot be seen when held before the eyes. Krakatau is wholly enveloped in smoke." This alas, was the last message sent to us from Anjer. In the evening at 4 or 4:30 the sounds became louder, however, and the rumble passed into variably recurring detonations much heavier than those heard some months ago during the earlier outbursts. Gradually these reports grew in strength, so that a thunderstorm which, coming in the meantime bestowed on us a few drops of the long-expected rain, was overborne completely by the threatening and terrific explosions from the volcano. When at 8 o'clock the gun was fired as usual from Fort Prins Frederick, the concussion from which had at other times proved so annoying to many old residents and newcomers at Batavia, the sound it produced resembled the report of a child's pistol in our ears, accustomed to these stronger explosions. . . . When Monday at length broke, everyone joyfully hailed the morning light, expecting it to dispel the dismal impressions unavoidably made during the night by such destructive natural phenomena. . . . The air was sluggish and the sky cloudy, and an ominous stillness and oppressiveness of the atmosphere prevailed; not a leaf, not a blade of grass stirred. . . . Suddenly at about 9 a.m., the sky became darker. . . . Soon twilight set in, and at 11 a.m., it became so pitch dark that, within the stores in town, people could not discern near objects, and candles and gaslamps had to be lighted. . . . Ashes then began to fall, while the sky on the western horizon assumed a strange dull yellow hue. Then it was that we received our first telegrams from Serang [halfway between Krakatau and Batavia] despatched at 11 o'clock that forenoon, running as follows:—"Yesterday afternoon at 3 o'clock an outburst from Krakatau was distinctly heard here. Flashes therefrom were plainly visible throughout the whole night. Since 11 o'clock last night the concussions have become stronger and more unbroken, until the sun this morning became invisible after a heavy shower of ashes fell, and it became then as dark as at 6:30 p.m. The China Camp at Pulo Merak has been swept away by the sea. Total darkness prevails here, accompanied by a shower of stones, it being dangerous to venture out without an umbrella." [The next day, August 28, another telegram from Serang brought the first news of Anjer.[56]]

"The shower of ashes since Sunday ceased at 11 last night. Today the sun became visible. Karang Antu (the port of Serang on the north coast of Bantam) has been laid waste, inclusive of warehouses. More that twenty corpses have been found. Many prahus have been destroyed. Anjer wholly laid waste. Several ladies and children from Anjer are at Chelegon [Tjilegon], several miles higher up in the mountains." [Subsequently, Lloyd's sub-agent from Anjer who had reached Serang, sent the following terse report[58] about Anjer:] "All gone. Plenty lives lost."

The above accounts and map (p. 110) show that Batavia Harbor and Tandjong Priok were separated from the main part of the city. The arrival of the main sea wave was particularly noteworthy in the harbor and we present three descriptions of the event. The first is from the master of a ship that anchored in Batavia Bay on the morning of August 28.[59]

I had never been here before, and everything was quite strange to me. I had been told earthquakes and volcanic eruptions frequently occurred, so that I was not much surprised at hearing the loud shocks and reports during the previous night. . . .

I decided to go on shore [by small boat], and had . . . not gone very far before the shower of ashes commenced. . . . Then the darkness came on—gradually at first, and then as black as night. I thought I had come to a strange place at last, but one of my men said he had heard it was often like this near Batavia. It soon grew so black that we could not make out how to steer. . . .

We had only just landed in Batavia, about noon, and had scarcely gone a hundred yards from the wharf when we heard shouts and cries behind us. Looking around we found the water in the canal leading from the sea breaking over its banks and flooding the streets. We had just time enough to get out of the way, but both of us had a narrow escape. Our boat was washed right up into the street, and the wave, when it broke over the quays, must have been quite three feet in height.

G.F. Tydemann, a lieutenant aboard the warship Koningin Emma der Nederlander, gives the following personal accounts of that morning and the arrival of the main wave.[60]

By 9:30 a.m. it was too dark in the long room to do anything so Goedhart and I tried to make the most of the diminishing light by sitting by the rear porthole reading. There was just enough light for that. We had only been there a short time when I felt a strange pressure in the ears. I had taken quinine the night before to counteract the influence of Onrust [the offshore island, 14 km NW of Batavia, where many large ships docked], but the effect of the quinine had never

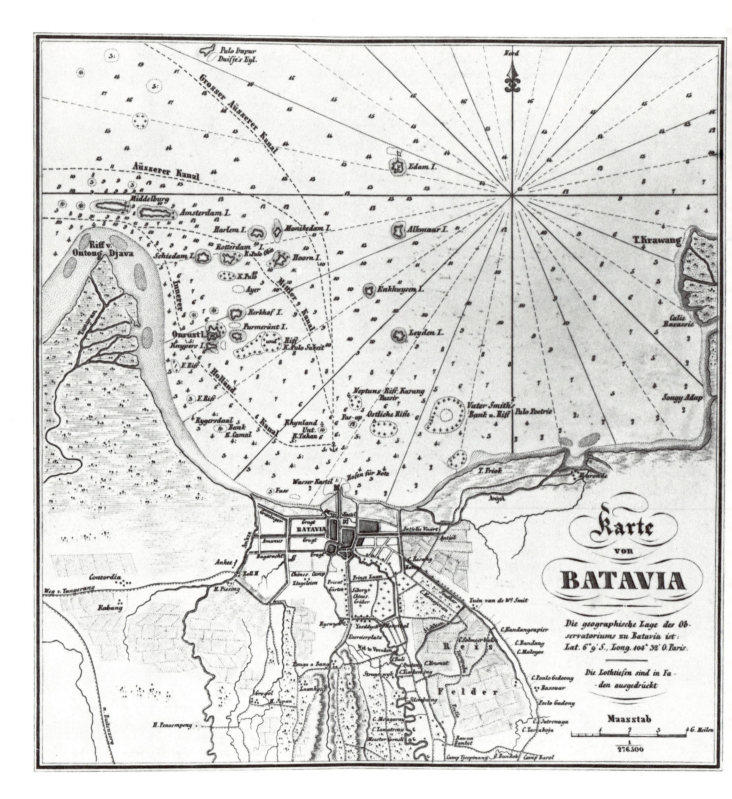

Karte von BATAVIA

Die geographische Lage des Observatoriums zu Batavia ist:
Lat. 6° 9' S., Long. 104° 32' O. Paris.

Die Lothtiefen sind in Faden ausgedrückt

Maasstab

$\frac{1}{276.500}$

110

been like this. A temperature maybe, I thought, and went on reading. A while, perhaps a quarter of an hour later, the same feeling of pressure came again, and as I looked up as if to study this sensation, Goedhart said, "What a strange feeling I have in my ears, as if something was pressing. I had it just now as well." "Me too. It must be the air pressure. Let's look at the barometer." Sure enough, this showed a lessening of pressure, 3 mm fall in a few minutes, then for half a minute steady, then again fast rising of about 7 mm again a short lull, then again a fall, and so on for some time in succession. A feeling of pressure in the ears with the rise; relief with the fall and a soft crackling noise. Gradually the times grew longer and the swinging shorter. By 12 o'clock they were no longer noticeable and the barometer remained quiet.

Meanwhile the ash rain fell thicker and it became darker. For something to do, and because the barometer was behaving so oddly, the Captain . . . ordered the yards and top-masts to be taken down. It was not wind pressure but water pressure which was turning the vessel. While the men were busy in the rigging, the water began to rise fast, just before noon, so fast and so high that the provision of the strongest mooring-rope was urgently necessary. Even higher came the tide, soon washing over the top of the jetty. Was it in fact water which rose? Was it not the bottom of the sea, the island itself perhaps, which was sinking before our eyes, perhaps for good?

Who, seeing the water rise every minute and creeping towards the houses, could answer that burning question? Who could say whether this unlucky bit of ground would not shortly be only a few feet high, with all the houses sunk many feet deep. Minutes of anxious tension followed, almost of paralysis, but also of the selfish awareness that those who stood on the deck of a good ship were safe for the time being.

Lamps had been lighted an hour before on the Island. Everything looked drab and reddish through the peculiar mist. People stared vacantly, not knowing what to do. Others walked fast, backwards and forwards. Roofs and trees were grey as from never-seen

Figure 25. Detail map of Batavia Roads and city, from 1835 German map of Java by J. Perthes. Scale is in geographic (nautical) miles, and width represented by map is 43 km. Tanjong Priok is about 5 km E of the main canal which projects northward from the city center. From the collections of the Library of Congress, Geography and Map Division.

snow. The floating dock with the three-master *Augusta* in it, an immovable threatening mass, loomed even larger than otherwise through the haze.

And suddenly, as the swelling of the water began to dawn on the inhabitants, there came cries of fear, at first far away and smothered, approaching and growing rapidly; a cry of distress from islanders and Chinese, mostly women and children who in panic tried to climb aboard anything that would float, into the sloops and on to the ships in the harbor, on to the Government steamer *Siak*, on to the floating dock, from which they were turned away, because its people had all they could do to keep the dock afloat, and finally also on board our ship.

A terror-stricken throng clambered aboard, causing terror thereto, where every moment we expected to see the mooring-ropes break, or the rails torn away. "Everyone aft. Everyone to the main deck," the officers ordered, trying to calm the terrified crowd. They had little difficulty in making room for the fear-driven people, till the ship was crowded to the half-deck. But they must hurry, for the ropes were taut like heart-strings.

One woman wished to leave the ship. But the quarter-master, standing at the gangway, pushed her back, instinctively wishing to prevent her rushing to her doom. "My children, my children," she cried. She had lost two children in the crowd, as she was pushed forward by the mass of people surging behind her. But the quarter-master still pushed her back. Maybe he did not understand what she tearfully said, busy as he was with the stream of refugees. One officer understood. "Let her go, quarter-master." Cynically but humanely he added, "Let her drown with her children if she wants to." But it was already too late. As she tried to push against the crush on the gangway, the pressure decreased, but only because the gangways were on the point of falling, and seconds later they slipped from the jetty and the ship was pushed forward by the rushing water.

For what the shocked islanders had not seen had already been noticed on board; the water had reached its highest level and had already started to fall, turning against the direction of the flow. With the rise of a moderate flow of water from the west, the port-side anchor, lying in the fairway of the channel, had provided us a safe anchorage. The launch and boat had already been smashed together, through the pressure of the ship against the jetty, so that the smaller boat was wrecked. The water flowing out towards the west gradually acquired a speed estimated at seven knots.

Bow rope and back spring parted, the bow spring pulled, and the stern of the ship sheered off. The strong tide came at an angle, under the starboard side of the vessel, and stretched the stern ropes tight on that side.

Carefully all those nearby moved forward, staring in fearsome expectation of what would break or yield, the ship's sides or the bollards, chain or the anchors? The balance lasted thus, only a few seconds, while the ship lay rudderless under the terrible pressure. Then suddenly there was a tremendous sweep of the stern to the offside of the channel, towards the Kuiper Reef; a sweep so impressive that everyone who watched it subconsciously set his shoulder against the expected jolt. And it was if it was turned by an invisible hand for, without a jolt, the ship now lay motionless but notwithstanding the water from a much wider flow. Only one stern chain, the mushroom anchor chain, now held. The other, from the buoys, lay loose in folds. The mooring-post, dug into the channel and held by a 30-lb weight, was torn out of the loosened coral base.

And now the bow chains were also ready to give; the mooring-posts were already floating. But just as they were about to sink, the order was heard, which so often gives seamen a feeling of temporary safety, "Stand by starboard anchor. Let out chain. Drop anchor."

Was the ship no longer bearing down on the Kuiper Reef, or had the mushroom anchor really found a favorable spot in which to fasten itself, just in time? The lead would perhaps provide the answer.

"Out with the lead to port." "Three and three-quarter fathoms," called the seaman. Five fathoms was the greatest depth. Surprisingly, the anchor had broken the strain. I could hardly believe it. But the lead sounding seemed doubtful on account of the strong current. Two minutes later our fears were calmed when a heavy downward drag on the chain caused the anchor to lose its grip. Three weeks later, when the vessel lay in dry dock, the zinc outer covering was found to be undamaged.

As terror rose in the hearts of the people as the water rose, so did it diminish with its retreat. For even the uneducated know that the first tidal wave is the biggest. [True only if there is but one generating shock. The noon wave that Tydemann describes so vividly here was preceded by nearly 24 hours of smaller, but nonetheless deadly waves described in many of the foregoing accounts.]

An hour later the sea reached its lowest level, some feet below the usual water-mark. The natives, who a few moments before had skirted death by drowning, jumped around the dried-out coral reefs, catching the silver white fish which swam around the shallow pools. Frantically the fish searched for greater depths, thereby betraying their presence.

In contrast to Tydemann's colorful account, Captain Visman, of the mailsteamer Princes Wilhelmina, describes the stranding of his own ship in most phlegmatic terms. He provides valuable observations on earlier ashfall as well, and we reprint below his full account of the two paroxysmal days.[19]

Sunday 26th. Covered sky wind northerly, light breeze the distant shakes become heavier, heavy blows and shakes causing doors and windows to clink.

The sky darker and darker; at 10 a.m. a very fine dust fell from the heavy clouds till 3 p.m. when a fresh sea-breeze cleared the sky again. From 6 to 9 heavy rain.

At short intervals heavy blows from Krakatau especially between 11 p.m. and 4 a.m. of 27 August, strong and nearly uninterrupted lightning in the direction of Krakatau.

The blows caused the whole ship (3500 tons) to shake heavily and give the idea of a battery of heavy guns being fired in proximity of the ship.

Barometer	8 a.m.	760
	12 noon	762
	7 p.m.	756.2

Monday 27 August. A heavy dark cloud came from the west. The dust falls again at 9 a.m. and becomes like sand and gravel falling with great noise on the tents. The sky darkening so much that we were obliged to light the lamps in the ship to keep the men at work.

The steam winches could not be used for the great amount of dust and stones, causing their metals to run hot.

After 12:30 the darkness was as intense as at midnight, with new moon and clouded sky. Wind W, WNW, light breeze, at clear glittering eastward. Carriages and tramways obliged to light their lanterns.

After 2 p.m. the sky became a little clearer, not yet quite day light from 10 o'clock until 2 p.m. the barometer very restless; sometimes up and down 12 mm within 5 minutes time.

At noon Thermometer: 24°C. Barometer: 763 to 749.

When the sand rain ceased at about 5 p.m. the ship was covered with 5 mm of dust of a blue colour just like ordinary lava stone.

Between 2 and 3 p.m. an unusual movement was noticed in the sea. The water rose about 5 ft within 10 minutes time, then it fell down again and so intensely that the difference between high and low water was 17 ft; so that the boats etc. used in the harbor and moored to the quay stand dry on the sands.

At about 2:45 the water came up again with tremendous force and went very soon over the top of the mole, making heavy whirlpools in the harbor.

However we dropped our second anchor with 45 fathoms of chain. The ship was pulled with irresistible force to the the western mole where it went ashore when the water was at rest, and could only get off by unloading the cargo.

Dust and sand rain now stopped, and the sea remained at its common height.

It is a remarkable fact that the 63 Javanese coolies who were at work on board when the darkness fell in on Monday insisted to be put ashore refusing any food, pretending to fear an inundation, when there was not yet any appearance of floods or high water.

Verbeek's account of his own observations during these two days (from his home in Buitenzorg, 45 km S of Batavia and, like Batavia, 160 km E of Krakatau) appears on p. 201, and he also reprints (p. 213) the detailed observations of the Controller at Kroë (194 km NW of Krakatau, on Sumatra's south coast). In a later section we reprint even more distant observations of the eruption's effects, but before leaving the vicinity of the eruption we move to the Aftermath section and the words of the first witnesses to view the devastation after August 27.

Aftermath; Accounts of Early Visitors to Devastated Areas

Accounts of the devastation, beyond the immediate stories of total destruction, were slow to appear. Transportation was severely limited in the affected areas, survivors were busy putting their own affairs in order, and residents of more distant cities no doubt had many disaster-related duties added to their normal work load. In this section we present first-person accounts describing the devastated areas in the months immediately following the eruption. As with the last section, we separate the accounts by region: Java, followed by Sumatra, and then the Straits.

Java Coast

Of the many descriptions of western Java, we present the accounts of coastal visits one week and six weeks after the paroxysm. But first we excerpt more of Tenison-Woods' story.[3] After a few words about Batavia itself, he provides some informative comments about the whole region.

I visited the [Batavia canal] a few days after the occurrence. The ruins along the [canal] wall were still visible, and there was much ash in the crevices and on the house tops, but all other traces had disappeared. No estimate could be formed of the loss of life. In an interview I had subsequently with the Governor-General he said that accurate statistics on the subject were as yet quite unattainable. But beyond what I have mentioned Batavia did not suffer. All the sensational accounts of the falling-in of part of the Government House, &c., which appeared in some American papers are pure fictions.

· · · · ·

It was a considerable time before the coastline could be visited and an approximate estimate of the damage done made. Even then the report was a series of negatives. Nothing was left. Not a house, scarcely a tree, not a road. All the divisions between the fields were obliterated, and the boundaries of properties destroyed. In fact, no one can tell where a house or a property stood. In Java generally there is no individual possession of the land. A certain area belongs to the village, or campong. It is tilled, or it is irrigated, by a certain stipulated division of labour, and the profits, after deducting the Government share, are divided amongst the various families, which form a kind of community. The mode of division is regulated by law. Boundaries are commonly watercourses; indeed, the whole country is parcelled out according to the wonderful Javanese system of irrigation. It is hard to say what might have been the difficulties arising from the disappearance of all landmarks by the earthquake. But with the landmarks, the crops and the population, all has been swept away. New colonies will have to settle on the locality to bring it again under cultivation, and all will have to begin anew.

· · · · ·

Confining our attention to [northern Bantam], we find that all the agricultural land of this country is on the slopes of Mount Kerang, over 6000 ft high. The extreme NW point of the island, terminating in St. Nicholas' Point, has another detached extinct crater, and in the valley between this and the Mount Kerang system is the town and bay of Anjer. North of this point there is more agricultural land than elsewhere, because it has a larger area of level alluvial soil. The actual extent of land inundated by the tidal wave was not comparatively large, but on it mainly was settled the whole, or very nearly the whole, population of that part of the country. It was principally cultivated in rice and sugar lands. On inspecting the maps of the district as it was before the disaster, we find that the area under cultivation was a narrow one, never exceeding four miles in width, and some not averaging a mile. It was only these lands that were affected by the tidal wave. The Dutch Government have issued a map on which the localities affected by the inundation are coloured, and this corresponds in an extraordinary manner with the portions marked off as under cultivation in their accurate and detailed agricultural maps. The exceptions are where a gentle slope favoured the cultivation and irrigation (inseparable things in Java) being carried up to higher levels than 100 ft above the sea. Thus south of Anjer the large rice-fields round the villages of Runtja-dering, Pamatam, and the two Sivings [all 3–4 km E and ESE of Fourth Point] were not touched, while the whole of the districts north of Anjer, comprising many thousands of acres, were laid waste. Fortunately most of the villages in this locality were built on the higher slopes of the hills. Between Anjer and Tjiringin the country may be described, at least the portions close to the sea, as a series of creeks emptying themselves into the ocean, and divided from each other by gentle

ridges covered with jungle. Only the portions very close to the sea were cultivated, as well as a few acres on the banks of the creeks. But in all, there were plantations of cocoanut-palms, with bread-fruit, jack-fruit, mango, and durian intermingled, and a very little teak-forest. All these were of course destroyed.

Between 40 and 50 villages were utterly swept away. It would be difficult to estimate the number of inhabitants who lost their lives in them on that memorable morning. Javanese villages are extremely populous. They are clusters of one-storied houses, built of bamboo, and a kind of plaited rattan woven between the posts to form the walls. There are no streets in such aggregations of houses, but they are clustered together without any apparent order, and enclosed by a slight bamboo fence. But they are all built under the thickest shade of fruit trees, of which cocoanut-palm, betel, and sugar palm (arenga) form the best part. Amidst these groves one might pass by many of the campongs or villages but for the swarms of naked children and glimpses of the highly-pitched roofs of palm thatch.

It is easy to understand how a tidal wave of any magnitude would sweep away all traces of such habitations. The trees might present a barrier for any ordinary rush of waters, but a wave 50 ft high would root them up, and carry trees, earth, and all with irresistible force, tearing the ground to great depth, and spreading the alluvial deposit and ruins on every side as it retired. It must be remembered, too, that the loose ashy or alluvial soil of Java is rarely stony. Not only would trees be easily uprooted, but the soil itself readily carried away and spread around in a finely divided state. These considerations will help to enable those at a distance to understand and realise the extent and nature of the catastrophe.

The first news from the inundated districts came from Tjiringin, about 30 miles S of Anjer. It was a large and populous town close to the seaside. It was entirely swept away. . . . The sea had scooped out a new bed for itself in some places. Thus the Chinese quarter at Tjiringin is now a portion of the ocean. At other places it had retired, and left a muddy flat strewn with seashells, the wreckage of boats, and huge blocks of coral. There are not many coral reefs in the Straits of Sunda; in fact, Java is on the NW and W side too muddy for the development of the coral animal. But still there are some reefs. Huge portions of these, several tons in weight, were broken off and borne inland, and now encumber the roads.

The post road between Arigu and Tjiringin ran

*Figure 26. Map of NW Bantam in 1886. Detail
from British Admiralty Chart to show locations
described by Neale, Gelpke, and others. From
Fourth Point Lighthouse, Merak (renamed New
Anjer) is 21 km NE, and Tjiringin (here Tyringin)
32 km SSW.*

Figure 27. Large block of coral, torn from off-shore reefs and thrown inland near Anjer. Man standing on right gives scale. Verbeek (see Figure 28) reported that this large block of coral had a volume of 300 m³ (corresponding roughly to a weight of 600 tons!). Photograph, dated 1886, from the archives of the Royal Institute for the Tropics, Amsterdam.

Figure 28. Sketch map of Java's Fourth Point Lighthouse (figure 41 in Verbeek's Atlas). Location "d" is position of 300 m³ block of coral, 6½ m high, that was swept 100 m inland by the tsunami of August 27, 1883. Old (destroyed) and new lighthouses are located by "a" and "b," respectively. Road to nearby Anjer is shown on right.

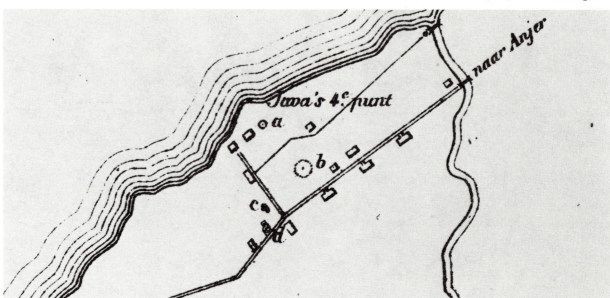

close beside the sea. It was a very good road, broad, well metalled, and fringed with trees. After the flood it was scarcely possible to discern a trace of it; the trees were, of course, laid level, and of the road a little patch of metal here and there showed where it had been.

The few who escaped to the high lands remained in the villages on the hillsides, fearing to return to the lower ground lest other tidal waves should engulf them. It was said that the natives manifested great animosity towards the Europeans, and blamed them as being the cause of this calamity. "This," they said, "is a judgement for your cruelty towards the Achimase." I doubt very much, however, if this was a feeling that was very general. The poor natives seem to have behaved with the utmost patience under the awful misfortunes which came so unexpectedly upon them. Crops, cattle, homes, and families were destroyed, and famine seemed inevitably before them. If, in the first instincts of self-preservation, they looked out for themselves, refusing aid to an alien and not very popular race, it would be no wonder. Yet very few such instances are recorded. One Dutch lady states that she was refused a drink of water except in exchange for a gold ring. On the other hand, one of the survivors stated to me that when he made his way to a village (Tjemangoe [45 km SSW of Tjiringin?]), clad only in a ragged sarang, the people took him in and gave him both clothes and food, and seemed to forget their own misfortunes in attending to his. Food of course was very scarce, and unless prompt aid had been rendered by the Government, no doubt many of those who crowded into the upland villages would have died of starvation.

When the first shock of fear was over the survivors began to descend to the plains; some to seek for the remains of their friends and relatives, others to try and recover some of their property from the universal wreck. Both objects were, of course, futile. . . . The Assistant Resident's house was still traceable by the foundations of the six rooms, which now formed six tanks of sea water. The Controller's house was quite effaced, as well as that of the native *Rajah* or Regent. It happened that there was a festival going on there, and all his family, to the number of 57, were assembled. Of these only his two nephews escaped. The exact number of Europeans who perished did not exceed 50, and of these it is said that some escaped the effect of the first wave, but in their anxiety for their relatives, or in attempting to remove property, they remained until the second wave overwhelmed them. The exact number of the Chinese who perished is not known, but it was very large, and only 20 escaped.

. . . . .

At Tjeringur [Tjiringin?] the harbour works had been washed away and the sea had rushed several miles inland. The same destruction had occurred at Karang Antoe [N of Serang], and further east two towns had entirely disappeared. The market was thronged just as the first wave broke over the shore, and when the Government pioneers reached it the market place was literally piled up with corpses— mostly of women, for these keep all the stalls in the Javanese bazaars. The number of those who perished there is estimated at 300.

The first observer dispatched to the west Java Coast by the Netherlands Indian Government was Dr. Sollewyn Gelpke whose report[61] appeared in the Batavia Handelsblad on September 8. He describes the horror of death and destruction along the densely populated coast. He also provides important insight as to the effects of airborne volcanic ash on various crops. His report begins in Tjiringin, the chief town among numerous villages some 31 km S of Anjer on a vast alluvial plain described above by Tenison-Woods:

As far as the eye can reach, the only thing that remains standing there is a solitary tree, a gigantic durian, maimed, branchless, and leafless. It forms the gravemark of a heap of corpses and carcasses lying under roofs, houses, and trunks of trees. Hundreds of such graves, though of smaller dimensions, may be seen over and over again on the plain. The turned-up earth often merely covers a corpse, alongside which a cocoanut branch or bamboo is stuck upright for the guidance of the authorities. Thousands of corpses of human beings and also carcasses of animals still await burial, and make their presence apparent by an indescribable stench. They lie in knots and entangled masses impossible to unravel, and often jammed along with cocoanut stems among all that had served these thousands as dwellings, furniture, farming implements, and adornments for houses and compounds.

The work of devastation did not last long. Only one tidal wave was seen. A second and a third probably followed, but were not noticed. The sea carried along coral rocks several hundred picals [probably *pikul*, slightly less than 1 kg] in weight and left them behind on the plain as if they had been so many shells. On the other hand it tore off extensive areas from the land, so that its bed now extends to the ground on which the market place and the Chinese quarter at Tjiringin once stood. The roads in that neighbourhood are unrecognisable. In the European quarter the foundations of houses serve as waymarks. The fields, strewn with corpses, offer an unusually animated scene in spite of their horrors. Controleur Tromp has taken vigorous action for burying the corpses at the rate of 5 guilders apiece. For this purpose, men are called up from each village separately. But along with the gravediggers, thousands of people come provided with handspikes or sharpened stakes to be serviceable to them as implements either in searching for their own property or in robbing what belonged to others. For robbery is the only object for which hundreds of all ages and both sexes are disposed to venture going to Tjiringin, where but few police are available. On my approach a group of them dispersed, to return forthwith, like hyenas scared from a battlefield, should the check on them be removed. Many gangs remained, robbing on as if they were owners of the articles which they dug up. Some of the robbers are aware of the whereabouts of the missing Government cash boxes. At least, this must be inferred from the considerable amounts of money found on several persons who were arrested near Pandeglang [32 km E of Tjiringin].

The affecting sight presented to spectators by the corpses and their gravediggers need not be described in a report like this, but it is worth mentioning that no corpse can be recognised, not even by its nationality, so that all the stories about recognition of corpses must not be believed. In that quarter, the limit of the havoc wrought by the tidal wave extends along the hill range between Tjiringin and Anjer 1 to 11 miles from the sea, and to 5 or 7 miles from it within the district of Penimbang. To villages on these hills, and even still higher ones, thousands fled, thinking that at any moment the wave might again come on, and hence were unwilling to return. But in fact, returning to these carrion fields with their pools and lagoons of rotting sea water is now impossible.

· · · · ·

Before I proceed with the description of the whole country, which, with the exception of the now devastated coast district, forms the seashore boundaries of the province of Bantam, the subject of the ash and mud showers must be dealt with. After a course of 22 miles in a straight line, the ashes cast out by Krakatau on the west coast of Java sunk to the stratum of air touching the firm ground. The quantities of ashes sank lower still, covering the ground and whatever stood thereon, but in the midst of this eruption a rain shower fell over a portion of the provinces of Bantam. The immediate consequence of it was that the ashy particles were carried along in the fall, and that the larger particles adhered together until no rain, but flakes of mud fell, which sometimes were several square inches in size. Where the ashes fell without rain, or with only a little they did slight harm, but where rain had clotted them into mud they destroyed leaves and branches by their weight. Moreover, the mud was accompanied by a moist heat which scorched everything green around, while on drying, it continued to stick to whatever it had struck on or against. After this explanation it will become plain how it is that in many tracts closely bordering on the devastated portion of Anjer and Tjiringin the trees have remained almost uninjured, while throughout the district of Serang they have heavily suffered; and how it is that, in the western portion of the province, they look again healthy after a little rain had relieved them of their ashes, while in some parts of Pandeglang and Rankasbetong and even on the private estates of Chikandie Udik [100 km E of Krakatau], where the ashy layers were thinnest, all the leaves have come off from the cocoanut trees, and not one banana stem has remained standing.

Now that a sounder judgement can be formed after the lapse of 8 days, and after a couple of heavy rain showers have fallen at the nick of time, the conclusion may be come to that the ash showers alone will have little harmful effect on fruit trees, but that where mud had fallen the crop therefrom will be very short. Growing paddy on the fields is in all stages of growth, from seedlings to ripening grain. Only ripening crops have been struck down and covered with ashes and mud, but at fifteen places I saw the ripe ears of paddy plucked out uninjured, though gathering operations were proceeding slowly. The paddy with young ears is damaged beyond recovery, from their growth being checked by the ashes sticking to them. The crops in other stages of growth are almost uninjured. Within the last few days they have grown several inches, and in some places the young plants have struck root or are looking luxuriant.

Finally, comes the coffee in Pandeglang [70 km E × S of Krakatau]. The trees there have suffered much injury, owing to branches from the shade trees falling on them when bent under the overlying ashes. They have lost their leaves, but new ones are appearing. The blossoms on them are, however, gone. The coffee plants in the nurseries may also be mostly written off, those with only two leaves being unable to bear up against the ash and mud showers. Not only are the prospects encouraging as regards the land under cultivation, from the circumstance that the root crops of all kinds are flourishing, but from the fact that all sorts of plants and, particularly grasses, live on the surface of the ground in soil mixed with ashes. Though the ashes, unchanged as they are, have had no effect, yet chemically they may in the end prove beneficial by making more porous the soil under the plough. Ploughing has not become more difficult on their account, as I saw myself and heard from many cultivators.

In conclusion, the foregoing notes lead consequently to the inference that the dreadful calamity which struck Bantam is, in its worst form, localised to the thickly peopled and productive tract along the north and west coasts, varying from 1 to 7 miles in breadth, and that, further inland, thus over the larger portion of the province, much damage has probably been done to the fruit trees, but the layer of ashes on the ground may shortly, or otherwise in the long run, prove beneficial rather than harmful to the soil.[62]

By far the most vivid first-hand account of the Java coast devastation is that of Philip Neale, the British Chaplain at Batavia whose words we have reprinted above (see p. 74). His journey began in early October.[63]

Six weeks after the catastrophe I found that I was the second European visitor who had been at Anjer. It would have been much more interesting, of course, to have gone earlier, but this was scarcely expedient until most of the dead bodies had been buried. When the great volcanic wave receded thousands of corpses were left behind exposed to the fierce rays of a tropical sun. Natives from the surrounding *kampongs* were called in to perform the melancholy work of burying their less fortunate neighbours. And what a task it must have been as day after day, for several weeks, they thus toiled! The single European who had been there previously to inspect the repairs to the Singapore telegraph cable could not bear the sight of his terrible

surroundings, and, we were told, had beat a hasty retreat. Fortunately the worst was over when we visited the district early in October. Lloyd's agent at Batavia [Mr. McColl] was my travelling companion. His errand was to find out the most suitable site for the new shipping station in the Straits of Soenda in place of ill-fated Anjer, and I gladly accepted the opportunity of going with him.

We made an early start from one of the suburbs of Batavia, and drove into the city at daybreak, there to commence our long journey by road to the western coast. [After two and one half hours in their carriage, colorfully described by Neale, they reached the town of Tangerang, 20 km W of Batavia. The carriage was drawn by teams of 4 ponies, changed at each posting station positioned 6 paalen (7.6 km) apart.]

The longer we travelled on the more noticeable became the various traces of damage along the road caused by the Krakatoa outburst. The dust from the showers of ash could be plainly seen by the roadside not many miles from the capital, and each mile made it the more distinct, until at length the road seemed completely covered with it. As this was exactly six weeks after the occurrence, its existence so many miles from the volcano is the more remarkable, and proves how thickly it must have originally fallen. About twenty miles from Batavia we came to some damaged palm and banyan trees. Heavy branches had been broken off by the weight of the ashes, and other large trees had been completely blighted, probably by the strong sulphuric fumes. There were many miles of these injured trees, the damage done gradually increasing the farther we journeyed on.

. . . . .

At length, fifty-eight paalen [73 km] from Batavia, we drew up early in the afternoon at the hotel at Serang, and after luncheon prepared to visit some of the ruined districts. We were now in the Residency of Bantam, a district which gives its name to the celebrated breed of fowls with which most of us are familiar. Bantam is the most ancient of the settled districts in the island, the Portuguese having formed a settlement there in 1524. It was not until seventy years later that the Dutch arrived upon the scene and founded their new home in Bantam and Batavia. The Portuguese had not been long in the island when they had their first experience of a volcanic eruption. Mount Ringgit, in Eastern Java, broke out in 1586, and one of their settlements was completely destroyed. [Neale and McColl then transferred to a small, two-wheeled cart, called a *ka-har*, for a 10 km side trip to the north.]

Karang-Antu is a small town on the north coast, and being the nearest port for Serang, was a thriving business centre. It is situated in the sheltered bay of Bantam, and, owing to its position, did not suffer so much as Anjer and the other places on the western coast, which we visited on the following day. As we drew near to the outskirts of the kampong we began to see a little of the ravages caused by the volcanic wave. Even here, between thirty and forty miles from Krakatoa, the water had dashed inland for a couple of miles, but the damage done was very small compared with what we saw later on in less fortunate districts. The first thing we noticed on the road from Serang was a picturesque village once embosomed in trees, but now partly in ruins. This kampong consisted of the usual cottages made of bamboo, and the roof thatched with dry palm-leaves, which naturally offered very little resistance to a great rushing torrent of water. Many of the cocoanut palm-trees were snapped off, just as a stick might be. Farther on we came to a broken boat lying by the roadside, washed in, two miles from the coast. From distinct marks on the trees the wave here must certainly have been some twenty feet high. It was only in a few places, however, that it had had fatal results. Some exposed parts of the district entirely escaped, while several of the more sheltered kampongs suffered severely.

Altogether, in the neighbourhood of Karang-Antu the loss of life must have been between two and three hundred. This, of course, was serious enough, but on the following day, in other parts of the Residency, we found the hundreds turned into thousands. Our driver soon came to an abrupt stop at the side of a river owing to the road having been washed away, and a bridge being too much damaged to bear even our light *ka-har*. We accordingly obtained a heavy boat, and sailed down the river and out to sea. Bantam Bay is exceedingly pretty, and has three or four small islands densely clad in tropical verdure down to the water's edge. None of these had suffered in the least, nor were the banks of the river much injured.

. . . . .

Leaving Bantam Bay—a spot more beautiful than healthy[64]—behind us, we retraced our steps to the little town of Serang. It was a long, dark drive, and we were very thankful when our tired ponies brought us back once more to the friendly shelter of the hotel from which we had started in the afternoon, and which we had then arranged should be our resting-place for the night.

. . . . .

Knowing that a hard day's work awaited us on the morrow, combined with a very early start, we were soon glad to creep into our mosquito-curtained beds, and get a good night's rest. . . . At any rate, on this occasion we found the night far too short, for it was scarcely four o'clock when we were summoned to prepare for our second day of exploration.

. . . . .

The first part of our journey lay along the main post-road once more, and so our travelling-carriage of the previous day was again brought into use. Our Batavian driver was still on the box, but the ponies and "runners" were provided fresh for each stage.

. . . . .

At Tjilegon, at the end of the second stage from Serang, [Tjilegon is 15 km NE of Anjer and 11 km SE of Merak], we came to the last of our posting. We could go no farther, for the best of all reasons, "because there was no road," as a Dutch official naïvely informed us, and on further inquiry we learnt that on the two remaining stages so much damage had been done as to render posting quite out of the question.

. . . . .

Whilst the choice of a suitable conveyance was being made we had been waiting in the hotel at Tjilegon, a building which bore serious traces of the damage caused by the eruption. . . . The official in charge showed us the marks, both inside and outside the building, which the eruption had caused. The pillars in the front portico were injured considerably, and the heavy ash rain had left some ugly stains on many parts of the whitewashed walls and outside verandahs. [Neale then transfered to another cart, shared with the young survivor from Anjer who gave Neale his personal account printed earlier on p. 74.]

With such a companion as this at my side our three miles drive in the *ka-har* seemed quickly over. And now at a turn in the road the scene of destruction suddenly came in view. Descending a little hill, we came into level country, and saw at a glance the terrible havoc which the inundation had caused. First came the destroyed roadway. The well-made road from Batavia to Merak—on which we had thus far travelled—now came to an abrupt ending. Its metalled track had suddenly disappeared, partly washed away at first, and a little farther on completely swept away. A ruined bridge was all that remained to show where once the road had been. Our *ka-har* could now proceed no farther, and the rest of our exploration had to be performed on foot. We were still several miles from the coast, but all the land between us was perfectly bare of timber. A few weeks before, the whole of the country we were gazing on was one dense forest of cocoa-nut palms, and beneath the shelter of tropical vegetation scores of native *kampongs* nestled, inhabited by many thousands of busy people. And now this immense district—fifteen miles long and four or five in width—was so completely ruined as to be nothing more or less than a huge cemetery. What a change had come over that thriving district on the western shore of Java in so short a period! The palm-trees were all thrown down—without a single exception torn up by the roots, lying in endless confusion one above another. The native houses—made of their frail materials of bamboo and leaves—were now on the ground, just as the receding waters had left them. Beneath the fallen *débris* lay all kinds of smashed furniture, broken cooking utensils, doors wrenched from their hinges, and every article of native costume in one great indescribable mass.

A more awful sight could scarcely be imagined. One great matter for thankfulness, as the fierce rays of a tropical sun beat down upon us, was that nearly all the bodies had been recovered and buried. It was well for us that our visit had not been made earlier, or else the sight would have been a still more terrible one. Now and again we detected decomposing matter near us, and the Malays who were accompanying us said that probably many a body still lay concealed beneath the immense fallen masses which lay on each side of us, and which they had not yet had time to examine. Closely following our guides, we made our way very slowly through the ruined district. A rougher piece of walking I never experienced. The road had completely disappeared, and there was no track or footpath in its place. Fallen trees lay everywhere, and every few yards they had to be scrambled over. By many a *détour* we tried to avoid the masses of fallen *débris*, and frequently these too had to be scaled, or else all further progress would have been stopped. Mile after mile we slowly picked our way amid these melancholy surroundings. Here and there we found ourselves hemmed in by pools of water, left in the hollows after the wave had receded. Whenever possible we waded through these, or if too deep for fording a long circuit had to be made.

But one of the most remarkable facts concerning the inundation remains to be told. As we walked or scrambled along we were much surprised to find great masses of white coral rock lying at the side of our path in every direction. Some of these were of immense

size, and had been cast up more than two or three miles from the seashore. It was evident, as they were of coral formation, that these immense blocks of solid rock had been torn up from their ocean bed in the midst of the Soenda Straits, borne inland by the gigantic wave, and finally left on the land several miles from the shore. Anyone who had not seen the sight would scarcely credit the story. The feat seems an almost impossible one. How these great masses could have been carried so far into the interior is a mystery, and bears out what I have said in previous papers as the height of this terrible wave. Many of these rocks were from twenty to thirty tons in weight, and some of the largest must have been nearly double. Lloyd's agent, who was with me, agreed in thinking that we could not be mistaken if we put down the largest block of coral rock that we passed, as weighing not less than fifty tons.

It seems very hard to imagine what a great volume of water would be required to carry such heavy masses so far into the adjacent country. The force with which they had met obstructions was very noticeable in several instances. In one case a bridge had been ruined by being thus struck. The keystone of the arch carrying the road over a little stream had been struck by a piece of rock some twenty tons in weight, and this mass had split the brickwork right through the centre just like a wedge, and lay finally jammed in half across the road. It is not at all probable that some of the larger of these coral blocks will ever be moved from the spots where the receding waters have left them, and they will thus remain a standing memorial of the Krakatoa disaster in August, 1883. To scientific men they will naturally be objects of no little interest, as being an index, to some extent, of the power which water has as an element of destruction, and also as gauging the immense height of the unparalleled volcanic wave.

Merak, the district through which our path thus far lay, was densely populated, and this will account for the great loss of life which here occurred. Our intelligent Malay guide told us something of the difficulties of his task in superintending the workmen who were engaged in recovering the bodies of the ill-fated victims. About three thousand he considered had been recovered in the neighbourhood where we then were. Most of them were buried as near as possible to the places where they were discovered, so that there should be as little carrying about as possible. In some cases it was found necessary to burn the remains. We could scarcely take a step anywhere in one part of the district without walking on a grave. Wherever we saw a stake driven into the ground we knew that some unfortunate victim lay buried beneath.

Nearer to Merak was the Chinese settlement. Their bodies were treated just the same as the Javanese—buried or burnt, as was thought best at the time. The great difficulty of the superintendent was in finding workers for this sad task. It was only by sending to distant *kampongs* that the services of a sufficient number of coolies could be obtained. Some of these soon fell ill and died, and thus added a few more to the long roll of victims.

Mile after mile, amid the most melancholy surroundings of death and destruction, had to be traversed before we reached our first halting-place at Merak. And very weary miles they were. It is most unusual in any part of Java for a European to be seen walking beneath the rays of the fierce tropical sun, but on this occasion there was no help for it. We must either walk or remain behind. Driving was, of course, quite out of the question; riding was equally impracticable, on account of the fallen *débris*; and even walking was a most difficult and fatiguing task.

Java—within six degrees of the equator—is no place for pedestrian exercise after the sun has risen, and though thinly clad, we had soon had enough of it. However, we still scrambled on as best we could. At one time we were clambering over the trunks of several fallen palm-trees, torn up by the roots and jammed together in one inextricable mass by the rushing torrent. At another, we found our progress barred by the huge blocks of coral rock, which had to be scaled in spite of their rough surface and meagre foothold. Then, again, we reached some heavy swampy ground many inches in depth, caused by the dense fall of grey ash having been turned into mud by the wave. Throughout our route lay the overthrown cottages and their scattered contents. Here a broken doorway, there a smashed bedstead; clothing, crockery, and furniture lying on all sides in hopeless confusion. Most of the least injured domestic articles had been already carried away by the natives, and this only served to make the scene of destruction seem more complete.

Such was the spectacle which met our eyes the whole of the distance towards Merak. Now and again a few feet of the old roadway could be traced, but for the most part it had completely disappeared, and the natives walking to and fro in their work of recovering the dead must have formed an entirely new track. At intervals we passed a few solitary Malays working amidst the ruin, but considering the large district we traversed there were comparatively very few about. Without a

single exception, the whole of the cocoa-nut palm-trees had been thrown down. Not one was left standing on the low ground near the coast, and it was not until the higher country was reached, several miles inland, that we found any trees which had escaped. The palm-trees have no depth of root, and consequently they offered but little resistance to the rushing waters. Stronger trees, however, on the rising ground, such as the Java *waringin*, were not so easily destroyed, and many of these had their trunks snapped off about twenty feet from the ground. The value of the timber and fruit destroyed was immense.

At length the first stage of our weary walk was coming to an end. We were now in sight of all that was left of the flourishing town and district of Merak. A few weeks before it had been the centre of teeming life and activity, and now not a single habitation remained. A solitary tent—pitched on an adjacent hill, with the Dutch tri-coloured flag floating above—was the only sign of life, and this was the temporary home of one of the few surviving Soenda Straits pilots. This man had fortunately been engaged in piloting a vessel to Batavia at the time of the eruption, and had thus escaped the effects of the volcanic wave on shore. It was in the Merak district that the greatest loss of life had occurred. Thousands upon thousands had here perished, and as many as 3,000 bodies had actually been recovered in the neighbourhood, in spite of the receding waters which carried all before them. To account for this immense loss of life it must be remembered that the island of Java is one of the most densely populated countries in the world. In calculating the average number of inhabitants to a square mile, there is only one country, I believe, which exceeds it. The following figures, published officially by the Dutch Government, will give some idea of the immense population and of its mixed character. Leaving out the Europeans and Chinese, there is in Java, at the present time, a native population of over 20,000,000. Next come the Chinese with 220,000, the Dutch with 37,000, the Arabs with 10,000, and last, as well as least, the English community of not more that 120 persons, all told.

There was an additional reason, too, why the Merak district had such a large resident population. In its neighbourhood were some very extensive stone quarries, employing a large number of hands, and these all perished in the midst of their work on that fatal Monday. They were engaged in preparing stone for the Batavia Haven-werken Company, who are constructing new docks at Tandjong Priok, close to the capital, and were swept away without any warning. As we approached the quarries a terrible scene of destruction again awaited us. The strong railway line, used for conveying the stone to the neighbouring jetty, was torn up for many hundreds of yards, twisted and bent just like wire [see Figure 16]. The fish-plates connecting the lengths of rail had held securely, and when the metals had been torn from the sleepers by the rushing water, the latter had been curved and bent in serpentine fashion, and carried a great distance from their original position. One of these lengths of torn-up rail must have measured a quarter of a mile. The railway trucks had fared very badly, having been dashed in all directions, and greatly damaged. Two of the locomotives employed on the quarry line, in spite of their great weight, did not escape so well as one would have imagined. One of them, a six-wheeled tank engine, was washed off the rails and thrown completely over on its side. The other, of similar size and construction, was more damaged, and had actually been carried right out to sea. There it lay, a battered wreck, some fifty yards from the beach, with the waves surrounding and breaking over it. This will give some idea again of the force of the torrent, but it is certainly not more remarkable than the huge blocks of coral rock which we found washed so far inland.

Passing on, we came at length to the little hill close to the ocean, on which, as before mentioned, the Dutch pilot had erected his temporary canvas home. Ascending it, we had a good view of the surrounding country. As far as the eye could reach there was the same sad scene of desolation and ruin. There too rolled the peaceful ocean, with its placid waves glittering in the dazzling sunshine. It was very hard to realise as the waters broke so gently upon the shore beneath that such a dreadful element of destruction could have risen so recently from their quiet depths. It was on this hill overlooking the sea at Merak that we were able to form a correct idea of the height of the volcanic wave when it first broke upon the Java coast, and this is how we came to our conclusion that the wave must have been at least 120 ft high. [McColl places the wave height at 135 ft, or 41 m.[65]] The ground on which we were standing was more than 100 ft above the sea level, and on the highest part of it had been erected a large brick house, occupied by the resident engineer connected with the quarries. It was very strongly built, as European houses in the tropics always are, with good solid foundations, and yet, although more than a hundred feet above the sea, this massive dwelling had been completely razed to

the ground by the passing wave. The walls had been washed away as neatly as if they had been sliced off with a knife, and nothing remained standing but the brick and marble floors, which rested on the strong foundation. There were marks on each side of the hill showing how the resistless torrent of water had escaped down the slope, bearing the ruined house and its contents far away.

At the time of our visit a vigorous search was being made by the natives for a large safe containing books and money connected with the quarry works, which having been carried away with the house, had up to that time remained undiscovered. The search for it was a hopeless task, and possibly it had been carried out to sea by the receding waters.

·····

A brief rest at Merak, and then we had to think of making a start for Anjer. We had hoped to have sailed down, the distance being only ten miles, but the wind was unfortunately against us, and we had to retrace our steps to the place where our ka-hars were waiting. Before leaving Merak we had a splendid view of the Soenda Strait. Turning our backs upon the land in the vain hope of shutting out the scene of horrors we had so lately been witnessing, we looked out to sea and found a beautiful scene before us [see Plate 1A]. Opposite to us lay the coast of Sumatra, with a hot misty haze rising from its sunny coast. Towering far above the dense green mass of vegetation were the wooded heights of Mount Radjah Bassa, 4000 ft above the sea. Half way across the strait lay a small island, clad in tropical verdure, rejoicing in the appropriate name of "Athwart the way." Krakatoa had found this island very much in its way during its outburst, and in a destroying mood had actually split up its little neighbour into four or five still more diminutive pieces. Not content with this, it had carried its work of destruction still farther, Poeloe Temposa [a small islet N of Merak Island] and several other smaller islands having totally vanished from the Soenda Strait.

Part of the walk back was saved by obtaining a boat and some natives to row us a mile or two along the coast. This was all very well as long as we kept out to sea, but when we wished to land we found it very risky work to again approach the shore. The coast was lined with coral rock—thrown up by the waves—and many a sharp-pointed block lay just below the surface. We had several narrow escapes of striking upon the latter, and owing to the great depth of water, an accident to the boat would have been very serious. The native boatmen, however, landed us in safety at last,

Figure 29. Destruction caused by tsunami at Merak. The wave reached its greatest height—135 ft by McColl's measurement—here near the stone quarry. Tenison-Woods (1884) recounted that "strewn about were massive iron trolleys, engines, locomotives, fragments of iron columns, and rails torn up, twisted, and broken like wire." Photographs taken in early 1886, presumably by the Batavia firm of Woodbury and Page. From archives of Royal Institute for the Tropics, Amsterdam.

and after a long walk we were glad to find ourselves back again at the spot where our conveyances awaited us.

With hands and face scorched and sunburnt, we again proceeded on our way, beneath the fierce rays of the midday sun. We were very tired and thirsty, and there was no water to be had. My companion, one of the Anjer survivors, who still rode with me, soon found a means of quenching our thirst. Stopping the ka-har, for a few cents he induced some of the coolies who were passing to climb a palm-tree at the roadside and throw down the fruit. Only the green cocoa-nuts were chosen, and when an opening had been cut in the thick outside rind, they were presented to us that we might drink the contents. [During this rest, one of the Javanese laborers from Merak gave Neale the eyewitness account reprinted above on p. 77.]

Soon after noon we were back again at Tjilegon, and at once, with fresh ponies, began our journey to the ruined and deserted town of Anjer. When within five miles of the latter place we came to the post-station of Tjigadieng. The buildings forming it had been clean swept away, the foundations of the brickwork alone remaining. The road soon after this became broken up, and we had some very rough travelling. Many of the bridges had been carried away, but most of them were repaired with a temporary bamboo covering, and, with many misgivings, we gently made our way across these frail and swaying structures. At length our damaged road got worse and worse, and our driver declined to proceed. A little coaxing and threatening combined induced him to make another start; but at last we were quite satisfied that the road was impassable, and two miles from Anjer we again had reluctantly to commence our pedestrian exercise beneath a burning tropical sun.

The same scene of ruin and death, such as we had just left behind us at Merak, again presented itself. Fallen trees and fallen houses were all that remained of what was once a well-built and thriving Dutch town. I had seen photographs of what Anjer had been in its original state six weeks before, but only one feature in it was at all recognisable, and that was a strongly-built fort, which now lay in a ruined state. [See Figure 14.] It had been too strong to be carried away bodily by the wave, but had nevertheless suffered severely. Only in a few places could the chief streets of the town be traced. The river had been strangely diverted in its course, and now took an entirely different channel, necessitating numbers of temporary bamboo bridges to be thrown over it. My companion, who had lived in the place all his life, was now so much out of his reckoning that he positively could not point out the street where his home had been. When I pressed him to give me some idea of where he had lived, he told me that he thought the river must now be flowing over the site, as he could not understand his whereabouts at all. One solitary tree, a huge waringin, was the only surviving one of the dense forest which had originally surrounded the town. Great masses of coral rock lay about in every direction, just as we had seen them, earlier in the day, near Merak. Being closer to the sea, they were if anything larger than the ones I have previously described. There was not a trace to be seen of the Anjer lighthouse, so complete had been its destruction.

Proceeding onward to the outskirts of the ruined town, we came to the European cemetery—a pretty spot, on slightly elevated ground, overlooking the sea. The destruction here had been very great. Not a single gravestone or monument remained to mark the last resting-place of those who had lived and died in Anjer's happier days. And in some cases, even, the more recent graves had been washed open, and the bodies interred had apparently been carried out to sea by the receding waters.

Very few of the thousands who perished in this neighbourhood were recovered. One of the few natives whom we found in the ruined town told us that not more than 300 had been buried in the whole town and district. It is the more easy to believe, therefore, the accounts of the captains, who reported on arrival at Batavia that their vessels in the Straits of Soenda had passed through hundreds of dead and floating bodies.

As we turned our faces homeward from this awful scene of devastation and death, we caught a glimpse in the distance of the famous Krakatoa. There it lay, quite out at sea, nearly thirty miles distant, a solitary island, with its cone-shaped mountain rising up to a height of 2,600 ft, not only uninhabited itself, but the terrible destroyer of fully fifty thousand souls. After careful inquiry, I do not think the loss of life could have been less than this, and possibly it may have been even more. The extent of coast destroyed or damaged between Karang-Antu on the north and Tjiringin on the west must have been fully twenty-five miles.

Finally we return to Seaman Dalby, whose June description of Anjer as "a real paradise" we reprinted above (p. 66). After a trip to Saigon, his ship Hope was anchored in Batavia Bay during the paroxysm, and then went to Singapore. They anchored at Anjer again on the day that the Reverend Neale was leaving Batavia on the trip just described.[66]

We left Singapore with a general cargo and arrived again in the Straits of Sunda on October 7, this time homeward bound. There were vessels of all nationalities surveying the Straits. Our charts were useless and a special pilot came aboard. It was my wheel and he told me that the navigation of the Straits was completely altered. We sailed near the spot where the city of Anjer once stood with its 25,000 [sic] inhabitants. The shores on each side looked burnt up and sterile. Java is known as the Garden of the East, but this bit looked more like the Sahara, absolutely desolate. On the top of a solitary cocoanut palm a flagstaff held a signal: "Call here for letters." It gave the most careless of us something to think of. In place of scores of bumboats loaded with fruit, only one appeared, but they had no fruit, only shells, coral and curios. One poor creature told me: "Mudder, Fader, kinde all gone!"

Sumatra Coast

Several accounts in the Paroxysm chapter described the devastation around Lampong Bay immediately after the August 27 tsunami. The story of the Beyerinck family, ended on p. 85 with their rescue. We start this section with a telegraph account of that rescue from Batavia.[67]

Steamer with Telegraph inspector back from Kalianda Lampong Bay brought Collector of revenues of that district with wife and two children whom he found few miles inland in a pitiful condition, fearfully scorched, lost one child. 8 a.m. Lampong natives evilly disposed attributing like Bantammers cause disaster to Achean war [Dutch war against Sultan of Achin, Atjeh, NW Sumatra]. Collector Kalianda escaped murder by promising to send rice. (not known?) what other Europeans saved, remainder in danger being murdered.

8:30 a.m. attempt to reach Telok Betong overland considered impossible without armed escort. 9 a.m. inspector reports heavily, in relating story (states) widespread misery. Thousands corpses floating about, many scorched to death, desolation over mainland extends three miles from beach. 10 a.m. collector describes eruptions as dull between mount Radjabassa and Krakatau, intervening ground upheaved, hot sand rose from under him whilst scalding feet of fugitives.

Controller Beyerinck's own assessment of the damage to Lampong Bay was reported in the newspaper Java Bode on 10 September.[68]

The havoc resulting at Katimbang in the Lampong districts from the eruption of Krakatau is officially reported by Mr. Beyerinck, Controleur there, on his arrival at Batavia, to be 32 villages devastated, one thousand persons drowned, and two thousand killed by showers of hot ashes.

At present Telok Betong and its immediate neighbourhood are unavailable for trade by sea. This in itself is a misfortune and an inconvenience so great that it would be sufficent, without taking other circumstances into account, to mark out the Krakatau calamity as one of the most dreadful visitations of the kind which have ever stricken Netherlands India.

Further news of the region in mid-September appeared in the Straits Times.[69]

The latest intelligence from the Lampong districts in Sumatra was that Telok Betong, the chief port, continued to be blocked up by pumice, and that corpses were still lying about in the neighbourhood on all sides, poisoning the atmosphere. The disposition of the people was reported to be excellent everywhere. At Katimbang, where hot ashes and pumice fell, seven to eight hundred corpses still remained unburied, eighteen days after the calamity. In villages numbering 250 inhabitants only twelve to forty of the latter have survived at each. Five thousand persons are officially estimated to have perished at Telok Betong. The tidal wave reduced that town to a heap of timbers and bricks, and carried a man-of-war, the *Berouw*, two miles inland, and left her behind some hills. Save the Resident, whose house was spared, from being on high ground, the Europeans there had been reduced to destitution, and had to be supplied by the relief committee with clothing and money. Swarms of flies, attracted by the corpses, had proved very troublesome to the survivors.

The *Kedirie*, a hopper dredger, had been dispatched from Batavia to Telok Betong. On their return those on board reported as follows:—After signals had been repeatedly blown from the steam whistle, several natives descended from the mountains to the beach, upon which Lieutenant Koster, along with Dr. Vorderman and several others, left the vessel in a boat, and proceeded towards the landing place. On reaching the latter, they, for the first time, beheld all the horrible results of the calamity—such as rotting and foul smelling corpses and carcasses, the few survivors all suffering from burns, the country around laid waste, and the houses gone. Of that of the headman, the foundations only were visible. A zinc roof, too, had remained and had been utilised to cover a hut on the beach. Taken as a whole, the scene presented was one which no pen can describe, and which must be actually seen to give any idea of it. But there is one bright side to this devastation, namely, that all the mosquitoes have been destroyed! In the Lampongs, at least in the stricken districts, not one of them can be detected. Have they been killed by the ashes or by the mud?

The Berouw, mentioned above, was first beached by an early wave on Monday morning and later transported inland by the largest wave (see p. 91). These unlikely resting places are shown on Verbeek's map of Telok Betong (p. 87). The ship was found behind a bend in the valley of the Koeripan River, 3300 m from its anchorage, and was described in September, 1883, by Lt. Koster of the Kedirie:[70]

I visited the ship on Saturday. It lays almost completely intact, only the front of the ship is twisted a little to port, the back of the ship a little to starboard. The engine room is full of mud and ash. The engines themselves are not damaged very much, but the flywheels were bent by the repeated shocks. It might be possible to float the ship again, sometime when the

Koeripan has enough water. But this is a question for the future.

The Berouw was never refloated. Fifty years later, photographs[70] *show only the heavy metal boiler remaining at the river bank illustrated in Figure 30. Photographs taken 95 years after the eruption*[71] *show the boiler in the same place, but in February, 1979, heavy flooding carried it 1 km downriver where it was cut up and sold for scrap.*

Nearly a month after the eruption, however, the area damaged by the waves remained grim, as reflected in the following accounts from Java newspapers.[72]

The Batavia *Dagblad* of the 25th September reports that by last accounts from Telok Betong, dated the 19th of that month, corpses were still lying unburied on the beach there, though 23 days had elapsed since the volcanic eruption, and the fee for burying them had been fixed at 2½ guilders each. Farther inland, corpses are described as still strewing the roadsides and lying in stagnant pools and morasses, where they contaminated the air so increasingly that travellers passing by had to avoid them, and there were great apprehensions of an outbreak of disease, several cholera cases having already occurred. The port was then still blocked up by pumice fields.

· · · · ·

Mr. Shuick, an official recently visiting the Lampong coast, thus sums up his experiences:—Lampong Bay, formerly so picturesque, is wholly changed in appearance since the volcanic eruption. All the trees are dead. The hills and mountains have all the same pale yellow or dark grey colour. The shores both of the islands and mainland, to a height of 10 to 120 ft above sea level, are quite bare, and covered with a grey coloured muddy deposit probably left behind there by the tidal wave. Where formerly hundreds of white sails on fishermen's prahus and crafts were charmingly reflected upon the blue surface of the water, the only living creature now visible is a solitary water bird which wanders by itself along the greyish plain.

By December, fortunately, the situation in the Lampong districts had improved. The official dis-

Figure 30. The steamship Berouw, torn from its mooring in Telok Betong Harbor, was swept inland by the wave and marooned almost intact in the valley of the Koeripan River, 2½ km from the sea. Etching by T. Weber, from a field sketch by M. Korthals (from Cotteau, 1886, p. 125).

trict report for November[73] closes this subchapter, and we then move to aftermath reports from the Straits.

The inhabitants of the villages laid waste by the tidal wave on August 27 last have reassembled in most places under their respective headmen. Housebuilding still underwent hindrance from want of *atap* [palm leaf thatch] for roofing. It had become more and more apparent that the fallen ashes had done no harm to the soil. All the growing crops bore a luxuriant appearance, particularly the pepper. On the other hand, many of the dammar trees to be found in the jungle have greatly suffered from the ash showers, so that about one-third of them must have died. It was the same with the durian trees. The coffee estates around Telok Betong, which also had suffered severely, had begun to recover, the trees again shooting out. Sufficient fodder had again become available for cattle.

The clearing of the ground at Telok Betong and putting the conduits there in order were steadily proceeded with. Everything necessary was done to restore communications. Only twice were vessels lying in Telok Betong roadstead enabled to communicate with the shore by means of boats. On the other hand, the bay of Semengka had been free from pumice since the 9th November. At two places in the district of Sekampong [on the east-facing coast of Sumatra, north of the entrance to the Sunda Straits] the tides on the sea coast were often unusually high. Trade everywhere had become brisker.

Official telegraphic advices to December 15 state that on that date, so far as could be seen from Telok Betong, Lampong Bay was free from the pumice fields which had blocked it since the outburst of Krakatau.

Straits of Sunda

The islands were described in the accounts of the Loudon and others immediately after the paroxysmal eruption (p. 90), but we include here the reports of ships passing through the Straits on following days. The events of August 27th dramatically changed the appearance of this important shipping route. Consequently, new surveys were quickly undertaken, and we include their reports here. We begin, though, with the log of the ship W.H. Besse,[48] as she continued southward through the Straits after weathering the eruption at anchor 80 km NE of Krakatau (p. 98).

Aug. 28.—Commences with light airs, and thick, smoky weather. Hove up starboard anchor, and hove short on port anchor. Dead calm throughout the day and night. Saw large quantities of trees and dead fishes floating by with the tide; the water having a whitish appearance, and covered with ashes. This day ends with a dead calm, and thick smoky weather.

Aug. 29.—This day commences with calms, and thick, smoky weather. Made all sail throughout the day. Moderate winds, and thick, smoky weather. Passed large quantities of driftwood, cocoanuts, and dead fishes. At 8 p.m., passed Anjer, and could see no light in the lighthouse (all except the foundation was destroyed), and no signs of life on shore. Furled all light sails, and stood under easy sail throughout the night. Day ends with moderate winds and cloudy weather. Barometer 30.14.

Aug. 30.—Commences with moderate winds and cloudy weather. At daylight made all sail with a fresh breeze from the westward. Found the water for miles filled with large trees and driftwood, it being almost impossible to steer clear of them. Also passed large numbers of dead bodies and fish. Kept a sharp lookout on the forecastle throughout the day. At 10 a.m., sighted Java Head lighthouse; but the wind hauling ahead, we kept away, and went round Prince Island. Latter part, fresh breezes, and thick, smoky weather. Friday and Saturday, passed large quantities of ashes in the water. Saturday, crew employed in cleaning ashes off masts and rigging. Water had a green color.

Approaching the Straits from the opposite direction, the steamer Graaf van Bylandt encountered more of the debris mentioned so laconically in the Besse's log book. On Sunday evening the Bylandt was anchored off Padang, 800 km NW of Krakatau on Sumatra's west coast, where explosions were heard in very short succession after 9 p.m. One of the ship's officers provided the following account of the trip toward the volcano on the culminating day of the eruption.[70]

The sky was hazy the whole day and the sun almost invisible. In the evening about 9 or 10 o'clock, when a land wind came up, ashfall was observed, which continued all night and which was so heavy that the ship was completely white with the deck covered by an ash layer about a thumb [inch] thick. About 6 in the morning of the 28th, arriving at Benkoelen [437 km NW of Krakatau], we found it covered completely with ash, so that it resembled a small city in the country after a snowfall. [The *Loudon* failed to keep her rendezvous at Benkoelen that day, and the *Bylandt* continued down the Sumatra coast knowing little more about the eruption.]

The next morning we arrived at Kroë and found this place also completely under the ash, it was there about half a foot thick. . . [That afternoon, the 29th, the] *Loudon* arrived at 3 o'clock. The ship looked terrible; the ash stuck to the portside with a thickness of at least a palm, and the deck was covered with half a foot of mud. . . The most important news they brought us was that probably nothing could have remained of Telok Betong and that Anjer and part of the coast there had been wiped off the map. By about

5 o'clock we were under steam and already at 8 o'clock we observed many thick ash streaks in the water. These streaks later grew into complete fields, but they were generally fairly thin, and not bothersome. In the morning at 5 o'clock, however, the layer was such that it was impossible to proceed, since the mechanic had difficulty with the [coolant] water supply. Thus we remained floating in this sea of pumice debris, which was about a foot thick. After the engine was made operational again, we steamed ahead, hoping to reach open water, but the pumice remained and became thicker. It was decided to find another route, since it was very probably that Telok Betong could not be anchored at. From the top, open water was observed under the Java shore, thus course was changed in that direction and open water finally was won.

However, another stop had to be made for the engine, since the condenser was full of pumice. Yes, pieces of pumice were even floating in the water gauge! Work was continued all night to be ready by the next morning. Then we steamed full speed, always sticking to open water and avoiding the uppermost tips of the pumice field. Thus we got the notorious Krakatau in view, or rather half Krakatau, since the other half no longer exists. . . . It smoked only very little, but the whole atmosphere seemed to have something oppressive.

Between Krakatau and Sebesie a newly-formed reef was discovered from which from time to time, steaming was discovered, similar to the blowing of a whale. Very probably there were small craters. Since up to Krakatau the water was open, it was decided to go to Telok Betong after all. It was a terrible sight; what must have happened there in a few minutes cannot be grasped! Along the whole Lampong Bay (now, I am speaking of what I have witnessed myself, the eastern shore of the bay) all kampongs had disappeared, trees uprooted, others broken in half.

From Varkenshoek to 1½ hours from Telok Betong there was a white stripe along the coast, about 4–5 m high, where everything was bare; that is how far the water must have risen. We passed by masses of dead fish, also numerous dead buffalo laying at the beach. All over bodies floated in the water.

We met the stonerunner *Kedirie* [on the mission that rescued the Beyerincks]. They had tried by all means to reach Telok Betong, but it appeared to be impossible. The water in front of Telok Betong was covered with pumice fields that could barely be seen across; for miles the coast was as if it were blockaded.

Death, which had celebrated its zenith here for days, would not admit anyone.

Also we had to steam past Telok Betong slowly, and without being able to assist in any way, continue our trip to Batavia.

After meeting the Bylandt and taking the Katimbang survivors to the Batavia hospital, the redoubtable Kedirie returned to the Straits. An anonymous passenger, not present on the earlier trip, wrote:[70]

On September 4, just after daybreak, we reached Sunda Strait. There we saw for the first time the scene of the destruction.

All the dry rice fields, which from the sea could clearly be seen laying against the mountains, had been remade into ash fields [see Plate 2A and others]. The trees were leafless. . . . Up to a height of 30–40 m, the sea had erased or knocked down every object, and covered it with a gray layer of mud and pumice-like material. On the island Peoloe Merak a few trees still stood upright. Dwars-in-den-Weg, which had been reported to be split in pieces, appeared to have had four pre-existing valleys scooped out deeper by the tidal wave. Thus from a distance, it gave the appearance of having been divided into five small islands. Toppershoedje was bare up to the height reached by the tidal wave.

At Merak one could clearly see the stone quarries, whose steep walls contrasted starkly with the lead-gray surroundings. At the spot of the community hill only six coconut trees were left standing.

The whole landscape was lifeless and much resembled a snowless winterscape in the north, the somber tint of which provided an unpleasant contrast with the splendid tropical sky and the fierce heat.

The shipping lane north of Dwars-in-den-Weg was free of pumice; at this point no bodies were to be seen. Closer to the Sumatra shore, however, where the stream from the Lampong Bay became noticeable, much pumice was encountered, mixed in with pieces of houses, trees, etc. Very remarkably, a large number of floating trees and bamboos stood straight up, a phenomenon for which we thus far have not received an explanation.[70] Concerning the bodies, Captain 't Hoen observed that all the men were floating on their stomachs with the legs pulled up, while the women and children always floated on their backs.

On the Zutphen Islands also the bottom side was completely bare up to a height of 30–40 m and had a light gray color. Especially the southern part of Poeloe Kandang had suffered much. Complete pieces of soil were washed away there and a layer of loose rock formed the surface.

. . . . .

Volcanic action was no longer anywhere to be seen, neither from Krakatau nor from Sebesie. Nothing was discovered of the 16 reported small volcanic islands. Everything was quiet. But all around the visible signs of the destruction brought to memory the terrible power, which had been active here.

After steaming around Varkenshoek, and arriving at the entrance to Lampong Bay, there was considerable up and down action of the water, so that even the hoppers on both sides took in water. The so-called Bochts [Bight] Islands [10 km ESE of Katimbang], whose surface appears to be less than 40 m above sea level, were completely bare and resembled ash-saddles. It seems that the most powerful action of the eruption was in the direction of Radjah Bassa. The kampongs on those islands and on the mainland were evidently destroyed less by the tidal wave than by the fallen ash and mud, and also by the preceding hurricane, which even far inland has uprooted giant tree trunks.

Sebesie is from the top down to the beach all ash. . . . Also Seboekoe is almost completely buried under ash. Only on a few of the highest points a few leafless trees can be discovered.

There again the *Kedirie* passed a colossal split-off tree trunk, in perpendicular position with its top 3–4 m above the surface of the sea. Certainly very puzzling.

The once so beautiful Lampong Bay has completely been altered in appearance. Where earlier hundreds of little white sails of fishing proas and other vessels happily contrasted with blue water surface, nothing but a single water bird is seen, circling lonely above the gray plain.

Passage through the Straits during that time was difficult enough for local seamen but provided extra measures of anxiety for those not familiar with the area. The debris persisted in the Straits for weeks. The following account, by Captain Morris of the Queensland Royal Steamer Cheyebassa, describes the ship's passage from Batavia through the Straits on Sunday, September 2, six days after the paroxysm.[74]

The awful news did not reach [us] until, I think, Wednesday, when a pilot came in whose wife had been washed up into a tree and left by the wave. He brought the intelligence that Krakatau had disappeared and the channel blocked. Here was news for me to get! Fortunately, a Netherlands India steamer was expected from the Straits, and we only had to wait. She did not arrive till Saturday afternoon. The commander's report was something awful. The big channel remained clear, he believed, as he came through it, but it was strewn with huge trees, bodies, and fields of floating pumice. Pleasant, was it not, for us? Our agents suggested going by Singapore, but I argued that if one ship could get through I could. We were ready for sea on Saturday evening, but I did not leave till two on Sunday morning, so as to have good daylight all through the Straits. Well, at seven on Sunday morning, September 2, we opened the Straits, and the sight was painful—bare rocks, nothing else, ruin everywhere. Anjer, that we had so often admired, the site not even to be recognised, a small bit of the lighthouse foundation standing, nothing more, and the sea more dreadful still with its awful burden, steering here and there to avoid all kinds of things, no danger apparent, which was to us the most important. At last we saw Krakatau, only the principal peak left, the whole north part cut down perpendicularly, and gone clean away. It was still smoking in places where it had not been smoking previously, so I am much afraid there will be more mischief. It was a lovely day, and I was able to get a series of angles, from which I have made a chart. After passing Krakatau things got thicker in the water, huge trees, roots and all, like islands, every conceivable thing that the awful wave could tear away. I got awfully anxious about this time. I could not find the man-of-war, and night coming on, the thought of having to cruise all night in such company gave me the cold shivers. At last, at six, I saw her masts in under the land. By seven I had fulfilled my commission, and was away to sea, with a big load off my mind; starting fair wind behind me, I did not leave the deck that night, you may be sure, for fear of trees, which I hoped to make out by the water breaking against them. However, all went well. Daylight came in with a dull, blowy day and torrents of rain, but anything was pleasant after those awful Straits. I am curious to hear further reports at Aden, because that morning, at eleven, when quite 140 miles away, we heard a most tremendous report like a heavy peal of thunder, right in the direction of the Straits. If the rest of the island is gone, Heaven save the ships we left there!

The dreadful debris was not limited to the Straits.[74]

The British ship *Bay of Naples* had called at these islands and reported that on the same day, when 120 miles from Java's First Point, during the volcanic disturbances, she encountered carcasses of animals including even those of tigers, and about 150 human corpses, of which 40 were those of Europeans, besides enormous trunks of trees borne along by the current.

Interest in the corpse-filled waters of the Straits remained strong, and nearly 3 months after the eruption a dispatch labeled "Netherlands India" from the Ceylon Times carried the following macabre paragraph:[75]

Recently a gentleman at Passar Ikan in Batavia bought a fish called *kakap* of middling size. On cleaning it, a gold ring was found in the stomach valued at 30 guilders. The wife of this gentleman was of opinion that the ring should be taken to the police office from its being likely to belong to one of the victims of the Krakatau calamity who may still be alive. This may prove to be the case on inquiry. In any case, one cannot help admiring the scrupulousness of the lady's conscience.

Several ships, in addition to the Kedirie, were dispatched to the Straits both to rescue survivors and to assist passing foreign vessels. Among these was the man-of-war Prins Hendrik, that successfully reached Vlakke Hoek lighthouse after the eruption. Mr. McLeod, whose account of Krakatau just 2 weeks before the eruption we reprinted above (see p. 68), used the Prins Hendririk to gather information shortly after the eruption. He was apparently the first to land on the island group and he prepared a map, not published until 1884, of the waters nearby. His account (curiously not cited by Verbeek, the Royal Society committee, or other compilers) is excerpted below.[76] *Under the heading "First reported ashfalls," McLeod noted:*

Figure 31. Fanciful view of ship passing through sea choked with corpses. Many corpses, of course, were accurately reported by ships in the Krakatau area, but these were generally associated with blankets of floating pumice and tangles of vegetation torn from the land by the tsunamis. (From "La Fin du Monde," by Flammarion, 1894).

All eruption materials should have cooled to nearly air temperatures, because of distances traveled, but on the NW coast of Verlaten Island, slowly hardening mud still had a surface temperature of 120°F on September 7. Also, vapor rising from cracks registered 132°F on the thermometer. Temperature of mud below the surface was higher than 155°F (the thermometer maximum). At Telok Betong, there were no reports about hot ash, however at Katimbang, people died of severe burns.[77] Anything closer, such as Sebesie (2000 inhabitants), suffered the fate of Herculaneum and Pompeii. The tree growth on the southerly slope of Krakatau peak (which remained) caught fire, was next covered by a layer of ash and mud, and remained smoldering beneath. Even on November 5, some light was seen on the mountain by the writer, who attributes it to this smoldering.

McLeod then discussed wave heights, listing 22 m for Toppershoedje, 36 m for Telok Betong, and 30–40 m for Merak. The maximum inland penetration of the waves was 10 km and the appearance of the land, as seen from the sea, was greatly changed.

Before the event it appeared that the coastline between Anjer and Tjiringin consisted of a strip overgrown with trees in front of high mountains. After the event it appeared for a while as though a row of dunes stretched itself along the coast. The low coastal strip was completely bare and lost itself in the rising land, which since it also was bare in most places appeared as dunes. Eight weeks later however, it appeared quite different. Everything had become green again; campongs once hidden by the trees showed picturesque against the slope. . . . Remarkable also was the change in the outlets of the small rivers. Earlier these outlets, as with most rivers in the Indies, had been closed off by shallows. However, the motion of the water had opened up these outlets and had normalized the banks, so that these rivers were now accessible to ships.

On the basis of bathymetric mapping by the Prins Hendrik and the Hydrograaf (see below), McLeod calculated that a mass of 6.29 km³ had been added to the sea floor near Krakatau and that

this was approximately matched by 6.74 km³ of material missing at the volcano itself. He calculated the collapsed portion of Krakatau as 2.72 km³ above sea level and 4.02 km³ below. In discussing the addition of material to Verlaten, and other areas north of the volcano, McLeod recognized that hot ejecta, when combined with cold seawater, produced secondary explosions. These "rootless eruptions" lack any source of molten magma at depth, but they can be quite violent in thick accumulations of hot pumice.

When we arrived September 3 . . . everything was still boiling hot. Verlaten Island appeared to steam out of thousands of cracks especially along the beach where the seawater contacted the hot mass; but also not too little on the slopes. On Steers Island and in the direction of Lang Island and Krakatau, steam clouds rose every so often, giving the appearance of small eruptions still taking place. It is very probable that these formed from water penetrating the hot bottom, converting to steam, which was then forced out again. Downwind the vapor had an unpleasant odor, resembling bitumen, sulfur, and phosphorus. [After a brief discussion of hell and religion, McLeod goes on to describe the materials themselves.]

The clay had a dark, almost black color, but was in turn covered over by a layer of gray mud; at the beach where the sea washed away the lighter material but attacked the clay less so, dams or heads (mounds) were formed, which because of their dark color contrasted with the light gray from quite a distance. North of Verlaten Island such clay banks also could be observed in the sea. The clay was hard enough to stand upon, but could be broken off with the hand. Between the clay dams on the beach were many pieces of a black lava type with conchoidal breaks and glassy grains; the stone was very hard, but breaks into pieces by itself. According to the description, it resembles obsidian. Its specific gravity is 2.52. Another piece of black stone, less splittable had specific gravity of 2.59. Very curious also were the balls consisting of a conglomerate of pieces of white rock, pumice and clay, apparently having become rounded or egg-shaped by rolling in the hot water of the crater. The specific gravity of such balls was 1.51. [These were later recognized to be concretions in the older bedrock of the volcano that were caught up in the eruption (see p. 253).]

McLeod ends his perceptive and valuable account by noting that the Spanish naval ship Gravina measured seawater temperatures of 28°C at 200 m depth near the volcano—far higher than should be expected so far below the surface. He suggested the addition of heat from below to explain the measurement and urged more research.

The secondary explosions described by McLeod continued, but most were probably "similar to the blowing of a whale," as quoted above from the Bylandt. A few, however, were larger, and aroused understandable apprehension, as reflected in the following newspaper account from Batavia.[78]

On the 26th of September last detonations [from Krakatau] were distinctly again heard, and tremors of the ground noticed in this city. This volcano still looms threateningly on the horizon of west Java, and the steadily increasing activity lately of the Merapi in Sumatra, as well as in its namesake in Java and of the craters on other volcanoes here, seems to indicate that we are at present in a period of more vigorous volcanic action. This discovery is not very tranquilising, and people sometimes wonder whether the Krakatau outburst is perhaps, only a foretaste of what awaits us here and elsewhere in Java.

These fears were not realized. A somewhat larger set of explosions took place from October 9th to 11th, with a wave reaching 75 m inland from normal highwater line at Tjikawoeng (60 km SSE of Krakatau), but there was no significant renewal of volcanism in the Sunda Straits. These and other events are discussed in more detail by Verbeek (see p. 218).

The U.S. Navy, having received notice of navigational hazards in Sunda Straits, ordered the U.S.S. Juniata to investigate. She left Singapore the next day, September 3, but was soon delayed by the Bay of Naples, the ship whose account of debris south of the Sunda Straits we quoted above. The Bay of Naples had run aground 300 km N of the Sunda Straits, and was not refloated until she jettisoned part of her cargo (coal from South Wales bound for Singapore). The Juniata reached Batavia on September 6 and we take up the account by Commander P.F. Harrington[79] *there:*

From various sources it was reported, (1) that the soundings between Kaik Point [35 km WNW of Batavia] and St. Nicholas Pt. were altered; (2) that Thwartway Island had been divided into five islands; (3) that the coast and soundings from Lileang River [10 km NE of Anjer(?)] to Tyringin were changed materially; (4) that a new island had appeared in Latitude 6°06'S, Longitude 105°31'E, approximately; and (5) that the Bezee Channel had been altered in many places, making it dangerous for vessels.

With these and some other reports of doubtful authority as guides to our examination, I sailed for the Strait on the 7th last. Passing into the inner or Dutch channel near the Menschen-eter [nearshore islands 35 km WNW of Batavia] the ship was kept westward, sounding carefully, and at night anchored [in Bantam Bay[80]]. On the following morning, soundings were resumed in a line from the anchorage to Sabrina Island and thence around St. Nicholas Point to Toppers Island. The trees and hills in the vicinity of St. Nicholas Pt. are covered with ashes. But I am satisfied from the bearings taken and soundings made that there has been no physical change in those parts.

From Toppers Island the ship proceeded to the southern end of Thwart-way, and beginning three cables length eastward of the reef at the point, passed around the island at distances of two to four cables, sounding, and with the steam launch sounding inside and upon the bow. Through the valleys of the island the sea appears to have rushed, tearing away the trees and leaving the land in several hills low and naked. When seen from the Northward and Eastward, or Southward and Westward and at a distance of 3 or 4 miles, these breaks in the line of verdure cause the appearance of 5 islands, but there is no change in the shore contour of the island, nor in any of the soundings adjacent.

On the afternoon of the 8th inst., the ship anchored off the site of Anjer. The buoys, which mark the line of the submarine cable to Telok Betong, Sumatra, and the base of the light-house at Fourth Point, are the only monuments of Anjer. The plain northward of Anjer Peak was swept by the flood of waters, and nothing remains but the vine-like roots of the cocoa palm and some scattered and ghastly relics of the inhabitants. The coastline about Anjer Point and the bank of soundings are not changed.

· · · · ·

At three o'clock on the afternoon of the 9th inst., twelve days after the earthquake, the *Juniata* was brought to anchor near the east point of Lang Island, in twenty five fathoms of water. I went with the steam launch and a cutter to examine the Krakatoa Channel. Upon the approach of the ship, the volcano appeared active. A nearer view in the boats proved that the appearance is due to scoria falling down the precipitous heights, and blown into dust by the wind. On entering Krakatoa Channel, some of the changes caused by the earthquake became apparent. The NW part of Krakatoa Island has disappeared. The line of fracture begins at a point south of Lang Island and forms an arc of a circle passing through the peak to the western side of the island. The boats passed into the crater-like area, concave to the northward, and sounded along the face of the heights, but no bottom could be found with 20 fathoms of line. Prior to the eruption, Verlaten and Lang Islands were covered with trees, and, refreshed by the rains of the SE monsoon, they presented a most pleasing view. With one slight exception these islands remain unchanged in contour, but both are covered with scoria. Eastward of Verlaten Island a small island has formed, as shown at *c* upon the enclosed plan [map, Figure 32] of Bezee and Krakatoa Channels as they now appear. Small necks of land have been thrown out from the eastern side of Verlaten, and the western point of Krakatoa, as shows upon the plan at *d* and *e*. The Polish Hat has disappeared, but a new rock, *f,* about 20 ft in height and as many in diameter now exists in Krakatoa Channel, nearer to the southern point of Lang Island. Within 10 yards of this rock there are 8 fathoms of water. At the place formerly occupied by the Polish Hat, no bottom was found with 20 fathoms of line. Islands and reefs have been formed in the Bezee Channel, the extent of which I was unable to find. Preparations were made to examine the Channel at daylight on the 10th inst., but the state of the wind and sea made it impossible to proceed. Cutters were sent later to examine and find the new islands in Krakatoa Channel and the eastern island in Bezee Channel. The southern end of the latter was approached by the cutter steering about East by North. At a distance of about a mile and a half, bottom was found in 8 fathoms and at half a mile 3 fathoms, hard bottom. Towards the southern end of the island further progress was barred by a reef and breakers. The boat then skirted the western side of the island, but was unable to approach nearer than a quarter of a mile. From the northern end of this island, marked *a* upon the plan, a reef extends in a NW direction, apparently connecting with the islands further westward. In the after-

noon, I landed upon Lang Island and obtained a good view of the new formation, from which the plan is partly drawn. The surface of the island was still warm, and steam rose through the fissures and holes in the uncooled scoria.

On the morning of the 11th, rough weather continuing, I weighed anchor and passed southward of Krakatoa in order to find by cuts the most western point of fracture upon that island. This was done by Lieutenant Sentzi, and also the ends of the island marked *a* by numerous tangents. The islands in Krakatoa Channel and the shoal at *k* were located by Midshipmen Roundstone and Rokebacher with the sextant. The islands at *b* and *h* and the breakers at *n* were plotted with less precision.

I regret that a more definite and full examination of Bezee Channel could not be made. But enough has been learned to mark the Pass as worse than useless for the present

. . . . .

The agreement of the plan made by the *Juniata* with the Dutch chart is worthy of note, the former having been made in rough weather and the latter under more favorable circumstances. The reefs at *k* and *n* are not marked upon the Dutch Chart.

On the 12th inst., I examined the coast of Java between Second Point and Fourth Point, taking bearings and sounding continually. This coast consists chiefly of a plain elevated but a few feet above the sea and extending inland for a mile to the hills. At intervals along the coast, the rising grounds abut upon the sea. Along these plains and upon the sides of the bluffs, the destruction worked by the *Bore* is plainly marked, and I estimate that the wave advanced to a height of 40 ft. The whole coast near the sea has been swept clear, but no changes in the coast lines and sounding have been found by the *Juniata*. At Telok Betong, the wave rose more than 100 ft, as marked upon the Government House.

I am informed that the loss of life upon the Java coast exceeds twenty thousand in number. Of this, Anjer contributed three and Tyringin ten thousand. The eastern side of Bezee Island was covered, prior to the earthquake, with pepper plantations, and several hundred people employed in the cultivation of pepper made their homes upon the little islands lying adjacent to Bezee. No trace remains of people or plantations. The loss of life upon the Sumatra side is supposed to have been greater than upon the Java coast. The situation and formation of Lampong and Semanka Bays with reference to the point of explosion

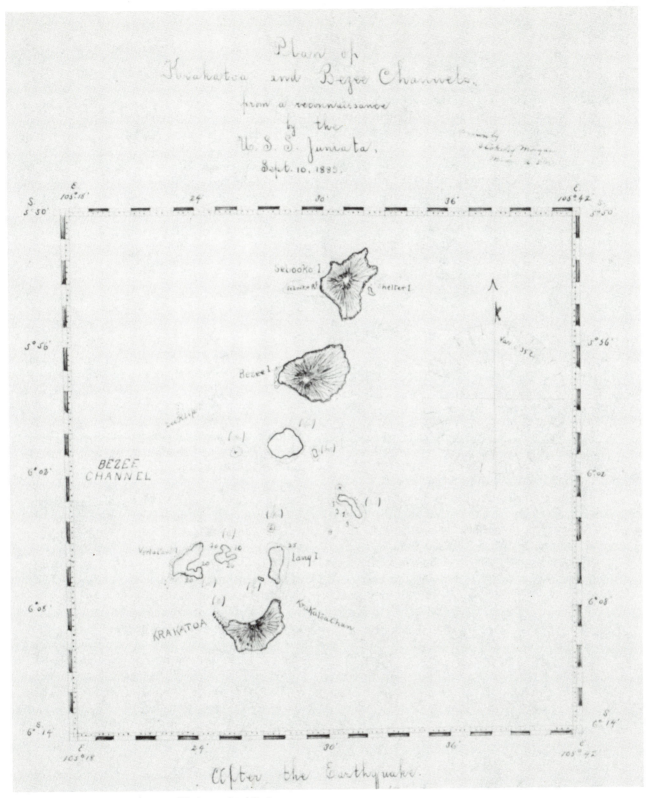

Figure 32. First post-paroxysm map of Krakatau, dated September 10, 1883. The crew of the Juniata documented the dramatic changes in the configuration of Krakatau within two weeks of the eruption and collapse. Comparison of this map with Figure 37, at the same scale, shows that the several small islands formed by the eruption's fragmental deposits were significantly eroded during the 3–5 weeks between the two surveys. This previously unpublished map accompanies the letter reprinted here from Commander P.F. Harrington, and is in the U.S. National Archives.

and the progress of the *Bore* explain the apprehensions as the effects upon that coast. Communication with Telok Betong is now interrupted by masses of floating pumice wedged in Lampong Bay.

The plan of Bezee and Krakatoa Channels transmitted herewith [Figure 32], shows the present condition as far as visible from the anchorage, but the depths in other ports of Bezee Channel have probably been materially altered. That part of Krakatoa which is missing, an immense mass, apparently occupied the place of the crater, and portions of it have probably made other modifications to the northward.

A more detailed survey was undertaken by the Dutch naval vessel Hydrograaf at the end of September. Although the Juniata had spent 5 days in the area, the Hydrograaf survey lasted nearly a month and provided the first detailed description of the physical changes to Krakatau and nearby islands. The following account is by the ship's commander, M.C. van Doorn:[81]

As we expected, our ship was soon ordered to survey the Sunda Straits. This survey was finished at the end of October, and the reader will probably feel interested to know what really has happened there.

Krakatoa has not entirely disappeared, while, till now, no new volcanoes are visible in the neighbourhood. But the report that new islands were said to

Figure 33. Krakatoa during the eruption of May, after a drawing of the Military Survey Bureau, Batavia. [This is figure 1 from van Doorn (1884).]

have arisen between Sebesie and Krakatoa is easily to be explained, for the new islands are like a mass of smoking and steaming rocks, and if seen from afar

they may easily suggest the idea of a great number of working volcanoes. But, when looked at closely, it appeared that the masses of rock were composed of hot pumice-stone, mixed with eruptive masses. In them there were a great many cracks and splits, in which by the heavy breakers, steam of water was continually generated. The northern part of the island has entirely disappeared. At what is now the northern edge the peak rises nearly perpendicularly from the sea, and forms a crumbled and rugged wall, and shows a vertical cutting (which is more than 800 m high) of Krakatoa.

Where was land before, there is now no bottom to be found, at least we could not fathom it with lines of 200 fathoms (360 m) long. When we had quite calm weather, and steamed slowly and cautiously to and fro along the base of the peak, or had turned off steam and let the ship drift, and were busy in measuring the depth, we could distinctly see the different strata and rocks of the bare, opened mountain. Only here and there a slight trace of melted volcanic matter was to be seen, which after half of the mountain had crumbled away, had flowed over the wall, which is still there. What remains of the slopes is covered with a grayish-yellow stuff (which, as plainly appears, had been in a melted or fluid state), full of cracks or splits from which steam is continually coming out.

In the same way steam is also coming forth from the deeper cracks of the steep wall, which is still remaining. Sometimes this is accompanied by slight explosions; at that time clouds of brown dust fly up from the cracks, and stones roll down which are often so big as to disturb the sea around the entire base of the mountain. Our entire survey of the north of Krakatoa suggested the idea that we were above a crater which had been filled with water and quenched by it, and this idea was still strengthened on observing that the decrease of depth, south of Sebesie, had principally been caused by matters which were cast out and flung away.

Figure 34. Krakatoa after the eruption in May, after a drawing of the Military Survey Bureau, Batavia. [This is figure 2 from van Doorn (1884).]

Almost in every place here the lead came up from the bottom, filled with black sand or carbonised dust, sometimes mixed with pulverised pumice-stone and

Figure 35. Peak of Krakatoa after the eruption in August [by M.C. van Doorn (figure 3)].

Figure 36. Peak of Sebesie and the volcanic rocks before it [by M.C. van Doorn (figure 4)].

. . . . .

little black stones, which apparently had been in a red-hot or melted state. Moreover, the soundings were very different, and the new rocks resemble clods of substances which, when in a melted or a very hot state, had contact with water. Probably such a whimsical shape of the rocks above the sea-level suggests the state of the bottom of the sea in the neighbourhood. The stones were still too hot to allow us to discover whether massive stones are under the pumice-stone also. It was not difficult, it is true, to knock off large pieces of these rocks by a hatchet or a chopper, but when a big block fell unexpectedly down, the sailors had often to flee on account of the gases which suddenly arose. The knocked off pieces which were brought on board were still warm after they had been in the boat for an hour.

It is also worth mentioning that a change took place in the figure of Verlaten Island; the area is now triple what it was before, though it is plainly visible that large pieces of the beach were there knocked off a short time ago.

Lang Island, in size and formation, has remained almost unaltered. The sight of these islands, which were formerly covered by a luxurious vegetation, is now very melancholy. They are now buried under a mass of pumice-stone, and appear like shapeless clods of burst clay (i.e. covered with cracks). After a torrent of rain, the coming forth of steam is sometimes so dense that these islands, when seen from afar, appear like hilly ground covered here and there with snow. If looking at these spots with the telescopes, one can plainly see that these white specks are formed by a

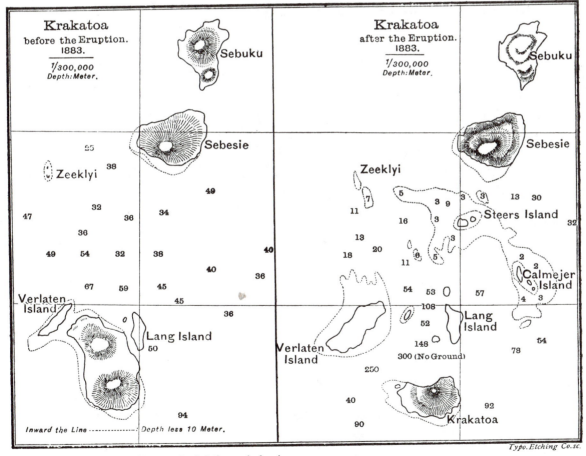

Figure 37. Krakatoa and neighboring islands before and after the eruption, from official surveys.

139

A

B

C

D

Figure 38. Earliest photographs known from Krakatau area after the eruption. Taken by R. Bréon, leader of the French expedition in May of 1884, these 4 photographs are from the Archives Nationales, Paris.

Figure 38a. Photograph of the NE side of Sebuku, 30 km NNE of Krakatau. Cotteau (1885, p. 104) says of this island "the magnificent vegetation which had been so often admired there remains nothing but a chaos of enormous trunks, whitened and dessicated, amidst the surrounding desolation." Most trees here have been toppled, although many stripped trunks remain standing, perhaps because this area was located on the leeward side of the island, somewhat protected from the direct effects of the eruption. Cotteau mentions "a layer of dried mud, 20 ft thick, ploughed up in deep crevices." Although it is difficult to determine from this photograph the original thickness of tephra here, much has certainly been stripped from the steep slopes by erosion during the intervening nine months and transported a short distance to form the alluvial deposit in the foreground.

Figure 38b. Krakatau as seen from the east. The shadowed cliff on the north (right) side of the island is the nearly vertical scarp formed by the collapse and engulfment of Krakatau during the paroxysmal eruption of August 26–27, 1883. A thick layer of tephra was deposited on the remainder of the island and can be seen as the light colored deposit at the top of the cliffs. Note that the thickness of this tephra layer increases on the lower and more gentle southern slope of the island.

Figure 38c. Krakatau as seen from the south. The original nearly symmetrical form of Rakata volcano is well displayed in this view. A layer of 1883 tephra blanketed this remaining side of the island, and the French mission estimated its thickness as 60 to 80 m at their landing spot on the west side. Cotteau (1885, p. 106) noted: "Notwithstanding all my researches, I was not able to observe any symptom of animal life. I only discovered one microscopic spider—only one; this strange pioneer of the renovation was busy spinning its web."

Figure 38d. The SE side of Verlaten Island, showing the 30 m thick layer of 1883 tephra that blanketed this area. This photograph, taken exactly 9 months after the paroxysmal eruption, documents very well the rapid erosion that carved deep gullies and transported large amounts of fragmental material to form the coalesced alluvial fan in the foreground.

great number of clouds, which issued like steam from the fissures.

Sebesie is also covered with ashes up to the top— 859 m—which appear like a grayish-yellow cloth. But it seems that the cover is already less thick here, for here and there one sees the stumps of dead trees peeping out from the crust.

Sebuku shows a dreadful scene of devastation. Perhaps all that lived here is not so completely destroyed as was the case on the southern islands, but the sight of the bare fields of ashes, alternating with destroyed woods, the trees of which are all either dead or uprooted, gives one a still better idea of the destructive powers which were here at work. It is not until we come to the small islands northward of Sebuku that our eyes are gladdened by little specks of green.

I do not try to describe the scene of destruction and misery which we saw at Anjer and the villages along the coast. The papers have already reported the full particulars, and therefore I do not care to repeat melancholy facts which are already known.

· · · · ·

It has been almost a month that we have been in the Sunda Straits, and even in this short period we could observe that the coasts of Bantam commence to revive. From many places from the heavy rain the ashes are washed down, and a fresh green appears again. Even on the beach young cocoanut trees and banana trees are shooting out between the chaos of dead trees, blocks of rocks, &c.

While the Hydrograaf was completing its survey of the region, R.D.M. Verbeek was making his first field studies on Krakatau since he mapped the island geology three years before the eruption.[82] His chromolithographs (Plates 1–8) were the first illustrations of the aftermath, and his accompanying descriptions provide a narrative to his field investigations 7 weeks after the eruption. Verbeek was designated by the government to lead the scientific investigation after the eruption and we later reprint his extensive observations (Part III). However, Verbeek's was not the only official investigation. At the start of 1884, the French government directed René Bréon and W.C. Korthals to visit the eruption site, which they did in May of 1884. They were accompanied by E. Cotteau, and several accounts of their week on and around Krakatau have been published.[83] We close this "aftermath" chapter with a summary of their report and their photographs (the first post-eruption photographs known to us).[84]

Messrs. Cotteau and Korthals, members of the French Mission sent by the Minister of Public Instruction to explore the Krakatoa volcano, write from Batavia on June 2 that the object of the expedition has been fully realised. Soon after their arrival at Batavia on May 14, the Dutch Colonial Government placed at their disposal a small steamer, on board of which they started for the Sunda Strait on the 21st. Along the west coast a well-marked line, running at an elevation of from 50 to 80 ft above sea-level, indicated the limit reached by the terrible wave that spread disaster far and wide towards the end of August 1883. The plantations had been swept away, and all the houses of this populous district, together with the town of Anjer, had completely disappeared. On the 23rd the steamer cast anchor at the head of Lampong Bay on the south coast of Sumatra, whence a visit was paid to the Telok Betong district. Here the extensive and thickly settled coastlands had assumed the aspect of a desolate swamp, relieved here and there by a few bamboo huts recently set up. Nearly three miles inland lay the steamer *Berouw*, which had been borne on the crest of the wave into the forest, where it now forms a sort of bridge across a small stream. On the 25th the formerly fertile and densely peopled islands of Sibuku and Sibesi were successively visited and found to be entirely covered by a deposit of dry mud several yards thick and furrowed by deep crevasses. Of the inhabitants, all had perished to a man. Continuing the trip on the 26th to Krakatoa itself, the mission was surprised to note the complete disappearance of the three islands of Steers, Calmeyer, and the islet east of Verlaten, which had risen above the

surface at the time of the eruption, but which are now covered by 12 or 14 ft of water [but see Verbeek, p. 174]. Approached from the north Krakatoa seemed wrapped in a whitish smoke, vapours apparently issuing from fissures on this side, and settling on the summit, which is at present 2730 ft high. It was at this point that the great convulsion took place on August 26–27, when about half the island was blown into the air. A closer examination showed that what had been taken for fissures were simply ravines, and the vapours were clouds of dust stirred up by stones

Figure 39. Three views of the north-facing scarp of Krakatau, formed by the collapse and engulfment of the volcano during the paroxysmal eruption of August 26–27, 1883. The collapse cut very near the former summit, and this remarkable 830 m cross-section reveals much of the volcano's internal structure. The upper photograph was the subject of Verbeek's only post-1885 publication on Krakatau. In a short 1908 note he wrote:

I visited the island on order of the government on 21 June, 1886 for the fourth time. About ten good photographs of that island were obtained then by [H. Busenbender of] the well-known Batavia firm Woodbury and Page, among which an exceptionally fine picture of the steep wall. . . .

This photograph, with a small note of explanation by me in French and dated Buitenzorg, December 1886, was offered as a loose page to all persons and institutions, who had received a copy of the work "Krakatau" for free. . . . I will repeat here part of the description which belonged with the picture. It went:

Our photograph shows rather clearly the system of concordant beds of basaltic cinders and lapilli alternating with flows of dense basalt and numerous cross-cutting dikes. From a point located beneath the summit, the beds slope on the left and right. At the foot of the mountain on the left, underneath the basaltic layers and discordant with them, one sees massive banks of an earlier rock (tridymite andesite) and beds of lapilli which cover them. Just beneath the summit one finds a large andesite dike that cuts the basaltic layers from sea level up to half the height of the mountain where it terminates in a large lenticular bulge.

The lower photograph, taken from a more distant (and westerly) position, shows more of the western cliff although the summit is obscured by cloud. Both photographs, taken June 21, 1886, are from the archives of the Royal Institute for the Tropics, Amsterdam.

The geologic profile at the bottom, by Escher (1919), shows the full cliff. In addition to the features described by Verbeek in the upper photo legend, the oldest lavas of the volcano are shown by the darker pattern at the left and at Zwarte Hoek near the right side. The prominent talus cones have grown by a third of a century of rockfalls since the 1886 photograph. The mantling 1883 tephra deposits thicken on the gentler lower slopes and make up all of the new addition to the island shown (in white) at the right side of the profile. The old coastline of the island was at the right side of Zwarte Hoek, the landing place shown in the 1886 photograph on the next page.

Figure 40. Landing party, June 20, 1886, standing on the beach just south of Zwarte Hoek. The old, dark lavas of Zwarte Hoek are to the left above the group, and 1883 tephra deposits are to the right. Another photograph of the tephra deposits near this spot, and taken on the same day, is shown on p. 425. R.D.M. Verbeek (see Part III of this volume) is near the center, wearing dark clothing. R. Fennema, Verbeek's geological colleague, is standing just to his left; and M. Treub, the first biologist to visit Krakatau in the nearly 3 years since the eruption, is far to his right, wearing both white hat and white clothing.

incessantly rolling down the steep slope of the mountain. This was accompanied by a continuous noise like the rattling of distant musketry, while stones of a certain size were seen whirling in the air, then falling and ricochetting down to the sea. Notwithstanding the evident danger, the boats of the expedition succeeded in approaching the foot of the volcano and collecting specimens of the rocks at several points. The same afternoon they reached the island of Verlaten, formerly one mass of verdure, now uniformly covered with a layer of solidified ashes about 100 ft thick. The deep crevasses, widened by the erosion of tropical rains, give the aspect of a glacier to this island, which has been doubled in extent by the deposits from the last eruption. Returning next day to Krakatoa the members of the expedition found a safe landing place, where it was possible to study the nature of the rocks and other matter ejected by the volcano. No trace was found of animal or vegetable life, with the exception of a solitary little spider, and the solidified bed of mud and ashes was estimated in some places to have attained a thickness of from 200 to 260 ft. A black rock rising a few yards above the surface about a mile and a quarter from the present shore represents a last fragment of the portion of the island engulfed during the eruption. After touching at Lang Island, which presented much the same appearance as its neighbour Verlaten, the expedition concluded its survey of the Strait, landing on the 28th at Merak at the NW extremity of Java. Merak had shared the fate of Anjer, and the coast-line in this district had been considerably modified. The expedition returned to Batavia on the 29th, after determining two new facts—the disappearance of the islands upheaving during the eruption, and the total cessation for the present of all volcanic activity at Krakatoa.

Distant Descriptions

The effects of Krakatau's eruption were witnessed by people thousands, and even tens of thousands of kilometers from the volcano: people who scarcely knew of the East Indies, much less of Krakatau, but people who recognized unusual sunsets, moon colors, or fluctuations in sea level. Such effects must have been produced by huge eruptions in more acient times, but the significance of the Krakatua eruption lies in the fact that global communications were sufficiently advanced in 1883 to speed news swiftly around the world.

144

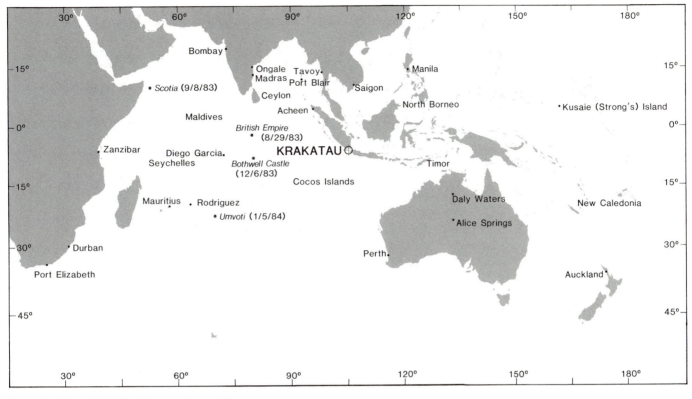

Figure 41. Map of the Indian Ocean and surrounding areas, showing the location of places mentioned in the text where the distant effects of the 1883 Krakatau eruption were observed, heard, and recorded (sounds, waves, airborne ash, floating pumice, and atmospheric effects).

People who had been puzzled by unusual effects learned of the eruption while interest was still strong, and news of other distant effects re-stimulated that interest, resulting in unprecedented communication between students of natural phenomena. In this chapter we reprint a sampling of accounts describing these distant effects. These are arranged in a roughly chronological sequence. We start with the sounds, heard swiftly over an area one-thirteenth of the earth's surface, and then move to the following waves that caused dramatic tidal fluctuations over an even larger area. Ashfall was perceptible in some areas 12 days after the eruption and masses of floating pumice were still being reported in 1885. The remarkable sunsets reached their peak in northern latitudes about 3 months after the eruption, and atmospheric effects were still visible in 1886. We then close this chapter with some comments on, and selections from, media coverage of this extraordinary eruption.

Sounds

No other historic explosion has produced sounds reported from greater distances. Rodriguez Island lies 4653 km WSW of Krakatau across the Indian Ocean. It is a small island 1600 km E of Madagascar, with local civil time 2 hours and 48 minutes behind Krakatau.[85] Normal sound would require about 4 hours to reach Rodriguez from Krakatau, meaning that an explosion heard on Rodriguez at 3 p.m. would have originated at the volcano around 1:48 Krakatau time. The account of Mr. James Wallis, Chief Officer of Police on Rodriguez,[86] follows:

On Sunday the 26th the weather was stormy, with heavy rain and squalls; the wind was from SE, blowing with a force of from 7 to 10, Beaufort scale. Several times during the night (26th–27th) reports were heard coming from the eastward, like the distant roars of heavy guns. These reports continued at intervals of between three and four hours, until 3 p.m. on the 27th, and the last two were heard in the directions of Oyster Bay and Port Mathurie.

Like the Rodriguez account, most reporters mentioned repeated sounds, rather than a single blast. Most likened the sounds to gunfire—from distant cannonading rather than nearby rifle shots—but some compared them to thunder. In South Australia, 3252 km (over 2000 miles) ESE of Krakatau, a resident of Daly Waters reported that "On Sunday, the 26th, at midnight we were awakened by an explosion resembling the blasting of a rock, which lasted for a few minutes."[87] The explosions were also heard in Perth, Alice Springs, and many other places in Australia.

Among those living near the sea, a common reaction was to interpret the sounds as the signal of a ship in distress. The most distant of these reactions was on Diego Garcia, an island in the Chagos Archipelago, 3374 km W of Krakatau. In a letter to the Meteorological Society of Mauritius, M. Lecompte[88] describes the sounds of the culminating eruption of 10 a.m., August 27:

Between 10:00 and 11:00 in the morning during lunch, we heard muffled but violent detonations. We so much believed it to be the call of a ship in distress that we ran out, and I sent several men to observe from different points on the shores. The captain of the Eva Joshua and his first mate had arrived . . . when they heard the same detonations. They immediately sent observers to the top of the mast. But, like those of mine, they did not see anything.

In Burma, 1480 km NNW of Krakatau, the Tavoy Police Superintendent reported unusual sounds, "resembling the boom of guns," all day on the 27th, and sent out the police launch to look for a ship in distress.[89] In Singapore, 840 km N of the volcano, the newspapers of August 27 reported:[90]

. . . that mysterious and unaccountable detonations have been heard here continuously during all last night and all this forenoon, and inquiries have been set on foot to ascertain the cause. These were first supposed to have been reports of heavy ordnance from some man-of-war in the neighbourhood, while others set them down to blasts, but their continuity,

Three Moorwomen, three children, and a man were crossing [the bar] about 3 p.m. A big wave came up from the sea over the bar and washed them inland. Soon after the water returned to the sea. The man said that the water came up to his chest: he is a tall man. These people were tumbling about in the water, but were rescued by people in boats who were fishing in the Kalapuwa (inland estuary). They lost the paddy they were carrying, and one of the women died two days after of her injuries.

Volcanic Ashfall and Floating Pumice

Molten magma deep within the earth, like carbonated beverage in a bottle, carries gas that is held in solution by the surrounding pressure. When that pressure is suddenly reduced, as in an eruption, the gas comes out of solution in rapidly expanding bubbles and the expansion can be, as in the opening of some bottles, quite violent. The molten magma is torn apart by the expanding gases at the same time that it is freezing to form solid glass fragments, and these fragments are carried high in the air by the eruptive process. The smallest fragments often retain little evidence of the bubbles that formed them, but when the explosive process is incomplete, a glassy froth of bubbles, or pumice, results. The Krakatau eruption produced large quantities of both pumice and fine ash (see Figure 42), and we reprint below some accounts of their distant distribution.

The larger fragments in an eruption naturally fall close to the volcano and the deposits there are thicker. Accounts of ashfall from these areas have been printed above in earlier chapters. Distant ashfall accounts are mainly in the form of letters from seamen responding to the Royal Society's request for information, and many of these are incidentally summarized in a 49 page chronological table compiled by Russell[101] to list observations of optical phenomena. "Showers of very fine sand" fell on the Brani, 1500 km W of Krakatau, from midnight on the 27th to the 29th, and Keeling (Cocos) Island, 1155 km SW of Krakatau accumulated ½ inch of fine ash between 4 p.m. on the 27th and midnight on the 29th. From the afternoon of the 29th through the following day,

with frequent combination of two or three reports almost in one and occasional rumbles like thunder, led to the inference that the detonations were volcanic. The sound, however, appeared to come from the westward, while there was an occasional vibration of the earth after an unusually loud report.

Similar reports of ships in distress came from Manila (2880 km NE), Timor (2175 km E), Port Blair (2440 km NW), and several closer areas. The sounds "like gunfire" were a different matter, however, when heard inland. Dutch soldiers in Acheen, 1725 km from Krakatau in NW Sumatra, thought their fort was under attack, and from St. Lucia Bay, North Borneo, 1800 km NW of the volcano, comes the following report[91] of what may be one of the more distant eruption-related fatalities:

The noise of the eruption was plainly heard all over Borneo. The natives inland, who murdered poor Witti, when they heard the noise, thought we were coming to attack them from the east and west coasts.

Waves

Moving at speeds of nearly 600 km/hr, about half those of the air wave,[92] the huge sea waves traveled throughout the Indian Ocean and beyond. Far from Krakatau, their height nowhere approached those that devastated the Sunda Straits, but they nonetheless caused damage and considerable consternation at great distances from their origin. An example of the latter is the following report[93] from the west coast of India, near Bombay, some 4800 km by sea from Krakatau.

An extraordinary phenomenon of tides was witnessed at Bandora on the morning of Tuesday last (August 28) by those who were at the time on the seashore. The tide came in, at its usual time and in a proper way. After some time, the reflux of the tide went to the sea in an abrupt manner and with great impetus, and the fish not having sufficient time to retire with the waves, remained scattered on the seashore and dry places, and the fishermen, young and old, had a

good and very easy task to perform in capturing good-sized and palatable fish, without the least trouble or difficulty, to their hearts' content, being an extraordinary event never seen or heard of before by the old men; but lo! suddenly the flux came with a great current of water, more swift than horse's running. The tide was full as before, and this flux and reflux continued two or three times, and at last returned by degrees as usual.

On Rodriguez Island, near the end of the time period when explosive sounds were heard, Mr. Wallis (quoted above on p. 146) noticed unusual behavior in the inner harbor. At 1:30 p.m. on August 27, as related by Dr. Meldrum,[94] Wallis observed:

It was then ebb tide, and most of the boats were aground. The sea looked like water boiling heavily in a pot, and the boats which were afloat were swinging in all directions. The disturbance appeared quite suddenly, lasted about half an hour, and ceased as suddenly as it had commenced. At 14 hr 20 min a similar disturbance began; the tide all of a sudden rose 5 feet 11 inches, with a current of about 10 knots an hour to the westward, floating all boats which had been aground, and tearing them from their moorings. All this happened in a few minutes. The tide then turned with equal force to the eastward, leaving the boats which were close in-shore dry on the beach, and dragging the Government boat (a large decked pinnace) from heavy moorings, and leaving it dry on the reefs. The inner harbour was almost dry. The water in the channel was several feet below the line of reefs; and, owing to the sudden disappearance of the water, the reefs looked like islands rising out of the sea. The tides continued to rise and fall about every half hour, but not so high, or with the same force, as the first tide. By noon on the 29th, the tide was about its usual height, and appeared to be settled.

Even farther across the Indian Ocean is the island of Mauritius, 5445 km WSW of Krakatau. Here Dr. Meldrum[95] gathered several accounts of the tidal disturbance at the harbor on August 27.

At about 13 hr 30 min the water came
round the point of the sea wall, and in abo
of minutes returned with the same speed
place several times, the water on one occ
2½ feet. The water was very muddy and a
quantities of jelly fish were thrown on sh
same time, but farther up the funnel-shap
the water, which was then unusually lo
rushed in with great violence, rising full
the former level. An alternate ebb and flo
tinued till nearly 19 hours, and the inte
between high and low water were about
There was no high wave or billow, but str
the estimated velocity of which was abo
10 minutes, or 18 knots an hour. Vessels
the Dry Docks swayed much, and at ab
min one of the hawsers of the *Touareg*,
circumference, parted. Buoys in the ne
were at times seen spinning round like t
ances were observed on the 28th also, a
unusual currents even on the 29th.

Farther yet from Krakatau, 7767 km
ESE, tidal disturbances were highly vi
New Zealand as described in the follo
paper accounts.[96] The timing of these
much smaller disturbances recorded b
in France, Panama, San Francisco, a
where—were difficult to correlate with
Ocean waves, as discussed in the later
section (p. 367–395), but the relation.
eruption was real.

The tidal wave, experienced in Auc
and in the different ports of New Zeala
of August, was at first observed at Merc
in a few minutes the tide rose fully 6 ft
receded again, leaving the vessels in
dry. Throughout the day the wave
times with equal strength.

The most detailed eyewitness acco
distant waves, however, come from
newspaper correspondent[97] from Ga

KRAKATAU

PAR

R. D. M. VERBEEK.

INGÉNIEUR DES MINES.

ALBUM

CONTENANT 25 PLANCHES CHROMOLITHOGRAPHIQUES DES RÉGIONS DÉVASTÉES

DU DÉTROIT DE LA SONDE,

PRISES DEUX MOIS APRÈS L'ÉRUPTION DU KRAKATAU.

Publié par ordre de Son Excellence le Gouverneur-Général des Indes orientales néerlandaises.

BRUXELLES.

INSTITUT NATIONAL DE GÉOGRAPHIE.

KRAKATAU

DOOR

R. D. M. VERBEEK

MIJNINGENIEUR

UITGEGEVEN OP LAST VAN ZIJNE EXCELLENTIE DEN GOUVERNEUR-GENERAAL
VAN NEDERLANDSCH-INDIË

BATAVIA
LANDSDRUKKERIJ
1885

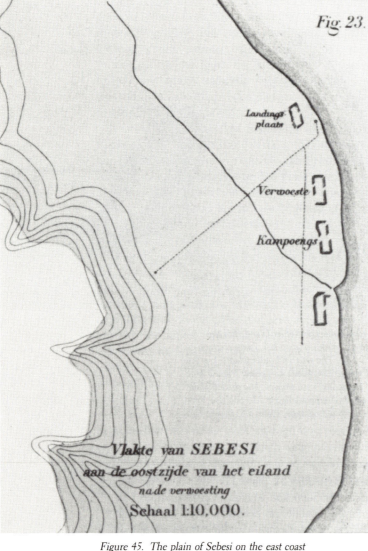

Figure 45. The plain of Sebesi on the east coast of the island after the destruction. Width of map is 1.0 km; contour interval is 5 m. The shaded area was flooded. The wharf ("landingsplaats") and a devastated kampong ("verwoeste kampoeng") are shown. (Verbeek's figure 23.) See also Verbeek's chromolithograph, Plate 3D.

four prosperous campongs on the plain near the beach, with good sawahs [rice fields] and pepper-gardens, I did not think to see it again as it is now.

From the present Huismans Island, or Mengoenang as it is actually called, appears the mountain, as Plate 3D shows. It is a singularly mournful scene, a picture of the most utter desolation. The forest has completely disappeared, the thickness of ash and pumice is 1 to 1½ m; there were everywhere deep narrow little gullies in the ash, which with their tributaries made the impression from afar as if the mountain were covered with dead wood on the plain, some tree stumps stuck out of the ash and on the place where before the main campong had been, we found here and there remains of furniture, but no cadavers.

Most of the people who lived in the campongs were apparently washed out to sea when the terrible wave rolled over the plain at 10 o'clock in the morning. The number of people who died here is estimated at 3000. According to our survey (see Figure 45), the plain is 700 m wide. Krakatau is in the background of the picture.

Plate 4A [Verbeek's plate 14]. The water between Sebesi and Krakatau, which was 36 m deep before, is now filled with ejecta, stones, ash and sand. Primarily two parts of this large mass are above the sea. They are called Calmeyer and Steers Islands. Their shape changes constantly, because the wash of the waves crumbles the loose ejecta and washes it away. Calmeyer Island is shown in Plate 4A, Steers in Plate 4B.

Plate 4A is from the north of Calmeyer, so that one also has a nice view of the peak of Krakatau and the collapsed walls on the north and east side of that island. The back side has its old shape, as shown on Plate 7A. Calmeyer is not one coherent island, but consists of 6, or if one includes those further away, 8 parts, as can be seen from Plate 4A and even better from map, Figure 46. The highest point rises only 6½ m above sea level. In August and September nothing of this island could be seen anymore above the sea.

Plate 4B [Verbeek's plate 15]. View of Steers Island from the east. It consists of three parts, the highest point rose at the most to 3 m above sea level in October 1883. The surf there is usually strong, so that our attempts to land failed.

In August and September 1884 Steers was still clearly visible as a sandbank above water during low tide. The report of the French Krakatau commission that this island had disappeared totally in May 1884 is therefore not correct. Possibly it was high tide when they were close to the island so that the sandbank could not be seen.

Plates 4C, D, and E [Verbeek's plates 17, 18, and 19]. We now return to Calmeyer. Plate 4E gives a good overview of that island. Here one is almost at the west end of the island and faces east. The sea, covered with pumice, penetrated into the different parts. The rise and fall of the water in these inlets is shown by the short white shorelines, which are colored by pumice fragments. The highest point of the island (6½ m above sea level) is to the left. On top of the fine pumice sand lies a 0.2 m thick layer of fine and darker colored ash, which must have gotten there as wet mud, because it developed many cracks while drying out on top of the hot ash. See Plates 4D and E.

From Calmeyer one has a beautiful view of Krakatau and Sebesi, and it is from here that Plates 4C and D were taken. Krakatau (Plate 4C) is shown here from almost the same side as on Plate 4A; however, this illustration is on a smaller scale. The island between Calmeyer and Krakatau is part of Calmeyer, and is island *a* on our map Figure 46. To the right of Krakatau lies Lang and completely to the right one still sees a part of Verlaten. Plate 4D shows Sebesi in morning light; the coloring of the mountain at that time is normally brownish at the bottom, blue at the top. The outline of both this mountain, and of Krakatau, as well as the one of Sebesi on Plate 3D, are taken with a Camera Lucida; the steepness of the slopes is therefore not exaggerated, as is normally the case, but agrees totally with the reality. To the right behind Sebesi the lower island Seboekoe appears, and still further to the right Radja Bassa. [The large, circular, water-filled depression in Plate 4E appears to be a secondary explosion crater, formed shortly after the main eruption by the interaction of seawater with still-hot tephra deposits.]

Plate 5A [Verbeek's plate 20]. Now in our mind we continue our journey further south, but first passing around Krakatau itself.

Semangka Bay also suffered significantly from the waves. Beneawang itself, the post of the Controller at the north end of the bay, and the flat strip at the mouths of the Semangka river were totally destroyed. The vegetation was ruined almost completely by the

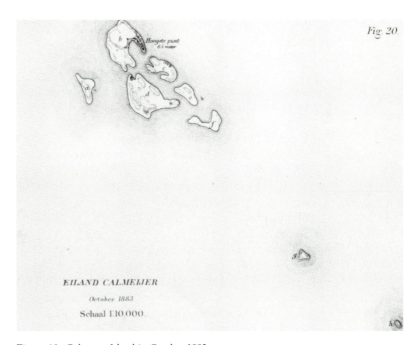

Figure 46. Calmeyer Island in October 1883. Width of map is 1.8 km. The highest point on the island is only 6.5 m above sea level. (Verbeek's figure 20.) See also Verbeek's chromolithographs, Plates 4A and E.

ash and mud rain, but less mud fell on this side than to the north of the volcano.

The SE side of the large island Tabuan suffered most from the waves. The N and NW half sustained a lot less damage, and fortunately the campongs were located on this side; most trees were leafless from the ash rain. In October I tried in vain to visit Poeti and the places further north, but the bay was already filled with pumice at a short distance from Tabuan, rendering a further penetration impossible. We therefore tried a western direction, visited first Tampang, the campong already mentioned in the description of Plate 5B, then continuing south of Vlakken Hoek to the Blimbing Bay.

Close to this place on Sumatra's SW corner stands a fine iron lighthouse built in 1880; 60 m high and a first-class light! Around the tower stood a building made of iron and stone, which vanished without a trace. The wave washed with great power over the flat southern portion of the peninsula and leaped 15 m high against the tower. Fortunately, the tower itself remained almost completely undamaged (see Plate 5A), but in the dense forest, between the tower and the campong Blimbing, such damage was done as one seldom sees; trees all over, among which were found iron parts of the building and bodies of the workers here and there, forming a chaos beyond description.

As one can see on the illustration, the trees which are still standing are totally leafless, nonetheless, this point is already 103 km from Krakatau.

Plate 5B [Verbeek's plate 16]. The Tampang Bay at Vlakken Hoek, at the SW end of Semangka Bay. The campong Tampang was destroyed by the big wave; it had been at the place in the picture where some wilted coconut trees can be seen. Although at a distance of almost 85 km from Krakatau, the rain of ash and relatively coarse pumice stones left the trees here almost completely without leaves. The white sections in the forest are so-called ladangs: parts of the forest where the large trees were cut down in order to make gardens. The ash layer gives them the light gray color.

Plate 6B [Verbeek's plate 21]. We now cross to the shore of Java and land first on the north side of the large Prinsen Island. There had been here a campong of 56 lumberjacks from Tjaringin, who all died. The barren strip is best visible at the left end (NE) of the island; however, the wave did not come any higher here than 10 to 15 m.

On Plate 6B at the south side of Prinsen Island one

sees a little mountain shaped like a volcano, the so-called "peak" of Prinsen Island.

Plate 6C [Verbeek's plate 22]. When we round now the Prinsen Island on the east side, we come before Java's First Point, west of Meeuwen Eiland.

From this anchor place a view of the little-known Goenoeng Pajoeng was taken, a mountain with the shape of a volcano, but only 471 m high. In front of that lies the Java shoreline, where the vegetation was only partly destroyed and the bare trees had already started to leaf out again.

Plate 6A [Verbeek's plate 23]. From the mooring place a very good road used to run in earlier days along the beach to the picturesque stone lighthouse, situated on a 40 m-high rock, also a first-class light.

The lighthouse had been higher before, but it was damaged so severely by the earthquake of September 1, 1880, that the top part had to be demolished.

The green, which is visible in Plate 6A, developed largely in the two months between August 27 and October 21; after the eruption not everything in the forest was leafless, but nonetheless a good part of it was. Especially the leaves of the banana trees developed with exceptional speed after the abundant rainfall.

On the road from the mooring place to the lighthouse and much further to the left in the forest, we found a large number of coral fragments, which were carried several hundred meters from the beach to the forest by the sea. Many tree trunks showed signs that they came in sharp contact with these coral fragments. The road was washed out in several places.

Plate 7A [Verbeek's plate 9]. Krakatau seen from the back (south side). As one can see, the back has not collapsed. It shows its normal slope, only without vegetation and thickly covered with ash. Trees had been growing here on August 11.

Plates 7B and 8 [Verbeek's plates 24 and 25]. After Java's First Point, we visited the coast of Bantam further north, to Tjaringin, Anjer and Merak, where large plains were swept completely bare, all houses and coconut trees were washed away and thousands and thousands of blocks of coral were thrown on land from the sea. At Java's Fourth Point, not far from the lighthouse, lies an enormous block of coral, with a measured content of 300 m^3, therefore having a weight of at least 0.5 million kg (see Figure 28 [p. 116]). No

Plate 1. Sunda Straits—North, October, 1883.

A. View west from Merak. Tip of Merak Island on left, with
Dwars-in-den-weg behind, and the volcanic cone of Sebesi in
the distance. The SE point of Sumatra makes up the right half
of the picture, with Toppershoedje in the foreground.

B. Dwars-in-den-weg from south. Vegetation stripped to
height of 35 m.

C. Varkenshoek and Zutphen Islands, Sumatra (see A). In the
distance is Sebesi on left and Radja Bassa on right.

D. Toppershoedje with Java coast in background.

illustration could
which gave an acc

We finally cross
much destruction
7B a view of the t
and pumice mate
name pumice sanc
of the beautiful st
side, formed by th
illustrations togeth
well as map, Figu
hope, of the mou

These plates ar
267], so that the f

Plate 7B was m
climbed the mou
out a survey at th

The deep gullie
of them is shown

They developed
eruption products,
our way to the to
gully bottoms. Bel
some places at th
thick, one sees th
the nearly vertica
also a part of the
has a slope of 30°
the back we did :
behind which to g
ing sun; the entir

On Plate 8 one
at the middle, as
crater was located
crater has not bee
least only in its up
of the steep wall b
crater is visible to
layers below (and
way that they do
layers belong to t
the same rock fou
different from the
are composed ma
fine ash. The loo
flows, and are cu
layers. Their col
contrast sharply w
ice material whic

At the borderl
finds dead tree tru

Foreword to Monograph

Plate 8. K cross-sectic 1883 rest c cano.

Verbeek's monograph begins with the above-mentioned "Short Report" of February 1884. This was translated in Nature and is not reprinted here. The Foreword to the main monograph, dated Buitenzorg, May 1, 1885, has been translated from the Dutch by J.A. Nelen.

When shortly after the large eruption of 1883 the Government ordered me to visit Krakatau and completely investigate the causes and consequences of the latest eruption, I originally thought I would have to perform an exclusively geologic task. But even before my departure, reports came in from Ceylon that on the day of the eruption a special movement of the sea had been observed on the beaches, which no doubt had to be ascribed to Krakatau. And I had barely returned from my trip to the Sunda Straits, when reports were added about barometric disturbances in Europe, about blue and green colorations of the sun and moon, and about exceptionally strange reddish phenomena before sunrise and after sunset. All these phenomena had already, soon after their first occurrences, been connected with Krakatau, and therefore had necessarily to be included within the reach of the research.

As with most volcanoes, the consequences of an eruption remain limited to the immediate area of the volcano, and while the research after a new eruption, as a rule, has to be of an exclusively geological character, it appeared already very soon that this was an exceptionally important eruption, whose consequences were observed over all of the earth, either as meteorological events, or as special movements of the air or the sea.

It is therefore not surprising that the interest in this eruption is exceptional, not only for geologists, but also for hydrologists, meteorologists, and astronomers.

Without any exaggeration, the Krakatau eruption of 1883, although not the largest, can be called the most important volcanic event of this century, and even the most interesting eruption witnessed by the human race up till now. No doubt earlier eruptions, as for instance the Tambora eruption in 1815, might have caused important atmospheric disturbances, but instruments to record these events were not available then, and therefore they went unnoticed and lost to science.

The Krakatau eruption makes a convincing case for the usefulness of self-registering barometers and tidal gauges; the number of these instruments, however, is still relatively small, and it is to be hoped that this description will make a contribution to the installation of larger numbers of self-registering barometers, which record the air pressure as a continuous graph, and also of more self-registering tidal gauges at appropriate points along the beaches and various islands in the ocean.

A very extensive correspondence with people inside and outside the country to obtain the necessary data was my immediate task and I must acknowledge that most have helped me as much as was in their power. The main difficulty was to obtain trustworthy data and to choose correctly from contradictory information. This cost me many an unpleasant hour and the incompleteness or inaccuracy of some information caused much disappointment.

[Verbeek goes on to mention the publication history of his investigation, summarized by us in the above introduction. He also notes that some tide gauge records, barometric charts, and other illustrations will be further delayed. These were published separately, with the other figures, as an Atlas distinct from the chromolithograph album and text. In a section of the foreword translated in *Nature* (April 15, 1886, p. 560), Verbeek corrects the minor errors in his earlier "Short Report."]

It is my hope that this book has everything in it necessary to describe this type of eruption; also, looking up a large number of references in various books and magazines and making numerous extensive calculations, which made writing this so cumbersome, will then not be necessary.

Hypotheses to explain the exceptional number of volcanic events in 1883 will not be found here, since in my opinion there is no basis for these. If water seeping from the surface into subterranean spaces is considered as the primary cause of earthquakes and eruptions, then it would be logical to think of formation or opening up of dislocation cracks or subterranean cave-ins, during periods of high frequency of these quakes and eruptions, since through both these causes the flow of water toward the depths is increased and the pressure in subterranean spaces is enlarged. But then, how to explain why just around the year 1883 such a change in the condition of dislocation cracks would have occurred will, in my opinion, remain forever an unexplained question mark.

Some have tried to see a connection between volcanic activity and the greater activity of the sun in that year. The maximum sunspot activity seemed to occur on 1884.0 [here Verbeek treats years in tenths], thus only a few months after the large eruption.

The elaborate research of Prof. R. Wolf, Zurich, has shown a connection between the number of sunspots and the size of the daily change of the magnetic declination. Maximum sunspot activity could lead to exceptionally strong earth magnetic currents, through which chemical activity inside the earth could occur, which would be favorable toward causing earthquakes or eruptions. It should not be forgotten however that, during the periods 1829.9, 1837.2, 1848.1, 1860.4 and 1870.6, there also was maximum sunspot activity. The events in 1837 and 1870 were almost twice as heavy as the maximum of 1884, while those years certainly could not be distinguished by exceptional volcanic activity.

Thus I cannot see any connection between the activity on the sun and on the earth in 1883; nor is there any connection between the position of the earth with respect to the moon and the sun regarding our large August eruption. This will be shown in the text.

Measures and weight in this report are expressed in metric; only for sea distances the minute mile is used; however, from references to other reports one comes across other measures. To avoid confusion I include a list of the most used measures for length.

1 geographic mile or German mile = 7420.44 m (abbreviated 7420.4 m).

1 minute mile = 1855.11 m (abbreviated 1855.1 m). In English magazines, this mile is sometimes unjustly indicated as "geographical mile."

1 sea mile = 1 mille or mille marin = 1 nautical mile = 1852.0 m. In this work the sea mile is mostly taken to be similar to the minute mile, since the difference is small, and since the two given measures are correct only for the equator and a meridian, but not for the distances in between. If more precision is required, the length is calculated independently.

1 English land mile = 1 mile or statute mile = 1760 yards = 1609.3 m.

1 English foot = 12 inches = 0.3048 m.

1 inch (English thumb) = 25.4 mm.

For g, the acceleration of gravity, a latitude of ϕ = 0° is used in the calculation, thus g = 9.781 m/sec/sec.

1 vadem [fathom] = 6 English feet = 1.829 m (abbr. 1.83 m). On some Netherland Indies sea maps, vadems of 1.8 m are also found.

N.B. If no date is given with reports, newspaper articles, etc., the year 1883 is indicated.

[Verbeek then devotes 3½ pages to the names of individuals and organizations acknowledged for assistance in his investigation.]

With a few words, let us review the most important points the eruption has taught us.

1. First of all, the exceptionally loud noises require our attention. The materials were blown out of the crater with large velocity to a considerable height. This blowout was accompanied by large explosions, which in loudness far exceeded all known noises. At no earlier event was the noise heard over such a large part of the earth's surface.

Only shortly ago there was talk at the French Academy (*Comptes Rendus* of March 9, 1885) about a progression of these sounds through the center of the earth, straight through the antipodes of Krakatau. According to Mr. F.A. Forel explosive sounds were heard on August 26 on the island Caïman-Brae, located in the Caribbean (south of Cuba, 80°W 20°N). The correct hour was not given, but from the report it is clear that they were heard during daylight hours. (The sky was clear. One ran to the beach to see if a ship was approaching, etc.)

For several reasons it does not appear probable to me that these noises originated at Krakatau. First of all, an eruption close to the antipodes seems to have taken place at the same time as the large eruption in the Sunda Straits, although the reports about this seem scarce. Second, probably for other reasons, an earthquake or eruption took place in the Caribbean at the same time. [Verbeek here references p. 435 and 455 of his text (not reproduced here), but we know of no volcanic activity in the Caribbean at that time.] Third, the time is not right, since the large explosions of Krakatau—assuming, as Mr. Forel does, one hour for the noise to proceed through the earth's core, which is probably too little anyhow—could not have been heard in the vicinity of the antipodes during the day, but only at first in the later evening of Aug. 26.

2. The air was made to vibrate so strangely by the tremendous detonations that many objects at large distances from the volcano started to vibrate to such an extent that one thought of earthquakes.

3. The formation of an atmospheric disturbance, which proceeded as large air waves around the earth's surface, has up till now not been observed as a phenomenon caused by an eruption, although other atmospheric disturbances which caused regular wave motions have already been observed prior to this.

4. The appearances of a green and blue sun and moon and the beautiful red glow have also been observed after earlier eruptions, but not to the extent

seen after August 1883.

5. If even before the huge blunted cones of many volcanoes had repeatedly been considered as ruins of earlier sharp-pointed mountain cones, having obtained their blunted or flattened-down shape by subsidence of the central portion, then here we have witnessed for the first time a subsidence comparable in dimensions to the "Tengger" in East Java, known to be one of the largest subsided crater voids in the world. The earlier explanation, which was doubted by some because they could not visualize subsidences of such often huge proportions, should now be considered without a doubt as the correct one since the catastrophe of Krakatau in 1883.

6. The conveniently formed, almost vertical cross-section of Rakata Peak has given us a much desired inside view of the internal structure of a volcano. Of course the composition of this volcano cannot be considered adaptable to all volcanic mountain cones. For instance, the existence of a hollow cavity as a compact nucleus might be considered very probable for many volcanoes, although the Rakata cross-section does not show this.

7. The toppling of a portion of the peak into the sea created waves which in height far exceeded the largest waves formed by storms. The largest number of victims of the Krakatau eruption can be attributed to this side event, and specifically to the flooding of the coastal areas of the Sunda Straits by these waves.

8. The procession of this wave motion is remarkable. These sea motions caused by the Krakatau wave have been observed not only throughout the Indian Ocean, but also in the Atlantic and Pacific Oceans. A portion of the disturbances in tide levels noticed on the coasts of America and Europe, and originally also ascribed to Krakatau, must however have had another cause.

9. As is known, from the speed of the proceeding wave motion the average depth of the sea along this passage can be calculated. For the route Krakatau–South Georgia a speed is found from the procession of the large Krakatau wave, which corresponds to an exceptionally large depth of 6340 m. Therefore along this route there is probably a deep trough, whose suspected existence, as I hope, will soon be certified by deep-sea measurements.

10. Finally an important result of the Krakatau ash research warrrants notice. This ash is the first rock type to contain a large number of different plagioclase types. While already earlier in many rocks of eruptive origin several triclinic feldspar types (usually two) were

suspected or indicated, the investigation of the Krakatau ash has shown, for the first time, that a rock type can contain "all" plagioclase from the most basic to the most acidic. In addition, a little sanidine occurs. All these feldspars are products of primary crystallization, since secondary crystallization was prevented by sudden cooling and solidification of the molten magma.

This co-occurrence of various plagioclases with specific gravities all the way from pure anorthite down to pure albite gives added support to the feldspar theory by Tschermak.

The occurrence of very different types among porphyritic feldspars, varying in specific gravity, and thus chemical composition, was here easy to prove by the isolated condition of the crystals. However, this also is true for many compact andesites and a large number of other erupted rocks.

Plotting the specific gravities along the abscissa and the corresponding quantities of plagioclase in a rock along the ordinate results in a number of points which form a curved line, which might be called the feldspar curve. This curved line must of course be different for the various acidic and basic rocks. It is a new and important project for petrographers to determine the feldspar curves of the most important erupted rocks.

An unusually detailed Table of Contents, running 27 pages, follows Verbeek's Foreword. His numbered pages begin with a chronological history of the 1883 eruption. These first three chapters of the monograph provide an enormously valuable narrative, filling in many of the gaps between eyewitness accounts reprinted above, and forming a coherent history gleaned from the wealth of material available to Verbeek in west Java.

Chronologic Narrative

Krakatau before May, 1883

Many, who in the good old days travelled by sail or later by Dutch mailboat from Europe to the Dutch Indies, will remember Krakatau as one of their first sights of the much praised *Insulinde* [Island Indies].

Krakatau is one of the numerous islands, which lie scattered in Sunda Strait, the narrow waterway connecting the Java Sea with the Indian Ocean, and separating the large island of Sumatra from Java. The island rises out of the sea as a steep cone, and from its shape, which on the southside is significantly steeper at the top than at the bottom, one recognizes from afar that the mountain is of the volcanic type.

The island was thus already known for a long time as a volcano. Vogel writes about an eruption which apparently occurred in May 1680 in his "Ost Indianische Reise Beschreibung."[1] He passed the Strait for the first time in July 1679, travelling from The Netherlands to Batavia, and for the second time in September of the same year, going to Sumatra; Krakatau did not seem to have shown anything unusual yet, at least in his narrative the island was not mentioned. In the beginning of 1681 he left Salida [46 km SSE of Padang], where he worked in one of the mines of the East Indies Company, for Batavia to seek medical treatment, and at this time he writes[1a]:

On January 26, 1681 we started to sail with the favourable East wind and, with God's help, we arrived February 1st at the mouth of the Sunda Strait, where I saw to my amazement that the island Krakatau—which was still very green and pretty with trees at my journey to Sumatra— presented itself to our eyes now completely burned and as a waste land and it threw out large lumps of fire at four places.

When I asked the ship's captain at which time this island had burst, he told me that it happened during May of the year 1680. While coming from a trip to Bengal, they had suffered a big storm and had noticed an earthquake in the sea about 10 miles from the island. This was followed by terrible thunder and noise for which he surmised that an island or another piece of land must have burst. A short while after, when they had sailed a little closer with the ship to the land, and closely approached the mouth of the Strait of Sunda, he had noticed that the island named Krakatau had burst, confirming his speculations. Also he and the entire crew had smelled a very fresh, strong sulfurous odor; and the sailors had collected with buckets stones from the sea which had drifted from the burst island, and which

resembled pumice, were very light and were collected as rarities. He showed me a piece which was a little bit bigger than a fist.

In November 1681, he returned to Sumatra, and in his description of that voyage we find included the journal of Elias Hesse, an author who wrote much about mountainous areas; the latter, when discussing the island, only mentions: "The Island Krakatau started to burn about during the year and is also uninhabited." He probably heard the story of the eruption from Vogel.

Finally Vogel once more went through Sunda Strait in October 1687 on the way to Batavia, and for the last time in December of the same year, when returning to The Netherlands. But in neither description of these voyages did he mention anything of importance about Krakatau.

Now the investigations by Mr. N.P. van den Berg of Batavia,[2] who took the trouble to read the *Daily Register of the Castle Batavia* of the years 1679, 1680 and 1681, showed that indeed the ship *Aerdenburg* of Bengalen docked at Batavia on June 12, 1680. Therefore there is little doubt about the credibility of the story that the captain of the ship, on which Vogel sailed in 1681, personally witnessed the eruption of May 1680.

However, it is impossible to explain why in the *Daily Register*, according to van den Berg, nothing is mentioned about the eruption, and also nothing in the reports from the ship *Aerdenburg* of Bengalen, while normally even the smallest events were noted. Mr. van den Berg concludes from this, and I agree wholeheartedly, that the eruption in 1680 could not have been a major one. The validity of the statement that Vogel himself in February 1681 had seen glowing rocks being spewed out, is therefore in doubt.

In November 1680 the Surgeon Christoper Frike travelled through the Strait,[3] but he was not aware of anything unusual. However, the ships might not always have passed close enough to Krakatau to really notice the island well; moreover the island most likely was obscured by fine ash during the eruptions. Therefore it seems to me not totally impossible that the eruptions of 1680 continued intermittently till the beginning of 1681, and Vogel's story therefore could be true. But it remains difficult to explain why nobody, except Vogel, mentions the eruptions.

Vogel's description of the eruption of 1680 is adopted by Leopold von Buch in his *Physikalische Beschrei-*

bung der Kanarischen Inseln, and this in turn was quoted in Berghaus' *Lander and Volkerkunde*, and after this in Junghuhn's *Java*.

From 1680 or 1681 to 1883 the volcano seemed at rest, at least no news of younger eruptions have come our way. The island was heavily vegetated, with the exception of a barren lava flow at the northern end, and in everybody's opinion it belonged to that group of innocent volcanos which were considered to be "extinct." How unreliable and how incorrect it is to describe some of them as "totally extinct" was proven only too clearly by Vesuvius in A.D. 79 and now by Krakatau in 1883.

Just as the name of Sebesi was corrupted by sailors to "Slebezee," so Rakata became "Krakatau." The latter name, which already was better known than Rakata, has become so generally used since the eruption, that I will use that name from now on, especially since Rakata already seemed to have been a corrupted name.[4] Only for the highest peak will I reserve the name Rakata. However, to corrupt the name Krakatau even further, to Krakataoe, Krakatoa or Krakatoea, as some do, should be condemned, as there is no valid reason for this.

The Krakatau group, in its earlier years, consisted of four islands, Krakatau proper, being by far the largest and highest of the four, Verlaten Eiland [Deserted Island] to the NW, Lang Eiland [Long Island] to the NE of Krakatau, and the small island of Poolsche Hoed [Polish Hat] to the west of Lang Eiland (see our maps, Figures 47 and 48).

No real map of Krakatau existed; size, location, and shape can only be evaluated by a couple of terrain sketches and from the Dutch and English charts of Sunda Strait. In 1849, Captain P. J. Buyskes, on board the navy frigate *Prins van Oranje*, made a sketch of Krakatau from the west-southwest, which recently was published enlarged by the former Chief Engineer C. de Groot.[5] A second sketch of Krakatau and its surrounding islands was made by me in 1880 from the NNW side; it can be found in the *Yearbook of Mining*, 1881, part 1. Because both sketches show the island from a different side, they complement each other nicely. One can see from both sketches (Figure 50) that there are three mountains on Krakatau; the most southern part, actually the steep cone-shaped mountain Rakata, was more than 800 m high; it was joined in the middle of the island by Danan mountain, with several peaks, which most likely belonged to a ring-shaped crater wall; to the north, to the end of the island was hilly terrain, with several peaks,

which was called Perboewatan. Several sloping lava flows were found here, one of which is shown on my sketch. They were only sparsely vegetated and appeared to belong to the newest and least weathered rock formations of the island. These lava flows of the Perboewatan developed most likely during the last eruption in 1680.

In 1854, a map of the islands of Krakatau was made by Master John Richards, commander of the English warship *Saracen*. His map is used in a reduced scale in the English chart of Sunda Strait[6] and also added, enlarged, on cardboard [?Dutch *carton*]. The Dutch chart of 1874 by Captain A.R. Blommendal,[7] shows slight differences in both shape and locations of the islands, compared to the English map. From the new map made of Krakatau, after the eruption of 1883, by Lt. First class M.C. van Doorn, it is clear that the location of both Verlaten Eiland and Lang Eiland was slightly further west than shown on the Dutch map, which agrees with the English map. The earlier east coast of Krakatau on the Dutch chart can not have been correct, because relocating Lang Eiland more to the west would have reduced to almost nil the width of the Strait between that island and Krakatau. I used for my maps, therefore, with only minor variations, Richards' map of the old coastlines of the four islands.

It can be concluded from our maps in Figures 47 and 48 that the length of Krakatau was 9 km, its width 5 km, its area at least 33 km^2, and the height of the peak 822 m, according to the chart. The geographical location of the peak is 105°26'36"E and 6°8'50"S while the crater of the mountain Danan was located at approximately 105°26'E and 6°7'S (see our map, Figure 49).

These are the most important topographic and geographic data about Krakatau, and now there is only left to tell what was known of the geology.

We already saw from Vogel's description that Krakatau is a volcano, which erupted in 1680, during which much pumice was ejected. As far as I could find out, nothing else was known about the rock formations of Krakatau. Therefore I stepped into a geologically completely unknown terrain when I visited the island in July 1880.

When the steamship *Egeron* went to Vlakken Hoek [Flat Corner] during that month in the service of Bebakening en Kunstverlichting [Beacons and Coastal Lighting] I used the opportunity to visit that place as well as the beautiful, recently built lighthouse. On my return trip to Batavia, I was able to pay a short visit to the small islands in Sunda Strait, i.e., Taboean, Krakatau, Brabantshoedje, the Zutphense Eilanden, and Toppershoedje. In 1877 I already had visited the islands of Seboekoe, Sebesi, and Lagoendi, while on board the steamship *Singkawang* of the Government's navy. As a result, I obtained a relatively complete picture of the geological state of the islands in the Strait. However, the *Egeron* had to return to Batavia, and I visited the islands for a couple of hours only.

My observations of the Krakatau group were reported in my description of South Sumatra.[8] When we approached Krakatau from the NNW, I sketched Figure 50, which shows the four islands. After this I went in a small boat to the NW end of Krakatau across from Verlaten Eiland to collect rock samples of the lava flow which runs into the sea there; then to Lang Eiland, where a light-gray lava is found which forms almost separate, nearly horizontal banks and which contains numerous small well-crystallized tridymite crystals; and finally to the Poolsche Hoed, where I found dark greenish-black glass-rich rocks. Microscopic investigation showed that these rocks are very glassy eqivalents of augite andesite and that the difference is caused mainly by the amount of glass between the crystals. They have a completely different habit than the normal augite andesites and pitchstones of the volcanoes on Sumatra and Java, and when chemically analyzed, they seemed to contain 72% to 73% silicic acid [SiO_2], while analyses of the regular augite andesites contain at most 61% SiO_2. They contain also alumina, iron oxide, calcium, magnesium, soda, no or hardly any potassium, and only 0.87% to 0.66% water. Although the dark rocks of the Poolsche Hoed resemble a water-bearing pitchstone, they are a water-free glass rock, a dark andesite obsidian. Thus, in my paper mentioned earlier I note on page 214 that these glass rocks and andesites of Krakatau are an exception among the volcanic rocks of Java and Sumatra.

There was no time to collect any rock samples from the southern part of Krakatau, that is of the peak, and of Verlaten Eiland, and even less time to make an excursion inland, which would have been very difficult anyway because of the dense vegetation. Little did I think that the places where I hammered rocks would disappear altogether 3 years later!

During the eruption of last year a collapse occurred which, in size, is not matched by any other in historic time. The older rocks remained largely intact; we must imagine Verlaten and Lang as the parts of an old crater wall, which are above the water, and which resulted

from the collapse of a large volcano.

The peak, which almost completely consists of different rocks, formed later at the south end of the collapsed crater; parts of the oldest crater wall mentioned above show up at its foot. Between these islands again formed through renewed eruptions the northern part of Krakatau, which finally became united with the peak. In this youngest part the volcanic eruptions occurred in 1680 and 1883, after which the central part together with the northern half of the older peak collapsed. Thus, until last year, Krakatau was a volcano like many others, consisting of an older crater wall and a younger central part. During the collapse, this last part disappeared, and as a result the volcano now has the appearance of Santorini (in the Greek archipelago), as it must have looked before the formation of the Kaimeni islands.

Eruption of May to August 26

On Sunday morning May 20, 1883, the inhabitants of Batavia, Buitenzorg, and vicinity were shaken by a dull rumbling sound, accompanied by explosions, resembling cannon fire. It started between 10 and 11 in the morning[9] and soon it so increased in severity that for many the initial surprise changed to worry. The explosions were accompanied by ground tremors and shaking of buildings and of objects in houses, but nonetheless it was soon agreed that this was not an earthquake, but vibrations in the air. No magnetic deviations of the instruments of the Meteorologic Institute in Batavia occurred; however, a magnetic needle, which was suspended from a cocoon thread, oscillated (with a mirror reading of 5 arc-seconds), but the movement was completely vertical, as any other non-magnetic bar would have done. The rumbling sounds and vibrations lasted also much longer than is normally the case with earthquakes, sometimes longer than 1 hour, and finally, people who put their ears to the ground, did not notice any sounds coming from the ground, even during the loudest bursts of sound. Therefore, one could only attribute the air vibrations and explosions to a volcanic eruption, and it is ironic that for more than two days it was totally uncertain which volcano was active. Indee' the explosions were coming from the direction of Krakatau, but telegrams from Serang, Anjer, and Merak (towns much closer to Krakatau than Batavia) indicated that no explosions or air vibrations were heard there. Furthermore, a

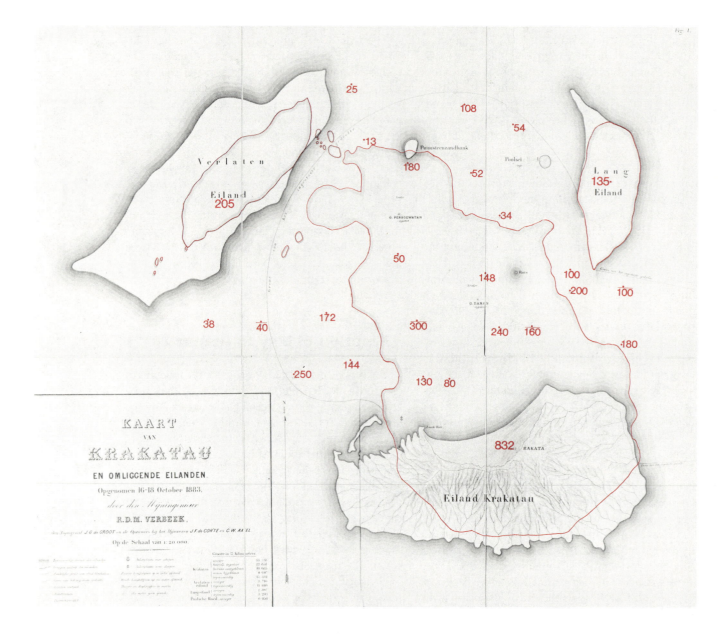

Figure 47a. Map of Krakatau and surrounding islands. Surveyed October 16–18, 1883 by Mining Engineer, R.D.M. Verbeek, surveyor J.G. de Groot, and employees of the mines, J.F. de Corte and C.W. Axel. The old shorelines of Krakatau, Verlaten and Lang Islands, and Poolsche Hoed are copied from the English sea chart of Richards, with minor changes to Lang Island from the new sea chart (Figure 37) by Lieutenant First Class, M.C. van Doorn.

Width of Verbeek's Atlas map is 72 cm, representing 14.4 km at his scale of 1:20,000, but we have been forced to reduce that size here. The old outlines of the islands are shown by red lines, and the present outlines in darker shades. The black line is the limit of the collapsed portion of the volcano, and the dashed

lines mark the measured outline of Perboewatan and Danan craters. The islet off NW Rakata and that labeled "puimsteenzandbank" are new pumice banks. Altitudes and depths are in meters. Depths greater than a given value are denoted by a line over that number.

Surface areas are shown in the table at the lower right side of the legend. The old surface area of Krakatau was 33.536 km², the collapsed portion is 22.851 km², with 10.685 km² remaining. The newly added area is 4.647 km², totaling 15.332 km² for Krakatau in October 1883. Verlaten's former area of 3.716 km² was increased to 11.810 km², and Lang's former 2.897 km² was increased to 3.203 km². Poolsche Hoed was formerly 0.056 km². (Verbeek's figure 1.)

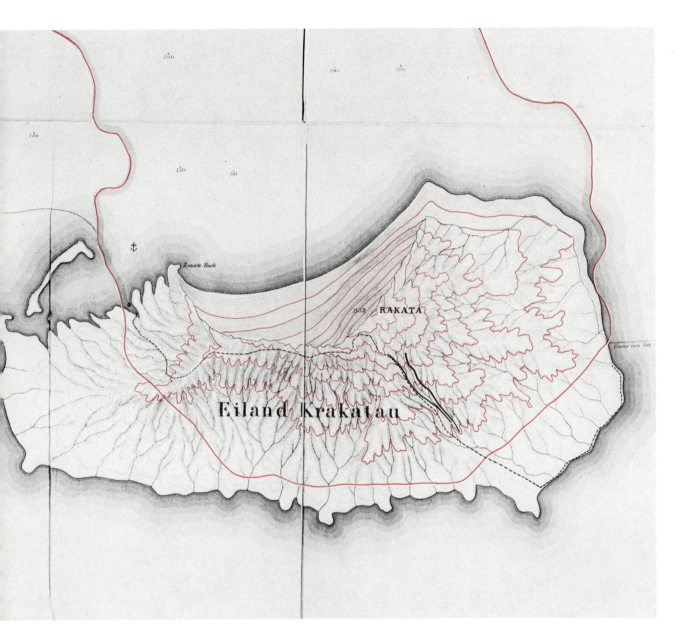

Figure 47b. Enlargement of Figure 47a showing Rakata, or Krakatau Island. The dashed line on Krakatau shows path of Verbeek's group in 1883. Anchorages for large ships and small boats are shown by large and small anchors, respectively. The 2 mud flows SSE from Rakata's summit are shown by bold lines. The black contour interval is 10 m and the red 100 m. On the north side of Krakatau, the crumbling rim is slightly overhanging, as can be seen from the contour lines. Verbeek's Atlas caption adds the note that the altitude of Rakata Peak should be 830 m, rather than the 832 m shown on the map.

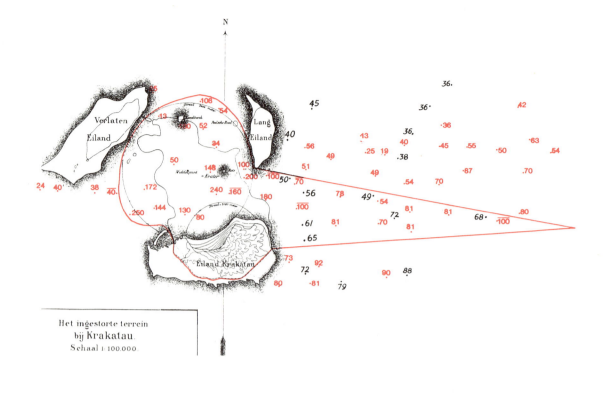

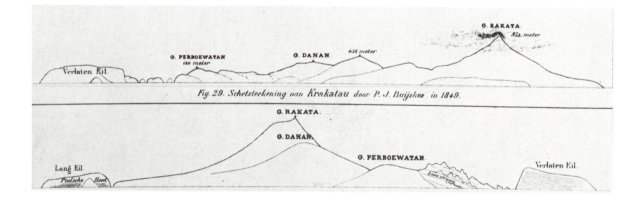

Figure 48 (above). Map of the collapsed area at Krakatau, indicated by the red line; width of the map is 42.3 km. Black and red numbers are former and present depths respectively, in meters. Numbers with lines over them are minimum depths. The old outlines of the islands are indicated by solid and dashed lines, and the present outlines are shaded. The arc north of Rakata Peak and the circle around the collapse center ("middlepunt") have radii ("straal") of 2080 and 3000 m, respectively. (Verbeek's figure 2.)

Figure 50 (below). Upper: Sketch of Krakatau in 1849 by P.J. Buijskes. Lower: Sketch of Krakatau in 1880 by R.D.M. Verbeek. A lava flow ("lavastroom") is shown. (Verbeek's figures 29 and 30.)

194

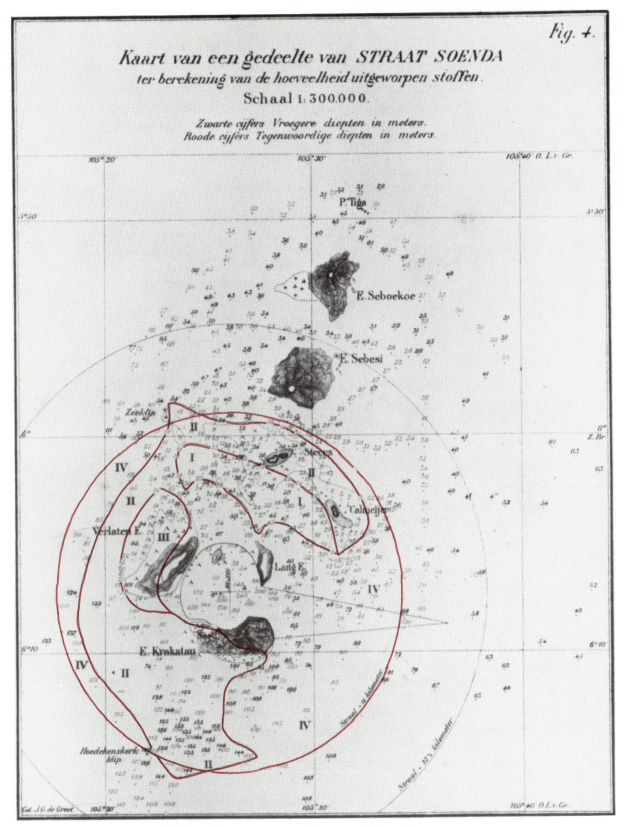

Figure 49. Map of a part of Sunda Strait, from the new sea chart and Verbeek's survey, used to calculate the volume of erupted material. Width of the map is 45 km; depths in meters. Old and present depths are given by darker and fainter numbers, respectively. Areas I, II, III, and IV are referred to in the calculation of ejecta volumes (see p. 235). (Verbeek's figure 4.)

195

passenger arriving in Anjer on the morning of May 20 (and who remained there till 1 p.m., then reached Serang at 3:30 p.m. and after a delay of 1 hour continued his journey to Tangerang) said that he did not notice any explosions or rumbling sounds. Because the volcano Karang in Bantam showed no sign of eruption, people started speculating that one of the volcanos of Sumatra had erupted, until the first telegram arrived on May 22, telling that Krakatau, after all, was active and the source of all the sounds.

In the meantime the explosions became increasingly loud in Batavia and became the loudest on the morning of the 22nd. According to the Batavian newspapers, explosions were most clearly heard on the following hours: May 20 from 10 a.m. to 1 p.m., 6:45 p.m. to 8 p.m., 11:30 p.m. to 12 midnight; May 21, 12 midnight to 1 a.m., 4 a.m. to 5 a.m., 7:50 a.m. (rather loud) to 9 a.m., 12 noon, 4 p.m., and 12 midnight; May 22, 3 a.m. to 4 a.m. and 5:30 a.m. to 6 a.m. (very strong, maximum detonation); hereafter weaker rumblings were heard, the latest in the night of May 22–23 from 12 midnight to 1 a.m.

In Buitenzorg[9a] the explosions started Sunday at 11 a.m. and continued intermittently till May 22.

In Tangerang the rumblings started at the same time, lasted till 3:30 and again were heard from 6:30 to 7 p.m.[9b] The explosions also were heard in Poerwakarta, the capital of the residency of Krawang [and 225 km E of Krakatau], while nothing was heard in the village of Krawang which is near. Along the coast of Sunda Strait the rumblings and vibrations were felt in different locations, only not in Anjer and Merak. A column of smoke from the direction of Krakatau was observed in Ketimbang on the morning of the 20th; Krakatau was not visible, and Sebesi and Seboekoe were only vaguely seen. Cannon fire and rumblings were heard from 6:30 p.m. to 9 p.m. and again at 12 o'clock at night to 1:30 a.m. May 21, and again from 8 to 9:30 in the morning; ash fell from 10 to 12 a.m. (May 21) in Ketimbang.[9c] Fishermen from Tjerita, north of Tjaringin, did not dare to set sail Monday morning (May 21), because they heard strange and heavy sounds, and a dark cloud was hanging over Krakatau. Vibrations were felt in Tjaringin Sunday night and explosions on Monday night as well as on Wednesday. The explosions also were heard in Madja [115 km ESE of Krakatau] during several hours on the 20th, 21st, and 22nd, for the first time at 11 in the morning of May 20.[9d] Most reports agree that the explosions best resembled cannon fire and that they were almost always accompanied by air vibrations.[10]

It became apparent from later reports that the explosions of the 21st and 23rd of May were heard in Bandar[10a] [320 km NW] and in Moeara Doea [230 km NW], on the 23rd in the capital city Palembang[11] [350 km N × W], and from May 21 to 23 in different locations in the department Kauer, residency Benkoelen[12] [270 km NW], while Batavia and Buitenzorg are 150 km from the volcano. The explosions were apparently also noticed in Singapore[13] (835 km from Krakatau).

During the May eruption the sounds did not seem to have travelled farther east than Poerwakarta, 225 km from Krakatau, but slower air vibrations, which shook buildings and objects in houses, were then already noticed in Semarang. In that city the rattling and shaking of windows, which were not closed properly, were clearly noticed on May 20 and 21, while no sounds were heard.[14] The report that in Soerabaja [820 km E] the astronomical clock in the observation house at the time ball on the Oedjong stopped, while the chronometers all jumped forward,[15] I found completely unfounded;[15a] I specially inquired about this.

In answer to the inquiry by the government about the volcanic phenomenon, the Governor of Sumatra's Westkust and the residents of Palembang, Benkoelen, and Bantam wrote that on May 21st and 22nd they did not notice anything unusual. In Teloeq Betoeng nobody knew which mountain was active, although they had an ashfall there on May 21 and 22, but already the same day telegraphic news came from Serang that on Sunday morning (May 20) volcanic symptoms were noticed on Krakatau by the American ship *A.R. Thomas* (name of captain was not mentioned), which had docked in Anjer. 1.5 inches of ash lay on deck, subterranean (?) sounds were heard, and smoke clouds rose from the top. The same symptoms were also noticed by fishermen.[16] The Resident of the Lampongsche districts also reported on the 22nd, after his arrival in Ketimbang, that it seemed to him that the mountain Roewatan (Perboewatan) on Krakatau had been active since Sunday morning; a rumbling sound was heard, occasionally accompanied by another sound, resembling cannon fire.[11] The next day the Resident of Bantam reported that the *djoeragan* [helmsman] Abdoel Wahab, on a boat anchored close to Krakatau on Sunday morning, had seen activity in the northern crater of Krakatau until roughly 10 o'clock in the morning (the Java newspaper *Java Bode* of May 24 writes from 6 o'clock to 10 o'clock in the morning); much fire and smoke came from the crater, also in the evening, accompanied by sounds, resembling cannon fire and the pulling of anchor chains. On the evening of the 22nd people in Anjer saw a fire in the direction of Krakatau; in Serang only a cloud of smoke was seen, but sounds or rumblings were not yet heard.[11,19] At Noord Eiland, south of the island Noord-wachter, underground vibrations were felt by Captain Meichle of the ship *Hallgerda*, while the sky was ash-gray in the direction of Krakatau.[20] A big smoke column, occasionally illuminated by lightning, was seen on the evening of the 22nd from the campong Makasser, 21 km S of Batavia.[20]

Thus it is that the quiet, unpopulated, densely wooded Krakatau suddenly became active again after more than 200 years of rest, and it is remarkable that this eruption did not announce itself very clearly. In the months from January to May of that year only 14 earthquakes occurred in the entire archipelago of which 4 were in the eastern part of the archipelago and 7 on Sumatra; earthquakes were reported from Sunda Strait, in Ketimbang on the night of the 15th to 16th of May and repeatedly between the 15th and 20th of May;[21a] a light tremor in Anjer was reported at 10:25 the evening of May 17,[11] and a tremor on Java's First Point[23] in the night of May 9th to 10th, just before midnight; but because earthquakes occur quite regularly at this last location and the tremors were not very severe, no one could have predicted an eruption on this basis even if the news of these earthquakes had been known in Batavia before May 20. Also the volcanoes of the archipelago were relatively quiet; only Lamongan ejected ash and glowing rock on April 13 and 14.[24]

In addition to the *Thomas* and the native vessel on which *djoeragan* Abdoel Wahab travelled, we also have reports from five ships, which passed Sunda Strait between May 20 and 23.

The steamship *Zeeland* departed Batavia by way of Padang [800 km NW of Krakatau] to the Netherlands on the morning of the 20th. At 6 o'clock in the evening the ship passed between Sebesi and Krakatau, and a black cloud was seen above the island, with continuous lightning accompanied by constant crackling, like machine gun fire; the lightning remained in the cloud and did not strike the earth. The compass kept on turning and showed a deviation of 12 degrees. A heavy ash- and rock-fall followed. In one of the two reports it was also mentioned that the water around and close to Krakatau rose sky high, as if there were waterspouts. Because it was already almost dark at that time, and the other report said nothing about this certainly remarkable sign, it is possible that it was an optical illusion. It is very unlikely that the waves were "skyhigh."[25,26]

The active volcano was also observed from the *Sunda*, which left Batavia May 22 and passed Krakatau between 8 and 10 o'clock in the evening. Dr. D. Sulzer, the medical doctor on board, talks about numerous flashes of lightning in the upper part of the cloud, and converging from the atmospheric clouds to the smoke cloud; but strangely enough the magnetic needles remained stable, which is totally the opposite of what was observed on the *Zeeland*. From the foot of the column of smoke, which rose from the crater opposite Verlaten Eiland, 10 to 15 dark red streaks of fire followed each other upward (most likely glowing ash streaks) which were followed by relatively strong explosions like cannon fire, resulting in a light shaking of the ship. Seven miles past Krakatau, a dense ash fell for half an hour; 10 miles past Krakatau floating pieces of pumice were seen, and another 20 miles farther, thus 30 miles from Krakatau (approximately south of the large island Taboean in Semangka Bay) the layer of pumice was so thick that a bucket lowered into the sea was filled with pumice, with hardly any water, when pulled up.[27,28]

Captain Grainger of the *Archer*, a steamship of the Queensland Royal Mail line, also encountered this floating pumice field on his way to Batavia on the 22nd at 5:35 p.m. at 6°6'S and 104°51'E [63 km W of Krakatau], therefore exactly at the place indicated by Dr. Sulzer, who arrived at this location only hours later. The *Archer* already experienced a fine dust cloud (ashfall) west of Vlakken Hoek from 6:30 a.m. to 1 p.m. Above Krakatau a dark cloud full of lightning rose.[11,29]

The Dutch mailboat *Conrad* arrived at the pumice field on May 23rd, after it had encountered a fine ashfall at Benkoelen; at 1:30 p.m. they saw the south point of Krakatau, and were severely hindered by a dense ashfall and sulphur fumes close to the island, at 7 o'clock in the evening. At a distance they saw the heavy smoke sharply cut by the east trade wind, as if it ran into a wall, while to the west the ash spread as far as one could see. The temperature was 38°C inside the ash cloud, and when the ship passed through it, it dropped immediately to 30°C; a remarkable difference. On May 24, the ship arrived at Batavia.[31]

During the first days after the eruption the wind seemed to have been mainly southeasterly (east trade wind); there are reports that on the 22nd in the afternoon fine dust particles resembling pipe clay were already whirling in the air in Moeara Doea.[11] In another report, it is said that from May 21 to 23 ash fell in the department of Kroë, sometimes so densely that it obscured the sun.[33]

The latest report certainly is not the least important. The German warship *Elisabeth*, captain Commander Hollmann, arrived from Singapore in Anjer on the morning of May 20 at 5 o'clock, after having been stationed in China and Japan for two years. The ship took on water and provisions, disembarking Mr. Herbing (who had travelled from Batavia to Singapore to meet his brother, an officer on the *Elisabeth*) and continued its voyage to Europe on May 20, exactly at 9:00 a.m.[33a] Soon it was noticed on board that a white steam column rose very fast from the island of Krakatau, together with some dark clouds. The height of this steam and ash cloud was estimated to measure not less than 11,000 m. A rain of very fine light gray, slightly yellow ash soon followed, which penetrated everything and continued into the night of May 21–22. On the morning of May 21, the sky resembled a large cap of nonglare milkglass in which the sun hung like a cone-shaped light-blue dish. Ash was still falling [556 km] from Krakatau. The sky was cloudy everywhere, but the ash fall had stopped on May 22nd.

This report is remarkable, in the first place, because it contains a description of one of the first, if not the first, important eruption of Krakatau; second, because it reports the height of the cloud, which enables us to estimate with a certain degree of accuracy the height to which the eruption products were ejected in August, when the eruptions and explosions were more severe than in May. Even if the height of the 11,000 meters is slightly incorrect, it is safe to put it at 10 km. Third, it is rather unusual that already on May 21st the description of a bluish sun is given, the same color which was observed in Ceylon, the British Indies, Paramaribo, and several other places in August after the big eruptions, and which led to different explanations among scientists. I include in the *Annotation* the most important part of the report by Mr. Heims, minister on board the *Elisabeth*, and a shorter report by Commander Hollman[34,34a] [reprinted here on p. 59].

The reports brought back by the steamships from Sunda Strait stirred such interest in the eruption of Krakatau in Batavia, that the Netherlands-Indies Steamship Company made the *Gouverneur-General Loudon* available for a visit to the island. It departed Batavia on the 26th with 86 passengers, at 5 o'clock in the evening, and arrived in Krakatau the morning of the 27th. That night earthquakes were felt in Sunda Strait. In Teloeq Betoeng a horizontal shock was felt on the night of the 26th–27th at 3:30 a.m., which lasted approximately 15 seconds;[35] in Tjaringin two shocks were felt at 2 o'clock and 3:55 a.m., the last was also felt in Pandeglang[23] [74 km E × N of Krakatau]; and at the lighthouse on Java's First Point three heavy jolts were felt at 3:30 and 4:20 a.m.; the lighthouse was not damaged.[33] Two shocks were noticed at Vlakken Hoek lighthouse, a relatively strong one at 4 o'clock and a second one at approximately 4:30 a.m., May 27.[37a] A vertical shock was felt in Painan [750 km NW of Krakatau] on the 27th, but only at 5 o'clock at night,[33] and thus is unrelated to the shocks of Sunda Strait.

The *Loudon* remained at anchor till Sunday evening to give the passengers the opportunity to visit the crater, and it returned on the morning of the 28th to Batavia. Because of this trip we have not only several descriptions, but also photographs of Krakatau made by Mr. Hamburg of Batavia [see p. 16 and 62]. The trip was described in the Batavian papers of May 28,[39] most extensively in the *Algemeen Dagblad*. From these reports and still others which I received by word of mouth, and from the sketches and photographs, I think it is safe to conclude that the location and shape of the crater were roughly as I depicted on the large map of Krakatau, Figure 47. The crater Perboewatan seems to have been surrounded in several places by high walls of lava flows, probably partly developed in 1680, which extended at most to 100 m above sea level, while the crater itself was located 40 to 50 m lower, in a bowl- or horseshoe-shaped depression, which was open to the north.

A large part of Krakatau and Verlaten were already covered by ash and were barren of woods, while the peak, Poolsche Hoed, and Lang still had beautiful forests which had hardly suffered at all from the ash. No people were seen; some Lampongers, who were temporarily on Krakatau on May 20 to collect forest products, had left the island earlier.[35,40a]

Following is a report by mining engineer J. Schuurman, who went on the trip. [Reprinted earlier, see p. 63–66.] I cannot give you my observations, as I was still in The Netherlands at the time of this eruption.

• • • • •

Another ship, the paddle steamer 3rd class H.M. *Sumatra*, departed for Sunda Strait on the 27th to investigate by soundings the state of the waterway around Krakatau[35] and on June 1, the Commander of the Navy already reported to the government that no rise of the bottom had occurred.[42]

Only two reports indicated movements of the sea during the May eruption.

The first report came from the hopper *Samarang* of the Batavian Port Authority, Commander Lourens, who on May 20th, travelling from Batavia to Merak, experienced a heavy swell from 10 to 12 in the morning, from NNE and NW, causing the propeller to come out of the water; before and after this event the water was relatively quiet. The commander did not think anything of it until he got the idea in Batavia that the swell could have been caused by the eruption, of which he did not hear anything during the trip.[13,43,44]

The swaying of the sea could not have been very important, because the indicator of the self-registering gauge in Tandjong Priok did not show anything unusual on May 20, as can be seen from [Verbeek's figure 10, not reproduced here].[46] Moreover, this movement of the sea had nothing to do with the eruption, because the swell came from a northerly direction (the report said NNE and NW).

The second report is from the hopper *Bintaing*, which, at the anchorage of Blinjoe (Banka) [500 km N of Krakatau] in the night of May 31–June 1 at about midnight, suddenly rocked in the water, causing the rudder to hit the ship, while it was dead calm and the sky clear.[47] The commander thought he was dealing with a seaquake, but this observation also stands alone, because no other reports of a sea or earthquake were received from around Blinjoe, so that a connection with the eruption here is also very unlikely.

Moreover, there were no reports at all about earth or seaquakes in or near Sunda Strait from May 27 to August 26.

We have reached with our eruption report the end of May, and now we continue with the events, after having reported what was observed at the lighthouses, in addition to the above-mentioned earthquakes in the first few days after the eruption. Originally, no sounds or tremors were experienced on Java's Fourth Point (Bodjong) near Anjer. A rumbling sound from the west was heard for the first time from May 29 to 31 in the evening from 7:30 to 9 or 10 o'clock.[47a] On Vlakken Hoek no sounds or tremors were heard; in the early afternoon of May 20 ash began to fall, which continued to May 23rd in the late afternoon when the wind shifted from the east to more to the north. On the windward side the mirror glass windows of the light had to be cleaned repeatedly.[47b] On Java's First Point nothing unusual occurred.[47c] On the island of Noordwachter muted rumbling and tremors were heard on May 20 at 11:15 a.m. and explosions and dull

bangs between 12 and 12:30 p.m.; these were also heard on May 21.[47d]

For the month of June, we find two reports from Anjer, indicating that Krakatau again smoked heavily on June 19 at 5:30 p.m., and a sound like thunder was heard from afar. A dense cloud which hung over the island only dissipated on Sunday, June 24, because of the easterly wind, and then two thick columns of smoke were clearly noticed, rising majestically. The northern smoke column was the heaviest.[48,49] This is the first report on the development of a second large crater on Krakatau. In his monthly report for June, the Controller of Ketimbang did not yet mention two craters but only said that Krakatau continuously expelled smoke, sometimes accompanied by heavy noises, being the loudest during the nights of June 28 and 30.[50] In the July report, however, the new crater was mentioned. During the few days that month that Krakatau was visible from Ketimbang, smoke was noticed coming from both craters. The oldest crater, the west one, was located at the foot of the mountain Perboewatan, the new one further east of the last one, at the foot of the mountain Danan. The appearance of Perboewatan had completely changed, the three masses of rock which earlier formed the tops of this mountain had disappeared[51] (probably because of a partial cave-in of the lava flows which surrounded the crater).

On July 3, I returned from The Netherlands to Batavia on board the Dutch vessel *Prinses Marie* and passed Krakatau on the east side on the night of July 2–3 at 3 o'clock in the morning. Through a dense hazy sky only a vague red glimmer was seen; no ash was noticed.

We still have to report one important observation, made in August by the Captain of the General Staff, H.J.G. Ferzenaar, chief of the surveying brigade in Bantam, about his visit to Krakatau on the eleventh of that month. The purpose of his trip was to investigate the possibility of surveying Krakatau. I quote from a private communication from Captain Ferzenaar to the Major, chief of the topographic service, to which is added the map Figure 11.[52]

[Reprinted earlier, see p. 67–68.]

. . . . .

All appreciation goes to Captain Ferzenaar who, as the last person to set foot on the northern part of Krakatau, made an excellent sketch in a very short time. Too bad that he did not peep around the corner on the south side, because we would then have had the complete contour lines, insofar as the smoke did not obscure the view. There were three head craters on the island on August 11, while from some other points steam and smoke escaped, mostly from the south slope of the Danan, which later, as Mr. Ferzenaar rightfully concludes, must have collapsed and thus formed the main crater during the eruptions of August 26 and 27. According to the earlier mentioned sketch of Buyskes, Danan must have measured approximately 450 m; the map indicates 400 m, which agrees perfectly, as the top B was higher before. The south side of the peak was still completely wooded, as were Lang and Poolsche Hoed. From the report, it also appears that all eruption centers were still on land, none were under the sea, that the thickness of the ejected materials was not more than 0.5 m, and that after the ejection of pumice during the first days of the eruption in May, only fine material (ash) was cast out and that it was blown mainly to the NW, so that on the north side of the peak and on Lang only a little and on the south side almost no ash at all had fallen. All this is very important in judging the immense eruption, which followed 14 days later. Although the eruption had already continued for almost three months, the total thickness of the ejected materials was not more than 0.5 m (1 m according to engineer Schuurman) at the eruption point. What a difference compared with the situation later when in a few hours at a distance of 15 km from the volcano, dozens of meters of ash had accumulated. We have only 3 reports of ships from August 12 to 26. The Dutch steamship *Madura* passed Krakatau on the 14th on its way to Batavia. It was seriously hindered by the ash falling everywhere. For miles the sky was so dense with ash, that it seemed almost pitch black, and one had to use lamplight to see the compass on the bridge. There was much concern about deviations of the compass; whether they really were observed is not mentioned. Dull explosions were also constantly heard. The *Madura* travelled in ash from 11 in the morning to 3 in the afternoon.[53]

The *Loudon* passed the island the afternoon of the 16th and it met with heavy ashfall.[54] The passengers on board the steamship *Prinses Wilhelmina* saw a thick column of smoke rising from the crater on the morning of August 23, and they were surprised by a dense ashfall.[54a] On the evening of the 25th, ash fell in Teloeq Betoeng, to nobody's surprise, because a fine dust rain had been experienced regularly after the eruption in May, and also from time to time in June, July, and August.[55]

These are all the reports I could locate regarding the eruptions from May 20 to August 26. They do not give a complete picture, but nonetheless give a sufficient idea of the prelude to the big spectacle that is now about to be shown.

In one of the next chapters I will return extensively to these first eruptions and to the nature of the eruption products. Following is only a summary of the results of the observations.

1. The eruption of Krakatau in May 1883 was preceded by several weak earthquakes in the coastal areas of Sunda Strait.

2. The first eruption started on May 20 in the morning. The steam and ash clouds had already reached a significant height at 10 o'clock in the morning. During the first four days, the eruptions were accompanied by rumbling and explosions, resembling gun fire, which were heard to the E up to 225 km, in the NW direction to at least 350 km, and probably to a distance of more than 800 km. In the east the vibration of air was felt more than the sound. Only in some places on Bantam were the explosions not heard (or heard weakly).

3. Pumice seemed only to have been ejected in any significant amount during the first 2 to 3 days, soon followed by ash.

4. The eruptions continued with varying power from May to August, during which time only ash and steam seem to have been ejected. The explosions were sporadically heard in places in the Strait of Sunda, but they were much weaker than in May, and were not heard at all in Batavia and Buitenzorg.

5. Repeated electrical discharges were observed in the ash cloud, namely in the upper part. Reports about deviations of compasses on ships disagree.

6. An earthquake occurred in Sunda Strait on the morning of May 27. After that date no earth- or seaquake is reported in the Strait until August 26.

7. In May, the crater Perboewatan alone was active; a second crater of the mountain Danan developed in June, and in August even three main eruption points were active.

8. The thickness of the eruption products was only 0.5 m close to the crater on August 11. Almost no ash covered the south slope of the peak at that time.

9. The ash was carried mainly to the NW by the wind; the pumice of the May 20 and 21 eruptions floated in the sea to the west. The pumice already reached Vlakken Hoek on May 22, after which it spread out more; the botanist H.O. Forbes reported that the steamship *Quetta* (Captain Templeton) constantly travelled through floating pumice from July 9

through the evening of July 12. The location of the ship on the afternoon of the 12th was 5°53'S and 93°54'E [1274 km W of Krakatau], in the evening of that day 1° more to the west. It is strange that at that time the current was constantly toward the Sunda Strait. [56] Large quantities of pumice were encountered by the P. and O. steamship *Siam* (Captain Ashdown) on August 1, at 6°S and 89°E, thus 960 nautical miles from Krakatau; the *Siam* sailed for 4 hours through the pumice. [56a] The steamship *Idomene* also encountered this pumice on August 11 and 12, between 6° and 8°S and 88°E [1870 km W of Krakatau]. [57]

Paroxysm of August 26–28, and Later Eruptions

It was again, as in May, on a Sunday that Krakatau chose to announce in a loud voice to the citizens of the archipelago, that although it was only a Lilliputian among giants, it did not have to be second to any of the volcanoes in Indonesia when it came to power.

We read that after May the sounds of Krakatau were sporadically heard, but never farther than the coasts of Sunda Strait. On August 26 at 1 o'clock in the afternoon a rumbling started in Buitenzorg, that I originally thought to be distant thunder, but at 2:30 it already became mixed with soft short explosions, convincing me that the explosions must be attributed to Krakatau, whose location was exactly in the direction from whence the noise came, i.e., WNW. Only a little later, the sounds were heard in Batavia, as was the case in Anjer, while they were heard at 3 o'clock in Serang and Bandoeng [268 km E of Krakatau]. Soon the explosions increased in severity, especially toward 5 o'clock in the afternoon, and it is established from reports received later that these explosions were already heard in all of Java.

The rumbling continued through the night, once in a while alternating with a loud explosion, during which time rumbling sounds and tremors were observed. These movements of the air will be discussed in detail in the next chapter; I only wish to remark here that, as was the case in May, no important earthquakes took place during this eruption. In the few reports about earthquakes, it was mostly said that the jolts were weak, and the movement vertical. The error was made especially when the sounds were weak but the tremors were noticeable. Most reports only indicated air vibrations, and some even reported specifi-

cally that no earthquakes occurred. Only in a few locations were some weak earthquakes experienced (see later). The explosions in the night from Sunday to Monday became so severe, that almost nobody in West Java dared to go to sleep. Not only were they frightened by the crashing sounds, but the unusual nature of the symptoms also caused great anxiety. It is very hard for anyone who was not present to understand what the impression is when a mountain located at a distance of not less than 150 km emits sounds resembling gunfire at close hand. This was so unusual and exceptional, that many doubted during the heavy explosions that Krakatau was the source, thinking that perhaps another, closer point was active.

Moreover, everything that was loosely attached in houses, especially hanging things, started shaking, with a rattling or cracking sound, which contributed to the feeling of discomfort among the citizens. At a quarter to seven in the morning, such a powerful explosion was heard, that even the last who had tried to resume their sleep jumped out of bed. In 4 houses in Buitenzorg, including mine, which were built with their front to the west, several lamps burst, plaster fell from the walls, doors and windows which were not properly closed jumped open; in short, it was a terrible racket. This was the loudest explosion in Buitenzorg; after 8:30 in the morning almost no sounds were heard, until the rumbling clearly started again at 7 o'clock in the evening; explosions were also heard between 10 and 11 in the evening and they were only a little less severe than in the morning; the sounds stopped at 2:30 on Tuesday morning.

After the loud explosion of 6:45 a.m. the sky was clear, only slightly cloudy in the west, from 7 to 10 it slowly grew darker, and after 10 the darkness fell fast, at 10:15 all lamps had to be lighted, and coaches started driving with lighted lanterns. The entire sky was then overcast and was grayish yellow in color. At 10:30 I saw in the back of my yard a dense yellowish gray cloud descend to the ground, standing out sharply against the surrounding sky, as is sometimes the case with smoke from a chimney. I went there immediately, hoping to find ash particles, but to my astonishment I found only steam, without any smell. It is likely that the ash cloud in other places had also been preceded by a steam cloud, but I was able to find only one report of such a cloud, namely from the Controller of Sekampong (Lampongs), van Hasselt, who noticed a cloud on the ground in Soekadana on August 27 between 10 and 11 o'clock. [58] However, he sees this in a different light, and attributes the cloud to condensation of the moisture in the place itself, although he also writes that a strong smell of sulphuric acid was observed, which proves that this steam also came from the crater, and only descended either due to pressure from above, or due to its own weight. According to him, a feeling of deafness was also experienced, a result of the high air pressure.

The ash cloud in Buitenzorg was not immediately followed by ash rain; it took more than half an hour before the first grains of ash were noticed, and the real ash rain only started at 11:20. This continued pretty strongly until 1 o'clock, and then less strongly till 3 o'clock. The ash fell in small round grains, which could be pulverized between the fingers, and had the consistency of a light gray flour; it was very damp and not less than 10% of its weight was water. A wet and cold fog hung everywhere after 3 o'clock, with a weak smell of sulphuric acid. It was notably colder than on other days after darkness set in, and also thereafter. It did not become completely dark in Buitenzorg, still it was so dark between 11:30 and 12 o'clock, that one could not distinguish objects such as trees or houses at a 25 m distance; it became much lighter after 1 o'clock and the roosters started to crow.[59]

Even further east, in Sindang Laja, Tjandoer, and Bandoeng [all 200-270 km E of Krakatau], it did not become completely dark, and the dark period was shorter further east. Here one reached the ash line, which was located west of Bandoeng.

The night from Sunday to Monday was not spent any more restfully in Batavia. Many citizens did not dare to go to sleep but walked around the Koningsplein. Several gas lanterns in the street and gaslights in the houses suddenly dimmed at approximately 1:30 at night (probably 1:55 a.m.) and this was repeated before 3 o'clock[60] (probably during the explosion of 2:38); several glass windows were broken in the stores in Rijswijk (downtown Batavia) as a result of the explosion of 1:55, and in Gang Chaulan the bulb of an unlit lamp broke.[61]

On the evening of the 26th, at 11:32 and 18 seconds central time Batavia, the astronomical clock stopped at the time ball[62] because of the continuous vibration. A very fine layer of ash covered the ground at 6 o'clock in the morning, but it must have been of no importance; nowhere was an exact time notation given for the ashfall. During the night one also clearly noticed a strong smell of sulphur, and Sunday evening one saw a red glow in the direction of Krakatau.

The heaviest explosion in Batavia occurred at 8:20[63] (according to others it was a little later; 8:25 or 8:30)

in the morning, during which strong tremors were felt and many buildings made crackling noises. After this basically nothing more was heard until 8 o'clock in the evening, when the rumbling was once again heard till late in the evening.[63a] It grew increasingly dark between 10 and 11 o'clock; at 11 ash started to fall, and it was almost completely dark till 12 o'clock, after which it became slowly lighter till 2 o'clock, when the ash rain stopped. According to calculations by the gas utility, 1500 lights were burning in Batavia that afternoon. A significant drop in temperature was also noted here, starting at 10 o'clock in the morning with temperatures at 12 and 1 o'clock reaching 7°C (approximately 12.5°F) below the temperatures of the days before or following.[64]

Suddenly, shortly after 12, when it was still dark, the sea rose to such a level that in short time part of the lower part of town up to the fishmarket was flooded. The highest level was reached in the Havenkanaal at 12:10, approximately 2 m above Batavia-Level [B.L.], while the day before the highest level at high tide at 4 o'clock only reached 0.67 m above B.L. Several flat- and rowboats were pushed up the river to the Heemradenplein, the water was temporarily still, but then turned in full force, because the wave had also reached Tandjong Priok at 12:30, and the water flowed through the Priokkanaal to the Heemradenplein. The bridge at the plein was damaged by the banging of the boats against it. The water gauge at the Tjiliwong River indicated 0.56 m above B.L. at the plein at 12 o'clock, at 12:45, 1.48 m, at 1 o'clock 1.38 m, and at 2, 0.83 m. When the water was receding in the Havenkanaal near the Kleinen Boom and the fishmarket, which had already taken place in the first half hour after the flood of 12:30, the channel almost completely dried up, stranding several ships and rowboats on the quay; fish could be caught by hand, as was done by many Chinese and natives. The water rose again twice at 2 and 4 o'clock in the afternoon, although lower than the first time; the exact times of its highest level seem not to have been reported.

The observations of the self-registering water gauge in Tandjong Priok, which we will discuss in great detail in the next chapter, are of great value. No fewer than 18 waves were registered here from the afternoon of the 27th at 12 o'clock to the night of the 28th at 12 o'clock; thus during a 36-hour period, the first and biggest wave reached its highest level at 12:30, namely 2.35 m above B.L.; after that the water receded to 3.15 m below B.L., which extraordinarily low reading was already reached at 1:30; at 2:30 the maximum level of the second wave was + 1.95 m, at 3:30 it was a minimum of 1.50 m below B.L., at 4:30 the maximum level of the third wave was 1.24 m above B.L., at 5:30 it was a minimum of 0.40 m below B.L. A very nice regular period of 2 hours can therefore be noted for these waves. No important damage was done by this flood; only the steamship *Prinses Wilhelmina* ran ashore [see p. 112].[64a] The coastline immediately eastward behind Tandjong Priok hardly suffered; because it was protected by the breakwater of the harbor, the water rose only 0.66 m at the market in Tjilintjing. However, in the beach towns farther to the east, from Sembilangan to the outlet of the Bloeboek [from 22 km E to 28 km NE of Batavia, respectively, on the E side of Batavia Bay (see Figure 54)], the water rose to 2 m; 6 campongs were partly, and Sembilangan completely, destroyed.[65]

Serious damage was also reported on the islands in the bay of Batavia. The difference in high and low water at the island must be said to have registered 4 m, a part of the island was flooded. I was not able to find the exact time for the first wave (probably approximately 12 o'clock); a second wave is said to have arrived at 3:30. The big dock, with the *Augusta* at it, was in danger, because the heavy chains, with which the ship was moored, broke like glass, and it bumped into the *Siak*, a ship of the Navy, whose paddlebox broke and chimney toppled. However, the drydock did not float away, because some chains and cables held the anchors. The drydock of Amsterdam Island [18 km NW of Batavia] broke loose and floated [4 km] to the south to the corner named Oentoeug Djawa, of the department of Tangerang.

On the north coast of the residency of Krawang, the wave reached the village of Tjilamaja [70 km E of Batavia] at 2:30, but did not cause damage; in the village of Pakies [40 km ENE of Batavia and 200 km from Krakatau], 8 houses were destroyed, drowning 2 children. The height of the water here is estimated at 0.66 m. The campong Sendarie [30 km] E of Pakies was also flooded, but only slight damage was done to a few houses.

East of Tjilamaja, in Krawang, the wave was noticed, but no damage was done on the Pamanoekan lands [270 km E of Krakatau].[66]

In the residency of Cheribon, the wave reached the Rambattan, the western outlet of the Tji Manoek [and 335 km E of Krakatau], at approximately 4 o'clock with a second wave arriving between 5:30 and 6:30 in the evening. A detailed description of time and height is not available; the height is estimated at 0.5

to 1 m.[67] Water flooded Japara [580 km E of Krakatau] at 6 o'clock in the evening, at a height of 0.5 m.[67a]

The wave was clearly registered on the water gauges in the Strait of Madoera, specifically on the one in Oedjong Pangha [796 km E of Krakatau] at 1:30 on the morning of the 28th, and on the one of the Oedjoeng in Soerabaja [35 km SE of O. Pangha, on the other side of the Strait] at 2:30 and the one of Tandjoeng Kleta at 2:45 on the same morning. However, the deviations were not very large; these water gauge data will be discussed again in the next chapter.[68]

In Tangerang, the western part of the residency of Batavia [and only 140 km E of Krakatau], one heard the first explosions at 4 o'clock in the afternoon on Sunday the 26th. Some ash started falling on the 27th, after 10 o'clock in the morning, and at 11 it grew darker and the ash rain increased, at 12 the lamps had to be lit and one was unable to see one's hand. At 4:30 in the afternoon the rain had stopped falling and it was light again. Between 11 and 12 a strange noise was heard from the north which soon turned out to be caused by the incoming tide. The entire north coast of this department [running nearly 50 km W of Batavia city] was flooded for 1 to 1.5 km; several people lost their lives; 9 beach towns were completely, and 5 partially, destroyed. The places on the west coast, which were protected by the protruding parts of the coast, were damaged the least; the height of the water, depending on location, was 1.75 to 3.25 m. Gentlemen Govijn, Frans, and Jacobs, who travelled to the campong Kramat [26 km WNW of Batavia] in the morning to hold an auction, saved their lives with great effort by climbing trees.[68a] In this department 1794 natives and 546 Chinese and other Orientals lost their lives.[68b]

The sounds started in Serang at 3 o'clock, Sunday afternoon. A sulphurous odor was noticed during the night and lightning came from the direction of Krakatau; some ash also fell. Monday morning the sky in the west had the color of lead, while continuously a fine ash was falling.[69] At 10:15 an explosion was heard,[69a] and soon thereafter, at 10:30, darkness set in, which was already so complete before 11 o'clock, that one could not even distinguish anything close at hand. A telegram from Serang reported at 11:10 that a rain of gravel (pumice stones) fell;[70] unfortunately the telegraphic connection between Serang and Batavia was interrupted from 11:30 until 12 o'clock in the afternoon of the 28th; following the hail of little stones, came a gray mud or wet ash, which attached itself to the leaves and branches of trees and broke them under its weight. At 12 o'clock the mud stopped and only drier ash continued to fall. No explosions were heard at all during that time in Serang; the reports mention a complete silence, which caused many a nervous depression; pets were also restless, they crawled as close as possible to the people in the houses near the light, and one couldn't get them to move. It remained pitch dark till 2 o'clock; then some light was seen in the east, the roosters started to crow, rumbling was heard again, the ash rain continued and the smell of sulphur was very strong and unpleasant; the lights were still on at 4 o'clock, although at that time a glimmer of light was filtering in.[54a] The ash rain finally stopped at 11 at night, according to the telegrams received after the connection between Serang and Batavia was restored on the 28th;[72] these also brought the first reports of the destruction of Anjer and the north coast of Java, and it soon became clear that the waves, resulting from the eruption which had already caused significant damage in the department of Tangerang and in Batavia, as expected, had wreaked havoc along the coasts of Sunda Strait, which were situated much closer to Krakatau.

The official Java newpaper of August 28, August 31, and September 4 and the Batavia papers of August 28 through September 1 are filled with reports about the disaster in Bantam. Among these are only a very few reports from eyewitnesses, as the coast villages of Merak, Anjer, and Tjaringin, the only places where Europeans lived, were totally destroyed, and of these Europeans only a very few who did not flee earlier were saved. If one also takes into consideration that complete darkness very quickly reigned, and that everybody was extremely tense under the circumstances, then it is quite understandable that the few time computations we received about the arrival of the waves on the coast of Bantam are not too accurate.

From Merak, we have a report from the accountant of the Batavian Port Authority, E. Pechler, the only European survivor. He was on his way to deliver a telegram, which he had received at 8 from the chief miner Naumann,[73] to a messenger to send to Serang. This report, the last to be sent from Merak, contained the message for the chief of the Port Authority in Batavia, that on the evening of Sunday the 26th and on the morning of the 27th, the low-lying part of Merak, namely the Chinese camp, the railroad, pier and corner Batoe Lawang, where the stones for the Port Authority were quarried, were destroyed; the cranes and pier were still intact, but the trailers were already floating in the sea, which at the time the telegram

was sent was still high.[74] According to another report, Mr. Pechler himself supposedly went to Tjilegon at 8:45, but this is not true, according to personal reports I received from Mr. Pechler himself in Batavia. Between 9 and 9:30 he was at the foot of the high hill behind the campong Merak, when the big wave came, and he hastened to climb the hill; but the water was faster than he and it came up to his knees, whereupon he fell unconscious, only the next morning (August 28) very early did he gain consciousness; and he found two natives close by. They soon saw the dredge Tegal arriving, the engineer Nieuwenhuijs on board; they hurried to the beach, where literally everything was ruined. The story the natives told the engineer was slightly different, and the reports of Pechler, as they were found in the official report of the Port Authority for August,[74] also do not agree with a report from engineer Nieuwenhuijs to the chief of the Port Authority about his findings in Merak on August 28, and with reports in the Java Bode of August 29. The time quotations of 8 o'clock for the telegram and 9 or 9:30 for the wave were probably both too early, the last one likely more than an hour; it must have been past 10 o'clock, because it is reported that it grew dark at about the same time the wave came in. It could not have been an earlier wave either, because then Pechler, who was lying on the hill, would certainly have been washed away with the higher wave of 10 o'clock.

Because a report was received in Tjilegon on Monday morning that part of Merak was destroyed Sunday evening, aspirant controller Abell set out for that place with the Wedana. At approximately 10 o'clock they reached the village of Sangkanila, close to Merak and situated very near the sea. Most inhabitants of the other campongs had fled to the higher Tjilegon or the mountains; only the ones from Sangkanila remained. After having been there for about 5 minutes, Mr. Abell suddenly saw a colossal sea coming toward him, perhaps as "high as a coconut tree." He narrowly escaped by speedily climbing the nearby hills with the Wedana. Looking back they saw the entire coastline under water, but soon afterwards it became pitch black and an enormous ash and mud rain fell; it grew lighter at 2:15 and the return trip could be started over the hills along slippery paths to Tjilegon, where they arrived at 1 o'clock at night. They spent 4 hours (from 10:30 to 2:15) in the hills in the dark and were completely soaked.[75]

The time quoted here seems to be correct; the big wave close to Merak was seen after 10 o'clock and shortly before the onset of darkness.

The following died in Merak: 1 chief miner, 2 supervisors, 1 store supervisor, 1 head mandoer, 13 mandeors (foremen), 4 carpenters, 10 machinists, 2 smiths, 3 fitters, 6 stokers, 135 coolies, most of them with families; only 2 natives and the accountant E. Pechler, whose family was in Tjilegon, survived. The engineer Nieuwenhuijs had left for Batavia on the 25th and thanks his life to this departure.[75a]

When engineer Nieuwenhuijs arrived on the morning of the 28th, he found nothing left of the earlier homes and work places; even his house, situated on a 14 m high hill, was washed away; only the cement floor was left. A locomotive was found completely bent out of shape 500 m away from its stand, and the rails were torn from their sleepers and bent like ribbons. Only 1 body was found then; the receding sea seemed to have taken along all victims. Several bodies were seen floating, washed ashore some days later, and were immediately buried. The height the sea reached was an average of 30 m according to him; the entire flat sea coast south of Merak was destroyed to the hills as far as one could see.[76] One may compare this with the map, Figure 15 [see p. 76].

One clearly heard the rumbling of Krakatau the afternoon of the 26th in Anjer, and fluctuations were already seen in the water; the first significant rise in the water was noticed at 5:30, although no flooding occurred at that time, but several vessels in the port channel broke loose and bumped into the drawbridge, severely damaging it. The height of this wave is estimated at 1 m, but by some at 2 m. Later in the evening and during the night the water also remained restless, but no reports of flooding or accidents were received. Some ash fell at 9 o'clock in the evening; some earthquake tremors (?) occurred during the night between 2 and 3 o'clock.[76a] The cable line, which had been snapped that evening by the masts of the schooner, was repaired early in the morning on Monday, when at 6:30 a big wave came in, almost completely destroying Anjer; several Europeans died and the survivors fled to Tjilegon, which is located 16.5 km from here. A second wave, higher than the first, must, according to a telegraph operator, have arrived at 7:30; thus, 1 hour after the first one,[69a] another report, probably from the same person[78] only mentions one wave; he fled as soon as possible, walking to Kares, which is located 4 km from Anjer. Here he wrote a note for the Governor of Bantam and the inspector of the telegraphic service about the destruction of Anjer, and then departed at approximately 9:30 for Anjer, to save what there was to save. After walking

1.5 km through a soft ash rain, he suddenly heard a loud bang, followed by a heavy ash rain and lightning. There followed four more such explosions, and a mud rain soon thereafter. Natives from Anjer ran toward him and yelled that the water was rising, so he joined them and they turned immediately into a side road to the campong Djahat, a small village of 4 or 5 houses located on a hill, and he arrived there in a heavy mud rain and complete darkness. One heard the cracking of trees and breaking of bamboo stems, but the wave itself was not seen here and thus apparently arrived after the darkness set in. How long it remained dark is not mentioned in the report; it seems to have been rather dark during the whole day; all the refugees remained in the place to which they had fled and only came together in the evening, when it became a little lighter.[78a]

The Governor of Bantam also mentions only one wave, in an official report, which would have destroyed Anjer at approximately 6 o'clock in the morning. It is certain that the big wave of 10 o'clock did not find anything left in Anjer but the fort, the jail, the house of the Patih and that of the Wedana;[76a] probably also the lighthouse on Java's Fourth Point, because it had not been toppled by the wave of 6 o'clock, according to the story of the wife of the lighthouse keeper Schuit, although it shook and trembled. The lighthouse is said to have been ruined at 9 o'clock (must likely have been after 10 o'clock).[78a]

The whole flat terrain around Anjer, which is about 1000 m wide right behind the place, seemed shaven; close to the waterline enormous blocks of coral were thrown on the beach; the largest block lies close to the old lighthouse and has a volume of 300 m³. The coastline from Merak to here and farther south to Tjaringin has hardly changed; of the capital Anjer, only a portion was washed away, as is shown on the new map of the Bantam coast.[80]

The pilot de Vries survived the first flood, which according to him occurred some minutes past 6 o'clock, by climbing a tree; when the water receded, he set out for Serang. Also in his report no mention was made about a second wave at 7:30; that wave must not have been very high between Anjer and Tjilegon, otherwise Mr. de Vries certainly would have noticed it, because he must still have been in the lower coast area at 7:30.[81]

In Anjer the following Europeans died:[81a]

1. Assistant Governor Th.W. Buijs.

2. A child of the above-named (died in the arms of his mother while fleeing; buried 1.5 km above

Anjer).

3. Portmaster P.F.M. van Leeuwen.

4. Supervisor of the Civil Public Works, H.J. van Rosmalen.

5. Mrs. Schuit, the widow innkeeper.

6. J. Schuit, lighthouse keeper.

7 and 8. Children of the above.

9 and 10. De Jongh (ship chandler and his wife).

11. Regensberg, clerk and registrar of Tjaringin.

12. Mrs. Schwalm (died September 2 in the hospital of Serang, from injuries resulting from the disaster).

13 and 14. Two children of Mrs. Schwalm.

The other 16 Europeans escaped the danger, by fleeing as was reported above.

South of the lighthouse on Java's Fourth Point, the low-lying coast area narrows; it only widens again in the area of Tjaringin. Between these places along the beach, several villages, such as Sirih, Pasaoeran, Tadjoer, and Tjerita [see Figure 54] were all destroyed.

Also not much is left of the populous city of Tjaringin itself; it was situated on a large, 1500 m-wide plain, behind which were the hills 20 to 30 m high, on which the few people who had the time saved themselves.

We received a report from Tjaringin from the Supervisor of the Department of Water Control Mr. Gaston.[82] According to him, several houses in that city in the dessa Tjaringin-Lor were already destroyed Sunday evening at 7 o'clock; the Governor of Bantam also reports that this happened at 5:30 or 6 o'clock, as was the case in Anjer, and that at that time the most populous fisher campongs in the capital, as well as the large *mesigit* [mosque], were destroyed; also that ash rain had been observed falling all day Sunday, not only in the capital, but in almost the entire department of Tjaringin.[76a]

Later in the evening between 7 and 9 o'clock, more houses were destroyed by the waves, and fire started three times because *palitas* (little lamps) had tipped over. At that time some women and children already moved to the house of the Controller in the campong Siroeng, which was situated higher in the hills and farther from the sea, while in Tjaringin itself the fires were fought by the Europeans till 2 o'clock at night.

At 6:30 in the morning the women returned from the Controller's house to Tjaringin, but fortunately did not stay long.

Mr. Gaston went by horse to Tjerita, situated on the coast 4.5 km north of Tjaringin, and found that here an iron bridge had been destroyed, probably also

Sunday evening. He wanted to report this in Tjaringin, therefore returned and about halfway between Tjerita and Tjaringin heard a tremendous explosion from Krakatau. Soon afterwards (he must have already been very close to Tjaringin) he noticed an increased activity of the water and saw an enormous wave nearing from afar. He ran as fast as he could to the house of the Controller and then with the other people present, to a hill nearby, where they luckily were safe. The water had reached a level of 15 m at and around that hill, which is located on the road to Menes, about 1600 m from the beach, as my measuring later showed. They were joined on that hill by 150 other natives; it was pitch black and a heavy mud rain fell; later in the day they felt their way, still in the dark, to Pandeglang, which they luckily reached.

In the flood died: Assistant Governor J.A.O. van den Bosch, 1st Lieutenant for the topographic service, A.F. Dessauvagie, Controller P. Schalk, Serviceman Hoffmann, Mrs. Berlauwt, also the entire family of the Regent, consisting of 55 members, the Patih [vice regent], whose body was found without its head, the Wedana [district chief] and his family, the Assistant Controller, who refused to flee and remained with his cash box, which he had in his possession for over 48 years, and finally a large number of natives, estimated for Tjaringin alone at 1880 people, for the entire department at 12,000.

In this report the hour at which the enormous destruction occurred is not mentioned. It is said by Mr. Gaston that it must have been around 10 o'clock that the large explosion was heard, soon followed by the wave and total darkness. The wave or waves, which caused so much damage in Anjer between 6:30 and 7:30, were apparently not observed in Tjaringin, or must have only reached a low level.

South of Tjaringin is a wide alluvial plain extending to Panimbang, capital of the district by that name, located about 9 km from the coast; then it narrows to Java's Third Point, where a high chain of hills extends into the sea. This flat stretch of land suffered severely because of its low level; the water forced its way onto land to Panimbang, caused significant damage and cost several people their lives. According to the story of a Panghoeloe [head of village], who fled to Menes [13 km ESE of Tjaringin], the beach was already flooded at a level of 2 m above normal at 6 o'clock Sunday night. Monday morning it became somewhat lighter until nine o'clock, then completely dark till Tuesday morning. Monday morning ash rain started to fall; later mud fell in addition. At approximately 8 o'clock (?) the big wave came, which flooded all the low land, destroying 9 large and small villages, and causing death for approximately 700 citizens of the subdistricts of Tjiseureuhum and Perdana. Only a very few citizens were saved.[84] The time estimates are likely to be very inaccurate.

South of Java's Third Point to Java's Second Point the borders of Welkomst Baai were also flooded; fortunately this coast was sparsely populated, as was the case with the whole SW portion of Bantam. According to a report from the controller van Heutz in Menes, the wave must have flooded the very low-lying land south of Wijnkoops Baii [160 km E of Java Head] to the campong Kaledjitan at the southern beach.

From Java's Second Point to the First Point, where a stone lighthouse is located [see Plate 6A], only a narrow stretch with 2 small campongs at the border of the Meeuwen Baai were destroyed. I received the following important observations from the journal of the lighthouse keeper M. van Mens:

Sunday, August 26. At 2:30 p.m. the sky in the north very cloudy. At 6 o'clock in the evening the sky dark everywhere, except for a clear view to the SW. At 6:10 dry ash rain mixed with coarse pumice pieces. At 7 wind changes to northerly. At 7:30 only fine ash rain, no more pumice. At 7:50 heavy earthquakes, everything shook. At 10 o'clock heavy weather with thunder and lightning until Monday morning.

Monday, August 27. At 1:30, 3 and 4 o'clock heavy tremors from earthquakes (?). At 4:30 wet ash rain mixed with rain; wind SW. At 5:30 wind west, slight breeze. At 6 o'clock; it did not become light; light in the lighthouse stayed on. At 7, wind north, rainy. At 7:30, partly cloudy. At 7:45, temporarily extinguished the light to change the wicks; ash rain damp, wind north. At 8 o'clock, lit the lamp; heavy thunder, completely cloudy sky. At 9 o'clock, weather becoming worse, completely dark, at approximately 11 o'clock (possibly somewhat earlier) heavy explosions were heard, and windows and doors banged open; and lightning hit buildings. At 11:10 the lightning hit the lightning rod, which broke; hereafter the lightning hit the entrance of the lighthouse, wounding 4 of the 10 convicts (only those wearing iron rings; they were burned from the ring down),[84a] opened up the floor of the lighthouse and then climbed the iron staircase up the tower to the service room. At 12:40 heavy thunder and earthquake (?). At 1:30 the weather slightly better, continually dark, wind very light. At 4 o'clock in the afternoon, wind SE. Continuous fine ash rain until Tuesday 1:30 a.m., August 28.

Tuesday, August 28. It was light at 6 o'clock, and one noticed for the first time that the coastal area was destroyed. The big wave had not been noticed, because of the darkness, at the lighthouse, which with its houses was located on a 40 m-high rock; judging from the violence, however, it must have arrived at approximately 11 o'clock. See map, Figure 51.

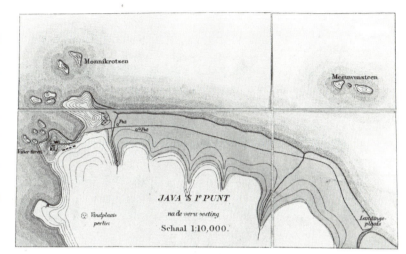

Figure 51. Java's First Point after the destruction. Width of the map is 1.8 km; contour interval is 5 m. The lighthouse ("vuurtoren") is on a 40 m-high rock (see Verbeek's chromolithograph, Plate 6A); a well ("put") and a perlite locality ("vindplaats perliet") are also shown. The shaded portion was flooded. (Verbeek's figure 26.)

There were 3 small campongs in the bay area, close to the lighthouse, Tjikoejah, Roemhatiga, and Oedjoeng-koelon, also nicknamed Djoengkoelan (the lighthouse itself was named Tandjoeng Lajaran); 12 people died there and later 2 more from exhaustion who were among the 120 people, who fled to the lighthouse.

North of the uninhabited Meeuwen Eiland [Seagull Island] a narrow stretch of land was flooded. The north and east side of the mountainous Prinsen Eiland was also destroyed; a hadji [one who has completed the pilgrimage to Mecca] of Tjaringin was entitled to cut wood here (and 55 other people who lived in a campong on the north side of the island) died; bodies were not found anywhere on the island. The height of the wave here was approximately 15 m.

The wave of 7:50 Sunday evening was definitely the result of an earthquake according to Mr. van Mens; the other rumbling could partly have been caused by the strong air tremors.

The south coast of Bantam was not seriously damaged, it was protected by the western corner of Java's First Point, which jutted out into the sea, and by

Prinsen Eiland [Prince's Island]. Still a wave of 1 to 2 m was observed in Binoeangan [65 km E of Java Head], where several proahs (river vessels) were destroyed.[85] Farther to the east in the south of Lebak [150 km E of Java Head], nothing was known about waves; only a great deal of ash fell in the entire department. This was also the case in the department of Pandeglang.

We return now to Merak and follow the coast to the border with Tangerang.

From Merak to St. Nikolaas Point, the hills stretch very close to the sea; the destroyed area was therefore very small and the few campongs there were saved by their high locations.

Eastward of St. Nikolaas Point to the campong Bantam the coast showed hardly any damage, because it was protected from the wave coming from the west. It is reported that the water rose to 2 m at most, while the height on the other side of St. Nikolaas Point was more than 30 m.

From the campong Bantam eastward, by way of Lonkar to Tanara, located at the Tji Doerian, the border river of Bantam and Tangerang [and 45 km ESE of St. Nikolaas Point], serious damage was done. The waves here reached more than 1.5 m in height, and in some places the land was flooded up to 2 km inland, completely destroying, for example, Karang Antoe (the landing place north of Serang in Bantam Bay), and farther eastward in the district of Tanara the campongs Lontar, Tanghoerak, Pasir Pandjang, and Pegadoengan [190 km E of Krakatau], and causing great loss of life. Also here the water apparently did not rise much higher than 2 or 3 m, but the wave was much more powerful than farther west and the destruction was therefore more complete.

On Java's south coast, except in Binoeangan in Bantam, the wave was observed in Wijnkoops Baii but did not cause much damage; the increase in the water level was insignificant.[85a] Farther, in the departments Soekapoera-Kollot and Soekapoera [300–400 km E of Java Head], the height is reported as 1 to 2 m, but the time—the afternoon of the 27th between 3 and 4 o'clock—was very indeterminate.[86]

In Tjilatjap [435 km ESE of Krakatau (and Java Head)], a wave apparently came ashore in the early morning of August 27, cutting loose a a dozen proahs; the water remained restless the entire day, until it rose to 2 m above normal high water at 5 o'clock in the afternoon, cutting loose all loading proahs and flooding part of the village to a height of ⅓ to ⅔ m. No damage was done in the Kinderzee[87,88] [400 km ESE of Java Head].

We now cross the Strait and follow the destruction along the coasts of the Lampong districts, where the sight was not any less sorrowful than in Bantam. As you know, Sumatra on the south is made up of three large land points, the western has the name Vlakken Hoek, the eastern Varkenshoek [Pigs Corner], and the middle one has no special name but extends into the sea across from the island of Lagoendi. Two bays were closed in by these three land spits; the eastern is called Lampong Bay and the western Semangka Bay.

The big wave coming from Krakatau flooded the entire coastal region of Vlakken Hoek along the Semangka and Lampong Bays to Varkenshoek and some of the lower campongs. We start our description on the east side, at Ketimbang.

I received a lot of personal information about this place from Controller Beyerinck [see p. 81–85], who, at my request, told me everything he remembered. He says that some of his times might be off, because he remembers the series of events of August 26 and 27 as a bad dream. The miserable situation, in which he, his wife, and 3 children found themselves on those and following days, makes this very understandable. According to him an exceptional fluctuation in the water level was observed on Sunday at 6:15 in the evening in Tjanti [2 km N of Ketimbang] and also at 6:30 in Ketimbang, causing a proah to hit the banks and sink. Between 9 and 10 in the evening more waves came in, this time higher, up to the yard of the house of the controller. This caused him to flee with his family and adjunct-recorder Tokaja to a small campong, named Oemboel Balaq, located above Tjanti against the slope of Radja Bassa. One of the servants remained in the house in Ketimbang, but was also forced to leave it at night, because at 2 o'clock it was lifted by a wave and ripped from its base. On the morning of August 27 around 6 o'clock, the Controller sent some natives for information; they soon returned with the message that Ketimbang was completely destroyed. Because the place was situated very close to the sea and at a low level, it is likely that the same wave, which had already destroyed Anjer at 6:30 in the morning, also flooded Ketimbang. Fine lapilli fell the entire night, but as a downpour till 11 o'clock Sunday night; at approximately 9 or 10 o'clock in the morning a hail of pumice stones started falling, with some the size of a [man's?] head. Explosions had been continuously heard since Sunday, sulphur had already been smelled at 6 o'clock Monday morning, the explosions were the loudest around 10 o'clock, soon followed by darkness; around 12 (?) o'clock it was pitch black, at that time hot ash started falling, causing a painful feeling on the skin; how long this lasted is uncertain, perhaps 15 minutes, a choking sulphurous smell was also in the air. This was followed by cold mud, which was very unpleasant, because it stuck to hands and face, but it was still a relief from the hot ash, which caused burns. Mud and ash rain continued all of Monday till midnight, possibly also Tuesday morning; daylight was not seen at all on Monday. Heavy electrical discharge was observed in the direction of Krakatau and later also closer by. Beyerinck, his wife, and 2 children spent five miserable days in a hut together with some wounded natives. They all suffered great pain because of untreated burns, and the youngest child of the Controller died from it. Finally they were saved from their terrible predicament by the hopper *Kedirie*, which docked Saturday morning September 1 in Kalianda [8 km N of Ketimbang]. Captain 't Hoen and several gentlemen went ashore and were informed that the controller and his family were in Oemboel Balaq, after which they went there immediately. They were brought to the beach on *tandoes* (carrying chairs made of bamboo or wood) and still on the same day the *Kedirie* left for Batavia, where the Beyerinck family was admitted to the hospital. It gives me pleasure to report that the entire family has recuperated.[89,90]

It is known from later reports that the entire coastal region from the Varkenshoek to Teloeq Betoeng was destroyed by one wave, which was an average of 24 m high; the number of victims is reported at almost 4900 for the department of Ketimbang alone or IV Margas (without the islands). The width of the flooded portion is minimal because the terrain soon rises everywhere.

Along the east coast of Sumatra, north of Varkenshoek, the wave was much less high, as would be expected because of its protected location; the campongs Laboean-Maringai and Tjabang at the mouth of the Sepoeti River [50 km N of Varkenshoek] were damaged by the water, but no lives were lost; however, a proah capsized at sea, drowning 5 people.[58] At the mouth of the Toelang Bawang River, at Teladas [170 km N of Varkenshoek], the water must have risen to 1.60 m; the estimations of time and height of the water are uncertain. On August 27, at 12 o'clock in the afternoon, the report for Laboean-Maringai gives a height of 1.5 m above the highest water level. In Tjabang 11 waves were seen between 3 o'clock on the afternoon of the 27th and 6 o'clock on the morning

of the 28th, with an average height of 0.75 m. In Teladas a wave was observed at 7 o'clock on the evening of the 27th (the report incorrectly mentions the 26th).[92]

The village of Kalianda, north of Ketimbang, was completely destroyed; here the water rose to the campong Kebang Teloeq, which is located 24 m above sea level (see map, Figure 52).

Teloeq Betoeng, the capital of the Lampongs, was almost completely wiped out by the wave; to compare how the place looked before with what is now, one should look at maps [Figure 19, p. 87]. The entire low plain [shaded in Figure 19] was flooded and totally destroyed; only the Residency house located on a hill [see Plate 2D] and the fort, to which fortunately almost all Europeans and many natives from the plain fled, were saved as were the jail and cemetery. However, these buildings were also almost destroyed as they are located only 24 m above sea level and the water reached 22 m up the hill, and judging from the wood found, the water must have come to within a distance of 30 m from the Residency house. None of the people who fled there noticed this, because, as was the case in so many other places, it was pitch dark when the big wave rolled in.

We have an official report about Teloeq Betoeng from the Resident N. Altheer[93] and a story from the Controller J.F. Wijnveldt.[94] Furthermore, I received personal impressions from two people who were in Teloeq Betoeng at the time of the catastrophe.[95,96] These reports differ significantly in their time quotations; according to two of the four reports the loud explosion took place at 8:30 or 9 o'clock, according to the two other reports at 10 o'clock. Two different explosions in this case are out of the question, as according to all witnesses, only one very intense explosion was heard, and only rumbling after that. Because the explosion was soon followed by darkness, it seems more likely that it was not before 10 o'clock when the explosion occurred, and therefore the other times must have been a mistake.

I will quote the following from the different reports. In the afternoon of the 26th at 4 o'clock one heard a loud bang; in one of the reports earthquakes are also mentioned, but these were most likely air vibrations and tremors of the houses. At 6 o'clock the first wave rolled in, flooding the pier, forcing people who were walking there to flee. Part of that pier (approximately 125 m) was already destroyed at that time according to some; according to others this did not occur till 11 o'clock at night. Some small vessels ran ashore, some

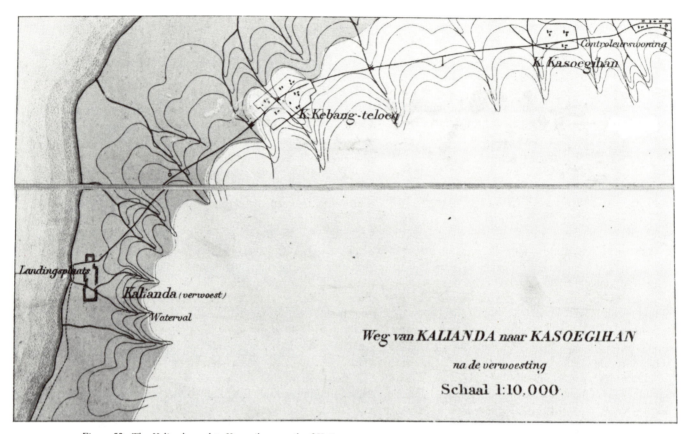

Figure 52. The Kalianda road to Kasoegihan, north of Katimbang, after the destruction, with the villages of Kalianda (destroyed), Kebang Telok, and Kasoegihan. Width of the map is 1.8 km; contour interval is 5 m. The Controller's house ("Controleurswonig") and a waterfall ("waterval") are shown. The water rose to Kebang Telok, which is located 24 m above sea level. (Verbeek's figure 25.) See Verbeek's chromolithograph, Plate 2B.

beach houses in the campong Kankoeng [NE of the river mouth] were washed away, and the bridge over the Koeripan or Teloeq Betoeng River was damaged by proahs, which floated against the bridge. The ash rain, which had already started falling on the evening of the 25th, increased in intensity at 6:30 (on the evening of the 26th) and the ash was mixed with pumice stones the size of beans; it is uncertain whether there were any large waves during the night. One of the reports mentions high water in the campong Kankoeng in the early morning of the 27th at 1:30. The steamship *Loudon* arrived Sunday at 7:30, but because of the rough sea could not communicate with land.

On the morning of the 27th at 6:30, a big flood wave came in, destroying the harbor light, the coal storage and the warehouse on the pier, and moving the steamer *Berouw* from the east side of the pier over

the pier into the Chinese camp. The salt warehouse was damaged, and the campong Kankoeng, together with all other campongs along the sea, was washed away.

The salt ship *Marie*, which was at anchor, capsized but righted itself. The destruction was witnessed by the passengers on board the *G.G. Loudon* (see later); one saw this ship leaving at 7 o'clock.

One of the reports mentions a wave at 7:45 during which the water must have been 1 m high in a stone *gardoe* (sentry box), as it turned out, when one ventured into the valley after the wave passed. The other reports do not mention this second wave. The escape to the higher places had already started at 6, but again and again some returned to the valley to save what they could; they should have been able to notice the waves, which the refugees farther away from the sea could not see. I was told that several Europeans still were in the valley at 9 or even 9:30 to see what the situation was like.

The sky was a copper color in the direction of Krakatau, continuous lightning was observed, and the ash rain continued, but the sea had become relatively quiet after 8 o'clock.

Suddenly at 10 o'clock (another report mentions 9:45, still another 9 or 8:45, and one even 8:30) an explosion was heard as if from a battery of guns going off very nearby, startling everyone. A ray of light and continuous lightning accompanied it from the direction of Krakatau. Soon after the explosion it started to become dark, and in addition to ash, pumice stones also started to fall again. At 10:30 or 10:45 it was already completely dark again, and the ash rain was replaced by a heavy mud rain, which continued for approximately 1½ hours, followed again by ash rain till 3 o'clock at night, August 28, when for the first time the moon lit the terrain of destruction.

What happened after 10:30 in the morning could not be seen because of a most complete darkness, which was described as being "blacker than the blackest night." The refugees in the Residency house only heard violent noises, mainly caused by a strong wind, breaking trees and branches, and throwing mud against doors and windows with great force. Because the wind overpowered all other sound, only a few thought they heard the roaring of the waves against the hill. But it is certain that nobody there saw the big wave, at a distance only 30 m away from them and only 2 m below the house. This proves the total darkness, which enveloped the area between 10 and 11 o'clock.

Only by Tuesday morning at 6 o'clock was one able to judge the size of the disaster. Let's look at our map [see p. 87]. Remains of houses, trees, driftwood, broken-up vessels, and bodies of people and animals were strewn about the entire valley to the foot of the hill; no house or tree had been spared, and I was able to convince myself of the truth of this story in October. Everything was swept away, nothing was left but the objects just mentioned, strewn about in a ⅓ m thick wet ash layer. The steamer *Berouw* had disappeared and was later found in the valley of the Koeripan River behind a bend in the valley [see p. 128] at a 3300 m distance from its anchoring place, and 2600 m away from the Chinese camp, where it had been swept at 6:30 in the morning. Many proahs were stranded along the borders of the valley, and a buoy was found on the slope of the hill, west of the cemetery [see map on p. 87, and color Plate 14B]. Only the salt ship

Marie, to everyone's surprise, had been saved and lay quietly in deep water.

As it later turned out, the entrance to the Lampoeng Bay was obstructed by large masses of floating pumice in the first days after the eruption. It did not take very long for the pumice to move to the bay, and it soon covered the whole water surface from Teloeq Betoeng to Gebang on the west side and the Tjondong Islands on the east side of the bay [or 12–14 km S and SE of Teloeq Betoeng]. Because of this, the capital could not be reached for several months by sea, and the transport of food and other materials from Batavia had to be made 35 km overland via Ratai Bay. It was December before the bay was opened up again by N and NW winds.[96a] I found the entire bay in front of Teloeq Betoeng still covered with pumice at the end of October, reminding me of dirty ice. This quiet and extraordinary sea surface, together with the deadly and barren valley of Teloeq Betoeng and the wilted leaves on trees which were left on the hills and mountains, made a tremendous impression on me, who had last seen the area in 1877 when it was very flourishing.

Only 3 Europeans died in Teloeq Betoeng, the 1st navigating officer, and the machinist, of the steamer *Berouw*, and one European private. The number of missing natives will be reported later.

The west coast of the Lampoeng Bay also was flooded, and several campongs were washed away completely. Only Menanga, along Ratai Bay, and the Hoeroen were not damaged seriously because of their protected location.

The Semangka Bay. All low-lying campongs along the beach were destroyed; and the flat delta land at the mouth of the Semangka River was flooded the farthest. The destruction of Beneawang, the capital of the department, on the north end of the bay, was described to us by Controller P.L.C. Le Sueur[97] [see also Le Sueur's own account on p. 89].

The first wave had already come in on Sunday, August 26, between 5 and 6 in the evening, flooding part of the campong, but no serious damage was done; it was followed by a rain of coarse ash (sand). A reddish light was seen in a large area between 4 and 5 at night. The sea was very low Monday morning (the 27th) after 6 o'clock, so that many rocks were visible. Some time after 7 (the correct time is not available) the water swelled, then apparently fell without causing a noticeable flood. However, a much bigger wave soon followed, washing away the house of the Controller and more than 300 natives who had fled there. The Controller was swept away by the flood, but gained solid ground under his feet when the water fell. He covered himself with clothing to protect himself against the mud rain; it seems to have already been dark at that time, but when darkness fell is not reported. Another wave rolled in soon after the first one, according to Mr. Le Sueur's report, but he told me personally in October, in Batavia, that it could have been later; it was impossible for him to determine the exact time. He was picked up by force, swirled around and hurled away, and he clung to a tree trunk and floated on it till he gained solid ground under his feet for the second time, when the water fell. (I assume that it was already past 10 o'clock when this last wave flooded Beneawang, especially in connection with what was observed in Vlakken Hoek, about which more follows). After he remained sitting there for about an hour in the mud rain and the dark, some natives passed him; they joined up and together they started their journey over fallen trees and bushes and through mud, until they met someone with an *obor* (torch) who brought them through the woods to the campong Kasoegihan, and further to Penanggoengan, where they arrived at approximately 8 o'clock in the evening. But after about an hour of rest they did not feel safe there either, and they set out for the village of Pajoeng, located on the slope of Keizerspiek (Goenoeng Tangkamoes) at about 2 hours distance from Beneawang [and 4½ km N].

Approximately 250 natives died in Beneawang, and almost all chiefs of the department, who had gathered here to meet the Governor who was expected to arrive on the 27th. Also the clerk-reporter, the only European in Beneawang besides the Controller, lost his life.

According to Controller Le Sueur's report all beach campongs on the east side and west side of the bay up to Vlakken Hoek were destroyed, most completely, some partially; in Tandjoengan and its neighbor Tandjoeng Bringin alone 327 people were missing, in Betoeng, not far from Tandjoengan [NW corner of Semangka Bay], 244. In Tampang on Tampang bay, which I visited in October, no house was left standing, and only a couple of coconut trees with broken branches and wilted leaves indicated the place where once the campong had been [SW mouth of Semangka Bay, near Vlakke Hoek].

The large island Taboean at the entrance of Semangka Bay had been visited then too; the wave came high up in the eastern and southern parts, but it fortunately did not do much damage in the campong, which was located near the NW end, because the height and power of the waves were here much less

than on the south side. Later reports mention that ash had fallen over the entire Residency of Lampong, but mud only in the southern departments; along the highway from Teloeq Betoeng [N] to Menggala, mud rain was observed up to Tegi Nenang which is situated on the Sekampong River; darkness set in between 10 and 11 o'clock in the morning (the 27th) over the entire Residency.[98]

We continue our journey along the coast to Vlakken Hoek and arrive in the territory of the Residency Benkoelen. The beautiful iron lighthouse withstood the force of the waves, although the water reached 15 m high against the tower; but the surrounding iron and stone buildings all disappeared [see Plate 5A]; the wave rushed over the flat terrain at the lighthouse to the campongs Laboean-Blimbing and Blimbing on Blimbing Bay and partly destroyed them, causing 34 people to lose their lives.[99] In October I found the forest to be a chaos of fallen and broken trees; at quite a distance from the lighthouse iron pieces of the establishment and bodies of convicts (who had been working at the lighthouse) were found.

The lighthouse keeper F. Hamwijk had been brought to Batavia on September 4 seriously injured. I visited him in Batavia and he told me the following, which coincides almost completely with what a mandoer lighthouse keeper told me in October. The journal was lost during the flood.

In the early morning of Monday at 1 o'clock after midnight the water had been high, but it was not a flood; the mandoer lighthouse keeper however thought that there already had been high water on that Sunday evening. On the morning of the 27th at 6 o'clock there was some daylight; the light was extinguished for a short while, but it was soon relit, because it turned dark again. At 10 o'clock lightning hit the lighthouse tower and thunder was heard from 8 to 12 o'clock that morning. At 10:30 the big wave rolled in, which took everything with it except the lighthouse tower. Mr. Hamwijk was trapped under the kitchen which had collapsed; he struggled free and fled to the lighthouse tower. The water rose and fell 3 times, and he seems to remember that this happened in not more than ½ hour. Ash started to fall at 6:30 Sunday evening and lasted till Monday evening at 10:30; it remained dark the whole day; he says that no mud fell there.

Among the lighthouse personnel, 1 mandoer and 10 convicts died; 2 of the 5 native lighthouse keepers and 4 convicts were injured and were brought to Batavia on September 4 together with Mr. Hamwijk.

North of Blimbing the wave only caused some damage in the campong Benkoenat [50 km NW of Vlakke Hoek], only a few houses collapsed; further north there is no report of damage.

At Kroë [115 km NW of Vlakke Hoek and 194 km NW of Krakatau] and on the neighboring island Pisang, nobody noticed the wave, but it was observed that the sea fell back farther than usual. Both the island and the village of Kroë are sheltered by the protruding corner at the south end of the bay; this may explain why the wave did not come here, although it had been clearly present further north.

From the Controller of Kroë, Dr. D.W. Horst, we received the following information about what had been observed there on August 27.[100]

August 26, 1883. Since 3 o'clock this afternoon continuous sounds like gunshots were heard from the SE, followed by and alternating with thunder. The sounds were accompanied by vibrations and tremors, causing doors to rattle.

August 27. A dense ash rain is falling at 3 o'clock at night (the 27th); the sounds are again increasing in power after they had diminished at sunset.

6 o'clock in the morning. A gray-yellow ash layer of 4 mm thickness covers everything. A sulphur smell is in the air. The sky is gray and the sun is obscured: a fine ash rain is falling.

8–10 o'clock. Fine ash is falling. No sounds are heard.

10 o'clock. Thermometer indicates 73°F, the sky is completely darkened. Inside the houses one is unable to write because of lack of light. Lightning is everywhere in the sky, accompanied by constant thunder. It becomes darker still.

10:30. It is as dark as at night. The thunder continues.

11 o'clock. It is darker than at night. A dense coarse ash rain is falling. Doors and windows are closed. All openings sealed to prevent the fine ash from entering.

12 o'clock. Dense darkness surrounds us. The falling ash is becoming finer and makes less noise while falling, constant thunder alternating with crashing explosions. Preparations are made inside the house to hold out as long as possible. Thermometer 73°F. The wind decreased. It is less cold. The ash rain diminishes, the wind has shifted to the west.

12:30. Intense darkness. The ash rain has stopped almost completely. An intense bolt of lightning cleaves the sky, followed by thunder.

1 o'clock. The wind is west. The ash is carried back from the west.

3 o'clock. The pause between thunderbolts is increasing. Ash rain diminishes.

4:30. Intense darkness. A tremendous explosion shakes everything.

6 o'clock. Intense darkness. Thermometer 73°F. Sounds are decreasing from 6 o'clock on the evening of the 27th.

August 28. 6 o'clock in the morning. Fine ash continues to fall, here and there some fireflies have fallen. It becomes lighter and slowly daylight returns; the sky is ash-gray; everything is covered with a grayish-white ash layer 5 cm thick,

from a distance resembling snow. Some roofs are in danger of collapsing under the weight.

8 o'clock. Ash is cleared from all roofs; a faint sun is visible.

9 o'clock. Fine ash starts to fall again from the SE. Thermometer 81°F.

If from all the places of Sumatra and Java, where Europeans were present, we had received such an excellent series of observations, written down at the same time of the events, we would not have received so many confused and incorrect reports on the phenomena themselves, and on the time of the most important events. Everything that was written down later from memory has only very limited value.

Waves were observed along the entire coast of Benkoelen, including Kroë which was mentioned above: At the mouth of the river Sambat [270 km NW of Krakatau], between Padang Goetji and Koedoerang [310–325 km NW], they were at least 2 m high because the road was flooded; in Manna [335 km NW] (11 o'clock ?), and a second wave came at 12 o'clock in the afternoon on the 27th; the sea receded only at 10:30, the height is reported as 1 m above the high-water mark, and at Pino [10 km NW of Manna], height 2–3 m, the *sawahs* (ricefields) at the banks of the Pino river were flooded to a distance of 2 km from the mouth. At Seloema [395 km NW of Krakatau]; at Poeloe Bay and Taba Badjau; at the capital Benkoelen itself [437 km NW of Krakatau], where the water is said to have risen 1 m above the high-water mark and said to have fallen 1 m below the low-water mark; at Lais and its vicinity; at Seblat and at Mokko-Mokko [630 km NW of Krakatau], the height of the water 1–1.5 m above the high water mark. The times, probably mostly given to us by natives, are apparently so wrong and imprecise (for example between 10 and 5 o'clock!) that it is not worth the effort to report them here; also the data on the height are not trustworthy.[101] In another report it is mentioned that the seawater at Benkoelen first withdrew at 11 o'clock, exposing the beach for a distance of 50 m. Many fish, turtles, and 2 specimens of the so-called sea calf (Malayan: *doejoeng* or *Halicore indica* Desmarest) were left dry and were captured by the natives. Afterwards the water returned again (when?) and this rise and fall occurred several times into the night of August 27–28. After 10 o'clock it became darker in Benkoelen; it was dark at 11 o'clock, and ash started to fall at 12 o'clock, continuing to 11 o'clock the morning of the 28th.[102] Ash fell in the entire residency, mostly in the department of Kroë and decreasing further to the north so that almost no ash was seen at the border of the department Mokko-Mokko and Indrapoera (Sumatra Westkust). Because, according to information from the Governor of Sumatra's Westkust, almost no ash fell in that department,[103] the ash line turns at Mokko-Mokko and runs through Sumatra to Bengkalis [920 km NNW of Krakatau (see Figure 55 and later discussion)].

In Painan [755 km NW of Krakatau], waves were reported: the first apparently reached its highest level, approximately 3 m above high tide, at 1:15 or 1:30 on the afternoon of the 27th; the water first receded at approximately 1 o'clock; the water level was low again at 1:30, approximately 2 m below the lowest level for normal low tide; at approximately 2 o'clock a second wave came which reached a level of 4 m above the high-tide mark. The rise and fall was noticed until 7 o'clock in the evening. The time and height data appear questionable to me.[104]

From Padang [800 km NW of Krakatau] we have an excellent series of observations on the rising and falling of the waves by the harbor master E. Roelofs.[105] The first wave reached its highest level at 1:25, the second at 2:20, the third at 3:12. This last one was the highest of all; the water rose up to 4 cm below the top of the riverside wall in front of the harbor office, and it was followed by the strongest retreat of the water; the difference between the highest and lowest level was 1.74 m. It is curious that the same phenomena are reported here as in many places farther away (see later), i.e., that not the first wave, but one of the following, was the highest. A total of 13 waves, slowly declining in size, were seen in Padang till 7:30 on the morning of August 28. They show a relatively regular period of 1 hour, between high and low water.

A rather important rise in the water appears to have been observed in Bangies [970? km NW of Krakatau] on August 27, flooding part of the village. Further information is not known.[106]

I have no further reports on the big wave from places farther north along the west coast of Sumatra.

Therefore, we now return to Sunda Strait and pause for a moment at the islands Sebesi and Seboekoe [20 and 30 km N × E of Krakatau]. We only can guess what happened here because nobody on these islands survived. The big wave of approximately 10 o'clock reached here a height of more than 30 m, washing away 4 prosperous campongs, located on the plains of Sebesi, and another campong at the northern corner of Seboekoe Ketjiel (Beschutters Eiland), with all their inhabitants. Compare maps, Figures 44 and 45

[p. 173 and 174]. The number of victims is estimated at 3000 for Sebesi, and 150 for Seboekoe Ketjiel; the big island of Seboekoe was not inhabited.

The big wave was not observed in the Residency of Sumatra's East Coast, and only some ash fell up to and slightly past the capital of Bengkalis.[107]

Neither were waves noticed along the coast in the Residency of Palembang; ash fell in the entire region; on the 27th it became dark in Moeara Doea [225 km NW of Krakatau] at 10 o'clock, in Batoe Radja at 11 o'clock and in Palembang [350 km N × W of Krakatau] around 1 o'clock, from which we may conclude that the density of the ash cloud was quite significant here.[108,109]

No unusual movement of the sea was observed on the islands of the Residency of Riouw; only on the island Lingga [660 km N of Krakatau] some ash fell.[110]

In the Residency of Banka, only in Taboali and on the Lepar Islands [both 360 km NNE of Krakatau] was the wave observed. It went unnoticed in Muntok [90 km farther N, on the W tip of Banka Island]. The island remained almost completely free of ash, only in the capital, Muntok, a very fine layer of dust on the furniture and on leaves of trees was discovered on the morning of the 27th.[111,112,113,114]

It is mentioned in a later report that the water in Toboali reached its highest point on the evening of the 27th at 4:15,[115] while on the same evening at 5:15 the water partly flooded the campongs Tandjoeng Laboe, Goenoeng and Penoetoek on the island of Lepar, causing slight damage to some bridges.[116]

On the island of Billiton, the big wave was noticed in Tandjoeng Pandan on the west coast and in Dendang on the south coast of the island; in both places [450 and 433 km NNE of Krakatau] the sea reached its highest mark at 5:30 on the evening of August 27.[117] In Dendang, the first wave rose 1.50 m above the spring tide mark, and it was followed during the evening of the same and the morning of the following day by 8 lesser waves. No significant damage was done.[118]

Only one wave was reported by the lighthouse keeper G. Hoedt on Ondiepwater Eiland [Shallow-water Island], SW of Billiton [see Figure 55]; it reached its highest level at 4 o'clock in the afternoon on the 27th.[119]

The information from the island of Noordwachter [145 km NE of Krakatau] by the lighthouse keeper H. van der Meulen is somewhat uncertain, because he was just in the process of stocking the lighthouse with food and water when the water reached its highest level. He reports that this happened at 11:30 in the morning on the 27th, but it could have been somewhat later (probably at 12 o'clock). The water flooded the entire island and also the lighthouse; the rise was 2.50 m. Ash started to fall between 10 and 11 o'clock and continued till 4, and the light had to be lit at 12 o'clock.[120]

The Duizend Eilanden [Thousand Islands], south of Noordwachter, were all flooded and most houses washed away. The citizens of the islands Klappa and Panggang, approximately 500 in number, saved themselves by climbing in trees. Only one woman drowned. The islands must have been 2 m under water.[85]

From the island of Edam, [15 km N] of Tandjong Priok, the lighthouse keeper L. Gerla reported that two waves were observed there, which reached their highest level at 1:30 and 2:45 in the afternoon on the 27th. His data do not agree well with the indications on the water gauge at nearby Tandjong Priok. Mr. Gerla reports: At 12 o'clock noon, very low water; at 1:30 in the afternoon very high water, coming up to 4 m from the house of the lighthouse keeper; at 2 o'clock low water; at 2:45 high water; at 3:30 low water; after 4 o'clock normal level.[122] The report from lighthouse keeper L. van Rooijen on Boompjes Eiland [Little Tree Island], north of Cheribon [and 330 km E of Krakatau], only mentions that he heard explosions at 4:30 p.m. on August 26 and during the following night, rattling doors and windows. A wave apparently was not seen.[122a]

On the other islands of the Indian Archipelago, Borneo, Celebes, etc., the Krakatau wave was not observed. There did occur a movement in the sea in the Moluccas that day; but this must be attributed to other causes and not to Krakatau; it will be discussed in section 12.

The explosions were heard on all islands of the Archipelago.

Reports from Ships

Ten ships were in or near Sunda Strait during the eruption; we owe some important information to them. [See map, p. 82, for location of most.]

1. The Norwegian bark *Borjild* was moored at Kombuis Eiland [Galley Island, 30 km WNW of Batavia, and 135 km E × N of Krakatau] on August 27; the ash which fell on board was later investigated microscopically by Mr. J. Joly in Dublin[122b] [p. 292].

2. The *Medea*, Captain Thomson, was in or near Sunda Strait from August 22 to 26; the exact location

of the ship during those days is hard to ascertain from the short communication in *Nature*.[122c] Captain Thomson [see p. 96] heard the first explosion on August 26, at 2 p.m., and afterwards several more, with regular intervals of 10 min. After the first explosion a smoke column rose into the air, apparently reaching a height of 17 miles (or 27 km) and, according to another measurement 3 hours after the explosion, even 21 miles (33.5 km). The last number is considered to be less certain.

This is the only estimate of the height of the ash cloud from the August eruption that I am aware of.

3. The *Bay of Naples*, Captain Tedmarch. The first mate W. Williams reported on September 2 from Toboali that they had already heard explosions in the night on Saturday and Sunday, August 25–26, at a distance of 120 miles S of Java's First Point. Ash fell on board on August 26, the sky was completely overcast; on the 27th they saw floating bodies of people and animals and heavy logs.[123]

4. The steamship *Annerley*, Captain Strachan, passed the Strait of Banka on Sunday, August 26, and dropped anchor at Noordwachter during the night on Monday [see p. 98]. Ash rain lasted till midnight August 27–28. Three aneroid barometers rose and fell an inch (25.4 mm) in short intervals; the exact time when this occurred was not reported. When the *Annerley* later (August 28?) passed Anjer, the lighthouse had disappeared.[124]

5. The steamship *Batavia* of the Rotterdam Lloyd, Commander Boon, departed Padang Saturday the 25th at 4 o'clock in the afternoon and reached Vlakken Hoek on the evening of the 27th. Already at a distance of 30 German miles [222 km] from the shore (?) (this most likely must have been 30 German miles from Vlakken Hoek, or 30 minute miles [55 km] from shore) many logs, wood and pumice were seen and in the evening after passing Vlakken Hoek many floating bodies were also seen. They did not steam at night; the following morning Krakatau was clearly visible and it was apparent that the northern corner of the island had disappeared.[125]

6. The steamship *Prins Frederik* passed Krakatau on August 25 on its way to the Netherlands. Explosions were clearly heard on the 27th, at a distance of 150 geographic miles (600 minute miles [or 1112 km]) from Krakatau. Fine ash fell on deck between August 27 and 29.[126]

7. The American bark *W.H. Besse*, Captain Baker, coming from Manila with destination Boston, struck a coral reef at Duizend Eilanden on June 24 and was

towed by the steamer *Generaal Pel* to Batavia on the 26th, where it remained under repair for 2 months. On August 26, the ship set sail again, and arrived in the Strait during the night; continuous heavy explosions were heard. The pilot left the ship at 9:30 in the morning on the 27th, at which time it was between Krakatau and Anjer, SE of Sebesi. [Corrected by Verbeek in an addendum at the end of his book. The *Besse* did not pass through the Straits until the 29th. During the 27th she was anchored 6 miles E of St. Nicholas Point.] Starting at daybreak a dark black cloud was seen in the west which rose slowly, obscuring the sun and blackening the sky. Captain Baker decided to drop anchor here and to take down all sails. This was hardly done when suddenly a gust of wind hit the ship with tremendous force; the starboard anchor with 80 fathoms of chain was ripped away. The sky in the meantime had become darker than the darkest night, and with the wind came a heavy rain of sand and ash. The wind soon increased to a storm and the water was in extreme turmoil. A heavy rumbling, mixed with explosions, was heard continuously and the darkness was made even more frightening by the intense bolts of lightning. The captain described the darkness as the most intense he had ever seen and, although it was day, one could not see a hand before one's own eyes. A suffocating sulphur smell penetrated the whole atmosphere and hindered breathing. The whole day the noises and sights were far worse than the most vivid imagination could produce: the screaming winds, the foaming and seething water, the dark and impenetrable veil above their heads, the ash, pumice and pieces of earth (probably mud) threatening to sink the ship in the abyss, all worked together to make the entire crew lose their senses. At 3 o'clock in the afternoon it became a little lighter, although ash rain continued to fall. The barometer was rising and falling rapidly and then remained stationary. The entire ship was covered with several inches of sand and ash.[127]

8. The English ship *Charles Bal*, Captain W.J. Watson, passed the Sunda Strait during the eruption on August 26 and 27, strangely enough without sustaining any damage. The story of his trip was published in a Hong Kong newpaper, a summary of which was printed in the Batavian papers.[128,129] A letter from Captain Watson about this trip is also published in the *Liverpool Daily Post*, which in turn was published in the magazine *Nature*.[130] [See p. 102.]

Captain Watson passed Prinsen Eiland on August 26 at 9 o'clock in the morning. Only a small portion of the island of Krakatau was visible, and most of it was wrapped in dark clouds. He saw smoke coming from the mountain from 2:30 to 4:15 in the afternoon and heard crackling noises as if from gunfire; the ship's location at that moment was roughly 10 minute miles [18 km] S of Krakatau. At 5 o'clock in the evening the noises increased, wind SSW; it grew darker and a rain of pumice which was still warm fell in large chunks, and feet and heads had to be protected with boots and sou'westers. The rain of large pieces of pumice ceased at 6 o'clock, finer ash started to fall, soon covering the deck with a layer of 3 to 4 inches; a deep darkness set in. Although they could not see a thing they continued to sail until they thought that they could see the light of Java's Fourth Point; they then stayed clear of the wall. At 11 o'clock in the evening Krakatau was visible again in the west, at a distance of approximately 11 miles [20 km]; chains of fire seemed constantly to move up and down between the sky and the island, the wind was warm and suffocating and had a sulphur smell. The sounding lead emerged warm from 30 fathoms [55 m] depth. (Did it lay around on deck in the warm ash for some time, so that it went down already hot?)

From midnight to 4 o'clock in the morning (August 27) heavy wind, changing between WSW and SSW; the same impenetrable darkness, sometimes alternating with bright lightning bolts, the sounds of Krakatau less continuous but more intense, the tops of the masts covered with St. Elmo's fire. The lighthouse of Java's Fourth Point was passed at 8 o'clock; the signaler's letters were not answered. They passed Anjer at 8:30 and so close to shore that they could see the houses, but no movement was seen on shore. At 10:15 they passed Toppershoedje [51 km NE of Krakatau in the Straits of Sunda], the ash rain had stopped, wind SE. At 11:15 a terrible explosion was heard, Captain Watson soon saw a wave heading straight for Toppershoedje, and running ashore on this island and also on Java; this wave was followed by two more. After the explosion everything became dark, and already at 11:30 (?) it was pitch black, while a rain of ash and mud fell, which continued till 1:30, under loud howling of the volcano and intense lightning. It became light between 2 and 5 o'clock, and a bearing could be obtained from West Island (one of the Duizend Eilanden, south of Noordwachter).

To this report I must add the following remarks. From our sources at Anjer, we know that after the first wave of 6:30, the fort, the jail, the homes of the Patih and of the Wedana, were still standing together with the lighthouse on Java's Fourth Point. It is therefore certainly possible that Mr. Watson saw these buildings at 8:30.[131] But the following time reports cannot have been correct, because darkness had already fallen everywhere in the area at 10:30. At 11 o'clock it was already completely dark in Serang, which is farther away and therefore a time of 11:30 for the darkness and the big wave is probably approximately 1 hour too late. It will remain uncertain whether the reported explosion at 11:15 is related to the 10 o'clock one, because at approximately 11 o'clock there was yet another big explosion, which was reported in Batavia (see later) and also was noted in Riouw, i.e., Tandjoeng Pinang on the island of Bintang. A heavy explosion was heard there at 11:38[132] and because the sound takes just 38 minutes to travel from Krakatau to Riouw (the civil time difference is unimportant), that explosion must have occurred at around 11 o'clock, and must have been heard 2 to 3 minutes later on board the *Charles Bal*. If this is so, then the wave must have come before and not after the explosion. It is curious that nothing was felt of the waves, which came so high against Toppershoedje; this can only be explained by the large length of the waves, causing the ship to be picked up very gradually.

9. The *Berbice*, Commander Logan, traveling with oil from New York to Batavia, was 20 minute miles [37 km] due S of Vlakken Hoek at 2 o'clock in the afternoon on August 26. At 6 o'clock in the evening an ash rain started to fall and just before midnight also small pieces of pumice [see p. 102]. Heavy electrical discharges were seen that night, several people received shocks and the copper-work of the steering wheel became hot. The ash was so warm that the larger pieces burned holes in the clothes and sails. Daylight was not seen on Monday morning, the ash rain increased and at 11 o'clock a heavy wind came from the SE, causing the ship to heel strongly.

At 3 o'clock in the afternoon the sea became heavy, overwhelming and shaking the ship, so that the chronometers stopped. The mercury and pointers of the aneroid barometers did not stop for a second, but moved constantly up and down from 28 to 30 inches. Afterward the weather calmed down, but daylight came only at 8 o'clock Tuesday morning. Approximately 8 inches of ash was lying on deck. When the ship passed Krakatau in the afternoon of that day (August 28), the Captain noticed that the island had split into 3 parts (Verlaten, Lang, and the remaining part of Krakatau itself, separated by the sea). It is curious that also on board this ship nothing had been noticed of the big

long wave of 10 o'clock. The wave, which shook the ship at 3 o'clock, appears only to have been a wild sea, but not in direct relation with Krakatau. Nowhere else was this wave reported.[133]

10. The tenth and last report from ships is that of the *Governor General Loudon*, Commander Lindeman, a steamship of the Netherlands-Indies Steamship Company, traveling from Batavia by way of Teloeq Betoeng, Kroë and Benkoelen to Padang. I possess the following reports from this voyage: 1. The verbal report of the G.G. *Loudon* given to the harbor master of Padang, after its arrival there at 1 o'clock in the afternoon on August 31.[134] 2. A telegram from Commander Lindeman to the steamship company in Batavia, mailed on August 28 from Bantam.[135] 3. Telegram from the resident of Bantam to the steamship company from August 29.[136] 4. Report from Mr. Lindeman to the steamship company, copied from the Batavian newspapers.[137,138] 5. Report from one of the passengers in the *Nieuwe Rotterdamsche Courant*.[139] 6. An essay from the same in French, with a map indicating the route of the *Loudon*.[140]

The *Loudon* departed Batavia on the 26th, 8 o'clock in the morning [see p. 90], and went to Anjer, to take on board some workers with destination Padang, left there at 3:30, steaming past Dwars-in-den-Weg and Varkenshoek, encountered ash rain, in Lampong Bay and arrived at Teloeq Betoeng at 7:25 in the evening. A small boat was sent to shore and came back empty-handed, because going ashore was impossible, due to the wild currents. At night it was again attempted, but the waves were too high and the currents too strong. It was clear that something unusual had happened at the anchorage, because the ships there sent alarm signals, but it was impossible to help.

At about 7 o'clock on Monday morning 4 successive high waves ran up the beach. One saw the harbor light disappear, and the steamer *Berouw*, a cross-boat and a few proahs were thrown on the beach. However, according to reports of the inhabitants of Teloeq Betoeng and also from the engineer van Sandick (in the French journal) this occurred not at 7 o'clock, but already at 6:30.

Commander Lindeman decided that to stay was too dangerous and left around 7 o'clock with the idea of reporting the destruction of Teloeq Betoeng in Anjer. But an increasing ash and pumice rain and upcoming darkness forced him to drop anchor at 10 o'clock near the little island of Tegal in 15 fathoms of water.

The following hours were really horrifying. Already at 10:30 it became totally dark, and heavy ash and mud rain started to fall, accompanied by thunder and lightning and a very strong wind, almost a hurricane, tearing away the sun tent and everything that had not been tied down securely. Bluish moving flames, the so-called St. Elmo's fire, were seen against the masts and spreaders. Extremely high seas rocked the ship in such a way that the Commander was afraid that it would capsize; in order to prevent drifting, he steamed slowly behind both anchors. Things calmed down around 1 o'clock, but it remained dark the whole day. It was already Tuesday morning at 4 o'clock before it became less dark when he prepared himself to continue the trip. When he reached Poeloe Tiga [between Ketimbang and Seboekoe], it appeared that a connection existed between Seboekoe, Poeloe Tiga and the shore of Sumatra near Ketimbang, so that it was decided to go [back westward] through the Strait of Lagoendi and then to round the south of Krakatau. After passing the Strait of Lagoendi, they encountered a large field of floating pumice, which was almost 2 m thick at the middle. Once they steamed through this field, they reached open sea, and reached Anjer at 4 o'clock in the afternoon. It only could be recognized by the stump that remained of the lighthouse on Java's Fourth Point; all other buildings, without exception, were gone. East of Krakatau, a large reef, from which steam rose, was seen between this island and Sebesi. Mr. Lindeman went ashore with a small boat in Anjer, found here Resident Spaan, brought him on board the *Loudon* back to Bantam and then continued immediately to Kroë, to meet there the mailboat *Graaf van Bylandt* coming from Padang to report the changes in Sunda Strait.

These are the most important reports on the eruption, as far as they concern the archipelago. What is observed outside the archipelago will be reported in one of the next chapters. A comparison of the here-reported information shows already that it contains many inaccuracies, exaggerated presentations and incorrect times, but I still am of the opinion that most reports must be given as completely as possible in their original form, especially to show what impression the catastrophe made on the eyewitnesses.

The following summarizes the reported observations:

1. The eruption of August was not preceded or accompanied by heavy earthquakes. Earth tremors were mentioned from only a few places, and these were not heavy.

2. The eruptions of Krakatau increased in severity on Sunday, August 26, in the beginning of the after-noon and especially around 5 o'clock, and they reached their maximum intensity at approximately 10 o'clock Monday morning, August 27, after which they decreased greatly in strength and ended completely on the morning of Tuesday, August 28.

3. Ash and pumice stones were ejected almost continuously, mud or mire only after 10 o'clock on the morning of August 27.

4. Several times the sea became quite turbulent, especially Sunday evening around 6 o'clock, and Monday morning around 6:30 and 10:30. The last wave was by far the biggest, and although the devastations caused by the first wave certainly were not unimportant, the large destruction of Tjaringin and Teloeq Betoeng must be mainly blamed on the last wave. Only this last wave travelled all along the entire north coast of Java; the first one was hardly noticed in Batavia. At the south coast of Java the wave had been noticed to Tjilatjap [135 km ESE of Krakatau], on the east coast of Sumatra to the mouth of Toelang-Bawang River, on the west coast of Sumatra to Ajer Bangies [970 km NW of Krakatau].

5. The sounds were heard in the entire archipelago.

6. The ash rain fell over entire South Sumatra, Benkoelen, Lampongs, Palembang and even to Benkalis, also in the Strait of Sunda, over all residencies of Bantam and Batavia and in the western part of the residencies of the Preanger Regencies and Krawang. It was dark for several hours on August 27, when the ash fell; the closer one comes to the ash line, the shorter the period of darkness lasted.

7. During the falling of the ash, the temperature in far-away places dropped; close to Krakatau, however, the air was hot and suffocating; the barometer acted irregularly, and intense electrical discharges were seen at and around Krakatau.

8. The large number of victims of Krakatau's eruption was caused almost completely by the tremendous flooding of the coasts of Sunda Strait and the north coast of Java and only a small portion by the hot ash falling in some places. Official reports indicate that 36,417 people died, as is specified in the [table on the facing page].

When discussing in more detail the phenomena in later chapters, I will try to give more accurate time computations for the different eruptions and waves than can be derived from the above reports.

Krakatau's Activity after August 28, 1883

As was already mentioned above, the sounds de-

Residency Department Place	Fatalities		Villages		Notes
	Eur	Other	Dest- royed	Dam- aged	
Benkoelen					
Kroë					
Vlakke Hoek	–	34	2	–	140a
Lampongsche Distrikten					
Teloeq Betoeng	–	714	9	1	141
Teloeq Betoeng Area	–	1546	24	4	
Sekampong	–	5	–	–	
Ketimbang (IV Marga's)	1	8037	46	–	
Semangka	1	2159	23	31	
Bantam					
Serang	–	1933	3	30	142
Anjer		7583	10	25	
Anjer	14				
Merak	13				
Tjaringin	5	12017	38	12	
Batavia					
City and Suburbs	–	2	–	16	68b
Meester-Cornelis	–	8	1	5	
Tangerang	–	2340	9	5	
Krawang					
Campong Pakies	–	2	–	3	143a
Total	37	36380	165	132	
Or also, according to the Residencies:					
Benkoelen	–	34	2	–	
Lampongsche Distrikten	5	12461	102	36	
Bantam	32	21533	51	67	
Batavia	–	2350	10	26	
Krawang	–	2	–	3	
Total	37	36380	165	132	

creased significantly during the night of August 27–28 and were heard only in Kroë till 6 o'clock Tuesday morning. After that rumbling sounds were heard sporadically in several places in the direction of Krakatau, but nowhere was an eruption noticed. During the first period after the eruption steam rose from the pumice heaps, and on Krakatau itself burned logs started to smolder (because of the hot ash) causing a glimmer of fire with smoke at night. A part of the ship reports about continuing activity at Krakatau can be attributed to these phenomena. In the meantime, I discovered during my visit to Krakatau that the volcano must have ejected mud for a long time after the August eruption; so that still some weak activity occurred after the big eruption.

I collected the following reports on Krakatau's activity after August.

September 17. At Antjol (immediately east of Batavia) as well as at Tanjong Priok, loud explosions too irregular to be a salute were heard between 10:30 and 11:30 that morning. The cause remains unknown, therefore it is attributed to Krakatau.[144]

September 26. In Batavia explosions were clearly heard and ground tremors felt.[145]

October 9. In the night of October 8–9 a strange light was seen in Serang. It remained light even after the moon had set at 11:25 (October 8), although it was foggy and cloudy, as if the moon continued to shine through a haze, so that one could see quite a distance and clearly could distinguish the outline of trees. It seemed like a haze which was lit for one reason or another; this phenomena continued till daybreak.[146] It still is uncertain whether we have to deal here with a strong zodiac light, or with one of the light signals, which were observed in all parts of the world during the last four months of 1883. The light hardly can be attributed to Krakatau itself, although it is likely that the following day (October 11)[146a] a small eruption occurred, because the eruption was submarine and a patch of light is unlikely. It seems to me most likely that ash particles were high in the air, illuminated by the moon when it had already set in Serang.

October 10. A big wave, which flooded the beach 75 m beyond its normal floodmark, was observed in Tjikawoeng [65 km S × E of Krakatau] in Welkomst Baii, around 10 o'clock in the evening. A rumbling sound from the direction of Krakatau had been heard both here and a little farther north at Soemoer. The wave was not seen anywhere else, because the beach was still totally deserted at night.[147] This wave most likely is related to an eruption of mud, which must have occurred that night, and which will be discussed further [on p. 229].

On board the ships, which were almost continuously present in Sunda Strait after the eruption in August, nothing like an eruption was noticed, either on October 10, or on another night. The cartographic vessel H.M. *Hydrograaf* was anchored 8000 m just N of the peak and 2000 m from the N end of Lang on October 10. Z.M. steamship *Koningin Emma* was moored that night at the "searock." Neither ship noticed anything unusual.[147a] The mud which covered the island of Calmeyer coming from above, therefore, cannot have been ejected that night.

Rumbling sounds from the west were sporadically heard from Friday the 19th to Sunday evening October 21 in Tangerang and Mauk (on the coast of Tangerang). They were attributed to Krakatau.[148]

Vibrations in the air and lightning in the direction

of Krakatau were observed in Tjilegon on Saturday and Sunday night, October 20 and 21.[149] Only a few days earlier (October 18) I left Krakatau in the afternoon, where I had been for two days and had not noticed anything resembling activity. I arrived at Vlakken Hoek on the 19th and at Java's First Point on the 20th during extremely bad weather, rain, and wind. I did not hear any rumbling sounds during my entire trip.

Krakatau supposedly had been active during the night of Nov 12–13, according to a report from Merak.[150] What type of activity is not even mentioned; such vague reports are useless.

February 20, 1884, and following days. The well-known sounds were heard in Batavia and in the evening one could see a flickering light periodically in a western direction. A commander, who had come with his ship through the Strait of Sunda reported that flames rose from the mountain (?) (probably burning logs).[151]

February 23, 1884. In Meester-Cornelis [12 km SSE of Batavia] in the evening, tremors of the ground and rattling of doors and windows were observed; also a red glow seems to have been seen in the west.[152]

I received information about this phenomenon from a person of that village. That evening between 8 and 8:30, he had noticed flickers of light and he had heard rumbling as from thunder, with sometimes a weak dull bang, but he did not notice any tremors or a red glow.[153] It seems most likely to me, that these were only signs of thunder and lightning.

This is the latest report received on the activity of Krakatau.

Discussion

The narrative portion above was completed by Verbeek within a year of the eruption and made available as an independent publication. When included in his 1885 book, however, he added numerous inserts to update the narrative and we have included these in parentheses.

Verbeek's more detailed discussion of individual aspects of the eruption follow in chapters based on his own subject divisions. They must be read with an understanding of the time in which they were written. Less than 100 years before Verbeek's book, many geologists believed that basalt and other lava flows had formed by precipitation from cold ocean waters. The most influential of these was A.G. Werner, who was until 1817 Professor at Freiberg, where Verbeek studied in 1865–66. A subsequent theory, that volcanoes were not built vertically by their own products but by the bulging upward of formerly horizontal flows, was not laid to rest until 1857. Seismographs had been developed, but the instrumental identification of a teleseism (distant earthquake) was not made until 1889. Understanding of earthquakes and volcanoes was not well advanced, and Alfred Wegner—recognized by many as the father of our contemporary understanding of tectonic processes and the way the earth works—was, at the time of the Krakatau eruption, three years old.

Causes and Theoretical Basis of Eruptions

As is known, volcanoes are not just scattered without some order over the surface of the earth, but most of them are aligned in longer or shorter rows. Examples are the volcanoes of South America, Middle America, Alaska and the Aleutian Islands, of Kamchatka, the Kuriles and Japan, of the Philippines and North Celebes (Menado), and finally of the smaller Sunda Islands, Java, and Sumatra.

This cannot be by pure chance: there must be a reason that caused the molten materials to appear preferably along certain directions, and it is obvious when looking for a reason to consider cracks and rips in the earth's crust.

As far as Sumatra is concerned, I tried to show that the initial development of fractures can be attributed to folding of the earth's crust, which occurred there almost always in the same direction, from the earliest times to the present. Not only the large volcanoes, but also the slightly older small volcanoes, lie in rows, which are parallel to the longitudinal axis of Sumatra (NW–SE). The early Tertiary andesite, the diabases, which appeared at the end of the Carboniferous, and the old granite mountains have the same direction, and this is even true for the sedimentary rocks of Sumatra.[154] The most simple explanation is by folding; if the force has been always in the same direction, then the cracks, which must be formed necessarily, lie generally parallel, so that mutual parallel lines of least resistance are developed. The molten matter will preferentially appear along these lines, but also small shifts of parts of the earth's crust, so-called slip faults, will occur mainly along these lines, usually resulting in earthquakes. Furthermore, water, either rain or sea water, can easily penetrate along the faults to molten material present under the crust, forming steam of high temperature and tremendous pressure, which, as we will see, can result in eruptions. Volcanoes, therefore, are normally found in regions where the original position of the rock formation is disrupted by folds or faulting, and earthquakes occur most frequently in that type of terrain; while large areas, where the position of the oldest layers is not disturbed, are almost completely free of earthquakes, such as, for example, the largest part of Russia. From what is said, it follows that in volcanic regions earthquakes can also occur, which are not directly related to volcanoes. It is possible that these can be attributed to steam, but they can be caused as well by other mechanisms.

The important role which cracks and faults play in earthquakes is repeatedly shown, e.g., at earthquakes in Northern Italy. A large arc of land, from Garda Lake via Roveredo and Ala, Belluno, St. Croce, Udine, Adelsberg and Klana to Fiume, which is very prone to earthquakes, probably forms the border of a slowly sinking terrain against the mountains further to the north, namely the Alps. In addition, earthquakes also occur along cracks which lie radially to the above-mentioned arc, and along these lines well developed faults were formed in the rocks, both in vertical and horizontal directions. Near the small lake at St. Croce, east of Belluno, for example, two parts of the mountain moved horizontally with respect to each other.[155]

Also in the reports on the latest earthquake of Ischia (July 28, 1883) it is mentioned that Casamicciola, the place where most damage occurred, was located very near the intersection of two faults in the earth's crust.[156–157a] This earthquake is attributed to activity of the volcano of Ischia, Epomeo.

Opinions on the causes of earthquakes still vary widely. Some scientists consider earthquakes to be the result of sudden development of steam in underground cavities, and this position is quite reasonable because warm water and steam are present under the surface of the earth, as is shown by hot springs and by the large quantities of steam, which come from volcanoes and fumaroles. Also, the existence of underground cavities can be assumed with certainty because the hot springs carry much material in solution, so that cavities form in the hard rock; and also at the region where the solid earth's crust meets the molten material caves must develop, whether it is assumed that the molten masses occur in special chambers not too far below the surface, or at greater depth in a continuous ring between the solid crust and core, which is probably also solid because of the enormous pressure. They therefore consider earthquakes as some type of volcanic eruptions which did not reach the surface. The sharp distinction between volcanic and nonvolcanic earthquakes does not exist for them.

Shocks resulting from the sudden development of steam, and the ones caused by a movement of the steam from one cave to another, which were separated by a rock wall but which suddenly breaks because of the pressure, are considered here to be the cause of the tremors which reach the surface as earthquakes.

Aristotle seems to have been the first who attributed earthquakes to penetration of water and the subsequent formation of steam. It must be noted that, if steam is always the cause, one should expect that at least with some earthquakes steam could be seen along cracks and faults of the earth's crust, but this is as far as I know never observed. In support of this hypothesis, it is noted that most volcanic eruptions are preceded by earthquakes, which decrease in severity, as soon as the volcano becomes active.[156] This may be correct in some cases, but before the big eruption of Krakatau, no important earthquakes were noticed during either May or August; the few earth shocks, which were felt along the coast of Sunda Strait, were very insignificant.

Other scientists attribute one category of earthquakes to volcanic activities, another—namely the ones which occur in nonvolcanic places—to underground cave-ins, which also cause shocks. Very recently even the strong earthquakes, which were felt over large areas, were explained this way, by assuming that the collapses in cavities took place at great depth.[159]

This theory, also very old, was later picked up by Boussingault, and developed further by Hopkins and others.

Also low and high tide of the liquid inner part of the earth is called upon to explain earthquakes and volcanic eruptions.[160,161] By investigating the earthquakes in Greece and Smyrna, and in Switzerland,[162,163] it is shown that a minimum occurs at the quadratures, a maximum at the syzygies, the same result Perrey had reached already for the earthquakes of Italy. Thus, although the position of the moon and sun in relation to the earth certainly must be considered, and for example an earthquake or an eruption could occur earlier, it is impossible for me to regard this as the main cause of these phenomena, for they should occur much more regularly and the time at which they were expected could be calculated beforehand. Up to now one has not succeeded in doing so, and as far as our eruption of Krakatau is concerned, this theory cannot be supported at all by the days of May 20–21 and August 26–27, 1883. According to calculations by engineer Melchior in Batavia, the theoretical tide was actually quite weak on May 20, and on August 26 so insignificant that a connection between tidal strength and this eruption definitely can be ignored.[164]

I will now consider the volcanic eruptions proper and limit my comments to only a short discussion of the most plausible way in which I think that the eruptions occur.

Most geologists nowadays assume that the force which pushes the molten matter in the crater pipes upward to sometimes several thousands of meters simply can be found in the steam which forms from water, as soon as it comes in direct contact with the molten matter, or when it descends in cavities which have a high temperature. They assume here that the earth is only partly converted to the solid state; the crust had become solid by cooling, and the core, where the heaviest material is collected, is probably also solid because of the high pressure, but in between lies a belt, or rather a zone, where molten matter is still present. It does not seem unlikely to me that this molten matter forms one connected mass, which does not, however, eliminate the possibility that in special higher-located cavities portions of this molten matter could be pushed up from this general reservoir, forming within the solid crust special lava chambers, underground lakes of lava. I visualize the so-called volcanic chambers this way, so that they stand alone, but still are connected with one another through the general, deeper-located reservoir. This way, for example, an important pressure in one of the centers is necessarily, also felt in the other chambers.

The penetration of the water to the underground cavities can occur by capillary action of the rocks, and also along the faults in the crust. Daubrée proved experimentally that water penetrates sandstone plates through capillary action, even when a significant opposing pressure is present.[165]

Larger quantities may suddenly penetrate when some movement occurs along a fault, so that first the crack opens a little and then closes again.

The water changes completely into steam when it comes in contact with the molten matter, which has a temperature certainly in excess of 1000°C,[165a] because no water can exist as a liquid above the so-called critical temperature. As is well known, there is for every gas a certain temperature above which condensation to liquid, even at the highest possible pressure, is not possible. The temperature at which this occurs varies widely for the different gases. For carbonic acid, it lies at 30.9°C, for ether at 196.2°C, for carbon disulphide at 276.1°C, and for water at 411.5°C.[166]

Thus, when water is heated to above the temperature of 411°C, in the underground cavity, it is completely converted to steam, and if the space available for steam is not much larger than the water originally occupied, then this steam will have a significant density and a tremendous pressure. Under these circumstances, steam can be compared to explosive gases, as is shown during experiments with superheated steam in closed tubes. Daubrée filled iron tubes, with an inside diameter of 21 mm and a wall thickness of 11 mm, with water and various materials, to investigate the working of water or steam on silicates at high temperature and high pressure. After the tube was sealed, and heated to 450°C, it happened regularly that the tubes exploded with a loud bang like that of a gunshot. Because the tube was filled for the most part with water, the density of the developed steam must have measured approximately 0.9 according to Daubrée; the pressure, which must have been very significant, cannot be calculated correctly.

When a few cubic cm of steam at 450°C is already capable of bursting a heavy iron tube, we can imagine that the pressure of the steam, heated to a much higher degree in the underground cavities, can become high enough to press lava from those cavities several hundred meters upward, and cause it to flow over the crater. Because the specific weight of lava averages 2.5, every 4 m-high lava column is equal to 1 atmosphere pressure, a column of 4000 m—as is at least the case for the lava which flows from the top of Aetna [Sicily]—therefore equals 1000 atmospheres.

At temperatures above 1000°C, still another phenomenon occurs by which the pressure in the underground cavities could further increase, that is, the dissociation.

Grove has already shown,[166a] that water vapor, when in contact with platinum wire which has been brought to glow by electric current, in part dissociates to its elements, hydrogen and oxygen, but it remained for Sainte-Claire Deville to explain this as dissociation, as he called it, meaning a stepwise splitting, depending on temperature and pressure.

The research on the associated phenomena[166b] has shown that dissociation can be reduced by increasing pressure, or can even be prevented almost completely.

In volcanoes, there is, as we saw, a very high pressure of the water vapor (with a height of the lava column of only 1000 m already 250 atmospheres). Furthermore, the temperature of the molten magma in the crater very close to the surface is approximately 1130°—for this is the melting point of rocks which resemble closely the composition of our Krakatau rocks—(see 165a) which is only 100° to 200° above the temperature where dissociation starts (slightly below 1000°C).

The dissociation in the lava chamber cannot be very significant for both reasons, and it is even open to question whether it occurs at all, because the temperature at which dissociation starts probably also increases when pressure increases. The increase of pressure in the lava chamber which obviously would be 50% for complete dissociation—for complete dissociation of 2 volumes of water yields 2 volumes of hydrogen and 1 volume of oxygen, and with constant pressure the volume would increase in the ratio 2:3, and, thus also with constant volume the pressure would increase by the same amount—can be expected to be small or none at all.

It is somewhat different in the crater pipe and especially in the upper portion, because here the effect of the pressure is partly cancelled. A bubble of water vapor which has a temperature of 1100 to 1200°C at the lower part of the crater pipe and a pressure of several hundred atmospheres, as a result of which only very little oxygen and hydrogen is mixed with the water vapor, will remain at about the same temperature, as it rises in the column of lava, but the pressure will continuously decrease. This will also result in an increase of the dissociation and when the bubble has reached the surface of the lava in the crater, the amount of the water vapor that has dissociated, will be what must do so at a temperature of about 1130°C and one atmosphere pressure. The escaping water vapor therefore must be mixed with hydrogen and oxygen, and it is shown from observations by Foqué on Santorini, that this is indeed the case.[166c]

No observations were made on the escaping gases from Krakatau's eruptions from May to August; furthermore, I am of the opinion based on the reasons mentioned above that also with this eruption dissociation plays only a very minor part. Whether the gases, hydrogen and oxygen, will recombine outside the crater during the rapid cooling and expansion at higher altitudes, appears exceedingly doubtful to me, because the rapid cooling of the gases formed from dissociation to below the lowest temperature at which they still can combine is exactly one of the mechanisms to prevent the combination of the dissociation products (Lothar Meyer, *die Modernen Theorien der Chemie*, 1884, page 412).

The very loud explosions which were heard during the eruptions, therefore, hardly can have been caused by a sudden explosive reaction of hydrogen with oxygen, but probably can be attributed to the same mechanism which makes the noise when guns are fired, that is the sudden strong expansion of gases, causing the rapid movement of the surrounding air particles.

The enormous strength of the explosions of Krakatau is sufficiently explained by the tremendous size of our giant volcanic gun and the very high velocity of the materials which were ejected.

During most eruptions lava not only flows quietly out of the crater, or from a crack at the side of the mountain, but fine materials such as ash and sand are ejected also from the crater with great force. During the youngest eruption of Krakatau no lava flowed out of the crater at all, everything was ejected in the form of pumice blocks, sand, and ash.

This violent action can be best explained by assuming that the steam suddenly found an escape path *through the lava*.

When in a lava chamber (see A–B, Figure 53) which is filled to *a* with molten matter, water penetrates, either by slow capillary infiltration or more suddenly by temporarily opening cracks, then the water will soon be transformed into steam, which will collect at the cavity C and exert pressure on the lava. If the pressure increases, then the level will drop from *a* to *b*, and obviously rise in all crater pipes, which are connected with the lava chamber, insofar as those

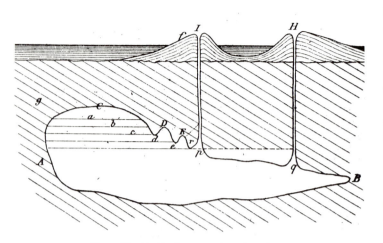

Figure 53. Idealized cross-section of a volcanic magma chamber. See text (p. 223) for discussion. Verbeek adds in a note that "H" should be "II." (Verbeek's figure 32.)

pipes are not clogged up. If the level of the lava drops to c by continuously increasing pressure, then suddenly a part of the steam will escape to D; this can result in an earthquake and even cause a small eruption. If the lava has already risen close to the mouth of the pipe f when the level reaches d, then again, a part of the steam escapes to E; but the really big eruptions will only occur when the lava is pressed down to e, because then a part of the highly pressured steam can suddenly escape from cavity C along p through the crater pipe to f. This pipe is not empty, however, but filled with lava to a certain level, perhaps even close to the surface, and therefore the steam must find its way through the lava. The steam and the gases created by the high pressure expand rapidly and carry with them the lava particles, which are ejected, or rather shot out, as fine dust. The process can be compared with shooting water from a gun or a pistol, thereby dividing it into small droplets. The power of the expanding gases must have been very large during the Krakatau eruption, because the ash particles were ejected several dozen km high.

After the eruption, the remaining portion of the lava sinks in the crater pipe, thereby automatically closing the lava chamber C off from the pipe at p. Again, steam develops anew, and when the pressure is sufficient to push the level down to p, a new eruption occurs, and so on. If the volume of chamber C to the level e is relatively large with respect to the crater pipe, then it can happen that the lava will rise to f before the steam can escape at p; in this case the lava will flow quietly from f and this lava eruption will be followed by an ash eruption only when the level in the chamber C has declined to e.

It seems that this explanation for ash eruptions first is given by Menard de La Groye and Morigand;[167] such a structure as is assumed here for the volcanoes has already been used to explain the activity of the Geysers on Iceland; Bunsen, as is known, has given later another and better explanation for the big Geyser.[168]

Cordenons recently gave the same explanation for the volcanic eruptions.[159]

If after one or more eruptions the remaining lava is no longer sufficient to close off the chamber C at p, then no more eruptions can occur because the steam and gases being formed can continuously escape at p; this is the period of the fumarole activity.

It is also obvious that it is not necessary that nearby craters which are connected with one and the same lava chamber are all active at the same time. However, the lava level will increase to a certain level in all pipes, if none of the crater pipes are obstructed, but when an ash eruption takes place in volcano I, in other words, if the steam can escape from C at p, no ash eruptions will occur in volcano II, because the point q lies so much lower than p and the steam therefore cannot escape at q. However, if the capacity of the crater pipes is so small that lava can flow out before the ash eruptions occur, then that volcano with the crater opening at the lowest level above the sea will become active first. Finally, it should be noted that an eruption can accelerate and also intensify when a portion of the lowest crater pipe at p, for example piece r, collapses, as we can easily see in our Figure 53.

If our assumption about the structure of the volcano chamber and the theory given above about eruptions are correct, then either only ash eruptions occur, as was the case at Krakatau from May to August 1883, or the ash eruptions must follow the flow of lava—this if no new lava is supplied to the underground cavities during a single series of eruptions. Our theory is certainly supported by the generally known fact that indeed very often the ash eruptions indicate the *end* of a period of activity; even where eruptions of lava occur from vents on the slope of the mountain, they sometimes are followed by ash eruptions from the top. [169a]

However, if a new supply of lava flows to the lava chamber after an ash eruption, then this can very well be followed by the extrusion of lava. Of course, I do not think that I have to point out here that I in no way consider the theory I have given here about the volcanic eruptions as the only one possible. I only think that it is a probable one for many cases because it often explains the observed phenomena more than adequately.

After these general observations, I return to Krakatau and the causes which could have resulted in the big eruption of this mountain.

The volcanoes of Sumatra are partly situated on a longitudinal crack, a slightly curved line, which almost coincides with the longitudinal axis of Sumatra, partly on smaller cracks, which cut the main lineament under different angles. The same is the case with the volcanoes of Java.

If one connects Atjeh-head, one of the most northern points of Sumatra, with the mountain Tangka (Kalambajan on the sea charts), on the middle of the three southern tips of Sumatra, then one can consider this line as the longitudinal axis of that island; the direction of that line is 138.5°–318.5°, thus approximately NW-SE. [170]

Connecting the western volcano on Java, Karang, with the eastern volcanoes of that island—Wilis, Keloet, Kawi, and Semeroe—then this line has a direction of 105°.

Both lines intersect at an angle of at least 33°, and the intersection coincides with the volcano Krakatau (compare our map, Figure 54). The volcanoes Radja Bassa on Sumatra, Sebesi and Krakatau in Sunda Strait, and Pajoeng [Java Head] on Java, and also the islands Seboekoe and Poeloe Tiga, which are composed of volcanic rock, lie on an almost straight line, a third volcano lineament which can be considered as a fracture intersecting both the longitudinal axes of Sumatra and Java. [171] The three lineaments intersect exactly at Krakatau and this volcano therefore is situated at the point where the three volcano centers of Sumatra, Sunda Strait, and Java meet.

It is likely that these lineaments coincide with faults, fractures in the earth's crust along which already several times, small movements of the adjoining parts

occurred. In favor of this argues strongly the greater depth of the sea SW of Krakatau compared to the adjoining points of Sunda Strait. On the old Dutch sea chart one finds to the W of the Sunda fracture mostly depths of 122 and 144 m, and E of the fracture 100 and 108 m; the area between the Sumatra fracture and the southern portion of the Sunda fracture, seems to have sunk deeper in relation to the rest of the sea bottom of the Strait, or less raised, and the mentioned fracture appears really to represent fault lines.

As far as the Sunda fracture is concerned, the areas which were lying in this direction, especially Java's First Point, were repeatedly subject to earthquakes in the last years. On September 1, 1880, the shocks there were so intense even that the stone lighthouse was seriously damaged. The upper portion snapped off and it was later removed. The cause of this earthquake cannot be established for certain, of course, but it does not seem very likely to me that this shock was caused by steam which suddenly shifted in the underground cavity. If one considers the shock as a preliminary eruption, which could not yet penetrate to the surface, then one would expect that these shocks would continuously increase in intensity, until the moment at which the eruption began. But this was not the case at all. Between 1880 and 1883, earthquakes were repeatedly felt, both on Java's First Point and in Ketimbang and Anjer, but they were much weaker than the one of September 1880. After the eruption of August 1883, again earthquakes occurred on Java's First Point, which were at least as strong as before the eruption.

It is always possible that these shocks were related to the underground volcanic chamber, but it is more likely that they should be attributed to other causes, such as either a sudden small movement of the earth's crust along the Sunda fault, or a collapse in the underground cavities. The collapse theory seems very plausible to me for cases of such very limited earthquakes, when it is difficult to attribute them to volcanic activities.

Whether a shift along the fault plane or a collapse is the cause of the rather strong earthquake of September 1, 1880, in both cases it could have caused changes, which resulted in easier access of water to the volcanic chamber under Sunda Strait than before. If, for example, a layer which was impenetrable to water formed the roof of the underground cavity, and possibly this layer collapsed, then the water would be able to seep through; or the seal between the sea and the underground cavity became less complete than

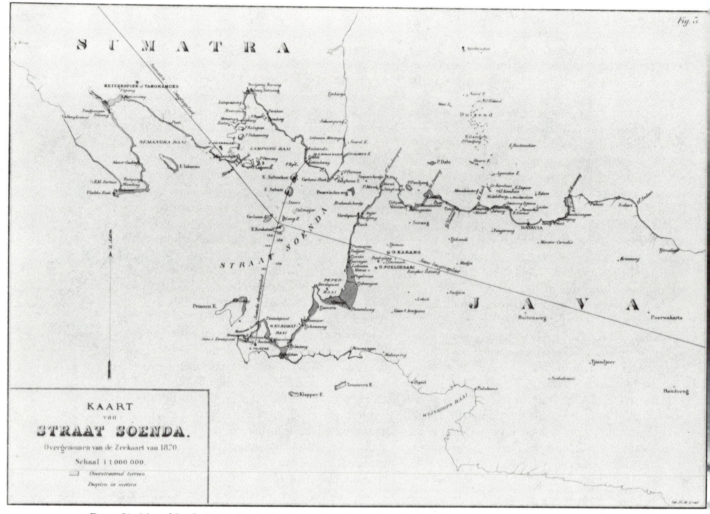

Figure 54. Map of Sunda Strait, after the Dutch sea chart of 1870. Width of map is 228 km; depths in meters. Shaded area shows land that was flooded and destroyed by waves. The three fault zones of Java, Sumatra, and Sunda Strait are shown. The lighthouses of Java's First ("eerste"), Second ("tweede"), Third ("derde"), and Fourth ("vierde") Points are indicated, as well as bays ("baai"), hills or mountains ("G" for "goenoeng") and islands ("E" for "eiland").

Verbeek adds, in a note that "Tjimalaja" in Krawang Residency should be "Tjilamaja;" and "Tjiligon" in Bantam Residency should be "Tjilegon." (Verbeek's figure 3.)

before, because of a shift in the earth's crust along the fault plane, and this could also result in a faster flow of the water. In these changes I see the main cause of the eruption of Krakatau of last year, which possibly was further helped along by an additional supply of the lava in the lava chamber located below Sunda Strait, through causes completely unknown to us. The 200 years of rest of the volcano makes it likely that during that time only a little water could penetrate to the molten matter; the motor, the steam at high pressure, was absent. After that time, however, it changed and already within 3 years the pressure was sufficient to create one of the most intense eruptions known in historic times. The eruptions of May 20 to August 26 formed only the prelude, the real eruption was the one of August 26 and 27.

The phenomena which occurred before, during, and after the eruption of 1883 are very different in nature; they consisted of movements of the earth's crust itself (earthquakes and collapses), movements of molten matter and gaseous products from the inner parts of the earth to the outside, movements of the air and movements of the sea; and at last electrical and magnetic phenomena. In the following chapters each will be discussed separately.

Earthquakes of 1883

It was shown [on p. 191–201] that before the eruption in May several earthquakes occurred in the region of Sunda Strait, but they did not stand out in either number or strength.

It cannot be said either that an increase in earthquake activity occurred for the period between May and August, nor that after the eruption a decrease could be noticed, so that I have concluded, as is already mentioned above, that these small earthquakes are not directly related to Krakatau, but are the result of shifts along the Sunda fracture, or from underground cave-ins.

The following shocks were observed in the year 1883 in the region of Krakatau.[172] [All the following place names appear on Figure 54.]

No. 1. May 9–10, 1883—Java's First Point. Just before midnight.

No. 2. May 15—Ketimbang, relatively strong. No. 2a. Between May 15 and 20. Repeated shocks felt in Ketimbang.

No. 3. May 17—Anjer, light shock during the evening at 10:25. May 20–21—first eruption of Krakatau.

No. 4. May 27—Java's First Point, in the early morning at 3:30, 4:02 and 4:20, rather strong shocks. However, the lighthouse did not suffer damage. May 27—Teloeq Betoeng, horizontal shock at 3:30 a.m. May 27—Tjaringin, 2:00 and 3:55 a.m., the last shock was also felt in Pandeglang. May 27—Vlakke Hoek, 4:00 and 4:30 a.m.—relatively strong.

No. 5. August 26—Java's First Point, heavy earth shocks at 7:50 in the evening. ?August 27—In Anjer some shocks of an earthquake (?) were felt at 2:00 and 3:00 a.m. (It is uncertain whether these were not rumblings resulting from air vibrations.) August 27—Again rumbling shocks (?) at Java's First Point at 1:30 a.m. and 3 and 4 a.m. These most likely were the result of vibrations in the air.

No. 6. September 1—Menes [13 km ESE of Tjaringin], two shocks, at approximately 4 o'clock at night.

No. 7. September 18—Rangkas Betoeng [50 km E of Tjaringin], 12:45 in the afternoon. September 18—Malimping (south coast of Bantam), 1 o'clock in the afternoon.

No. 8. September 19—Java's First Point, 2 o'clock in the afternoon, two smaller shocks.

No. 9. December 6—At 7:30 in the evening, an earthquake felt over a large part of the Residency of Bantam, in the entire department of Tjark and Goenoeng Kentjana (department of Lebak), and in Pasaoeran (department of Anjer).

No earthquakes were reported from the coastal villages of Sunda Strait during the first 4 months of the year. They started in May on Java's First Point and Ketimbang, both located on the Sunda fracture. Approximately one week after the first eruption began, and while the volcano was active, earth shocks were felt on Java's First Point, Vlakken Hoek, Teloeq Betoeng, and Tjaringin; after this there was a period of rest for 2 months. The reports on the earth shocks of August 27 during the big eruption are very unreliable, only the shock at Java's First Point on the evening of August 26 appears to have been a real earthquake.

In September, on the 1st and the 18th, thus after the eruption, shocks were felt twice in Bantam; the last one was also rather strong on Java's First Point. It seems that the condition of the lighthouse, which always suffered considerably from earth shocks, has not improved after the big eruption of Krakatau. Likely, we will hear more about this unfavorably located place.

On December 6 an earthquake occurred over a large part of Bantam, and in January and February 1884 (not reported in this list) shocks were felt at the lighthouse in Vlakken Hoek [1/31, 2/6, and 2/10. All were listed as "light shocks" by Verbeek in his later table on p. 537.] Therefore it cannot be said that it was especially quiet after the eruption. [However, only one other earthquake is listed by Verbeek (p. 537–542) for 1884 that was felt within 200 km of Krakatau, a shock felt in Menes on 4/29.]

Concerning the causes, one should recognize two types, the limited shocks along the Sunda fracture and the more extensive earthquakes in Bantam, which apparently are not related to the fracture.

Whatever else is reported on earthquakes from various places of the archipelago during the eruption of August 26 and 27, probably are rumbling sounds resulting from air vibrations. It is remarkable that the movement of these so-called earthquakes, which mostly were noticed together with shot-like explosions, often were reported as being vertical, while the shocks themselves were weak. Apparently the vertical trembling of hanging objects, such as lamps, were thought to be the result of weak earthquakes.

Ejecta of 1883: Volumes and Atmospheric Effects

From the reports of the mining engineer Schuurman, who visited Krakatau May 27, and of Captain Ferzenaar, who visited it on August 11, it appeared that the volcano up to that time almost only ejected pumice pieces and ash. Three layers could be distinguished on the island itself; the lowest consisted of pumice fragments, followed by gray ash and finally by dark-gray ash. The pumice appeared to have been ejected mainly during the first days of the eruption, followed thereafter till August 26 almost only by finer material, so-called sand and ash; the combined thickness of the eruption products on August 11 amounted to not more than 0.5 m near the active craters. Engineer Schuurman also found some glass-rich rocks, among them a grayish-black piece of obsidian, which showed on one side a porous pumice-like surface, probably where the dissolved gases, mainly steam, could escape from the molten mass. I agree completely with Mr. Schuurman, who considers these pieces parts of a continuously broken and newly forming crater crust, the uppermost solidified portion of the material in the crater.

Concerning the olivine-containing andesites he found, I am of the opinion that they originated from older Krakatau rocks, which were present there earlier, or which were broken up by the eruption and ejected by the crater. In any case, I did not find any rock with olivine among the materials ejected in 1883 (except in olivine-containing older fragments), and this mineral cannot really be expected in the relatively acid younger Krakatau rocks.

During my investigation on Krakatau in October, I found tremendous piles of coarse pumice material, the size of the fragments varying from 1 m³ to very small, with sand and ash in between; the very fine material there occurs in much smaller quantities than on the surrounding islands. On the east side of the island, a yellow, coarse pumice ash mixed with pumice pieces is found lying directly on the old surface of the mountain, and cannot be distinguished from the products of the highest layers. I did not find any chunks of pumice larger than 1 m³. At that time

nothing could be found anymore of the products which were ejected by the volcano from May to August 25, for little or nothing of those products fell on the southern part of the peak at all and the rest of Krakatau had collapsed.

Except for this very monotonous yellowish-gray pumice field, the only thing catching the eye was here and there a black pitchstone-like fragment of which it was not always certain whether it was newly formed; possibly some were fragments of the older glass-rich andesites of the island, which had fallen into the crater during the collapse of parts of the island and were ejected also. Finally, some fragments of obsidian having a pumice-like crust and also pumice pieces with a broken glassy crust offered some variety. In the mass of eruption products, for which we use the name *pumice sand*, which covered the mountain to a height of several dozen m, nowhere was a sedimentary layering noticed, neither a difference in color nor in any other aspect of the products: actually, this is quite reasonable because it formed in only a few hours. The dark blocks of obsidian, pitchstone, and glass-rich augite andesite are randomly distributed in the gray mass. In this pumice sand, partly mixed with seawater, and ejected in a very wet condition, very deep and steep canyons had been eroded already in October; the rainwater apparently is aided by the wetness of the materials themselves, during erosion. The canyons were up to 6–8 m deep, the sides steep, sometimes sheer vertical, so that climbing up or down the mountain caused great difficulties.

On the back side (south side) of the mountain, on top of the pumice material, lie two mud flows, with a thickness of 0.2 to 0.3 m and a width of 1 to 5 m, consisting of a very fine, dark-colored ash; they begin at approximately 200 m below the top, thus 600 m above sea level, and continue over a length of 1300 m, to 100 m above sea level [see Figure 47]. They flowed partly over the ridges, partly in the already-present valleys and canyons in the pumice; therefore they could have occurred only after the channels were formed, for which several weeks must have been necessary. The mud was still damp on October 17, and it could be molded by hand; so it is likely that this mud eruption occurred only on October 10 and is related to the wave, which was observed that evening in Tjikawoeng at Welcomst Baii, and with the rumbling sounds, which were heard (see the report note 147). This wave is the only one observed after August 27 and the mud eruption also appears to have been the last (and only) one after the main eruption of

August.

The same fine black mud I also found on the island of Calmeyer, where it covered the pumice sand with a thickness of 0.20 m. The mud had numerous cracks on the surface, which developed during drying (see color Plates 18 and 19). However, I did not find the fine mud on Sebesi. Mud did fall there after the big eruption at 10 o'clock August 27, as was the case over the whole region up to 100 km distance from Krakatau, but this was normal ash and pumice mixed with seawater, which after drying had exactly the same gray appearance as the dry material which had been ejected earlier, and thus it is easy to distinguish from the fine black mud.

On ships which were then in Sunda Strait, among which were the survey vessel H.M. *Hydrograaf* and the steamship H.M. *Koningin Emma*, nothing was noticed of an eruption either on October 10, or any other day between August 28 and October 10.

The mud on Calmeyer, which was already completely dry on October 17, cannot have come from the eruption of October 10, because the *Hydrograaf* was anchored between Calmeyer and Krakatau that evening, as was already mentioned. It was likely ejected by the underwater eruptions, which occurred after the big eruption of Monday morning and which lasted till Tuesday morning, thus during the evening of the 27th or the night of August 27–28.

Also the island Steers was covered with black mud which we noticed when we passed this island with a small boat. This mud therefore has been thrown to a distance of 15 km from Krakatau, while that from the eruption of October 10 appeared to have been limited to the back side of Krakatau and the immediate surroundings of this island.

Except for these products of a [lithic] volcanic nature,—which for a small part are derived from older fragments of the volcano, but mainly are only in the 1883 solidified liquid crater contents in the form of compact or porous fragments—one can find among the ejected material fragments which do not belong to Krakatau itself, but originate from the floor on which the volcano rests. These samples from the bottom of Sunda Strait show that the same rocks exist there, which are already known from the southern part of Sumatra and the western part of Java; among these samples, one can find older (Miocene) andesite, fragments of marl and mudstone of diluvial and Recent age, and marl concretions, some with irregular shape, but not seldom also of a purely spherical shape. All these ejecta will be discussed in detail below.

The thickness of the ejecta is quite substantial at the western foot of Krakatau and amounts at some points to 60 m and more, with an average thickness of at least 30 m. Towards the top the thickness decreases, so that in the washed out ravines near the top, the old surface of the mountain and the toppled and charred tree trunks are visible.

The size of the ejected fragments decreases with the distance from Krakatau; on that island itself and on Verlaten Eiland some pieces of pumice reach the size of 1 m^3, the glassy rocks at most half that size. On Calmeyer and especially Sebesi, pieces the size of a head are already rare, and it can be said in general that the big and heavy pieces did fall within a circle of 15 km radius around Krakatau. Whatever fell outside this circle consists for the largest part of ash, but bean-size fragments of pumice, in Ketimbang even up to fist-size (the Controller Beyerinck reports fragments the size of a head, but I did not find these), still had fallen on Java's First Point, and at Teloeq Betoeng on Sunday evening, in Ketimbang, Serang, and Menes on Monday morning, thus at distances 40 to 80 km from Krakatau. For the larger fragments, for example, those which fell in Ketimbang at 40 km distance, one cannot think of material that was transported by the wind, as is the case with the finer ash particles, which remain in suspension for a long time. These were projectiles, which were fired from a gun barrel to that distance, and the initial velocity was so large, that the wind direction had hardly any effect on them. The following considerations may serve to appreciate the tremendous velocity which the pumice fragments must have had when leaving the crater, and thus to reach some reasonable understanding of the enormous forces, which were active during the eruption.

To throw an object a certain distance in a vacuum, the necessary initial velocity is dependent upon the angle of elevation under which the object is fired. It is the lowest for 45°; for either larger or smaller angles the velocity is higher. We, therefore, will consider three cases, with a small (10°), an average (45°), and a large (80°) elevation angle. For a distance of 40 km, the distance from Krakatau to Ketimbang, the velocity in the first second must have been 1070 m for an angle of 10°, 625 m at 45°, and again 1070 m at 80°, the same as at 10°. The highest altitude which the projectile reaches amounts, in the first case, to 1763, in the second to 10,000, and in the third to at least 56,700 m, and the time needed to reach that distance in the three cases is 0.5, 1.5, and 3.5 min.

These numbers are only valid for the parabolic path in the vacuum, and are subject to a substantial change when the resistance of the air is taken into account. This is fortunate too, because, considering that the final velocity in a vacuum is equal to the initial one, nobody would have survived the bombardment in the area of Ketimbang if the resistance of the air had not slowed the projectiles. But what mainly concerns us here is the initial velocity, and with the resistance of air, this must have been even higher than in vacuum, in order to throw the objects over the same distance;[173] the numbers given above for the velocity, therefore, are clearly smaller than in reality; with a higher velocity the altitude reached also should have increased, but the resistance of the air again slows the projectile and decreases the altitude; because most paths must have been nearly vertical (approximately 80°), for which elevation angle we found a maximum altitude of approximately 57 km in vacuum (and this number increases at a higher speed, but decreaes again because of air resistance), the real attained altitude cannot have been that different from the one mentioned and one can assume with some confidence that the material ejected by Krakatau reached a height of 50 km. This is valid mainly for the coarser ash particles, while the finest particles probably were thrown even higher into the atmosphere. When one considers that at the explosion of 2 o'clock in the afternoon of Sunday, August 26, the ash cloud already reached a height of between 27 and 33 km, according to Captain Thomson of the *Medea* [see p. 96], then a height of 50 km for the ash particles which were ejected during the much stronger eruptions of Monday morning and especially during the heaviest explosion of 10 o'clock in the morning cannot in the least be regarded as exaggerated.

The initial velocities for different kinds of large cannons are normally between 300 and 425 m/sec, and only for a few more recent cannons values of 500 m/sec are reached (Krupp caliber 30.5 cm, 460 m/sec; Woolwich 40.6 cm, 460 m/sec; Krupp 35.5 cm, 500 m/sec);[174] therefore, the velocity with which the Krakatau projectiles were ejected far exceeds that of the largest cannons. However, these velocities are not incredible, especially if one considers that the ejection is caused by steam at high pressure, which in its action can be compared to explosive gases. The explosion velocity of guncotton lies between 5000 and 6000 m/sec, according to Abel and Nobel,[175] a velocity we certainly do not need to explain the Krakatau projectiles.

Still another phenomenon has to be discussed here, that is the fall of *hot ash* in the region of Ketimbang. Although warm pumice fragments and ash particles also fell in other areas, it appears that only the ash which fell in the region of Ketimbang, before the mud rain began and thus before the underwater eruption took place, was so hot that it caused burns.

The explanation for this seems to me in that the material, which is always hot when coming from the crater, was mostly ejected at large elevation angles, but that the ash in the direction of Ketimbang was ejected at an especially low angle, for example 10°. The time necessary to reach Ketimbang, both for large and small angles, is so short that the time difference cannot be the cause for the cooling of the ash particles, but, in the first case, the particles reach a much higher altitude and thus are cooled in the higher atmosphere by the low temperature existing there. If we compare, for example, the numbers given above for a vacuum; at 10° only a height of 1763 m is reached, at 45° already 10,000, at a larger angle still more; therefore, at a somewhat large angle, the ash particles must have been already relatively cool when they fell down. When, during a new burst, an opening on the side of the mountain is formed, it is very possible that occasionally a blast occurs in a sideways direction at a very low angle; I did observe such a blast at the volcano Kaba in Palembang.[176] It seems to me that this also explains why so little hot ash has fallen *north* of Ketimbang; the mountains Sebesi (859 m above sea level) and Seboekoe lie in the direction of the path and must have caught a large part of the ejected material, because the height of the ejection path must have been minimal.

Tephra Distribution and Volume

The large fragments of pumice thus are confined to Sunda Strait and its immediate vicinity, while the finer ash particles were transported over a large area of Sumatra by the wind, which was primarily from the SE and NE during the days of the eruption.

According to the information I obtained, the border of the area within which ash has fallen, must have been as shown on the map, Figure 55. The northernmost border is located in the Residency of Sumatra's East Coast.

A little north of the capital city Bengkalis the borderline curves east to Singapore, then south to the island Lingga, next passing Muntok and north of Noordwachter to the Residency of Krawang; runs directly south just east of Dawoean, Tjikao, and Poerwakarta [225 km E off Krakatau] and west of the volcano Boerangrang toward Bandoeng, which town, however, remains just outside the borderline; then past the volcano Patoea [245 km ESE of Batavia] and the Breng-Breng mountain chain [220 km SE] to the mouth of the River Boeni on the south coast of Java. Its farther course in sea is not exactly known, on Kokos Eiland [Cocos (Keeling) Island, 1155 km SW of Krakatau] and between this island and Krakatau, ash still had fallen, so that I placed this island within the ash line. I drew the line from Keeling to the northern part of Benkoelen, and then E of the Government of Sumatra's Westkust back to Bengkalis, because no ash had fallen on Sumatra's Westkust. [177-186]

The area enclosed by this line has an irregular shape, which one can visualize as two overlapping ellipsoids, with Krakatau roughly at the focal point and with the long axes directly to the NW and SW, corresponding to the prevailing SE and NE winds during and after the eruption. The area of this figure measured by the planimeter is 827,000 km^2 or 15,019 square geographic miles (1 geographic mile = 7420.4 m) and thus more than 23 times larger than the Netherlands.

In order to calculate the quantity of the ejected material, I made observations everywhere on the islands and along the coasts of the Strait of Sunda; the thickness of the materials deposited in the sea corresponds with the difference in depth of the sea and after the eruption. The Director of Education requested information from the Residents of the Residencies of Bantam, Lampongsche Districts, Benkoelen, and Palembang. However, most of the data received are too large; only the observations which were made immediately after the eruption can be trusted.

About the thickness I received the following information:

Residency Department Place	Thickness	Observer
Krawang	Insignif.	–
Preanger-Regentschappen		
Parakan-Salak	½ mm	Mundt[187]
Batavia		
Buitenzorg	½ mm	Verbeek[188]
Bantam		
Tjaringin		
Menes*	15 mm	O.R.[76a]
Tjaringin*	10–20 mm	O.R.[76a]
Panimbang*	30–50 mm	O.R.[76a]
Tjibalioeng*	15–30 mm	O.R.[76a]
Anjer	40–60 mm	O.R.[76a]
Pandeglang		
Kolelet*	20 mm	O.R.[76a]
Baros en Pandeglang*	25 mm	O.R.[76a]
Tjiomas en Tjimanoek*	30 mm	O.R.[76a]
Lebak		
Paroeng-Koenjang en Tjilangkahan*	15 to 1 mm**	O.R.[76a]
Rangkas-Betoeng*	15–20 mm	O.R.[76a]
Lebak*	15 m avg.	O.R.[76a]
Sadjira*	5–12 mm	O.R.[76a]
Serang	10–30 mm	O.R.[76a]
Merak	20 mm	Verbeek[190]
Java First Point	10 mm	Verbeek[190]
Lampongsche Distrikten		
Krakatau	1–60 m	Verbeek[190]
Eiland Sebesi	1–1½ m	Verbeek[190]
Eiland Seboekoe	0.6 m	Verbeek[190]
Ketimbang	0.3 m	Verbeek[190]
Kasoegihan	0.16 m	Verbeek[190]
Teloeq-Betoeng	0.20 m (uncertain)	Verbeek[190] Verbeek[190]
Vlakke Hoek	0.20 m	Verbeek[190]
Semangka	Uncertain	O.R.[191]
Soekadana	7 mm	O.R.[191]
Goenoeng Soegi	6 mm	O.R.[191]
Menggala	15 mm (??)	O.R.[191]
Benkoelen		
Kroë	50 mm	Controller Horst***[192]
Kauer	50–60 mm (?)	O.R.[192]
Pasar Manna	50 mm (?)	O.R.[192]
Ommelanden van Benkoelen	10 mm (?)	O.R.[192]
Benkoelen	10 mm	O.R.[192]
Lais	10 mm	O.R.[192]
Mokko Mokko	Insignif.	O.R.[192]
Palembang		
Moeara-Doera	15–20 mm	O.R.[193]
Labat	3 mm	O.R.[193]
Bandar	7 mm	Stammeshaus***
Tandjoeng-Radja	10 mm	O.R.[193a]
Palembang	7 mm	O.R.[193b]
Talang-Betoetoe	5 mm	O.R.[193c]
Sekajoe	5 mm	O.R.[193c]
Tebing-Tinggi	15 mm (?)	O.R.[193c]
Soeroe-Langoen (Rawas)	5 mm	O.R.[193c]
Djambi	1–2 mm	O.R.[193]
Sumatra's East Coast		
Bengkalis	V. Insig.	O.R.[194]
Riouw		
Lingga	Not much	O.R.[195]
Banka		
Muntok	Nothing	O.R.[196]

Key: O.R. = Official Report
* = District
** = Less towards S Coast
*** = Good observation made immediately after ash rain.

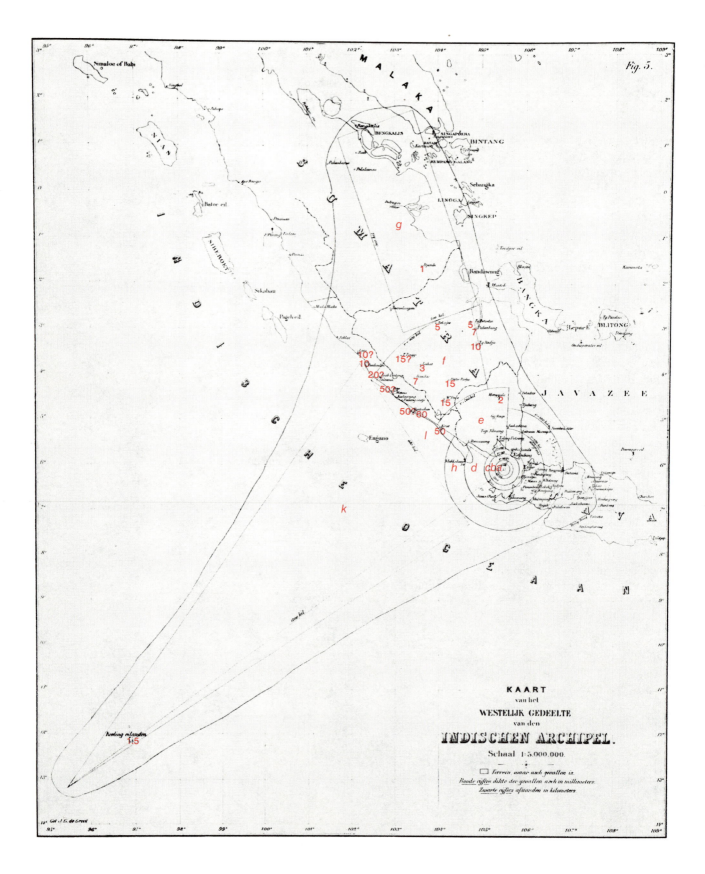

Fig. 5.

KAART
van het
WESTELIJK GEDEELTE
van den
INDISCHEN ARCHIPEL.
Schaal 1:5.000.000.

☐ *Terrein waar asch gevallen is.*
Roode cijfers dikte der gevallen asch in millimeters.
Zwarte cijfers afstanden in kilometers.

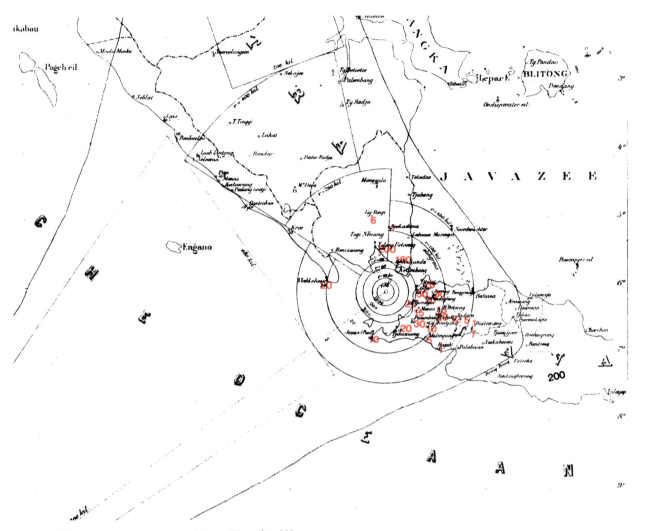

Figure 55b (above). An enlargement of Figure 55a within 200 km of Krakatau. Thickness of ash layers (in mm) shown by red numbers.

Figure 55a (at left). Map of the western section of the East Indian Archipelago. Width of the map is 855 km. Red numbers indicate thicknesses of ash layers in mm; but thicknesses near Krakatau are shown only on Figure 55b enlargement. The outermost solid line describes the area that received ashfall; it has an irregular shape with long axes to the NW and SW due to the prevailing NE and SE winds during and after the eruption. The concentric circles around Krakatau have radii of 22.5, 40, 50, 100 and 150 km respectively. See text (p. 235) for discussion of areas "a" through "l," which were used to calculate the volume of material erupted. (Verbeek's figure 5.)

233

As is explained further in the notes, most numbers are not very reliable, because only very few observations were made immediately after the eruption, and, moreover, not the thickness of compacted ash but that of the loose ash layer was reported. As the specific weight can be put at 2.2, the data of the weight of the ash, which fell on a known surface is, of course, more reliable, but I obtained only very few reports on the weight. However, a few better observations on the thickness enable us to obtain an average for the various regions that at least approaches the real value.

We now take a look at map, Figure 49; it is mainly a copy of the new sea chart made by Navy Lieutenant 1st Class, M.C. van Doorn, Commander of the surveying vessel H.M. *Hydrograaf* [see p. 138]; the shape and location of the islands are copied unchanged, only Krakatau itself was slightly modififed following our survey. The fainter figures indicate in m the present, the darker figures the earlier depths, taken from the sea chart of Blommendal of 1874.

Comparing these numbers shows that the largest quantity of material fell within a circle with a radius of 15 km around Krakatau, using the crater Danan as center.

The thickness of the materials, however, are not everywhere the same. Where the islands Steers and Calmeyer are located, the sea which was 36 m deep has now an average depth of 6 m; these islands are only the highest points, sticking out of the sea, of a large bank of sand and ash mixed with pumice fragments, which fills almost completely the sea between Krakatau and Sebesi. At other points on the part of the map marked II, the depth was formerly 43, now 13 m; more to the south formerly 122, now 97; formerly 74, now 54; formerly 128, now 97 and at Hoedekenskerkklip formerly 144, now 112. On still other points of section II the difference is sometimes more, sometimes less, but as an average difference in depth one can take 30 m for the entire section II.

Between Steers and Lang is part I, where the earlier depth averages 40 and the present depth 20; of course, here the differences are also not everywhere the same; however, 20 m can be assumed as an average difference here.

To the west of Krakatau the thickness of the ejected material is substantial; only a few depth measurements were made here, so that the difference cannot be determined with accuracy. In the northern part of Section III the depth was formerly 59, now 18, thus a difference of more than 40 m; the difference seems to be larger still in the southern part (70 and 75 m)

but because of a lack of sufficient data, I put the difference in depth in Section III everywhere at only 40 m.

Finally, considering section IV, being equal to the area of the circle with a radius of 15 km, less the area of the sections I, II, and III, one here finds differences of 2, 5, 9, and 18 m. In the collapsed part, the present depths, of course, are much larger than the earlier ones. I think that I cannot assume more than 6 m as an average difference in depth for section IV.

The differences in depth cannot be attributed to an uplift of the sea bottom, or the development of new cones under the surface of the sea, but only to the enormous volumes of sand, ash, and rocks, which have fallen into the sea there. If the ejected materials had consisted only of pieces of pumice, these would, of course, have been afloat and thus could not have formed islands or banks; but, because it consisted mainly of fine material, with a specific gravity of approximately 2.2, the materials can sink into the sea, even when mixed with a considerable amount of pumice fragments.

The thickness is considerably less outside the first circle of 15 km radius. In order to calculate the volume of the ejected materials, I drew concentric circles around Krakatau, Figure 55, with radii of 22.5, 40, 50, 100 and 150 km. I calculated averages for the thickness of the ejected materials in the successive circles using the numbers given above: for the first circle, in which lies Sebesi, 1 m, for the second 0.3 m, for the third 0.2 m, for the 4th 0.02 m; outside this circle almost no mud fell, therefore the circle with a 100 km radius forms the "mud" line, with only Beniawang slightly outside of the line; for the 5th 0.005 m. For the last two rings, only ⅚ was calculated with the thickness mentioned here, ⅙ with the thickness of 0.05 m, because the wind direction has to be considered, causing the ash particles to drift to the NW. In part *e*, ⅙ of the entire ring between the circles with a radius of 50 and of 200 km, the average thickness is put at 0.05 m. In part *f*, being ⅛ of the entire circle between the circles with a radius of 200 and 400 km, the thickness is assumed to be 0.01 m, and what fell outside of it toward the NW, with a rectangle 200 km wide and 500 km long, only at 0.001 m.

In the direction of Cocos Island, I assumed a triangle with a base of 480 and a height of 1200 km; the thickness is very hard to determine here, and the figure of 0.005 m (5 mm) assumed by us, is rather too low than too high.

All this results in the following calculation from Figure 49:

Area of section I	54 km²
Area of section II..............................	243 km²
Area of section III............................	36 km²
Total................................	333 km²
Area of circle 1 with r = 15 km =	707 km²
Minus I, II, and III =	333 km²
Remains for section IV =	374 km²

Regarding the volume in:

Section I..........	54 × 10⁶ km² × 20 m =	1080 × 10⁶ m³
Section II........	243 × 10⁶ km² × 20 m =	7290 × 10⁶ m³
Section III.......	36 × 10⁶ km² × 40 m =	1440 × 10⁶ m³
Section IV........	374 × 10⁶ km² × 6 m =	2244 × 10⁶ m³
	707 km²	Circle I = 12054 × 10⁶ m³

r (km)	#	Area (km²)	Area of the rings
15	1	707	Ring a: 883 km²
22½	2	1,590	Ring b: 3434 km²
40	3	5,024	Ring c: 2826
50	4	7,850	Ring ⅚d: 23550 − ⅙ × 23550 = 23550 − 3925 = 19625
100	5	31,400	Ring e: ⅙ × 94200 + 3925 = 15700 + 3925 = 19625
200	6	125,600	Ring f: ⅓ × 376800 = 47100
400	7	502,400	
100	–	31,400	Ring ⅚h: ⅚ × 39250 = 196250/6 = 32708
150	–	70,650	

Rectangle g	200 × 500 =	100,000 km²
Triangle k ½ ×	480 × 1200 =	288,000 km²
Piece l	=	15,000 km²

For the Volume in:

Surface × thickness

a	883 × 10⁶ × 1	= 883 × 10⁶ m³
b	3,434 × 10⁶ × 0.3	= 1030 × 10⁶ m³
c	2,826 × 10⁶ × 0.2	= 565 × 10⁶ m³
d (⅚)	19,625 × 10⁶ × 0.02	= 393 × 10⁶ m³
e	19,625 × 10⁶ × 0.05	= 981 × 10⁶ m³
f (⅛)	47,100 × 10⁶ × 0.01	= 471 × 10⁶ m³
g	100,000 × 10⁶ × 0.001	= 100 × 10⁶ m³
h (⅚)	32,708 × 10⁶ × 0.005	= 164 × 10⁶ m³
k	288,000 × 10⁶ × 0.005	= 1440 × 10⁶ m³
l	15,000 × 10⁶ × 0.005	= 75 × 10⁶ m³
Sum	529,201 km²	6102 × 10⁶ m³ = 6.102 × 10⁹ m³ = 6.102 km³

Add to this Circle 1:

707 km²	= 12.054 km³

Surface:

529,908 km²	= 18.156 km³

Remaining surface: Volume:

297,192 km²	Negligible

Total: 827,000 km²   18 km³

As will be shown the figures everywhere used for thickness can hardly be considered too large, so that a volume of 18 km³ is probably not too large, but is most likely too small. The possible inaccuracy of this calculation, I think, is not more than 2 or at most 3 km³. Of this quantity, ⅔ or 12 km³, is located within the circle with a radius of 15 km around Krakatau, ⅓ or 6 km³, on the outside.

Junghuhn calculated the amount of material ejected by the volcano Tambora on Soembawa in 1815, at 318 km³.[197] The ash was several meters thick close to the volcano, on Lombok at 90 minutes distance from Tambora, 2 feet thick, on Banjoewangi, 210 minutes away from the volcano, still 8 rhineland inches thick. Junghuhn draws a circle with a radius of 210 minutes around Tambora and assumes that the average thickness of the ash within this circle was 2 feet. That results in a probable quantity of: $\pi r^2 \times \text{thickness} = \pi \times (210 \times 1855)^2 \times \frac{2}{3} \text{ km}^3/10^9 = 317.8 \text{ km}^3$.

But because the wind was mainly from the E, and the finer material was therefore largely carried to the W (Lombok, Bali and Banjoewangi), the assumption that two feet of ash fell everywhere is too high for the areas situated E, N, and S of Tambora. Also, I found a report in the *Javasche Courant* (newspaper) of 1815, that the ash layer was only 0.1 m thick in Bima, 40 minute miles E of the volcano, and only 0.03 m in Makasser, 217 miles north of Tambora.[197a] Junghuhn's calculation therefore gives apparently much too high a figure. It is more likely that the ash, with an average thickness of 2 feet, only fell in a rectangle of approximately 150 minutes wide and 300 minutes long, with Tambora located close to the eastern end of this rectangle. We then obtain: $J = \frac{2}{3} \times 150 \times 300 \times (1855 \times 1855) \text{ km}^3/10^9 = 103 \text{ km}^3$; and if we take another 50% for the material falling outside of it, which definitely is high, then we still only come to 150 km³. We can give the same comment on this calculation as on the one of Junghuhn, that is, it is based on too few data; but the figure of 150 km³ is more likely than 318 km³.

In any case the quantity of the ejected ash was considerably larger than that of Krakatau. Indeed, this must have been so, because according to the report it had been dark for three consecutive days on Madoera at a distance of more than 500 km from Tambora, while the darkness lasted only a few hours (2 to 8 hours) in most places after the Krakatau eruption. In most places along the coast of Sunda Strait it became dark soon after 10 o'clock in the morning, at the lighthouses of Vlakken Hoek and of Java's First

235

Point it was dark during the entire Monday, and according to the story of Commander Logan of the *Berbice* (see 133) no daylight was seen by him from Sunday evening 6 o'clock to Tuesday morning 8 o'clock. The ship was 20 English miles directly S of Vlakken Hoek.

Tephra: Ship's Reports and Atmospheric Effects

Very fine ash particles were carried in the higher atmosphere to the west by eastern winds and fell into the sea outside the area, indicated in map Figure 55. We possess the following ship reports [with distance and directions from Krakatau added in brackets] about this:

1. Ash fell on board the steamship *Ruby*, travelling from Palembang to Singapore, on August 26.[198] This ship was just within the area shown on map Figure 55.

2. Captain Knight of the brig *Airlie* heard heavy explosions on Sunday, August 26 at 3 o'clock in the afternoon; the following morning he found fine dust on deck. The ship's location was north of Banka, at 0°32'S and 105°57'E [622 km N].[124]

3. The ship *Charlotte* was south of Java at 8°3'S and 106°E [226 km S] on August 27. The explosions were clearly heard; ash fell on deck at 8 in the morning, and at 2 o'clock in the afternoon the lights had to be turned on (at what location?). Also this ship was still within or very close to the ash area as shown on the map Figure 55.[200]

4. On board the ship *Tweed* from Mr. Ross of Keeling Eiland, 7 inches (?) of ash fell at a distance of 320 miles from Krakatau.[201]

5. On board the steamship *Prins Frederik*, which passed Krakatau on August 25, one heard explosions 600 miles away from Krakatau on August 27, and ash fell on deck from August 27 to 29. Neither latitude nor longitude are given.[126]

6. An ash rain fell for several hours on the *Salazic*, Captain Loyseau, on a journey from Calcutta to Reunion, from 5:30 in the morning of August 28 to the 29th. First, relatively coarse sand fell, then, fine ash. The ship was at 9°15'S and 90°30'E (from Paris?) [1430 km W × S, assuming Paris meridian].[203]

7. The *County of Flint*, Captain Rowland, experienced an ash rain on August 28 at 8°20'S and 92°4'E [1494 km W × S].[124]

8. On the Bremer ship *Barbarossa*, ash fell on August 27 (?) at 93°15'E and 1°41'S [1437 km WNW]. This ash was chemically and microscopically analysed by K. Oebbeke and A. Schwager.[204a] Ash still fell on deck on August 28 and 29 until the afternoon (93°25'E 5°0'S [1334 km W]); according to Dr. Neumayer a sample of the ash, which fell on deck the morning of the 28th, probably the same ash which Oebbeke investigated; the ship journal does not mention anything about the ash which presumably fell on August 27.[204b]

9. Ash fell from midnight on the 27th to 11 o'clock in the morning of August 28 on board the French brig *Brani*, Captain Perrot, at 1°39' to 2°59'S and 89°56' to 89°50'E of Paris [1541 km WNW to 1509 km W × N]. Explosions were also heard, and ash fell again on the evening of August 28–29.[124]

10. Captain Robert Williams, of the bark *Arabella*, reports that sand started to fall on the morning of August 28; this continued the entire day and the following one. Latitude 5°37'S 88°58'E, in the afternoon of August 28, thus 970 miles [1821 km W] from Krakatau.[206]

11. At 2°37'S and 79°52'E [2859 km W × N], ash fell from the afternoon of the 29th to the evening of August 30, on board the ship *British Empire*.[207]

12. In of the night of August 30–31, an ash rain fell on board of the *Meda* between Ashburton River and Perth, at 50 to 100 miles distance of the W coast of Australia, and approximately 1000 miles away from Krakatau in a SSE direction.[208]

The locations of these ships are indicated on the map Figure 56; it shows that the heavier ash particles were carried by the winds prevailing in the lower atmosphere first to the NW, then to the SW, and the finer ash in the higher atmosphere was carried by eastern winds to the west. The ashfall occurred gradually; the easternmost ships received ash already in the evening of August 27, the ones farther west on the 28th, and the ship *British Empire* at 80°E first on August 29.

That not only eastern winds but also NNW winds were prevalent in the upper atmosphere is shown by ash, which fell on the *Meda* close to the Australian coast, between August 30 and 31.

The ash particles thus were carried westward up to 80°E and fell here into the sea at a distance of almost 1600 minute miles [2965 km] from Krakatau. One can pose the question whether the still finer ash particles remained in suspension even longer and therefore were carried even further westward. This appears to have been indeed the case. The finest particles, mixed with a considerable amount of water vapor, passed over the Seychelles and Africa to Cape Coast Castle on the Gold Coast, farther to Paramaribo, Trin-

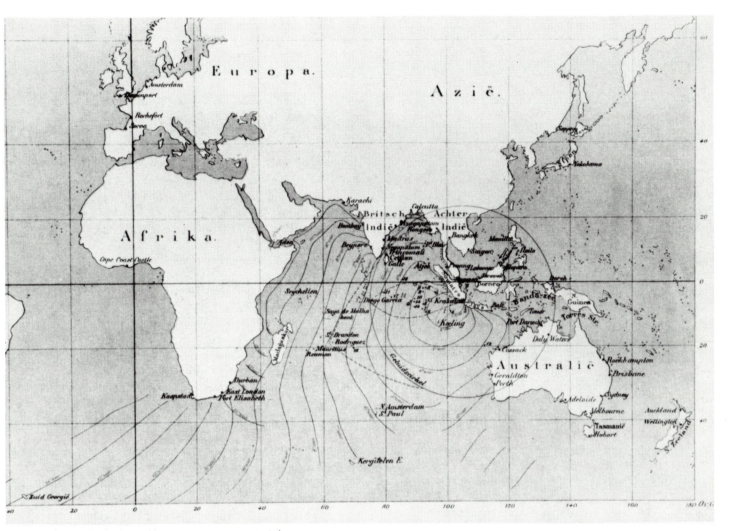

*Figure 56. Portion of a world map (Mercator projection) show-
ing the spread of the sounds, ash, and sea waves. Width of map
at equator is 25,000 km. Ships that received ash were (1) Ruby,
(2) Airlie, (3) Charlotte, (4) Tweed, (5) Prins Frederick, (6) Sala-
zie, (7) County of Flint, (8) Barbarossa, (9) Bram, (10) Arabella,
(11) British Empire, and (12) Meda. Ships that encountered
floating pumice were (13) Quetta in July, 1883; (14) Siam on 1
August, 1883; (15) Idomene on 11–12 August, 1883; (8) Barbarossa on 31 August, 1883; (16) Cleomene on 1 September, 1883;
(17) Gipsy on 9 September, 1883; and (18) Umvoti in February
1884.*

*The sounds of the explosions were propagated to the periphery
of the solid circle ("geluidscirkel"), and a little farther to the west
of Krakatau to the dashed line. The area of this circle is 1/15, and
the entire area to the dashed line is 1/14 of the earth's surface.*

*The pumice and heavy ash fell within the area indicated by
"I." Fine ash fell on the decks of ships and in the ocean to the
west of Krakatau on 27–30 August in the area marked by "II."*

*The black lines indicate the propagation of the sea wave, hour
("uur") by hour. The numerals indicate the number of hours
passed since the beginning of the big wave, on 27 August at
10:00 a.m. Krakatau time. (Verbeek's figure 6.)*

idad, Panama, and the Sandwich Islands to Ceylon and British-India, and summoned in all these places blue and green colors for the sun and moon just after rising and before setting, and also created intense red skies after sunset and before sunrise. The dates on which the blue- and green-colored sun first was seen in the various places, are as follows (see map, Figure 56):

Cape Coast Castle [now Ghana], September 1 and 2, color blue.[209]

Paramaribo [now Suriname], September 2, indigo blue.[210]

Puerto d'Espana (Trinidad), September 2, blue; after sunset the sky was so red, that people thought that somewhere there was a fire.[211]

San Christobal (Venezuela), September 2, color blue.[211a]

Medellin (Colombia), September 2, blue.[211a]

Bogota (Colombia), September 2, nice blue.[211a]

Cartagena (Colombia), September 2, color green.[211a]

Panama, September 2 and 3, green.[212]

Maracaibo (Venezuela), September 5 (?), sky blue.[211a] (Footnote: This date can hardly be correct, because the phenomena were already observed on September 2 in places nearby.)

On board the vessel C. Southard Hurlburt at 125°W and 17°N on September 3, only a red sky was seen, but no green sun.[213]

On board the Jennie Walker at 155°28'W and 8°20'N on September 4, 5 o'clock in the evening; green sun.[213]

Fanning's Island, 159°22'W 3°52'N, September 4, copper-colored sun.[213]

At Maalaea, on the island of Maui (Sandwich Islands) [Hawaii], red skies were seen in the morning of September 5, but no green sun.[213a]

. In Honolulu, on the island of Oahu (Sandwich Islands), red skies were seen in the evening of September 5 and the following days; one report also mentions a green sun.[214,213]

On board the Zealandia, 3 days after after leaving Honolulu, on a journey from San Francisco to Sydney, a blue sun was observed at approximately 5°N in the evening of September 5, and also in the morning of September 6.[214a,215]

On the Gilbert Islands, September 7, copper-colored sun.[215] (Footnote: The Sandwich Islands are located E, the Gilbert Islands W of the meridian of 180°, causing the date to leap. September 7 on Strong's Island and the Gilbert Islands is therefore the same as September 6 on the Sandwich Islands.)

On Strong's Island (on the English sea chart, named Kusaie or Ualan Island), 163°4'E 5°10'N; September 7, sun silver-blue.[215]

Ceylon and the southern part of English India. In a number of places, a blue, blue-green or green sun was seen from September 9 to September 14.[216,217]

At 87°E and 15°S at sea; September 14, color appeared green-yellow. (Report from the ship Ida.)[217a]

At 10°W and 11°N at sea; September 14, light green. (Report from the German warship Carola.)[217a]

At 27°W and 11° and 12°N; September 15 and 16, grass green. (Report from the bark Frieda Grampp.)[217a]

Captain Penhallow of the bark Hope saw the red in the sky on September 18, at 140°29'W 24°N.[217b]

In Honolulu, red skies were reported again on September 20.[214]

The phenomena of a green sun and moon reappeared again in several places in the British Indies from September 22 to 24 (see 217).

In Deum (Sudan) the sun was light-green on September 24.[218]

During the second half of September, beautiful sunsets were reported in South Australia and the Cape of Good Hope; in October, in California and the United States of America; in November, December, and even in the first months of 1884 in almost all of Europe. It is, however, remarkable that after September only a very few reports mention a clearly green color of the celestial bodies. I only found mentioned that the moon from Karachi had a green hue during the first half of October,[219] that the moon rising on December 4 from York and Worcester had a green color,[220] that the sun in Krakau [Poland] had a beautiful green color on January 24, 1884,[220a] and some others(?); but further reports mainly mention red colors in the sky.

It is clear from the above about the blue and green sun that this phenomenon moved from the E to the W after August 27, and it is obvious to attribute this unusual phenomenon to the the finest ash particles and water vapor ejected by Krakatau floating in the atmosphere.

During the last days of August, this phenomenon could not have been seen in Ceylon and the British Indies, because the "ash cloud" passed south of Ceylon and even south of the equator.

It should be noted, however, that between September 7 and 9, the green sun was not seen at places between Strong's Island and Ceylon, e.g., in Manila or Saigon. However, it has been reported on Iloilo [Philippines] that the sun had a greenish color, but the reported date is not September 8, but September

9 and 10.[221] In Elopura, on the north coast of Borneo, the sun was dull green during sunrise and sunset 14 (?) days after the eruption. This could also have been approximately on September 10.[221a] The phenomenon might have occurred 1 or 2 days earlier, but was just not noticed.

The date of the green sun on Laboean [1685 km NE of Krakatau] is not reliable (see below). I haven't heard any mention of a green sun in Saigon.

If we assume that these ash particles were carried over Africa and America to Ceylon, from the morning of August 27 to the evening of September 9, they must have travelled at a very high speed, more than 37 m/sec, or 134 km = 72 minute miles per hour, this being equal to the speed of the wind during a heavy storm.

It also appears to have been possible for some of the particles to have travelled to the east, because already very soon after the eruption the sunlight had been weakened and had an unusual appearance, on Bali, on Laboean and on some places in Japan.

The Resident of Bali reported that during the first days after the eruption (the exact date at which this phenomenon began is not mentioned; probably already on August 28 or 29) till September 2, the sun had been obscured somewhat in Boeleleng, so that one could look into the sun without hurting the eyes until 8 o'clock in the morning. It had a yellow glow. The Resident explains the phenomenon as the result of ash particles from Krakatau drifting in the air.[98]

A letter from Commander the Hon. Foley C.P. Vereker of HMS *Magpie*, dated Laboean Island, October 1, mentions that the sun when was low, had a greenish color for several days after the eruption. The exact date was not given.[222a] (Was this possibly on September 8 and following days?)

In Yokohama on August 30th, the sun appeared to diminish in strength just after noon and an even yellow-gray haze seemed to spread in the sky. Two hours before sunset the sun resembled a full moon surrounded by a weak halo. On the 31st, the sun rose behind a dense mass of clouds, and appeared only after 8 o'clock, having the same appearance as in the afternoon of the day before. Thin clouds resembling smoke were seen passing the sun at quite a distance from the surface of the earth. The same was observed on September 1st, only on the 2nd the obscuring haze moved away, probably in a northern direction. The phenomenon was attributed to smoke and ash ejected by Krakatau.[223] The ash particles then must have travelled the 3149-mile-long route from Krakatau to Yo-

kohama (measured along the earth's surface, therefore not counting the altitude of the particles) in 3 days, which agrees with a speed of 22.5 m/sec, or 81 km/hr.

Another report from Yokohama indicates that this phenomenon started 2 (?) days after the eruptions and continued for 2 days, after which the sun had become blood red.[224]

It is reported from Tokyo that the sun had a copper color during the last 2 or 3 days of August.[225]

The particles were carried to Japan by a SW wind, those travelling westward by an east wind, and those going to Australia by a NNW wind, while in the lowest air layers in the Strait of Sunda during the eruption, as we saw, NE and SE winds prevailed.

This dispersion of the ash particles in all directions is in complete agreement with the prevailing winds at various higher altitudes.

During the month of August the so-called East Monsoon, which is nothing but a regular SE *passat* [trade] wind, rules Java. The direction of the winds then is mostly SE and SSE, also pure E or even NE, and as we saw the heavier ash particles travelled with these winds to Bengkalis and Singapore to the NNW and to Keeling Eiland in a SW direction; according to the report from Cocos Island (see note 184) the wind direction there was NNE and NE during the time the ash fell, from Monday evening August 27 to the night of August 29–30.

As is well known, the winds in the upper atmosphere in Java always come from the east (SE, E, seldom NE), regardless whether the winds at low altitudes come from the W or E. One can assume 2000 m as the lowest limit for these winds, so that the smoke clouds, coming from the craters of the volcanoes, almost all of which are higher than 2000 m, always drift to the W. The strength of these eastern winds appears to increase with their height and they must have had a high velocity, for not only the transport of the ash particles, which fell on ships and in the sea west of Krakatau, but also the phenomenon of the blue and green sun are to be attributed to them. Earlier this velocity was given as 134 km/hr; however, a small portion should be attributed to the apparent speed of the ash to the W, because it trails the movement of the earth. At the time they left the crater, the ash particles possessed a speed equal to the rotating speed of the earth at the equator so that they travelled the speed $2\pi r$ in 24 hours, assuming that r is the radius of the earth. If the particles were ejected to a distance R from the center of the earth, then they must travel the distance $2\pi R$ in 24 hours in order not to lag behind the world. Because they retain their original speed, they lag behind in 24 hours $2\pi R - 2\pi r = 2\pi(R - r)$, which amounts to $2\pi \times {}^{50}/_{24} = {}^{314}/_{24} = 13$ km/hour at a height of 50 km. Of the 134 km, $134 - 13 = 121$ km can be attributed to the wind, if indeed the height of ash particles was 50 km, which is still considerable. Had the height of the ash particles been only 30 km, then they lag not more than 8 km/hr behind, so that the wind velocity must have been 126 km.

In the upper atmosphere of the northern hemisphere, SW winds prevail, and on the southern hemisphere, NW winds prevail as a result of the hot air rising from the equator and then moving to a certain altitude to the poles. The S and N winds, which should develop, become SW winds in the northern and NW winds in the southern hemisphere as a result of the earth's rotation. To these winds must be attributed the transport of the fine ash, which fell on the ship *Meda* near the Australian coast in the night of August 30–31, and also the transport of the even finer ash particles, which caused the ususual appearance of the sun on Bali, Laboean, and in Japan during the first days after the eruption.

Also the dispersion of the ash and vapor particles of the volcanic cloud, which at first went W very close to the equator to not more than 20°N, can probably be attributed by and large to these NW and SW anti-*passat* [anti-trade] winds. The phenomenon of the beautiful sunsets, which originally were only seen in places of minimal latitude, as a result were soon observed in numerous places at moderate latitudes, while a blue- or green-colored sun and moon only very rarely were seen after the end of September, which in my opinion undoubtedly must be attributed to the dispersion of the ash and water vapor particles.

Although, therefore, a very strong air current from the E to the W must be assumed at a certain elevation above the equator, an air current, which most likely only developed as a result of the eruption of Krakatau, because of the enormous quantity of highly heated material (ash and steam), which were suddenly injected into the high and cold air layers during the explosion of Monday morning at 10 o'clock—it does not seem in doubt to me that the green sun and the red skies should be attributed to Krakatau, not only because the phenomenon started only after August 27 and moved from E to W, but principally because it was observed in the British Indies and Ceylon not once, but twice, and the observed duration of both

trips around the earth yields the same velocity, if one assumes that August 27, 10 o'clock in the morning was the starting time.

From August 27, 10 o'clock in the morning to September 9, 6 o'clock in the evening (at which time the phenomenon had been clearly observed) thus in $13\frac{1}{3}$ days, our ash cloud travelled the route from Krakatau, via Trinidad, Fanning's Island, and Strong's Island, to Galle and Madras, a distance of approximately 23,000 miles [Verbeek uses nautical, or "minute," miles here and below]; we ignore here initially the elevation of the ash cloud above the earth. Hereafter the ash cloud travelled once around the earth, from 6 p.m. September 9 to 6 a.m. September 22, thus in 12 ½ days. We therefore find a speed of 23000/$13\frac{1}{3}$ = 1725 miles/day [3197 km/day] for the first revolution.

For the second revolution the cloud most likely did not follow a great circle—in which case we would have obtained a velocity of 21600/12½ = 1728 miles—but the parallel circle at 10°N (the average latitude between Galle and Madras), because the direction would have remained E-W, and the center of the cloud already was at 10°N of the equator on September 9. For the second revolution we find therefore a speed of: $(21600 \times \cos 10°)/12\frac{1}{2} = 21270/12\frac{1}{2} = 1702$ miles/day. On the 22nd the phenomenon could be observed only shortly after sunrise, but the ash cloud certainly could have arrived already on the night of September 21–22. Assuming, therefore, for example, not 6 o'clock, but 2 o'clock in the morning (at night), then our travel time changes from 12½ days to $12\frac{1}{3}$ days and the speed to 21270/$12\frac{1}{3}$ = 1725, the same as at the first revolution.

Considering the uncertainty of the number 12½, the obtained velocities for both revolutions agree remarkably well, and one therefore cannot doubt, in my opinion, that the time at which the ash cloud was formed can be set at August 27 and that the cloud must have come from Krakatau during the big eruption of 10 o'clock.

The data from Strong's Island, from the *Jennie Walker,* and from Fanning's Island (see above) enable us to check the derived speed of 1725 miles/day.

The distance from Strong's Island to Krakatau (in the W-E direction) amounts to 18100 miles; this distance was covered in: 18100/1725 = 10.49 days = 10 days, 12 hours. Add to: August 27, 10 a.m., Krakatau time; which gives then: September 6, 10 p.m., Krakatau time. Add time difference (3h 50m), or 4 hours which results in September 7, 2 a.m. local time.

According to the report, the phenomenon was observed "September 7."

The *Jennie Walker* location was at 155°28'W and 8°20'N. Distance to Krakatau (from W to E): 15600 miles. 15600/1725 = 9.04 days = 9 days and 1 hour. Add to: August 27, 10 a.m., Krakatau time; which gives: September 5, 11 a.m., Krakatau time. Subtract time difference (17h 14m) or 17½ hours which results in September 4, 5:30 p.m., local time. The green sun had been observed on board on September 4, 5 o'clock in the evening.

Fanning's Island is 15900 miles away from Krakatau (from W-E). 15900/1725 = 9.22 days = 9 days and 5 hours. Add to: August 27, 10 a.m., Krakatau time, which results in: September 5, 3 p.m., Krakatau time. Subtract time difference (17h 39m) or 17½ hours, so we obtain September 4, 9:30 p.m., local time. The cloud arrived here on September 4, late in the evening; the report does not mention a green sun, but only a copper-colored sun that day; nothing was said about the sun's appearance on the following day, September 5.

In places, further away from the equator, the phenomenon of the green sun did not appear, or it was very vague, while on the other hand the skies were beautifully red. In this light, the reports from the *Southard Hurlburt* at 17°N, from Maalaea on Maui, at 21°N and from Honolulu at 21°N, mention mainly the red skies; only one single report from Honolulu also mentions a green color of the sun.

West of America, the center of the ash cloud therefore seems to have travelled over the 8° or 10°N parallel so that, especially in places not too far from this latitude, the blue and green sun was observed; on the other hand the red skies were clearly seen in places with a more northern latitude, which were situated under the much thinner end of the cloud, where the ash particles were much smaller in number and the water vapor was more important.

The average speed of 1725 miles per day or 71.88 miles per hour is slightly lower than the actual speed, because the cloud did not travel along the surface of the earth, but high above it. At a height of 30 km, the speed changes to 72.21, at 50 km height to 72.44 miles per hour.

As is well known, the scientists in Europe do not yet agree on the explanation for the green sun and the red skies. Some assume that very fine ash particles from Krakatau are the reason, others that the red skies result from a high water vapor content in the air, still others that this high content of water vapor should be attributed to the eruption of Krakatau; some also consider "cosmic" dust as the cause of the red skies.

I already explained above that I consider the ejected materials of Krakatau the cause for the green sun and for the red skies; but because the "volcanic ash cloud" consisted of both ash particles and water vapor, I still have to explain what the contribution was of each of these to these two phenomena; because, as Prof. Michie Smith already rightly remarked, based on the different spectrum, one deals here with 2 different phenomena.

As far as the blue and green hues of sun and moon are concerned, which were observed mostly during the first month after the eruption and only in places which lie close to the equator, it appears reasonable to me that solid particles in the air play a major role here, on the basis of the following observations.

[On p. 191–201] and notes 34 and 34a we find the description of what was observed on board the *Elisabeth* on May 20 and 21, 1883 close to Sunda Strait. During the morning of the 21st, when ash still was falling, and the air everywhere was filled with ash and vapor, the sun was light blue.

The eruption of Cotopaxi [Ecuador] on July 3, 1880, was observed by Mr. Edward Whymper. He was at 16,000 feet above sea level on the west side of Chimborazo, at a distance of approximately 100 km from Cotopaxi. At 5:45 in the morning a big smoke column rose from the top, reaching a height of 20,000 feet in less than 1 minute. This estimate was made possible because only the highest 10,000 feet were visible of the 19,600-feet-high Cotopaxi, and the smoke rose to double its height. The top of the smoke column therefore was 40,000 feet above sea level. Here the ash was first carried by an easterly wind to the W, and then by a wind from the N toward the observer. When the ash came between the sun and the observer, the sun became very clearly *green*. The clouds looked green-gray, then blood-red or stone-red, finally copper-colored. At 1:30 a very fine ash started to fall on the peak of Chimborazo.[226]

Dr. Budde of Constantinople writes that the sun is sometimes blue when seen through fine dust in the Sahara.[226a]

Also in China the sun is sometimes a dull blue, because the atmosphere contains dust from the "loess" areas.[226b]

In the two first cases much water vapor was mixed in with the ejected ash; in the remaining cases it was mostly dry dust. These observations seem to indicate clearly that the solid dust particles are here the main cause for the special absorption of the light, so that the sun turned blue and green; the water vapor could have reinforced the phenomenon, for it is known that the sun can also take a blue hue because of fog.

That Mr. Lockyer saw a green sun because of vapor, coming from the chimney of a little steamship, cannot be taken as counter-evidence, because it is very likely that from that chimney also several ash and rust particles were released, and it is certainly possible that the sun was seen as green, because just then there were many dust particles present in the vapor. This vapor therefore was completely in the same condition as our volcanic cloud.

The red skies after sunset, which began very soon after the eruption, e.g., already on August 28 on Rodriguez, Mauritius, and the Seychelles,[124,228] and hereby already indicate a connection with the eruption, were also noticed in 1831 and 1863, shortly after the submarine eruptions between Pantellaria and the coast of Sicily in those years.[229–232] An exceptional appearance of the sun was also observed in 1783, after the big eruption of the volcano Skaptar Jökull [or Lakagígar] on Iceland.[232a]

I was not able to find reports, however, on red skies after the big eruption of Tambora in 1815; the *Javasche Courant* (newspaper) of that year, for example, was searched fruitlessly.

It occurs to me that in all these cases the water vapor, which was released by the volcanoes, played a more important role than the solid particles.

In the first place, it should be mentioned that the surface over which the red skies were seen simultaneously, for example at the end of November, was much larger than the narrow band in which the blue and green sun was successively observed. Only in the beginning, when the ash particles were not widely scattered, could they give green hues to the sun within a limited area. Soon this phenomenon stopped, the ash particles were spread over a much larger part of the world, namely in the northern hemisphere by SW winds and in the southern hemisphere by NW winds, and a portion probably slowly fell to earth. It is not really likely that the extremely thin layer of ash which resulted, could have caused by itself the unusual light effects. Dr. J. Hann calculated that a quantity of fine ash of 6.4 km^3, divided equally over the entire atmosphere, would only supply a layer of 0.01 mm thickness; divided over the warm and temperate latitudes, the layer would be 0.03 mm, and when spread over the temperate latitudes only 0.05 mm thick.[233] Because the ejected material near the volcano does not amount to more than 18 km^3, and already in the first 3 days after the eruption a considerable amount of ash fell westward in the sea from the dust cloud which reached the higher atmosphere, it seems to me that even 1 km^3 is far too much for the amount that remained in the upper atmosphere. This amount agrees with a layer of 0.002 mm thickness divided over the entire surface of the earth, or of 0.01 mm over the temperate zone alone.

Therefore, it is not likely that this extremely thin layer of dust was the main cause of the unusual light effects, for which we therefore should turn to the huge masses of water vapor which were released by Krakatau, a quantity that is impossible to calculate, unfortunately. This water vapor, which formed by far the largest part of our "volcanic cloud," caused the exceptionally beautiful sunsets, after it condensed and froze in the higher and colder upper atmosphere. The role which was played by the ash particles in this was two-fold: first, they could have reinforced the phenomenon; second, the ash particles served as centers of condensation for the vapor. The actual cause of the red skies, therefore, was probably the same as that of normal sunset glow, and the exceptional intensity only the result of the unusually large amount of vapor in the higher atmosphere, ejected by Krakatau.[233a]

Also small salt crystals, as some have suggested, could have been mixed with the ice crystals, being derived from sea water that reached the volcanic hearth, partly through infiltration, partly by entering from the top, and ejected together with the lava. Nevertheless, the content of salt in the volcanic vapor and ash cloud must have been insignificant, so that for our explanation of the red skies the salt crystals can be excluded.

Several reports seem to indicate that some time after the eruption in the atmosphere dust was present, which slowly fell on earth.

On November 17, snow in a valley in central Norway, the Storelfdal, was covered by a gray and black dust.[234] On the same date, rain with dust fell in the vicinity of Worcester [U.S.].[235,236]

On November 29, a white ash (?) fell (matter having a white sulphurous appearance) in Glen Grey at Queenstown, South Africa.[237]

On December 12, rain fell in Highfield, Gainsborough [England], leaving a gray sediment; also on the 22nd of December in York.[238]

On December 7, snow fell in Madrid, which was analyzed microscopically by Joseph MacPherson. Aside from mineral particles which could have come from the Madrid area itself, he also found brown rhombic pyroxene, one of the components of the Krakatau ash.[239]

Messrs. Beijerinck and van Dam in Wageningen [Netherlands] investigated the gray deposit that rain left behind on the window sills on the morning of December 13. They think that they saw in it the same components as in the ash from Krakatau. When I requested samples of this ash, Messrs. Beijerinck and van Dam answered that they did not save any samples.

The same gentlemen also analyzed the sediment of rain of January 11, 1884; the crystals partly dissolved in water (salt), partly not.[240]

In the night of December 18–19, snow with a black dust fell in Sauerland, between Agger and Lenne, in Gimborn, Ludenscheid and vicinity [Germany].[241]

It seems highly questionable to me that these particles can be attributed to Krakatau. All kinds of dust particles are usually present in the atmosphere, and the salt crystals as shown by Beijerinck, and the so-called "andesitous mineral," probably feldspar, cannot be evidence that they originate from Krakatau.

The rhombic pyroxene which Mr. MacPherson found proves a little more, although in more recent research this mineral has also been found in very many Tertiary eruptive rocks, and in no way belongs to the rare group of minerals; but it is remarkable that the lightest particles, porous glass fragments (pumice), were not found in significant quantities, or even in such significant quantities as the pyroxene, because one would expect that ash particles, which fell so far from Krakatau would consist almost completely of microscopic pumice particles. Because this was nowhere the case, I am of the opinion that the finest particles from Krakatau, which were at the highest altitudes, were slowly spread out over such a large area that they escaped observation after having fallen to earth. The quantity also cannot have been large, and the dust particles found in rain and snow probably must have had a different origin.

Finally, it must be recognized that the particles in suspension in the atmosphere, even when they are volcanic in nature, and also the light effects in the sky after October 6, should not be attributed solely to Krakatau, because on that date an important eruption of the mountain Augustine in Alaska occurred, during which pumice, ash and vapor were ejected.

Also, a point in the proximity of Bogoslof Island (Aleutians) was active, creating a new island. The ash which fell on Unalaska (Alaska) on October 20th came probably from this volcano. Also ash appeared to have fallen on October 13 in Sapporo on Jeso, the northernmost island of Japan; the large distance to Bogoslof, 2050 minute miles, however, makes it doubtful that this ash can be attributed to that volcano. All the same, I have no reports on any activity of volcanoes in Japan itself for the month of October.[242,243,243a] [Tarumai, 40 km S of Sapporo, erupted in the autumn of 1883, with ashfalls reported in October and November.]

Geology of Krakatau

It was already mentioned in a few words [on p. 191] that after the large collapse of 1883 only a part of Krakatau, the older rim, was left, while the younger central portion completely disappeared with the exception of a very small island, which on our map is called "rots," and on the new Dutch sea chart of Sunda Strait "Bootsmansrots".

Because the central portion was visited only very briefly in 1880 and only a few rock samples were collected, our knowledge of the geology of this younger part of the volcano is of course very limited. Still, the remaining parts provide sufficient data to deduce the main aspects of the history of the volcano Krakatau.

Partly on the basis of the relative position of the rock units and partly on the basis of the differences in composition, we can divide the products of this volcano into three groups which were formed during successive periods. Each period represents a phase of activity during which a series of eruptions occurred from one main crater, and during which the petrographic character of the ejected material remained constant; within such a period, of course, the eruptions could be and would be separated by small and even by large time intervals.

The rocks of Krakatau form only two petrographic groups: a pyroxene andesite with about 68% SiO_2 and a basalt with only 48% SiO_2. The acid products were always ejected from a central crater, while the basic products erupted from satellite or excentric craters.

Because the basalt, as far as age is concerned, lies between two pyroxene andesites, we achieve a differentiation of our three groups mentioned above:

a. First: an oldest andesite eruptive period.

b. Second: a basalt eruptive period.

c. Third: a younger andesite eruptive period.

The last group includes also the two known eruptions of the volcano, namely the one of 1680 and the one of 1883. Because the last eruption is of such

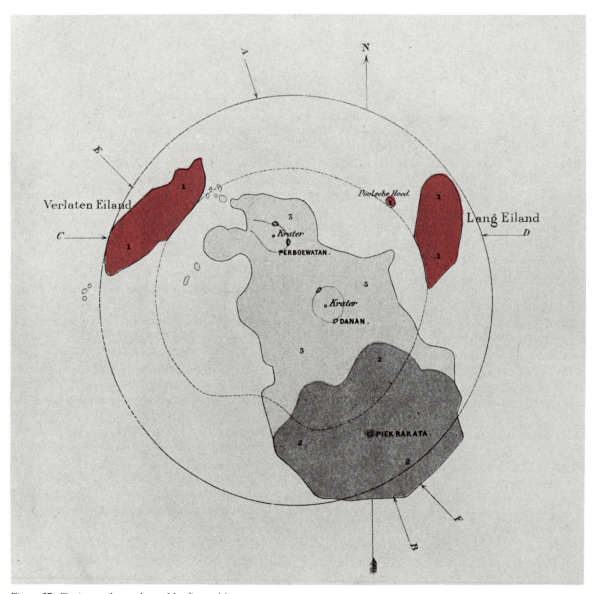

Figure 57. Tertiary rocks are denoted by diagonal lines, and very recent sediments (Quaternary and modern) by closely spaced horizontal lines; (1) old hypersthene andesite with tridymite crystals; (2) basalt; (3) very young hypersthene andesite; (4) 1883 products (hypersthene andesite pumice and ash). The + pattern indicates lava within the volcanic conduit and the crater, and "zee" is the sea. (Verbeek's figures 42, 43, 34, 35, 36, and 37, respectively.)

Figure 57a. Geological map of Krakatau before the 1883 eruption. Two concentric dashed lines indicate the portion of the oldest cone which remained after a huge collapse. Diameter of the largest circle is 10.7 km.

geological importance, and the products formed at that time could be analyzed much more accurately than those of earlier eruptions, it is preferred to described this eruption and its products separately. We, therefore, distinguish this one from the third group's, as:

d. A youngest andesite eruption of 1883.

a. First Period

The activity of our volcano began with the eruption of hypersthene andesite lava flows, along a point of the already described fracture [see p. 225]. Slowly a

large cone was built up, which finally became much higher above sea level than the highest point of the present island.

Of that oldest cone only a few parts are still there; because of a huge collapse, the central portion, which must have been at least 2000 m high following a conservative calculation, disappeared to the depths. A more or less circular rim of eruption products—the foot of the volcano—remained, the latter I schematically indicated on the map of Figure 57a by two concentric dotted lines, because the number of earlier made depth measurements is not sufficient to follow accurately the course of the collapse at the inner rim.

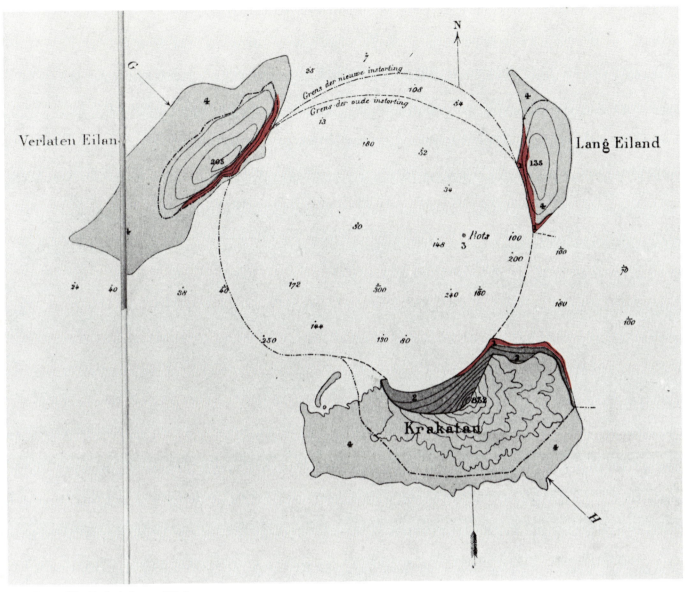

Figure 57b. Geological map of Krakatau after the 1883 eruption. Same scale as Figure 57a, depths in meters. The dash-dot-dash line is the limit of recent collapse and the dashed line the limit of old collapse. Note: In the portion of Verlaten Island colored red, the number 1 was omitted.

On the profiles Figures 57*c* to *e* the perimeter of the old volcano is indicated with a dotted line; the crater must have been about at the center of the circle shown on the map (Figure 57*a*), that is almost, if not exactly, at the place where later the volcano Danan was located.

The rim of eruption products that remained after the collapse did not form a continuous wall above the water line, but several parts formed islands. Before 1883 only three parts of the rim could be seen above the water—Verlaten, Lang, and Poolsche Hoed; after the collapse of 1883, a fourth part of the rim became visible, namely as the foot of the peak Rakata on the

NE and E part of the present island. The upper parts of the peak cover the underlying older rocks in a different direction and slope, thus discordantly. (See the map Figure 57*b*, and Plate 8). Finally, a very shallow place with a depth of only 7 m was found between Verlaten and Lang in August 1884 (see map, Figure 57*b*), indicating that here also the old rim is present close to sea level.

After the first collapse the volcano looked almost the same as nowadays (Figure 57*b*), but without the rocks of the peak, and with Poolsche Hoed.

In favor of the collapse are: the steep talus slopes on the inner sides of Lang and Verlaten; the gentle

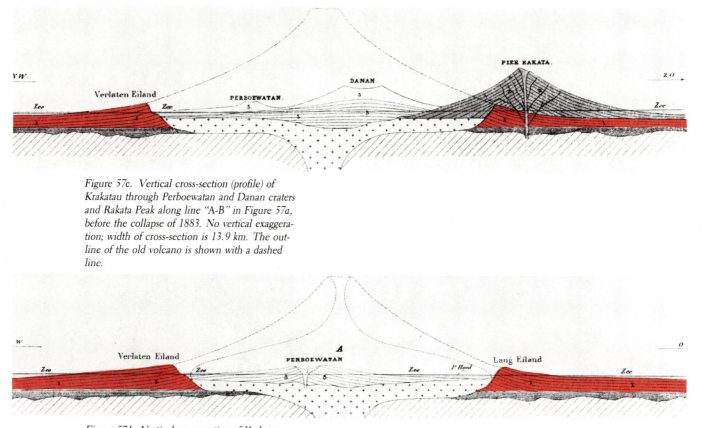

Figure 57c. Vertical cross-section (profile) of Krakatau through Perboewatan and Danan craters and Rakata Peak along line "A-B" in Figure 57a, before the collapse of 1883. No vertical exaggeration; width of cross-section is 13.9 km. The outline of the old volcano is shown with a dashed line.

Figure 57d. Vertical cross-section of Krakatau through Verlaten and Lang Islands from west to east along line "C-D" in Figure 57a, before the collapse of 1883. No vertical exaggeration; width of cross-section is 14.0 km. The outline of the old volcano is indicated with a dashed line.

outward slope of the lava flows; and especially the curious petrographic character of those oldest parts, as will be shown below.

The circular space, formed by this collapse, has a diameter of approximately 7 km, thus being one of the largest collapsed craters of the world [known in 1883].

The crater of Tengger on E Java, which is still considered to be the largest of the world, was formed in the same way as the collapsed craters of Krakatau and of Santorini in the Greek Archipelago. If one wants to call the almost completely horizontal plane at the top of Tengger simply a "crater," then the space encircled by islands at Krakatau and Santorini must be named similarly, and then the crater of Tengger is certainly not the largest in the world.

The dimensions of the old collapsed craters are:

	Dimensions	Shape
Krakatau	7 km diam.	Almost circular
Tengger	8 km (N–S) and (E–W)	Square, the dimension of 8 km is the diagonal of the square[243b]
Santorini	6.5 km (E–W) 10 km (N–S)	Elongated (irregular elliptical)
Peak of Tenerife	7.5 km (N–S) 10 km (E–W)	Oval

All these sizes are far exceeded by the collapsed crater of the Manindjoe volcano in the Padang Highlands on Sumatra, which has an irregular elliptical shape with a 23 km long axis (N–S) and an average

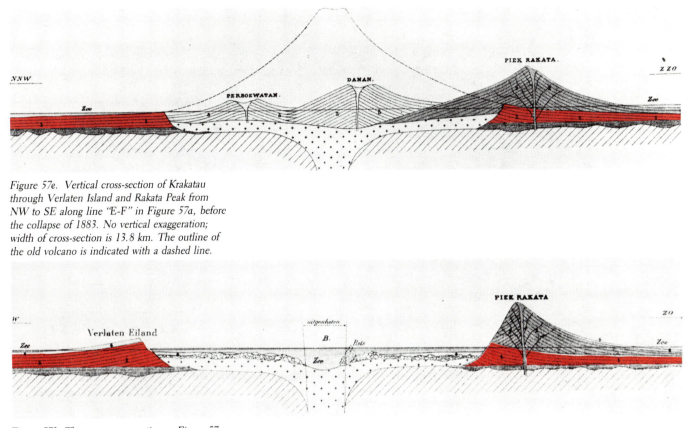

Figure 57e. Vertical cross-section of Krakatau through Verlaten Island and Rakata Peak from NW to SE along line "E-F" in Figure 57a, before the collapse of 1883. No vertical exaggeration; width of cross-section is 13.8 km. The outline of the old volcano is indicated with a dashed line.

Figure 57f. The same cross-section as Figure 57e, after the collapse of 1883, along the line "G-H" in Figure 57b. No vertical exaggeration; the width of the cross-section is 14.0 km. The 1883 vent ("uitgeschoten") literally "ejected region" is bound by two dashed lines.

11 km short axis (W–E). The area enclosed by the rim is about 200 km². Inside the ring lies Lake Maninjoe, which is 16,600 m long (N–S) and with an average width (W–E) of 6,000 m, and a surface area of nearly 100 km².[243c]

This is, among all carefully surveyed volcanoes, the largest collapsed crater; the one of Lake Toba in the northern part of the residence of Tapanoeli on Sumatra is probably even larger, but until now only the southern rim has been surveyed [dimensions ~30 × 100 km].

Rocks of the First Eruptions of the First Period

The main mass of the old rim is composed of a series of banks of massive gray to a weathered brown-gray hypersthene andesite on top of each other, without interlayering of loose material. The rock has a largely dull so-called stonelike groundmass, only at the west side of Lang did I find in 1880 a few dark glassy rocks, thinly layered, which appeared to alter-nate with the much thicker stony andesites. Poolsche Hoed was completely composed of this pretty dark green glass, while it was found neither on Verlaten nor at the foot of the Peak Rakata, so that it is present in only a small quantity, and probably only formed during a very small eruption.

The layers of lava which can be observed on the inner side of Verlaten and Lang in bare steep walls at elevations of 50, 80, and even 100 m, show only very little variation from top to bottom. Because of this monotonous petrographic character, and the lack of intermediate positioned weathered layers (which would indicate an old, vegetated, and weathered surface), they give the impression of one unit, and formed by a sequence of eruptions which were not separated by long time intervals. They form layers of several meters thick, but contain also a large number of joints which are parallel to the layers and which divide the lava in relatively thin plates of 1 cm or less, which is very characteristic of this lava. These joints are not the boundaries of individual lava flows, but apparently were caused by cooling and contraction of the rock; they have a weakly undulated surface, often branch out, and occasionally even intersect feldspar crystals, so that one can observe under the microscope thin platelets which are cut perpendicular to the joints. The joints themselves are colored brick-red due to a thin alteration crust, and furthermore filled with beautiful tridymite platelets which are clear as water, so that the surface of the lava plates sparkle as if covered with frost. These deposits of tridymite on the joints of the rock are found mainly on Verlaten; on Lang the thin-plated lava contains numerous cavities [vesicles], just as at the foot of Rakata, and these cavities are almost without exception completely lined with the most beautiful highly sparkling tridymite platelets; most crystals are clear as water; in some cavities they are colored brown-red by a later infiltrated iron oxyhydrate. The occurrence of this mineral in our Archipelago was found the first time macroscopically in the cavities on Lang (mentioned already in 1880 in my description of south Sumatra[244]). Tridymite is almost completely confined to the cavities and the joint planes, and represents only a small part of the composition of the rock. The old hypersthene andesite is often very rich in tridymite, only a few dense lava banks of Verlaten are slightly poorer in this mineral. While also in some younger rocks of the volcano tridymite crystals were encountered, the content of that mineral here is always very minor, and the abundant occurrence of tridymite can be considered a good characteristic property of the oldest hypersthene andesite. Therefore, we will henceforth call this rock the "tridymite rock," in order to differentiate it from the younger andesites.

Rocks of the Last Eruptions of the First Period

On top of the upper compact lava flows of the tridymite rock on the NE and E side of Krakatau, lies a 2–3 m thick layer of fine ejecta—weathered ash and sand including fist-size lapilli—having the same direction and slope of the underlying lava layers, but discordant to the layers of basalt material which cover it, and which form the largest part of the island Krakatau.

The lapilli, which thus were ejected from the same point as the old lava flows, are also hypersthene andesite. The boundary with the underlying solid lava layers can be seen already at some distance because of the lighter brown color of the most upper layers of these lava plates, which contrast with the yellow and brown-yellow lapilli layers, while these in turn contrast with the younger layers by the browner hue of the basalt ejecta.

Thus, at the termination of our first period the occurrence of lava flows is replaced by the ejection of loose material, but it will remain uncertain whether these two phases of activity followed each other soon, or whether these were separated by a longer period of time. It is not completely impossible that the large collapse occurred between the two phases, and thus that the lapilli layers were formed only after the collapse.

b. Second Period

After the old Krakatau had collapsed, and only the currently existing crater wall was left, and likewise after the above-mentioned layers of lapilli were formed (for these could have been younger than the collapse), a renewed eruption took place at the southern end of the volcano, outside the ring of the oldest products which completely covered the most southern of the four islands mentioned above. These younger products originated from a side eruption, or a so-called flank eruption of the volcano; they are both chemically and petrographically very different from the other rocks of Krakatau, contain olivine which is visible to the naked eye, and belong to the basalts; thus, they are a much more basic rock than our andesite lava. From these rocks the peak Rakata was successively built up to an altitude of 832 m, the highest point of the Krakatau group as we have known it.

During the collapse of 1883 this mountain was cut through almost perpendicularly, so that the internal structure of this basalt volcano is eminently visible (Plate 8) [see also the 1886 photograph, p. 143]. When looking at the steep wall from the north, one sees at the bottom, on the left (E) side, the old massive banks of the tridymite rock, and the lapilli layers lying on top of these, but appearing discordant under the basalt layers.

The entire volcano is further built up to the top by a system of concordant layers of basalt ash and lapilli, alternating with basalt flows, and intersected by numerous dikes. All layers lead downward to the left and the right from any point below the top; the slope diminishes with distance away from the top—the center of the mountain. The cross-section is symmetric with regard to a line going from the top straight down, which indicates that the crater must have been in a vertical plane passing through the top of the mountain. A crater pipe, however, is not visible, as can be suspected from Plate 8, showing the steep wall as it looked in October 1883. In the center, below the top, was a lot of dark-gray, wet ash, produced by the most recent eruption, which had oozed downward. Also nearby was a yellow sulphur stain, on which basis it was thought that a small pipe could be seen, but this was soon after found to be incorrect.

When I visited Krakatau again in August 1884, recent erosion had removed the ash coating, and both the bedding and the dikes were much more visible than earlier. Just below the top one can now see a wide dike, which cuts the basalt layers almost vertically from sea level to ⅔ of the height of the mountain where it terminates in a much thicker lens-shaped body. The width of this dike, composed of hypersthene andesite, is about 2 m at the bottom and 1 m at the top.

Between this dike and Zwarte Hoek (Black Corner)—the westernmost tip of the island (see Figure 47)—several small dikes can be seen, all of basaltic composition, between ⅓ and ¼ m thick, with a usually steep-to-vertical orientation, but a few with more gentle slopes which cut the basalt layers sometimes at considerable elevations. No dikes were found in the tridymite rock lying below; however, fragments of this rock were found in basalt.

Special attention was given to determine the location of the summit crater, but I was not completely successful in this. The crater was not cut through by the collapse, but whether it lies south of the wall, or lay north of the wall (and collapsed) is not clear from the position of the layers. In the first case, the layers which are exposed in the steep wall must slope to the N, and in the second case to the S; thus, when seen by an observer who is located to the N of the wall, they must descend toward him in the first instance and away from him in the second. However, only the ends of the layers are exposed, and from that, of course, one cannot see a slope.

Also the fault face at the eastern side does not provide conclusive information, because it intersects only the base of the volcano. Had this fault been more to the W, near or through the crater, (in other words, had not a half but only a quarter of the Peak remained), then of course the problem would have been solved.

So there was nothing else to do but to look for a crater opening at the top. There exists at the backside of the mountain, a little below the top, a small depression which indeed may indicate the location of the crater vent; but in October 1883 the ash cover was too thick to establish this with certainty. Furthermore, the crater mouth of a non-active volcano, which at the top is composed of loose material, is not rarely completely filled with ash and lapilli by slumping and down-washing from the crater walls, making the opening difficult to find. I hope to visit this place again sometime in the future.

In the profiles, Figures 57c, d, and e the crater is still assumed to be present. This is also the most reasonable supposition, because the basalt differs strongly in composition from a hypersthene andesite, and it is therefore not likely that the crater of the Peak terminated in the large lava chamber, which appears to have contained always a rather acid magma. From what is shown on the profiles, one can imagine that the crater is connected with a separate lava chamber which contained a more basic magma.

Regardless, the cross-section on the basis of the layers shows clearly that the collapse occurred close to the crater, and therefore almost exposed the center. We hereby can establish the geologically important fact that at this volcano neither a large hollow chamber nor an extensive solid core exists [within 800 m of its summit].

The Peak once formed a steep cone without a collapsed rim. Because the cause of collapse is the melting of the inner walls of the volcano, it appears to me not unlikely that only at volcanoes with a central collapse has substantial melting occurred of the inner parts of the volcano, while for volcanoes which retain a regular cone shape, such melting either does not occur or occurs only to a small extent.

It will be difficult to ascertain whether this rule is generally valid, because such highly instructive cross-sections as the one of Krakatau certainly will remain extremely rare.

The basalt flows which occur between the layers of loose basaltic material are often lens-shaped and are locally irregularly swollen as the result of periods of blockage of the liquid matter. The flows usually have, both at the top and at the bottom, brick-red crusts, caused by the escaping dissolved gases. The central part of the flows are compact and fresh. Their thickness varies, not including the swollen portions, between ⅓ and ½ m; that of the layers of lapilli between ¼ and 2 m.

Finally, as far as the material is concerned, the flows as well as the lapilli and dikes appear to be the same type of feldspar basalt. Only in one of the dikes accessory melilite occurs, a mineral that all the numerous other samples lack.

c. Third Period

The basic basalt eruptions again were replaced by those of a more acidic composition material, namely hypersthene andesite. These renewed eruptions actually occurred at the center of the volcano, between the islands. During these, the mountains Danan and Perboewatan were built successively; probably at first they formed one or two islands, which finally united with the peak Rakata to form one island. The craters of Danan and Perboewatan and possibly also those of other eruption centers nearby can be considered as chimneys of one and the same large central lava chamber, so that the products of this period, even when coming from different craters, are all derived from the same main crater [magma chamber]. Danan attained a height of approximately 450 m, Perboewatan approximately 120; the crater of the latter lay much lower on a horseshoe-shaped floor, 50 to 60 m above sea level.

The boundary of the basalt with the younger rocks from Danan is shown schematically on the geologic map, Figure 57a. A survey of that boundary was not made before.

Of the period in which all the parts of the volcano mentioned thus far were formed, we know hardly anything; everything happened in pre-historic time, although we should not forget that here in the Indies, the so-called pre-historic period occurred more recently than in Europe, for we have only a few credible reports on events in the Archipelago that are older than 300 years.

From Vogel's reports (see note 1 [and p. 284]) we only know that Perboewatan had erupted during May 1680; but whether that crater already existed before or was active for the first time is not certain.

Our volcano was composed then out of an older rim and a younger central part—just as Tengger with Bromo in E Java, Monte Somma with Vesuvius [Italy], the island Thera, Therasia and Aspronisi with Kaimenen of the Santorini group [Greece], and a number of other volcanoes.

On the rocks of which the cones Danan and Perboewatan were composed, we have only very few data. During the month of July 1880, I collected samples only from the lava flow on the N side of Perboewatan, which leads to the sea. This flow was not weathered at all, and therefore had no plant life, the only barren spot on heavily vegetated Krakatau, which indicates the relative youth of that lava, and suggests that it was formed during the 1680 eruption.

This lava is, like the rock of the old crater rim, a hypersthene andesite, but differs from it by the absence of macroscopic tridymite. The upper part of the flow was very porous, the remainder compact, glass-rich, and dark in color. Other samples, however, are light-gray with a stone-like groundmass.

Also Bootsmansrots, now the only remaining part of Danan, consists of a layered stone-like hypersthene andesite, also without crystals of tridymite. The layers of lava all have a steep slope, 60°–70° to the west; and since they were not deposited at such a steep slope it is clear that this rock, a fragment from Danan sticking out of the sea, is not in its original position.

Furthermore, the earlier-mentioned hypersthene andesite dike of 2 m width, which cuts the basalt layers vertically near the top of Rakata, should be considered to belong to this period. The rock is dark-gray in color and has numerous cavities in which gypsum crystals are formed. Probably Danan, just as Perboewatan, consisted of alternating layers of solid and loose andesite material, cut by numerous radial dikes of the same rock. One of these dikes appears to have gone beyond the Danan mountain to the adjoining Rakata cone, and is exposed now by the most recent collapse. In addition to the gypsum crystals, some crystals of tridymite could be seen with a magnifying glass, the only known occurrence of this mineral in the younger rocks from Krakatau.

Furthermore, I assign to this period the fragments of the olivine-bearing, hypersthene andesite collected in May 1883 at the foot of the then-active Perboewatan, by the mining engineer Schuurman.

This remarkable rock, of which nowhere else a trace was found, certainly does not belong to the material of the May eruption, because the products of 1883 do not contain olivine and are also much more glass-rich. It is, therefore, probably a fragment from the Perboewatan substructure, ejected at the same time.

Finally a few fragments of hypersthene andesite were found among the 1883 ejecta which resemble neither the rocks of the old crater rim nor the products of 1883, and thus must belong to this third period. Some pieces have cavities containing beautiful dolomite crystals.

As is seen, all that is left us of the rocks of the third period are a few fragments, completely insufficient to compose, even for a general outline, a history of the consecutive eruptions.

The common feature of the rocks of this period is that they all consist of hypersthene-andesite; still they show not insignificant variation, so that we may conclude with confidence that they are the products of very different eruptions from different locations in the central part.

d. The Eruption of 1883

After the eruption of 1680, the volcano was dormant for 203 years, until May 20, 1883, when Perboewatan became active. In June, Danan became active too, and probably soon after it formed the main crater, located at the center of the old volcano, probably almost exactly on the same place as the earlier crater. The most intense activity occurred on August 27th, late in the morning; the entire central part of the volcano collapsed. The rim, being composed of solid layers of lava (Lang and Verlaten) and also the part of the peak that rested on the old andesite layers (see the profiles, Figures 57e and f) remained. The northern half of the peak, however, which was not supported by the old crater rim, but by the upper part of the old lava in the lava chanber (weakened by heat and partial melting), disappeared in the depths.

From the measurements of the depth of the sea, while unfortunately few in number, it can be seen that the recent collapse must have approximately the same outline as the old almost-circular one. I have indicated both on the map, Figure 57b. The collapse of 1883 is thus only a repeat of the old pre-historic collapse. Here and there a part of the old rim broke off as well; Poolsche Hoed became a victim of such collapse.

On the late morning of August 28 the eruption of 1883 can be considered terminated, even though another small submarine eruption occurred during September or October at an unknown date. The solid matter ejected during the eruption of 1883 again consists of hypersthene andesite as glassy rocks, pumice, and ash, the latter two in much greater quantity than the glasses. Lava flows did not occur. Everything was either as large or small fragments, even very fine powder, thrown exposively out of the crater.

These newest products of Krakatau strongly resemble the older hypersthene andesite mineralogically, but are generally much more glassy.

So we see that the large central crater always produced hypersthene andesites, while the basalt only appeared from a side crater. Thus, while by chance the basalt peak has the name Rakata, the actual volcano Krakatau is a real hypersthene andesite mountain, from the oldest to the youngest products. Because the basalt eruption occurred very close to our volcano, the basalt mountain forms together with Krakatau one topographical unit, and therefore they must be considered together.

Had the basalt appeared a little farther to the S, then we would have had two volcanoes, one built from hypersthene andesite, the other from basalt; the same combination of acid and basic rock we also find on other nearby islands of Sunda Strait, without any regularity in the occurrence of these different rocks.

It possibly could be thought that the basalt appeared only along the cross fault of Sunda and the hypersthene andesite only along the length of Java and Sumatra (see Figure 54), or possibly the reverse. This is absolutely not the case. Along all the eruption belts, centers of both acid and basic material are found; furthermore, several islands are distributed in such a way that they cannot be related to the three fracture directions. The occurrence of these two rocks thus is not related to certain directions.

Whether the basalt, found everywhere in Sunda Strait, was formed in the same period in between the two andesite eruptions, as on Krakatau, is not certain, because the rocks have not been observed in direct contact at the other locations.

We can, therefore, distinguish in the history of our volcano the following important periods, or consecutive events:

1. Formation of the volcano at a point along the Sunda fault. Eruption of hypersthene andesite lava.

2. Collapse of the central part of this volcano which was at least 2000 m high. The remainder forms a circular-shaped crater [caldera] wall of which 4 pieces emerge above sea level.

3. Formation of Rakata Peak as the result of a basalt eruption at the side. It is built up by a sequence of loose material alternating with lava flows.

4. Formation of the craters Danan and Perboewatan at the center of the main crater. They are built of alternating layers of loose and solid hypersthene andesite.

5. Eruption of Perboewatan during May 1680. Fragments of pumice are ejected; possibly lava flows of hypersthene andesite were also formed.

6. Eruption of May 20 till August 28, 1883. Hypersthene andesite is thrown out, largely as ash and pumice with a small part as glassy rocks in loose large fragments.

7. Collapse of the central part of the volcano in the late morning of August 27, 1883.

It can be expected that with a renewed activity of the volcano, in the center of the sea bordered by Rakata Peak, Verlaten, and Lang, islands will appear, just as the Kaimeni of the Santorini-group, and just as in earlier days the craters Danan and Perboewatan were formed in the sea surrounded by the old crater wall.

Regional Geology

Krakatau ejected in 1883 several fragments which did not come from the volcano but from the older rocks on which it was built.

In order to derive the age of these partly volcanic, partly sedimentary fragments, I would like to discuss briefly what is known nowadays about the geology of the western part of our Archipelago, with emphasis on Sunda Strait.[245]

On a basement of strongly folded Paleozoic sediments intruded by igneous rocks, mainly granites and diabase, lies directly the Tertiary, with the Mesozoic rocks absent. Only in the east of our archipelago some Cretaceous rocks occur.[245a]

The Tertiary sediments can be divided into two groups, a pre-andesitic, in which no andesitic material can be found and which contain among others a quartz sandstone with coal beds, and a post-andesitic, which is mainly composed of andesite material. The first is probably Eocene, the latter Miocene in age. Both groups of the usually folded Tertiary rocks are separated from each other by extensive outpourings of massive, partly pyroxene, partly hornblende andesites, while also later in the Miocene of W Java extrusions of a quartz andesite occurred.

On the Miocene (partly perhaps also Pliocene) rocks the volcanoes sit; they already began to become active in diluvial times, and continued to be so until today. Because of their cone shape and especially because of their structure, most are real strato-volcanoes, sharply different from the homogeneous Early Miocene andesite massifs. Several islands in the Strait, and some rows of hills along the coasts, do not show the characteristic cone shape, but probably they too consist of younger (Quaternary) rocks considering the very fresh and young volcanic appearance of the rocks. Most islands were visited only briefly, and it is not improbable that by a careful geologic study a crater or at least an old volcano shape could be found, which through partial collapse lost its cone shape. It is also possible that some never had a cone shape, because the material did not extrude from a single point but from a shorter or longer fissure.

During diluvial and Recent times, sediments were deposited in Sunda Strait which are composed of volcanic ejecta. Microscopically they can be distinguished from Tertiary rocks because they contain porous glass fragments (pumice) which are absent in older rocks.

It was already mentioned casually that the islands and coastal areas of Sunda Strait are not yet geologically mapped in detail, for which several months should be needed; in general we can obtain an idea of the geology on the basis of samples which were collected from numerous locations most of which were studied microscopically.

The sedimentary rocks found are:

Shales near Tarahan, on the east coast of Lampong Bay [18 km SE of Teloeq Betoeng]; also on 3 of the Zutphens Eilanden near Varkenshoek, these are Kadang, Hoog Eiland, and Klein Eiland. The strike of the layers is 145°, dipping SW. They are brown and gray quartz-rich shales without concretions. Formerly these were thought to be Paleozoic. Recently, on Java, Miocene shales were found, so that possibly the ones from Sunda Strait are also Tertiary in age.

Very quartz-rich white rocks are found in the area of Teloeq Betoeng (Apenberg) and near Tandjoeng Karang, to the N; they are usually poorly layered. The same rock is found on the island of Brabandshoedje [Brabant's Hat], off of Anjer, strike 135°, dip approximately 60° NE. Microscopically they show a cloudy groundmass with poor mosaic polarization and some spherulites. It is similar to the groundmass of some Miocene quartz andesites, especially when weathered. These rocks are probably quartz andesite tuffs of Miocene age.

Tertiary marls, mudstones and sandstones, probably Miocene in age, are found on Meeuwen Eiland, the large island in Meeuwen Baii, near Java's First Point.

Diluvial sediments, mainly white and light-colored pumice tuffs, are found over an extensive area in the central parts of the Residency of Bantam and on the E coast of Sumatra near Ketapan, E of Radja Bassa.

The eruptive rocks are:

Old Miocene andesites. These occur in a long ridge, called Boekiet Sawah, on the west coast of Semangka Bay. The pyroxene, usually strongly pleochroic with red brown and green colors, is generally rhombic, the rock is a hypersthene andesite.

On the N coast of Taboean, the large island near

the south end of Semangka Bay, a rock very similar to that of Apenberg near Padang (Sumatra's Westkust) occurs in banks. It also occurs at numerous other localities of the long andesite belt, which terminates at Boekiet Sawah mentioned above. It is similar to an old diabase, because of a high chlorite content, and lesser epidote; even dark spots around iron ore (leucoxene?) can be seen, as in some rocks from Apenberg, an alteration product which is not usually found in Tertiary rocks. The pyroxene is monoclinic augite. If these rocks are Early Tertiary, thus augite andesites (which is not certain), then it seems that leucoxene occurs also in the oldest Tertiary extrusive rocks of the Archipelago.

Even in the Miocene quartz andesites of the W parts of the Residency of Preanger-Regentschappen, one can find in very weathered rocks dull spots around ore crystals which I think are leucoxene.

Younger Tertiary andesites. The Monnikrotsen (Monk rocks) and the main rock on which the lighthouse on Java's First Point is built are composed of a dark quartz porphyry-like andesite with a dense groundmass; the rock is a quartz andesite or dacite which occurs especially in the W of Preanger and is interlayered with Miocene beds, indicating that they are Miocene.

In the rocks of the Monnikrotsen, quartz occurs only very sparingly among the large crystals. On the E side of the Monnikrotsen [see Figure 51] a very nice perlite occurs, which I already described in the "Nieuwe geologisch ontdekking op Java." The green to red pleochroic "augites" are again "hypersthenes." The rock is a hypersthene andesite perlite.

The exposure is not good enough to see whether the perlite occurs as a dike in the dacite or whether it is just a glassy part of it. Several samples of the glass-rich rock contains spherulites; the perlitic fractures occur also in this rock.

Basalt (Quaternary and younger). This rock occurs in flows near the hot spring at the foot of Tangkamoes (or Emperors Peak) which rises as a cone to 2280 m near the N end of Semangka Bay. The top of the mountain has not yet been visited.

On the island of Lagoendi I found basalt among the pebbles in a river which ends in the beautiful Patappan Bay, at the N coast of the island.

Also at the NE foot of the beautiful cone-shaped Sebesi, basalt is found on the small [offshore] island Mengoenang (Huisman Eiland). The mountain has

an old [somma] rim which can be seen from the west side of the island, and where a younger eruption cone was formed which is 859 m high, according to the charts. No rocks have been collected from the top.

A fine-grained basalt is found on Seboekoe Besar.

Finally, on the N side of Rimau Besar, a sharp cone-shaped island of the Zutphen Eilanden, a very fresh dark black basalt lava occurs.

Hypersthene andesite (probably Quaternary and younger). This is the most common rock of Sunda Strait. It is found on the N side of the large Prinsen Eiland, in small hills; in the ridge connecting the volcanoes Tangkamoes and Pesawaran (Lampongs); on the island Lagoendi (in the same river in which the lava fragments mentioned above were found); on Seboekoe Besar and Seboekoe Ketjiel; near campong Tjanti at the foot of the 1300 m-high volcano Radja Bassa; on Varkenshoek; on Hout Eiland, one of the Zutphen Eilanden; on the island Dwars-in-den-weg; and on Toppershoedje.

One can see from this review that the basalt and the hypersthene andesite occur often close together, and even on the same island, so that their occurrence is not determined by certain directions, as I already mentioned above.

[Verbeek then discusses at some length his earlier misidentification of hypersthene andesite as augite andesite before returning to summarize the geologic setting of Krakatau.]

The volcano Krakatau is surrounded by sea so nothing can be seen of its base. The fragments ejected during the youngest eruption (partly sedimentary, partly extrusive) that are not related to the volcano are the same rocks we listed above [from nearby locations], so we may assume that the subsurface is composed of similar rock.

The fragments of sedimentary rocks are partly calcite(?)-bearing, partly calcite-free mudstones and sandstones of volcanic material. In all Krakatau material the porous glass, pumice, is present in varying quantities.

These rocks thus belong to a diluvial, or Recent, already-lithified marine deposit; a young volcanic tuff(?).

Of special interest are the calcium-rich concretions which are present in these rocks. The shape varies from pure spherical to irregular. Sometimes they occur isolated lying loose on the pumice sand; I did not find these within the sand so that they must have been ejected during one of the later eruptions. [In Verbeek's initial short report published in early 1884, he considered these concretions to be products of the 1883 eruption.]

The extrusive rocks from Krakatau itself do not contain andesites that weather to white rock and contain small pyrite crystals similar to the Miocene extrusive rocks of W Java. Pyrite that was found in small quantities in the ash is probably derived from these [foreign] rocks.

From the above, we may conclude that the base of the volcano Krakatau, and in general the bottom of Sunda Strait, is composed of Miocene extrusive rocks covered with horizontal layers of diluvial and Recent deposits, which are derived form the current volcanoes of Sunda Strait. Fragments of Tertiary or older sedimentary rocks were not ejected by the volcano.

Macroscopic and Microscopic Petrography of Krakatau

This chapter, from p. 178 to 290, is the longest in Verbeek's book; nearly twice the length of any other chapter. There is some repetition from the geology chapter above, and much of the petrography has since been redone by Stehn (see our p. 311–340) with the benefits of additional field work and an important 44 years worth of advances in petrographic techniques. This is not to demean Verbeek's talents as a petrographer—his work was characteristically excellent and has stood the tests of time well—but limitations of time and money have prevented us from translating all of the monograph and this long section must be reduced to a summary with only a few sections quoted in full. Translation of this and following chapters is by J.A. Nelen (with the exception of the chapter on collapse, translated in full by E.M. and A.G. Koster van Groos). Verbeek begins with 17 pages describing the pre-1883 products: the hypersthene andesites of the First Period, the basalts of the Second Period, and the hypersthene andesites of the Third Period. The remaining 97 pages are devoted to the ejecta of 1883. He starts on p. 195 with an important observation:

Among the products of 1883 one finds only pumice, ash, and dense glassy rocks; the first two comprise at least 95% of the total quantity ejected, the compact glassy rocks, together with a few chunks of the old

volcano and of the underlying base, forming at most 5%.

After a brief macroscopic description of the glassy rocks, pitchstone, and obsidian, Verbeek discusses the porosity of pumice (see Figure 42, p. 150–151) and describes some of the ships' observations of floating pumice at sea. The great bulk of petrographic description from Verbeek's p. 201 to 290 is devoted to ash, rather than pumice. Macroscopic examination showed that the ash fragments consisted of glass (formerly molten liquid that essentially froze upon expulsion from the volcano) and crystals that had grown in the liquid before its expulsion. Verbeek discusses these components in ash collected near his home in Buitenzorg:

The ash from Buitenzorg contains 91% glass and 9% crystals. The quantity investigated is taken from the total quantity of ash which fell [on the 27th] between 11 and 3 o'clock, and can be considered to represent the average of the total ashfall there. The ash which fell between 11 and 1 o'clock and between 1 and 3 o'clock was not collected separately; the latter has a somewhat finer grain size and thus probably contains fewer crystals than the ash which fell between 11 and 1 o'clock.

The crystal content was also determined for a few other ash species, from which it was evident that they primarily contain less than 9% crystals.

A fine ash collected from the upper layer on Sebesi, which apparently fell last, consists almost completely of glass, with only 1.5% crystals, of which 1.3% are lighter and 0.2% heavier than the specific gravity of 3.00. Thus the ratio of feldspar to the heaviest crystals is here [at Sebesi] 7:1, and in the ash from Buitenzorg 2:1, which shows that the finest ash contains the smallest number of crystals, and that the heaviest crystals (magnetite and pyroxene) are present in relatively smaller quantity than the light crystals (feldspar) in the finer ash. The ash is a mixture of glass and crystals, which have a very different chemical composition. Thus it is evident that chemical analyses of ash species which fell at different places, or which fell at the same place but were collected at different hours, or were collected at different spots in the same ash layer, can differ considerably from each other. This explains in part the differences which we will find later among the ash analyses.

All Krakatau products of 1883 are very glass-rich rock materials of the hypersthene andesite group. They do not differ in their large (porphyritic) crystals from the old hypersthene andesites; their much larger glass percentage is explained by the rapid solidification of the material during the ejection from the crater, so that there was insufficient time for crystallization of the groundmass.

Microscopic descriptions of the various products then follow, with the most detailed work again centering on the ash. This description begins on Verbeek's p. 212:

All the ash types of 1883 are contents of the crater reservoir, fragmented into a fine powder, which belong to the hypersthene andesite group. The color is light to dark gray; the powder is finer-grained and lighter-colored at greater distances from Krakatau; the light-colored, porous particles make up a greater percentage of the ash with increasing distance from Krakatau, and finally become almost 100% of the ash.

However, this very fine ash occurred also on Sebesi and other places close to Krakatau; it formed the upper layer and thus fell *last*, the coarser ash somewhat earlier. Therefore, ash samples collected from the same locality differ both in grain size and crystal content fairly significantly depending on whether they were collected at the beginning or the end of the ashfall.

The main components of the ash are: porous glass; dark, granular, non-porous glass; feldspar, hypersthene, augite, and magnetite. Here it seems we have the various Krakatau rock types in the separate components of the 1883 ash. This rare opportunity to study (microscopically) whole crystals, rather than thin-sections of them cut in different directions, made it seem opportune to study in detail the crystalline parts of one of the ash samples. The ash which fell on August 27 was chosen for this since the crystals are larger than in other ash samples. Furthermore, I can vouch for the cleanliness of the ash, since it was collected by myself on clean papers and plates. A very extensive investigation of the ash sample by Mining Engineer J.W. Retgers, will also be found below [in Verbeek's book, but not here]. In my description of the other ash samples I can thus be brief, since they differ only in quantity of crystals and glass particles and crystal size.

Ash collected by Mr. Schuurman near Perboewatan crater on May 27, 1883. Consists of evenly fine, sandy gray powder, mixed with a few 4 mm-size pumice pieces.

The *suspended* ash, which produces cloudy preparations because of its extreme fineness, appeared under the microscope to consist mostly of pumice particles, water-clear glass with numerous round and elongate vesicles, sometimes drawn out to fine capillaries giving the glass a fiber-like structure. The glass fibers are often wound like rope. Because of many vesicles, in addition to iron ore grains and very few rod-like microlites, the thicker pumice pieces are often cloudy and opaque. In addition to this porous glass, there are glass pieces without bubbles (but filled with rod-like microlites and iron-ore grains) were observed in lesser quantity, usually making thicker pieces of this glass opaque and dark like the microlitic, devitrified matrix of many pyroxene andesites. The color of the glass is either water clear or brown.

There is a fair quantity of crystalline material with the glass particles. However, the crystalline components could be better studied in the *settled* ash, which contains less fine material and porous glass.

The *settled* ash also contains many pumice and dark glass particles, but mixed with more crystals than in the suspended ash; the largest percentage of the crystals are fragments, average size 0.15 mm. Glass was observed on the rims of many crystals, probably part of the glass crust which surrounded the crystals before fragmentation. Round glass droplets often found in volcanic ash *are absent* in all Krakatau ash types. The crystals consist of clear plagioclase, partly banded, often with rim structure, with very different extinction angles indicating many different compositions; brown hypersthene, strongly pleochroic, with parallel and 90° extinction angles on both sides; green augite with large extinction angles; magnetite and apatite. The inclusions in these minerals are the same as those already described in the rocks, pitchstone, obsidian, and pumice of 1883. As a foreign component pyrite must be mentioned, occurring as dodecahedrons or cubes and must be derived from older rocks. For further properties of these minerals, crystal shape, specific gravity, etc., we refer to the investigation of the ash from Buitenzorg.

Ash collected 11 August, 1883 at the foot of Perboewatan by Captain Ferzenaar. Bottom layer.

One might remember that on August 11, three different layers of ejecta were observed, first a layer of pumice fragments, on top of that fine gray ash, and on top of that darker colored ash. The ash from the bottom layer probably resulted from the May, and possibly June, eruption similar to that collected by Mr. Schuurman. Meanwhile it is not completely the same because the color is brownish gray and also under the microscope it appeared that this ash contains more brown microlitic devitrified glass particles. Otherwise the ash is similar to the previous one. Average size of crystal particles 0.15 mm.

Ash collected 11 August, 1883, at foot of Perboewatan by Captain Ferzenaar. Upper layer. Probably ejected in July and first half of August.

This ash is dark gray and finer than the previous ash. It also deviates microscopically from the previous ash because porous glass particles, microscopic pumice fragments, are not present. The non-porous microlitic devitrified glass particles contain (along with the microlites) very many fine magnetite crystals and dark, black and brown transparent grains, and to this the dark color of this ash must be attributed, because the loose magnetite crystals are not present in greater quantity than in the other ash types. This ash contains much fine powder that is removed by washing. The remaining glass and crystal fragments again are 0.15 mm in size. Most crystals are also fragments.

Ash collected by the writer, August 27, 1883, between 11 and 3 p.m., at Buitenzorg, 150 km from Krakatau. This ash very probably was ejected by the largest explosion on Monday, 10 a.m.; the first grains fell at Buitenzorg soon after 11 a.m.; from 11:20 until 1 p.m. ashfall was fairly heavy, diminishing continuously from 1 to 3 p.m.

The light gray ash fell in damp small grains of average size 0.6 mm. A harder crystal or pumice fragment was occasionally found by rubbing the ash between one's fingers, but otherwise the ash is very fine. The biggest proportion here also consists of pumice, in addition to lesser quantities of slag particles, nonporous light yellow or brown glass fragments with numerous microlites and ore grains. It did not appear unlikely that these microlitic devitrified glass particles *for a small part* could have originated from the groundmass of the old Krakatau rocks, which got into the molten mass and were partially mixed with it. However, the largest part no doubt separated from the molten magma in the upper part of the crater near the surface; because of lowered pressure the water content could slowly escape there and the microlites in the glass had time to crystallize before the mass was ejected. This supposition is probable, since the ash ejected in the month of July and the first half of

August is exceptionally rich in slag particles; during this period the eruptions were much less violent than in May and August and most likely only the *upper* part of the crater content was ejected or rather carried out with the steam which escaped with force from the crater. The largest part of the microlites in the dark glass particles probably was formed in the upper part of the crater itself.

The crystals are the same as in the ash from May, but reach considerable size between 0.3 and 0.5 mm, a few elongate pyroxenes even up to 1 mm. Also at the edges of the crystals sharp glass fragments were usually observed. Sauer[249d] assumed that the rapid cooling of the crystals and glass particles by sudden ejection to a height of several tens of km produced a great tension, causing explosion and collision of the particles while falling. The fragmentation thus would be the consequence of the explosions of the already solidified particles outside the crater, which appears probable.

The ash of August 27 contains more whole crystals than the ash from May, but by far the largest part are broken.

For a detailed investigation of the crystals, see the investigation by Mr. Retgers.

Ash collected by writer on 14 October, 1883, in the plain on the north side of Sebesi.

Is light gray in color but finer grained than ash from Buitenzorg. Crystal grains are very few (1½%) and average 0.10 mm in size, which must be attributed to the fact that ash collected from the *upper* layer consists of the lightest particles which fell last.

Ash which fell at Bandar [320 km NW of Krakatau] during the night of 27–28 August, 1883. Collected by Dr. A. Stammeshaus.

Very fine, flour-like, white-gray in color, contains more pumice and less crystals than ash from Buitenzorg; the relative proportions of crystals however is fairly much the same. Average crystal size 0.15–0.10 mm, pumice fragments in part much smaller; otherwise ash similar to ash from Buitenzorg.

Ash which fell at Talang-Betoetoe [375 km NW of Krakatau], 28 August, 1883. Collected by Controller J. Peelen.

Ash finer than previous and whiter in color. The content of crystals less here and magnetite content proportionally smaller.

Crystal size 0.10 mm, pumice is mostly dust size; otherwise similar to previous.

The detailed microscopic investigation of the Buitenzorg ash sample by Verbeek's colleague J.W. Retgers follows for 68 pages. Verbeek then returns for a brief description of foreign rocks— fragments of pre-existing rocks such as carbonate concretions caught up in the 1883 eruption products—before moving on to the next chapter.

Chemical Compositions of Krakatau Rocks

Chemical analyses of volcanic rocks provide valuable information about the liquids deep inside a volcano that produce eruptions. Verbeek quickly sent specimens of the 1883 ejecta to Professor Winkler in Freiberg, Germany, for analyses, and in this 22-page chapter he discusses the results. He compares them with other andesites of the archipelago, noting a relatively high silica content for the Krakatau rocks, but devotes most of his discussion to the relationships between different products of the 1883 eruption and pre-existing rocks of Krakatau. On page 312 he summarizes the results of the chemical investigation as follows:

1. The old hypersthene andesites of Krakatau and the rocks of 1883 are very close in composition: for the old rocks the silica content falls between 68¾ and 70½%, and for the new between 66½ and 69%. A single ash species, which contains no porous glass, but only dark-colored, microlitic, devitrified glass (probably because of the melting of basic basaltic rocks), contains only 61% SiO_2. The water content of all the new rocks is either very small, or they are completely without water.

2. The basalts of Krakatau are much more basic than the hypersthene andesites and have an average SiO_2 content of 49%.

3. The ash of August 27 contains *all* feldspar compositions, from the most basic to the most acidic. The average feldspar is an acidic andesine with 57.76% SiO_2, consisting of 51.71 weight % albite, 41.206% anorthite and 7.223% microcline.

4. The clean pumice glass contains about 69% silica; the further from Krakatau the ash has fallen, the poorer it becomes in crystals and the more the composition of the ash approaches that of pure pumice with 69% SiO_2.

5. The water-soluble salts in the ash originate from seawater with the exception of some of the gypsum, which is derived from the older rocks of Krakatau.

Meteorological and Magnetic Phenomena

Through the cooperation of Dr. J.P. van der Stok, Director of the Magnetic and Meteorological Observatory in Batavia, I am able to give a listing of observations of air pressure, temperature, humidity and magnetic disturbances at Batavia on the day of the eruption. The first three are only hourly observations; those for August 26, 27, and 28 are plotted in Figure 58. In contrast, the magnetic disturbances are a continuous record; the graph for the 27th is given in Figure 59.

One might remember that the eruption was already heavy during the night of August 26–27, but magnetic disturbance was observed in Batavia only between 6 a.m. and 5 p.m. on the 27th. During that time, there was ashfall, which was heaviest between 11:00 a.m. and 12 noon, when the magnetic variations were also the greatest; therefore, it is clear that the magnetic iron in the ash was the cause of the disturbances here. *The eruption itself did not influence the magnetic variations.*

Dr. van der Stok was good enough to add a few remarks to the following table [shown graphically on Figure 58, but not reproduced here as a table], which I quote here:

1. *Status of meteorological observations.*
a. Highest barometer reading = 764.05 mm, the highest reading observed since 1866.
b. Thermometer rises until 10 a.m. on the 27th, then goes down. It is self evident that this can*not* be ascribed to radiation; blocking out the sun's rays would at best cause no change in temperature. From the *Relative Humidity* data, it is evident that evaporation could not be the cause either. It does not increase after 10 a.m., but remains about constant. Since 8 this morning [the 27th] the atmosphere has become drier, rather than more humid, while the water vapor pressure and the temperature have decreased considerably; thus, with the temperature drop, moisture from the atmosphere must have condensed, rather than the atmosphere taking up moisture from the humid ash and therefore cooling off.

2. *Status of magnetic disturbances.*
The time of greatest declination cannot be given with great precision, since the photography is incomplete. The largest deviation observed is 2°20.8′ at 11:25 a.m. Even with very large disturbances in the earth's magnetic field, the declination needle is never deflected this strongly.

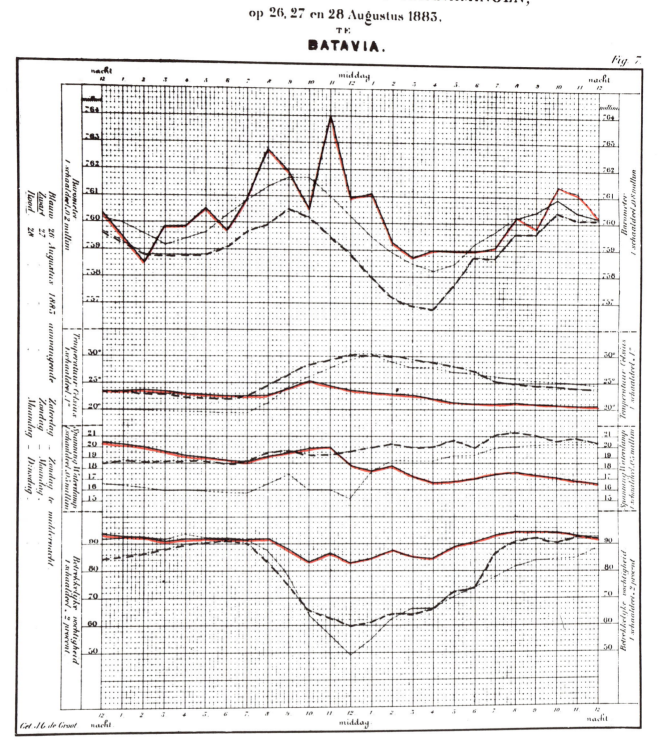

Figure 58. Hourly meteorological observations at Batavia on August 26 (dashed), 27 (red), and 28 (black). Horizontal scale in hours from midnight ("nacht") through noon ("midday") to midnight.

From top to bottom: barometric pressure (mm); temperature (°C); water vapor pressure (%); and relative humidity (%). (Verbeek's figure 7.)

With most major disturbances in the earth's magnetic field, the horizontal and vertical pull deviate together without short-term up and down variations. But in this instance the horizontal pull stays on the average fairly normal, while the vertical pull decreases.

The total magnitude and inclination are calculated only for the following times: 6 p.m. as normal value; 12 noon (minimal horizontal pull) and 12:35 p.m. (maximum horizontal pull); 11:10 a.m. (minimum vertical pull); since for the latter the horizontal pull is missing, it is deduced from the average horizontal pull of four values at 11:05 and 11:15 a.m..

The normal value of inclination 27°23' appears too low. The cause of this might be that the assumed value for the zero-line of the vertical pull is too small; or (and this is more probable) because of the disturbance. a decrease has taken place in the location of the balance magnet, which can be determined only later, after comparing a complete series of absolute observations. If the needle returns by itself, then such an instrument at fault cannot be traced back, this is a fault particular to the instrument. Possible however, is that the inclination then was small.

Concerning the barometer indications, it is to be deplored that no continuously recording barographs were available. Earlier a barograph was installed at Batavia, but it had fallen into disuse and was sent back to Utrecht because the barometric pressure here was always so regular. The hourly observations, which normally would suffice, are a disadvantage here, since it cannot be determined what happened between the readings. Thus, the big air wave, which started from Krakatau at about 10 a.m. and arrived a few minutes later at Batavia, was not read. At 11:00 a.m. the barometer was already on the way down; the time of maximum was between 10:00 and 11:00, but cannot be determined any closer. No one had expected such a large and exceptional disturbance during the eruption; otherwise, the barometer would have been read every 5 minutes during that day.

According to the humidity observations, the considerable temperature decrease, observed not only at Batavia, but also at Buitenzorg, Kroë, Moera-Doea, Bandar and numerous other places, cannot be ascribed to the evaporation of water from the ash.

In my opinion it was caused by the low temperature of the ash particles falling from considerable heights, which had cooled to the temperature of the higher atmospheric layers. In the vicinity of Krakatau, the temperature did not decrease. Ship reports (*Besse, Charles Bal,* and G.G. *Loudon*) speak of a warm suffocating air, which certainly proves that the ash which was ejected to high altitudes and which fell at great distances from the volcano, caused the lowering of temperature.

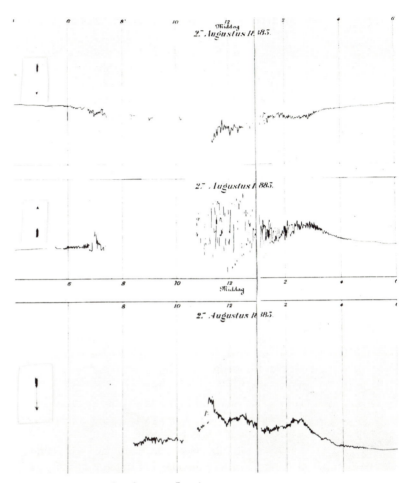

Figure 59. Magnetic disturbances at Batavia on August 27 from 4 a.m. through noon (midday) to 6 p.m.

Upper: Declination, with the beginning of the graph at 0° 59' 44" E, reaches a minimum of 0° 36' 24" E about 11:20 a.m. E declination increases in the direction of the arrow.

Middle: Horizontal intensity, with the starting point of the graph at 3.68406 mg-mm-sec (mms), reaches a maximum of 3.69708 mms around 12:30 p.m. Intensity here (and below) increases in the direction of the arrow.

Lower: Vertical intensity. The graph begins at 1.88493 mms, and reaches a minimum of 1.86263 mms around 11 a.m.

Portions of the curves are missing due to insufficient sensitivity of the photographic paper. (Verbeek's figure 8.)

At Batavia the average temperature was 23°C between 12:00 and 4:00 p.m. on August 27, 30°C on the 26th, and 29°C on the 28th, thus differences of 6° and 7°C [11–13°F] with the preceding and following days; at Kroë the temperature was 75°F = 23°C for the largest part of the day (See p. 213, report from Controller Horst); at Bandar [320 km NW of Krakatau], Dr. Stammeshaus observed 18.2°C [65°F] at 2:00 p.m., an exceptionally low temperature.

Movements of the Air

See also [p. 201–220] about explosions heard in west Java during the eruption.

Reports were received about rumbling noises and short explosions from all the residencies in Java. In connection with this, it should be mentioned that in middle and east Java the loudest explosions were heard between 10 and 12 o'clock; many reports mention 11:30, when nothing was heard any longer in Batavia and Buitenzorg. This must have been caused by the ash cloud, then hanging between Krakatau and Batavia. Already after the explosion of 7:00, but especially after 10:00, an ash cloud filled with dust particles spread eastward from the volcano in the shape of a lampshade and wrapped itself around every place between Krakatau and Bandoeng.

It appears that the noises were transmitted very poorly or not at all within the cloud of millions of ash particles; even at Serang, no noises were heard after 10:15. However, shots were heard at the lighthouses of Java's First Point and Vlakken Hoek and on board ships (W.H. Besse and Charles Bal) in the Sunda Strait. Only on the Loudon nothing was heard [but 2 of the ship's 3 eyewitnesses quoted on p. 90–96 reported "thundering"]. Thus a certain thickness of ash seemed necessary to damp the sound completely. The suspended ash particles are such a simple explanation (at least from a superficial view) for the transmission of the sounds, that, in my opinion, other hypotheses are unnecessary. Interference of the sound, from directly transmitted and reflected air waves, can hardly have played an important role. Of course such interference can take place; thus, for instance, a single noise can be weakened or even amplified at a location, but it is highly unlikely that all noises would be completely deadened at one place for several hours. In addition, through interference of sound waves at nearby locations, the noise can be alternately weakened or amplified. I specifically mean to imply that the extra strong explosions heard at Buitenzorg (still loud in the early evening of the 27th) can be explained by its location against Salak and the reflection of noise from that mountain.

Above the ash cloud explosions were transmitted in all directions and, of course, were heard most clearly in the direction from which the wind was blowing. At 10:00 a.m. on the 27th, when the explosions were heaviest at Buitenzorg and Batavia, no noise or rumbling was heard at Kroë; the cause of this must have been the W or NW wind. Later rumbling was heard at Kroë, but only one loud explosion at 12 o'clock, probably because ash was still suspended in the air; at 4:30 in the afternoon, when the ashfall was considerably diminished, a tremendous explosion was heard. All this seems to me to be explainable by the suspended ash particles, without having to go to explanations about force and direction of wind, as has been observed for instance with signals in a fog.

As will be explained below, the heaviest explosions took place before noon at 5:35, 6:49, 10:07, and 10:57, Batavia time. To avoid confusion, I will give all times in Krakatau time and use it in all my calculations. Thus the mentioned explosions were at 5:30, 6:44, 10:02, and 10:52, Krakatau time.

Verbeek gives a 16-page table listing places where eruptive sounds were heard and notes that most fall within a "noise circle with a radius of 30°" (3333 km). He then discusses the non-audible airwaves—the rising and falling of ships' barometers, the feeling of deafness and buzzing in the ears described by many witnesses, the measurements of the gasometer in Batavia (see Figure 109 and caption to the gasometer trace on p. 371), and the many reports of atmospheric disturbances reported from recording barographs around the world. Verbeek uses the barogram from Sydney, Australia, to confirm the explosion chronology he developed from the Batavia gasometer trace, and then goes on to discuss the velocity of the airwave. Although aware of the wave's multiple passages around the earth, described later in more detail by Strachey in the Royal Society Report (see p. 368), Verbeek notes that the wave's return to Batavia was not recorded. The first return, at 9:45 p.m. on the 28th, was at a time when gas pressure was too high to sense external pressure changes on the gas line, and gasometer records during subsequent wave passages were missing.

Collapse Volumes

Significant movements in parts of the solid earth's crust occurred during the eruption. However, they remained restricted to the immediate vicinity of the crater.

Nowhere could any evidence of an uplift, either of the sea bottom, or of the crust, be found on Bantam and the Lampongsche districts; the sections of the gravel roads along the coast which had remained after the eruption were at the same height above sea level as before.

Depth soundings in Sunda Strait showed that also the sea bottom at some distance from Krakatau had remained unchanged, and that the lesser depth in the immediate proximity of Krakatau (and between Krakatau and Sebesi) probably should be attributed only to the materials which were deposited there.

I paid much attention to whether anything like a crater or solid lava was present on the newly formed islands, Calmeyer and Steers, because it was certainly possible that a satellite crater had been formed during the activty of Krakatau and that a submarine eruption of loose materials or solid lava had occurred, as had been the case with the birth of Nyöe (New Island), SW of Iceland in 1783; the island Sabrina in the Azores in 1811; the island Julia (Graham Island), SW of Sicily in 1831; the Kaimeni islands of the Santorini-group[388,389] in the years 1546, 1650, 1707 and 1866; the island Bogoslof in the Aleutians in 1795 and 1796; a new island at 0.5 miles NNW of Bogoslof, and another one close to Augustin[390] or Chernaboura Island (Alaska), in 1883.

However, I have not been able to find anything at all that could suggest that anyplace, except Krakatau itself, had been active. The islands Steers and Calmeyer consist of horizontal and not sloping layers of ash, sand, and pumice fragments; as can be seen from the contours of the new sea chart; they are not cones rising steeply out of the sea, but only the highest points of a large mass of ejected material, stretching from these islands W and then S in a circle around Krakatau, and which are above sea level. On Calmeyer, one finds several funnel-shaped depressions, which are the result of local sinking of the originally wet ash, and the bottom of these wells usually is at sea level. Some lie in a straight line and because of renewed sinking they form a canyon, which soon will be widened further by sea water. There is no doubt that soon the islands will have disappeared and that also the part of the bank which lies under water will

slowly be removed. Probably everything consists of loose eruption products, although I obviously was not able to see the islands' lowest parts. It is therefore quite possible that, after some time, the sea between Sebesi and Krakatau will become about as deep again as before, and can again be used for ship traffic.

During my second and third visits to Krakatau, in August and September 1884, Steers was still visible as a very low sandbank with a strong surf. Calmeyer was no longer above water, although we steamed closely south of the place where the island had been.

However, a permanent change occurred between Verlaten, Lang, and the southern portion of Krakatau (see the maps, Figures 47, 48, and 49) [see p. 192–195]. The northern part of Krakatau, which earlier extended from the Peak nearly to Verlaten Eiland, and consisted of the craters Perboewatan and Danan and the northern part of the peak, has completely disappeared. Where the island had been before is now a deep sea, mostly 100 to 200 m, and at some places more than 300 m deep. The Commander of the *Hydrograaf* reports that in several places not even with lines 200 fathoms [366 m] long lead soundings could be taken of the bottom[391] [see p. 138].

Outside of the part that disappeared, but between the three islands, one still could find significant depths, 144, 172 and 250 m, and farther N 108 m, so that not only the N part of Krakatau, but also the neighboring sea floor had collapsed.

The part of Krakatau that disappeared, therefore, must either have been blown into the air, or collapsed. I must admit that I only consider the latter likely and possible. In the first place, one only very seldom can find a piece of basalt among the ejected materials at the W end of Krakatau; one can find several pitch-like glassy fragments of andesite, although also these are fairly rare. Had the peak been blown into the air, then undoubtedly much more basalt should have been present, because the peak consists of this type of rock. Furthermore, it is unlikely that suddenly an almost purely circular area with a 3400 m radius, thus more than 36 km^2, would have been blown into the atmosphere. Moreover, the sea had become very deep not only between the islands, but also E of Krakatau. On the map, Figure 48, I marked both the old and new depths, from which is shown that the earlier depth was between 50 and 70, now between 80 and 100 m or more in most locations. On the map I depicted the triangular area where depths are now greater than before as small as possible; it is likely that it extends a little further E, but sufficient old and new data to confirm this are lacking.

This triangular area also would have to have been thrown into the atmosphere. Both form and size of the area make this assumption improbable.

In the past, the so-called "Maare" of the Eifel [Germany] were explained by explosions, but the theory of the "Explosions-Kratere" must be considered highly unlikely, based on Vogelsang's research.[392]

Moreover, the dimensions of these craters are much smaller than those of Krakatau. The mountain range which encircles the "Laachersee," the largest of the Eifeler Maare, has an average diameter of 3.5 km; the area of the crater encircled by that mountain range, therefore, is 4 times smaller than at Krakatau.

On the other hand, a collapse can be expected in all volcanic regions. The lava, during its ascent in the crater pipe, partly melts the inner wall of the volcano which remains as a hollow dish once the lava recedes, and obviously it will easily crumble, as von Hochstetter observed with his little sulphur volcanoes.[393]

One therefore can imagine that part A of the large volcano (Fig. 57d [p. 246]) had melted away by the continuously ascending lava, and that the first large collapse occurred when the lava receded, so that only the four border areas, Lang, Poolsche Hoed, Verlaten, and the area beneath the Peak (Figure 57c) remained. The minimal depth (7 m) between Verlaten and Lang indicates that here an old rim had remained below sea level (sea chart, Figure 57b). The lava solidified below sea level, not only in the crater pipe, but also outside, and later it served as the foundation, on which a part of the peak came to rest (Figure 57c).

Also the ejected materials from the craters Danan and Perboewatan, which were formed still later, were deposited on the old lava flow, which was broken up either by molten matter or in itself was again melted by fluid lava, which circulated in the cracks and joints of the old lava.

During the lengthy activity of 1883 it appears that the whole surface of the old lava slowly softened because of total or partial melting and thus finally everything that rested on the old lava formation collapsed. As can be seen from Figures 57e and f, not only the craters Perboewatan and Danan disappeared, but also the N part of the Peak, while the S portion, which rested on the old lava banks, remained intact.

The seawater seems to have had access to the lava before the collapse occurred. Both events probably took place very soon after one another, if not at the same time. The collapse of the massive part of the peak caused a tremendous movement in the water,

resulting in a big wave.

Because of penetration of water to the lava and the following collapse, and because of the significant amount of crust developed on the lava, the pressure on the lava column increased significantly, but only for a short moment. With a power which by far exceeded the preceding explosions, the central part of the lava at B (Figure 57f [p. 247]) was blown away, mixing with seawater and forming a mud, which was thrown to a distance of 100 km around the crater. Hereafter some still lesser explosions occurred, but soon the activity ended.

The lava, now loaded with fragments of the collapsed mountains, sank back, as I have shown in Figure 57f.

It is certainly possible that later, by renewed activity, islands will again form within the now collapsed crater. In order to ascertain this, one has to take some soundings from time to time.

The change of Krakatau was already noticed on August 28, on board the G.G. Loudon and the Berbice [see p. 91 and p. 271], thus, the collapse undoubtedly occurred on August 27 and probably at approximately 10 o'clock during or before the loudest explosion.

A more exact time will be given during the discussion of the wave movements [see p. 264].

The center of the almost circular collapsed space is located near the place where the crater Danan had been, which indicates that this point must be considered as the actual center of activity during the eruption of August 27. The eastern collapse outside Krakatau shows that, here, a space under the bottom of the sea existed, probably completely or partly filled with lava and connected with the lava space under Krakatau. This eastern offshoot can be seen as the beginning of the magma chamber which probably extends underneath all of Java.

It seems that the highest top of Krakatau has remained intact and that the collapsed area passes exactly over this point. According to our measurements the top is 832 m high. The old sea chart shows only 822 m, which cannot be correct, because the top certainly has not increased in height, for the thickness of the eruption products is very minimal near the top. [In 1929, Stehn measured a pumice thickness of 5 m at the top.[393a]]

The earlier peak must have had a nearly circular base, with a radius of 2080 m (see Figure 48 [p. 194]). The part of this cone that disappeared must alone have been approximately 1 km³ in size above sea level.[394] How large the volume of the more northern part of Krakatau was cannot be calculated, because (besides the fact that the exact height of the terrain is unknown) probably not much more than a hollow dish had remained in the area of the big crater because of melting of the inside, so that the land mass thus was no longer solid, either above or below sea level.

The collapsed, nearly circular area between the 3 islands is 41 km², inside the eastern triangular piece 34 km², thus together 75 km². I have to state here that the collapsed space, as shown on the maps, Figures 47, 48, and 49, has been slightly changed by my research on Verlaten Eiland in August 1884, as can be seen by comparing the maps, Figures 48 and 57b. The collapse on the latter map is more correctly shown than on the other maps, which were made earlier.

The sizes of the islands at both earlier and present stages are summarized in the table below. Krakatau's outline is taken from Richards' map of 1854 (see p. 190). The increase in size of the islands is caused by loose eruption products, which were deposited around the islands. The heights of Verlaten and Lang also increased slightly, because of a thick coating of pumice sand. Since the growth consists completely of loose material, it is to be expected that the islands of the Krakatau group will change somewhat in appearance in the coming years, and will decrease in size, until they have regained their old outlines.

The little island Poolsche Hoed, a part of the old rim, also collapsed, but on the other hand two new islands have formed in the deep sea north of the present Krakatau. The first consists of loose sand at its surface and is located east of Verlaten. The collapse was not significant here, for a sounding between this point and Verlaten indicates a depth of only 13 m. It is therefore likely that part of the island remained beneath this sand bank and that loose material is piled on top of it, forming the upper part of the island. In October 1883, and still in September 1884, this island was hardly 0.5 m above the sea; it soon will be washed away. A second remnant of Old Krakatau is named *Rots* [rock] on the map, and it lies between the earlier crater Danan and Lang. This rock, which rises 5 m above water, I could not visit in October 1883, due to the heavy swell which was present; however, I succeeded in August 1884. The rock is composed of an andesite lava, which is separated into parallel slabs which slope toward the W with a dip of 60°–70°. Because lava slabs cannot form at such a large dip, the "rock" therefore represents a fragment tilted from its earlier position, a remnant of the Danan mountain range.

With the exception of these two points, the sea is everywhere very deep; nowhere can rocks be seen, and the steamships coming from Europe can now take the route N of Krakatau and S of the other two islands, at least during the day. This newly formed "Krakatau passage" does not hold any dangers for navigation.

The black numbers showing the depth on our maps, Figures 47 and 48 [p. 192–194], are a copy of the old Dutch sea chart of 1874, and the red numbers shown in Figure 48 are those from the new sea chart of Lieutenant van Doorn. Added are three soundings [130, 240 and 200 m], made by Mr. J.A. 't Hoen, commander of the hopper barge *Kedirie*, on October 17, 1883, during our visit to Krakatau.

Finally, one finds on the map, Figure 57b, another sounding made in August 1884 by Commander D. Nolles, of the steamship *Argus*, of the Government's Navy; it indicates a very shallow place of only 7 m, between Verlaten and Lang, which is the old crater rim under the sea surface.

The height of Rakata Peak has been established by our measurement; the heights of Verlaten (205 m), and of Lang (135 m), were determined by the Lt. H.J. Ferguson of the survey vessel *Hydrograaf* (see 391).

Size[395] in km²

Krakatau	Before	33.536
	Of which collapsed	22.851
	Of which remains	10.685
	Newly added	4.647
	Present	15.332
Verlaten	Before	3.716
	Newly added	8.094
	Present	11.810
Lang	Before	2.897
	Newly added	0.306
	Present	3.203
Poolsche Hoed	Before	0.056
	Of which collapsed	0.056
	Of which remains	0.—

This collapse produced a very nice and interesting cross-section of the peak, shown from the north side in all its imposing splendor in Plate 8, that has already been discussed extensively in the geological section.

Sailing from the north coast further along the east coast of Krakatau, then, it can be seen from the steep rock face, that the collapse took part of the island here. The old rocks along the coast soon become lower, and where they reach sea level we find the boundary between Old and New Krakatau. Everything south of here has been newly added. The location of this point according to the English sea chart and to our measurements do agree well (see map, Figure 47).

Finally, a small part of Lang, opposite Krakatau, also disappeared in the depths, recognizable by the steep rocks at the coast.

These last two areas, the east section of Krakatau and the west section of Lang, border the east triangular collapsed area, which is shown on the map, Figure 48.[395a]

Movements of the Sea

The coastal areas of Java and Sumatra, which were flooded by tremendous sea waves and about which we provided some information in the eruption history [on p. 201–220], are pictured on the map, Figure 54.

Only where large alluvial plains lay at the coast, namely at the mouth of the Semangka River, near Teloeq Betoeng, Anjer, Tjaringin, and Panimbang did the water penetrate far inland. Otherwise the flooding was restricted to a very narrow strip at the coast. However, because most of the kampongs were right at the sea, very many lives were thereby lost.

Concerning the cause of the largest wave, it was remarked above that it was caused by the cave-in of Krakatau, the sudden submerging of a tremendous rock mass into the sea.

Verbeek goes on to say that the exact origin time of the water wave is more difficult to calculate than that of the air wave, since its speed through the sea depends on the locally variable (and in places uncertain) depth of the water. The only recording gauges in the archipelago were at Tandjong Priok and 800 km E of Krakatau in the Madura Staits. He recounts the reports of witnesses at Anjer, Tjeringen, Merak, and Vlakken Hoek (all given above) and concludes:

These are the only data, which are trustworthy. As can be seen, they are few enough in number and in addition the times reported are very uncertain.

For the wave to reach Tandjong Priok from Krakatau should take *about* 2½ hours, assuming an average depth of approximately 35 m. According to the

reports (see p. 202) it arrived there about 12:30. This also indicates the moment of formation of the wave at about 10 o'clock and thus there is no doubt, *that the largest sea wave formed about the same time as the heaviest explosion, by which also the largest air wave was formed.*

The only question now is: Did these two events occur entirely together or not?

Verbeek provides a one-page table, with calculations of speed and arrivals at various locations. He added 15 m to the measured depth in Sunda Strait, assuming that the water level there rose by that much because of the wave.

Assuming, for the moment, the calculation of the time of flooding at Vlakken Hoek as correct, then the wave would have left Krakatau at 10:30 − 42 min = 9:48, which would give the following arrival times: Sangkanila, 10:29; Anjer, 10:21; and Tjaringen, 10:17. This clearly shows that the wave did *not immediately* follow the large explosions, but, according to this time calculation, arrived ¼ hour later, even at the most nearby location, Tjaringen; and we will see below that the time span between hearing the explosion at Tjaringen and the arrival of the wave there was still larger, namely 27 minutes.

This all agrees well with the report[82] of Mr. Gaston [see p. 206]. He heard the explosion about halfway between Tjerita and Tjaringen, thus at least 2 km distant from the place and thus never would have been able to reach Tjaringen had the wave arrived immediately or only a few minutes after observing the explosion. The time span *must* necessarily have been at least a quarter hour, thus also at Anjer and Sangkanila. The report that the wave followed "soon" after the explosion at those towns should not be taken too literally.

The time calculations above are still fairly uncertain, not only because they are dependent on the time the wave arrived at Vlakken Hoek, which we put at 10:30, but also because the sea depth between Krakatau and Vlakken Hoek (approximately 150 m), to which the progression time of the wave (42 min) is related, is not precisely known.

In the following 4 pages (385–388 of the original), Verbeek calculates the speed of the wave from Krakatau to Tandjong Priok and evaluates the harbor records for exact arrival time there. He concludes:

Because 12:36 Batavia time corresponds to 12:31 Krakatau time, and because the wave, according to our calculations, needed 151 min or 2 hr and 31 min to cover the distance between Krakatau and Tandjong Priok, *the wave was formed at 12:31 − 2 hr 31 min = 10:00 a.m.*

Therefore, it now appears that the cave-in of part of Krakatau, which caused formation of the sea wave, took place at about the same time as the big explosion which formed the large air wave. Since the first calculation can be wrong by only a few minutes, the only uncertainty still remaining is whether the cave-in preceded or immediately followed the big explosion.

Both assumptions are independently possible. However, the ejection of a tremendous quantity of *mud*, formed from the mixing of the ejected ash with seawater, clearly shows that the explosion took place underwater and thus that penetration into the crater of seawater from above and, very probably, simultaneous cave-in of Krakatau must have happened before the materials were ejected. In addition, the calculation of 10:00 o'clock for formation of the wave is more likely too late than too early, because we did not calculate the influence of the current, which was opposite to the movement.

Collapse of the walls of the active craters, weakened on the inside by melting; penetration of seawater onto molten lava in the crater void; and cave-in of part of the peak occurred at 10:00 Krakatau time, immediately followed by ejection of molten materials and sea water. The maximum air pressure, caused by the explosion, was reached at 10:02 at a considerable height above the crater. The remaining lava fell back into the crater and crater pipe, 200–300 m below the surface of the sea, and solidified.

After a short listing of arrival times for the large wave, Verbeek discusses the wave and its heights. He points out at the start that the wave was not caused by an earthquake (he believed that there were no earthquakes associated with the eruption) nor was it a tidal wave (having nothing to do with the tides). He believes, rather, that the waves

started the same way as when a stone is thrown in the water: a sort of ripple effect. First a primary wave, followed by several smaller secondary waves.

The rise of the large wave in the ocean must have been about 15 m, from which it follows that the total wave height was about double, or 30 m. This is an exceptional height; even the largest waves caused by a long and severe storm[398a] have a height of only 15–18 m, thus half of the Krakatau wave.

A calculation of the wave caused by the collapse of a cubic kilometer into the sea cannot be given, because this is governed by the force of the collapse and the space into which the collapse takes place, and we do not have enough data.

According to our measurements, the wave ran up against the steep coasts on the south side of Dwars-in-den-weg and at Anjer, 48 and 53 km from Krakatau, to a height of 36 m, at other localities much less; only at Sangkanila near Merak, 64 km from Krakatau, the water ran up to 35 m; but this must be ascribed to the narrow passage between Merak Island and the mainland forcing the water higher. Against the south side of Toppershoedje the water reached 30 m, on the north side only 24 m. Near Kalianda, north of Ketimbang, the water ran up a sloping plain to a height of 24 m; at Teloeq Betoeng, up to the Resident's house, 21.7 m; against Apenberg (Goenoeng Koenjiet), 24.2 m; at the Vlakken Hoek lighthouse, 15 m; on Prinsen Island and Java's First Point, 7–10 m. At Sebesi the water line could not be seen too well, because, after the big wave of 10 o'clock, much ash fell, which covered everything. On Seboekoe the height of the wave was not measured; it amounted, however, to no more than 25–30 m, which is surprising since Seboekoe is so close to Krakatau, but it was somewhat protected by Sebesi.

Thus the heights differ and depend on the steepness and shape of the coastline, depth of the sea along the coastline, distance from Krakatau, and degree of protection of the coastline by islands.

Having discussed mainly the largest wave, Verbeek goes on to the smaller waves that preceded it. These include the waves observed between 5:30 and 6:00 on Sunday evening at Tjaringen, Anjer, Ketimbang, and Telok Betong as well as the one which destroyed part of Anjer after 6 a.m. Monday and the lower part of Teloeq Betoeng at 6:30. Verbeek argues that these could not have been caused by collapse of the volcano because seawater would then have had access to the active vents, resulting in wet, muddy ejecta. Mud rain, however, did not start until 10 a.m. Monday, mud being thrown as far as 100 km. If mud had been ejected during the fairly severe eruption of 5:30 a.m., it likely would have been noticed, he feels, at Ketimbang or Tjaringen, about half the distance of 100 km. Verbeek concludes that the smaller waves were caused by large quantities of ejecta falling into the sea. He calls attention to his earlier calculations that there are about 12 km³ of ash and rock in the surroundings of Krakatau, almost all of it ejected from the evening of the 26th until the next forenoon. This ejection was not continuous, but occurred mainly during severe explosions, of which 15 have been mentioned. Thus some of these explosions might have ejected 1 km³ at once, more than enough to cause waves of 1–3 m.

Verbeek goes on to discuss the effects of barriers, water-borne debris, and other factors interfering with the simple progression of these smaller waves (and explaining why not all waves were observed at all places).

The record of the Tandjong Priok tide gauge is then described in detail. Verbeek notes that the gauge is unfavorably located (at the mouth of a canal, the Zindergracht) and that its range was exceeded by several waves. However, by observations in the inner harbor, he was able to add dashed lines to the record indicating the approximate high and low watermarks during the event.[399] These dashed lines are retained on the copy of the Tandjong Priok record reproduced below on p. 378. Verbeek's discussion of the smaller waves on the Tandjong Priok record follows:

It appears that the sea became unruly at 6 o'clock Sunday afternoon. Small variations lasted the whole night and continued into the forenoon of the 27th, until at 11:35 a very sharp rise suddenly started, caused by the first big wave.[399a] The amplitude of the preceding small waves amounts to at most 0.10 m and of the first big wave not less than 5.50 m, which clearly shows the big difference in height between the wave of 6 o'clock Monday morning, which flooded part of

Anjer and Teloeq Betoeng, and the large wave of 10 o'clock, which was the main cause of the destruction of the coastal areas in the Sunda Strait.

The most important waves were marked at the following hours: 4:05; 5:00; 5:36; 5:56; 6:23; 6:33; 7:13; 7:38; 8:14; 8:28; 8:40; 9:17; 9:28; 9:39; 10:24; 11:00; and 11:24. Among these are probably several repetitions of the same waves, the figures clearly indicate a period of 2 hours with some. The most important waves are those of 7:38; 8:28; 8:40; 9:39; and 10:24 and for the first four a correlation with the same number of explosions is indicated.

After more discussion of wave speeds and variation in tides during the year, Verbeek moves on to discuss the only other tide gauge records in the Netherlands Indies. These three gauges marked the Straits between Madura Island and Java, some 800 km E of Krakatau.

From the drawings it can be seen that, although small disturbances preceded it, the first main disturbance took place at Oedjoeng Pangka at 1:30 a.m. August 28, at Soerabaja at 2:30, and at Karang Kleta at 2:45. On the tide gauge at Soerabaja two waves which arrived one hour apart were observed. The amplitude of the disturbance there was fairly unimportant and varied between 0.10 and 0.20 m.

On page 406 of his text, Verbeek introduces a 6-page table listing places and times where the wave was observed, mainly beyond the Netherlands Indies. His remaining text for this chapter (through his page 442) discusses these distant observations, covered in somewhat greater detail by Wharton in the 1888 Royal Society Report (see our pages 374–382). Verbeek did note, however, that several more distant wave records (San Francisco, Kodiak, Panama) could not be from waves that travelled a direct sea path from Krakatau's culminating explosion. This problem was not solved for over 70 years (see p. 382).

266

Volcanic and Seismic Activity Beyond Krakatau in 1883–4

In his last chapter, Verbeek moves beyond Krakatau to consider geophysical phenomena elsewhere that might be related, in some way, to the great eruption. He searched the Javasche Courant between 1 January 1883, and 31 December 1884, for earthquake reports, and added some data received from officials and others, to construct a 10-page table reproduced as his note 423. We have not reprinted this table, but have incorporated from it all eruption and all earthquakes felt within 200 km of Krakatau in our Chronology (p. 26–53). In discussing these data on p. 443, Verbeek observes:

From this compilation if appears that in 1883 60 earthquakes and in 1884 even 78 smaller and larger earthquakes were osberved, against only 47 in the year 1882.[424] [But in 1883, only 24 took place before August 26, converting to 37/year for 1883 before the great eruption.] From these figures it thus seems to follow that the earthquakes have strangely increased in number from 1882 to 1884, but for the most part, this only appears to be so. While before the eruption usually only rather important earthquakes were reported officially, after the catastrophe (which made a tremendous impression through all of the East Indies) reports were given with the greatest care for all earthquakes, no matter how insignificant. Thus their number now seems considerably larger than before. Because of the mostly insufficient data on magnitude, it is hardly possible to distinguish the mild from the severe earthquakes. Thus it is even possible that the proportion of important earthquakes for these three years is reversed from that indicated by the figures.

However in the last 4 months of 1883, following the large eruption, exceptionally many earthquakes have been observed, including several important ones. The maximum of volcanic activity no doubt occurs in the latter part of August, but after that time the earth's surface had by no means quieted down. In a previous chapter (see p. 227) a report was made of 9 earthquakes, which were felt in 1883 on and near the shores of the Sunda Straits. We pointed out there the remarkable fact that the lighthouse at Java's First Point, together with a part of Bantam, was visited by an earthquake far more severe than the other earthquakes for that year. On the other hand an earthquake felt widely in Bantam on December 6 was not at all noticed at Java's First Point, indicating that this shock had a different origin than those of our cross fissure.

After noting that the Sunda Straits were seismically quiet in 1884, Verbeek goes on to discuss 1883 volcanic activity elsewhere in the East Indies. Eruptions early in the year were not particularly noteworthy, but on August 26–27 Krakatau was not alone in experiencing geophysical unrest. On Banda Api, 2700 km to the E, there was a major landslide submerging nearly 10,000 m² of the SE coast that had stood 2–5 m above sea level. An earthquake was felt at nearby Ambon, and a "seaquake" experienced through most of the Mollucca Archipelago. August 27 eruptions were reported on Sumatra's Merapi and on Goenung Api. Verbeek goes on to mention other events that he regards as insignificant before moving, on p. 451, to geophysical events beyond the East Indies. He believes Krakatau may have had some connection with Australian earthquakes August 26–29, and he notes eruptions around the same time of Cotopaxi (Ecuador) and Izalco (El Salvador) near Krakatau's antipodes. The only large eruption during this time period was that of Augustine, Alaska, on October 6th, 1883. Verbeek feels that these distant events are more than coincidental, but he does not venture a connective hypothesis. However:

The [nearer events] make me consider likely a cohesion of the different subterranean spaces of the Indian Archipelago (Java, Sumatra, the Molluccas) and also Australia; thus an increase or decrease of pressure in one of these spaces necessitates changes in the other spaces, through which sudden displacements of steam and molten lava take place, which can make themselves felt through widespread earthquakes or volcanic eruptions. These large spaces speak for a partly molten condition of part of our globe.

The remaining two pages of this, Verbeek's concluding chapter, are devoted to a discussion of the difficulties experienced by those wishing to explain "the heat of the volcanic hearth" solely on local chemical action, such as the mixing of water with calcium or alkali metals, deep "in the inner earth."

Notes and References

Verbeek's notes, a combination of reference citations and extensive footnotes, were set in small type but nonetheless took up 14% of his numbered pages. We have shortened this section by listing only author and year when the full citation appears in our Bibliography and by referring the reader back to the first citation of a commonly cited reference rather than repeating it each time in the notes (e.g., 6 references to Javasche Courant of 25 May are all renumbered to reference 11, the number of the first citation.) We have otherwise retained Verbeek's consecutive numbering, to facilitate comparison with the original text, but have added a few notes of our own (e.g., 1a) by adding a letter to Verbeek's previous note. The notes have been translated from the Dutch by J.A. Nelen.

[1]Vogel (1690).

[1a][Translated from the German by Professor H.-U. Schmincke.]

[2]N.P. van den Berg (1884). The ship *Hollandsche Thuijn*, with Vogel aboard, did not arrive, as he indicates, on June 17, but on July 27, 1679 in Batavia. (Later communication of Mr. van den Berg.)

[3]The descriptions by Hesse, Frike, and a third person, Schweitzer, are found together in one binding, translated [in Hesse (1694)]. The second edition is from 1705; I have not been able to look at the German edition.

[4][Verbeek here quotes from van den Berg (1884, p. 19) concerning the names Rakata and Krakatau, which we reprint in translation on p. 291 (van den Berg's footnote 11).]

[5]C. de Groot (1883).

[6]*Sunda Strait and its approaches*, from the latest Dutch Government Surveys, with corrections by various officers of the Royal Navy. Published 1868. Corrections August, 1870, Nov., 1875 (scale 1:314,000).

[7]*Map of Sunda Strait and the SW area of Java Sea*, by A.R. Blommendal, Sea Captain. Scale 1:300,000, 1874.

[8]Verbeek (1881).

[9]*Batavia Handelsblad* of 21 May gives just after 10 o'clock; the *Algemeen Dagblad* of 21 May gives 10:30; the *Java Bode* of 21 May, 10:55; the Resident of Batavia in an official report to the Government mentions 10:45.

[9a]Telegram from the Assistant Resident of Buitenzorg to the Resident of Batavia on 20 May.

[9b]Message from the Assistant Resident of Tangerang to the Resident of Batavia on 20 May.

[9c]Message from the Controller of Ketimbang to the Resident of the Lampong District on 21 May.

[9d]Addition to the message from the Resident of Bantam to the goverment on 26 May.

[10]*Algemeen Dagblad, Java Bode, Bataviaasch Handelsblad* of 21, 22, and 23 May.

[10a]Report of Dr. A. Stammeshaus in his description of the August eruption.

[11]*Javasche Courant*, 25 May.

[12]*Javasche Courant*, 13 July.

[13]*Java Bode*, 23 May.

[14]According to particular communication of Mr. Dietrich at Semarang. From a collection of 234 newspaper and magazine articles made available to me by Mr. Dietrich. "Similar movements of the air were very clearly noticeable in Semarang on May 20 and 21. The upper window latch of my work room had not been closed; this created a very annoying long-lasting clatter of the windows on both days after 1 p.m." (C. Dietrich).

[15]*Het Indisch Vaderland* (edited at Semarang), No. 122.

[15a]Mr. W.H. Dittlof Tjassens, Sea Lieutenant First Class, was kind enough to obtain the indicated information at my request. According to reports of Mr. Pennink, ship-building engineer, who reviewed the registers of the overseer of the time-ball in Surabaja, the astronomic clock did not stop either in May or in August during the eruption; nor is anything noted about a jump of the chronometers. [A time-ball is an instrument used for indicating mean time and consists of a ball on a vertical rod which, usually by the closing of an electric current, drops from the top to the bottom of the rod at a certain time each day.]

[16]*Javasche Courant*, 22 May.

[19]*Java Bode*, 24 May.

[20]*Java Bode*, 26 May.

[21a]Message from the Controller of Ketimbang to the Resident of the Lampong District, dated 21 May.

[23]*Javasche Courant*, 1 June.

[24]*Javasche Courant*, 1 May and 4 May.

[25]*Java Bode*, 30 May. Report of Commander MacKenzie of the Dutch steamer *Zeeland*.

[26]*Algemeen Dagblad*, 8 June. Report copied from *Nieuw Padangsch Handelsblad*.

[27]*Java Bode*, 30 May. Report of Dr. D. Sulzer (incorrectly written here as Lubzer), medical doctor aboard the Dutch steamer *Soenda*.

[28]*Locomotief*, 1 June. Report of Dr. Sulzer.

[29]*Algemeen Dagblad*, 23 May. Report from Captain Grainger of the steamer *Archer* to the agents of the Queensland Royal Mail Line, Maclaine Watson and Co., Batavia.

[31]*Algemeen Dagblad*, 25 May.

[33]*Javasche Courant*, 12 June. Wrongly mentioned as April 21 to 23; also in *Algemeen Dagblad*, 13 June.

[33a]Special report by Mr. Herbing, from Batavia.

[34]From the *Tagliche Rundschau* (Berlin), 1883. No. 255 and 256. [Verbeek here gives three pages of German text reprinted by us (in translation) on p. 59 of our Narrative section.]

[34a]*Jahresbericht der Deutschen geographischen gesellschaft*, Berlin, 1884. [German text reprinted by us (in translation) on p. 59.]

[35]*Javasche Courant*, 29 May.

[37a]Report of Light Supervisor First Class J. Sparenberg, sent to me by Sea Lieutenant Second Class J.J. Poortman.

[39]*Algemeen Dagblad, Java Bode, Bataviaasch Handelsblad,* of 28 May.

[40a]Through mediation of the Resident of the Lampong Districts, I have requested a report of the experiences of the nine persons who had left for Krakatau in April, to collect *kekaret* and *tahoei* (types of tree gum) for a certain Hadji Soleiman of this Betong. The Controller Lux received from five of the nine persons a very much embellished and apparently incorrect story which I do not quote for these reasons. According to their story, after they had remained for three days without food or drink they were picked up by a *djoekoeng* (native vessel) belonging to Hadji Soleiman.

[42]*Javasche Courant,* 5 June.

[43]Special report from the Chief of the Batavia Harborworks.

[44]Extract from the journal of the *Samarang* of 20 May.

[46]The tidal readings of May 20 and 21 received from the Chief of the Batavia Harborworks.

[47]*Javasche Courant,* 22 June.

[47a]Report of Lighthouse Supervisor Second Class J. Schuit.

[47b]Report of Lighthouse Supervisor First Class J. Sparenberg.

[47c]Report about the time by Lighthouse Supervisor Fourth Class J. Stemlé.

[47d]Report by Lighthouse Supervisor First Class de Groot. All of these [47a through 47d] sent to me by Sea Lieutenant Second Class J.J. Poortman.

[48]*Algemeen Dagblad,* 20 June.

[49]*Algemeen Dagblad,* 26 June.

[50]*Javasche Courant,* 20 July.

[51]*Javasche Courant,* 21 August.

[52]Letter and map from Captain Ferzenaar lent to me through the cooperation of the Major of the General Staff F.C.E. Meyer, Chief of Topographic Service.

[53]*Bataviaasch Handelsblad,* 16 August.

[54]*Algemeen Dagblad,* 17 August.

[54a]*Java Bode,* 27 August.

[55]Special report from Captain of the Infantry, G.J.A. Beunk, Military Commander of Telok Betong.

[56]Forbes (1883).

[56a]Ashdown (1883).

[57]*Nature,* Oct. 25, 1883, [28:626–627]. Report from Mr. C. Meldrum of Mauritius.

[58]*Javasche Courant,* 2 October.

[59]Observations at Buitenzorg performed by writer.

[60]According to Mining Engineer Schuurman at Batavia.

[61]*Algemeen Dagblad,* 27 August.

[62]Official report from the keeper of the time-ball to the Harbormaster of Batavia on September 22.

[63]According to Dr. van der Stok of the Meteorological Observatory.

[63a]*Bataviaasch Handelsblad,* 28 August.

[64]Observations at the Meteorological Observatory at Batavia.

[64a]Further particulars about Tandjoeng Priok can be found in the report of the Batavian Harborworks for August, *Javasche Courant,* 18 September.

[65]Official report from the Resident of Batavia to the Director of Education and Industry on 14 March, 1884.

[66]*Javasche Courant* of 4 and 11 September. Official report from the Resident of Krawang to the Director of Education on 19 October.

[67]Official report from the Resident of Cheribon to the Director of Education on 28 December. Special information from the Controller Steinmetz to Lobener and from the Engineer of the Waterworks de Meijier.

[67a]Special report from the Resident of Japara. [Later in his text (p. 414 of the Dutch original) Verbeek noted that the wave's arrival time at Japara did not agree with that at Rambatan and Soerabaja. He believed that the Japara time was wrong.]

[68]Copies of graphs of the tidal scales in Madoera Strait were received by me from Chief Engineer J.J. Dijkstra of Soerabaja.

[68a]*Algemeen Dagblad,* 28 and 29 August.

[68b]Report of the Resident of Batavia, 21 May, 1884.

[69]*Javasche Courant,* 28 August.

[69a]*Javasche Courant,* 31 August.

[70]*Java Bode,* 27 August.

[72]*Java Bode,* 28 August.

[73]K.A. Naumann was an old and faithful official of the Department of Mines; he had been temporarily detached by the Harborworks to supervise the drilling and blasting of rock at Merak and would have returned the next day to Batavia, since his work at Merak had been finished.

[74]*Javasche Courant,* 18 September. The telegram is: "Last night (26 August) and this morning (27 August) earth- and seaquakes have taken place, partially destroying Merak; among others railway, pier and *Batoe Lawang* destroyed; Chinese camp wiped away. Cranes, pier still standing, trucks in sea; sea still always high."

> Engineer Sec. 3,
> In absence;
> Chief Mineworker,
> (signed) Naumann.

[75]Letter of acting Assistant Controller Abell. Reported in the *Locomotive* of 1 September.

[75a]This paragraph condensed by us.

[76]Official report from Engineer Nieuwenhuijs to the Chief of Batavia Harborworks on 29 August and 24 September, 1883.

[76a]Official report from the Resident of Bantam to the Director of Education on 12 October, 1883.

[78]*Bataviaasch Handelsblad,* 8 September. Story about a telegraph operator at Anjer (A. G. Schrok) [Schruit?] who was saved.

[78a]*Algemeen Dagblad,* 3 September.

[80][Verbeek here cites the detailed "before and after" map of Sunda Straits sold in Batavia in October, 1883 for 3 guilders. See our Bibliography under Topographic Bureau of Batavia.]

[81]*Bataviaasch Handelsblad,* 3 September. Story of a pilot (de Vries) at Anjer who was saved.

[81a]Report from the Resident of Bantam of 25 April, 1884.

[82]*Algemeen Dagblad,* 5 September. An eyewitness (Th.A. Gaston) account of the destruction of Tjaringin.

[84]*Javasche Courant,* 7 September.

[84a]This interesting fact was later confirmed to me by Dr. A.G.

Vorderman, city doctor at Batavia, who at my request collected information at the hospital. The four forced laborers had burn wounds over all of their bodies except on their heads. They all were released from the hospital completely healed.

[85]*Javasche Courant*, 4 September.

[85a]Report from the Head Engineer of the States Railroads, J.W. Ijzerman.

[86]Official report from the Resident of the Preanger Regencies to the Director of Education on 5 November, 1883.

[87]*Javasche Courant*, 4 September. Here, the arrival of the tidal wave is given as from 3 to 5 in the afternoon.

[88]*Javasche Courant* 7 September. Arrival of the wave given as 5 p.m.

[89]Special report from the Controller W. Beyerinck.

[90]The report of the Captain of the *Kedirie*, J.A. 't Hoen, is taken up in the *Javasche Courant*, 4 September.

[92]Official report from the Resident of the Lampong District to the Director of Education, 14 December, 1883.

[93]*Javasche Courant*, 11 September.

[94]*Algemeen Dagblad*, 10 September.

[95]Oral report by the Captain of the Infantry, G.J.A. Beunk, Military Commander of Telok Betong.

[96]Oral report by Mr. H.C. Stuivenberg, Captain of the steamer *Barouw* of the Government Navy.

[96a]*Javasche Courant*, 18, 24, and 28 December.

[97]*Algemeen Dagblad*, 11 September; *Bataviaasch Handelsblad*, 11 September; *Java Bode*, 12 September.

[98]*Javasche Courant*, 14 September.

[99]*Javasche Courant*, 5 October.

[100]*Algemeen Dagblad*, 1 September.

[101]Official report from the Resident of Benkolen to the Director of Education, 7 December, 1883.

[102]Official report from the Resident of Benkolen to the Government on 28 August.

[103]Official report from the Governor of Sumatra's West Coast to the Director of Education, on 26 December, 1883.

[104]*Nieuw Padangsch Handelsblad*, 1 September.

[105]Observations at Padang on 27 August, 1883, by Harbormaster E. Roelofs (Report to the Governor of Sumatra's West Coast on 28 August). [In the table below, "low" indicates the start of the rising (flood) wave, and "high" the start of the outgoing (ebb) wave. Δt = difference in time in minutes.]

low	Δt	high	Δt	Comments
12:50				Speed ± 4 miles, increasing.
	65	1:25		
1:55			55	
	55	2:20		
2:50			52	Speed ± 12 miles.
	56	3:12		
3:46			59	
	68	4:11		a little less.
4:54			66	
	58	5:17		
5:52			55	
	62	6:12		
6:54			63	Speed ± 6 miles.
	61	7:15		
7:55			70	
	64	8:25		
8:59			65	Speed ± 4 miles.
	90	9:30		
10:29			84	Strongly decreasing, until weak.
		11:54		

Still, after the last wave, three long but very weak waves were observed, the last one on the morning of the 28th at 7:30. The strongest rise took place with the third wave, about 3 p.m., followed by a strong backwash by which, among others, the River Mati (a small creek at Padang which runs into the right bank of the Padang River) emptied like a waterfall.

[106]*Sumatra Courant*, No. 107, 1883.

[107]Official report from the Resident of Sumatra's East Coast to the Director of Education, on 29 December.

[108]Official report from the Resident of Palembang to the Director of Education, on 8 September.

[109]Official reports from the Resident of Palembang to the Director of Education, on 24 December 1883, and 17 January 1884.

[110]Official report from the Resident of Riouw to the Director of Education, on 28 December.

[111]*Javasche Courant*, 21 September.

[112]Monthly report on the artificial lighting at Muntok during August by the Harbormaster at Muntok, J.W. Nix.

[113]Official report by the same to the Inspector of Beacons and Artificial Lighting, on 1 December.

[114]*Soerabajaasch Handelsblad*, No. 205, 1883.

[115]Official report from the Administrator of Toboali to the Resident of Banka, on 16 March, 1884.

[116]Official report from the Postal Official of the Lepar Islands to the Administrator of Toboali, on 16 March, 1884.

[117]Message from the Head Administrator of the Tin Mines, C.F. Michielson, to the representative of the Billiton Corporation of Batavia, on 31 August.

[118]Extract from the monthly report of the Administrator of Dendang K.A. Begemann about August 1883.

[119]Extract from the monthly report about August from the Light Supervisor on Ondiepwater Island.

[120]Extract from the monthly report about August from the Light Supervisor on Noordwachter Island.

[122]Extract from the monthly report of August from the Light Supervisor on Edam Island.

[122a]Extract from the monthly report of August by the Light Supervisor on Boompjes Island.

[122b]*Nature*, 1 May, 1884, 30:23.

[122c]*Nature*, 15 May, 1884, 30:72.

[123]Official report from the Administrator of Toboali to the Resident of Banka, on 3 September. *Javasche Courant*, 21 September, where the wrong date (29 August) is given. In the report from the Administrator of Toboali it was stated that the ship sailed 120 miles distant from Java's First Point S to W. This apparently is a mistake, it should have been N to W or possibly the ship was located S to W of Java's First Point. In either case, the ship was south of the Strait.

[124]*Nature*, 8 November, 1883b, 30:32. [Editorial condensation of a contribution by Meldrum to the Mauritius *Mercantile Record*.]

[125]*Bataviaasch Handelsblad*, 5 September.

[126]*Algemeen Dagblad*, 2 November.

[127]*Bataviaasch Handelsblad*, 9 February, 1884; taken from a Boston newspaper. [Verbeek's addenda notes that the Batavia newspaper report mentioned "Bezie" Island (Sebesi) to the NW of one of the *Besse*'s positions when it should have read "Babie Island" (N of Bantam Bay).]

[128]*Algemeen Dagblad*, 9 October.

[129]*Java Bode*, 9 October. In this report it is wrongly reported that the deck was covered with ash 3 to 4 ft thick; this should be 3 to 4 English thumbs. (In the original it says 3 or 4 inches.)

[130]Watson (1883). [We reprint a slightly different version, see pages 102–105 in our Narrative section and note 55.]

[131]Mr. E Metzger of Stuttgart declared that he was unable to compare the story of Captain Watson with the reports from Anjer [(Metzger, 1884, p. 241)]. In the morning, however, not all of Anjer was destroyed, but only a part; the last buildings were destroyed only after 10:00.

[132]Official report from the Resident of Riouw to the Government on 28 August. *Javasche Courant*, 7 September.

[133]*Algemeen Dagblad*, 4 September. Here, I copy also this item from an eyewitness in its entirety.

In Sunda Strait during the eruption.

A more terrible experience than the one experienced by the ship *Berbice* certainly was experienced by few seagoing persons. The ship *Berbice*, Captain Logan, was in the Sunda Strait, loaded with kerosene from New York, from Sunday afternoon until Tuesday night.

Following is the report of the alert captain.

Sunday (26 August) 2 p.m. Were 20 English miles straight south of Vlakken Hoek. In front of us very dark and threatening and the sun was burning hot. All small sail taken in.

4 p.m. The weather remains threatening, the top sails taken in.

6 p.m. Heavy thunder and lightning, suddenly fairly heavy ashfall. It was already completely dark then.

[Captain Logan's account of the next 24 hours is quoted in its original English by Tenison-Woods (1884) and we have reprinted it on p. 101–102. The *Algemeen Dagblad* continues Logan's account, however, and we print below the remainder of Verbeek's note 133, translated back into English by J.A. Nelen. The report resumes August 28:]

Midnight. The weather showed a tendency to subside, the lightning stayed more at a distance.

Tuesday 4 a.m. The weather somewhat calmer. Raised the lower main topsail.

8 a.m. Again saw daylight. The weather was calm and clear. The whole ship was covered with ash at least 8 English thumbs [inches] thick, on the booms and ropes was a crust of ash somewhat hardened by the dust rain which occurred between the ashfall. In all, well over 40 tons of ash must have been removed from the ship. I increased sail.

12 noon. Under full sail steered for Java Head. The thick layer of pumice prevented us from making much progress.

Midnight. Saw the light of Java Head. When we passed Princes Island we saw large banks of pumice between 18 English thumbs and 2 feet thick.

In the afternoon we passed east of Krakatau. As far as I could see, the island was separated into three parts by two gaping openings.

The sea remained covered with pumice and every so often we saw bodies float by.

Near Dwars-in-den-Weg I thought I saw a bank which had formed from that island up to Anjer. [Verbeek suggests this was floating pumice.]

The Captain declared that after what he had experienced with this ship of which really only the sails had been damaged, he would not be afraid to to go through any weather with that ship.

No one had thought about eating or drinking during those terrible twenty four hours.

Besides the *Berbice*, during that time, two other ships were in the Sunda Strait, which were seen from a distance from* Merak on Sunday. They were seen leaving and therefore maybe had the luck to get outside the ring of action in time.

[*This must have been an error in translating from the original English to the Dutch reprinted by Verbeek. The correct word is probably "near," rather than "from," because the *Berbice* was far to the SW of Merak at the time. We have not found the English original to resolve this problem.]

(These must have been the American barque *W. H. Besse* [but see inserted note on location of *Besse* (east of the Straits) on p. 165] and the English ship *Charles Bal*, the latter one however not leaving but arriving.)

[134]A copy of a report turned in on 31 August by the Harbormaster to the Governor of Sumatra's Westkust, and by him, on 11 September to the Government.

[135]*Bataviaasch Handelsblad*, 30 August.

[136]*Algemeen Dagblad*, 29 August.

[137]*Algemeen Dagblad*, 30 August, same in *Java Bode*, 31 August.

[138]*Bataviaasch Handelsblad*, 31 August.

[139]*Nieuwe Rotterdamsche Courant*, 23 October, 1883; report sent by the Engineer of Waterworks, R. van Sandick.

[140]R. van Sandick (1884a). This report gives a fairly good review of the eruption, but it contains the old errors about the disappearance and formation of islands, which were given by the first confused newspaper reports. (The island of Tempoza, near Merak, has entirely disappeared, while the island of Dwars-in-den-Weg has been divided into 5 distinct parts, etc). See also the same report in *la Nature Française*, 29 December, 1883. [On p. 92–96 we reprint a slightly later account by the same author.]

[140a]*Javasche Courant*, 5 October. Among the 34 persons were ten forced laborers of the lighthouse and one native supervisor. The reports of the *Javasche Courant* of 11 September and 18 September mention 39 persons.

[141]Official report from the Resident of the Lampong Districts, *Javasche Courant*, 19 October. Here it is given 5 Europeans and 12,539 natives, Chinese and other easterners, while our list indicates 12,456* persons. The latest count received by me from the Resident of the Lampong Districts in April 1884 is the correct one. According to estimate, 3000 persons have perished on Sebesi, of which 1000 were on the island temporarily. On Seboekoe, 150, of which 70 were temporary. These 3150 are included in the number 8037 for Ketimbang. *Except 5 persons of the Sekampong District who drowned when their proa capsized at sea [note added by Verbeek at end of book].

[142]Official count from the Resident of Bantam, *Javasche Cour-*

ant, 6 November. Here it is given 21,538 persons, our list, according to the count from the Resident of Bantam of 23 April, 1884, gives 21,533. Among the 1933 persons of the section Serang, are included 161 Chinese; among the figure for Anjer are included 7 Chinese at Anjer and 12 at Merak, together 19 Chinese (men and women). At the capital Anjer besides Europeans and Chinese, 568 natives perished, at the capital Tjaringin 1880 natives.

[143a]*Javasche Courant*, 4 September. In the kampong Pakies [200 km E by N] 2 children drowned.

[144]*Java Bode*, 17 September.

[145]*Java Bode*, 6 October.

[146]*Javasche Courant*, 12 October.

[146a][Verbeek gives this date as October 11, but he is describing the day following October 9.]

[147]*Javasche Courant*, 26 October.

[147a]Special report from Mr. D. Coops, First Assistant at the Hydrographic Bureau in Batavia. The information about the *Hydrograaf* is given by Sea Lieutenant First Class M.C. van Doorn.

[148]Official report from the Resident of Batavia to the Government, on 31 October.

[149]*Algemeen Dagblad*, 25 October.

[150]*Java Bode*, 15 November.

[151]*Java Bode*, 22 February, 1884.

[152]*Bataviaasch Handelsblad*, 25 February, 1884.

[153]Special report from Dr. H. Onnen of Salemba.

[154]Verbeek (1883a, p. 541–550).

[155]R. Hoernes. Erdbebenstudien. *Jahrb. der K. K. Geol. Teichsanstalt*. 1878. Page 387.

[156]Daubrée. Rapport sur le tremblement de terre ressenti a Ischia, le 28 Juillet 1883; causes probables des tremblements de terre. *Comptes Rendus de l'acadamie des Sciences*. Vol. 97, 8 October, 1883.

[157]H.J. Johnston Lavis. The Ischian earthquake of July 28, 1883. With Map. *Nature*, 6 September, 1883, 28:437–439.

[157a]G. Mercalli. *L'Isola d'Ischia*. Milano, 1884.

[159]F. Cordenons. Etude sur les tremblements de terre et les volcans. *Archives des sciences physiques et naturelles de Genève*. Vol. 10, 1883, p. 119–150 and 244–270.

[160]A. Perrey. *Propositions sur les tremblements de terre et les volcans*. Paris, 1863.

[161]R. Falb. *Brundzüge zu einer Theorie der Erdbeben und Vulkanausbrüche*. Graz. 1869–1871.

A short compilation of Falb's theory in: *Siruis, Zeitschrift für pop. Astronomie* 1868, No. 23 and 24.

[162]J. F. Schmidt. *Studien über Erdbeben*. Leipzig 1875.

[163]F.A. Forel. *Archives des Sciences Physiques et Naturelles de Genève*. Vol. 6, 1881, p. 487.

[164]Personal communication of the engineer of Public Works A. P. Melchior in Batavia, who carried out the mentioned calculations at my request.

[165]Daubrée. "Expériences sur la possibilité d'une infiltration capillaire au travers des matières poreuses, malgré une forte contrepression de vapeur; applications possible aux phénomènes géologiques." *Bulletin de la Société géologique*, Vol. 18, 1861, p. 193–202.

[165a]Erhard and Schertel have determined the melting point of several rocks with the aid of gold platinum alloys, whose melting points had been determined with porcelain air thermometers:

Rocks	Melting temperatures
Nepheline basalt from Neudorf near Annaberg	1080° to 1106°C
Melaphyre from Mt. Mulatto near Predazzo	1106°
Pitchstone from Arran	1106°
Leucite basalt from Pohlberg near Annaberg	1130°
Syenite from Edle Krone near Tharand	1130° to 1160°
Porphyritic pitchstone from Leissnig	1130° to 1160°
Quartz porphyry from Travignolo valley near Predazzo	1130° to 1160°
Asbestos	about 1300°

(Th. Erhard and A. Schertel. Die Schmelzpunkte der *Prinsep*'schen Legirungen und deren pyrometrusche Verwendung. *Jahrbuch für den Berg- und Hüttenwesen im Königr. Sachsen*, 1879, pages 154-170. A reference of this publication can be found in *Neue Jahrbuch für Mineralogie* etc. 1880 I, p. 188 of reference.)

[166]Joh. Müller. Lehrbruch der Physik und Meteorlogie. 8 Auflage, bearbeitet van L. Pfaundler 1879. vol. 2. Pages 259 and 291. The critical temperature for steam given by Cagniard de la Tour is somewhat uncertain, since during the tests the glass tubing was attacked by the highly heated steam.

Prof. J.D. van der Walls in Amsterdam estimates it to be 390°C on theoretical grounds and the critical pressure at 280 atmospheres. (Communication from Prof. Bosscha from Delft.) Daubrée says in his above mentioned publication (see note 156) that the critical temperature for steam according to Clausius is near 332°. [Critical temperature for water is now taken to be 374.1°C.] Thus here we have 332 Réaumur = 415°C [Réaumur = ⅘°C].

[166a]Grove. *Jahresbericht für Chemie für 1847 und 1848*, p. 326; *Ann. der Chemie und Pharm*. Band 63, p. 1; *Poggend. Annalen*. Band 76, p. 447. H. Sainte-Claire Deville. *Comptes Rendus*, vol. 45, p. 857; *Jahresbericht für Chemie für 1857*, p. 58; *Ann. der Chem. und Pharm*. Band 105, p. 383. H. Sainte-Claire Deville. *Comptes Rendus*, vol. 56, p. 195; *Jahresbericht für Chemie für 1863*, p. 27.

[166b]See above: Alex. Naumann. *Thermochemie*, Brauschwieg 1882, p. 107-167.

Also: Lothar Meyer. *Die modernen Theorien der Chemie*, 5th Edition, 1884, p. 411 and p. 479.

[166c]Fouqué (1879).

[167]F. Naumann. Lehrbuch der Geologie 2nd Auflage vol 1, p. 130. Brieslak. Lehrbuch der Geologie, vol. 2, p. 126.

[168]Bunsen. *Annalen der Chemie und Pharmacie*, vol 62, 1847, p. 1. Also in: *Pogg. Annalen*, vol 72, 1847, p. 159.

[169a]G. Bischof. *Die Wärmelehre des Innern unseres Erdkörpers*. Leipzig 1837. On page 276 in the note one finds: "The observation at Vesuvius as well as at Pic von Tenerife show that most of the ash was ejected last, and that it indicates the end of the eruption." And on p. 277 in the note: "In close relation to these general remarks we also have the condition that the large lava flow which

at Etna and Vesuvius does not come from the crater itself, and that the mix of molten material is usually in reverse proportion to the height at which the fissure which ejects the lava has formed. But with both these volcanoes a flank eruption ends every time with an ejection of ash from the crater, in other words from the summit of the mountain itself."

[170]Verbeek (1883a, p. 402).

[171]Verbeek and Fennema (1881, p. 12 and 15). Also in Verbeek (1881, p. 152).

[172]Taken from the *Javasche Courant* and from offical Government reports.

[173][This note, covering 3 full pages of Verbeek's book, gives detailed calculations for his ballistic models. We have not reproduced this note "since the laws of air resistance," as Verbeek himself admits, were "still only incompletely known."]

[174]Information supplied by the Chief of General Staff in Batavia, Colonel A. Haga.

[175]*Nature*, 25 October, 1883, 28:612.

[176]Observed on 5 June, 1876. *Jaarb. Mijnwezen*, 1881, I, p. 171.

[177]At Bengkalis [920 km NNW of Krakatau], Siak, Pakan and at Poeloe Lawan (Pelalawan) an extremely thin ash layer fell. At the mouth of the Rokkan River [1020 km NNW] no ash fell. Official report of the Resident of Sumatra's East Coast to the Director of Education, Worship, and Industry on 29 December, 1883.

[178]At Singapore [840 km N × W of Krakatau] a thin layer of dust was observed on the furniture on 27 August at 8 in the evening. *Java Bode* 4 September (taken from the *Straits Times*). *Soerabaja Handelsblad* No. 209 (also from the *Straits Times*).

[179]At Tandjoeng Pinang, the capital of the Residency Riouw, located on the island Bintang [and 70 km SSE of Singapore], no ash fell. Also from Batam and Karimon no ashfall is reported, but an extremely small quantity of dust must have fallen here, as well as at nearby Singapore. On the island Lingga [S of Singapore] on the 27th in the afternoon at 3 o'clock it became very dark, but no ash fell. Tuesday the 28th, a very fine ashfall. (Personal communication of the Resident of Riouw; official report of same to Director of Education on 28 December; offical report of the Assistant Resident of Lingga to the Resident of Riouw on 30 August.)

[180]According to the Resident of Banka (offical report to the Director of Education on 8 December) no ash fell in this residency; only a very fine dust blew in the air at Muntok in a quantity not worth mentioning. (Letter of the Resident of Banka to the undersigned on 15 December.) According to the harbormaster, however, a fine ash layer was observed at Muntok in the morning of August 27 (from the monthly reports for August from the coast lighting of Muntok.)

[181]Ash fell on the island Noordwachter. (See [p. 215] and note 120 [p. 271].)

[182]In the Residency of Krawang no ash fell on Pamanokan [270 km E by S of Krakatau] and Tjisaelanden. The border runs from kampong Tempoeran, near the coast, in a nearly straight line to the volcano Boerangrang. The towns Dawoe [220 km E by S], Poerwakarta [230 km ESE] and Wanajassa [250 km ESE] thus are within the boundary. (Personal report from the Resident of Krawang).

[183]In the Residency Preanger Regency ash was observed at 6 places, Tjipadalarang, Batoe-Djadjar, Tjililin [250 km ESE], Tjisandaoet, Goenoeng Haloe, and even a little easterly, nothing however at the capital Bandoeng [258 km ESE], nor in the district Tjisondari. (Personal communication of the Controller of West Bandoeng, H.V. Baron Bentinck, of Tjipadalarang; official report of the Resident of Preanger-Regencies to the Director of Education on 5 November, 1883).

The ash boundary thus runs from Boerangrang closely along Bandoeng to the volcano Patoea and its northerly foothills; next the ash hit the northerly slope of the Breng-Breng mountains so that south of the mountain range, for instance at Sindang-Farang, no ash fell.

The ash border reached the southern coast near the mouth of the Tji-(river) Boeni. (Personal communication of the Assistant-Resident J. J. Bischoff at Tjandjoer.)

[184]On the Cocos Islands, ash fell from Monday, August 27 at 4 p.m. until the night of Wednesday to Thursday, August 29–30; the wind direction during that time was NNE to NE; the ash was very fine, the thickness is estimated about half a thumb [inch], probably considerably too high. A ship belonging to Mr. Ross, *The Tweed* which was 320 miles from Krakatau received up to 7? thumbs [inches] ash on deck. The estimate of the thickness must have been quite exaggerated. (Personal communication from Mr. Ross of Keeling Island, communicated to me by Mr. P. Landberg of Batavia.)

[185]Ash fell in the whole Residency of Benkoelen. In the section Mokko-Mokko the ashfall, however, was of very little significance. (Official report of the Resident of Benkoelen to the Director of Education on 7 December, 1883.)

[186]Ash fell neither in Indrapoera nor in the 12 Kota's, the two most southern subsections of the government of Sumatra's Westkust [650 km NW of Krakatau]. (Official report from the Governor of Sumatra's West Coast to the Director of Education on 26 December, 1883.) The ash boundary thus runs from Mokko-Mokko south and east of Padang Highlands back to Bengkalis, our starting point on the east coast of Sumatra.

[187]Per bouw (or bahoe) of 500 square rods (or 7096.5 m²), 2160 kg has been calculated to have fallen (information of the Assistant-Resident O.A.B. Lautier of Soekaboemi.)

Thus assuming a specific gravity of 2.2 for the porous ash:
$7096.5 \times x \times 2.2 = 2160$ (x in mm)
$x = \frac{1}{7}$ mm.

[188]At Buitenzorg an average of 315 g dried ash fell per m². Thus:
$x \times 2.2 = 0.315$, or $x = 0.143 = \frac{1}{7}$ mm.

[190]Own observations at the locations themselves in October.

[191]Addenda of the Controllers [of Semangka, Sekampong, Sepoeti, and Menggala] to the official letter of the Resident of Lampongs to the Director of Education on 14 December, 1883.

At Teloeq Betoeng the thickness could not be measured very well in October.

The Controller van Hasselt at Soekadana [120 km N of Krakatau] reports that 16 kg/m² of ash fell, which corresponds to 7 mm thickness. The Controller of Sepeoti reports 25 Amsterdam pounds, thus 6 mm.

Comparing the figures in the *Javasche Courant* of 2 October, the thickness of the ash is found to be the "width of a hand" at Sepoeti (Goenoeng Soegi), 0.03 m at Soekadana, and even 0.2 m at Goenoeng Raja, figures which do not correspond to the 6 and 7 mm values given above, and which no doubt are much too high; in general, determination of weights is of greater value than the figures for thickness, the latter are almost always overestimated. The figure for Menggala is probably considerably too high.

[192]With the exception of Kroë, where the thickness of the ash was measured immediately, all the figures for Benkoelen are probably much too high.

Nowhere was the weight correctly determined. Official report of the Resident of Benkoelen to the Director of Education 7 December, 1883.

[193]Addenda of the Assistant-Resident and Controllers to the official letter of the Resident of Palembang to the Director of Education 24 December, 1883.

[193a][Official report of the Controller of Ogan-Ilir.]

[193b][Official report of the Assistant-Resident of Palembang.]

[193c][Official report of the Controller of Iliran and Banjoe-Asin.]

[193d][Official report of the Controller of Moesi-Ilir.]

[193e][Official report of the Assistent-Resident of Tebing-Tinggi.]

[193f][Official report of the Controller of Djambi.]

[194]Official report of the Resident of Sumatra's East Coast to the Director of Education 29 December, 1883, and *Javasche Courant* 30 October.

[195]Official report of the Resident of Riouw to the Director of Education 28 December, 1883.

[196]Official report of the Resident of Banka to the Director of Education 8 December, 1883.

[197]Junghuhn, *Java.* 1854 German translation, vol 2, p. 819–828.

[197a]*Java Government Gazette*, vol. 4 May 20, 1815, No. 169. Here a rather extensive piece is found in English and in the following number of May 27, No. 170, the Dutch translation, copied from a personal letter of the Capt. of a ship, which was at Makasser during the eruption of Tambora. Already on April 5 there were shots heard. During the night of April 10–11, again shots were heard but now much louder than before and which became especially heavy or severe in the morning of the 11th, so that the ship and the houses at the fort vibrated strongly. Between 10 and 11 a.m. ash began to fall. At 11 it was almost completely, and at 12:00 completely, dark. The next morning (April 12) after 7:30 it slowly started to get light; in the afternoon the sun very faintly came through the dust-loaded atmosphere. The ash continued to fall in small quantity during this and the next day (April 13). At Moressa, going ashore, the Captain found the earth covered everywhere with an ash layer which was 1¼ English thumbs (0.032 m) thick. [Makasser is 373 km NNE of Tambora.]

From the 12th to the 15th the sky remained dark and overcast; April 15 the Captain went under sail, arrived in the view of the island Soembawa on the 18th, where large banks of floating pumice where encountered, and arrived on the 19th at the roads of Bima. The thickness of the ash layer in the vicinity of Bima amounted to 3¾ English thumbs (0.095 m). The ashfall started here, 40 minute miles E of Tambora, on the morning of April 11 at 7:00 and lasted 12 hr longer than at Makasser (thus until the 14th of April in the morning?). Also the sea had been in heavy motion so that the water stood up to one foot high in the houses at Bima and numerous proas were thrown on the beach.

See also a short report in the *Algemeene Konst- en Letterbode* for the year 1815, 2nd part. The thickness of the ash at Makasser is given here as 1½ thumbs.

[198]*Java Bode*, 4 September.

[200]*Tägliche Rundschau* No. 292, 1883. *Meteorologische Zeitschrift*, February 1884, p. 54.

[201]Personal communication of Mr. Ross of Keeling Island, received by intervention of Mr. P. Landberg at Batavia.

[203]Daubrée (1883).

[204a]*Neues Jahrb. für Mineralogie*, 1884, II, p. 32.

[204b]*Meteorologische Zeitschrift*, 1884, p. 55.

[206]*Nature*, 13 December, 1883, 29:152. [Letter to the editor from H. Fox.]

[207]*Weekly Ceylon Observer*, No. 40, Colombo, 13 October. From the *Ceylon Observer*, 1 October.

[208]*Nature*, 13 December, 1883, 29:154. Report from Perth. Probably the same ship is meant in the same number of *Nature*, p. 150.

[209]*Gold Coast Times*, 14 September, copied in *Nature*, 6 December, 1883, 29:133.

[210]Report of Mr. Zaalberg, minister at Paramaribo, copied in *The Locomotive*, No. 262.

[211]*Nature*, 11 October, 1883, [28:?].

[211a]*Meteorologische Zeitschrift*, February, 1884, p. 56.

[212]*Nature*, 13 December, 1883, 29:152. [Letter to the editor by H. Clarke.]

[213]*Nature*, 10 April, 1884, 30:549. Report of Mr. Sereno E. Bishop at Honolulu.

[213a]*Nature*, 17 April, 1884, 30:573. Report of the same.

[214]*Nature*, 20 December, 1883, 29:174. Reports [by the editor] of the same.

[214a]*Nature*, 20 December, 1883, 29:181. Report of Mr. G.F. Burder, passenger aboard *Zealandia*.

[215]*Nature*, 2 October, 1884, 30:537. Reports of Mr. Bishop.

[216]*Ceylon Observer*, 10 and 11 September. Green sun at Colombo and other localities at Ceylon during those days.

Ceylon Observer of 17 September. Manipay, Jaffna, 10 September; Madulsima, 11 and 12 September; Batticaloa, 11 September.

Ceylon Observer of 18 September. Madras, 9–12 September.

Ceylon Observer of 20 September. Amblantota, 9–11 September.

Weekly Ceylon Observer, No. 37, Colombo, September 17. Green sun at Colombo, Puleadierakam, Batticaloa and all the rest of Ceylon of Sept. 9–12.

The heat at Colombo during the days of 9–12 September was determined to be less than usual.

The *Weekly Ceylon Observer*, No 38, Colombo, 29 September. Calcutta, Bellary, Karnool and other places in south English India. All reports speak of bluish and greenish colors of the sun.

[217]*Nature*, 11 October, 1883, [28:576–577]. Report of W.R. Manley of Ongole (east coast of English India, north of Madras). After 4:00 he observed the sun first bluish-green, then green, next yellow-green; after sunset a yellow, then orange and red reflection in the west, visible until one hour after sunset [see p. 157 for his account].

Nature, 18 October, 1883, 28:597. Reports of a green sun on Ceylon taken from the *Ceylon Observer*.

Nature, 25 October, 1883, 28:611. At Ongole the light effects of 22–24 September were observed a second time, but much weaker than the first time.

Nature, 1 November, 1883, 29:7. About the green sun at Colombo 9–11 September.

Nature, 8 November, 1883, 29:28 and 15 November, 1883, 29:54. Reports of C. Michie Smith at Madras that the sun, moon and stars had green colors after rising and before setting, from 8(?)–14 September and for the second time from 22–24 September. The spectrum indicated much water vapor. The phenomena spread over all of southern India up to Vizagapatam, was not visible at Bombay, but was in the west up to Aden.

Later Mr. C. Michie Smith has given more extensive reports about the green color of the sun at Madras and other places in British India. (The report was read at the meeting of the Royal Society of Edinburgh, 7 July, 1884, and printed in *Nature*, 7 August, 1884, 30:347). The green sun appears to have been seen on Ceylon and in the southern part of the Presidentship Madras up to Ongole in the north, not before 9 September in the evening, and in the eastern part of the Presidentship not before 10 September in the morning. Thus, the date of 8 September is faulty. At numerous places in British India the green color reappeared on 22 September.

The phenomena of the the green sun and moon should, according to Prof. Michie Smith, be separated from the beautiful red sunsets, first of all, because the horizon in the case of the latter was very clear and transparent, while with the setting of the green sun the horizon was so hazy that the stars became invisible there; also since it appeared from spectroscopic research that during the green sun a very strong absorption of the red end of the spectrum took place, which during the red sunrises was not observed at all.

Although Prof. Smith ascribes the absorption of the red to water vapor, it can, according to him, also be caused and explained by little dust (ash) particles floating in the air. At Muttum, south of Madras, the sun was seen as green on 10 September and several days thereafter; at Bellary the sun was emerald green during rising and setting from 10 to (and including) 14 September.

Also at Coonoor in Nilgiris green tints were observed.

Aboard the ship *Cleomene* the sun and moon were seen as green on 9, 10, and 11 September, between 8° and 16°N and 83°30′ to 88°40′E. Also a green moon was seen on the night of 9–10 September and a green sun 10 September in the morning, aboard the steamer *Pelican* at 10°4′N and 64°12′E.

[217a]*Meteorologische Zeitschrift*, February 1884, p. 58.

[217b]*Nature*, 20 December, 1883, No. 174; and No. 742, 17 January, p. 259. Reports of Mr. Bishop.

[218]Report of Hicks Pasha dated "Duem, 24 September." *Nature*, 20 December, 1883, 29:181.

[219]Report of F.C. Constable dated "Karachi, 16 October." [Letter to the editor.] *Nature*, 15 November, 1883, 29:55.

[220]Reports of J. Edmund Clark at York, and J.L. Bozward at Worcester. *Nature*, 6 December, 1883, 29:131–132.

[220a]Report of van Karlinski in *Zeitschrift der Oesterreich Gesellschaft für Meteorologie*, vol. 19, 1884, p. 124. (Distinct from *Meteorologische Zeitschrift* mentioned above.)

[221]*Java Bode*, No. 252 of 25 October, taken from the paper *Comercio* of 4 October, appearing at Manila.

[221a]*Java Bode*, of 12 November, taken from the Hong-Kong *China Mail*.

[222a]*Nature*, 13 December, 1883, 29:153.

[223]*Java Bode*, of 17 October, taken from the *Yokohama* (Japan) *Gazette*.

[224]Report of Mr. Hamilton from Yokohama. *Nature*, 13 December, 1883, 29:153. [In a letter from W. Hamilton.]

[225]Report of Prof. James Main Dixon at Tokyo. *Nature*, 27 December, 1883, 29:196. [In a letter to the editor by L. Campbell.]

[226]Letter of Mr. Edward Whymper to Mr. Norman Lockyer dated 21 December, 1883. *Nature*, 27 December, 1883, 29:199.

[226a]*Nature*, 20 December, 1883, 29:177.

[226b]*Nature*, 17 January, 1884, 29:260. Report taken of the great work of China by van Richthofen, part 1, p. 97.

[228]About the dates on which exceptional phenomena were observed for the first time the following can be found in "Ciel et Terre" 15 February, 1884 p. 553, copied from *Science*, Vol. 3, No. 49.

1883	August	28	Rodriguez Island
	"	28	Mauritius Island
	"	28	Seychelles
	"	30	Brazil
	September	1	Gold Coast
	"	1	New Ireland
	"	2	Venezuela
	"	2	Antilles
	"	2	Peru
	"	5	Hawaiian Islands
	"	8?(10)	southern part of British-India
	"	8?(9)	Ceylon
	"	15	South Australia
	"	15	Tasmania
	"	20	Cape of Good Hope
	October	8	Florida
	"	19	California
	"	20	southern part of United States
	November	9	England
	"	20	Turkey
	"	21	United States
	"	25	Italy
	"	26	Frankfurt
	"	27	Belgium
	"	28	Germany
	"	30	Spain
	"	30	Sweden

I am sorry to say I am unable to give extensive observations about the light reflections in Dutch East India. The phenomena were very clear at Buitenzorg and Serang in the last week of November and in the beginning of December. In addition at Serang in the night of 8–9 October a very clear sky was observed, after the moon set at 11:25 p.m. (See note 146).

[229]*Zeitschrift der Oesterr. Gesellschaft für Meteorologie*, Vol. 19, 1884, p. 72–74. W. van Bezold. Ueber die ausserordentlichen Dämmerungserscheinungen.

[230]*Comptes Rendus de l'Académie des Sciences*, Vol. 98, No. 3 (21 January, 1884), p. 164. A. Angot. Sur les crépuscules colorés. Here the fact is mentioned that such light effects already have been observed in 1831 and were explained that time not by volcanic dust or vapor but in the normal way by water vapor and very high-lifted snow particles.

[231]*Comptes Rendus de l'acádamie des Sciences*, No. 4 (4 February, 1884) p. 317. G. Tissandier. Sur la cause des lueurs crépusculaires de 1883. In July 1831 an eruption took place in the sea between Sciacca, Sicily, and the island Pantelleria. The newly formed island (Graham, according to the English, Julia according to the French) was later washed away by the sea.

[232]*Comptes Rendus*, No. 5, 1884, p. 318. M. Perrotin. Sur les lueurs crépusculaires des derniers mois. Also in Barbados [?] an eruption and earthquake took place 10 and 11 August, 1831. The sky reflections of 1831 thus definitely cannot be against volcanic theory.

[232a]Communication of G. Karston, from Kiel, *Science*, Vol. 3, No. 55, 1884, p. 231.

[233]*Zeitschrift der Oesterr. Gesellsch für Meteorologie*, Vol. 19, 1884 p. 78. The contents of Krakatau which are used as the basis for this calculation, however, do not matter here, since not Krakatau itself was blown into the sky, but the materials which were in molten condition in the crater, the crater pipe and the subterranean lava cavity.

[233a]The morning and evening red appears to be mainly a diffraction phenomenon, and partly a breaking phenomenon, because of the fine water and ice particles floating in the higher air layers. Solid particles in the air seem to be necessary for the condensation of water vapor. One sees, thus, that after the eruption of Krakatau the conditions for exceptionally strong red reflection were very favorable: large quantities of water vapor which were ejected into the high and highest air layers and solid dust particles, which served as nuclei of condensation.

See the important article of Prof. Kiessling (1884).

[234]*Nature*, 6 December, 1883, 29:135.

[235]*Nature*, 6 December, 1883, 29:130-131. Also 14 July rain with dust must have fallen at Worcester, thus before the large eruption of Krakatau.

[236]*Nature*, 20 December, 1883, 29:178.

[237]*Nature*, 10 January, 1884, 29:252.

[238]*Nature*, 3 January, 1884, 29:225.

[239]*Nature*, 20 December, 1884, 29:174; and 3 January, 1884, 29:224.

[240]*Nature*, 20 December, 1883, 29:175; and 31 January, 1884, 29:308, with picture of crystals.

[241]*Cölnische Zeitung*, 4 January, 1884; *Tägliche Rundschau* (Berlin), No. 5, 1884.

[242]*Nature*, 3 January, 1883, 29:225. Taken from the *Japan Weekly Mail*, published at Yokohama, 20 October, 1883. "The official *Gazette* (the editor, in a Japanese-edited paper) states that since the 13th (October) a constant haze has pervaded the atmosphere of Sappora (Yeso, 43°N and 141°E); and that the sun and moon are of a blood red colour; clouds of ashes fall continuously. The phenomenon is ascribed to some volcanic eruption." [Tarumai, 40 km S of Sapporo, erupted at that time.]

[243]*Nature*, 24 January, 1884, 29:284.

[243a]*Nature*, 22 May, 1884, 30:91.

[243b]During the new topographic survey of the Tengger mountain range it has been shown that the map by Junghuhn is very incorrect: the crater is even larger than Junghuhn reports.

[243c]Verbeek (1883a, p. 423–429).

[244]Verbeek (1881, p. 155 and 180).

[245]Concerning this see Verbeek (1881), Verbeek (1883a), and Verbeek and R. Fennema (1881).

[245a]Verbeek (1883b, p. 39–43). This last sentence, with reference 245a, was added as a footnote on p. 169 of the original text.

[249d]Die Krakatau-Aschen des Jahres 1883. Report of *Naturf. Gesellschaft* of Leipsig, 1883. Copied in *Chemisches Centralblatt*, 1884, p. 129–135.

[374]Description and picture of the regulator used at Batavia (English governor) can be found in *King's Treatise on the Science and Practice of the manufacture and distribution of Coal Gas*. Vol 2. London, 1879, p. 309, Fig. 173.

[375]Description and picture of the indicator used in Batavia (French mouchard, English pressure register) can be found in above named *King's Treatise*, Vol. 2. London, 1879, p. 309, Fig. 189.

[388]Lyell. *Principles of Geology*. Vol. II, 10th Edition. 1868, p. 58–74.

[390]*Science*, Vol. III, 1884, p. 89–93. W.H. Dall, A new volcano island in Alaska.

[391]Report about the survey of the changes in Sunda Strait after the eruption of Krakatau in 1883, dated 22 October, to the commander of sea forces in Dutch East Indies, by Sea Lt. First Class M. C. van Doorn.

[392]H. Vogelsang. *Die Vulkane der Eifel*. Haarlem, 1864.

[393]*Neues Jahrb. für Mineralogie*, etc., 1871, Vol. 469.

[393a][Docters van Leeuwen (1936, p. 24).]

[394]From Figure 48 [p. 194], and [Verbeek's] figures 39a and b [see opposite], it appears that the radius r = 2080 m, the height h = 832 m, AC = 3840 m, KD = 770 m, angle AKC = 136½°, and G = content of triangle AKC = ½ × 3840 × 770 m². The contents of the piece which disappeared BDK ([Verbeek's] figure 39b) thus is = content KABCK − content prism

$$\text{KACK} = \frac{\pi r^2 h}{3} \times \frac{136\frac{1}{2}}{360} - \frac{1}{3}Gh = 1.019 \text{ km}^3.$$

[395]Determined planimetrically.

[395a]The steep collapsed coast areas of Lang and the east side of Krakatau can be seen from some explorations (sketches) produced on 20 April, 1884, aboard the German warship *Prinz Adalber*, Commander Sea Captain Mensing I, and published in the *Annalen der Hydrographie*, Vol. 12, 1884, Chapter 8.

[398a]*Almanach für die K.K. Kriegsmarine*, 1883, Internationale Scala für Höhe des Seeganges. See also: *Handbuch der Oceanographie, etc.*, Vienna, 1883, p. 401.

L. Franzius, *Der Wasserbau*, Chapter XIV, p. 697, gives 12 m as the greatest height of the waves. The reports vary greatly, since the wave heights are, of course, difficult to measure during storms in open sea.

[399]Personal communication from Engineer van Bosse, Acting Chief of Harborworks at Tandjong Priok.

[399a]These and subsequent time measurements were made on the original water level records, not on the smaller copy (figure 9 of the Atlas [not reproduced here]). The reduced copy allows an uncertainty of several minutes.

[463]These photographs are available from Mr. Schultze and Mr. Thomas, photographers at Batavia, and the interesting photographs of the May eruption (see [p. 16 and 62]) by Mr. Hamburg of Batavia.

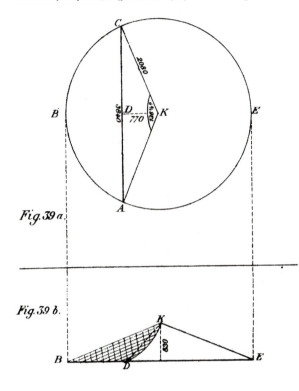

Fig. 39 a.

Fig. 39 b.

Biography of R.D.M. Verbeek (by Ir.C. Blotwyk)

As we read more of Verbeek's important contribution, our curiosities grew about this man whose name was so closely linked with Krakatau yet whose life was virtually unknown to readers of English. We asked Ir. C. Blotwyk, of the Mineralogical Geological Museum at the Delft University of Technology, to tell us about the man, and he kindly provided the following biography. A more extensive biography, from which we have taken Figure 60, was written by Wing Easton in 1926 at the time of Verbeek's death.

Rogier Diederik Marius Verbeek
April 7, 1845—April 9, 1926

Verbeek was born in Doorn, near Utrecht, the son of a clergyman of the local Dutch Reformed Church. At the age of 16 he was admitted to the Delft University of Technology, where he graduated in 1866 as a mining engineer. His final year of academic studies was spent at the Bergakademie of Freiberg in Germany, the 19th century European academic center for mining and geology. After graduation he married Helene Fritsche, the daughter of one of his professors in Freiberg.

In 1867 Verbeek started his career with the Mining Department of the former Dutch East Indies, as Holland had practically no mining industry of its own. During his initial years as a junior mining engineer at the East Borneo coal mines, he dedicated all his spare time and (limited) private means to a geological study of the whole area. His first paper, "The nummulites of the East Borneo limestone," published in 1871, drew much attention, as it brought new field evidence that changed some of von Richthofen's concepts of the extension of Tethys.

From then on Verbeek was a recognized geologist, and the Mining Department transferred him to Sumatra for a geological evaluation of the recently discovered Ombilin coal fields. Here again he extended his fieldwork over the whole area, first the southern part of Sumatra and then its west coast. At that time,

there was no topographical base for geological fieldwork, so topographical mapping was always part of the job. Verbeek, himself, prepared such maps as well as thin sections for microscopic rock studies. The printing of the report and the maps was done in Holland under Verbeek's supervision when on home leave in 1882–1883. The final result earned him an honorary degree from the University of Breslau in Germany. Back again from home leave, while preparing for a new assignment, the eruption of Krakatau occurred, and Verbeek received government orders to study "the cause, extension and effects of the eruption." The publication of his report in May 1885 made him world famous.

After this "interruption," Verbeek started a geological survey of all Java and Madoera. Ten years later this work, covering some 130,000 km² (over 30 million acres), was finished.

From 1896 to 1901 Verbeek continued his fieldwork in the eastern part of the archipelago, retiring in 1901 after 34 years of service in the tropics. Back in Holland he started a complete bibliography on mining and geology in the Dutch East Indies. This work he carried out in yearly publications which he continued until he was 80; one year later he died from a stroke.

Verbeek was a man gifted with an enormous zest for work; his working day stretched until two or three o'clock in the morning. Not everyone could keep his pace, and Verbeek, not understanding why others lacked his energy, preferred to work with only a few trusted people who could keep up with him. Nevertheless he was a gregarious man who particularly enjoyed hosting musical parties. He was an enthusiastic piano player and loved operas, Wagner being his favorite composer. Characterizing this old Dutch master of geology, one may rightly call him a Wagnerian hero in his field.

Figure 60. Photograph of R.D.M. Verbeek and his great-grandson taken shortly before his death in 1926. From biographical memorial of Verbeek by Easton (1926).

Smithsonian Institution

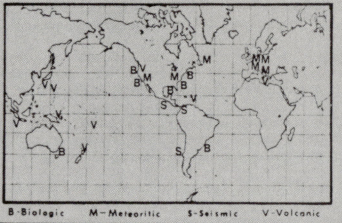

B-Biologic M—Meteoritic S-Seismic V-Volcanic

SEAN
Scientific Event Alert Network

BULLETIN

VOLCANIC EVENTS
Mt. St. Helens (Washington): Lava extrusion ad
Krakatau (Indonesia): Small ash clouds ......
Langila (New Britain): New lava flow descend

natur

Vol 294 No 5843 24 Dec 1981 6 Jan 19

SCIENCE

AN ILLUSTRATED JOUI

PUBLISHED WEEKLY

VOLUME IV

JULY–DECEMBER 1884

THE 1883
ERUPTION
OF KRAKAT

PHILOSOPHICAL TRANSACTIONS

OF

THE ROYAL SOCIETY

OF LONDON

A. MATHEMATICAL AND PHYSICAL SCIENCES

VOLUME 266   PAGES 425-533   NUMBER 1178

2 July 1970   Price £2 17s (U.S. $7.40)

Volcanic dust in the atmosphere;

with a chronology and assessment of its
meteorological significance

THE ERUPTION OF KRAKATOA,

AND

SUBSEQUENT PHENOMENA.

REPORT OF THE KRAKATOA COMMITTEE

OF THE

ROYAL SOCIETY.

VIZ. :—

ABERCROMBY, THE HON. RALPH.   RUSSELL, THE HON. F. A. ROLLO.

Verbeek's monograph—from his own observations at Buitenzorg, through his collation of other narrative accounts, to his conclusions on the causes of the various 1883 events—provides the natural transition from our own compilation of eyewitness accounts (Part II) to subsequent scientific interpretations (Part IV) of the phenomena so vividly described by the eyewitnesses. Below we present a succession of excerpts from the scientific literature selected in an attempt to provide the reader not only with authoritative explanations, but also with an appreciation of the historic development of these explanations through the last hundred years. Within each of the four main disciplinary approaches—geologic, acoustic/oceanographic, meteorologic, and biologic—we have sequenced these selections chronologically, in order to show the development of ideas, and we have inserted some of our own words to provide context and continuity. To retain footnote and reference information in a manner unobtrusive to the general reader, we have used superscript numbers in each text that guide the reader to footnotes and references at its end. Source reference titles and full citations are listed in our Bibliography. We have sequenced the references alphabetically and added footnotes after the references, a practice that requires renumbering of some originally-numbered references, but one that helps the reader to see quickly which references have (and have not) been cited by an author. We have renumbered all illustrations consecutively, but retained the original author's identification in the legend.

Many questions about the events of 1883 will not be answered by the interpretations appearing below. The critical question of when and how the northern half of Rakata Island collapsed into the sea during the paroxysmal eruption has never been convincingly answered, and the absence of seismic records at the time may mean that it will never be answered. The generating mechanism for the devastating seawaves remains controversial, and modern petrochemical studies of the eruptive products have, surprisingly, not yet been undertaken. We must also candidly state that we have not read each of the many works that have been written on Krakatau, and we have no doubt missed important references, particularly those in other languages and in non-geologic publications. What follows, then, is a personal selection of papers that should help the reader whose interest has been piqued by

the descriptions reprinted in preceeding sections. It should be clear from this selection that understanding of these events has developed substantially during the last hundred years, but that many questions remain to be answered about this most important eruption.

Geology

Verbeek's geological training no doubt prompted him to emphasize the geological aspects of the 1883 events, and we confess to the same bias. The geologic section below is the longest of our interpretive sections, and it has been difficult for us to limit our selection to the 13 papers presented here. For a concise summary, though, we recommend the paper by Williams (p. 341–350). For even more geology, readers are referred to our Bibliography for additional references on subjects such as regional geologic history,[1, 6] and tectonic setting,[5] the volcanoes of Indonesia,[7,8] tectonic rotation of Sumatra with respect to Java at the Krakatau "hinge,"[9] chemical comparison of Krakatau rocks to those of Sumatra,[10] gravity studies of Krakatau,[11] and the development of Anak Krakatau.[3,4,7,12] The more exhaustive bibliography of Brodie et al.[2] lists 317 references under their "geology" section.

[1] Van Bemmelen (1949b).
[2] Brodie, Kusumadinata, and Brodie (1982).
[3] De Nève (1981, 1982).
[4] Decker and Hadikusomo (1961).
[5] Hamilton (1981) and Katili (1975).
[6] Hutchison (1982).
[7] Kusumadinata (1979).
[8] Neumann van Padang (1951, 1971).
[9] Ninkovitch (1976).
[10] Westerveld (1952).
[11] Yokoyama and Hadikusomo (1969).

The A.D. 1680 Eruption of Krakatau
(Van den Berg, 1884)

Some of the world's most violent eruptions have come from unremarkable volcanoes not previously recognized as a threat to surrounding populations. Many volcanoes undergo slow subsurface changes, building inexorably toward eruption conditions, but on a time scale that is very slow when measured in terms of human lifetimes. When a previously unrecognized volcano erupts violently, though, there is an immediate rush to learn its earlier eruptive history, much like a physician taking the medical history of a new patient before going on to examine the symptoms of illness. After the Krakatau eruption, Professor N.P. van den Berg explored historical resources in Batavia at the same time P.J. Veth was doing the same in

Holland. Both discovered accounts of the 1680 eruption and published their findings in 1884. We reprint here a translation from the Dutch, by J.A. Nelen, of the more detailed report by van den Berg which includes much additional background information about Krakatau and the surrounding region. It was submitted for publication on 4 November, scarcely two months after the paroxysmal eruption, and was referenced (above, p. 268) by Verbeek.

In spite of the heavy traffic through the Sunda Strait since the beginning of the great shipping to the East Indies, reports about the scattered islands there are very scarce. Usually they were passed by and lyrically described as picturesque; it was described that the "Sunda Strait was similar to the Rhein River on a larger scale."[1] But the islands were seldom landed on. What has been written about them belongs more to the category of legends than true history.

Javanese folklore talks about Hanoman, a servant of the gods, walking around in the form of an ape, who came carrying two large heaps of sand and rocks to fill in the Sunda Strait; but as a little rhyme[2] goes, the good friend had barely arrived when he discovered Krakatau already there in the middle of the Straits.

Furious that someone else had preceded him in the execution of his plan, he threw down his sand, thus forming the Karang, and the Poeloesari, the cone-shaped mountains in the interior of Bantam. The Karang, the story goes, was then so high that it reached the stars. This encouraged the apes to climb to the top and eat the stars, which infuriated the king of Bantam, Loera Dalam, who took scissors and cut off a large piece of the mountain. When the top fell, it created numerous small hills, which surround the foot of the Karang to the present day as convincing evidence for all unbelievers.

From early on, Dutch seamen suspected that Krakatau and neighboring islands were inhabited by all kinds of bad ghosts, "which let themselves be heard both day and night by yelling and screaming." Out of this belief developed the seaman's legend about a boatsman, who as punishment for his misdeeds was doomed to work without cease until he had sewed the islands Krakatau and Sebessi together, and whose moaning and sighing could clearly be heard by all who sailed by. ...

It is very probable that still more legends concerning Krakatau exist among the population of the coastal areas of the Sunda Strait, and especially of the Lampongs. Its inhabitants supposedly had to thank for their origins a large dragon or snake which, after landing on the south side of Sumatra, produced a number of eggs, from which came the fathers of the different tribes, which still separate the inhabitants of the Lampong Districts.[3]

The research of this, however, is outside my field and I want from here on to remain only with what the history of Krakatau has to tell us.

The oldest report in our language concerning the islands in the Sunda Strait can be found in the 28th Chapter of "Reijs-geschrift van de navigatien der Portugaloysers in Orienten" ("Travelogue of the navigation of the Portuguese in the Orient") by Jan Huyghen van Linschoten, first published in 1595. On page 57 of the 1644 reprint the following can be read:

To reach the mouth of the Sunda Strait stay close to the mainland of Sumatra, always keeping a good eye out for the islands and cliffs, of which there are many ahead, for one does not know where one will find the mouth of the Strait except only by the knowledge of the islands; look for a high island located straight across from a land tip on the north side of Sumatra, which with the island of Java Major forms the Strait ends here. On the northwest side of the coast are two or three small islands about one mile away from land. On the island closest to land a ship with Frenchmen[4] was run aground once. Its guns went to the king of the Island Bantam (?) and the one from Calapa. And a mile from land toward the South is an island with a high top or pointed mountain.

This "pointed island" was not mentoned by name by van Linschoten, but it cannot of course be any other than Krakatau, mentioned as Poeloe Carcata on the map of the Sunda Straits on p. 168 in "Rerum et urbis Amstelodamensium historia" by Johannes Pontanus, published in Amsterdam in 1611.

Van Linschoten himself never visited the Indian Archipelago and his reports quoted here are strictly from other sources, the observations and notes put down for him by the Portuguese pilots; however in the same year that "Reijsgeschrift" was published, a direct trip to the East Indies was begun by the Dutch, thus, soon they would be able to see with their own eyes what, until now, was known only from stories by strangers.

With regard to our present subject not much can be learned from the Journals of the Dutch travelers. The journal of the first trip was maintained by Cadet Frank van der Does[5] on the ship *Hollandia* and started on April 2, 1595, the day of departure from Texel, and continues until June 18, 1597, just after passing the equator on the return trip to Amsterdam, where

the remaining ships arrived on Aug. 14. One reads under the date June 11, 1596:

In the evening we arrived in the vicinity of the Sunda Strait, which contains numerous islands, so that it is difficult to recognize the right entrance to the Strait. We held close to the coast of the mainland of Sumatra and running parallel noticed that it was bad land and deserted. We anchored next to an island on 25 fathoms of blue clay, from which we saw the islands in such a multitude that they seemed impossible to count.

The names of these islands however were not mentioned on this first trip to the East Indies, neither here nor in any other journal.[6] Also in the following trips things are discussed only in general terms, as far as we can determine. One of the first reports, in which the name Krakatau occurs, is probably in Pieter van den Broecke's "Wonderlijcke historische end journaelsche aenteijkeninghe" ("Beautiful historic and journalistic notes"), published in 1648 in Amsterdam. He describes that in January 1620 he, "with Willem Jansz, had been in a fleet of 12 ships at Cracatouw in the Sunda Strait to watch the English and at the same time to cut as much wood as the ships could load."

Joh. Sigismund Werffbain, who in August 1632 saw for the first time the Sunda Strait, mentions in his otherwise very extensive journal[7] only "the many unfruitful and thus uninhabited islands and dangerous cliffs, with which the Strait is covered," and in none of the travelogues of that time is anything else of interest mentioned. Only Wouter Schouten mentions with a single word "the high tree-covered island Krakatau", which he passed in October 1658.

The first more extensive report about Krakatau is found in the travelogue of Johan Wilhelm Vogel, first published in 1690;[8] it relates the volcanic eruption of the island, which according to Vogel's report would have taken place in the month of May, 1680. We will therefore purposely spend more attention on this travelogue, because only through Vogel's reports do we know of the event. Johan Wilhelm Vogel, provided with an appointment as Mayor at the newly opened mines at Salida on Sumatra [756 km NW of Krakatau, near Padang] by the Governors of the Company, started his trip to Batavia in December 1678 with the ship the *Hollandsche Thuyn*. He arrived there safely on June 17, 1679 after having been retained in the Sunda Strait by opposing winds and counter currents between the 8th and the 16th of that month. Vogel remained about 2½ months in Batavia, waiting for an opportunity to travel to Sumatra. The opportunity came in

Figure 61. East Indies as they were known carto-
graphically around the time of Krakatau's 1680
eruption. This map was prepared by Giacomo
Cantelli, of Vignola, Italy, in 1683, and is in the
collections of the Library of Congress, Geography
and Map Division.

September with the ship *Wapen vau ter Goes*. With him on board were the mountain masters Th. Bijlander and Jacob, meanwhile arrived from The Netherlands with the ship *Azia*, together with their personnel numbering about 60 men, mostly Walloons. This time the Strait was passed without any delay and evidently nothing out of the ordinary was noticed at Krakatau, since on that occasion not a word was mentioned about the island, just as in June before, when Vogel sailed by for the first time.

However, a good year later it was different with Krakatau. Vogel, for reasons of health, was forced to leave the mines at Salida to get medical attention in Batavia. He left for that destination on January 26, 1681 with the yacht *de Zijp* and concerning that trip his diary contains the following:

On January 26 we went under sail with a favorable east wind and kept steady course to Batavia, holding about a mile away from Sumatra. We passed Serantie, Piaman Para, Cambangh, Palangii, Sangii toenoe, Moere Langan, Ayerhadja, Inderapoura, and Sillebar all close to the mainland of Sumatra on our left or to the east of us; the islands Engano, and large and small Fortun, however, to our right and west of us.

On Feb. 1 we arrived with God's help at the mouth of the Sunda Strait. I saw with amazement that the island Cracketovv, on my first trip to Sumatra completely green and healthy with trees, lay completely burned and barren in front of our eyes and that at four locations was throwing up large chunks of fire.

And when I asked the ship's Captain when the aforementioned island had erupted, he told me that this had happened in May, 1680. That time also he had made the trip from Bengal, had run into a heavy storm, and about 10 miles away from the island had experienced an earthquake. This was followed by a tremendous thundering crash which had made him think that an island or otherwise a piece of land had split apart. Shortly afterwards, sailing the ship a little closer to land and coming close to the mouth of the Sunda Strait, he became aware that the already mentioned island Cracketovv had split and that his suspicion had not fooled him. He and the whole ship's population had smelled a strong and very fresh sulfur odor. Also the sailors had retrieved with water pails from the sea some very lightweight rocks, very much resembling pumice stone, which had been thrown from the island. They were scooped up as a rarity. He showed me a piece of island. They were scooped up as a rarity. He showed me a piece of it a little larger than a fist.

During this conversation we sailed in God's name into the Sunda Strait and since the wind was very favorable all during the night, we left behind the islands Slepzee, Dwars in de wegh, Tobbershoetje, etc. and fortunately arrived the next day at 2 p.m. in the harbor or at Batavia roads.

Vogel came immediately under treatment of Dr. Andreas Kleyer, who as castle doctor during almost all of the second half of the seventeenth century had an excellent reputation here. Also in Europe he was well known by his colleagues because of the papers he published there. Still, it took quite some time before our patient could enjoy the desired recovery and his return to Sumatra could not be undertaken until the fall of 1681.

He left on November 12 with the ship *Middelburgh* in the company of the headman of the mine works, Benjamin Olitsch, who arrived from Patria in June, and the mountain writer Elias Hesse, whose task it was to accurately record all events of the voyage. Vogel had his journal incorporated into Hesse's writings to save himself the trouble of reworking his own original notes written in Plat-Deutch. After leaving Bantam on November 15, the *Nieuw-Middleburgh* anchored at Anjer on the 16th and Hesse's journal from that time reads as follows:

The 19th we again lifted anchor and proceeded first to the north of us, to the island Sleepzee, or as some desire Zibbesie, uninhabited, densely covered with high trees and a home for bad ghosts, whose crying is heard day and night;[9] and then still north of the island Cracatou, which erupted about a year ago and which is also uninhabited. [Van den Berg surprisingly does not continue with the next sentence of Hesse's journal which reads:[19] "The rising smoke column of this island can be seen from miles away; we were with our ship very close to shore and we could see the trees sticking out high on the mountain, and which looked completely burned, but we could not see the fire itself."]

This time, the rest of the trip did not proceed as well, since not until December 19 could the *Nieuw-Middelburgh* drop anchor at the roads of Poelo Tjinko near Painan. On the 11th a heavy seaquake was observed aboard, which made the ship bump and sway badly, a phenomenon which repeated itself 6 days later, although to a somewhat lesser extent; but arriving ashore they heard, that on the first mentioned day an earthquake had been felt, which "had not only made the sky high mountains to shake and move" but also had done considerable damage to the buildings of the Company.[10] [The Dutch East Indies Company: founded in 1602 and dissolved in 1799.]

This time Vogel remained a number of years at Sumatra; in 1685, for his faithful service, he was put in charge of the minework at Salida; but in 1687 he could no longer resist the desire to return to his beloved homeland, in order to, as he expressed himself: "to attend the public religious service, and to take part in receiving the holy absolution and celebration of the last supper, for which I long very much and which I have had to live without the whole time." Thus he requested and received permission to resign, left on October 15, 1687 for Batavia and passed on the 24th of that month "Cracketow, Sleepsee, and Tobbersho-etjen"; but neither on that occasion, nor on the home voyage to Patria, which was undertaken in the later half of December, 1687, can anything further special be found about Krakatau. He limits himself on this voyage to the notations that they dropped anchor on December 25 under the Java shore and "that we had the island Crackatouw right opposite us on the side."

In August 1688 Vogel arrived safely in Amsterdam and returned as soon as possible to the land of his birth, where he in 1690 published a first edition of his travelogue. The information given above about Krakatau and the eruption which the island must have witnessed, are taken from a much larger second edition, which appeared in Altenburg in 1716. Other data concerning this, besides the ones contained in the travelogues of Vogel and Hesse, I have not been able to trace, and the question now remains how reliable these data are. In this regard I allow myself the following remarks.

Neither Vogel nor Hesse were eyewitnesses of the eruption noted by them and very likely the latter would not even have spoken about it, had he not happened to be aboard the same ship with Vogel, when he sailed through the Sunda Strait in November, 1681. What he then noted in his journal, that Krakatau "had ignited itself a year ago" (thus sometime during 1680) must have been at Vogel's instigation, because in May, 1681, when Hesse, on the voyage from Amsterdam to Batavia, saw the island for the first time, he limits himself to the notation, that "Cracatouw" and the other islands "which are all located in the middle of the Sunda Strait are overgrown with high trees and wilderness".

It seems that he did not notice anything of the consequences of the event supposed to have taken place earlier and which he mentioned half a year later. Hesse apparently was the spokesman of Vogel and what Vogel himself put down about the eruption of May 1680, he obtained, as we saw above, from the Captain's story with whom he made the trip from Padang to Batavia in January 1681, and who, according to his declaration, was aboard a ship from Bengalen, destined for Batavia, which passed through the Sunda Strait only a few days after the eruption.

In reality according to the "Dagregister van het Kasteel Batavia" ("Day Register of the Castle Batavia") the ship *Aerdenburgh* arrived at the roads of Batavia from Bengalen on June 12; and under that date the register contains extensive notes about reports carried along from Bengalen; but nothing is said about any special event during the passage through the Strait. Also, one searches in vain for any report prior to or after that day about the event mentioned by Vogel, and this is that much more surprising since in the year 1680 the Sunda Strait was visited and cruised by more ships of the Company than ever.

Tensions between Bantam and the Company ran high at that time; and when, after the first few days of January 1680, reports were received that the Bantammers in the vicinity of the island Groote Kombuis had overrun (captured) the *borgersloep* (a civilian sloop) of Pieter van de Voordt, manned by two Dutch and three native sailors, a boy and two slave girls, and that all aboard had been murdered by the "godless natives", following the resolution of the eighth of that month, the yacht *Alexander*, the frigate *Tigjer*, the hooker *Baars* and the sloops *Massangboom*, *Kalkoen*, and *Vlieger*, thus altogether six vessels, were sent to the Sunda Strait to "prevent as much as possible the pirating of the Bantammers and to cruise the shipping lanes between the islands" and with the expressed orders "to kill all pirates" but otherwise to let pass all other "trade vessels provided with passes."

A few months later, in the latter part of April, "the ships *Odyck* and *Pynacker*, besides the *chialoupen Orangieboom* and *Zalm*, left from here for the Sunda Strait to reinforce our cruisers and to prevent all attacks and to safeguard the shipping waters;" and shortly thereafter it appeared with what courageous enemies one was dealing, because on the 7th of May, the yacht the *Tigjer* arrived "returning from cruising the Strait," with news about the capture of the sloop *Orangieboom* by the Bantammers' "murdering the helmsman Isaak de Rijke and three sailors," after which "these natives fired two shots with our own pieces of the *Orangieboom* on the ship *Swanenburgh*," wounding two men, one of which was assistant cooper Arent Suijck, and then further sailed for the wind to the coast of Bantam with the captured *Orangieboom* where they however were overtaken and where the captured vessels were taken away from them.

In the same month of May the reports from the Strait were exceptionally frequent. Thus, on the 12th, the commander of the cruisers, Reynier Reynierz reported that again "two pirate vessels, manned with 16 head mixed thieves, coming from Cheribon, without passes and provided with 6 *bassen* [weapons]" had been overtaken, that all occupants had their "feet rinsed" and that the vessels themselves had been sunk. In the morning of the 16th the *Vlieger* returned from the Strait with "six head of Malayan womenfolk, which with our recapture of our *chialoup* the *Orangieboom* had been found therein", and the 20th this aforementioned vessel itself appeared here at the roads. This was two days after a letter was delivered by a native proa from the Assistant of Bantam to the Resident Willem Caeff, temporarily remaining at Batavia, which contained the announcement of the departure to the Lampongs of several influential personalities, banned there by the King of Bantam.

Nearly a week passed, when there was not any report from the cruisers in the Sunda Strait, and how faithfully they kept the government here informed about what went on shows in a piece of information from the Lampongs that "a good quantity of pepper was delivered in Bantam." During August reinforcements again were sent to the Strait, "since a few pirates had been reported in the shipping waters again", but a week or so later things had completely changed, for by resolution of September 7 it was decided "to end the cruising in the Sunda Strait with the present quiet of the Bantammers and to recall the ships".

While in the Day Register of the Castle, from which the above is taken, faithful notation was made of even the least significant happenings, such as the appearance of a tiger in the immediate vicinity of the city, the catching of a crocodile, the running amok of a couple of natives, yes even the appearance of a comet in Tagal. There is nowhere any report of an eruption on the island Krakatau and this, in my opinion, warrants the conclusion that the eruption can be of only little significance and that Vogel's report has to suffer from great exaggeration.

In any case his story about the fire is very suspect, the fire which he claimed to have seen coming out of the crater in February 1681, thus eight months after the eruption, which so altered the appearance of the island. In addition only six months after the event, namely in November 1680, another traveler, Christoph Fricke, hired by the Company as surgeon or wound-healer, passed Krakatau, and the only thing catching Fricke's attention, sailing through the Sunda Strait, were the "the Javanese proas or little boats, which sail with exceptional speed," this according to his "Aenmerckelijke reijzen nae en door Oose-Indien" ("Remarkable travels near and through the East Indies", p. 24, translated in Utrecht in 1694). Thus, nothing special was to be observed on the island then, and therefore the reports of Vogel about what he claims to have seen himself are either pulled out of the air

or the eruption of May 1680 (of which the ship's captain coming from Bengal told) must have been followed by a second eruption in January 1681.

Had this been the case, then Valentijn, who passed the Strait in December 1685 on his first trip out, certainly would not have remained unaware of this; but far from it, he only notes, how a few days before reaching Batavia he "had to suffer such sharp coldness" that he and several others "suffered chapped winter heels," a thing "that seems almost unbelievable and is really absolutely correct". In his "Beschreijvinge ran het eijland Groot Java of Java Major met de eijlanden en rijken daaronder behoorende" ("Descriptions of the island Groot Java or Java Major with the islands and kingdoms belonging to it") he does speak of Prinsen Island, but not at all of Krakatau, and only in his "Beschreijvinge van Sumatra" ("Descriptions of Sumatra"), he mentions at the end of the second chapter among the islands located in the Strait, besides Dwars-in-den-weg and Sibessie, also "the burning island Krakatau". This is all he says about it, and I do not feel strange about the idea that he speaks here less about his own view of it than about the travelogue of Vogel, which certainly would not have been unknown to him.

Since then the story was forgotten until Leopold von Buch recalled it again in a review of the most important volcanoes of the world, added on to his description of the Canary Islands. According to the translation of this work published in Paris in 1836 ("Description physique des Iles Canaries, suivie d'une indication des principaux volcans du globe") von Buch notes about Krakatau the following:

Cracatou in the Sunda Strait. Vogel ("Ost-Indische Reisebeschreibung", Altenburg, 1704) recounts that when he had previously visited this island it was covered with trees and greenery. He was very astonished on February 1, 1681, to find the ground burned and devastated and great quantities of flames rising from certain points. The ship Captain informed him that in May 1680 the island opened itself up with a noise resembling that of thunder which followed an earthquake that was even felt by the ships on the high seas. At the same time, one was suffocated by the strong odor of sulphur, and the sailors, with the *sceaux*, drew out pumice-stones which covered the surface of the ocean, some of which were the size of a fist.[18]

In connection with this, Professor Henrich Berghaus wrote on p. 718 of the second part of his "Allgemeine Länderund Völkerkunde":

Cracatou, or Rakata, in the Sunda Strait . . . An eruption in 1680 is known, which covered the sea with pumice stones, many of which were larger than a fist. . . . Since that time the volcano has been at rest, no sea goer of the newer times

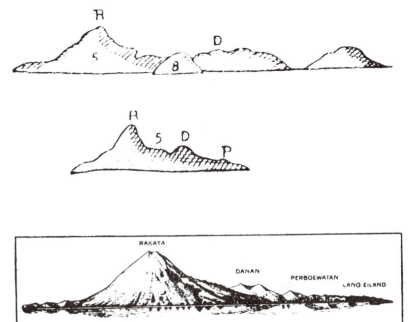

has seen it burning, although it is located along the large lane from China to Europe, one of the most traveled shipping lanes of the world.

And from this report Junghuhn finally got his information about the eruption of Krakatau in 1680, which we find on p. 5 of the second part of his "Java; deszelfs gedaante, bekleeding en inwendige structuur" ("Java; Its shape, covering and internal structure").

The particulars concerning the eruption came to us through Vogel's writing and whatever is taken from that by present day writers agrees too much with the phenomena observed lately to completely doubt the reliability of his report; but that that eruption, compared to the one the Sunda Strait has witnessed recently, had little or no significance, may in my opinion be assumed on the grounds mentioned above.

Not much more of interest about Krakatau can be gleaned from travel stories dated later than 1680. Father Guy Tachard was one of the six Jesuits who on orders of Louis XIV accompanied the Knight of Chawmont on his trip as ambassador to the King of Siam. The purpose was to satisfy the wish of the newly formed Academy of Sciences to make observations in the fields of physics and astronomy. In August 1685 they encountered many adverse conditions in the Strait, even to the extent that there was great danger of being shipwrecked on Prinsen Island; however, concerning Krakatau, which they had in view for days, he mentions only that "Cacatoua", as he writes the name, "is thus named because of the white parrots, which live on the island and continually repeat its name."[11] Neither in "Historische reizen door d'oostersche deelen van Asia" ("Historic travels through the Eastern parts of Asia") by A. Bogaerts who arrived in Batavia in October 1702 nor in the "Reizen over Moskovie door Persie en Indie" ("Travels via Moscow through Persia and India") by Cornelis de Bruin, arriving in February 1706, is there any purposeful mention of Krakatau, and the best proof that during the course of the eighteenth century nothing more is known about volcanic activity on Krakatau to the scientists is certainly the circumstance that in the travel story of the Swedish naturalist Peter Osbeck[12] not a word is mentioned about it. Several pages of his journal, of importance especially to naturalists, are dedicated to a description of the flora and fauna of Prinsen Island, Meeuwen Island and the environs of Anjer. Osbeck, on his trip to China in July 1751 could remain here for a while. On occasion of his visit to Meeuwen Island on the return trip in January 1752 he brings to memory, how about 10 years earlier, in 1743, the

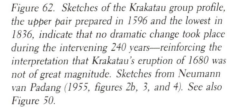

Figure 62. Sketches of the Krakatau group profile, the upper pair prepared in 1596 and the lowest in 1836, indicate that no dramatic change took place during the intervening 240 years—reinforcing the interpretation that Krakatau's eruption of 1680 was not of great magnitude. Sketches from Neumann van Padang (1955, figures 2b, 3, and 4). See also Figure 50.

crew of the Swedish ship *Bitterhaus* had remained there for months. Evidence of that was still to be found in the numerous names which he found carved in the trees; but concerning Krakatau there is only the notation that they passed by on the right side on July 15, 1751.

Thirty years later in February 1780 the ships with which Cook started his trip in 1776 which ended so badly for him, remained for ten days in the Sunda Strait. On that occasion Krakatau was visited as well, resulting in the following notation in the daily-book of the trip:

The island of Cracatoa is the southernmost of the group of islands situated at the entrance to the Sunda Strait. . . . The coastline which forms the western margin of the roadstead has its direction to the northwest. One sees a coral bank that extends into the sea approximately a third of a cable length, which rendered the landing of canoes difficult, when it was not high tide. But the anchoring was very good, and there were not any prominent points of rock. The *Resolution* refilled its barrels at a stream located on the southern extremity of the little island, a short distance from the shoreline. A little to the south, one finds a heat source, where the islanders bathe. While we were on a level with the southern extremity of this island, the Master went to find a *aiguade*, but he disembarked with difficulty, and he returned without having discovered sweet water.

The island of Cracatoa is considered very healthy in comparison to those thereabouts.[13] She offers elevated ground which rises little-by-little from the shoreline on all sides; she is covered with trees, except in several places where the islanders have cleared them for growing rice. The population is not very considerable. The chief is subject to the King of Bantam, just as those of the other islands in the Strait. One finds on the coral reef a large quantity of little turtles, refreshments which elsewhere are very rare and have an enormous price.[14,18]

Thus not a word occurs about earlier volcanic eruptions in this report, one of the most extensive about Krakatau known to me. Apparently none of the scientific people, who were aboard the *Resolution* and the *Discovery* knew anything about the event. Apparently, this also was the case with a military captain, Stavorinús, who according to the story of his trips to India in the years 1768 to 1778, visited the Sunda Strait on several occasions. Nor was this the case with the scientists (Dr. Gillan, Dr. Dinwiddie, and astronomer Barrow) who accompanied Lord Macartney on his trip to China in 1792 as special ambassador for the King of England. These scientists used their delay in the Strait in March 1793 to make observations and to do surveying. Concerning the little islands Toppershoedje and Brabandshoedje they note that, among others, "from some distance one imagines seeing

the remains of old decayed castles, on the tops of whose ruins already grow large, tall trees; but approaching closer it is evident, that these imaginary ruins are nothing else than the products of a fire spitting mountain."[15] To these remarks they still add a few considerations about undersea volcanoes in general; however, about the eruption of Krakatau, which had to have taken place a good hundred years ago, not a word is mentioned.

What is said above in the report of Cook's travel companions concerning the inhabitants of Krakatau, agrees in general with the information in "Beschrijving van Bantam en de Lampongs" ("Description of Bantam and the Lampongs") dated 1787 by a trader and at that time administrator to Bantam, J. de Rovere van Breugel.[16] According to him the islands Cracatoa and Poelo Besie are inhabited "by a small number of people living in miserable huts." He remarks further that "earlier a reasonable quantity of pepper was cultivated here", but presently, he continues, "there occurs no further supply of that kernel from these islands."

Horsburgh also speaks in his "Directions for sailing to and from the East-Indies", London, 1809, Part II, p. 90, of a village on Krakatau, located near a brook, where the ships can supply themselves not only with water and firewood, but also goats, poultry and fruit; in later times however the islands seem only to have served as a place for lawbreakers exiled there from Lampong,[17] and since this also has come to an end the island remained completely deserted and is visited only occasionally by fishermen from shore.

What now, after the destructive eruption of August, remains of the island formerly so rich in trees is an inhospitable mountain top, covered by ash and pumice, denuded of all flora and fauna, and of importance only to geologists, who can find here such a field for their observations as is only rarely offered to them.

[1]Dr. Strehler, "Bijzonderheden wegens Batavia en deszelfs omstreken," Haarlem, 1833, p. 105.

[2]"Bataviasche Courant" of 25 August, 1821, No. 34.

[3]An extensive review of these legends can be found in a contribution about the Lampongs from the hand of J.H. Tobias, included in the "Nederlandsche Hermes", 1830, No. 7.

[4]More particulars concerning the tour of the French sailors, mentioned by Linschoten, who were shipwrecked (in 1529) on the south coast of Sumatra, can be found in the study of Mr. P.A. Tiele, "de Europeërs in den Maleischen Archipel", second part, 1529–1540, included in the "Bijdragen tot de taal- land- en volkenkunde van N.I.", Sequence IV, Part III, p. 28.

[5]Edited by Jhr. Mr. J.K.J. de Jonge in the second part of "De opkomst van het Nederlandsche gezag in Oost-Indië", p. 287.

[6]For as much as I have been able to consult namely these; these being the journal included in the first part of "Begin ende voorgeng van de Verrenigde Nederlandsche Geocroyeerde Oost-Indische Compagne", and the story occurring in the 1614 translation of the work of J. Pontanus, quoted in the text "Historische beschryvinghe der seer wijt beroemede coopstad Amsterdam", p. 180–237.

[7]Joh. Sigismund Wurffbains "Vierzehen Jährische Ost-Indianische Krieg- und Ober- Kauffmans-Dienste in einem richtig gejührten Journeund Tage-buch"; the first edition, edited without the knowledge of the writer, appeared in Nurnberg, 1646.

[8]Under the title of "Journal einer Reise aus Holland nach Ost-Indien"; Franckfurt and Leipzig, 1690. The newer much enlarged edition, which appeared in Altenburg in 1704 and 1716 has the title "Johannes Wilhelm Vogel's Zehen-Jährige, jetzo auffs neue revidirte und vermehrte Ost-Indianische Reise Beschreibung, in Drey Teile abgetheilet. Nebst einem Anhange oder kurtzen Beschreibung derer vornehmsten Länder und Königreiche in Indien, deroselben Zustand und Gewohnheiten, samt der Inwohner Lebens-Art und Sitten, etc."

[9]To Hesse's notation about ghosts, on Sebissi, Vogel adds the following (p. 236): "The mad ghosts which supposedly inhabit the island Zibbesie, are nothing but orangutangs or apes, which sometimes produce a terrible howling, especially when the weather is about to change, which I also have often observed on Sumatra and where many a night I could not sleep because of their howling."

[10]No mention is made of this earthquake in the chronological review of earthquakes and eruptions in the Indian Archipelago, composed by Junghuhn and printed in the "Tijdschrift voor Nederlandsche Indie" of 1844, Part I, p. 30, nor in the compilation appearing in his "Java", Part III, p. 1381.

[11]"Reis na Siam, gedaan door den Ridder de Chaumont; in't Fransche beschreven door den" by Father Guy Tachard, and translated into Nederduitsch [low German] by G.V. Broekhuizen. Amsterdam, 1687.
It does not need noting that Tachard's name explanation has been completely fabricated, since Kakatoes belong only in the eastern part of the Archipelago and do not occur in the Sunda Strait. See A.F. Wallace's "Insulinde", translation by Prof. Veth, Part I, p. 18. The notation of Guy Tachard thus carries the same weight as the following story. Once upon a time an Indian prince sailed through the Sunda Strait, and the shipper answering his question about the name of the pointed island in the middle of the Straits would have said "Kaga tau" ("I don't know"). The prince not familiar with the Malayan dialect, would have understood the name Krakatau. About the real meaning of the word Krakatau I have not been able to obtain anything certain. Also the official native name Poeloe Rakata, appears to be an altered form, because in Malayan writings, among others, in a recently published ballad by a certain Kiagoes Moehamad Arsat, containing a rhyming description of the destruction of Telok Betong in August, the writer speaks of Kalkata, thus the same name, except for a very common exchange of r to l as in Karkata, with which we already became familiar from the little map of the Sunda Strait, dated before 1611. According to a communication from Dr. J.G.H. Gunning at Soerakarta, to whom I turned to for further information, it is not improbable that the name of the island originated from the Sanskrit words Karta Karkata and Karkataka, which mean lobster and crab, and which also indicate the similar sign in the animal rhyme. Thus Krakatau could be translated as lobster or crab island if the above mentioned conjecture was correct, but neither Dr. Gunning, nor other language experts dare to give a definite opinion concerning this. The Malayan word resembling Krakatau the most is, according to Mr. Gerth van Wyjk, the word Kelakatoe, meaning flying white ant (laron).

[12]Peter Osbeck, "Reise nach Ostindien und China. Am dem Schwedischen übersetzl von J.G. Georgi", Rostock, 1765.

[13]In the "Topografische en geografische beschrijving der Lampongsche districten" by F.G. Steck, included in the "Bijdragen tot de taal-land-en volkenkunde van Nederlandshe-Indie", Nieuwe volgreeks [follow series], Part IV, p. 69, just the opposite is argued. There it is mentioned that Sibezie, Kalagian, Kadogan and Laboean are known among the Lampong people as places of good health, even so much so that they serve as a refuge during outbreaks of epidemic diseases, while Krakatau and Seboekoe have just the opposite fame; it is even argued by many people that no one can remain on these islands for longer than fourteen days without being attacked by a fever.

[14]"Troisième voyage de Cook ou Voyage à l'Océan pacifique exécuté sous la direction des capitaines Cook, Clerke et Gore sur les vaisseaux la Résolution et la Decouverte en 1776/1780, Traduit de l'Anglais", Paris, 1785; vol. IV, p. 460.

[15]"Reis van Lord Macartney naar China door George Staunton. Uit het Engelsch", Amsterdam, 1799, Vol. II, p. 166.

[16]"Bijdragen tot de taal-land-en volkenkunde van Nederlandsch-Indie; Niewe volgreeks", vol. I, p. 309.

[17]According to the report, quoted of F.G. Steck in his description above, of the Lampong districts, p. 81. Here is found the surprising announcment that Krakatau had its latest eruption in 1680, "and Sebesie a couple of years earlier." I have not been able to find the source from which this information could have come, and I ask to be allowed to entertain the opinion that it has been completely picked out of the air.

[18][This quotation translated from the French by E. Nielsen.]

[19][Hesse (1690, p. 152), translated from the German by J.A. Nelen.]

Pumice from Krakatau
(Iddings, 1884)

*The area surrounding the Sunda Straits was in
such a state of chaos immediately after the paroxysmal eruption, that it was to be many weeks before trained observers would be able to penetrate
the area on land and begin to piece together what
had happened. Thus, it is not surprising that the
first published interpretations of the events dealt
with descriptions of ejecta collected by passing
ships and returned relatively swiftly to their home
ports in Europe and America. The first of these
accounts that we reproduce here appeared as a
brief letter to Science, written January 30, 1884,
by J.P. Iddings who was at the time a young pe-
trologist with the U.S. Geological Survey. Iddings
was a leader in the growing field of igneous petrology—the study of rocks formed at high temperatures—and when the first professorial chair of petrology was created, at the University of Chicago
in 1893, it was given to Iddings. After his retire-
ment there he spent the last four years of his life
as Curator of Petrology here at the National Museum of Natural History.*

Capt. A.W. Newell, of the bark *Amy Turner* of
Boston, has brought in some pumice which was washed
aboard his vessel, Sept. 17, 1883, in latitude 7° 25'
south, longitude 103° 21' east, about a hundred and
sixty-five miles [271 km] south-west from Krakatoa,
Sunda Straits. It covered the sea in windrows, and
was observed as fine ashes as far distant as thirteen
hundred and fifty miles [2170 km] from its source.

A piece about seven inches by five, which came to
my notice, is of a reddish-gray color, and very much
inflated: it carries porphyritic crystals of plagioclase
felspar, in many cases surrounded by dark-brown glass,
forming small black spots in the gray mass, which
might at first sight be mistaken for augite or hypersthene. There is, besides, dark-green augite and brown
hypersthene, which is strongly pleochroic, and resembles closely that found in the lavas from the volcanoes
of northern California and the Cascade Range.[1]

The percentage of silica for this pumice was found
to be 62.53, and is almost identical with that of the
hypersthene-bearing pumice from Mount Shasta, which
is 62. It is undoubtedly the pumice of a hypersthene
andesite, and is especially interesting because of its
similarity to rocks found on the western coast of North
America. The observations of Rénard on the ashes

that fell in Batavia soon after the eruption of Krakatoa[2]
show the same component minerals, and have doubtless been made on similar material.

[1]Notes on the volcanoes of northern California, Oregon, and
Washington Territory, Amer. journ. sc., September, 1883.
[2]Nature, Dec. 6, 1883.

Volcanic Ash from Krakatau
(Joly, 1885)

*Another description of ejecta from Krakatau—this
time volcanic ash that fell on shipboard rather
than floating pumice, and transported to Dublin
rather than Boston—was read by J. Joly on March
17, 1884, and published with some later additions
in early 1885. Joly was at the time a young assistant to the Professor at Trinity College, Dublin.
The examination of volcanic materials under the
petrographic microscope was still in its youthful
stage of development, having begun in the 1850's,
and Joly's enthusiastic description conveys the excitement of discovering this new world of the microscopic.*

On the 26th of August, 1883, the Norwegian barque *Borjild* (Captain Amundsen), on her way from
Cherribon to Anjer, cast anchor off the east coast of
the Great Kombuis Island, some seventy-five miles to
the north-east of Krakatoa. Here she remained during
the period of the eruption; volcanic ash falling on her
decks from 6 a.m. to 6 p.m. on the 27th. On that
day, at 2 p.m., the darkness, due to absorption by the
great layer of dust above them, was described as being
so intense that mutual recognition by vision was impossible.

In the month of February, during the stay of the
Borjild at Dublin, a portion of this ash was, through
the kindness of Mr. Hogg, of Trinity College, obtained by the author. The examination of this ash
forms the subject of the following notes.

Mere inspection with a lens shows the ash to consist
principally of vesicular fragments of pumice inter-
spersed with vitreous and crystalline particles. Before
dealing with these it is interesting to note the presence,
as of accidental origin [probably from the ship's deck
where the ash was collected], of

Sodium Chloride.—The presence of this substance
may readily be demonstrated by taste; or by immersing

in distilled water and testing. Mr. Moss, who first called attention to it, estimated it to be present to the extent of 0.8 per cent.

Organic Marine Remains.—Those noticed were foraminifera, of which some quite perfect shells were found, and also fragments of starfish (identified by Professor Sollas). Similar remains were removed from the external cells of a speciment of the "floating pumice," picked up by the *Borjild* in the Straits of Sunda.

Perfect identity, mineralogically, seems to exist between this floating pumice and the ash. Larger crystals may, however, be obtained from the former than occurred in the latter. Feldspars 3 mm long were found protruding from the abraided surface of the block pumice. In the dust they rarely exceed 1 mm in length. The formation of the dust by mere pulverization of the pumice seems a most likely supposition.

With regard to the *modus operandi* of preparing this dust for the microscope, it may be useful to note that while it was found that mere shaking up with water, and pouring off before complete settlement, served to remove the lighter fragments of pumice, complete separation was only readily effected by the following method:—

Into a glass tube 1 m long and about 4 cm in diameter, closed at one end and filled with water to the brim, the partially cleansed dust is introduced and allowed to settle. A slip of glass is now pressed on the open end, and the whole rapidly inverted into a shallow dish containing water. The denser particles descending most rapidly through the column of water in the tube reach the dish first. When the more slowly moving particles are observed to have nearly attained the dish, a movement of the tube to one side effects the desired separation.

One and all the constituents of this ash present under the microscope a spectacle of the most extreme interest and beauty. The almost unlimited minuteness of the vesicular structure of the pumice, the endless variety in form and colour of the amorphous fragments, the exquisite perfection of form exhibited by the minute crystals of magnetite, of pyrites, of pyroxene and of feldspar; the nebulae of enclosures in these last, and their delicate overspreading lace-work of still adhering vesicular glass. Here are seen small crystals enclosing many others, and these again, still others; while often with the symmetry of the crystal the vitreous inclusions, amber-yellow, range in concentric zones in the translucent depths.

But if this be a wonderful spectacle viewed by ordinary transmitted light, the beauty and wonder of it

are a thousandfold increased when, rotated in polarized light, each feldspar crystal reveals its molecular symmetry in flashes of changing colour beside which the richness of the emerald, ruby, or saphire, would pale. The abundance of twinned crystals add much to the effect: and now, also, many fragments passed over before as less interesting put in their claim to symmetry, and shine not less brightly than those displaying facet and angle. Many hundreds of square miles were thickly covered with this ash around the scene of the eruption, and these miracles of structural perfection doubtless abundant in every grain of it.

Dealing with the constituent minerals in the order of their abundance, the *Feldspars* first claim attention. They will be at once identified by their colourless transparency; specimens exhibiting a milky decomposed appearance, or showing diffused iron stains of brown-yellow tint being rare. In the latter case, also, a few moments' immersion in hydrofluoric acid generally shows the colour to be confined to the covering of pumice glass adhering to the surface of the crystal.

This covering of pumice, most noticeable in the feldspars, but also overspreading pyroxene crystals, is obviously the remains of a former matrix of highly vesicular glass; being occasionally even recognisable as the fragments of bubble walls; sometimes projecting along the edges of the crystal, giving a fringed appearance, or, again, overspreading the more developed faces forming a hexagonal pattern often of great beauty and regularity. The appearance, indeed, suggests at first sight such markings, cohesion figures, as are formed when two flat surfaces compressing a viscous material are suddenly separated. It will be found, however, that crystals removed from the block pumice carry with them just such remains of the matrix.

Optical examination could not safely be undertaken till this coating had been removed by hydrofluoric acid. This operation demands care, as the feldspars themselves are soon decomposed by the acid.

Two principal forms of feldspar crystals occur; a columnar and a tabular, the latter most abundantly.

That the tabular variety is in general plagioclastic is certain. Polysynthetic lines of twinning are frequently observed with polarized light, sometimes crossing at right angles. More generally these lines traverse the crystal longitudinally. Carlsbad twinning is common, extinction occuring at some 8 or 9 degrees at either side of the medial line. This form of twinning is seldom absent in crystals of the columnar variety. If such tabular crystals as exhibit this medial twinning line be considered as of the same nature as the col-

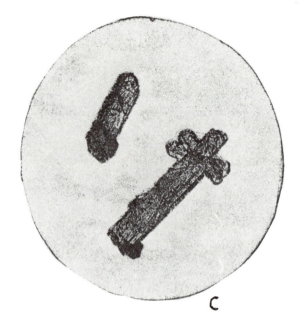

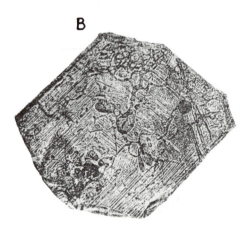

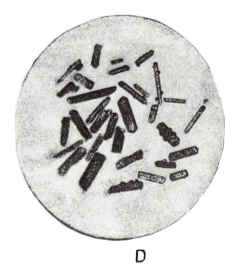

Figure 63. Photomicrographs of crystals separated from Krakatau pumice. Plagioclase (a and b) and hypersthene (c and d) enlarged 15 to 35 times (see text). (Joly's plates XII and XIII.)

umnar crystals, a plagioclastic character might be ascribed to the latter, as just such tabular crystals will be met superimposed and twinned with others exhibiting undeniable plagioclastic characteristics. At the same time, many orthoclastic peculiarities are, as will be seen presently, noticeable in the columnar crystals.

Little or no cleavage is apparent in these tabular crystals. Extinction does not occur parallel to the edges of the dominant faces—apparently macropinacoids. Want of properly furnished instruments forbids the author entering at present further into the anomalies presented by these plagioclastic feldspars. They are quite insoluble in boiling hydrochloric acid—or after some days' cold digestion in the same.

The second variety, if it may be considered as such, may be described as columnar, with nearly equally developed faces seemingly at right angles to each other. Four pyramidal faces terminate one or both ends. This pyramidal termination is occasionally truncated, giving a fifth terminating face at an angle other than 90° with the zone axis of the prismatic faces. Marked rectangular cleavage on one set of these faces; direction of cleavage apparently parallel to pyramidal planes: generally a single medial twinning line on the other set of prism faces. Extinction for the first set of faces (those showing cleavage), parallel to the longitudinal axis of the crystal. For the second set, symmetrically on either side of twinning line; seldom more than 15° on either side. A specimen wanting the twinning line extinguished on these faces at 16° with the longitudinal axis; parallel to it on the adjoining faces of the same zone.

Viewed when resting on one of its longitudinal edges, characteristic border lines displaying vivid prismatic colours become apparent between crossed nicols. Polysynthetic surface striations might account for this appearance.

The photograph (Figure 63a), taken with nicols crossed, contains a couple of these crystals removed from the floating pumice. The crystals, adhering together, rest on their edges and display well the border lines just mentioned.

Flame tests indicate for such crystals a percentage of potassium comparable to that of orthoclase. If they, indeed, are sanidine, there is evidently a peculiarity in twinning. Although good crystals are scarce, fragments are numerous. They will be detected by their marked cleavage.

The tabular variety is represented in the photographs by the remaining crystals shown in the photograph (Figure 63a), which is taken at an enlarge-ment of about 20 diameters. A very good specimen is shown, magnified 35 diameters, in Figure 63b: enclosures, vitreous, containing crystals, will be noticed. Growth striations and the lace-like pattern of adhering-glass are also shown. The presence of growth striations or zones, very common in these feldspars is generally assumed to indicate a more or less tranquil formation.

The *Pyroxenes* are a noticeable feature in this ash. The rhombic variety is by far the most abundant, indeed the monoclinic is scarce, and present usually in badly developed or small crystals. A group of the rhombic pyroxenes is shown in Figure 63d. Enlargement 15 diameters.

These crystals are olive-green to brown in colour; translucent. Their pleochroism is well marked, the colouration following the order assigned to *Hypersthene*, by MM. Fouqè and Levy (Minéralogie Micrographique): that is, parallel to their principal axis dark-green, parallel to the macrodiagonal, red, with intermediate tints of brown.

This mineral will be found to extinguish parallel to its pinacoidal faces, not alone when viewed longitudinally, but also when placed with its principal axis in a vertical position between crossed nicols. Treating in this way the nearly central crystal, the one exhibiting a pointed termination at each end in the group (Figure 63d), the exquisite perfection of its minute form became apparent.

This crystal, which parallel to its longitudinal axis shows pinacoidal and prismatic faces, the former dominant, shows four principal terminating planes, apparently octahedral. Two other faces, brachydomes seemingly, are well defined. Other minute faces are visible, scarcely determinable. The adjoining woodcut, a sketch of its appearance viewed in a direction inclined a little upwards, and to the left of the brachydiagonal, shows some of its faces.

The photograph (Figure 63c) conveys but a faint idea of a very beautiful specimen—consisting of three interpenetrating crystals. Their faces are very perfect, and extinction for each crystal is parallel to its longitudinal axis. These are soluble in hydrofluoric acid after long immersion. Just such crystals are depicted in the Minéralogie Micrographique of MM. Fouqè and Levy, as extracted from the lavas of Santorin of 1866.

The monoclinic pyroxene, *Augite*, which so closely resembles the hypersthene in appearance will be found to be only feebly or not at all polychroic. Extinction occurs at some 30 to 37 degrees with the principal

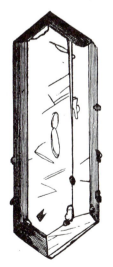

axis. This angle is stated to vary with the amount of iron present in the mineral. It is never so low as to confuse it with hornblende.

In general its crystals are of a brighter green colour than the greenest of the hypersthene. They, also, are slowly soluble in hydrofluoric acid. Crystals of hypersthene 4 mm long were picked up: the augite rarely was found above 1 mm in length. Similar crystals fell in Norway in a volcanic ash from Iceland (Fouquè and Levy, *op. cit.*).

Magnetite occurs not alone abundantly as inclusions in the various crystals, but is plentiful as minute octahedrons exhibiting the usual twin forms with octahedral composition face. It shows a fine black, splendant, metallic lustre; occasionally bluish and even like that of anthracite. An electro-magnet enclosed in a long test tube was found of much service in removing it from solutions, and also in isolating the pyroxene containing this mineral.

Iron Pyrites is present in such characteristic forms as to leave little room for doubt as to its identity. It will be observed not alone in isolated fragments, little aggregations of cubes showing the striations at right angles on adjacent faces, and exhibiting the brassy lustre of pyrites, but also, imbedded in and protruding from the surface of some of the rough amorphous fragments scattered through the ash. In good light the faces of these crystals are seen to be generally pentagonal, and the crystals in fact to be principally pentagonal dodecahedrons.

It was thought that this substance might be foreign to the real constitution of the ash. The discovery, however, of a crystal with the lustre and appearance of pyrites imbedded deeply in the interior of a feldspar rendered it impossible to suppose this mineral to be merely blown up from local rocks, and so intermingled with the ash. Remarkable deposits of it, having the appearance of infiltration along cleavage planes, occur occasionally in feldspar crystals.

Among the amorphous fragments, *Olivine* was not observed; many fragments picked up on suspicion being found to be easily soluble in hydrofluoric acid.

One of the most interesting features of this ash is the nature of the various *enclosures* in its principal minerals. They obviously give us a means of judging of their relative order of formation.

Classifying on this basis, *Magnetite* would come first in order of formation. It occurs as an inclusion in all the silicates present. It will be noticed protruding from the crystals of hypersthene in Figure 63c.

Pyrites might be of contemporary origin.

The *Pyroxenes* would in that case be second in order, for while including magnetite they are themselves included in the feldspars.

The *Feldspars* were probably the last minerals formed.

Vitreous inclusions are abundant, generally iron-stained to a light-brown tint and enclosing the bubble which probably started their formation. Very often these inclusions are ranged parallel to the outline of the crystal; often again the vitreous mass has had the symmetrical form of the containing crystal impressed upon it. Sometimes then by their individual form, sometimes by their disposition, it is possible to judge of the former crystalline symmetry of a mere formless fragment containing such enclosures.

Additional Notes

Subsequent to the reading of the foregoing, the author received many additional samples, both of the ash and of the block pumice. To the courtesy and kindness of Mr. T. Brewis the author owes these specimens in the first instance. Through information received from that gentleman samples were obtained from Captains who were in the neighborhood of Krakatoa during the period of the eruption. To Captain Ralston, of the *Niobe*; Captain Calangich, of the *Jafet II*; and, above all, to Captain Thomson, of the ship *Medea*, the author's best thanks are due.

The specimens of block pumice received bore, one and all, remains of marine life, incrusting the walls of the larger surface cells. Mineralogically they were not found to differ; many, however, showed veins or layers of black vesicular glass, giving a stratified appearance. The specimens, some of which are now in the Museum of Science and Art, Dublin, were picked up considerably to the south-west of the Straits of Sunda.

Dust from Batavia did not, on examination and comparison with that gathered at half that distance from Krakatoa, indicate any such sifting of its constituents in the course of its journey as M. Renard assumes in his paper, read before the Académie Royale de Belgique (November 3, 1883). The probable explanation is that the dust was thrown so high, and in such quantities, that for many miles it was descending almost vertically, and was not, therefore, subjected to such a sifting process as it would have experienced had it been travelling horizontally.

Bearing on this point, the following computation respecting the height to which the dust, &c., was projected may be of interest:—

[Captain Thomson's report from the *Medea*, of 17 mile cloud height measured at the time of the initial eruption on the afternoon of August 26, is reprinted on p. 96 of our "Narrative" section.]

With regard to the presence of *Pyrites* in the ash, nothing was said about it by M. Renard in his original paper (which was not, however, known to the author of these notes at the time of preparing his communication to the Royal Dublin Society); but in a note appended to a paper appearing in *Nature* (April 17th), as the joint production of that distinguished mineralogist and of Mr. Murray, its occurrence is mentioned and dismissed as "accidental." It is, however, not alone present, free, as aggregations of cubes and dodecahedrons, but also as an inclusion in the feldspars and in the hypersthene. Again, its abundant occurrence in the ash received from various localities is observable. Fifty specimens were counted by the author in one of three slides prepared from about half a gramme of the dust from Batavia. The dust had been treated for the removal of glass, feldspars, and free magnetite. It is hard to see why, under the circumstances, it should be considered accidental.

Hematite in thin, blood-red, semi-translucent flakes occurs in the ash. It is neither cleavable perceptibly, nor elastic, and is soluble in hydrochloric acid. It shows no trace of dichroism.

The very great abundance in the ash of *Hypersthene*, compared to *Augite*, suggests that the original rock should be considered more of the nature of a hypersthene andesite than an augite andesite. In connexion with this point the results of Mr. Whitman Cross' examination of a hypersthene andesite, kindly brought under the author's notice by Professor V. Ball, are of much interest. (Bulletin of the United States' Geological Survey, No. 1, 1883.)

Volcanic Phenomena of the Eruption (Judd, 1888a)

The classic English-language account of the Krakatau eruption and related phenomena is the massive report of the Krakatoa Committee of the Royal Society of London, published in 1888. The Committee was appointed on January 17, 1884, following two meetings at which the Royal Society heard reports on the great air-wave and physical changes to the Krakatau region (and following two

months of remarkable sunsets that attracted much attention in London itself). John W. Judd was a member of that original committee. At the time he was Professor of Geology at the Royal School of Mines and President of the Geological Society. His book, Volcanoes, had just been published in 1881. Judd's chapter entitled "On the Volcanic Phenomena of the Eruption and on the Nature and Distribution of the Ejected Materials" was the first in the multi-disciplinary Royal Society Report. We have excerpted the interpretive, rather than descriptive parts of his account, including those dealing with (1) his "check and rally" hypothesis relating access of seawater to intermittent explosivity, (2) the interpretation that disruption of the old Krakatau cone and creation of the submarine caldera was the result of enormous explosions, and (3) the hypothesis that large volumes of water were incorporated into the magma, lowering its melting point and resulting in the production of large volumes of glassy pumice and ash.

During the closing days of the month of August, 1883, the telegraph-cable from Batavia carried to Singapore, and thence to every part of the civilised world, the news of a terrible subterranean convulsion—one which in its destructive results to life and property, and in the startling character of the world-wide effects to which it gave rise, is perhaps without a parallel in historic times.

As is usual in such cases, the first reports of this tremendous outburst of the volcanic forces appear to have been quite misleading and altogether unworthy of credence. Nor is this to be wondered at. The towns and villages along the shores of the Sunda Strait were, during the crisis of the eruption, enveloped in a terrible darkness, which lasted for many hours, and, while thus obscured, were overwhelmed by a succession of great sea-waves; those who succeeded in saving their lives amid these appalling incidents were, it need scarcely be added, not in a position to make trustworthy observations upon the wonderful succession of phenomena occurring around them.

· · · · ·

The scene of this terrible catastrophe lies in the very heart of the district which has long been recognised as being at the present epoch the greatest focus of volcanic activity upon the globe. The Island of Java, with an area about equal to that of England, contains no fewer than forty-nine great volcanic mountains, some of which rise to a height of 12,000 feet above

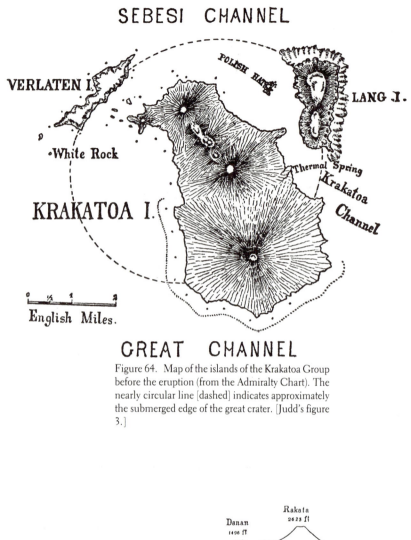

SEBESI CHANNEL

VERLATEN I.

POLISH HAT

LANG I.

·White Rock

Thermal Spring

KRAKATOA I.

Krakatoa Channel

0 ½ 1 2

English Miles.

GREAT CHANNEL

Figure 64. Map of the islands of the Krakatoa Group before the eruption (from the Admiralty Chart). The nearly circular line [dashed] indicates approximately the submerged edge of the great crater. [Judd's figure 3.]

Rakata
2623 ft

Danan
1496 ft

Verlaten I.

Perboewatan
399 ft

Lava Stream

Figure 65. Outline-section viewed from SW showing the position of the volcanic cones upon the Island of Krakatoa previous to the eruption. [Judd's figure 4.]

the sea-level. Of these volcanoes, more than half have been seen in eruption during the short period of the European occupation of the island, while some are in a state of almost constant activity. Hot springs, mud-volcanoes, and vapour-vents abound in Java, while earthquakes are by no means unfrequent. The chain of volcanoes which runs through the whole of Java is continued in Sumatra on the west, and in the islands of Bali, Lombok, Sumbawa, Flores and Timor on the east.

The marked linear arrangement in this immense chain of volcanic mountains points to the existence of a great fissure in the earth's crust, along which the subterranean energy has been manifested. The Strait of Sunda, which separates Java from Sumatra, is a shallow one, having a depth of rarely more than 100 fathoms. Along the line of this Strait we have evidence of a transverse fissure crossing the main one nearly at right angles. [Judd's figure 1, referenced here, is a sketch-map simplified from Verbeek's figure 3, our Figure 54, p. 226.] Upon this transverse fissure a number of volcanoes have been thrown up, namely— Pajung, in Java, with a height of 1,500 feet; the cone of Princess Island, 1,450 feet; Krakatoa, 2,623; Sebesi, 2,825; and Rajah Bassá, in Sumatra, 4,398 feet.

In spite of the significance of its position at the point of intersection of these two great lines of volcanic fissure, Krakatoa had, until the year 1883, attracted but little attention. Amid so many volcanoes of more striking appearance and more frequent activity, it, in fact, remained almost unnoticed.

Krakatoa does not present the regularly conical outlines characteristic of volcanoes, a form which is so well exhibited by the neighbouring island of Sebesi[1] [see Plate 3D]; it is, indeed, only a fragment of a great crater-ring rising out of the Sunda Strait. The general relations of the islands of the Krakatoa group and the outlines which they exhibited prior to the great eruption are illustrated by the accompanying sketch-map and section (Figures 64 and 65).

By the great eruption of August, 1883, the volcano of which Krakatoa and the adjoining islands form parts was completely eviscerated. The admirable descriptions given by MM. Verbeek and Bréon of the splendid sections now exposed enable us not only to determine the nature of its materials, but to study all the details of the internal structure of the volcanic mass. Guided by the principles which have been established by the study of numerous volcanoes in different stages of their development, we are able from the data thus obtained to re-construct the whole his-

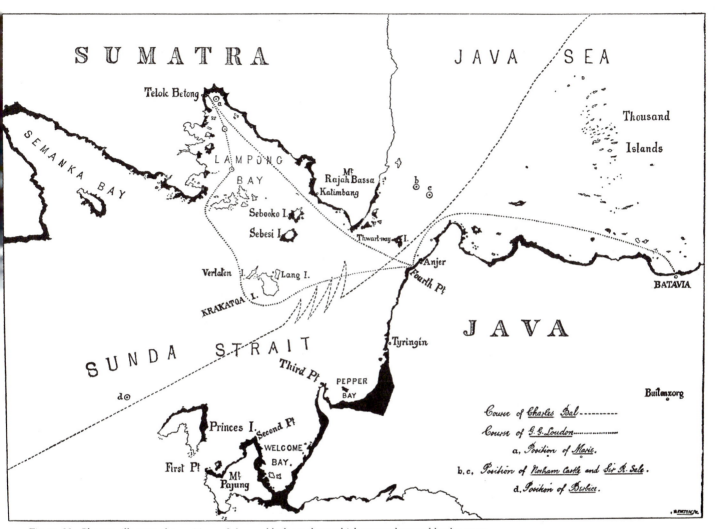

Figure 66. Chart to illustrate the positions of the towns and the tracks of the vessels where the most important observations bearing on the great final outburst at Krakatoa were made. The areas shaded black are those which were submerged by the great sea-waves. [Note that ship tracks differ from those plotted by us (Figure 17, p. 82) from ship's logs and other eyewitness accounts. Judd's figure 9.]

tory of this interesting example of volcanic architecture. [Judd devotes the next 16 pages to a sketch of the history of Krakatau through the events of August 26, a history already covered by Verbeek and others above. We rejoin Judd's discussion of the culminating 1883 eruption on p. 20 of the Royal Society report.]

All these details prove conclusively that Krakatoa had arrived at the paroxysmal phase of eruption. The explosive bursts of vapour beginning on the afternoon of Sunday and continuing at intervals of ten minutes, increased in violence and rapidity, and from sunset till midnight there was an almost continuous roar, which moderated a little toward early morning. Each explosive outburst of steam would have the effect of removing the accumulating pumice from the surface

of the melted lava, by blowing it into the atmosphere, and the cauldron of white-hot lava would then have its glowing surface reflected in the clouds of vapour and dust hanging above.

The numerous vents on the low-lying parts of Krakatoa, which were recorded as having been seen by Captain Ferzenaar on the 11th of August, had, doubtless, by this time become more or less united, and the original crater of the old volcano was being rapidly emptied by the great paroxysmal explosions which commenced in the afternoon of the 26th of August.

All the eye-witnesses are in agreement as to the splendour of the electrical phenomena displayed during this paroxysmal outburst. Captain Wooldridge [of the *Sir Robert Sale*, see Figure 66], viewing the eruption in the afternoon from a distance of 40 miles, speaks of the great vapour-cloud looking like "an immense wall with bursts of forked lightning at times like large serpents rushing through the air." After sunset this dark wall resembled a "blood-red curtain, with the edges of all shades of yellow; the whole of a murky tinge, with fierce flashes of lightning." Captain O. Sampson [from the *Norham Castle*], viewing the volcano from a similar position at the same time, states that Krakatoa "appeared to be alight with flickering flames rising behind a dense black cloud; at the same time balls of fire rested on the mastheads and extremities of the yeard-arms."

Captain Watson [of the *Charles Bal*] states that during the night the mastheads and yard-arms of his ship were "studded with *corposants*," and records the occurrence of "a peculiar pinky flame coming from clouds which seemed to touch the mastheads and yard-arms." [See Figure 66 and our somewhat different map of the ship's position on p. 82. More of Captain Watson's account is reprinted above on p. 102.] From the G.G. *Loudon*, lying in the Bay of Lampong, 40 or 50 English miles north-west of the volcano, it was recorded that "the lightning struck the mainmast-conductor five or six times," and that "the mud-rain which covered the masts, rigging, and decks, was phosphorescent, and on the rigging presented the appearance of St. Elmo's fire. The natives engaged themselves busily in putting this phosphorescent light out with their hands, and were so intent on this occupation that the stokers left the engine-rooms for the purpose, so that the European engineers were left to drive the machinery for themselves. The natives pleaded that if this phosphorescent light, or any portion of it, found its way below, a hole would burst in the ship; not that they feared the ship taking fire, but they thought the light was the work of evil spirits, and that if the ill-omened light found its way below, the evil spirits would triumph in their design to scuttle the ship."

This abundant generation of atmospheric electricity is a familiar phenomenon in all volcanic eruptions on a grand scale. The steam-jets rushing through the orifices of the earth's crust constitute an enormous hydro-electric engine; and the friction of ejected materials striking against one another in their ascent and descent also does much in the way of generating electricity.

Up to late in the afternoon of the 26th of August, the phenomena exhibited by Krakatoa were precisely similar to those witnessed at every great paroxysmal volcanic eruption. But at that time the effects of the somewhat peculiar position of the Krakatoa crater began to be apparent. Lying as it does so close to the sea-level, the work of evisceration by explosive action could not go far without the waters of the ocean finding their way into the heated mass of lava from which the eruption was taking place.

It is often assumed that if a mass of water come into contact with molten lava a terrible outburst of steam, producing a great volcanic eruption, must be the consequence, and some vulcanologists insist that the admission of water by fissures into subterranean reservoirs of lava is the determining cause of all volcanic outbreaks. But careful observation does not give much countenance to this view. Lava streams have frequently been seen to flow into the sea, and although a considerable generation of steam occurred when the molten mass first came in contact with the water, yet none of the prolonged effects which are popularly supposed to result from the conflict of fire and water were found to occur. The surface of the lava-current becoming rapidly chilled, a layer of slowly conducting rock is formed at its surface, and then the gradual cooling down of the whole mass ensues, without further disturbance.

By the lowering of the mass lying within the old crater-ring of Krakatoa, and the diminution in height of the crater-walls, water would from time to time find a way to the molten lava below; each such influx of water would no doubt lead to the generation of some steam with explosive violence, and the production of small sea-waves which would travel outwards from Krakatoa as a centre. From the reports made by the officials at Anjer and other places on the shores of Java and Sumatra, the production of such waves, which were only a few feet in height, began to be observed about 5.30 p.m. on Sunday, the 26th of August, and continued at irregular intervals through the night. Towards morning, however, the chilling effects of the water which had from time to time found its way to the molten materials below the volcano began to be felt, and as a result a diminution in the activity of the volcano is recorded.

If, as I shall show when I proceed to discuss the nature of the materials ejected from Krakatoa, the cause of the eruptive action was due to the disengagement of volatile substances *actually contained in those materials*, the checking of the activity, by the influx into the molten mass of vast quantities of cold sea water, would have the same effect as fastening down the safety-valve of a steam-boiler, while the fires below were maintained in full activity.

N.W.   S.E.

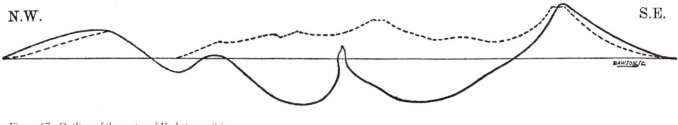

Figure 67. Outline of the crater of Krakatoa as it is at the present time. The dotted line indicates the portions blown away in the paroxysmal outburst of August, 1883, and the changes in form of the flanks of the mountain by the fall of ejected materials upon them. [Judd's figure 10.]

The constant augmentation of tension beneath Krakatoa, in the end gave rise to a series of tremendous explosions, on a far grander scale than those resulting directly from the influx of the sea-water into the vent; the four principal of these occurred, according to the careful investigations of Mr. Verbeek, at 5:30, 6:44, 10:02,[2] and 10:52, Krakatoa time, on the morning of August the 27th. Of these, the third, occurring shortly after 10 o'clock, was by far the most violent, and was productive of the most wide-spread results.

Although no one was near enough to Krakatoa during these paroxysmal outbursts to witness what took place there, a comparison of the condition of the volcano and of the surrounding seas before and after these terrible manifestations of the subterranean forces, leaves little doubt as to the real nature of the action.

In the first place, we find that the whole of the northern and lower portion of the Island of Krakatoa disappeared, with the exception of a bank of pumice and one small isolated rock, about 10 yards square, which was left standing above the ocean with deep water all round it. This rock consists of solid pitchstone,[3] and probably represents a dyke or plug filling the throat of one of the volcanic cones that formerly occupied the old crater. At the same time a large portion of the northern part of the basaltic cone of Rakata was destroyed and a nearly vertical cliff formed, giving rise to a magnificent section which afforded a perfect insight into the internal structure of the volcano.[4] [See p. 143.] The depth of the great crateral hollow which was produced, where the northern part of Krakatoa formerly rose to heights of from 300 to 1,400 feet above the sea level, in some places exceeds 1,000 feet below that same level. (See Figure 67.)

In attempting to judge of the effects produced around the flanks of the great crater of Krakatoa, we have the two new and very detailed charts prepared by the Royal Dutch surveying vessel Hydrograaf, under Commandant C. van Doorn. The first of these was the result of a careful survey made immediately after the eruption, and was published on October the 26th, 1883, while the second appeared somewhat later, after the new Islands of Steers and Calmeyer had been reduced to sandbanks. These are reproduced[5], but it is a very unfortunate circumstance that the old charts of the Strait of Sunda are far from accurate, and thus considerable difficulty arises when we attempt to make an exact estimate of the changes produced by the eruption. (See Figure 68.)

Certain it is that the portion of the Island of Krakatoa which disappeared during the eruption was equal to about two-thirds of the original area, the part that remained consisting only of the southern moiety [half] of the volcanic cone of Rakata. Of this fragment the southern outline, according to the new charts, differs considerably from that of the southern shore of the original island, and its height, if the old charts can be depended upon, was increased from 2,623 to 2,750 feet.[6] But the top and sides of this fragment of the cone of Rakata are so covered by masses of ejected materials that the alteration in its form and height are, it appears to me, sufficiently accounted for without requiring us to call in any theory of general upheaval of the mass.

Of the other islands of the group, Poolsche Hoedje (Polish Hat) has entirely disappeared; Lang Island has been increased by an addition to its northern extremity, and its height above the sea seems to have been

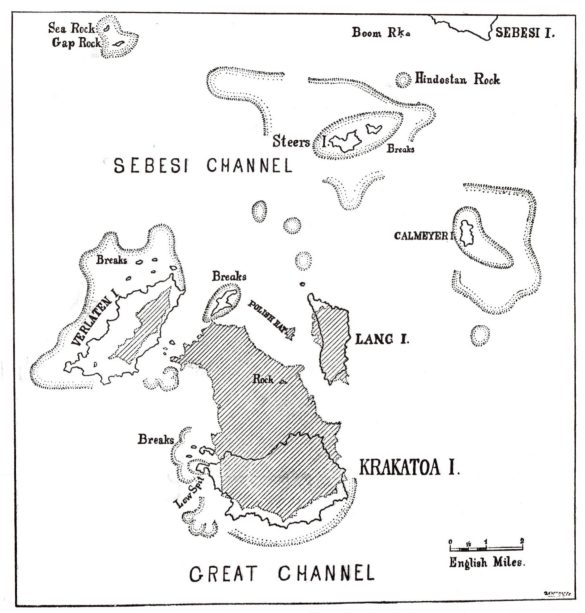

Figure 68. Map of Krakatoa and the surrounding islands, from the Chart prepared immediately after the Eruption. Later charts show the islands of Steers and Calmeyer reduced to sandbanks. The shaded areas show the form of the islands according to the old chart. Much of the discrepancy between the southern limit of Krakatoa in the two maps is due to the imperfection of the old survey. Dotted lines show sandbanks and lines of breakers. [Judd's figure 11.]

302

augmented, the whole of the vegetation that formerly covered it being deeply buried by ejected matters; and lastly, Verlaten Island has, by accretions on the side farthest away from the central crater, been enlarged to more than three times its former area, while a considerable addition has been made to its height.

In judging of the alterations in the form of the sea-bottom around the Krakatoa group, we have to rely upon the few and not very accurate soundings in the old chart of the Strait. From a comparison of these with the depths given in the new chart, we can scarcely doubt that over a circle with a radius of 10 or 12 miles from the centre of the Krakatoa volcano, the sea-bottom outside the great crater has been raised by an amount which varies from 10 to 60 feet. Mr. Verbeek concluded however, that along a line 8 or 9 miles in length, and extending westward from the great crater, an *increase* of depth has taken place, and this is not improbably due to the opening of a fissure on the flanks of the submerged cone.

In the so-called New or Sebesi Channel, between Krakatoa and Sebesi Islands, the original depth of water was much less than on the other sides of the Krakatoa group, seldom, indeed, exceeding 20 fathoms; and several rocks in this chananel rose above the sea-level. After the eruption it was found that this channel was completely blocked by banks composed of volcanic materials, and two portions of these banks rose above the sea as islands, which received the name of Steers Island and Calmeyer Island. By the action of the waves, however, these islands were, in the course of a few months, completely washed away, and their materials distributed over the sea bottom.

The changes which took place in the forms of the islands and in the depth of the sea around them, have been supposed by some to indicate a general elevation of the islands of the Krakatoa group, accompanied by a great subsidence of the central or crateral area. A careful study of these changes in the light of what is known to have taken place at other volcanic centres leads me to adopt a wholly different conclusion.

The action going on within a volcanic vent during eruption is in all essential features identical with that which takes place in the throat of a geyser. In both cases we have a mass of heated liquid, in the midst of which large quantities of gaseous materials are being disengaged so as to escape into the atmosphere as the pressure is relieved, and these escaping gases carry up with them portions of the liquid in which they have been confined. Now just as the throwing of sods and earth into the tube of a geyser, by causing a check in the escape of steam and water and thereby leading to an augmentation of the tension of the elastic fluids below, gives rise to a more than usually violent explosion, so the interruption to the regular ejections going on at Krakatoa, consequent on the chilling of the surface of the lava in the vent by inrushes of sea-water, caused *a check and then a rally* of the pent-up force of gases seeking to escape from the molten mass. The serious catastrophic outbursts that produced such startling effects both in the air and in the ocean appear to me to have been the direct consequences of this "check and rally" of the subterranean forces.

In these last terrible outbursts, in which the volcano rapidly expended its remaining force, we are evidently dealing with the breaking up and ejection of solid lava constituting the framework of the volcano, and not with the simple dissipation of the lava-froth (pumice) as during all the earlier stages of the eruption. That the materials were not carried far from the centre of ejection is shown by the fact that no falls of coarse materials are recorded from any of the vessels that were within or near the Strait at the time, but the bulk of the solid fragments thrown out during these great explosions must have fallen back into the sea, upon and immediately around the flanks of the volcano itself. This is proved by the alteration in the forms of the islands of the Krakatoa group, and by the change in the height of the floor of the surrounding ocean. By these grand explosive outbursts the old crater was completely eviscerated, and a cavity formed, more than 1,000 feet in depth, while the solid materials thrown out from the crater were spread over the flanks of the volcano, causing the alterations in their form which have been noticed.[7]

It was the rush of the great sea-waves over the land, caused by the violent evisceration of the crater of Krakatoa aided by the impact upon the water of the Strait of the enormous masses of falling material, that caused the great destruction of life and property in the Strait of Sunda. By the inrush of these waves on to the land, all vessels near the shore were stranded, the towns and villages along the coast devastated, two of the lighthouses swept away, and the lives of 36,380 of the inhabitants, among whom were 37 Europeans, sacrificed. The first waves reached both the Javan and the Sumatran coasts between 6 and 7 on the evening of August the 26th, and these probably mark the time of the first influx of water into the igneous focus. A succession of small oscillations of the sea continued all night, but the waves that followed the four great explosions of 5:30, 6:44, 10:02, and 10:52 in the morning of August the 27th, were undoubtedly the highest and most destructive of all. The question of the nature and height of these waves, and the phenomena which accompanied them, are discussed in a subsequent part of this report. The areas submerged by these great waves is shown on the Chart, Figure 66, above.

· · · · ·

The soundings after the eruption indicate, as already pointed out, that a great depression or fissure had been formed in the sea-bottom, extending eastward of Krakatoa for a distance of about 7 or 8 miles, and extending nearly in the direction of the great line of volcanic activity which traverses Java and Sumatra. The formation of the islands of Steers and Calmeyer appears to be most naturally accounted for if we imagine that two or more parasitical volcanic cones had grown up on the northern flank of the Krakatoa volcano and had increased in size till they rose above the sea-level. In this state they appear to have been seen by those on board the G.G. *Loudon* on August the 28th; and in a later stage of degradation by those on board the *Prins Hendrik*, on the 3rd of September. These cones[8] of loose pumice on rising above the sea-level were soon attacked by the waves, and as in the analogous well-known cases of Graham's Island and Sabrina, were gradually reduced first to sand-banks and then to shoals. [Judd adds the following two sentences as a footnote here.] The excessive quantity of material which must have been deposited in the channel between Krakatoa and Sebesi, to cause the formation of the two new islands and the surrounding shoals, has given rise to the suggestion that large portions of the volcano were actually hurled bodily into the air, and fell into the channel in question. But it is not necessary to adopt so improbable an hypothesis as this, when we remark the frequency of lateral eruptions upon volcanoes, and that we have in this case some direct evidence that small parasitical cones did actually exist at this point immediately after the great outbrust.

There is considerable doubt as to whether several small eruptions did not occur in and about Krakatoa after the great outburst had died out on the 28th or 29th of August. The investigations by Mr. Verbeek, however, have established the fact that a not inconsiderable explosion, accompanied by a rumbling sound, the ejection of large quantities of black mud, and a heavy sea-wave certainly took place at 9:30 p.m. on the 10th of October. The materials thrown out in this

last exhibition of activity were afterwards clearly seen covering the slopes of the peak of Krakatoa, and the Island of Calmeyer, and the outburst must have been a by no means insignificant one.

Judged by the quantity of materials ejected, or by the area and duration of the darkness caused by the volcanic dust, the eruption of Krakatoa must have been on a much smaller scale than several other outbursts which have occurred in historic times. The great eruption of Papandayang in Java, in 1772, of Skaptar Jökull (Varmárdalr) [Lakagígar] in Iceland, in 1783, and of Tomboro in Sumbawa, in 1815, were all accompanied by the extrusion of much larger quantities of material than that thrown out of Krakatoa in 1883. The special feature of this last outburst of the volcanic forces was the *excessively violent though short paroxysms* with which it terminated. In the terrible character of the sudden explosions which gave rise to such vast sea and air-waves on the morning of the 27th of August, the eruption of Krakatoa appears to have no parallel among the records of volcanic activity. The peculiarity of the phenomena displayed during this eruption is, I believe, to be accounted for by the situation of the volcano, and its liability to great inrushes of the waters of the sea, as the evisceration of the crater opened a way to the volcanic focus. The manner in which these influxes of cold water would first moderate the volcanic action, and as a consequence give rise in the end to tremendous and exhaustive explosions of abnormal violence, I have already endeavoured to explain.

[After 14 pages describing the materials ejected from Krakatau, Judd comes to his final section entitled "General Conclusions".]

The thoughtful consideration of some of the facts which have been detailed in the foregoing paragraphs is calculated, I believe, to afford an important insight into the nature of the forces which give rise to volcanic outbursts, and to the causes of the variation in character of these phenomena, in different places and at various times.

All the materials ejected from the *central* vent of Krakatoa have been wonderfully similar in their chemical and mineralogical constitution. At one period of the volcano's history, it is true, basaltic lavas and tuffs were thrown out from a *lateral* vent, and of these the parasitical cone of Rakata is built up; but both before and since this episode in the history of Krakatoa, the materials ejected from the central crater have always belonged to the remarkable class of enstatite-dacite rocks. [Judd was the first to apply this more accurate name to these rocks. In an earlier footnote he points out: "This rock has been called by many authors 'enstatite-' or 'hypersthene-andesite' but although the minerals present in the rocks are the same as those found in the 'enstatite-andesites' it has a silica-percentage of over 70, and it, therefore, belongs to the class of acid lavas. It bears, in fact, the same relation to the andesites that the rhyolites do to the trachytes, and on this account the name 'dacite' may be conveniently applied to it."] The composition of these rocks may be represented by the following general averages:—

Silica (with Titanic Acid)		70
Alumina		15
Oxides of Iron		4
Lime and Magnesia		5
Potash		2
Soda		4
	Total	100

In this magma apparently, by a first consolidation, well-developed crystals, equal to about 10 percent of the whole mass, seem to have been separated, these crystals consisting of 6 percent of felspar, 2 percent of ferriferous enstatite and augite (the former mineral being twice as abundant as the latter), and 2 percent of magnetite. Making a calculation on the basis of the composition actually found by analysis for rocks would have the following composition:

Silica (with Titanic Acid)		72.8
Alumina		14.7
Oxides of Iron		1.8
Lime and Magnesia		4.4
Potash		2.2
Soda		4.1
	Total	100.00

This magma exhibits a greater or less degree of devitrification in different cases, microlites of felspar, pyroxene, and magnetite belonging to a second period of consolidation, separating from it sometimes in small quantities, at other times to such an extent as to convert the glassy base into a stony one.

It is scarcely possible to doubt that the separation of the larger and porphyritic crystals from the magma, must have taken place under totally different conditions from those of the second consolidation; in all probability, when the mass existed at great depth and under intense pressure. And it is by no means certain that the proportion of glassy matrix to the included minerals has not been altered since the crystallization of the latter.

Now the startling fact which comes into prominence when the lavas of the earlier and later periods of eruptive activity at Krakatoa are studied in the field is that, in spite of this identity in chemical composition and of the included minerals, their mode of behaviour has been strikingly dissimilar.

During the earlier period, massive lava-streams flowed from the central vent, almost unaccompanied by any explosive action, and these lavas gradually accumulated to build up a bulky cone. In these massive lavas the slow cooling down of the molten rock permitted of the imperfect crystallization of the felspar, pyroxene, and magnetite from the base; where the cooling was somewhat rapid, magnetite and felspar were the chief minerals formed, as in the pitchstones; where less rapid, felspars and pyroxenes, as in the stony lavas.

But during the later period a lava having precisely the same chemical composition exhibited perfect liquidity. Occasional lava-streams composed of this material are found, as at Perboewatan, but the greater portion of it, on being relieved from pressure by coming into the outer atmosphere, at once became distended into pumice, through the escape of the volatile materials imprisoned in its midst.

Now, what is the cause of the difference of behaviour of the same chemical compound in these two cases? It might, at first sight, appear that the cause of this difference is to be sought in variations of temperature, and that the later lavas were more liquid because at a higher temperature, and more thoroughly fused than the earlier ones.

But if we examine the porphyritic crystals of the same minerals which have floated about in the magma in both cases, we shall find that all the evidence points to exactly the opposite conclusion, namely, that the pitchstone-rock was actually at the higher temperature, for the crystals of felspar in the obsidian-rock are often almost uncorroded, while in the pitchstone they have been attacked by the fluid in which they floated, and have indeed been to a great extent dissolved by it.

If we now try the actual fusibilities of the magmas in the two cases, we shall find the inference derived from the condition of the felspar-crystals to be strikingly confirmed. In the case of the pitchstone, portions of the substance held in the flame of a jet urged by a strong blast are hardly affected, while in the case of the obsidian the material under the same conditions rapidly becomes liquid.

But this production of liquidity in the obsidian is attended with the disengagement of a large quantity of volatile materials by which the rock rapidly passes into the condition of a pumice. It is, therefore, impossible to avoid connecting the presence of these volatile matters in the rock with the production of its liquidity.

I have in another place[9] pointed out that the leucite-basalts of similar composition ejected from Vesuvius at different periods exhibit just the same differences. When, as in the lavas of 1872, the quantity of steam and gas given off from them was large, their liquidity was perfect; when, as in 1858, the quantity of volatile matter was small, the lavas exhibited the greatest viscosity.

That by admixture with varying quantities of water many salts have their fusion-points proportionately reduced has long been known. Indeed, the late Dr. Guthrie, F.R.S., by his interesting experiments upon nitre, was able to demonstrate that there is actual continuity between the two states of fluidity known by the names of *solution* and *fusion* respectively. For, as there is a perfectly gradual rise in the temperature at which liquidity is produced when more and more nitre is added to a definite quantity of water, it becomes impossible to decide when the proportion of the water becomes so small that we can no longer regard the case as one of "solution," and we must begin to call it "fusion."[10]

That the silicates, like other salts, have their fusion-points lowered by admixture with water, we have many proofs. Most of the felspars are minerals of difficult fusibility, while the zeolites, which are analogous compounds of the silicates of alumina and the silicates of potash, soda, and lime, with the addition of water, are remarkable for their easy fusibility and for the manner in which they swell up and lose their waters at a comparatively low temperature. And this is true, not only of definite hydrous silicates, like the zeolites; the colloids of indefinite chemical composition, such as tachylyte, hydrotachylyte, and palagonite, appear to have their fusion-points lowered according to the proportion of water that they contain.

In the case of the Krakatoa-lavas we have the clearest evidence that when the mixtures of silicates of which they consist contain water, then very fusible glasses are formed. In these circumstances, the earlier

formed porphyritic crystals are but little liable to be attacked by the liquid magma in which they float. As the interesting synthetic researches of MM. Fouqué and Lévy have shown that any particular mineral is liable to separate from a magma when the latter is kept for a long time at a temperature just below the point of fusion of the mineral, we can understand how small is the chance of devitrification taking place in magmas which are liquified at low temperatures, and which, by a small reduction of temperature, become solid.

In other magmas, however, consisting of precisely the same admixture of silicates, *but without water*, we find the fusion-point far higher. The excessively heated magma in such cases exercises the strongest solvent action on the crystals of felspar immersed in it; and in cooling down, much magnetite, augite, enstatite, and felspar separate out from it before it solidifies.

I am convinced that this is a class of questions to which petrologists will have to give much greater attention than they have hitherto done. The characters assumed by an igneous rock depend not only on the peculiar admixture of silicates which compose it, but also on the temperature at which liquifaction and solidification could take place in the mass; this being to a great extent dependent on the quantity of water that was present. The temperature at which fusion could take place would largely determine not only the minerals which separated out from the magma, but also the degree and nature of their crystallization. In other words, the texture as well as the mineralogical constitution of the rock would be greatly influenced by the proportion of water present in the magma from which it was formed.

In the same way the actual nature of the volcanic manifestations at any particular vent are seen to be determined, not so much by the mineralogical constitution of the lava, as by the circumstance of the quantity of water contained in the magma. Where this is great, the lava will be perfectly liquid, and will be almost wholly thrown out in the form of pumice and dust. On the other hand, lavas containing little water will require a very high temperature for their fusion, and they will be characterised by great viscosity rather than perfect liquidity.

If, as seems highly probable, the younger ejecta of Krakatoa were formed by the re-fusion of the older lavas, then we can trace the cause of the introduction of water by which their liquefaction by heat was rendered more easy. These older lavas, by the presence in them of hydrous compounds, and by the existence in their cavities of tridymite and other secondary minerals, betray the fact that they have been greatly acted upon by percolating waters. It is through the introduction of the sea and other surface-waters into the rock-masses by slow percolation from above, and the consequent formation of new compounds, more readily acted upon by subterranean heat, that I am disposed to regard volcanic phenomena as being brought about. In this we find an explanation of the proximity of volcanoes to great bodies of water, which it seems to me is far more in accord with the actual phenomena than the suppositon that water finds access to volcanic foci by means of actual open fissures.

Note.—It is very greatly to be regretted that no accurate survey of Krakatoa, and of the surrounding seas was made prior to the great eruption of 1883. Had such been done, a splendid opportunity would have been afforded us for determining whether elevation and subsequent subsidence of the whole mass of the volcano actually occurred. The existing statements concerning the height of the peak of Rakata before and after the eruption are so confused and contradictory (see p. 301 and footnote[6]), while both the outlines and soundings on the old charts appear to be so untrustworthy, that I fail to detect certain evidence of any movements of the kind. As the phenomena observed at Krakatoa seem be be reconcilable with principles aready well established by the study of other volcanoes, I have felt it incumbent on me to adopt such interpretations in preference to those which depend on movements of the volcanic mass which are of a conjectural character.

The theoretical questions, suggested by the study of the Krakatoa-lavas have been more fully discussed by the author in a paper read before the Geological Section of the British Association at the meeting in Manchester in 1887. The paper is published in the "Geological Magazine," Dec. iii, vol. v. (1888), p. 1.

[1][Judd's figure 2, referenced here, is an engraving from Verbeek's chromolithograph of Sebesi, plate 4, number 13, reprinted as our Plate 3D.]

[2]Corresponding to the wave mentioned on p. 69 [of the Royal Society Report and p. 370 here] as 9 h. 58 m. Krakatoa time = 2 h. 56 m. G.M.T.

[3][Compare Verbeek's description of this rock on p. 250.]

[4][Judd's plate II, referenced here, is an engraving of Verbeek's plate 9, number 25, the chromolithograph of the Rakata wall re-

printed as our Plate 8. See also the 1886 photographs of this face on p. 143.]

[5][Plates XXXII and XXXIII of Royal Society report reproduced at the end of Captain Wharton's report. These are British Admiralty Charts of 1868 and 1886, the Krakatau areas of which are reprinted by us in Figure 69.]

[6]According to Verbeek, the height previous to the eruption was 2,697 feet. After the eruption he says the height was 2,730 feet, but was reduced by June, 1886 to 2,677 feet.

[7]It is probable that lateral eruptions contributed to the alterations produced by the ejection of materials from the central crater.

[8][Contrast this description of "Cones" with Verbeek's on p. 261.]

[9]Judd (1875, p. 68), (1888c, p. 92).

[10]Phil. Mag., 18:22 (1884).

Legend of A.D. 416 Eruption Chronicle (Judd, 1889)

The appearance of the Royal Society's report in 1888 rekindled widespread interest in Krakatau and its earlier history. Furthermore, the Royal Society's committee had already established itself as a clearing center for information on Krakatau. In 1889 Professor Judd received a fascinating account, from ancient Javanese chronicles, suggesting a huge eruption and collapse of Krakatau nearly 15 centuries before the events of 1883. In a letter to Nature, Judd quotes some of his own words on prehistoric eruptions and subsidence in the Sunda Straits before moving on to the Javanese account quoted below, remarkable in its closeness to modern conceptions of what the catastrophic prehistoric collapse of Krakatau must have been like.

I am greatly indebted to Mr. C. Baumgarten, of Batavia, who, through Dr. R. Rost, the Librarian to the India Office, has called my attention to some ancient records. . . . Mr. Baumgarten writes as follows:—

In a Javanese book called 'Pustaka Raja,' the 'Book of Kings,' containing the chronicles of the island, kept secret during centuries in the Royal Archives, and only recently made public, we find the following interesting and curious account of an eruption of the mountain Kapi:—

'In the year 338 Saka [i.e. A.D. 416], a thundering noise was heard from the mountain Batuwara,[1,2] which was an-

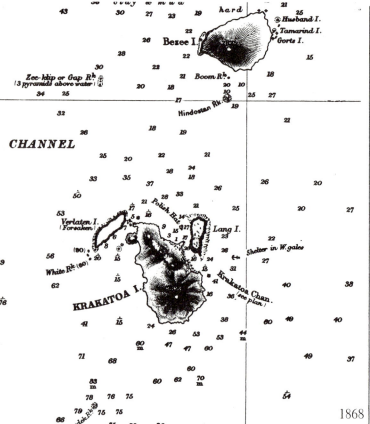

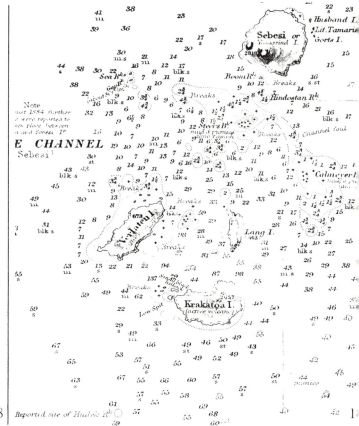

Figure 69. Changing bathymetry of the Krakatau area. The same area, measuring 36 × 39 km, shown on four British Admiralty Charts of the Sunda Straits. The first two are before (1868) and after (1886) the 1883 collapse, and the later two show further redistribution (after 41 and 73 years, respectively) of the 1883 fragmental deposits that formed such a thick layer on the

swered by a similar noise coming from the mountain Kapi, lying westward of the modern Bantam. A great glaring fire, which reached to the sky, came out of the last-named mountain; the whole world was greatly shaken, and violent thundering, accompanied by heavy rains and storms, took place; but not only did not this heavy rain extinguish the eruption of fire of the mountain Kapi, but it augmented the fire; the noise was fearful, at last the mountain Kapi with a tremendous roar burst into pieces and sunk into the deepest of the earth. The water of the sea rose and inundated the land. The country to the east of the mountain Batuwara, to the mountain Kamula,[3] and westward to the mountain Raja Basa,[4] was inundated by the sea; the inhabitants of the northern part of the Sunda country to the mountain Raja Basa were drowned and swept away with all their property.

'After the water subsided the mountain Kapi and the surrounding land became sea and the Island of Java[5] divided into two parts.

'The city of Samaskuta, which was situated in the interior of Sumatra, became sea, the water of which was very clear, and which was afterwards called the lake Sinkara.[6] This is the origin of the separation of Sumatra and Java.'[7,8,9]

[1]Footnotes 2–7 are from the original article by Judd.

[2]"Now called Pulosari, one of the extinct volcanoes in Bantam, and the nearest to the Straits of Sunda."

[3]"Now called the 'Gedé' mountain."

[4]"The most southern volcano of Sumatra, and situated in the 'Lampung' country."

[5]"The Sanskrit Yawa-dwipa."

[6]"The well-known Lake of the 'Menang-Kebo' country."

[7]See the "Krakataō Eruption and the Javanese Chronicles" in Trübner's Record for August 1889 (third series, vol. i, pt. 3).

[8][The anonymous article cited in footnote 7 appeared in the July 1889 issue of Trübner's Record and carried the same words (including footnotes 2–6) attributed here to Mr. Baumgarten. Trübner and Co. were the publishers of the Royal Society's report on Krakatau. Professor Judd's article, excerpted here, appeared in the August 15, 1889 issue of Nature (40:365–366).]

[9][De Néve (1983) points out that the Sunda Strait is a recent feature first navigated in 1173 and not known to 13th and 14th century European explorers such as Marco Polo. Geol. Mag., vol. 2.]

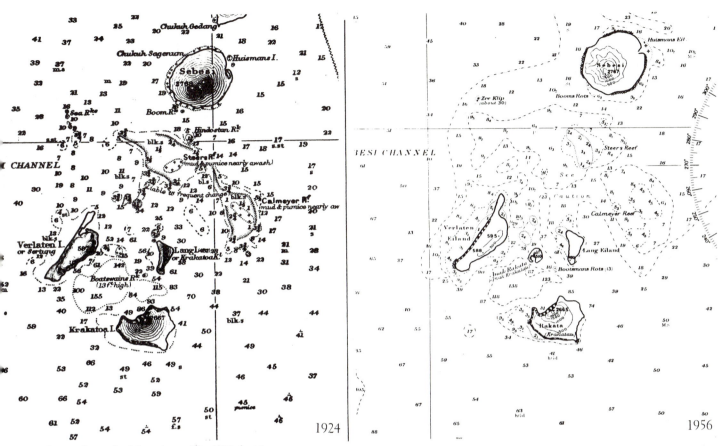

sea floor to the north of the volcano. The 1924 chart incorporated much of the detailed surveying of the early part of the century, but not the growth of Anak Krakatau which began in 1927.

Explanation of the 1883 Eruption—Engulfment Hypothesis (Dana, 1890)

Judd's concept of explosive disruption as the principal mechanism of Krakatau's evisceration was widely influential, particularly among English-speaking scientists to whom Verbeek's Dutch monograph was not available. However, James Dwight Dana, the eminent mineralogist and pillar of American science, published a book in 1890, just 5 years before his death, that briefly mentioned Krakatau but with a dramatically different interpretation. Noting the paucity of coarse lithic debris in the near-vent ejecta, Dana reasoned that the eruption of such large volumes of magma, in the form of pumice and ash, resulted in the evacuation of a shallow magma chamber and in subsequent collapse and engulfment of parts of the pre-eruption volcanic edifice. This is the modern concept of caldera collapse (see Williams, below, p.

341), but the word caldera was not even introduced to the geologic literature until the year after Krakatau's famous collapse. Dutton, in his 1883 book-length report on Hawaiian volcanoes, recognized the collapse origin of their great summit depressions and suggested the word caldera, Spanish for cauldron, to distinguish them from the generally smaller craters formed by explosion. Dana's 1890 book Characteristics of Volcanoes also concentrated on Hawaiian volcanoes, and the following appears under his discussion of explosive eruptions.

At Krakatoa, in 1883, the projectile discharge was equally sudden, and far more terrible and destructive. The height to which the dust was carried was made by Professor Verbeek fifty thousand feet. It began in the early morning of one day, made day into night (by its ejections of ashes) for thirty-six hours, and left the sky clear by the close of the next day. Nothing is said of an outflow of lavas.

The earthquakes at Tarawera [New Zealand, a major eruption there in 1886 is compared to Krakatau] were not violent; they were felt to a distance of fifty or sixty miles only; and a dozen miles from Tarawera Mountain, at Rotorua, on the geyser plains, no shock was able to upset a chimney or jar down crockery from a shelf. They were manifestly local, and had their centre near the surface, —an effect, not a cause; and they thus prove that the immediate cause of the eruption was local. The facts as to the Krakatoa earthquakes are similar. The deafening roar in each was made chiefly by the violent projectile action, the incessant detonations, and the ragings and thunderings of a storm.

Such eruptions are of a wholly different cast from the ordinary outbreaks and discharges of Hawaii. The projectile agent must gain access to the conduit lavas to produce so extraordinary projectile violence.

The eruption of Tarawera Mountain was probably brought about by the opening of a fissure that let subterranean waters *into* the reservoir of lavas; for Lake Rotomahana, situated on the line of fracture, and only three or four miles distant, lost its waters, and probably in the process of supplying water for the projectile work. The volcanic mountain had been long extinct; but the widely distributed geysers and boiling springs were testimony to the existence of liquid lavas just below the reach of descending atmospheric waters. The geyser lakes of Rotorua and other localities became hotter during the night of the eruption, and continued so afterward. Under such conditions an old volcanic mountain, perhaps hollow from former discharges, might be burst open again. Had the ingressing waters passed into the lava-reservoir *at a great depth* below the surface, the generated vapors would almost necessarily have added outflows of lava.

The volcano of Krakatoa was probably started into action by a similar incursion, but of marine waters.

In both cases there were enormous chasms and crater-like depressions made, with a loss of the old foundations, and of the rocks that occupied the depressions. But the facts, while they include the projection of large stones over the vicinity, show positively that the stones were few compared with what would be needed to fill the great cavities left in the region. The explosive eruption threw to great heights fragments of the liquid lavas in the shape of scoria and sand or ashes, but did not blow off the solid rocks of the mountain. The disappearance of these and the making of the cavities are explained by the engulfment or down-plunge of material *to fill the space left empty* by the projectile discharges.

Rockfalls on Krakatau's Cliff: The Pseudo-eruptions (Cool, 1908)

Following the initial studies of Verbeek and the French mission, there was surprisingly little geologic field work at Krakatau for the next two decades. In 1908, however, W. van Bemmelen attempted a more detailed bathymetric map of the caldera and he described his findings in a report to the local scientific society the next year. During the initial survey in May, "brown smoke" was reported from a fissure on the steep north face of Rakata, and when van Bemmelen returned to the island on August 7, he was accompanied by geologist H. Cool, whose excerpted account (1908, p. 245–246, translated from the Dutch by J.A. Nelen) follows:

In the evening the ship steamed along this steep wall and fissure, where the phenomenon was said to have taken place. We observed the cliff with field glasses under exceptionally good light conditions without seeing any smoke rising from the openings.

What looked like openings in the May photos, turned out to be shadows of protruding parts. The so-called fissure appeared more like a slit. The next morning we landed at the foot of the rubble piles; both were climbed and in addition the steep cliff was partly climbed at a spot above the western pile. Nowhere could a trace of smoke nor larger or smaller openings be seen. During the day this point of the cliff was watched continuously, without anything happening. Toward evening about 6:15, however, two dull bangs were heard and brown clouds, which looked like dust clouds appeared along that part of the mountain. They slowly rose and cleared, while there was a noise of rolling rock and splattering water. Probably a rockfall had taken place, rocks loosened by the cooling of evening after exposure to the sun during the day. These normally are accompanied by loud noise.

On the morning of the 9th further observations were made from a sloop near the middle of the Krakatau cliff, when suddenly a virtual bombardment was heard and a heavy rockfall occurred along the slit and the wall above the rubble piles, partly landing on these and partly in the water. Dust clouds formed along the slit, the cliff, and the rubble piles.

It was just at this moment that the sun started to hit the upper part of the slit.

Immediately we rowed closer, the dust cloud disappeared and the rest of the day nothing more was observed. In the evening we started on the return trip.

The above phenomenon, as is shown, should be attributed to rockfalls, not volcanic action.

The Juniata, two weeks after the paroxysm, and the French mission, 9 months later, both reported rockfall dust clouds that were initially mistaken for volcanic activity (see p. 136 and 142, respectively). Such clouds were also observed[1] in 1896 and 1897. The 1968 collapse of Fernandina caldera, in the Galápagos Islands, was volumetrically smaller than the 1883 Krakatau collapse, but formed comparable cliffs—12 years later rockfalls down these oversteepened cliffs still produced occasional dust clouds rising as much as 1 km above the rim and appearing from a distance like eruptive clouds.

[1]*Java Bode (1933).*

Geology and Volcanism of the Krakatau Group (Stehn, 1929a)

Additional field work at Krakatau resulted in papers by de Jongh, in 1918, and Escher, in 1919, but it was not until 1927 that the geological spotlight again focused prominently on Krakatau. In that year the volcano awoke, after 44 years of quiet, and repeated eruptions from the middle of the submerged caldera swiftly aroused fears that paroxysmal events might again devastate the region. The Netherlands East Indies Geological Survey quickly initiated detailed field observation with the requisite logistic support. A young geologist, Dr. Ch.E. Stehn, spent much of the years 1928–1929 on the islands and carried out the most detailed field study known to us of Krakatau geology.

He summarized the results of this work for the Fourth Pacific Science Conference, which met in Batavia in 1929, and we reprint his full report below. In addition to his detailed field work, Stehn had the benefit of nearly half a century of petro-graphic advances since Verbeek's work. He also describes the birth of the new volcano, Anak Krakatau or child of Krakatau. In addition to exceptionally detailed observations of submarine volcanism, this paper provides the first seismic study of the area and adds some interesting observations on water waves produced by submarine eruptions.

Situation and Morphology

Krakatau, which required a world-wide notoriety because of its most catastrophic eruption in 1883, and which has recently excited fresh interest by the activity of a submarine volcano, lies in the Sunda Strait between the Great Sundas, Sumatra and Java. It belongs to the long series of volcanoes, which follows the longitudinal axis of Sumatra and is continued in the volcanic group of West Bantam (Java), in Goenoeg[24] Peolosarie, Goenoeng Karang and others, and also to a second series which begins with the solfataralike Goenoeng Radjabasa in the Lampong District (South Sumatra) in the NE and is continued in the islands of Peoloe[25] Tiga, Seboekoe and Sebesi, which are built up out of volcanic material, terminating in Prinsen Eiland in the SW. It is only 12 km from Poeloe Sebesi but 40 km from Prinsen Eiland.

Krakatau embraces a group of three larger islands viz. Krakatau or Rakata, Lang or Peoloe Rakata Ketjil and Verlaten or Poeloe Sertoeng and a small rock known as Bootsmansrots. The highest island is Rakata. The Peak has an elevation of 813 m, Verlaten Eiland of 182 m and Lang of 172 m. In extent Verlaten today has more than 8 km, as a result of phenomena to which we shall presently revert. All three show the peculiarity that the highest portion is situated towards the central space between the islands. The sole exception is the southern part of Verlaten where the greatest uplift is centrally situated. The cause of this lies in the geological structure. The three islands lie on the edge of a circle of about 7 km diameter.

Geology and History

Thanks to the researches of R.D.M. Verbeek,[22] H. Cool,[5] A.C. de Jongh,[10] B.G. Escher[6,7,8,9] a large amount of material has been collected pertaining to the geology and history of Krakatau, and that has been supplemented in 1922 and 1928 by the Staff of the Volcanological Survey. The observations of the latter have made it possible to collect additional information and to modify former conceptions of the structure and history of the volcano in a few details.[26]

Figure 70. Rakata NE. 1 Products of the first, 2 products of the second and 3 products of the third period. [Stehn's photo 1.]

The following constructive and destructive periods can roughly be distinguished.

I. Formation of a hypothetical single volcano about 2000 m high, after Verbeek and Escher of which the latest lava streams and ejecta consist of *hypersthene andesite with tridymite* and a microlithic devitrefied glass (Escher) (The "pitchstone" of Verbeek).

Destruction of this volcano leaving four remnants, which form the socle of Rakata, Verlaten, Lang and the Poolsche Hoed ("Polish Hat"). Formation of a seabasin of unknown depth in the centre.

II. Formation of an eccentric *basaltic* volcano, covering the Rakata remnant, a little over 800 m high.

III. Submarine activity of two *andesitic* volcanoes, Danan and Perboewatan. Formation of an island which joins up with the basaltic volcanic cone of Rakata. The same magma penetrates into the Rakata cone through a fissure.

Fresh activity in May 1680.

IV. May 20th 1883 commencement of a new eruption which continues with short pauses.

August 26th–28th 1883 the greatest activity. Considerable increase in magnitude of Rakata, Verlaten and Lang from ejecta of a *andesitic* magma, obsidian, pumice stone and rocks dating from before 1883. Terminating with destruction of the volcanoes Perboewatan and Danan and half the basaltic cone of the

Peak of Rakata. Formation of a 279 m deep basin between the three islands.[27]

V. Severe abrasion by ocean waves especially on the west coast, of the three islands. Silting up of the low northern portion of Verlaten.

VI. Submarine activity since December 29th (June?) 1927. Out of *basaltic* bombs and ashes and old material a submarine volcanic cone is built up, which appears above the surface on January 26th 1928 and later disappeared by the action of the breakers. Submarine lava streams.

The crater rim appeared again on January 28th 1929. A new island of *basaltic* magma was formed "Anak Krakatau".

The First Period

Between E and N Krakatau and along the east side of Verlaten and west side of Lang, there are light grey rocks exposed, which must be classed among the hypersthene andesites and contain a good deal of tridymite in clefts and hollows. Verbeek and Escher take these for the oldest rocks in the Krakatau group. The latest researches have shown, however, that there are still older rocks on Verlaten. These are exposed along the steep coast, beginning at the point to eastward of the highest point (182 m) of the island, in a SW direction to an extent of about 100 m.

The deepest layer in this profile is formed by coarse-grained andesite (No. 2341), which contains much glass of a dense black colour. The rock does not lend itself to an accurate chemical analysis, being greatly subject to the effects of the sea water. The percentage of silicic acid has been found by analysis in the Volcanological Research Laboratory to be 65.6%. The same rock was found again on Lang in the two block horizons (see p. 316 and 320).

On Verlaten this rock is covered by several layers of red, black, and also lighter-hued, rough-grained volcanic ashes, and a basaltic porous lava (No. 2496) on which lies the tridymite andesite lava referred to above.

The implication from this profile, therefore, is that the supposition of N.J.M. Taverne[18] ([his] p. 19) "that we shall have to regard the andesite with tridymite as a lava-shield, which had served as the foundation for the original Krakatau volcano" is proved incorrect.

This tridymite-lava attains a very great thickness. In the northern part of Rakata (Figure 70) and on Lang the steep andesite wall has a height of about 50

m. On Verlaten it is still thicker. For the chemical analysis of a sample (No. 2298) taken on Rakata see Table (p. 337).

According to Verbeek there is on the NE and E side of Rakata above the rock "a layer 2–3 m thick of fine, loose ejecta disintegrated ashes and sand containing lapilli of the size of the closed hand", distinguishable by its yellow and brownish-yellow colour. It has been found, for example, that above the tridymite andesite there follows first a tuff-series, which is covered by the series determined by Escher, comprising "yellow glassy lava with black glassy streaks and foreign matter held in it" (SiO_2 67.14 %), a "bluish-grey lava", "alternate layers of black and red lava", a red fluid lava, of which the foundation consists of dark-red glass (SiO_2 65.94 %), "bluish-grey lava" and a "white tuff layer". That completes the andesite substructure of Rakata.

Do the other two islands show the same succession of layers?

On Lang the latest researches have shown that the typical light-grey tridymite-andesite, revealed on NE Rakata, occurs only in the SW of this island and in the deepest layers (to westward of the highest point 147 m) and that above this there follows the series above described in Rakata. In the NW of Lang (Figure 71), westward of the highest point 87 m, is a steep lava-coast with no beach; the rock probably contains some tridymite but its presence is rare. The colour is darker and is like the bluish-grey lava in Rakata. The lava-mass is covered by a red lava-bank rich in glass. The dark bluish-grey lava is absent in this profile. The series closes, on the other hand, with dark grey-green silicious rock devitrified by augite microlites (Analysis No. 2283 see Table (p. 337)) from which according to Verbeek, the island known as the Poolsche Hoed to west of Lang, which existed before 1883, was also formed.[28]

This glassy rock has penetrated into fissures of the red lava of Lang, thus forming a permanent junction with it. There were but little contact effects. The glassy rock laid bare about 2 or 3 m thick in the profile here described, has near about the middle, a perlitic structure. Numerous spheroids the size of a pea lie close together. Near the surface these spheroids become more rare, until the rock acquires a dense structure.

After an old conception a part of Lang before the 1883 eruption was rather low, at least near the inner side of the present basin there were not high and steep walls of rock everywhere. It is now established that the middle part of the lava mass, as well as the north-

erly portion, has steep walls, which form the old coastline, now 75 m inland. West of the triangulation-point "P-68" lies the upper limit of the blue-grey lava at a height of 45 m and of the darker glassy rock at 56 m (see also Figure 72).

The lava-mass referred to above begins WNW of the summit 87, the strata disappearing into the depths with an inclination of 12° to northward, thus establishing the NE boundary of the oldest volcano (Formation I). Escher[8] has pointed out on [his] p. 209 that in the most southerly part of Lang, above an adhesent [adjacent?] pumice tuff of 1883, andesite appears again. This andesite, as our researches show, is formed out of the series bluish-grey lava to dark glassy rock, which like the red lava, which Escher did not see, re-appears on the steep east coast of Lang South. Moreover, the surface of the glassy rock could be followed from the east coast to far above it, in the latest barranco which can be reached along the coast, coming from the north.

The inclination of this rock is 16° to the ENE. In the middle of the east coast also, where the wide plain ends, the glassy rock is revealed as a mass that has been burst into blocks.

On Verlaten, unfortunately, the profile is less clear. The high and steep walls are more difficult of access. But the blocks lying at the foot of the old easterly mass indicate that the darker glassy rock is not lacking here either. What we know, however, is that it forms the uppermost layer of the old rock in the SE part of Verlaten. The grey lava containing tridymite emerges out of the sea a little more to the north. The floor of the glassy rock here, too, is the red lava, partially cut through by the dark glass.

On Lang there follow, above the silicious rock, four shallow strata of clayey sand, one with white pumice, covered over with a, likewise shallow, white pumice layer which passes upward into a layer, about 30 cm thick, of old weathered soil. The volcano must, therefore, have lain dormant for a long time. The weathered soil has not, however, been found yet on the two other islands.

Examining this fine profile of Lang West further (Figure 71), we find above this old humus-layer, first a white and pink pumice with sharp edges and, next, a yellow pumice which diminished upward and passes into a shallow and greatly weathered stratum. These two strata, about 2 m thick, which are laid bare also at various points on the coast of Lang, we regard as the last ejecta of the central volcanic cone.

The volcano was destroyed by collapse. There are

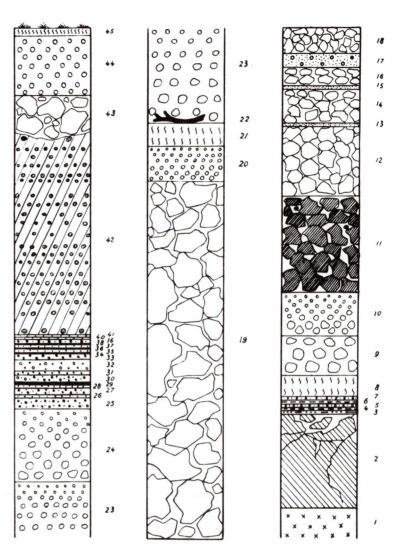

45. LATEST MOULD-LAYER.
44. pumice with fragments of other pyroclastic ejecta.
43. BLOCK-LAYER with pumice.
42. black pumice.
41. very small pumice-lapilli and pumice-ash.
40. small pumice-lapilli and ash.
39. small pumice-bombs and pumice-lapilli.
38. pumice-ash.
37. very small pumice-lapilli.
36. pumice-ash.
35. very small pumice-lapilli.
34. pumice-ash.
33. pumice-lapilli.
32. small pumice-bombs and pumice-lapilli.
31. small pumice-lapilli.
30. pumice-lapilli.
29. grey-white pumice-ash.
28. very small grained pumice-lapilli.
27. pumice-lapilli and sand.
26. small pink pumice-lapilli and pink pumice-ash.
25. pumice-lapilli.
24. coarse grained pale-pink pumice, upwards becoming finer grained.
23. coarse grained white pumice, upwards becoming finer-grained.
22. charred trunks. Vegetation of before 1883.

21. SOIL-FORMATION OF BEFORE 1883. (Old land-surface) MOULD-LAYER.
20. pumice and small fragments of other pyroclastic ejecta, upwards weathered.
19. BLOCK-LAYER.
18. scoriae, the size of an egg.
17. fine-grained pumice-sand with some coarser-grained lapilli.
16. red-gray scoriae. Also pumice.
15. fine lapilli.
14. red-gray scoriae. Also pitchstone.
13. fine lapilli.
12. red-gray scoriae.
11. black, more or less consolidated scoriae.
10. yellow pumice, upwards smaller and weathered.
9. white and pink coloured, angular pumice-fragments.
8. SOIL-FORMATION (Old land-surface). MOULD.
7. coarse-grained, sand, with white pumice.
6. fine-grained, clayish sand.
5. gray clay, with white pumice.
4. gray, clayish sand.
3. brown-red, clayish sand.
2. pitchstone, upwards changing into blocks.
1. tridymite-andesite (solid).

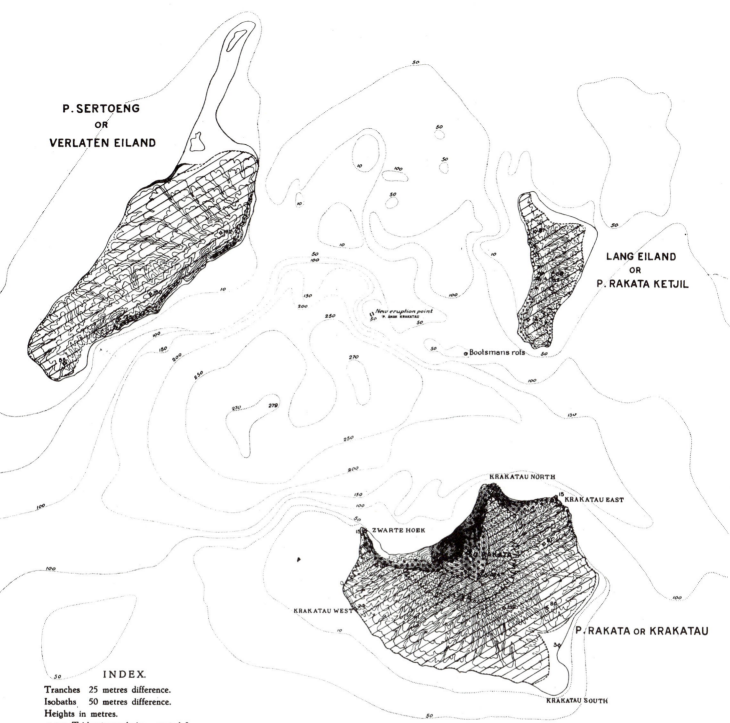

P. SERTOENG
OR
VERLATEN EILAND

LANG EILAND
OR
P. RAKATA KETJIL

New eruption point
P. ANAK KRAKATAU

Boolsmans rofs

KRAKATAU NORTH

KRAKATAU EAST

ZWARTE HOEK

KRAKATAU WEST

P. RAKATA OR KRAKATAU

KRAKATAU SOUTH

INDEX.

Tranches   25 metres difference.
Isobaths   50 metres difference.
Heights in metres.
.ˣ.ˣ.ˣ. Tridymite andesite   period I.
。。。。。 Basalt   period II.
||||||||| Hypersthen andesite period III.
///   Products of the eruption of 1883.
White: Beach.

Figure 71 (left). Columnar section of the layers of
NW Lang Eiland. (Border of Former- and Late Lang
Eiland). [3 columns total 40 m in height. Stehn's
plate II.]

Figure 72 (above). Geological Map of the Krakatau
Group. Reduction of the 1:25,000 map, published
by Dr. B.G. Escher in 1919, with topographical
corrections and geological complements by the
Netherlands East Indian Volcanological Survey in
1928. [Stehn's plate I.]

315

four remnants left viz. Rakata. Verlaten, Poolsche Hoed and Lang. Its activity did not cease, however. Eight layers, 5.40 m thick altogether, of cinder alternating with small lapilli, are evidence of that. The cinder and the small lapilli, however, are black or red, as a result of strong oxidation, as I think during the contact with sea-water. They were, therefore, thrown up by a submarine volcano. The black pumice-like cinder welded together by heat. The reddish-grey cinder have been chemically analysed (Nos. 2264 and 2313, see Table (p. 337)). They differ little from the composition of the tridymite andesite. Apparently the volcano emerged above the water once more, for the next two layers consist of white pumice, the upper one with lapilli the size of a hen's egg.

A violent explosion followed. Young rock and old were hurled out obliquely and covered Lang to a depth of 9 m (Old Lang North. See Figure 71) to 12 m (Old Lang South). Very numerous in this block layer are, besides the tridymite andesites and the covering cinder, old rock from the substratum, comprising breccias, cemented with quartz, silicious slates, sandstone, pitch-stone, dacites and highly propylitic rock.

This block-layer was found again on Verlaten but not so thick; on Rakata, however, it has not been found so far.

The Second Period

Over the remnant Rakata of the oldest volcanic island a new cone is formed eccentrically. Lava streams alternate with ejecta of loose substances, bombs, lapilli and fine ashes until a mountain more than 800 m high was produced. In the section of the Peak the interchanging conformable strata are easily distinguished. All the products of this cone consist of basalt rich in olivine. For two analysis of rocks (Nos. 2081 and 2289) from Zwarte Hoek (Black Hook) see Table (p. 337). Unfortunately, on account of the many severe landslides in the couloirs to east and west of the central area caused by the numerous earthquakes in the earliest eruption period, it has not been possible to determine the number of lava-banks and layers of loose material and to examine them more closely, with a view especially to solving the problem whether the basaltic peak was built up in a short time or whether longer intervals of inactivity, distinguishable by the weathered crusts, were interposed between the different effusiva and explosive activities of the Peak. Until these lava-banks and layers of loose material have been carefully examined, it will be impossible to ascertain

whether the lava-banks to east and west of the central area correspond to each other, that is to say whether the lava flowed out simultaneously in these two directions.

Besides these lava-banks formed by breaches or overflows, we notice in the section of the cone numerous dikes running through the deposits of loose material and the solid lava-banks, right up from the sea-level to great heights. (Figure 73). Escher counted more than 25 in the west half of the section. We favour his idea that these dikes, which reach no greater heights than 400 m (most of them terminate at 200–300 m), were formed after the formation of the 800 m high mountain. They must be regarded as a final attempt on the part of the basaltic magma to overcome the pressure of the congealed pipe, origining radial fissures in the volcanic mantle. Along these the magma forced its way upward. The tension ceased and the magma was congealed in the fissures. Whether the lava of a dike forced its way to the surface we do not know yet. The possibility is not precluded that basaltic lava-streams which have their point of emergence in one or other of these basaltic dikes, lie hidden under the covering of pumice-tuff.

Figure 73 shows the exterior of one of these basaltic dikes in the western half of the scarred face of the fallen Peak. One can distinguish clearly the difference between the centre and the flanks of the dike and the "Salband".

The Third Period

In the basin between the three islands there began a fresh activity from submarine eruption-points. There appeared slowly in the space between them two new volcanoes, Perboewatan in the north and Danan more towards the centre. We do not know which of the two volcanoes formed first, or whether there was yet a third. The depth from which the activity came is not known. When the volcanoes appeared above the water, they slowly merged together into one island. Danan, which must have been the more active—it was 450 m high in 1883, while Perboewatan had reached only 120 m—, joined with Rakata to form one island whose greatest length was 9 km and greatest breadth about 5 km.

The eruptive activity of the two volcanoes and of a few smaller parasites comprised the ejection of loose matter and the outflow of lava. Verbeek collected in July 1880[21] samples of lava streams on the NW end opposite Verlaten, which belong to the hypersthene

Figure 73. Rakata N. A basaltic dike. [Stehn's photo 3.]

andesites without tridymite. The older lava was a dense light grey normal andesite; the younger which flowed over this was found to be a darker andesite with a pitchlike glassy groundmass. This being entirely devoid of vegetation and not at all weathered, Verbeek regards it as a product of the eruption of May 1680, which is the only one known in this volcanic group in historical times, when probably it was Perboewatan that was in action. Large quantities of pumice were then ejected.

Of the same rock as Danan and Perboewatan, namely hypersthene andesite without tridymite, is the wide dike [see p. 143], which can be followed in the cross section of Rakata below the Peak almost perpendicularly upward from the sea, (for chemical analysis see Table (p. 337)). Verbeek thought that the andesitic magma rose along a radial fissure proceeding from Danan. Escher[8] ([his] p. 210) has proved convincing that this is not possible. The dike, which according to Escher[8] ([his] p. 211) terminates at 320 m, continues according to this author, Verbeek, and Cool[4]([his] p. 26), in a lens-shaped thickening, which Escher regards as a sort of diatrema in Daubree's meaning and the dike as a radial branching-out therefrom.

In a hitherto unpublished report in 1922 N.J.M.

Taverne[17] questions Escher's view: "that the oval section at the end of the andesitic dike belongs to that. It seemed much rather as if the oval section comprised not one and the same sort of rock and that only the edge of the left part of it showed a continuity with the andesitic dike. The rest of this oval section, as it is called, appears to cohere with a large black-coloured mass of rock, with scaly cooling surfaces, which extends to summit and can very well be a part of the real volcano-pipe".

During our long sojourn on Krakatau in 1928–29, we saw the dike and the oval every day. Each change in the light produced a different effect: every photograph from different points of view and at different times of the day appeared to provide grounds for a different conception of it. We tried to climb the dike as high as possible, in order to solve from close quarters the two problems: "Is there coherence or not?" and "Is the lens formed of andesite or basalt?", but at 125 m up one comes to an almost perpendicular wall.

To attempt a conclusion from the various observations made by us, it seems to me probable that the two formations, dike and oval, have nothing to do with each other and that the dike terminates below the oval. In the photo [see p. 143] published by Verbeek in 1908,[23] too, there is, I think a clear division to be seen between the two.

Whether the lens, which with Escher I regard as a diatrema, i.e. as a vent filled up with lava, has its continuation downward in the portion of the island that has been preserved or whether it lays in the portion destroyed, only the future can decide, after some further subsidences of the wall and a re-survey of the height of the upper and lower limits of the oval. Since the elevations taken by Baron van Lynden, 2nd. Class Sea Lieutenant, in 1919[8] ([his] p. 210), the middle portion of the wall has not changed. Severe subsidences in recent times, especially on the east side of the summit, have slowly isolated this middle portion, so that I think it is possible that one day large masses may be dislodged by severe earthquake shocks.

Of products of the third period there is in the profile of Lang West (Figure 71), above the block-layer, a 90 cm thick layer of pumice and small rocks of former eruptions, which can probably be associated with eruption of the Danan-Perboewatan group. They pass upward into a layer of weathered soil about 60 cm thick, viz. the *vegetation-zone before May 1883*. Thick, carbonized tree-trunks and branches and humus testify to this.

This vegetation-zone was found again in various

places on Lang. It forms a sort of impermeable layer, at the outcrop of which small springs originate. The only powerful spring on Lang is situated above the steep south bank. From this, even in the driest period of 1928, the water descended in a shower of spray. The spot cannot always be reached along the bank, however.

The vegetation-zone is exposed on Verlaten, too, above the old rock on the SE bank. In Rakata we have so far found the old vegetation only above the basalt between the Peak and Zwarte Hoek.

The Fourth Period: The Eruption of 1883 May 20th to August 25th

On May 20th 1883 opened the fourth period in the history of the Krakatau Group, which completely changed the whole aspect of it and finally brought it world-notoriety after the paroxysm in August of that year.

Men of science, when this eruption is mentioned, always recall with great appreciation the work of R.D.M. Verbeek.[22] English scientists, too have described in detail the eruption and its accompanying phenomena.[16]

Before the beginning of the 1883 eruption there were a few weak tremors, which were felt on the shores of Sunda Strait, but it is not certain whether they were connected with the approaching eruption, because Sunda Strait is often the centre of tectonic tremors.

In the forenoon of May 20th Perboewatan began working. By 10 a.m. the steam and cloud or ashes had already reached a height of over 11 km. Detonations were heard more than 200 km away.

While in the first few days large quantities of pumice were ejected, in a short time that phase changed to the ejection of ashes, which, probably owing to hot noxious gases, caused great damage to vegetation, especially on Rakata and Verlaten, being borne over by the east monsoon, while Lang and Poolsche Hoed did not suffer much.

On May 27th the volcano in eruption was visited by the mining engineer Schuurman, who made his way to the edge of Perboewatan and collected several samples of ash and other ejecta [see p. 63–66 for Schuurman's report]. Schuurman[22] and Verbeek[22] [see p. 255], too, mention a grey, and again a dark-grey, ash. In the exhibits of the Sumatra party of the Geological Survey there are 3 samples of ash of different colours, collected by Schuurman on the same day.

The first sample (No. 8231) is dusky-black. The

chemical analysis showed the surprising result that the ashes contained only 51.04 % SiO_2; moreover, it was established petrographically that olivine is present and that the ash is basaltic.

The second sample (No. 8232) has an SiO_2 content of 56.23%. The third (grey) sample (No. 8233) corresponds to the normal andesitic pumice ash, with a content of 65.14 % SiO_2.

These samples were collected not far from Perboewatan, for only the northern part of the island was visited on that occasion. Unfortunately, the stratigraphic order of the samples and the exact spot where they were found are not known. Sample 8231 has nothing in common with the sample No. 7 collected later by Capt. Ferzenaar in the coast-profile (dark ashy-grey according to Ferzenaar, a lighter hue according to Verbeek), because the SiO_2 content shows a great difference (No. 7 SiO_2 = 60.13 %).

Besides the ashes and the pumice there are also blocks of a greenish-black glassy rock, which resembles a great deal the rock on Lang and Poolsche Hoed referred to above. It is not impossible that there were blocks of older material also ejected. Near these, Schuurman found a piece of obsidian, which was partly swollen into pumice, a find which later gave rise to the experiments carried out by A. Brun[3] ([his] p. 122) and repeated by Prof. Alphen de Veer at Bandoeng[8] ([his] p. 216).

Excepting a short break in the first half of June— at any rate records of observations are lacking for that eruptive phase—the eruptions continued with varying degrees of severity from May to August. Only gas, steam and ashes were produced. While in May only Perboewatan was active, in June the Danan too commenced.

As early as August 11th Rakata was re-explored by Capt. Ferzenaar [see p. 67–68 for Ferzenaar report]. The eruptions had proceeded from 3 main craters, while steam and gases had escaped at many points. The crater of Danan was wider because of collapses.

The thickness of the ejected products on August 11th 1883, in the immediate vicinity of the crater, was not more than ½ m. In the period from August 12th to 26th ash eruptions were observed on August 14th, 18th and 23rd by ships passing Krakatau.

The Paroxysm of August 26th–28th 1883

The paroxysm of the 4th phase of eruption took place in the period August 26th to 28th. No earthquakes were felt on the shores of Sunda Strait before and during the paroxysm. After 1 p.m. on August 26th the severity of the eruption increased and reached its maximum on August 27th at 10:02 a.m., after which it diminished very greatly in intensity. Submarine eruptions took place, according to Verbeek, in the evening or night of the 27th. On the morning of August 28th the volcano was quiescent once more. Nothing is known for certain about any eruption after August 28th. It is possible that a few phenomena observed in September and October 1883 and February 1884 can be connected therewith. Verbeek states, for example, that on October 17th there was again a small submarine eruption, when mud was ejected, and a small wave in consequence.

As we proceed to consider further the phenomena and the consequences of the paroxysm of August 1883, we must draw attention to the fact that the mightiest scene of the whole eruption-period, the disappearance of the greater part of the island of Rakata, with half the Peak, and the tidal-wave which destroyed the population of the neighbouring coasts, was played before no human spectator. The events had to be reconstructed from conditions after the eruption.

Verbeek thinks a mass of rock, which he estimated at 1 km^3, sank first into the ocean-depths, and with the collapse of the Peak arose the tidal-wave, when the latter phenomenon was over, short as the interval may have been, came the terrific explosion.

Verbeek opines, further, that this severest explosion took place in the central portion, and therefore, that only material from Danan and Perboewatan and from subterranean depths was shot out. He confirms that opinion with the fact that among the ejecta basalt corresponding to the rock of the Peak was found only rarely.

The question now arises:

Are there positive indications regarding the consecutive order of the eruptions during the paroxysm?

We have said above that the thickness of the layer of ejected matter up to August 11th was not more than ½ m in the immediate vicinity of the Danan crater and that, the first days excepted, the products chiefly consisted of ashes. Must we now regard the great mass of pumice, which lies, for example, about 45 m thick in the northern part of Lang, as the result of a single explosion or of several explosions, and was it ejected simultaneously with or after the main explosion?

Above the vegetation-zone before 1883 there follows in the section of Lang West (Figure 71) the mass of the ejecta which extend the length of the island to northward by about a quarter.

Escher in his panorama[8] sketches already the stratification in the north portion of this mass of pumice but does not go further into the question, also not in Escher[6] ([his] p. 4).

Kemmerling and Taverne[17] drew a profile in 1922 but dealt with the pumice mass only so far as to subdivide it into two layers of finer lapilli. Nor were any comparative researches carried out then on the other two islands.

The stratification of the pumice in Lang NW can be marked from a great distance in the steep face where the wall has fallen away. The lower layers run obliquely from the most northerly point at an angle of about 10° and, reaching their greatest height after about 200 m, are continued horizontally for the most part. Irregular against the background of light yellowish-white pumice. These lenses can attain considerable lengths in the profile. They occur both in the N and NW of Lang. Besides these darker lenses, the steep wall shows thin bars and lenses of stratified and unstratified pumice. Even cross stratification occurs not seldom. Rough material alternates with fine, with a sharp demarcation between them. Other strata show the slow change from rough bombs to the finest ashes. The difference in the structure of the deposit and the thickness of the strata are evidence of severe eruptions following each other in rapid succession after long intervals of rest during which even the finest part of the ejecta could settle.

In the whole mass of the ejecta of 1883 in this profile there are three layers which compel interest.

As one proceeds along the strand of NW Hook on Lang Eiland, one notices in the pumice wall, especially if there have been fresh landslides, a layer about 10 cm thick and coloured through cinnabar-red, which runs obliquely southward from the beach at an angle of about 10°. This layer is found again farther southwards 6 m above the old vegetation-zone, that is at a total height of 29.5 m above sea-level.

Under this cinnabar-red layer there are on Lang tuffs of large fragments of pumice. Considerable landslides of great length and depth, resulting from a few severe earthquake shocks, have laid bare fresh material, unaffected by the spray. This pumice-tuff was found to be of a light pink colour, which means that it has been subject to a slight oxidation, which reached its maximum in the cinnabar-red layer. A further striking fact is that in this red layer there are a very large number of small fragments of dense eruption-rock while such ejecta are scarce in the horizontal mass.

Figure 74. Verlaten Eiland NE. Stratified pumice-tuff of 1883. The darker layer is cinnabar-red. [Stehn's photo 6.]

The same cinnabar-red layer appears in the pumice mass of Verlaten NE (Figure 74). Here the thickness of the layer is greater (15–20 cm). Here too, through thin white layers of the main-stratum, and mutually separated, two more thin bands are exposed. These too run obliquely southwards from the shore. They have so far been traced to above the old tridymite-andesites. For chemical analysis (sample No. 2339) see Table (p. 337).

In the central part of Lang and of Verlaten they have not yet been found, however.

According to the researches of Verbeek[22] and Brun[3] the pumice acquires this red colour by oxidation of ferrous minerals as a result of contact with sea-water.

On Lang the cinnabar-red layer is succeeded first by a mass of unstratified rough fragments of pumice, white and yellowish in colour and about 3.60 m thick.

The second layer of special interest is the lens of a darker material already referred to, which appears to be dark greyish-brown pumice (sample No. 2083). The rock was collected by earlier explorers on the beach of Lang in the shape of boulders but the spot where it is exposed was not known to them.

The darker pumice, the undermost limit of which is almost horizontal, has a very irregular surface. The greatest thickness is about 11 m.

The fragments of pumice adhere together firmly and form in that way a sort of pumice breccia. While great subsidences of the coast have caused the pink and white pumice to disappear very quickly, the darker pumice breccia still lies on the shore in the form of large blocks, offering a stout resistance to the action of the waves. The darker pumice No. 2083 (for analysis see Table (p. 337)) was found again over a large part of Lang, but is absent from the southermost part. No trace of this rock has been seen on Verlaten.

The third and most interesting part of this profile of Lang is a light-coloured pumice-tuff, in which is a layer, greatly varying in thickness, of blocks of various eruption-rocks. This tuff, which, with the block-layer it contains, was found over the whole length of the island and is present on Verlaten and Rakata as well, is the highest stratum, and therefore, the last deposit of the eruption-period of 1883, which passes into the disintegrated soil of the present day.

Before proceeding to explain these strata, the deposit on Verlaten and Rakata will have to be further examined first.

It has been stated above that the cinnabar-red layer is to be seen in the northern profile of Verlaten. Here too light pink pumice lies below this layer and here again tuffs succeed upwards, which however, are all in fine layers and consist of whitish pumice. As on Lang more solid components, like obsidian and dense hypersthene-andesites or other rocks are rare and mostly no larger than a hen's egg. But there was another important discovery made here, namely the occurrence of two block-strata separated by a white pumice tuff about 2 m thick.

Entirely different is the aspect of the pumice mass in the south of Verlaten.

Instead of any stratification the pumice mass presents up to about $\frac{1}{5}$ of its height a chaos of blocks of all possible dimensions (Figure 75). Snow-white pumice obsidian, the lustreless, dark, microlitic devitrefied glass, eruption-rocks of younger and older date, clay rocks and other sediments occur in this mass. Obsidian and the dark glassy rock however form the principal components.

Escher[8,9] ([his] pp. 208 and 734 respectively), on the ground of the presence of the large blocks on the south-coast, thinks that these form a special layer, are continued beneath the tuff-wall and were probably the result of the first explosions of August 1883. Since

Figure 75. Verlaten Eiland S. Unstratified products of 1883. [Stehn's photo 7.]

Figure 76. Rakata W. The steep pumice-walls. Only in the uppermost portion are these deposits somewhat stratified. [Stehn's photo 8.]

1919 the action of the waves has thrown the steep coast a good way back. There was no particular block-stratum observed at the foot of the wall. The large blocks are strewn, instead, over the whole pumice mass. Specimens of the glassy rock were seen, for example, in the middle of the steep wall, with a surface of 4 by 3 m. Often the rock is broken into fragments or ground down to a core. Here too, there is present in large quantities the obsidian of 1883, the motherstone of the pumice, frequently swollen into the latter. According to Escher[8] ([his] p. 216) it appears from the experiments of Prof. W.M.A. van Alphen de Veer that the change takes place at a temperature between 783° and 1000°C., not however under genuine phenomena of explosion according to Brun[3] ([his] p. 122) but gradually under the escape of gases. At 1170°C. the surface of the pumice is remelted into a "dead" glass.

The profile of the greater part of the West-Coast of Verlaten Eiland shows the same aspect as the south. Here too, the large blocks of the microlitic devitrefied glass, washed out of the fallen pumice tuff, lie at the foot of the wall.

In the top fifth part of the profile lies the block-stratum referred to under Lang, but it is much less thick.

The steep coast of Rakata W. (Figure 76) fairly corresponds in its composition to that of Verlaten S., that is to say a great layer of unstratified tuff, covered over in the highest part by a tuff that has been sorted in the air according to its weight, with a shallow block-stratum at the base.

The gentle slopes of Verlaten N. and Rakata S. show plainly in their profiles the action of the atmospheric water, viz. by the flowing together of gravel washed out of the uppermost strata of the interior of the island.

In general there are in the NW of Verlaten more solid remnants of rock than in the south, thus giving a darker hue to the steep wall.

The atmospheric water has caused further the formation of the "barrancos", the rain-water rills, which on all three islands run from the summits or the highest ridges down to the shore. Where steep walls are formed along the coast by the action of the waves, the barrancos often terminate in the form of "Hänge-

Scientific Accounts: Geology

Their bed is mostly covered with boulders and blocks washed down by downpours of rain. During the period of observation on Krakatau in 1928 a downpour sufficiently violent to carry down such a freight was registered only once. Generally, the water sinks too rapidly into the soil.

After the great eruption of August 1883 the atmospheric water could at first cause much more erosion of the loose pumice. To that is due also the mudstreams which are exposed at the end of a few barrancos in the steep coasts. On Rakata W. the fine mud, which was covered later by pumice washed down with or without blocks, formed layers containing water, the limits being clearly shown by a slight dampness. A powerful spring that arose in this manner is found in the south-east of Verlaten. The fine layer of mud is here about 1½ m thick. While the dense vegetation on the three islands greatly counteracts erosion, there is at the present time another factor that assists in the process of remodelling that their surfaces undergo, and that is the subsidences of the steep walls in the barrancos caused by the numerous tremors during the recent active phase of the volcano.

The Relief of the Sea-bottom between the Three Islands

(Figure 72)

Thanks to the numerous soundings, which were commenced shortly after the 1883 eruption by the survey-ship *Hydrograaf*[22] [see p. 138 and Figure 37 on p. 139] and were continued by Dr. W. van Bemmelen[20] in 1908, and more especially to the many soundings taken in 1919 by the survey-ship *Van Gogh*, published by Escher[8] and a few supplementary soundings taken by the survey-ship *Orion* in 1922–1923, also published by Escher,[9] the relief of the sea-bottom between the three islands is to some extent known.

With Escher[8] ([his] p. 203) we distinguish two main basins:

1. One between Lang and Verlaten of an average depth of about 70 m, in which however are two hollows with depths of about 120 m;

2. The other nearly centrally situated with a level bottom about 270 m deep.

In the former an eccentric uplift was found about 60 m higher than the bottom of the basin and in the latter a more central ridge only 25 m above the bottom.

Starting from the second basin two depresssions extend E and SW.

Verbeek knew only the second basin and the lateral depression between Lang and Rakata.

The question how the basins and the lateral extensions of the central one arose has received the attention of Verbeek, and afterwards especially of Escher. He dealt with the problem in 1919 and recently again in a publication entitled "Krakatau in 1883 en 1928".[9] Verbeek explains the origin of the basins by melting and subsidence, Escher by explosion and subsidence (on the strength of observations made by Frank Perret on Vesuvius in 1906).

Verbeek supposes further that one subsidence on August 27th at 10 o'clock in the morning created the basin with the easterly branch, when half the basaltic Peak collapsed, and at 16 hours 38 minutes another subsidence of the wall followed. Both subsidences were succeeded by tidal-waves. The prior tidal-waves on August 26th and 27th Verbeek explained by the large masses of ejecta that fill [fell?] into the sea. Escher, on the other hand, thinks the explosions on August 26th, 27th and 28th also were the cause of subsidences and waves.

Conclusions

Escher's opinion that the central island and environs were destroyed or altered by several subsidences, explosions and waves, I can accept on the strength of the geological profiles of the three islands. The difference between the stratification in the north of Lang and Verlaten and absence of stratification in the south of Verlaten and the west of Rakata is so great, and the composition of the deposits varies so much, that these cannot be explained by a single explosion. I think it can be concluded further that the depressions started in the north, that is the vicinity of Perboewatan. That the collapses were preceded by explosions is demonstrated nowhere.

The products of the eruptions of the period May-to-August 1883 remained in the immediate neighbourhood of the active craters. The paroxysm came on August 26th and after. Perboewatan and perhaps other parasitic but unknown craters threw out large quantites of pumice.

It is a striking fact that at the spot where Poolsche Hoed was situated (which disappeared by subsidence, according to Verbeek) a depth of 25 m only is found at the present day. But the soundings have shown that to the west of the old site of the island lies the basin of about 120 m depth in 1919, which Escher regards as a crater of an unknown period. It seems, in my opinion, not so improbable that a submarine volcano was in eruption here for a short time during the paroxysm in 1883 and that *it was this* which produced the ejecta that have acquired a pink and cinnabar-red colour by oxidation. Attention has been drawn above to the fact that this red stratum contains much solid lava blocks. Further examination has shown that it corresponds to the older lava from Perboewatan, which therefore probably flowed out from under the sea, too, while there was found besides in that red stratum an indeterminable fragment of coral from the old sea-bottom. By subsidences into the original crater, which was much deeper then, Poolsche Hoed disappeared into the sea.

The mass of the ejecta was great and could be deposited on the abrasion terrace, which was situated (according to the old charts) off the north-coast of Lang, thus enlarging that island as early as then.

That the eruption point for these pink and red products must have been situated to northward is proved by the fact that the red stratum is found only in the north of Lang and Verlaten.

Numerous minor eruptions occur on the central island, the ejecta of which, small white lapilli and white or greyish-white ashes are deposited in different layers.

At 4:40 a.m. on Monday August 27th occurred the destruction (by subsidence) of Perboewatan or more correctly of the northern portion of the central island. A severe explosion followed, which was directed obliquely eastward, and deposited the greater part of its ejecta on the new portion of Lang in the form of mud. This is the darker pumice mass which forms a solid bank in the profile of Lang and which is absent from the other two islands. Its altered structure as compared with the former white pumice ejected by Perboewatan is due to contact with sea-water.

Fresh subsidences took place, associated with tidal-waves, which caused landslides of the pumice deposits on Lang resulting in the formation of a bluff, such as the coast exhibits at the present day.

Now followed the collapse and explosion of 10 o'clock, in my opinion eccentric to west of Danan, where there lies at the present day the great level floor of an average depth of 263 m. In consequence of this explosion, the detonation of which was heard in Singapore and Australia, there was ejected the mighty mass of pumice, which attained thicknesses up to 100

m on Verlaten South and Rakata and which was deposited without any sorting according to the size of the component fragments; pumice, the fine particles of which rose to the incredible height of 70 to 80 km in the atmosphere. The products of this explosion covered a surface of 827,000 square kilometres. Simultaneously arose the tongue-like fracture to southwest. The collapse was followed by subsidences of the basaltic Peak. The tidal-wave caused by the former dashed against the coastal bluffs of the islands. On Lang N quantities of water were flung in, which washed away large masses of the pumice. It is in this way, I think, that the irregular surface of the darker pumice and the apparently capricious thickness of this layer are to be explained.

There was left of the large Rakata island part of the Peak and a portion of the Danan area.

According to Verbeek another severe detonation was heard at 10:52 a.m., which was not much less violent than that of 10:02 a.m.

In my opinion, it was at this moment that Danan was destroyed by explosion. The solid rock of which Danan was built up, products of the first eruptions in 1883 and of the recent explosions, which had been deposited here also, were hurled high into the air and distributed over the three islands.

The heavier material fell first and formed the block horizon; the lighter pumice descended later. Thus the sifting according to weight took place in the air. The white pumice filled up the spaces between the blocks and formed the last layer of the products of 1883. Blocks of several cubic metres have been found on Lang. They are chiefly the hypersthene andesites without tridymite, and next the microlitic devitrefied rocks and rocks of the old substratum. Basalt was only rarely found among the blocks on Lang and Verlaten. The hypersthene andesite contained, according to our analyses, an average of 62.76 % SiO_2 and scarcely differs in composition from the stone of Bootmansrots (63.22 % SiO_2), which is regarded as the remnant of Danan. The steep gradient of the rocks of the latter I suppose to have been caused by the violent explosion upwards. The Danan explosion hurled into the air not only part of the land but also part of the old sea-bed between Danan and Lang. We found as evidence of that in the block-stratum and in the pumice above it remnants of shells and coral, which Dr. J.H.F. Umbgrove of Bandoeng assigns to recent species. No fossil-containing Tertiary rocks having been found hitherto among the ejecta, a *Favia Pallida* Dana, which occurs from the Miocene to the present day,

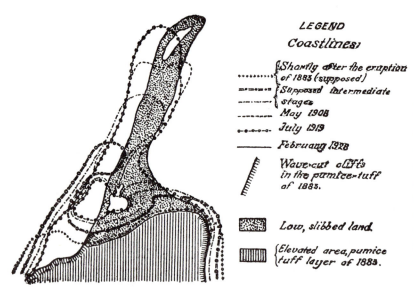

LEGEND

Coastlines:

········· {Shortly after the eruption of 1883 (supposed)

━·━·━· {Supposed intermediate stages

─ ─ ─ ─ May 1908

─·─·─· July 1919

───── February 1928

╱ Wave-cut cliffs in the pumice-tuff of 1883.

▨ Low, slibbed land.

▥ {Elevated area, pumice tuff layer of 1883.

Figure 77. Coastline changes of northern Verlaten Island, 1883–1928. (From Stehn, p. 26.)

would be a recent specimen. By supposing two subsidences and explosions at different points it seems to me that the presence of the ridge between the two deepest portions can also be explained and Escher's assumption that this must be regarded as a plug rendered unnecessary.

According to Verbeek and Escher too, yet another subsidence occurred at 16 hours 35 minutes.

After the explosion of Danan remnant there followed the fracture between Lang and Rakata, the subsidence of the portion between the present capes of Krakatau N. and Krakatau E. and of a small part of Lang S. causing the last tidal-wave observed in August 1883.

The Fifth Period

Immediately after the products of the explosion had been deposited, with the resultant increase in the magnitude of the three islands, the waves began their destructive action upon the coasts and the rains worked deep into the loose material. The two islands, Calmeyer and Steers, which came into existence by the deposit of loose material, quickly disappeared beneath the surface once more. On the west coast of Rakata and the west and south coast of Verlaten, especially, there were great losses of land by the erosion of the waves. The floating material was carried by the current and partly redeposited in the north of Verlaten, where it formed fairly soon a broad tongue of land. The coast-line here changes from year to year, however. Since 1918 the loss of land by crumbling has been

exceptionally great and we find already (see Figure 77) what Escher foretold in 1919 viz. "crumbling of the low west coast, shrinkage of the lake, and acquisition of new land towards the north". And it will certainly not be many years before his second prophecy is realized, namely the disappearance of the saltwater lake in the low spit. At the present day there is a lake also in the northern extremity of Verlaten, which came into existence between 1922 and 1928 but is already diminishing as a result of the pumice washed in.

The Sixth Period: The Latest Eruption[14,15,19]

"In any renewed activity of the volcano it is to be expected that islands will arise in the middle of the seabasin that is surrounded by Rakata Peak, Verlaten, and Lang, just as the Kaimeni arose in the Santorin Group and just as formerly the craters Danan and Perboewatan formed in the sea within the old craterwall". Thus did Verbeek prophesy in 1885 [see p. 251].[22]

After a rest of about 44 years Krakatau has shown fresh activity. On December 29th fishermen from the coast of Java in the Bantam residency saw steam and smoke issuing from the sea between the three islands. At night a glow was seen which probably emanated from glowing bombs ejected. There must [have] been a slight eruption of gas before, for the fishers report that as early as June 1927 gas-bubbles had been seen at the spot where the new eruption was to take place. It is possible that even the welling up of sulphur gases at three points between Krakatau and the Bantam coast, which the fishers have been familiar with for many years, can be associated with the resuscitation of the Krakatau. (These points are known to the natives as the Sea of "Gegemping, Sea of "Lelempah" and Sea of "Djangkol", they are remote from one another and occupy an area of about 400 m² each).

The Location of the Submarine Volcano

The first astronomical bearings taken on January 4th 1928 indicated 105°25′27″E and 6°6′6″S as the location of the submarine volcano, which would correspond to an old sea-depth of 28 m. According to bearings taken on January 20th, however, by the Government steamer *Cycloop* from land and from boardship, the eruption-point lies a little more to the west. When these soundings were entered on the chart of the *Van Gogh*[6,8] it was found that the position of the eruption-point corresponds nearly to the depth-point of 188 m. Rapid soundings at the end of January by Sea-Lieut. Jhr. Berg of H.M. Minelayer *Krakatau* showed at about 360 m W of the eruption point depths of more than 200 m. According to the soundings taken in 1919, the new volcano lies immediately off the steep NE wall of the basin formed by the collapse of Perboewatan and Danan (see p. 323), about midway between the former craters of Perboewatan and Danan (see Figure 78). As a result of the numerous and violent eruptions in the first period from December 29th, the volcano built up a cone in the course of January, which appeared above the water on the 26th of that month. On Figure 79 the situation at the scene of the eruption is compared with that of 1919 on February 2nd 1928, the soundings taken in the middle of March by the Volcanological Survey being used. The isobaths of this chart must be regarded as tentative. In the first place, the various phases of eruption and of inactivity have since altered the situation and, secondly, in view of the renewed activity it has not yet been possible to take soundings from a survey ship. The western slope of the volcano is considerably steeper than the eastern. That is not only the consequence of its position right off the steep wall of the basin. When the crater-wall rose to about 28 m below the surface, the material being ejected was caried SW to NE by the strong current that was generally running in this direction during the first eruption period.

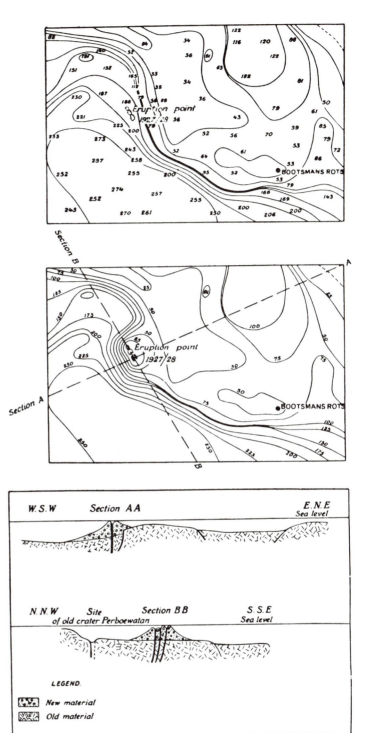

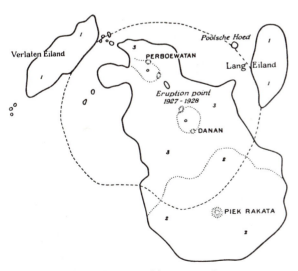

Figure 78. Krakatau. Situation of the new eruption point 1927/28, and of old craters Perboewatan and Danan, which were blown up in 1883. Map after R.D.M. Verbeek, Krakatau, 1887, atlas. [Dashed caldera diameter is 7 km. Stehn's plate III.]

Figure 79. *Upper:* Surroundings of the new submarine volcano according to the latest official survey (by Her Majesty's *Van Gogh*, June 1919). Isobaths 25 meters difference. *Middle:* Probable situation on February 2nd, 1928, according to some preliminary soundings taken by the Volcanological Service in the month of March 1928. *Lower:* Sections through the eruption point of 1927/28. [Width of map is 4.1 km. Stehn's plate IV.]

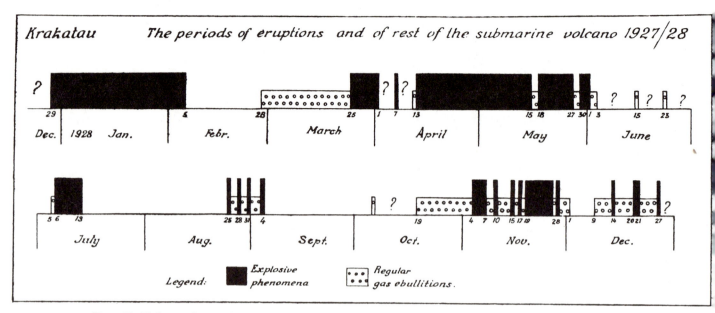

Figure 80. Krakatau. The periods of eruptions and
of rest of the submarine volcano 1927/28. [Stehn's
plate V.]

On January 3rd it was already established that the
eruptions were not proceeding from a single point but
that rather there were six crater openings arranged in
a line about 500 m long in the direction NNW–SSE.
In the later eruption-period the situation was altered
and there were at first three craters, later only one,
active.

The Phases of Activity and of Rest

The first phase of eruption December 29th, 1927–February 5th, 1928.

The first phenomena of eruption were observed on
December 29th 1927. This phase lasted until February 5th with a break of only a few hours on January
28th. While the eruptions on January 3rd and 4th at
the time of our first visit on the Government steamer
Wega, did not reach a greater height than 200 m,
after January 10th they increased in height and strength.
Several times heights of 1000 to 1200 m were measured from the observation-post on Lang Eiland.[29] The

number of eruptions was also less at the beginning
than in the latter part of January. Eruptions reaching
a height of about 60 m followed each other at intervals
of half to one minute. Nearly every 10 to 15 minutes,
after a somewhat longer interval, a higher eruption
occurred. Within the space of two hours 103 eruptions
were counted altogether. On January 14th the average
for two hours was 176 eruptions.

On January 26th 1928 the crater-edge appeared
above the surface of the sea in the form of a low
elongated island. In the course of the following days
the island grew to a height of 3 m above high tide
and a length of 175 m. On February 2nd another
portion of the crater-edge was visible as an island to
the west of the former.

From February to March 25th the volcano was
apparently quiet. On February 28th gas-bubbles appeared in the water above the point of eruption, and
these continued to be visible during the following
month. The waves and the strong current running
made short work of the little islands, built up of loose
material, and they quickly disappeared below the surface. A broad dirty yellowish-green band, starting from
the point of eruption, showed the route taken by the

finest material in the direction of the current. [In] February the depth of the crater floor was found to be 34.5 m; on March 13th and 14th 37.8 m. The height of the crater-wall on these two days was about 26 m below the surface of the sea.

The second phase of eruption, March 25th–June 1st.

On March 23rd the gas-bubbles effervesced much more violently. In the night of the 24th dull detonations were heard. On the 25th at 1:55 p.m. a cloud of steam arose above the eruption-point, which marked the commencement of the second phase of visible eruptive activity that continued until April 1st. On April 7th detonations were heard during the night. On the 12th floating pumice was observed above the eruption-point and large gas-bubbles rising out of the sea. From the 13th there were eruptions again which continued without a break until May 15th. On the 16th and 17th of May the activity comprised only the bubbling up of gasses. On the 18th the scene of the eruptions was sounded and the depth of the crater-wall was found to be only 5 m below the surface. On the same day at 12:39 the visible activity of the volcano was resumed. The first eruption reached a height of 500 m. On the 28th and 29th of May there was no manifestation; on May 30th and 31st and June 1st minor eruptions. Since that date there was rest again. During soundings on June 15th and 23rd gas-bubbles were seen to rise.

In this second phase of eruption the height of the eruptions was generally small, with a very few exceptions. A peculiarity of this period of activity is a number of eruptions following each other in quick succession in separate series. Thus on May 13th from 5:40 to 6 a.m. 330 eruptions were counted in one series. Water-fountains also occurred frequently. The largest number of eruptions was counted on May 14th, viz. 7164 in 14 hours.

Unique phenomena hitherto were the lava flow on May 1st and the emergence of flames on the 1st and 2nd.[30] On June 15th the spot was again sounded. Two areas of gas-effervescence were found, rising from a depth of 8 and 18 m.

The third phase of eruption, July 6th–13th.

A period of weak activity. It commenced on July 5th with a strong effervescence of gases. On July 6th at 12:10 eruptions were again observed. Their number was small. The greatest height was not more than 130 m. Besides ashes and bombs, waterfountains and bubblings were seen and detonations heard. On the 13th this third phase terminated.

The fourth phase of eruption, August 25th–Sept. 4th.

Only a few days of volcanic activity, alternating with intervals of rest. The activity comprised a very little bubbling and detonations heard on the 25th, 28th and 31st of August. Only once on September 4th, there was sufficient force for an eruption, but it did not attain a height of more than 30 m. A period of complete inactivity succeeded.

The fifth phase of eruption, November 4th–28th.

On October 6th the effervescence of gases was again seen. It is not known whether this continued without interruption up to the 19th. On the 19th, however, it was so strong that it could be seen through a telescope four kilometres away at the observation post on Lang. On November 3rd detonations were heard at 10:45. The ejection of gases grew stronger. On November 4th, for instance, 20 bubblings were seen and many detonations heard. On the 5th the ejecta reached a height of 30 m in a few minor eruptions at quick intervals. A small eruption occurred again on the 6th. Days of rest alternated with days of very slight activity (bubblings or only detonations) until from the 19th to the 26th there were daily phenomena of eruption observed. On the 21st steam was formed at the foot of the column and the ejecta reached a height of 80 m. Though there was stronger activity than in the fourth period, it was not of the degree as in the third. From November 28th to December 2nd effervescence of gases was telescopically observed.

The sixth phase of eruption, December 14th–27th.

This opened with a detonation on December 14th. Gas effervescence was observed on the following days. On December 20th at 1 a.m. both components of the seismograph (see following section on seismic observations) register a strong disturbance for 23 minutes. At 19:35, preceded by a brief shock half a minute before, visible eruptive activity was resumed in the form of an 80 m high eruption of ashes [and] glowing bombs. The base of the eruption column was wreathed in steam. No further eruptions occurred, though on

Dec. 20th, 21th and 27th detonations have been heard. On Dec. 28th, at 19ʰ41ᵐ, a very strong tremor was felt.

The seventh phase of eruption, January 12th, 1929–February, 18th.

In the beginning of 1929 the submarine volcano showed no visible action, but tremors of local origin were daily registered by the seismograph on Lang; many were also felt. After January 7th the number of tremors increased considerably. The seismogram of 11th–12th January shows an almost continuous series of very slight vibrations.

On January 12th at 12ʰ53ᵐ a new eruption-phase began, with ebullitions and steam-forming above the eruption point. Some bombs appeared on the surface of the sea and floated round so long as they remained hot and comprised gases. During the first days the action increased slowly. Steam eruptions, and eruptions of ash and bombs were seen. The number and height of these eruptions became gradually greater, till from January 20th–21st during 24 hours from 6–6 a.m., 6817 eruptions were counted and 1100 m was measured as the greatest height of the compact eruption-column.

On the same day a part of the crater-rim appeared east of the eruption point, consisting of ashes, lapilli, loose blocks and bombs lying one on top of the other. It formed an island above the water and was named "Anak Krakatau" (Child of Krakatau). On the night of January 20th–21st submarine land-slides had evidently occurred, for the next morning the crater-rim had disappeared again under the water.

The action thereupon decreased till January 23rd. On January 22nd–23rd from 6–6 a.m., 303 eruptions were counted, the greatest height being about 150 m. Many detonations were heard without visible action. Before noon of January 24th an increase of action was ascertained. Even though it was but slight during the following days, the number and force of the eruptions after January 25th became at least equal to those of January 1928. Tremendous amounts of solid material (Figure 81), were ejected from 2 or 3 crater-openings which fell back again into the sea in the immediate surroundings. Eruption-columns of 900, 1000, 1100, and even 1200 m in height, and up to a width of 250 m were seen, which were surounded at the foot by a still wider wreath of steam.

The result of the powerful eruptions was the reappearance in the afternoon of January 28th of the east-erly crater-rim above water, and a rapid increase in height and length. The height on January 30th was only 1½ and on the 31st only 4 m, but on February 1st the height of the Anak Krakatau was already fixed at 12 m (Figure 82). The action still continued to increase. The greatest number of eruptions was recorded from February 3rd to 4th, i.e. 11791 within 24 hours. On February 9th the island was already 21 m high. From February 15th the action gradually became less. A few eruption columns however still reached a height of 800 m. On February 18th at 20h the eruptions were no longer visible, [the new island] was shaped like a sickle, opening to the SW, and which had reached a height of 38 m above sea level and a length of about 275 m. The westerly part of the crater-rim was then invisible above the water. During a local survey, on February 20th and 24th the crater-rim was, during lowest ebb, visible as a closed ring. The westerly part rose to about 1½ m above the water. The crater space was not deep and comprised muddy water and also great blocks here and there. On the northerly outside of the rim, forcible gas-ebullitions were seen.

The Phenomena of Eruption

The visible phenomena of eruption comprised bubblings and fountains of sea-water, eruptions of steam, and eruptions of ashes and bombs. There was also a flow of lava seen and flames appeared above the point of eruption. We may include gases rising out of the sea during periods of rest, that is periods when there was no explosive activity.

The phenomena of the first group were generally accompanied by detonations or rumblings but these sounds were also heard without any visible eruptive activity.

Ebullitions of Gases.

There is little to be said about the ebullitions of gases. The gases that rose out of the sea during periods of inactivity did not always issue from the same place. That is connected with the shifting of the point of eruptive activity in the different periods. It has been said [above] that in the first phase activity was observed at no less that 6 points of a fissure. The same was true of the ebullition of gases. The greatest quantity of gas escaped above the midmost crater, which in the later periods was generally the only active opening. Unfortunately there were factors which militated against the collection of samples of gas. In the first place there

Figure 81. An eruption of 500 m on January 23rd, 1929. [Stehn's photo 10.]

Figure 82. Eruption 1929. The northwestern part of the new island "Anak Krakatau" on February 2nd, 1929. [Stehn's photo 11 by Petroeschevsky.]

was the comparatively great depth from which the gases rose, so that owing to the current the bubbles never reached the surface at the same point. Secondly there was the ocean-swell and the strong current between the Krakatau islands, which rendered it impossible to keep the boat above the spot. Nor has the anchoring of apparatus for the collection of gases been successful so far. To judge by the smell, sulphur gases formed a large part of the ebullition.

It was observed in November that the ebullitious gases could also be thrown out in jets. In such cases the strength of the large bubbles was sufficient to stir up the fine mud at the bottom and to render the water turbid with "mud-clouds". In a short time the fine mud settled and the colour of the water became normal again until another powerful ebullition repeated the phenomenon once more.

The rest of the phenomena, the welling up of water, fountains, eruptions of steam, eruptions of ashes and bombs are immediately associated with explosions.

Upwelling of Water.

This arises from weak explosions. The force of the explosions is only sufficient to cause a strong wavelike movement of the water above the crater. The welling-up is the effect of a force transmitted from molecule to molecule in a perpendicular direction upward, which is the line of least resistance. It can be eccentric, however, in a strong current.

The same effects have been frequently observed with an exploding mine.[1] One difference, however, between the effect of a mine and an explosion in the crater pipe of a submarine volcano consists in this, viz. that in the former case the pressure can be transmitted laterally without hindrance whereas in a submarine volcano the pressure of the explosion finds escape in only one direction, that is upwards. But when the crater-pipe changes into the funnel, the transmission of pressure takes place in spherical concentric movements, part of the pressure is absorbed and diverted by the sides of the funnel. That accounts for a phenomenon observed from time to time, viz. after the first disturbance of the surface by the perpendicular pressure the formation of a vortex above the point of eruption.

On our first visit to the active volcano on the Government steamer *Wega*, the ship approached to within 300 m of the eruption-point. On the upper-deck we felt the first pressure of the explosion as a slight vibration. Down in the hold, however, the shocks were felt like hard blows.

Water-Cones.

In a more violent explosion the water is lifted into a dome or cone, rounded at the top and forming an acute angle with the surface of the water in expansion of the gases. Figure[31] 83 shows such a water-cone with a height of about 21 m and a base of about 3115 m^2. Two others photographed from Lang have heights of 17.5 and 26.3 m and bases of about 6000 and about 3530 m^2 respectively. The commencement of another eruption shows a height of 13 m and a base of about 4580 m^2.

Such cones are also known in the case of exploding mines.[12,13] According to Bertelli,[2] whom Rudolph[13] quotes ([his] p. 287) the terminal conoid of a cylindrical mine exploding 3 m below the surface approximated to the shape of a cylinder. While the final shape of the above mentioned water-domes, observed from the 12th to about 20th January 1928, is a truncated cone, there is one of January 24th which shows a cylindrical shape (Figure 84). This most probably is connected with the fact that the crater was then a short distance below the surface. On 26th January, as has been said above, part of the crater-wall appeared above the water.

Rudolph[13] ([his] p. 329) compares the cylinder of water above the mine-discharge with the projectile discharged from a cannon; the angle of the water-cylinder is thus explained by the tapering shape of the projectile.

The surface of the water-cone is white with foam-flakes.

Fountains.

These arise in different ways. In the first place, they can be the first effect of the explosion to be visible above the surface, as Abbot and Rudolph have noticed. In such cases they do not reach a great height and might better be spoken of as spurts of water. In the second place, they are the natural sequel to the welling-up of water or the formation of a water-cone in an explosion of gases, without any ejection of solid matter. The mass of water rises high and thus loses in breadth.

On one of the observation cruises round the eruption-point on May 2nd 1928 when 41 fountains were observed, it was noted that mud appeared at the back of the eruption-column behind the water ejected. This mud has, in my opinion, nothing to do with the phenomena of eruptions of ashes and bombs referred to below. After the exploding gases have been hurled out, the water rushes in with great force from the sides to fill the vacancy. A first-wave is formed, which shoots upward laden with the material deposited on the inner slopes of the crater. This pehonomenon is only possible, however, if the crater-floor does not lie too deep down below the surface. Indeed, soundings taken on May 1st showed that during the second eruption-period the crater-wall had again risen to 5 m below sea-level.

Eruptions of Steam.

If the gases thrown out by the explosion have high temperatures the particles of water carried along with them are brought to boiling-point. Hence a great cloud of steam.

Eruptions of Ashes and Bombs.

These, too, were often preceded by the formation of a water-cone. That was generally the case after longer intervals of rest. On January 13th 1928 between 8 and 12 a.m. there were 31 water-cones observed from Lang out of the 294 eruptions counted, of which two (at 9:13 a.m. and 14:19 p.m.) reached a height of about 60 m with a base of 500 m (as measured from Lang).

If the eruptions follow in close succession, the formation of water-cones does not occur.

After the cone has reached its greatest height, the mass of the ejecta first shoots through the point of the cone in the form of fine rays (see Figure 81) and then assumes a more irregular surface. The succession of ashes [and] bomb eruptions is best illustrated by the six photos of Figure 85.

A dense black column rises high in the air. Immediately after its appearance above sea-level, there is formed at the foot of the column, as a result of the contact of the hot mass of ejected matter with the sea-water, a wreath of steam, which rapidly grows in breadth and height as the mass shoots up and plumps down again. The force of the explosion is exhausted; the highest point has been reached. The appearance of the column changes; the solid matter descends. The gases, however, and the steam formed by the particles of water carried along with them higher with strong eddies. Each bomb as it falls leaves a trail of steam and gas, which takes a spiral form as a result of the spinning motion of the bombs. In a short time the

Figure 83. Eruption 1928. A water cone 21 m high. The magma is beginning to shoot through the top in fine rays. Taken at a distance of 4 km from the observation station on Lang Eiland, a telescope [(magnification ×36) being used as a telelens. Stehn's photo 13].

Figure 84. Eruption 1928. A cylindrical water-dome. Flecked surface. The magma shooting through appears black. [Stehn's photo 14.]

Figure 85. Eruption 1928. Six photos taken at intervals of 6 seconds from the eastern coast of Verlaten Eiland [4500 m distant] on January 24th. Height about 1000 m. [Stehn's photo 16.]

whole is transformed into a white column, surrounded at its foot by a white wreath. The cloud of steam and gas rises slowly but the relation of column and wreath can be distinguished for a long time. The finest ash is carried up in the cloud and descends slowly curtainwise in fine bands. The current carries it great distances in a dirty yellowish-green ribbon of mud.

Rains of ashes were observed only in eruptions of a height exceeding 600 m.

In the night most of the eruptions exceeding 100 m showed bombs glowing a dark to light red. The bombs were also seen to burst and cast a sharp white illumination.

Outflow of Lava.

On one occasion only did we observe, as we believe, a stream of lava. On May 1st 1928 shortly after 7 p.m., after some eruptions, the water was illuminated from below and the illumination was strongest about the crater. It took a south-westerly course, in which direction it slowly diminished in brightness. On the other hand the demarcation between light and darkness in other directions was very sharp. We suppose that lava flowed over the south-west edge of the crater and down the south-west slope. The luminosity disappeared at 7:30 p.m.

Flames.

In the third phase of eruption flames of inflammable gases appeared after the lava flow on May 1st at 20 hours 5 minutes and 20–19, on May 2nd from 1:49–2:35, at 2:42–45, at 3:21–22½, 4:09–4:22½, 4:50–51, 5:06, 5:18–21, 6:04–06, 19:44 and 45, 20:02, 30 and 38, 21:05, 21:11–17, 21:47 to 22:04. The last flames were seen on May 3rd at 0:12 and 1:26. The flames were preceded by eruptions during which large quantities of faintly glowing bombs were ejected.

On May 2nd the phenomena of 21 hours was observed from close quarters. The flames were orange-yellow. The entire surface of the water above the crater was like a sea of flames. Seen from a distance of about 200 m the flames were about 10 m high. There was no report heard. By day the presence of flames could only be concluded from the heat-haze above the eruption-point. No smoke emanated from them. After May 3rd no more flames appeared.

Methane and hydrogen were found by the researches of Fouqué on Santorin volcano. Judging by the colour of the flames the same gases were probably present in this case also though the probablity is not precluded that the salts in the sea-water affect the colour.

Electrical Discharges.

During the first period a few electrical discharges were observed in the eruption-columns, but only in the very tall ones. Unfortunately after January 27th, the day on which the Naval Wireless Station on Lang was opened, they were no longer seen, so that it was not possible to hear as atmospheric disturbances. In the succeeding period the eruptions were not powerful enough to create the necessary conditions for the discharge of electricity viz. dry particles of ashes.

Lightning-phenomena were however noticed several times during the seventh phase. These electric discharges occurred under two different circumstances. On January 22nd 1929 at 8^h 50^m and 8^h 57^m, during a thunderstorm the lightning struck the top of the eruption-column, which had respectively reached a height of 700 and 875 m. At 9^h 5^m a light yellow coloured thunder-bolt was seen above the top of the column, which exploded with a tremendous bang. The second time that electric phenomena occurred during a thunderstorm, was on February 2nd at 7^h 9^m, 7^h 16^m and 7^h 29^m. The respective heights of the eruption-columns were 150 m, 50 m and 250 m. In the first two cases the lightning struck from the top of the eruption cloud upwards; at 7^h 29^m the lightning came from above. During the night of February 12th–13th electric discharges were at last noticed while there was no thunderstorm. These discharges occurred at the following times — between brackets are ciphers indicating the height of the respective eruption column —: On February 12th at 21^h 9^m (150 m), 21^h 17^m (100 m), 21^h 50^m, 2 flashes (150 m), 22^h 13^m (600 m), 22^h 26^m (90 m), 22^h 51^m (250 m), 22^h 52^m (70 m), 22^h 55^m (500 m), 22^h 57^m, 3 flashes (175 m), 23^h 12^m, 4 flashes (300 m), 23^h 32^m (150 m), 23^h 57^m (150 m) and on February 13th at 0^h 12^m (600 m), 0^h 29^m (150 m), 0^h 31^m, 2 flashes (180 m) and at 2^h 14^m, 3 flashes (300 m). All these struck upwards.

Steam-Spouts.

In the second half of the first eruption-phase we noticed the formation of steam-spouts, which arose out of the eruption-cloud. We know that most steam-

Figure 86. Eruption 1928. Several eruptions in close succession. Right: eruption-cloud lifting to form a spout. [Stehn's photo 19.]

the falling ejecta (b-wave). The former waves are the higher. On January 18th 1928 at 9ʰ 27ᵐ 13ˢ we observed that with the fall of a water-cone 45 m high a wave was formed that was 4 m higher than the normal sea-level.

Waves caused by the falling of ejected material are a little lower.

During the seventh eruption-phase attempts were made to complete these observations made from the observation post. Lang even proved to be too low to allow of any exact measuring, especially as it was often impossible to make out whether the wave, boiling on the shore, emanated from the eruption point, or originated from the normal ocean swell. For this reason an expedition to the 813 m high top of the Rakata, was decided upon, with the hope that from there the propagation of the wave could be studied to more advantage. This expedition took place on January 25th. At 11:30 o'clock the top was reached, after a climb of 4½ hours. The view from above of the eruption point and of the sea between the islands was surprising. As there was no wind the sea was fairly calm, only the ocean swell coming in from the SW, could be seen as flat broad waves. The surroundings of the eruption point were also calm, only a white circle was observed, caused by a number of hot bombs floating about while developing steam. Fine mud prevented anything of the bottom relief under the sea being discovered.

spouts have their origin high up in the atmosphere, from where they sink to the land or the sea. Those which we observed began immediately after the ascent of the eruption-cloud, the lower extremity remaining in contact with the hot gases of a succeeding eruption emerging above the eruption-point. The steam-spout thus assumed a crooked shape (Figure 86). Only after it reached a greater height did it work free of the eruption-point. The spinning spiral now hung down almost vertically. It slowly grew thinner and disappeared from sight. On January 21st the length of a steam-spout was found to be about 600 m. It drifted very slowly in a northward direction. Just six minutes after it was formed it vanished, at a distance of 4½ km from the point of eruption. In every case the strength of the wind at the time of these phenomena was very weak. Before January 20th and in the later eruption-periods there were no steam-spouts. The phenomenon was known during the eruption of Santorin. H. Reck[11] has recently published further details.

Waves.

Waves arose in two different ways; firstly by the collapse of the water-cone (a-wave) and, secondly by

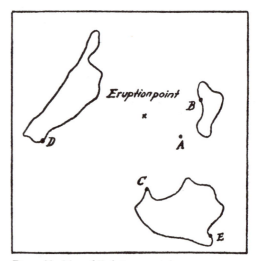

Figure 88. Map of Krakatau group showing positions used in determining velocities of waves generated by Anak Krakatau submarine eruptions. See text and Figure 89. (From Stehn, p. 42.)

Figure 87. Eruption 1929. Eruption point seen from the top of the Rakata (813 m). Very clearly are the concentric eruption-waves emanating from the eruption point. On the left is the northern part of Verlaten Eiland. January 25th, 1929. [Stehn's photo 20.]

The fact that on that day the eruptions followed one another at long intervals was very favourable for the following observations.

An eruption occurred, beginning by the pushing up of a water-dome. When this fell back shortly after the solid eruption material shot through [see Figure 84], a high circular wave originated round the eruption column, which rapidly propagated to all sides. Smaller waves followed. (Figure 87). A new higher wave was observed when the mass of ejected material fell back into the sea. The sea resembled a water surface into which two stones had been thrown at the same point, quickly one after the other. With the aid of a telescope and a stop-watch, the speed of the propagation of the waves towards known points was now studied. The following fixed points were selected [see map Figure 88]: A. "Bootsmansrots" 2150 m distant from the eruption point, B. the west coast of Lang underneath the observation-post, distance 3700 m, C. Zwarte Hoek on Rakata, distance 4280 m, D. Verlaten South distance 5950 m. Finally E, the bay of Rakata South, distance 10675 m to where, with a favourable light, the eruption waves could be observed.

The height of the water-dome and of the eruption-column were measured from the observation-post on Lang.

At this place only the velocity of progress of some a- and b-waves emanating from the eruption-point will be recorded.

335

wave		I	II	III	IV	V	VI	VII	calculated
Height of the water-dome.		15 m	15 m	5 m	55 m	c.a. 5 m	10 m	5 m	
Time of the first great wave. / Fall-down of the water-dome	a	$11^h45^m05^s$	$11^h52^m46^s$	$12^h27^m19^s$	$12^h44^m02^s$	$14^h00^m02^s$	$14^h20^m23^s$	$14^h49^m31^s$	
Height of the eruption-column		175 m	150 m	100 m	600 m	80 m	100 m	20 m	
Time of the second great wave. / Fall-down of blocs and bombs	b	$11^h45^m11^s$	$11^h52^m51^s$	$12^h27^m22^s$	$12^h44^m08^s$	$14^h00^m05^s$	$14^h20^m27^s$	$14^h49^m34^s$	
Point A, distance 2150 m,	a	1^m50^s	1^m52^s	1^m51^s	1^m49^s	1^m51^s	1^m51^s	1^m53^s	1^m49^s
was reached within min., sec.	b	1^m52^s	1^m58^s	1^m58^s	1^m52^s	1^m59^s	1^m58^s	1^m59^s	
Point B, distance 3700 m,	a	4^m27^s			4^m26^s				4^m25^s
was reached within min. sec.	b	4^m32^s			4^m30^s				
Point C, distance 4280 m,	a		2^m07^s	2^m09^s	2^m05^s	2^m07^s		2^m06^s	1^m51^s
was reached within min., sec.	b		2^m14^s	2^m17^s	2^m09^s	2^m14^s		2^m13^s	
Point D, distance 5950 m,	a			2^m50^s	2^m51^s				2^m42^s
was reached within min., sec.	b			?	?				
Point E, distance 10675 m,	a				7^m02^s				6^m44^s
was reached within min., sec.	b				?				

Figure 89. Wave velocities from submarine eruptions of Anak Krakatau. Seven waves timed from observation post on peak of Rakata, January 25, 1928 (see Figures 87 and 88). Calculated velocities are based on the relation $V = \sqrt{gh}$, and Stehn's text includes the bathymetric data used in making each of the 5 calculations. (From Stehn, p. 44.)

Comparing the observed rapidities of transmission of the waves and the calculated ones after the chart of 1908, we see that they now need a longer time to traverse the distances from the eruption point to Zwarte Hoek (C) respectively to Verlaten South (D). [See table, Figure 89. The original paper also presents the calculations for wave travel times based on the formula $V = \sqrt{gh}$, with distances and mean depths (h) taken from Escher's chart.[8]]

Therefore we must deduce that important changes of the relief of the bottom of the caldera have taken place. It would be of great interest to control this supposition by new soundings in these two directions.

The difference in time to Rakata South (E) must be seen in changes in the relief of the bottom of the sea caused by waves and currents. Such changes we observed in the preceeding year along the east coast of Lang, where a difference of 11 m was stated near the buoy of the motorboat within a week.

Acoustic Phenomena

The eruptive phenomena were generally accompanied by loud reports or rumblings, which sounds were also heard without any visible manifestations on the surface of the sea. The rumblings were caused by a number of eruptions occurring in rapid succession.

Effect of the Eruptions on the Temperature of the Sea-Water

The temperature of the sea-water in the vicinity of the eruption-point was taken several times.

On January 4th at 300 m distance a temperature of 39.5°C. was found, which was 10.5°C. higher than the normal temperature of the sea taken on the same day about two miles distance from the eruption point.

[Stehn also presents a table with chemical compositions of seawater collected at these two points and, nearly two months later, above the new crater floor.

	2298	2283	2264	2085	2081	2289	2304	S.K. 8231	S.K. 8233	2317	2339	2083	2088
SiO$_2$	70.43	71.50	65.55	65.58	50.25	53.63	64.00	51.04	65.14	67.64	63.75	66.38	51.81
Al$_2$O$_3$	15.21	14.48	16.41	16.18	18.16	18.01	19.21	19.77	15.28	14.54	17.01	16.94	18.48
Fe$_2$O$_3$	1.96	1.00	0.55	2.02	3.36	4.03	2.28	4.80	2.57	2.26	1.93	1.35	2.95
FeO	1.76	1.58	3.76	2.56	8.52	6.09	1.57	5.10	1.79	1.89	2.67	2.65	6.64
MnO	0.05	0.08	0.05	0.16	0.17	0.08	0.14	0.18	0.14	0.06	0.13	0.08	0.21
MgO	0.64	1.02	1.08	0.19	5.25	4.37	0.56	4.00	1.38	0.99	1.48	1.14	5.97
CaO	2.54	2.56	3.32	3.43	9.32	8.13	4.62	9.43	3.17	3.02	4.24	3.11	9.05
Na$_2$O	3.92	4.21	4.03	4.52	2.46	3.05	4.09	2.89	3.77	4.03	4.22	4.09	2.97
K$_2$O	3.08	2.89	2.82	2.24	1.02	1.06	2.20	1.37	2.89	2.91	2.36	1.78	1.07
TiO$_2$	0.42	0.60	0.47	1.01	1.28	1.20	0.43	1.05	0.48	0.57	0.92	0.64	0.93
Cl	none	0.08	trace	trace	none	trace	trace	none	0.13	none	0.06	0.25	0.003
SO$_3$	none	0.03	none	none	none	trace	trace	none	0.15	0.42	0.13	none	trace	0.05
P$_2$O$_5$	trace	trace	none	0.10	0.28	0.19	0.12	trace	0.06	0.06	0.10	none	none
H$_2$O+	0.15	0.035	1.90	0.68	0.28	0.23	0.30	0.20	2.24	2.06	0.82	2.12	0.14
H$_2$O—	0.04	none	0.11	none	none	none	0.28	0.02	0.74	0.08	0.25	0.30	none
Totaal.	100.20	100.065	100.05	98.67	100.35	100.07	99.80	100.00	100.20	100.24	99.94	100.83	100.273

			Norms according to Niggli.						Magma
			si	fm	c	al	alk	k	
No. 2298	Tridymite andesite, Rakata NE		330	18.2	12.9	41.9	27.0	0.34	plagioclase-granitic
No. 2283	Andesitic pitchstone, Lang Eiland NW................		344	17.6	13.3	40.9	28.2	0.32	plagioclase-granitic
No. 2264	Black andesitic cinders, Lang Eiland NW		273	21.4	14.7	40.2	23.7	0.32	plagioclase-granitic
No. 2085	Redblack andesitic cinders, Lang Eiland NW		286	23.1	15.2	41.6	25.1	0.24	quartz-dioritic
No. 2081	Basaltic lava, lowest layer. Zwarte Hoek Rakata		123	43.0	23.4	26.1	7.5	0.21	gabbro-dioritic
No. 2289	Basaltic lava, uppermost layer. Zwarte Hoek Rakata ..		143	39.3	22.7	28.2	9.8	0.19	normaldioritic
No. 2304	Andesitic dike. Central part of the northern side of Rakata		253	15.6	18.7	44.6	21.1	0.26	plagioclase-granitic
No. 8231 S.K.	Basaltic ash of the year (?), Perboewatan		130	36.6	25.6	29.6	9.2	0.25	gabbro-dioritic
No. 8233 S.K.	Andesitic pumice ash of 1883, Perboewatan		281	24.3	14.8	38.9	22.0	0.36	quartz-dioritic
No. 2317	Andesitic pumice of 1883, Lang Eiland NW		305	21.6	14.6	38.4	25.4	0.33	quartz-dioritic
No. 2339	Red andesitic pumice of 1883, Verlaten Eiland E		245	23.0	16.9	38.5	22.6	0.27	quartz-dioritic
No. 2088	Darkgreybrown andesitic pumice of 1883, Lang Eiland NW		287	21.6	14.3	43.1	21.0	0.23	plagioclase-granitic
No. 2088	Basaltic ash of January 1928, Lang Eiland. NW........		148	41.1	23.3	26.4	8.7	0.21	gabbro-dioritic

Analyses of rocks from the Krakatau group. Analyses by R.G. Reiber, Volcanological Survey. Westerveld (1952) presents 45 analyses of Krakatau rocks, including 10 from 1883 material and 7 from 1928–1935 products, and Kuenen (1935, p. 328–329) compares Stehn's analyses to others from the East Indies by variation diagrams.

Compositional differences are small.]

The Ejected Material.

The ejecta consisted of bombs, lapilli and ashes. Only four bombs could be fished up. While they were still hot and contained gases they floated on the surface. The gases escaped slowly and their place was taken by the water which found its way into them. When they have cooled, which can take rather a long time, the bombs sink to the bottom. The greatest part of the ejecta disappeared immediately into deep.

Closer examination of the bombs fished up showed that they consisted of two kinds of matter. The inner portion is a white pumice mass of glass, originating from eruption of 1883, as the chemical and petrographical analysis showed. This was surrounded by a darker blackish-brown to black porous crust, the product of the most recent magma.

The ashes, which fell on Lang on some days in the latter part of January also had this dark colour.

Chemical analysis shows a great difference between the magma of 1883 and 1928, as can be seen from subjoined analyses.

	No. 2317	No. 2088
SiO$_2$	67.64	51.81
Al$_2$O$_3$	15.65	18.48
Fe$_2$O$_3$	1.62	2.95
FeO	1.42	6.64
MnO	0.06	0.21
MgO	0.99	5.97
CaO	3.02	9.05
Na$_2$O	4.03	2.97
K$_2$O	2.91	1.07
TiO$_2$	0.57	0.93
Cl	—	0.003
SO$_3$	0.13	0.05
P$_2$O$_5$	0.06	—
H$_2$O$^+$	2.06	0.14
H$_2$O$^-$	0.08	—
	100.24	100.27

No. 2317 Pumice of 1883, Lang Eiland NW 50 m above sea level.

No. 2088 Ash of 1928 which fell on Lang Eiland on January 24th 1928.

Analyst: R.G. Reiber, Volcanological Survey, Bandoeng.

Specific gravity of the 1928 ashes: 2.6.

The supposition, based on the chemical analysis, that the magma of 1928 is basaltic was confirmed by the petrographical analysis made by Dr. Ch.E.A. Harloff.

The result of the findings[31] may be briefly reproduced here.

The feldspar test showed that the percentage of anorthite fluctuates between 83 and 94%. The ashes contained, further crystals and crystal fragments of monoclinic pyroxene, i.e. diopside, and of rhombic pyroxene, i.e. hypersthene. Fine idiomorphic individuals and fragments of olivine, in which the proportion of Mg_2SiO_4 (forsterite) to Fe_2SiO_4 (fayalite) is about 7:3. This composition corresponds to that of olivine occuring in basalts. Further, there is magnetite present. Lastly there were large quantities of glass fragments found with a refraction index of about 1.555, which corresponds to a basaltic glass.

Dr. Harloff found further, in the white pumice-like mass of the interior of the bombs fished, cordierite, which he describes as follows: ". . . This rock consists of a porous mass of glass, which contains very numerous and generally fine, idiomorphic, small individuals of cordierite. . . ."

We may supplement the above by stating the significant fact that there is no cordierite in the pumice of 1883 collected on Lang Eiland NW, so that it seems not impossible that the cordierite was formed by contact effect.

Seismic Observations

For the period before January 28th we have to depend on the records of the Wiechert seismographs in the Royal Observatory at Weltevreden [suburb of Batavia] which is 150 km distant from Krakatau.

In the Seismological Bulletin for 1928 of this Observatory the following tremors were published as probably emanating from Krakatau. January 24th 10^h 48^m 21^s, January 25th 8^h 4^m 12^s, 10^h 5^m 24^s, January 26th 11^h 4^m 40^s, January 27th 3^h 30^m 34^s, Greenwich time.

In 1927, according to the Seismological Bulletin there were no tremors recorded with an epicentrum in the Krakatau Group or even in the Sunda Strait.

A portable seismograph with two horizontal components weighing 12½ kg was put into commission on Lang, but unfortunately not till January 28th. The distance from the eruption-point is about 4 km. The correct time was furnished by the Wireless Station fitted up on the 27th by the Royal Navy next to the observation-station of the Volcanological Survey. It was now possible to compare the tremors recorded by the instrument with the visible and audible phenomena.

We noted, in the first place, that seismic movements occurred not only during eruptive activity but also in periods of rest. A few days before the commencement of fresh visible manifestations of eruption there was great increase of seismic disturbance. Similar observations were made in Japan before the great eruption of Sakura-jima on January 12th 1914.

It was noted, further, that the time of the largest number of tremors, and the greatest amplitudes do not correspond to the time of the most severe eruptive activity, the former being on the contrary very few then. This is shown by the fact that at the time of the tremors registered at Weltevreden there were no violent explosions. It appears further (for instance) from the registrations of May 4th 6 p.m. to May 5th 6 a.m., when 2696 eruptions, 111 bubblings and 163 fountains were counted, while 211 tremors were registered by the N-S component and 51 by the E-W component. It is supposed that these tremors are manifestations of the efforts of the magma to break through and are therefore preparatory to and not caused by the visible eruptions.

Tremors that accompany the explosions are not altogether absent but they never equal the strength of what I have called preparatory tremors.

As far as the relation between tremors and eruptions is concerned the results fairly correspond to what was experienced in Japan in several eruptions e.g. that of Usu-san in 1910 and Asama-yama in 1911.

Yet another peculiarity was noticed in the way the two components registered.

Up to the end of March they were either uniform or the registration in the N-S component were more powerful than those of the E-W. The direction of the disturbance in respect of the seismograph was about SW-NE. It was different however, after the rest at the beginning of April. After a fairly uniform distribution of the tremors in the two registrations for six days, those of the E-W component were more numerous after April 11th.

Plate VI

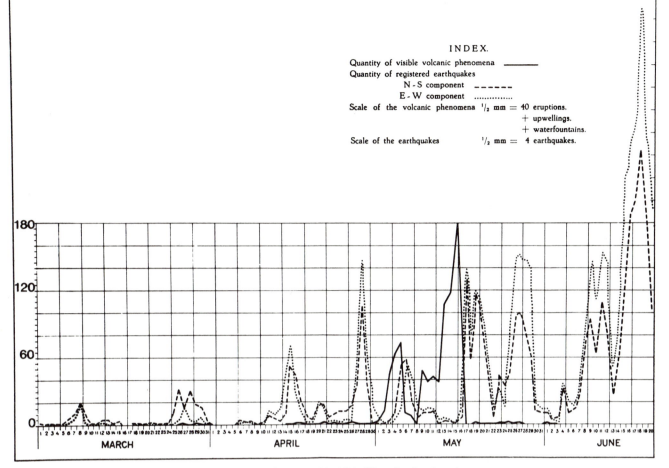

Figure 90. Krakatau eruption of 1928. Diagram showing the daily quantity of visible volcanic phenomena and the daily quantity of earthquakes observed seismographically at Lang Eiland (Krakatau). March 1–June 20, 1928. [Note that late June increase in seismicity was followed in early July by renewed volcanism (see Figure 80). Stehn's plate VI.]

This difference and change are connected with the situation of the magma bed. In the first period when there were on the whole more tremors registered by the north component, the strain of the magma was either vertically below the point of eruption or perhaps a little to the south in the direction of the old Danan. The supposition is that during the interval of rest in February or at the beginning of March the magma worked more in the direction of Perboewatan. At the beginning of March both components registered fairly uniformly. In support of the theory that the magma-bed spread northwestward is the fact also, that on the 25th and 27th of March that is at the commencement of the second eruption-period, a cloud of steam was seen above the sea at the site of old Perboewatan.

The new eruption-point is situated almost midway between Perboewatan and Danan. When the gases in the magma had again acquired sufficient force, the magma sought the easiest way to break through, finding it in the fissures and vents of the first eruption-period.

Since that date the preparatory tremors were chiefly recorded by the E-W component.

The area where the explosions in the depths took place is not too far below the crater mouth, i.e. more southward.

That is the reason why the N-S component was more affected by the disturbance and registsered more and more strongly, than the E-W component.

In the interval at the beginning of April there were no tremors registered at all for three days. On the 5th a new seismic activity began and it was now the N-S component which was more affected by the preparatory activity or, in other words, the exertions of the magma took place more southward.

Visible volcanic activity commenced on April 13th and at that moment the registrations of the E-W component were more numerous and more powerful. Measurements from Lang showed that the eruptions came into view from openings in the fissure situated more northward (azimuth 117½ to 120°). On May 15th the telegram reports 170 tremors N-S and 81 E-

W and azimuth between 121 and 123° or more southward. Since that date this has been the relation between the components.

What the seismic disturbance can be like during the intervals of inactivity between the eruption periods, appears from the period the 2nd to 6th of June. At first there was slight seismic activity, which gradually increased, reaching its maximum on June 17th when the N-S component registered 979 tremors and the E-W as many as 1504. The seismic activity then declined again but continued to be high until the commencement of the third phase of eruption. On July 3rd there were 40 N-S and 61 E-W tremors. At [the] moment of the fresh eruptions the number of registrations considerably declined.

After the termination of the third phase of eruption no tremors were registered from July 13th to August 23rd. They commenced again on the 24th. On the 25th at $14^h 7^m$ there was visible volcanic activity.

After the end of October the tremors were more powerful. Before, during and after the termination of the fifth phase strong tremors were felt from time to time, which had their epicentre in the Krakatau itself. The seismograms are however those of tectonic tremors. The numerous miner aftershocks of volcanic tremors were absent.

On December 20th, as already dated, the seismogram showed great disturbance at 18 hours for the duration of 23 minutes. The mighty shock that occurred at 19 hours 34½ minutes was followed after half-a-minute by an eruption of ashes and bombs which reached a height of 80 m.

These examples will suffice to illustrate the relation between the preparatory and explosive volcanic tremors.[32]

[1]Abbot (1881).
[2]Bertelli (1890, 1891).
[3]Brun (1911).
[4]Cool (1908).
[5]Cool (1909).
[6]Escher (1919a).
[7]Escher (1919b).
[8]Escher (1919c).
[9]Escher (1928).
[10]Jongh (1918).
[11]Reck (1926).
[12]Rudolph (1887).
[13]Rudolph (1898).
[14]Stehn (1928a).
[15]Stehn (1928b).
[16]Symons (1888).
[17]Taverne (1922).
[18]Taverne (1926).
[19]Umbgrove (1928).

[20]Van Bemmelen (1908).
[21]Verbeek (1881).
[22]Verbeek (1885).
[23]Verbeek (1908).
[24]Goeneng = Mount. Pronounce Dutch oe as ou in would.
[25]Poeloe = island.
[26]It should be borne in mind that during the recent eruption the time of the Volcanological Survey Staff was too fully occupied with continuous observation and recording of the phenomena of the present activity for adequate surveys of the three islands. The difficulties caused by the landslides because of the numerous earthquakes in 1928 have made it necessary to maintain for the present in the sketchmap of Rakata in Figure 72 the results of Escher's researches in 1919.
[27]Escher has made a series of very instructive diagrams (though rather sketchy as regards distances), which he has reproduced in Escher[6,7] and which also appear (e.g.) in Rutten's "Geologie van Ned. Oost-Indië" Groningen, Den Haag 1927, and in Umbgrove.[19] [We present a modern version of these diagrams, as modified by A. Sudradjat, on p. 360.]
[28]The socle of this island apparently consisted of tridymite andesite, for there is a sample collected by Verbeek in the Geological Museum of the Department of Mines; Verbeek says nothing about it, however, neither in Verbeek[21] ([his] p. 155) nor in Verbeek.[22]
[29]It is a deeply felt want to express at this place my feelings of appreciation to the sense of duty of the European as well as of the native observers of our Survey, and to the punctuality and the patience with which they noted day and night for more than a year now, every volcanic phenomenon and so contributed in bring together the great amount of material about the new eruption of Krakatau.
[30]See the section on *Flames*, p. 333.
[31]They will appear in greater detail in No. 11 of the "Vulkanologische en Seismologische Mededeelingen" with the other results of the research of Krakatau and the youngest eruption.
[32]In total 22358 volcanic tremors in 1928 were registered on Lang Eiland.

The 1939 Eruption of Anak Krakatau (Neumann van Padang, 1963)

Anak Krakatau's battle with the sea continued, with vigorous volcanic explosions repeatedly building a small island that was then destroyed by waves after the activity declined. Finally, three years after the eruptions began, volcanism won: An island emerged that has continued to grow to this day by intermittent Strombolian eruptions [see Plate 16C]. The growth and development of Anak Krakatau through 1982 is summarized in a paper by Sudradjat that we reprint at the end of this section, but here we extract an account of 1939 activity that illustrates both the nature of Strombolian eruptions and the difficulty of predicting them. The author, M. Neumann Van Padang, has had a long and distinguished career, with his first paper on Krakatau published in 1933 and others continuing into the 1970's. He pioneered the Catalog of Active Volcanoes of the World series published by the International Association of Volcanology, and authored the first Catalog, on Indonesia, in 1951. The following account is extracted from a paper discussing the problems of predicting eruptions by surface thermal measurements.

From June 1 till 7, 1939, Anak Krakatau had weak volcanic activity. The eruptions did not reach higher than 500 m.[1] Then the volcano was quiet again.

From June 14 till 17 the island was surveyed by personnel of the Volcanological Survey. On June 14 dense steam was still rising from the crater. The next day the colour of the lake was dark grey and numerous gas ebullitions were seen along the NE and SSE border. Steam rose from the lake water which had a temperature of 55°C; weak fumaroles with a temperature of 50°C were found on the NE shore.

The next day, on June 16, the temperature of the lake water had decreased to 47°C; the gas ebullitions were less and the development of steam was feeble.

On June 17 the temperature of the lake was less again, being 30°C. Steam was scarcely visible, gas ebullitions were feeble. It is worth mentioning that it had not rained during this time, so that rain water could not have been the cause of this fall in temperature.

At 16 o'clock of that day the surveyor Umar Ali climbed to the summit of the crater rim to have a look at the crater. *There was not the least activity, neither steam, nor gas ebullitions.* Then he continued his work.

About an hour later, at 17:20, the magnetic needle of the *boussole tranche montagne* [transit compass? alidade?] began to swing to and fro. This suspicious phenomenon was the reason why the instruments were packed at once, and why the surveyors fled to the motor boat, which was waiting near the northern coast of the island. Feeble tremors were felt on their way to the coast, and a noise as from a big surf was heard.

When waiting for the other members of the group who were working at other points, the first eruption cloud rose from the crater, followed by others. By leaving back some instruments, all the survey personnel reached the boat safely, and steamed away. The activity lasted till 17:50 with eruption of some hundreds of meters height. The bombs, ashes and hot gases

covered the island, so that the surveying personnel left Anak Krakatau just in time.

From 17:59 till 1:10 o'clock in the night the volcano was quiet. Then a new phase of strong activity followed with eruptions of more than 3000 m height, cracks, electric discharges, glowing bombs, etc.

It is not the intention to describe the volcanic activity which followed. These phenomena are only mentioned to show that the new activity *did not begin with a rise in temperature, nor with an increase of fumarolic activity.*

Looking back on what happened, we see that the eruptions of Mount Merapi in 1930, 1932 and 1942–43, of Mount Papandajan in 1924–25, of Mount Slamet in the time of 1923 and 1932, and of Anak Krakatau in 1932 and 1939 were not preceded by a distinct increase in temperature of the summit fumaroles.

[1]Stehn (1939).

Calderas of the Krakatau Type (Williams, 1941)

The late Howel Williams was a giant in volcanology. His first paper was published in 1921 and his authoritative textbook, co-authored with A.R. McBirney, was published only the year before he died in 1980. Among his many contributions to volcanology, his 1941 classic monograph on "Calderas and their Origin" is particularly outstanding. It was written after visiting Krakatau, and no other volcano figures more prominently in his global review of young calderas. Williams establishes the 1883 Krakatau eruption as the type example of collapse of a pre-existing volcanic edifice being caused by large-scale eruption of silicic magma from a shallow reservoir. He discounts the importance of tephra falling back into the sea as a mechanism for generating tsunamis.

Krakatau

As the type of a caldera produced by collapse following the evisceration of a magma chamber by explosions of pumice, it seems best to select that of Krakatau, both because of the recency of its origin and the clarity of the evidence. It especially deserves description here because of the many misconceptions that have crept into writings on the subject, and the widespread belief that the caldera was formed directly by the great explosions of 1883 rather than by engulfment. These erroneous views date back to the writings of Judd[6] and have been handed on in spite of the admirable study of the problem by Verbeek[12] and the recent work of Stehn.[11] All who have carefully examined the caldera in the field are convinced that collapse was the dominant process.

The present appearance of the Krakatau group is indicated in Figure 91. There are three main islands: Rakata, the largest, which rises to a height of approximately 2700 ft, and Lang and Verlaten islands, neither of which exceeds 600 ft in height. These three islands lie on the edge of a caldera nearly 7 km in diameter, from the floor of which rise the rocky islet of the Bootmansrots and the basaltic cinder cone of Anak Krakatau, which first appeared in 1927. Four periods in the evolution of the island group may be distinguished.

First period.—On the three main islands the oldest rocks include flows of andesite, some of which are unusually rich in tridymite, associated with many thin layers of pumice and scoria. Possibly these formed part of an original cone about 2000 m high. According to Stehn, the central part of this old cone disappeared by collapse, leaving four small islands on the periphery of the caldera. Subsequently, there were repeated explosions, at first submarine and later subaerial, which deposited ejecta to a thickness of 60 feet.

Second period.—A new cone, Rakata, then developed on the SE margin of the original caldera, erupting lavas and fragmental debris until it reached a height of 800 m. In contrast to the products of the older cone, which were dominantly andesitic, Rakata erupted only olivine-rich basalt. After it had attained its present height, the new cone was injected with swarms of basaltic dikes, which now are beautifully exposed on the precipitous north wall of the island, converging toward the peak (Figure 91).

Third period.—Two smaller cones of andesite, Danan, 450 m high, and Perboewatan, 120 m high, then rose within the caldera and ultimately united with the basaltic cone of Rakata to form one large island measuring 9 by 5 km. In 1680 a flow of andesitic pitchstone escaped from the vent of Perboewatan. Then followed more than 200 years of quiescence.

Fourth period: the catastrophe of 1883.—On May 20, 1883, Krakatau began the historic and destructive outbreak which culminated on August 26–28 in the formation of the present caldera by foundering on a tremendous scale.

The initial explosions issued from Perboewatan and were not especially violent. When the volcano was visited on May 27, it was found that the main island and Verlaten Island were in large part covered with fine ejecta and that the vegetation, though not burnt, had been killed. Toward the northeast, however, on Polish Hat and Lang Island, very little debris had fallen. Nowhere, in fact, did the products of the first four days' activity accumulate to a thickness of more than about a meter, and few of the erupted fragments were larger than a man's head. For the most part they consisted of pumice and crystal ash, admixed with pieces of old lava.

After these preliminary explosions, the activity died down until June 19, when a column of steam was seen to rise from the crater of Perboewatan. Five days later, two columns could be distinguished, signifying that a new vent had opened at the foot of Danan. By this time the summit of Perboewatan had been greatly modified, doubtless by caving of the conduit walls. There are no records of any activity during July, but when the islands were visited on August 11, for the last time before the final paroxysm, there were three main vents in a mild state of eruption. It is clear, however, that little fragmental material had been added to the thin layer left by the explosions of May. Between August 12 and 26, passing vessels reported falls of cinders. Exactly what happened during the fateful three days, August 26 to 28, when 98% of the total ejecta was erupted and the whole configuration of the islands was utterly transformed, will long remain a matter for debate, but the main events can be deduced from records obtained on Java and Sumatra and from a consideration of both the ejecta and the present topography.

The paroxysm.—At 1 p.m. of the 26th a noise like thunder was heard 100 miles away, at Buitenzorg on Java. At 2 p.m. a black cloud rose to a height of 17 miles above Krakatau, and at 2:30 many short, sharp explosions could be distinguished, the noises increasing until about 5 p.m. It was probably at that time that the first collapse and tidal wave occurred. The noise of explosions continued all night, accompanied by severe air shocks, though not by quakes. At Buitenzorg, lamps and plaster fell in the houses and windows flew open. No one could sleep anywhere in western Java because of the incessant noise. Between 4:40 and 6:41 a.m. of the next day, August 27, several large tidal waves emanated from Krakatau, probably propelled by further collapses of the northern part of the main island. Stehn believes that these were followed by submarine explosions from vents in that

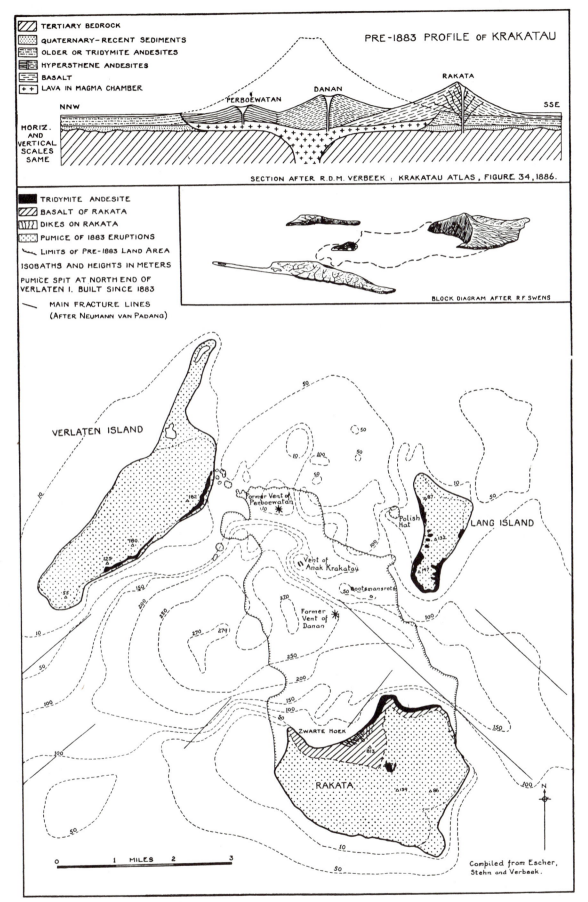

Figure 91. The Krakatau caldera. [Williams' figure 2.]

vicinity, when a thick layer of dark gray pumice was deposited on Lang Island.

At 10 a.m. of the 27th occurred the most violent explosions of all. Ejecta rose to a height of 50 miles [50 *km* in Williams' 1979 textbook with A.R. Mc-Birney] and were spread over an area of more than 300,000 square miles. So loud was the detonation that it could be heard even in Australia. About half an hour later, a tidal wave 120 feet high overwhelmed the neighboring coasts of Java and Sumatra, drowning more than 36,000 people. By 10:30 a.m. rain was falling at Batavia, and by 11 a.m. it was accompanied by moist ash and pisolites of mud. This was the first time that such ejecta had been observed.

At 10:52 a.m. a second gigantic explosion occurred, hardly less violent than that of 10 a.m., but this does not seem to have been attended by a tidal wave. At 4:35 p.m. there was still another loud explosion, followed by a small wave. Throughout the night of the 27th and early morning of the next day the noise of the explosions recurred with diminishing intensity, and then virtually ceased. Detonations were heard in Batavia, however, on September 17 and 26, October 10, and finally on February 20, 1884. From that date until 1927, when Anak Krakatau commenced to erupt on the floor of the caldera, the volcano seems to have been dormant.

The preceding chronicle of events shows that the activity which led to the formation of the Krakatau caldera lasted only a little more than three months. All but an insignificant fraction of the eruptive energy was spent within the short space of 24 hours almost at the close of the episode. After weak and intermittent preliminary explosions the activity rose suddenly to a climax and as quickly came to an end.

Products of the eruptions.—Verbeek[12] calculated that at least 18 km³, or somewhat less than 5 cubic miles of ejecta, were blown out of Krakatau in 1883, of which two-thirds fell within a radius of 15 km. The deposits show their maximum thickness of 200 ft on the south part of the main island, Rakata. Of fundamental importance for the problem of the origin of the caldera is the fact that 95% of the ejecta consists of new magma in the form of pumice, and only 5% of old rock fragments torn from the former cones of Danan, Perboewatan, and Rakata. It follows, beyond question, that these cones did not disappear by explosive decapitation, but by some other process.

Much can be learned from a study of the ejecta of 1883, which are perfectly exposed on the cliffs of Rakata, Lang, and Verlaten islands. Stehn's careful examination[11] has shown how the various layers of pumice can be correlated with recorded explosions, and has thrown much new light on the sequence of events. The observer is at once impressed by the contrast between the well-bedded pumice deposits of the first eruptions and the thick piles of almost unstratified pumice left by the paroxysmal explosions of August 27. Clearly the earlier eruptions were chiefly of vulcanian type, the ejecta being thrown high into the air and drifted northward by winds, whereas the culminating explosions were of pelean type, the overwhelming mass of pumice being deposited with great rapidity as glowing avalanches (*nuées ardentes*), so that sorting was prevented.

a) The bedded pumice.—Prior to the paroxysm of August 27, the active vents were at the northern end of the main island, near the old cones of Danan and Perboewatan. From the first eruptions of May until August 11, only a thin layer of ejecta, scarcely more than a meter thick, was laid down and this was virtually restricted to the northern islands, Lang and Verlaten. It rests on an old soil layer the thickness of which testifies to the long period of quiescence which preceded the activity of 1883. Here and there stumps of trees may be seen lying prone on the old soil, most of those on Lang Island being uncharred although others near the summit of Rakata are thoroughly carbonized. In many places the pre-eruption surface is made evident by seepage lines on the cliffs, where the water, percolating through the overlying pumice, drains from the contact with the impervious layer of soil beneath.

The first ejecta, from the northernmost vent on Perboewatan, are composed chiefly of fine pumice dust and lapilli, admixed with crystal ash and a few small fragments of lithic debris. These are succeeded on both Verlaten and Lang islands by a thick series of pumice sheets, most of which exhibit perfect stratification and a grading from coarse pumice at the base to fine dust at the top. These must be the products of a rapid succession of mild explosions. Changes in wind direction are suggested by cross-bedding in many of the deposits. A few of the layers, up to 25 feet in thickness, show no internal stratification and carry lumps of pumice up to 2 feet in diameter. These represent the deposits of more violent eruptions.

Two distinctive layers have been given especial consideration by Stehn. The lower of these is a sheet of pink pumice approximately 10 cm thick, which may be seen on Lang Island about 6 m from the base of the 1883 deposits. On Verlaten Island the corresponding pink pumice reaches a thickness of 20 cm. Accepting the opinion of Verbeek and Brun that the color is the result of contact with sea water, Stehn suggests that the pumice is a product of the first submarine eruption. The tiny chips of coral found within the pumice lend support to the suggestion. Accompanying them are small pieces of lava comparable with the lavas that formed the cone of Perboewatan. These facts seem to imply that an early and minor collapse permitted access of sea water to a vent of the northern cone just west of the former site of Polish Hat.

Above the pink layer, and separated from it by a quickly alternating series of fine pumice and lapilli layers, is a bank of smoke gray, compact pumice, up to 11 m in thickness, confined to the northern end of Lang Island. Apparently this also is a product of a submarine explosion, one that was directed eastward from a vent near the northern end of Perboewatan after than cone collapsed at 4:40 a.m. of the 27th. Though the lower contact of the smoke gray pumice is almost horizontal, the upper surface is deeply channeled, probably, as Stehn believes, owing to the inrush of the great tidal wave of 10 a.m.

On Verlaten Island the pink pumice is overlain by well-bedded pumice sheets the grading of which indicates more than 30 successive explosions. One of the sheets contains pumice lumps up to 2 ft across, but in most the fragments are less than an inch in diameter, and include no more than about 2 or 3% of lithic debris. Clearly all but an insignificant fraction of the bedded pumice deposits is made up of fresh magma.

b) **The pumice of the culminating phase.**—The two paroxysmal explosions of 10 a.m. and 10:52 a.m. of the 27th originated from a vent or vents well to the south of the earlier vents and just west of Danan, where the present floor of the caldera has a depth of more than 270 m (Figure 91). More than 90% of all the ejecta of 1883 were thrown out in the course of these two violent eruptions. Little fell on Lang Island and on the north end of Verlaten; almost all fell on Rakata and on the south end of Verlaten or out to sea.

So vast a mass of pumice was ejected in a short time that it fell virtually *en masse* as an avalanche and accumulated close to the source as a chaotic, almost wholly unstratified pile up to 60 m thick. Only the finer particles of pumice were shot high into the air, and these were drifted away by winds for thousands of miles. Figures 92, 93, and 94 show the typical appearance of these pelean deposits.

On Rakata, near Zwarte Hoek, the deposits of white pumice form precipitous cliffs in which the lack of sorting is strikingly displayed. Few of the pumice bombs exceed 3 feet in diameter; by far the greater number are less than 1 foot in maximum dimension. Between these, and making up the bulk of the deposit, are small pumice lapilli and chips of the size of sand and gravel. Approximately 90% of the mass is pumice lightly sprinkled with feldspar and pyroxene crystals; 5% consists of lumps of black obsidian, many of which have pumiceous crusts; and the remaining 5% is made up of fragments of old lava, few of which are more than a foot across while most are even less than 3 inches in longest dimension.

At the south end of Verlaten Island the proportion of old lava fragments is considerably larger, increasing southward from about 10–30% of the total mass. Though most of these lithic blocks are less than a foot across, several are up to 10 feet in diameter, and one was seen to have an exposed surface measuring 15 by 35 feet. A decided majority of the blocks are of black, resinous, andesitic pitchstone, many of which are in an extremely crumbly condition, possibly owing to reheating in the course of the eruptions. Together with these are abundant chips of black obsidian, generally with a skin of gray pumice but occasionally with a nucleus of it. Other lithic ejecta include blocks of varicolored, porphyritic andesite, buff sandstone, and blue-gray concretionary mudstone. The pumice itself is almost wholly composed of pieces less than an inch across; few exceed a foot in diameter; and much of the material is as fine as sand or even finer.

At the foot of the pumice cliffs, both on Rakata and Verlaten islands, the beach is littered with piles of large lithic blocks. Escher has interpreted these as part of a block layer that passes beneath the pumice sheet, but there is nothing to substantiate this idea. On the contrary, the blocks are merely a result of avalanches from the cliffs. On Rakata the chaotic pumice lies directly on the old basaltic substratum, without a trace of an intervening sheet of lithic debris. On Verlaten Island, for a distance of fifty yards south of the southern-most exposures of tridymite andesite, the unbedded pumice deposits of the 10 a.m. explosion rest immediately on 50 feet of fine, well-bedded pumice deposits of the earlier eruptions (Figure 92).

The cataclysmic explosion of 10 a.m. was accompanied or followed at once by the engulfment of much of the old cone on Rakata, and the consequent tidal wave which wrought such devastation on the coasts of Java and Sumatra. At this time also a large sub-

Figure 92. Bedded pumice beneath massive pumice. East coast of Verlaten Island. (Photograph taken by Ch. E. Stehn.) [Williams' figure 3.]

Figure 93. Cliffs of massive unbedded pumice. East coast of Verlaten Island. Note large lithic blocks on beach. [Williams' figure 4.]

Figure 94. Massive pumice on Verlaten Island. White bombs of pumice; darker blocks of lithic debris. [Williams' figure 5.]

marine graben was formed to the west of Rakata, leading out of the caldera (Figure 91).

The last important explosion occurred at 10:52 a.m. of the 27th. Stehn believes, with good reason, that the remainder of the Danan cone was then demolished. On all three islands, Rakata, Verlaten, and Lang, the topmost layer consists of large lithic blocks, mostly andesites like those that once formed the cone of Danan, accompanied by pieces of sediment, coral and shells. The pumice erupted at the same time settled gradually from the air, infilling the interstices between the underlying blocks and forming a continuous blanket over them. No collapse seems to have accompanied these explosions, but about 6 hours later, to judge from the time of arrival of the last tidal wave on the coast of Java, there was yet another engulfment. It was this that probably caused the disappearance of the last remnant of Danan and also produced the submarine graben running east between Lang Island and Rakata.

Form of the caldera.—The present caldera of Krakatau has a diameter of approximately 7 km, and its floor includes two principal basins (Figure 91). The smaller basin lies between Lang and Verlaten islands and has an average depth of 70 m, though in two places the depth increases to approximately 120 m. The larger depression lies to the south and has a flatter floor, the maximum depth of which is 279 m. Between these two basins is a NW-trending ridge that passes through the Bootmansrots and the new cinder cone of Anak Krakatau, built since 1927. Leading out of the caldera toward the SW and SE are elongated graben with floors deeper than 100 m. Clearly this submarine topography bespeaks the dominant control of engulfment; it does not suggest a series of explosion funnels. The SW-trending submarine graben runs parallel to the main volcanic chain of Sumatra, and the SE-trending graben is on the tectonic line which passes through the volcanoes of Sebesi, Seboekoe, and Radjabasa. There is little doubt that the position of Krakatau itself is determined by the intersection of these two fissures. Neumann van Padang has suggested[7] that the magma chamber prior to 1883 extended for some distance from the present caldera beneath the radial graben.

Cause of the tidal waves.—Wharton, in the Royal Society Report on the eruptions, maintained that the collapse of the old cones of Rakata, Danan, and Perboewatan would have produced tidal waves vastly larger than those observed, and concluded that the waves were produced by an elevation of the sea floor and by the fall of ejecta into the water. Later studies show that there was no upheaval of the sea floor, and probably the falling of even great masses of pumice into the sea could not have given rise to a wave exceeding 120 feet in height. Verbeek argued that some of the waves were caused by collapse of the old cones, but that most were produced by falling ejecta. Escher thought that only the former was important. The four principal means by which tidal waves may originate in connection with volcanic eruptions are: the formation of submarine graben, as suggested by Sieberg;[10] the avalanching of material from submarine slopes or from land into the sea; the eruption of ash and gas from submarine vents; and the falling of great masses of ejecta into the water. Of these, the first two were by far the chief causes of the Krakatau waves of 1883.

Cause of the eruptions.—The origin of the eruptions has been discussed particularly by Verbeek,[12] Judd,[6] and Brun.[3] All three emphasized the importance of the reheating of old rocks as a motivating factor. Brun, impressed by the finding of many blocks of pumice-crusted obsidian among the 1883 ejecta, and knowing from his own experiments that when obsidian is heated to a certain temperature, dependent on its composition, it froths suddenly and violently into pumice, concluded that the prime cause of the eruptions was the reheating of obsidians within the old cones. Few volcanologists nowadays would be willing to attribute more than a trivial role to this rejuvenation of "live" rocks. Besides, the fragments of obsidian were proably not derived from the old cones, but represent new magma, first chilled and then reheated between successive explosions.

Judd supposed that the old lavas had been decomposed by water action and thus made more easily fusible, as the following quotation shows:

> If, as seems highly probable, the younger ejecta of Krakatoa were formed by the refusion of older lavas, then we can trace the cause of the introduction of water by which their liquefaction by heat was rendered more easy. These older lavas, by the presence in them of hydrous compounds, and by the existence in their cavities of tridymite and other secondary minerals, betray the fact that they have been greatly acted upon by percolating waters. It is through the introduction of the sea and other surface waters by slow percolation from above, and the consequent formation of new compounds, more readily acted upon by subterranean heat, that I am disposed to regard volcanic phenomena as being brought about. In this we find an explanation of the proximity of volcanoes to great basins of water.

There is no need to recapitulate here the many arguments against the view that the occurrence of volcanoes close to the sea is a matter of cause and effect. Moreover, a study of the Krakatau ejecta lends no support to the idea of widespread refusion of older lavas. There is no hybrid pumice comparable with that erupted by Katmai, where the evidence of assimilation is undeniable. The blocks of andesite and pitchstone within the Krakatau pumice display no signs of resorption, and the pumice itself presents no features that bespeak contamination.

Judd seems to have been in error also in attributing an important role to the action of sea water rushing into the craters in intervals of quiescence between eruptions. He pictured the sea sweeping over the vents after each explosion, chilling the magma and causing it to crust over so that gas could accumulate beneath until it developed explosive pressure. In this way he sought to account for repeated checks and rallies during the activity. But many pumice eruptions occurred before the sea could have gained access to the vents. Besides, the chilling effect of sea water could not develop a crust on the magma thick enough to delay the explosive process. The progress of the recent submarine eruptions of Santorin and Anak Krakatau shows that the sea has almost no damping effect.

Turning now to Verbeek's picture of the causes of eruption, we find that he invokes three processes:

1. Percolation of sea water through fissures into the magma chamber. There the water is vaporized and by increasing pressure the vapor forces the magma level up the conduits.

2. The rising magma dissolves the overlying lavas until the cones are reduced to thin shells enclosing a molten, hybrid core.

3. Collapse of the conical retaining shells into the magma, permitting the sea to rush into the craters and generate violent explosion of the magma as pumice. Then withdrawal of the remaining magma to approximately 200 or 300 meters below sea level.

Reasons for doubting that much internal liquefaction of the old cones took place prior to the eruptions have already been mentioned in the discussion of Judd's views. Further, the paucity of lithic ejecta does not harmonize with the concept that the collapses immediately preceded the explosions. Surely, if such had been the sequence of events, there should be vast quantities of coarse blocky detritus admixed with the pumice.

Two alternative explanations of the activity may now be noted. Prior to 1883, Krakatau had been quiescent for more than two hundred years. Doubtless, during that long interval of repose the magma at depth was undergoing differentiation. As crystallization proceeded, the vapor tension increased by retrograde boiling and the residual melt became progressively more siliceous. A stage was finally reached when the vapor pressure exceeded the resistance of the overlying rocks; then the eruptive cycle began. Drilling of the vents further released the pressure on the magma, so that gases escaped from solution with increasing rapidity. Not until the gas-rich top of the magma chamber was exhausted did the eruptions come to an end. By that time so much magma had been emptied from the reservoir that the solid roof was left with too little support and suffered a succession of tremendous collapses. Against this explanation of the eruptions it may be said that the pumice, which makes up 95% of the total ejecta, is predominantly composed of glass, and therefore the vapor pressure of the magma cannot have been greatly increased by crystallization before activity commenced. On the other hand, it may be that the bulk of the early-formed crystals sank to deep levels in the reservoir and so escaped eruption. Besides, if the magma lay at shallow depths, as seems probable, a slight amount of crystallization would create explosive pressures.

A second explanation of the activity may be based on the assumption that the magma prior to 1883 was potentially explosive owing to a high content of dissolved gases, perhaps absorbed from the walls of the reservoir. If the magma were saturated throughout, its potential explosivity would increase with depth because of the greater solubility of gas at deeper levels. Supersaturation of the upper layers of the magma, either by diffusion of gas or by incipient crystallization, may have been adequate to open new vents. Gas fluxing of the conduits and release of pressure by the opening of an eathquake crack may have hastened the catastrophe. Once the vents were opened, the eruptions would grow gradually to a climax as deeper and therefore more gas-rich layers of magma were tapped; the end would come only when the reservoir was virtually exhausted. The poverty of the pumice in crystals and the intensification of the explosions as activity continued would accord with this explanation. But as between the hypothesis of a magma increasingly charged with dissolved gas at depth and of one increasingly rich in gas in its upper layers owing to crystallization, it does not seem possible to decide which is applicable at Krakatau.

Origin of the caldera.—Judd, as we have noted, came to the conclusion that the caldera was formed directly by explosive decapitation of the old cones,

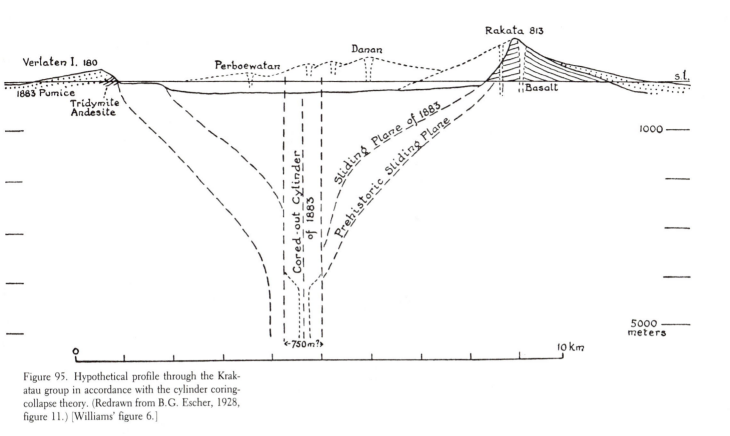

Figure 95. Hypothetical profile through the Krakatau group in accordance with the cylinder coring-collapse theory. (Redrawn from B.G. Escher, 1928, figure 11.) [Williams' figure 6.]

aided by an earlier internal melting. This view has been handed on in most English and American texts—Russell,[9] Bonney,[1] and others. Verbeek,[12] impressed by the scarcity of lithic detritus, was the first to suggest that collapse was the dominant factor involved and that it was preceded by internal melting of the cones.

Escher[4,5] sought to explain the caldera as a result of an inward sliding of the old cones along funnel-shaped glide planes, following the coring out of an immense explosion cylinder during the eruptive cycle. This process had occurred at Vesuvius in the great eruption of 1906, and Escher believed that the events at Krakatau were analogous though on a much grander scale. Apprehending that the coring of a deep and wide cylinder must leave its traces in an imposing accumulation of lithic ejecta, and having in mind that Verbeek had been able to calculate that only 5% of the 1883 ejecta is composed of old detritus, Escher supposed that most of the lithic debris formed a thick, blocky layer beneath the chaotic pumice sheet erupted at 10 a.m. of August 27. Field studies show that no such layer exists. In his diagram (redrawn here as Figure 95) he shows a cored cylinder 4 km deep and approximately 800 m in diameter, having a volume of about 2 km³. Had the explosions originated at such a depth, there should be a thick pile of debris derived

from the Tertiary sediments which form the foundations of Krakatau; actually, only a very trivial percentage of the ejecta is made up of such material. Nor does Escher's mechanism account for the two submarine graben leading from the caldera.

Already in 1890 Dana had correctly surmised that the caldera was produced by engulfment resulting from the formation of a subterranean cavity left by the rapid eruption of pumice. Subsequently, Neumann van Padang,[7] Reck,[8] van Bemmelen, van den Bosch,[2] Stehn,[11] and the writer have supported his opinion that collapse was caused by withdrawal of support from the roof of the magma chamber by hurried evacuation. Reck points out that the arcuate bay on the west coast of Rakata, between Zwarte Hoek and Krakatau North (Figure 91), cannot have been formed by explosion, but resulted from the foundering of the old cone of Rakata into its feeding reservoir, and is thus analogous in mode of origin to the scalloped bays so well displayed along the margins of the caldera of Santorin. Calculations by van Bemmelen have also shown that the volume of pumice erupted in 1883, when recalculated as magma, approximates closely the volume of material that disappeared by engulfment. This, together with the paucity of lithic debris, is a powerful argument in favor of the collapse hypothesis.

Changes in the caldera since 1883.—The subsidence which produced the caldera did not cease when the eruptions came to an end. Soundings made in 1923, forty years later, show that drastic changes had occurred in the interim. At two places close to what was in 1883 the deepest part of the caldera the depths increased from 162 and 210 m to 279 and 270 m, respectively. Close to another point where the depth had been only 80 m the soundings showed 255 and 274 m. A short distance north of Zwarte Hoek on Rakata the depth increased from 80 to 171 m; and between Rakata and Lang Island, at the head of the SE-trending graben, the depth increased from 180 to 188 m. Examination of the submarine profiles has convinced Neumann van Padang[6] that this deepening of the caldera floor cannot be ascribed to an inward sliding of material, as suggested in Escher's theory of caldera formation, but must represent a vertical sagging. For this, several possible explanations may be offered. It might have been produced by a change of volume resulting from crystallization of magma at depth, or by a movement of magma toward the new vent of Anak Krakatau, which began to erupt in 1927, four years after the later soundings were made. Again, it might have been caused by readjustment of the blocks forming the collapsed roof of the magma reservoir, aided by assimilation below or by a redistribution of stresses in the roof consequent upon injection of magma into fissures. Certain it is that the deepening cannot be attributed to submarine explosions. It seems rather to be due to a continuation of the engulfment by which the caldera itself came into being.

A new stage in the history of Krakatau opened in December, 1927, with the rise of the basaltic cinder cone, Anak Krakatau, from the caldera floor. It will suffice here to refer the reader to the careful records of this activity presented by Neumann van Padang and Stehn in the Monthly Bulletins of the Volcanological Survey of the Netherlands East Indies.

[1]Bonney (1912).
[2]Van den Bosch (1929, 1930, 1931).
[3]Brun (1911).
[4]Escher (1919b).
[5]Escher (1928).
[6]Judd (1888a).
[7]Neumann van Padang (1933a).
[8]Reck et al. (1936).
[9]Russell (1897).
[10]Sieberg (1923).
[11]Stehn (1929a).
[12]Verbeek (1886).

In 1968, Williams and McBirney revised Williams' 1941 classification of calderas. The mid-1960's was a time of greatly increased interest in pyroclastic flows—explosively fragmented materials entrained in gas and vapor capable of moving laterally down slope at hurricane velocities—and the 1968 paper reflected that increased interest. The discussion of Krakatau was short, but carried an important modification of Williams' 1941 interpretation. The paroxysmal eruption was described in the following four sentences:

During the fateful days of August 26–28, the pumice falls were followed by tremendous pumice flows, some of the coarse, unstratified and unsorted deposits of which can still be seen lying on the bedded pumice-fall deposits on the adjacent islands. Most of the pumice flows swept across the floor of the Sunda Straits; hence their volume cannot be calculated. There can be no doubt, however, that their total volume was vastly greater than that of the earlier pumice falls, even through they issued within less than two days. Whether the pyroclastic flows issued from the old vents of Danan and Perboewatan or from new fractures opened during the eruptions, cannot be told.

The 1883 Eruption of Krakatau (Self and Rampino, 1981)

The most recent published account of the large 1883 pyroclastic eruptions is by two young geologists who visited the volcano in 1979. Stephen Self and Michael Rampino bring numerous modern volcanological concepts to bear in reinforcing the interpretations of Verbeek (1885), Stehn (1929a), and Williams (1941) that Krakatau caldera was formed by collapse due to voluminous magmatic eruptions. They also introduce the hypothesis that the destructive tsunami were formed when large pyroclastic flows entered the sea. A report by Yokoyama (1981), excerpts of which are included in this volume (see p. 386), offered a different interpretation of events at Krakatau, prompting published discussions of the issues involved (Self and Rampino, 1982; Yokoyama, 1982).

Abstract

The 1883 eruption of Krakatau was a modest ignimbrite-forming event. The deposits are primarily coarse-grained dacitic, non-welded ignimbrite. Large explosions produced pyroclastic flows that entered the sea, generating destructive tsunami. Grain-size studies of the ignimbrite suggest that these explosions were not driven by magma-seawater interaction. The total bulk volume of pyroclastic deposits, including co-ignimbrite ash, is estimated to be 18–21 km.[3]

Although the paroxysmal eruption of Krakatau (or Krakatoa) in 1883 was very spectacular there are little data relating to the mechanism of the eruption, or to interpretation of the pyroclastic deposits in terms of modern volcanologic theory. Studies have concentrated on Anak Krakatau, a young cone growing in the 1883 caldera,[1] and not on the 1883 deposits. The idea of caldera formation by explosive removal of cone material has been revived[36] but we dispute this mechanism.

We report here results mainly from new field investigations at Krakatau during September 1979. We attempt to correlate the eruption sequence reported previously with the stratigraphy of the deposits to re-evaluate proposed mechanisms for the eruption.

Most interpretations of the Krakatau event rest on the studies of Verbeek.[25,26] He is the first to propose that the huge explosions were caused by seawater coming into contact with the magma within the volcano. Deposits resulting from such phreatomagmatic activity for other eruptions are described elsewhere.[14] Verbeek also suggested that reaction with seawater caused the magma to froth, thus forming the extensive pumice ejected in the 1883 eruption. Although this latter interpretation is now seen to be incorrect, the question of interaction of the magma with seawater as a possible cause of the catastrophic explosions is still being debated.[29,36] However, the eruption is usually ascribed to such phreatomagmatic activity.

Later workers have recognized that the near-source deposits of the 1883 eruption were largely emplaced by pyroclastic flows. Williams and McBirney[34] suggested that these flows may have swept for some distance across the floor of the Sunda Straits. We now present evidence that the culminating event of the Krakatau eruption was the generation of pyroclastic flows by gravitational collapse of the eruption column after several large magmatic explosions. We discuss here the role of magma-seawater interaction during the eruption and suggest that the major tsunami that accompanied the eruption were produced when the

pyroclastic flows entered the sea.

Before the eruption of 1883, Krakatau consisted of a large island 9 km long and 5 km wide constructed of three volcanoes, Perbuwatan, Danan and Rakata, situated along a fissure with a prehistoric caldera 7 km in diameter.[33] The surrounding smaller islands of Sertung (formerly Verlaten Island) and Rakata Kecil (Lang Island) are remnants of the rim of the prehistoric caldera (Figure 96). Krakatau Island largely disappeared during the 1883 eruption, leaving only the southern portion of the cone of Rakata volcano (and a small rock pinnacle) exposed above sea level. The consensus of opinion is that the main vent or vents for the 1883 eruption lay between the vents of Perbuwatan and Danan. Our results are consistent with a vent location in this general area; the location of Anak Krakatau may be controlled by the 1883 vent and conduit.

The foundation of the Krakatau volcano is largely basaltic andesite to andesite composition.[31] The 1883 eruption produced a widespread deposit of non-welded dacitic ignimbrite which covers major portions of the present Rakata, Sertung and Rakata Kecil Islands.

Stratigraphy of the 1883 Deposits

We have compared the stratigraphy of the pyroclastic deposits examined in the field with the contemporary eruption records compiled by Verbeek,[25,26] and with the later work of Stehn[23] and Williams.[33] The chronology of the eruption, tsunami, stratospheric effects, and the global spread and transport of long residence time 'dust' were documented in the Krakatoa Committee Report of 1888.[24]

A composite section of the pyroclastic deposits of the 1883 eruption is shown in Figure 97. The stratigraphy of the airfall and pyroclastic surge beds is based primarily on two localities on Sertung and Rakata Kecil Islands (Figure 96), and the stratigraphy of the pyroclastic flow deposits (ignimbrite) is based on several cliff exposures on the western coasts of Rakata and Sertung Islands.

The 1883 eruption began with a period of intermittent mild explosive activity on 20 May 1883. Contemporary reports suggest that on 26 August 1883, at about 13h 00min LT the volcano went into an increasingly explosive phase of eruption, producing a more or less continuous eruption column through explosions at brief intervals (10 min) (see Judd in ref. 24). The largest explosions during this stage of eruption were recorded at 17h 07min on the evening of

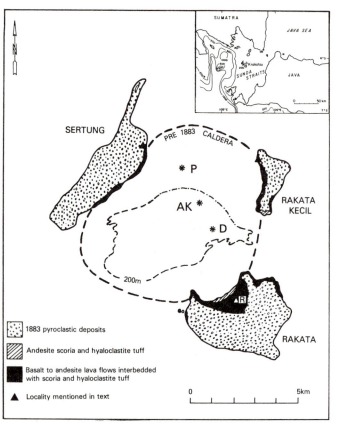

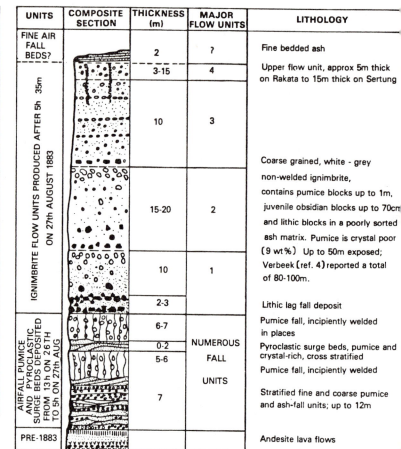

UNITS	COMPOSITE SECTION	THICKNESS (m)	MAJOR FLOW UNITS	LITHOLOGY
FINE AIR FALL BEDS?		2	?	Fine bedded ash
IGNIMBRITE FLOW UNITS PRODUCED AFTER 5h 35m ON 27th AUGUST 1883		3-15	4	Upper flow unit, approx 5m thick on Rakata to 15m thick on Sertung
		10	3	
		15-20	2	Coarse grained, white - grey non-welded ignimbrite, contains pumice blocks up to 1m, juvenile obsidian blocks up to 70cm and lithic blocks in a poorly sorted ash matrix. Pumice is crystal poor (9 wt%) Up to 50m exposed; Verbeek (ref. 4) reported a total of 80-100m.
		10	1	
		2-3		Lithic lag fall deposit
AIRFALL PUMICE AND PYROCLASTIC SURGE BEDS DEPOSITED FROM 13h ON 26TH TO 5h ON 27th AUG		6-7	NUMEROUS FALL UNITS	Pumice fall, incipiently welded in places
		0-2		Pyroclastic surge beds, pumice and crystal-rich, cross stratified
		5-6		Pumice fall, incipiently welded
		7		Stratified fine and coarse pumice and ash-fall units; up to 12m
PRE-1883				Andesite lava flows

Figure 96 (above). Sketch map of Krakatau Islands showing prehistoric caldera, possible 1883 caldera outline (200-m isobath, lighter dashed line, dash-dot where conjectural) and simplified geology. R, Rakata cone; P and D are positions of Perbuwatan and Danan vents on pre-1883 Krakatau Island; AK, vent of Anak Krakatau. Outline of islands is from Indonesian Geological Survey map (1940). Inset: location of Krakatau Islands; isobaths in metres (after ref. 36). [Self and Rampino's figure 1.]

Figure 97 (above right). Composite section through the 1883 pyroclastic deposits. Layers of fine ash at top of section were observed from the boat in cliff sections but were inaccessible to examination in the field. [Self and Rampino's figure 2.]

Figure 98 (below right). Sequence of reported explosions and tsunami during 26–27 August 1883 (all times are local). Data from refs. 24, 25, and 26. Relative magnitudes of explosions, as recorded by the Batavia gasometer, are indicated by lengths of arrows. Approximate eruption column heights given at left are not accurate to more than ± 5 km. Travel times of tsunami from Krakatau to Java and Sumatra coasts estimated at between 30 min and 1 h (ref. 24). [Self and Rampino's figure 3.]

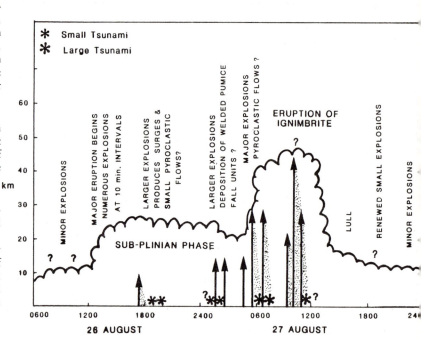

352

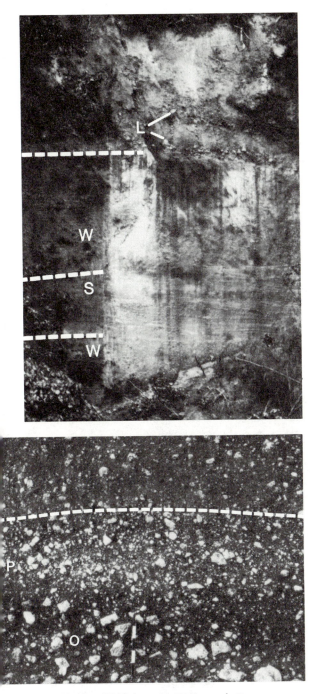

Figure 99. *Above:* Welded pumice ("W"), pyroclastic surge ("S") and lag ("L") deposits on Rakata Kecil Island at locality shown in Figure 96. Cliff section, 15–18 m high. Above and between lag layer is 1883 ignimbrite. *Below:* 1883 Ignimbrite exposed on Rakata Island. Dashed lines, flow-unit boundary; "P," indicates pumice concentration at top of flow unit; "O," juvenile obsidian clast. Scale is 50 cm long with 10 cm bars. [Self and Rampino's figure 4.]

26 August and 1h 42min, 2h 25min and 4h 43min on 27 August (Figure 98; see Judd in ref. 24). The eruption column is reported to have been up to 25 km high during this interval. Ships within 20 km of the volcano reported heavy ash fall, with large pumice clasts (up to 10 cm diameter) (Judd in ref. 24).

The explosions produced fall units of dacitic pumice up to 20 m thick that are exposed on the islands of Rakata Kecil and Sertung. Pyroclastic surge deposits, found interstratified with the fall units, indicate that minor eruption column collapse during this stage of the eruption produced thin, low-density turbulent pyroclastic surges.[4] All outcrops of the fall/surge deposits are very close to the source (only 2 or 3 km from the supposed vent) and it is inferred that the surges were fairly localized (with much material probably flowing onto or into the sea). The fall deposits were probably of sub-plinian type[13,28] and also of modest dispersal. For example, there were reports of only minor ash fall in southern Sumatra and western Java before the climax of the eruption of 27 August[24] ([his] p. 14). No pumice fall deposits were found beneath the pyroclastic-flow and surge deposits on Rakata Island, only 6 km south-east of the vent, even though exposure was excellent. However, the axis of dispersal of the ash fall may have been directed to the west or south-west.[26]

On Rakata Kecil Island, an estimated 3 km from the source vent, two uppermost 5–6-m thick pumice fall units are welded to form a dark-grey coherent deposit, differing markedly in colour from the over- and underlying white dacitic pumice (Figure 99a). Sparks and Wright[19] have described similar welded airfall tuffs of silicic composition; such tuffs are localized around the vent and indicate high rates of eruption and accumulation of pumice, but imply perhaps only moderate (2 km) heights for the gas-thrust part of the eruption column. This combination allows the hot, plastic pumice to sinter and agglutinate under its own weight on deposition. Grain-size analyses of the incipiently welded fall unit show it to be rather poorly sorted ($\sigma\phi = 3.2$), and similar to many previously studied non-welded proximal pumice-fall deposits (Figure 100).

That the pumice-fall deposits are relatively coarse grained compared with phreatoplinian[14] deposits (Fig. 100) suggests that, during the sub-plinian phase of the eruption, the Krakatau explosions were largely magmatic and did not involve significant interaction with seawater. The lithic-poor nature of most of the fall

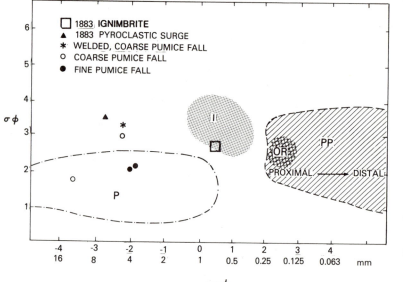

Figure 100. Grain-size characteristics of Krakatau 1883 pyroclastic deposits, summarized on a plot of median diameter $Md\phi$ ($= \phi_{50}$) against graphical $\sigma\phi$ ($= \sigma_{84} - \sigma_{16}/2$), a sorting parameter. The Krakatau pumice-fall deposits are compared with the field of proximal plinian fall deposits ("P") and the field of phreatoplinian deposits ("PP"), after ref. 14. The Krakatau ignimbrite (plot shows area of four analyses) is compared with the field of normal subaerial ignimbrites (layer 2b in ref. 20), ("I") and that of ignimbrite produced from a phreatomagmatic eruption, the Oruanui ("Or") ignimbrite (S.S., in preparation). [Self and Rampino's figure 5.]

deposits also suggests that, during these early stages of the eruption, large-scale break-up and collapse of the volcanic edifice into the conduit (to allow access of seawater) did not occur. The surge deposits at Krakatau are also lithic poor and similar to the thin pumice-rich ground-surge deposits associated with other ignimbrite-forming eruptions and described from several other localities.[20]

At about 5h 30min on 27 August, the style of the eruption changed dramatically (Figure 98). The first of five enormous explosions took place. Wharton[24] gives the times of the largest explosions as 5h 30min, 6h 44min, 9h 29min, 10h 02min and 10h 52min LT on 27 August; Verbeek[25,26] gives slightly different times (3–5 min later) based on a different reading of the gasometer tracing from Batavia, which fortuitously recorded the air waves from the explosions.

We suggest that each large explosion yielded a pyroclastic flow, almost instantaneously, by large-scale gravitational collapse of the eruption column. These flows moved rapidly off the island and into the sea. The four thick major pyroclastic flow units observed in the field (Figure 97) probably correspond to the four largest explosions[23] (Figure 98).

Material came from the vent between explosions, but was probably finer grained and not of significant volume. We may compare this with the Mt. Ngauruhoe, New Zealand eruption sequence of 19 February 1975 (ref. 8) where after an initial period of more or less continuous magma flux, activity declined, then began again with a series of large explosions, each producing a small pyroclastic flow. We propose that the Krakatau eruption sequence was similar but on a much larger scale.

Characteristics of the 1883 Ignimbrite

The Krakatau pyroclastic flows apparently moved preferentially to the north and north-east and covered the islands and surrounding sea floor with dacitic ignimbrite (Figure 101). The biased distribution could be due to directed explosions and/or the topographical control of Rakata volcano (813 m) on the collapsing eruption column, forcing material northwards. The only reports of burns caused by hot ash and gases come from the area around Kalimbang in southern Sumatra, 40 km north-east of Krakatau and 25 km in a direct line from temporary islands produced by the pyroclastic flows. The destruction to the north may have been at the outer edge of a directed blast zone, or perhaps due to ash-cloud surges generated off the

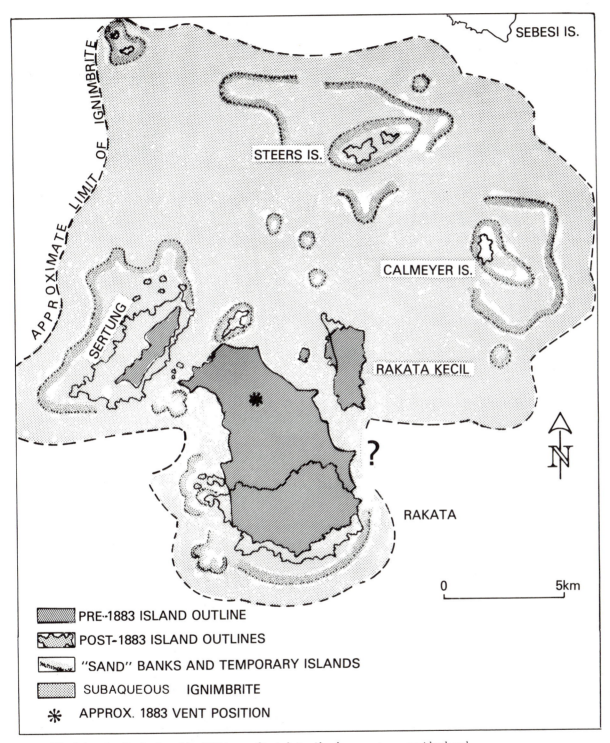

SEBESI IS.

STEERS IS.

CALMEYER IS.

SERTUNG

RAKATA KECIL

APPROXIMATE LIMIT OF IGNIMBRITE

?

RAKATA

N

0   5km

//// PRE-1883 ISLAND OUTLINE

POST-1883 ISLAND OUTLINES

"SAND" BANKS AND TEMPORARY ISLANDS

SUBAQUEOUS   IGNIMBRITE

✳ APPROX. 1883 VENT POSITION

Figure 101. Submarine distribution of the 1883 ignimbrite, inferred from maps and charts in refs. 24
and 26. Hatched area shows outline of the Krakatau
Islands before 1883. Stippled pattern shows extent
of ignimbrite. Also shown are temporary islands and
shallow banks where ignimbrite protruded above sea
level (outline of islands after ref. 24). [Self and Rampino's figure 6.]

tops of moving pyroclastic flows.[4] Such ash-cloud surges can apparently move across water as they did in the St. Pierre disaster in 1902.[5]

Deposition of ignimbrite extended Sertung and Rakata Kecil Islands and the southern and eastern parts of Rakata (Figure 101). Shallowing of the sea floor as far as 15 km to the north of Krakatau[25] was caused by submarine pyroclastic flows that largely filled the 30–40-m deep basin in the sea floor; two new temporary islands, Steers and Calmeyer Islands, were portions of the 40-m thick ignimbrite exposed above sea level (Figure 101). Judd[24] ([his] p. 28) erroneously attributed these pumice banks to the growth of parasitic cones on the flanks of the Krakatau volcano.

Yokoyama[36] suggested that these temporary islands were composed primarily of lithic material derived from the explosive removal of the missing portions of Krakatau Island. However, the field descriptions of Verbeek[25,26] and his chromolithographs of these islands[26] clearly show them to be composed of light-coloured pumice and ash similar to the ignimbrite exposed at Krakatau. The >15 km 'run out' distance of the pyroclastic flows was a result of the vast momentum of several km[3] of pyroclastic debris collapsing from a height of perhaps >5 km (ref. 22).

The 1883 magma was a sparsely porphyritc dacite with 65–68 wt. % SiO_2; the small phenocrysts are plagioclase, augite and minor opaques.[26,31] A small amount (<5 wt.%) of grey and white-streaked, mixed pumice is also present.

The ignimbrite is composed of non-welded pumice and ash with 5 wt. % lithic fragments (Figures 97 and 99b). A small but significant component (<5 wt. % of the deposit) is non-vesiculated to poorly vesiculated obsidian that we consider to be juvenile. The Krakatau ignimbrite has the typical grain-size characteristics of a sub-aerially erupted ignimbrite (Figure 100). This contrasts with fine-grained phreatoplinian deposits[14] and associated ignimbrites (S.S., in preparation), which were apparently erupted through water. These ignimbrites are much finer grained than the Krakatau ignimbrite, especially in their lack of large-sized components near source (Figure 100). This again indicates that magma-seawater interaction did not have a significant role in the fragmentation of the magma during the 1883 Krakatau eruption.

Initiation of Ignimbrite-forming Explosions

Verbeek[25,26] suggested that the Krakatau eruption became submarine at about 10h on 27 August as a result of foundering of the volcanic edifice, and that the largest explosions were caused by seawater rushing into the vent, making contact with the hot magma and causing it to froth explosively into pumice. By contrast, Judd[24] argued that entry of large amounts of seawater into the vent would chill the magma and cause it to crust over. Gas would then accumulate below this crust until explosive pressures were reached. These ideas both assume that the volcano was collapsing before the explosions. However, the evidence suggests that this was not the case, and that the subsidence of Krakatau and formation of the caldera took place late in the eruption sequence.

First, lithic debris makes up only ~5% of the deposits which suggests that large-scale collapse of old cone material into the vent was not taking place during the eruption.[33] Second, the coarse-grained nature of both the pumice-fall deposits and the ignimbrite suggests that fragmentation was not caused by magma-seawater interaction. Third, the pyroclastic flow deposits that cover the southeastern part of Rakata Island, and which must have come from one of the vents to the northwest, would be cut off from their apparent source by the caldera wall collapse (Figure 101). Thus we propose that the large pyroclastic flows were erupted before major collapse of the volcano.

The 1883 caldera lies within the prehistoric Krakatau caldera (~7 km diameter; Figure 96), and seems to be a graben-like feature extending along two intersecting zones of fractures.[33] The 'missing' portion of the cone of Rakata may represent a large-scale slump of material into the east-west elongated caldera. The > 250-m deep caldera was apparently not extensively filled with deposits of 1883 ignimbrite, also suggesting caldera collapse after the eruption of the major pyroclastic flows and emptying of the magma chamber.

We propose that seawater in large quantities did not gain access to the vent during the most explosive stages of the eruption but that seawater may have leaked slowly into the conduit area, sparking small phreatomagmatic explosions. Such explosions would have broken a cap of viscous magma and allowed sudden, explosive release of large batches of vesiculated magma from beneath the upper conduit system.[12,15,35] Contemporary accounts indicate that the explosive activity subsided in the early hours of 27 August before the large explosions started (Figure 98). This may have allowed a partly solidified plug to develop in the vent, facilitating the above mechanism. The presence of juvenile obsidian clasts in the ignimbrite might indicate partly solidified magma in the vent.

It has been suggested that some large volcanic explosions can be triggered by magma mixing.[3,23] Sudden mixing of rhyolitic and basaltic or andesitic magma might lead to violent exsolution of dissolved volatiles. A small percentage (< 5%) of grey and white-streaked pumice occurs in the Krakatau ignimbrite, suggesting some mixing of magmas. However, we cannot envision a magma-mixing process that would adequately explain the sequence and timing of the large explosions of Krakatau as alluded to by Rice.[11] Magma mixing may have had a role in initiating the eruption, but we do not believe that mixing events were the prime cause of the major explosions on 27 August.

Co-ignimbrite Ash

During the eruption of the pyroclastic flows, much vitric dust was dispersed in the atmosphere and formed a widespread thin, fine ash-fall deposit.[26] Considerable distal ash fall did not occur until the large explosions of 27 August, and we suggest that the widespread ash fall was mainly co-ignimbrite ash.[18]

Mechanisms envisaged for the generation of the high-altitude column of fine vitric dust and gases that accompanies many events involving production of pyroclastic flows are: (1) rise of selectively fine (low terminal fall velocity) material above the vent; (2) generation of ash from the moving pyroclastic flows; and (3) secondary explosions that may occur as hot pyroclastic flows enter the sea.[29] Evidence for this type of secondary explosion was not found at Krakatau, possibly because of the lack of lateral exposure. However, the expected airfall layers produced by such secondary explosions are not present between the ignimbrite flow units at Krakatau in the outcrops we examined.

All large ignimbrite eruptions are accompanied by the production of co-ignimbrite ash.[18] This fine ash consists of the vitric component—pumice shards and fragmented shards commonly from 50 μm down to a few μm in diameter. The finest ash was capable of significant stratospheric residence times varying from days to months (depending on size). This dust may have been partly responsible for the widespread atmospheric optical phenomena observed after the August 1883 eruption,[2,24,32] although the sulphate aerosols generated by the eruption were probably more important.[6]

Volume of the 1883 Eruption

Calculations of the total volume of ejecta from the 1883 eruption must include the volume of widely dispersed dust and ash as well as the subaqueous ignimbrite. Volumetric estimates range widely from Verbeek's 18 km^3 for the total ejecta,[25,26] to the Royal Society's value of 14.4 km^3 for the fine distal ash fall alone,[24] to recent estimates of 13 ± 4 km^3 (ref. 36) and only 5 km^3 (ref. 7) for the total ejecta based on the volume of the caldera.

Close to Krakatau, Verbeek[26] estimated from field investigations and depth soundings of the sea bottom before and after the eruption that 12 km^3 (bulk volume) was ejected. This is a reasonable figure for the volume of ignimbrite produced, based on a sheet of ignimbrite averaging ~40 m thick and covering an area of ~300 km^2 (Figure 101). Verbeek also considered the volume of widely dispersed ash and estimated this to be 6 km^3. This value must be a minimum because it only considers a portion of the total dispersal area, which the Krakatoa Committee estimated to be 1.1 × 10^6 miles^2 (see [his] ref. 24, p. 448). Our recalculation of the volume of widely dispersed ash from data in ref. 26, using an area against thickness plot and extrapolating to 1 mm thickness[30], gives 8.5 km^3. Recent studies of co-ignimbrite ash volumes compared with the volume of the parent ignimbrite indicate that up to 50% of the magma erupted can be co-ignimbrite ash.[17,18] Applying the methods for estimating crystal concentration in ignimbrites,[18,27] preliminary studies suggest that the Krakatau ignimbrite must have lost at least 40% of the vitric component into the fine co-ignimbrite ash, which therefore has a minimum volume of ~5 km^3. The above calculations suggest a bulk volume of fine, dispersed ash between ~5 km^3 and 8.5 km^3.

The pre-27 August sub-plinian fall and surge deposits are thought to be of small volume, probably < 1 km^3. Analysis of samples suggests that only 8% of fine vitric material in these deposits is missing. Therefore, the volume of fine ash produced during the sub-plinian phase of the eruption is very small compared with that emitted during the ignimbrite-forming phase. When the amounts of ignimbrite, co-ignimbrite ash and sub-plinian deposits are added up, the total bulk volume of the 1883 Krakatau deposits is 18–21 km^3. The equivalent volume of dense rock may be roughly estimated as 9–10 km^3.

Generation of Tsunami

The Krakatau eruption also produced tsunami that inundated coastal areas around the Sunda Straits. These tsunami are generally attributed to submarine explosions or to caldera collapse[9,33] although ejecta falling into the sea has also been suggested.[24,25,26] The evidence indicates that the tsunami were caused by several cubic kilometres of pyroclastic flow material entering into the sea immediately after each of the large explosions.

The early small explosions of 26 August were followed by small tsunami (Figure 98). For example, an explosion occurred at about 17h 20min on 26 August, and the first destructive waves reached the Java and Sumatra shores 40 km from Krakatau soon afterwards, between 18h and 19h. This early wave or waves may have been due to surges or small pyroclastic flows entering the sea. No other destructive waves were observed until the morning of 27 August (Wharton[24]). At about 6h 30min a large wave swept over much of the Java coast; another wave followed at about 7h 30min. At about the same time a wave hit low-lying areas of Sumatra. These waves followed the large explosions at 5h 30min and 6h 44min (Figure 98).

At some time after 10h a gigantic wave (or waves) inundated the coasts bordering the Sunda Straits. This wave is reported to have been the largest, and was the last recorded in the straits; most survivors of the earlier waves had by this time fled from the coastal areas. The tide gauge at Batavia (Jakarta) also recorded waves that correspond to the large explosions.

The sequence and timing of tsunami suggest that the major tsunami were generated at the times of the explosions (Wharton[24]). Pyroclastic flows resulting from column collapse would have entered the sea within about ~30 sec of the explosions[22] and initiated the tsunami. The slumping of large parts of the volcano, for example the segment of Rakata cone that probably slid into the caldera, could have been a factor in generating tsunami late in the eruption. The idea that tsunami can be caused by pyroclastic flows entering the sea is supported by a study of the huge eruption of Tambora in 1815 during which tsunami were generated which flooded the nearby coasts of Sumbawa to a height of 4 m, and Java to a height of 2 m (ref. 27). These waves could not have been produced by magma–seawater interactions or caldera collapse, as the volcanic crater lies some 15–20 km inland at an elevation of about 2,850 m. Pyroclastic-flow deposits from the 1815 eruption entered the sea at the base of the volcano (M.R.R. and S.S., in preparation), and this was the most likely cause. The large tsunami that are inferred to have accompanied the Minoan eruption of Santorini[9] may have been generated in the same way.

We conclude that the 1883 eruption was an ignimbrite-forming event of modest volume. The deposits are largely coarse-grained non-welded dacitic ignimbrite and show little support for a phreatomagmatic origin. The occurrence of welded pumice-fall deposits beneath the ignimbrite also seems to argue against water–magma interaction in the early stages of the eruption. The presence of mixed pumice clasts indicates some magma mixing and supports the contention that welded airfall deposits result, in some cases, from superheating of magma during a mixing event.[19]

During the paroxysmal phase, four or five large-volume explosions driven by magmatic gases led to collapse of the eruption column, and to the production of pyroclastic flows that entered the sea. The blasts and ensuing pyroclastic flows seem to have been directed preferentially towards the north and northeast. The times of the explosions correlate with the times of tsunami generation, and we propose that the entry of the pyroclastic flows into the sea caused the major tsunami. Caldera collapse probably came late in the eruption.

The total volume of the deposits of the Krakatau eruption is estimated to be 18–21 km³ (bulk volume), including 12 km³ of ignimbrite and up to 8.5 km³ of distal co-ignimbrite ash fall. When compared with prehistoric ignimbrite-forming events, ranging in volume up to 10³ km³ (refs. 10,16), the volume of the Krakatau eruption was very modest.

We thank Adjat Sudradjat and Rudi Hadisantono of the Indonesian Volcanological Survey, Bandung, for their support and assistance. G.P.L. Walker critically review the paper, and J.V. Wright supplied useful ideas and constructive criticism. This work was supported by NASA grant NSG 5145. M.R.R. was a National Academy of Sciences Research Associate during this study. We thank the Indonesian Institute of Sciences (LIPI) for permission to work at Krakatau.

[1]Decker and Hadikusomo (1961).
[2]Deirmendjian (1973).
[3]Eichelberger (1978).
[4]Fisher (1979).
[5]Fisher et al. (1981).
[6]Hansen et al. (1978).
[7]Kent (1981).
[8]Nairn and Self (1978).
[9]Neumann van Padang (1971).
[10]Ninkovich et al. (1978).
[11]Rice (1981).
[12]Schmincke (1977).
[13]Self (1976).
[14]Self and Sparks (1978).

[15]Self et al. (1979).
[16]Smith (1979).
[17]Sparks and Huang (1980).
[18]Sparks and Walker (1977).
[19]Sparks and Wright (1979).
[20]Sparks et al. (1973).
[21]Sparks et al. (1977).
[22]Sparks et al. (1978).
[23]Stehn (1929a).
[24]Symons (1888).
[25]Verbeek (1884).
[26]Verbeek (1886) [French edition of Verbeek, 1885].
[27]Walker (1972).
[28]Walker (1973).
[29]Walker (1979).
[30]Walker (1980).
[31]Westerveld (1952).
[32]Wexler (1951).
[33]Williams (1941).
[34]Williams and McBirney (1968).
[35]Wilson (1980).
[36]Yokoyama (1981).

Most Recent Activity (SEAN Bulletin, 1981)

When the above paper was published, Anak Krakatau was continuing its Strombolian activity. We reprint here the description reported in the December 1981 Bulletin of the Scientific Event Alert Network, a monthly review of contemporary volcanic and other geophysical events around the world published here at the Smithsonian (and available through the American Geophysical Union, 2000 Florida Ave. NW, Washington, D.C. 20009). This is the most recent report known to us of the on-going activity at Anak Krakatau.

KRAKATAU VOLCANO, Sunda Strait, Indonesia (6.10°S, 105.42°E). All times are local (= GMT + 7 hours).

Explosions from Anak Krakatau resumed 20 October after several months of fumarolic activity. Guy Camus and Pierre Vincent visited the volcano for 4 hours during the afternoon of 19 October, but noticed no premonitory activity. Explosions began between 0300 and 0400 the next morning. From Rakata Island (about 3 km SE of Anak Krakatau), Camus and Vincent noted 19 explosions in the 2 hours just after sunrise, before leaving the island. They had seen several others by midafternoon during discontinuous ob-

servations from a boat. Most were initiated by a "cannon-like" explosion from the main cone, followed by convective growth of an eruption column, (typically to 400–600 m, but occasionally to 1 km in height). No noise could be heard on Rakata Island. The explosions usually lasted from one to several minutes, but the last one observed by Camus and Vincent as they left the area began at 1511 and continued until 1525. Most of the eruption columns were dark, containing abundant ash but few blocks and no incandescent material. Water vapor could be seen condensing at the top of several eruption columns and lightning was occasionally observed. Ash fell on Sertung Island, about 2 km W of Anak Krakatau.

Information Contacts: Guy Camus and Pierre M. Vincent, Département de Géologie et Minéralogie, 5, Rue Kessler, 63000 Clermont-Ferrand, France.

Development of Anak Krakatau (Sudradjat, 1982)

One of the most recent publications on the volcanology of Krakatau is the 1982 review of Anak Krakatau's development by Dr. A. Sudradjat, Director of the Volcanological Survey of Indonesia. We reprint much of this paper here, including the important observation that pre-1927 activity at Anak Krakatau is indicated by bathymetric charts of 1919. We also supplement this paper with three illustrations from a much longer and more detailed 1981 review of Anak Krakatau by G.A. de Nève, Professor of geology at Padjadjaran and Hasanuddin Universities, who has been reporting on Krakatau volcanism for the last 30 years.

The Development of Submarine Anak Krakatau Volcano

After the gigantic eruption of 1883 several investigations were carried out. The first surveys immediately after the eruption[8,11] recorded the new configurations of the islands of the Krakatau complex (Figure 102) [see also p. 137]. Volcanic deposits consisting mainly of pumice surrounded the surviving islands. The three volcanic bodies of Rakata, Danan and Perbuatan were partly or completely destroyed by the eruption, but Sertung [Verlaten] and Panjang [Lang] became larger. Sertung Island located NW of Rakata

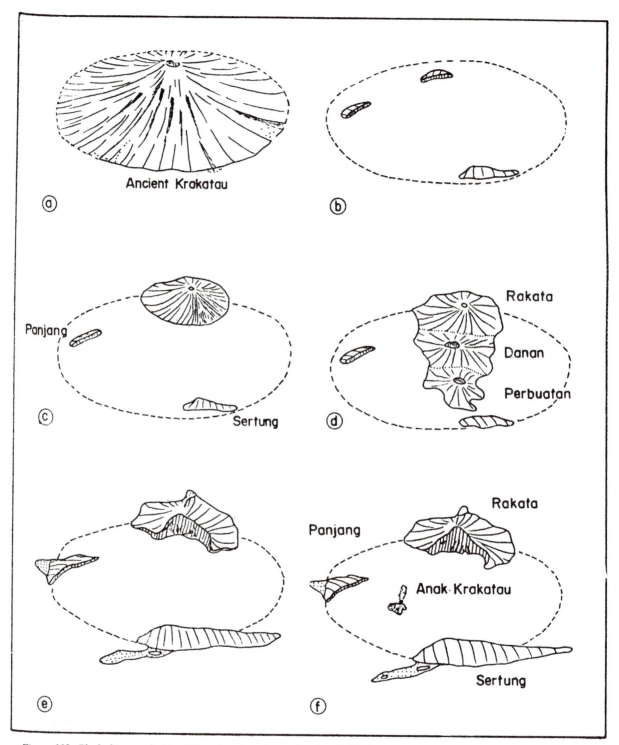

Ancient Krakatau

(a)

(b)

Panjang

Sertung

(c)

Rakata

Danan

Perbuatan

Panjang

(d)

Rakata

Anak·Krakatau

Sertung

(e)

(f)

Figure 102. Block diagrams looking SE-wards at Krakatau volcano complex showing schematic development of Krakatau Volcano before (a to d) and after (e to f) the 1883 outburst. The latest post-eruption diagram shows the present situation of Krakatau volcano after the Child of Krakatau was born in 1927. (Figure adopted from and after Escher, 1919, completed for recent situation by Sudradjat, 1981). [Sudradjat's figure 1.]

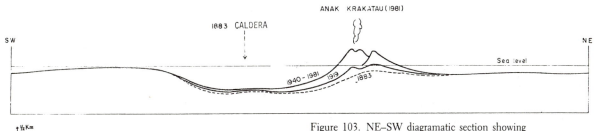

ANAK KRAKATAU (1981)

1883 CALDERA

SW

NE

Sea level

1940 - 1981

1919

1883

Figure 103. NE–SW diagramatic section showing the sea floor development of Krakatau Complex after 1883 eruption. [Sudradjat's figure 4.]

had grown almost three times as large as it was before the eruption, while Panjang Island, NE of Rakata, was partly destroyed and partly enlarged. The twin volcanoes Danan and Perbuatan completely disappeared, as did the northwestern part of Rakata. On the other hand the western and southern coasts of Rakata grew almost 1 km to the southwest and south respectively.

The steep wall created by the eruption on the NW coast of Rakata island revealed the inner geological formation of the dormant Rakata volcano. This natural section is well exposed across the middle part of the volcanic body. Escher[1] and later van Bemmelen[9] studied the section.

Typical strato deposits intruded by dykes were readily observable across the wall. Escher[1] noted that more than 25 dykes were counted.

A bathymetric chart was first prepared by Symons[8] and then by Escher.[1] It appears that a caldera with a depth of more than 250 m and elongated approximately SW was formed NW of Rakata Island. This submarine caldera at the depth of 100 m below sealevel was approximately 9–10 km long and 2 km wide. Volcaniclastic deposits probably consisting mainly of volcanic sands or base surge deposits were found scattered around Sertung and Panjang islands.

The bathymetric survey by Escher[1] indicated morphology of a parasitic cone that grew from the caldera floor. However, an accurate position of Anak Krakatau determined later by Neumann van Padang[3] revealed the central activity to be north of the cone, which was supposedly the embryo of the volcano as based on submarine morphological account. Apparently the submarine Anak Krakatau volcano had grown up to an orifice on the inner NE slope of the 1883 caldera, or slightly north of the line connecting the earlier central Danan and Perbuatan. The survey has also revealed that the caldera had become deeper as it compared with the situation in 1888 (ref. 1). This perhaps very closely related with the subsidence of the crater's floor due to the compaction and bedding-in of the crater.

An underwater shoe-shaped ridge with a small rock island (Bootmans Rock) sticking out was discovered

during the 1919 survey SW of Panjang Island. This tiny island perhaps represents a NE orifice of the caldera or it may be a relief part of the old Danan volcano.

The initial activity of Anak Krakatau had not been noticed in the 1919 survey. There were no underwater topographic signatures marking the initial development of the submarine Anak Krakatau volcano, before the eruption was noticed at the surface.

The activity of Anak Krakatau was first noticed in December 1927 until January 1928. It mainly produced steam that rose several tens of meters high. The first air reconnaissance was carried out in January [1928] by Nash[2] to locate the activity. A new island was observed in the location of the activity forming a sand dune-like shape with the concave steeper slope facing southwest. The lateral extension was approximately 8–10 m. The survey carried out later measured the height of the crest at 8.93 m above sealevel. This was the birth of Child of Krakatau that was witnessed. The development was then studied through a series of topographical surveys carried out regularly by Neumann van Padang[3,4,5] and then by van Bemmelen[10] and by the Volcanological Survey of Indonesia since 1950. The location of Anak Krakatau Volcano and the bathymetric chart of the 1919 survey are shown in [Figure 72, see p. 315].

The development of the submarine caldera after the eruption was significant due to the sedimentation of volcanic materials supplied by Anak Krakatau. The deepest part of submarine caldera's floor had become shallower from 279 m to approximately 250 m while the shallower part of the floor was found to be between 200–250 m below sealevel. In general the caldera had been filled with approximately 20–30 m of volcanic materials during the period of 1919 to 1940; in the NE part of the caldera, closer to the vent, the thickness of deposits ranged from 20–70 m. The rate of deposition thickening, therefore, is estimated to be approximately 1 to 3.5 m annually. A recent bathymetric chart has not yet been obtained in order to compare the rate for the last 40 years. However, from the periodicity and magnitude of the eruption of Anak Krakatau it is very likely that the rate has remained stable during this period (Figure 103).

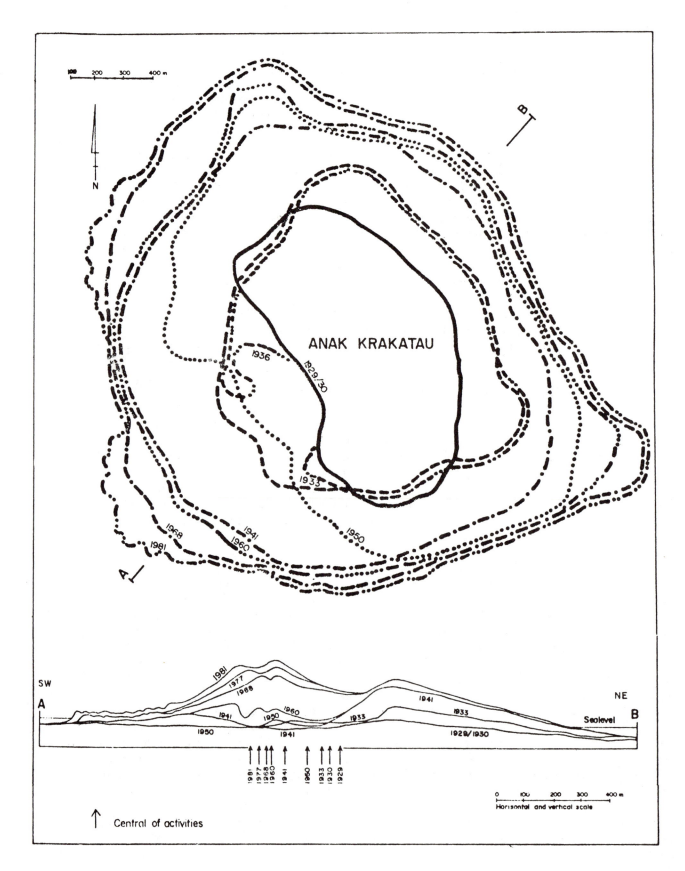

ANAK KRAKATAU

Year	Island size		Highest elevation above sealevel (m)	
	SW-NE (m)	NW-SE (m)	Old crater's rim (OCR)	New volcano summit (NVS)
1930	450	900	8.93	submarine activity
1931	550	1000	47,2	submarine activity
1932	750	1000	37,6	craterlake
1933	1000	1500	66,8 92,7)	craterlake
1934	1000	1150	88,19	craterlake
1935	950	1250	88,47)	craterlake
	1150	1250	59,8	
1936	850	1250)	62,49	submarine activity
	600	1250		
1941	1400	1600	132,32	craterlake
1950	550	1700	138,70	new volcanic cone started to emerge; elevation 3,33
1960	1450	1700	166,70	elevation ± 30; lake started to dry
1968	1600	1900	169,67	159,46
1977	1900	2000	154,657	181,445
1981	1950	2000	151,66	199,29

Figure 105. Topographic development of Anak Krakatau (1930–1981). [Sudradjat's table 1.]

Topographic Development of Anak Krakatau

The newly born Anak Krakatau was intensively surveyed in the 1930's for the fear of a recurrence of the hazardous 1883 eruption. An observation post was set up in Panjang Island to observe the volcano, and regular visits were carried out by volcanologists and observers. Accurate topographical changes, therefore, were recorded, particularly in the initial stages of development of the volcano.

The sand dune-like shape of the newly born island, with an elevation of 8.93 m, grew relatively fast in the first decade of its existence. The island had grown from 8.39 m elevation to 66.8 m in 1933, and 132.32 m in 1941, and eventually to 169.67 m in 1968. The elevation changes were accompanied by increases in the islands lateral dimensions (Figure 104). Figure

Figure 104. Coastline development of Anak Krakatau Volcano Island since its birth in 1927/1929 and vertical development across NW–SE section (below). Center of activity seemingly has moved SW-wardly to the submarine caldera of 1883 eruption. [Sudradjat's figure 5.]

105 shows the topographic development of Anak Krakatau island from 1930 to 1981. Measurements have been made on the development of the NW-SE and SW-SE diameter of the island to record the development of the coastline. The NW-SE diameter shows the continous development of the island. A minor break was encountered during the period of 1950 to 1960, perhaps related to the building up of a new volcanic cone during this period. The irregular development of the coastlines was well observed in the SW-SE diameter of the island. Within this period three significant breaks had been encountered, namely in 1934, 1935, and 1950. During this period a destructive coastline development occurred, very likely related to the submarine sliding toward the SW where the volcano's submarine basement was relatively steep facing the caldera's floor, as suggested by Neumann van Padang.[5]

The volcanic activity controlled very closely the development of the coastline and the elevations of the island as a result of the piling up of volcanic products. The regular increase in elevation during the first stage of Anak Krakatau volcano was accompanied by the increase in diameter of the island. A collapse occurred in 1934, which was reflected in decreases in the SW-NE diameter and in the elevation. A similar situation occurred in 1935, whereas by 1950 collapse had greatly reduced the SW-NE width of the island but not the elevation itself.

The elevation development of the island decreased in the early 1960's, perhaps after it exceeded the culmination point, due to the development of a new cone that started in 1950. Here the development has been progressing very smoothly since its birth within the last 30 year period. The present rate of increase in elevation of Anak Krakatau has been estimated at approximately 4–4.25 m a year.

Based on the island outline map and elevation chart a rough claculation was compiled to estimate the volume of volcanic deposits that built up the island. Ignoring the materials deposited on the seabed and washed away from the volcanic body, and also the materials carried out by wind, the volcanic material produced in the first 20 years was estimated to be 26.2 × 10^6 m^3 or a rate of 1.3 × 10^6 m^3 a year. The development of a new cone since 1950 has produced 42.6 × 10^6 m^3 of materials or approximately 1.4 × 10^6 m^3 a year. It seems the development was stable with a rate of 1.3 × 10^6 m^3 a year.

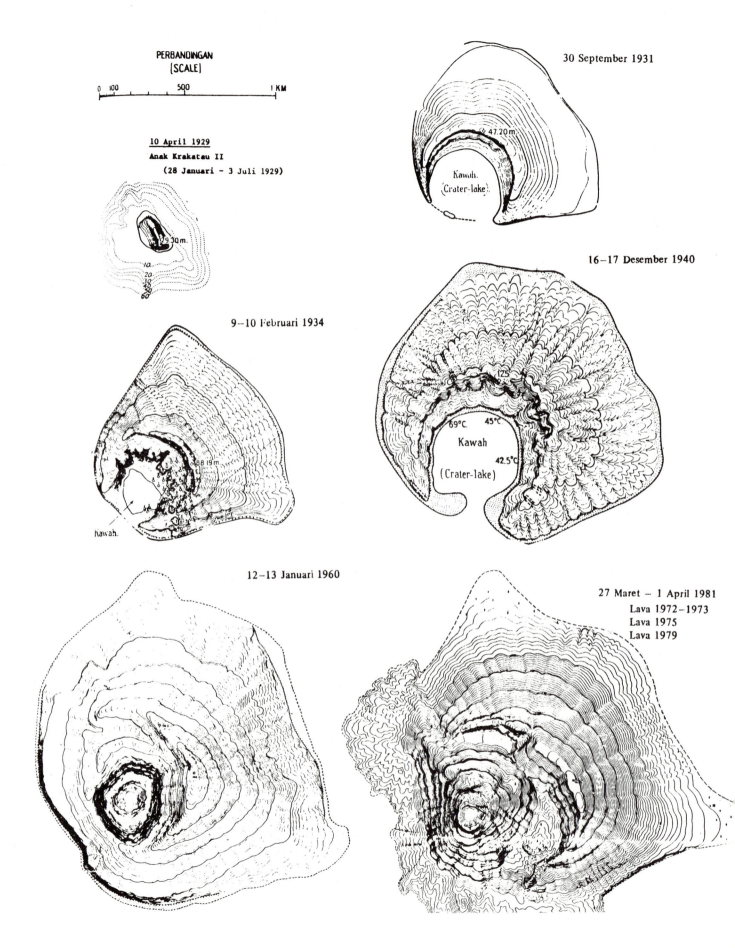

PERBANDINGAN
(SCALE)

0   100   500   1 KM

10 April 1929
Anak Krakatau II
(28 Januari – 3 Juli 1929)

179.30 m.

30 September 1931

47.20 m.

Kawah.
(Crater-lake).

9–10 Februari 1934

88.19 m.

Kawah.

16–17 Desember 1940

125

69°C.   45°C.

Kawah

(Crater-lake)   42.5°C.

12–13 Januari 1960

27 Maret – 1 April 1981
Lava 1972–1973
Lava 1975
Lava 1979

364

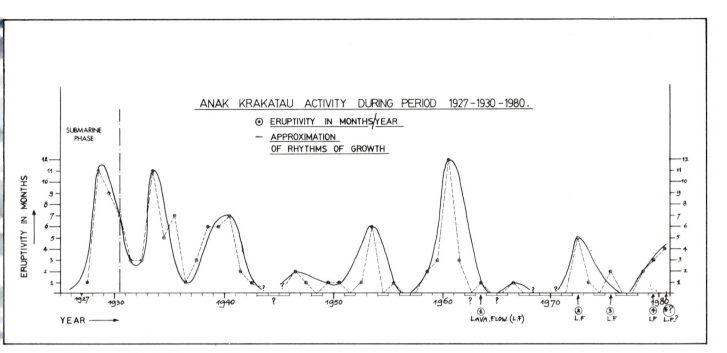

Figure 107. Overview of Anak Krakatau's activity [also from de Nève, 1981, diagram I] from the time of its submarine birth in 1927 until the end of 1980. For each year the "eruptivity" is indicated by number of months in which the volcano was active; the solid line gives an approximation of the evolutionary rhythms of developmental growth.

Figure 106. Selected topographic maps of Anak Krakatau, all at the same scale, to supplement the preceding illustration. These maps, from the 45 maps neatly assembled and presented by de Nève, 1981, illustrate the volcano's growth. The early stages were characterized by phreatomagmatic activity—the explosive fragmentation of hot lava upon contact with cold seawater. By 1960, however, the cone had grown large and the vent area became sealed off from the sea, permitting the non-explosive emission of basaltic lava flows in 1961. The most recent map, in 1981, shows many more lava flows having pushed out into the sea on the SW side, ensuring the survival of this island in its long battle with the waves.

Discussion of the Morphologic Development of Anak Krakatau

The submarine caldera that existed after the destructive eruption of 1883 was formed in the caldera of the Ancient Krakatau of Escher [see Figure 102, p. 360].[1] A hypothetical gigantic volcano destroyed itself several centuries before the twin volcano of Danan and Perbuatan came into being. A speculation envisaged by de Nève[13] suspects the ancient caldera formation perhaps took place in the third century AD based on the available historic documents and the sea floor volcanic deposits found in the Java Trench. If the assumption is true, the development of Rakata, Danan, and Perbuatan had taken place around 15 centuries ago until they destroyed themselves, and later Anak Krakatau volcano came into existence after the 1883 eruption.

The 1883 caldera, formed within the ancient one, was somewhat elliptical in a SW direction. The caldera formation has been discussed by several authors. Stehn[7] [see p. 322] assumed the caldera formed as a result of volcano collapse due to the space left by removal of gas and magma while Yokoyama[12] concluded that the caldera was formed by the ejection of materials (based on geophysical results of a gravimetric survey). On the generation of tsunamis that swept the

365

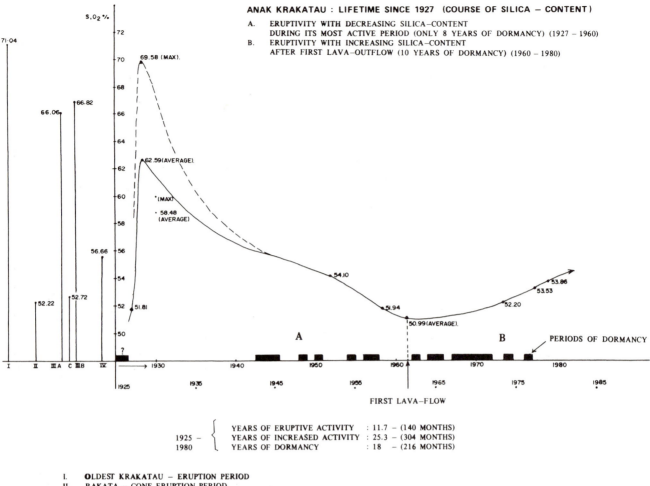

A. ERUPTIVITY WITH DECREASING SILICA–CONTENT
    DURING ITS MOST ACTIVE PERIOD (ONLY 8 YEARS OF DORMANCY) (1927 – 1960)
B. ERUPTIVITY WITH INCREASING SILICA–CONTENT
    AFTER FIRST LAVA–OUTFLOW (10 YEARS OF DORMANCY) (1960 – 1980)

FIRST LAVA–FLOW

1925 –
1980
{
YEARS OF ERUPTIVE ACTIVITY : 11.7 – (140 MONTHS)
YEARS OF INCREASED ACTIVITY : 25.3 – (304 MONTHS)
YEARS OF DORMANCY   : 18 – (216 MONTHS)

I. OLDEST KRAKATAU – ERUPTION PERIOD
II. RAKATA – CONE ERUPTION PERIOD
IIIA–IIIB. PERBUWATAN – DANAN ERUPTION PERIOD – PAROXYSM OF 1883 KRAKATAU ERUPTION / C. XENOLITH AVERAGE SILICA–CONTENT.
IV. ANAK KRAKATAU ERUPTION PERIOD (AVERAGE SILICA–CONTENT).
(1927 – 1980)

Figure 108. Chemical changes in Anak Krakatau's ejectamenta (again from de Nève, 1981, diagram II) during fifty years of its growth (1930–1980). Silica content is plotted against time, and earlier phases of Krakatau's development are shown by vertical lines (not to time scale) to the left of the 1930 start of Anak Krakatau's data.

Java and Sumatra coasts Stehn accounted that the tsunamis had been caused by the volcano collapse during the caldera formation. He also gave other arguments such as the energy release during the eruption or perhaps the submarine landsliding. Yokoyama suggested that the tsunamis were generated by the energy released when volcanic material totalling 18 km³ was ejected. His analysis was also supported by the signatures of the wave records available in places.

The location of Anak Krakatau was at the orifice on the upper part of the NE inner slope of the submarine caldera. This influenced the development of Anak Krakatau and perhaps the shifting of location of activity. Based on the development of the island it may be noticed that there was an apparent shifting to the SW of the center of activities since 1930 to 1981 (Figure 104). The previous activities of Rakata-Danan-Perbuatan located along the linear zone trending NW-

SE, whilst the 1883 eruption supposedly also occurred at this lineament.[6,12]

It is speculated that the activity center will continue shifting towards the Rakata-Danan-Perbuatan line. The fact is that the development of the Anak Krakatau's volcanic body has been towards the SW, including the lava outpourings that occurred several times in the last 20 years. This may also have been the result of the seafloor configuration. The landsliding evidence noted by Neumann van Padang[5] in the early stages of Anak Krakatau contributed to the idea of the seafloor influence in the development of Anak Krakatau island.

[1]Escher (1919a).
[2]Nash (1929).
[3]Neumann van Padang (1933b).
[4]Neumann van Padang (1935).

[5]Neumann van Padang (1936a).
[6]Self (1979).
[7]Stehn (1929a).
[8]Symons (1888).
[9]Van Bemmelen (1934).
[10]Van Bemmelen (1941).
[11]Verbeek (1885).
[12]Yokoyama (1981).
[13]Oral communication (1981) [see also de Néve, 1981].

Waves: Air and Sea

The culminating explosion at 10 a.m. on August 27 sent shockwaves through the atmosphere that were recorded by barographs throughout the world and heard by human eardrums over 4600 km from Krakatau (see p. 146). Murray-Aaron, emphasizing the size of the explosion in a popular 1900 article,[3] writes:

If a man were to meet a resident of Philadelphia and tell him that he had heard an explosion in Trenton, thirty miles away; he might be believed, although there would be some doubt as to his powers of imagination. If, however, he should make the same assertion of an explosion in Wheeling, West Virginia, three hundred miles away, all doubts of his accuracy would vanish. But if, with every sign of sincerity and a desire to be believed, he should earnestly insist upon his having heard an explosion in San Francisco, *three thousand miles away*, he would receive a pitying smile, and his listener would silently walk away. Yet just this last marvelous thing was true of those who, on the island of Rodriguez, over toward Madagascar, two thousand nine hundred and sixty-eight miles away, heard clearly and beyond doubt the faint sound of the ear-splitting detonation in the Strait of Sunda. In India, in Australia, and in every direction, literally for thousands of miles around, this sound was carried.

But the distribution of sound was surprising. The reported sounds seemed unusually loud at some distant locations while, as in many eruptions, some areas quite near the volcano reported little or no noise. Sound waves from large explosions are reflected back to earth from air layers in the atmosphere. As explained by Bolt,[1] "Because the sound velocity in the atmosphere first decreases and then increases with altitude, at some distances the sound may focus, like rays of light through a lens. At short range, the zone of silence is disturbed only by weak sound waves diffracted along the ground." Furthermore, as anyone who has walked through a gentle snowfall knows, the presence of particles in the nearby atmosphere wonderfully muffles sound transmission, and the areas experiencing heavy ashfall from Krakatau must have been similarly quiet.

In addition to the dramatic sound waves, the much lower frequency air wave detected by meteorological stations around the globe aroused widespread scientific interest. This great wave, reflected back and forth around the earth, taught meteorologists much about atmospheric wave propagation and was widely referenced after World War II when study of large, man-made explosions increased. The Krakatau air wave also proved critical to understanding the far-traveled sea waves, as will be described below, and the relationship between air and sea waves—the only two phenomena for which we have instrumental records—has been important in developing a well-timed chronology of the paroxysmal events of 1883. Therefore we have combined interpretations of air and sea waves in this section.

The devastating sea waves, or tsunami, were much emphasized in the narrative accounts of Part II, but their scientific understanding remains the most puzzling aspect of the 1883 events at Krakatau. The wave mechanics, however, are reasonably well understood for these long-period waves where crest-to-crest distances often exceed 100 km. In a popular article on tsunami, an anonymous author[3] writes that:

Its speed is proportional to the square root of the depth of the water: a tsunami wave in water 18,000 feet deep travels about 500 miles an hour; in water 900 feet deep, 115 miles an hour; and in 60 feet, 30 miles an hour. When a tsunami approaches shore, shoaling causes its waves to telescope by increasingly restricting their forward motion as the water becomes shallower. Also, the waves grow taller and the distance between them shrinks. In this fashion, a 2-foot wave traveling 500 miles an hour in deep water becomes a 100-foot killer traveling 30 miles an hour when it approaches shore. Throughout, however, the time interval between crests tends to remain large; this is one of the most significant characteristics of a tsunami at any stage. The effect of the same tsunami wave may be vastly different from one point on shore to another. Local topography is usually responsible: a bay or an an estuary has a funneling effect, which accentuates the height of the wave; an offshore shoal or sandbar diminishes it. This is why in one area the wave may be 50 feet tall, while at a point a few miles away it might be only 5 feet in height.

What remains uncertain about the Krakatau waves is their cause. Williams (p. 347) has summarized 4 wave-forming mechanisms, all of which undoubtedly operated during the paroxysm: (1) huge masses of Krakatau Island thundered down into the sea during the collapse; (2) submarine faulting extended around the submerged margin of the caldera (and probably in the formation of radial graben as well); (3) enormous quantities of material fell back into the sea from the gigantic eruptive cloud columns; and (4) after the vents were submerged, subsequent explosions must have burst upward through the ocean surface creating water-domes and waves that dwarfed those observed by Stehn during the 1928 submarine eruptions of Anak Krakatau (p. 330). The 1883 waves ranged in size from the gentle oscillations observed by the Anjer telegraph master on Sunday afternoon (p. 72) to the calamitous killer wave late the next morning. The problem, then, is to understand which mechanism was the dominant one, and papers presented below argue for different mechanisms without reaching a consensus.

[1]*Bolt (1976, p. 15).*
[2]*Anonymous (1978, p. 18)*
[3]*Murray-Aaron (1900, p. 889–890).*

Explosive Air Waves and Sounds (Strachey, 1888)

At the December 13, 1883, meeting of the Royal Society of London, a paper was read by Robert H. Scott, Secretary to the Meteorological Council, and a note was appended by Lieutenant-General R. Strachey, Chairman of the same Council. Both noted the "temporary derangements of atmospheric pressure" recorded by European barographs between the 27th and 31st of August, and related them to the Krakatau eruption. This meeting led directly to the formation of the Royal Society's Krakatoa Committee, and both men were appointed to the sub-committee investigating the air waves and sounds. Reports of the sounds were gathered along with traces of all continuous recording barogaphs. Strachey's report forms Part II of the Royal Society's 1888 publication, and begins with a summary of the 46 barographic stations that supplied data. European records dominate these 46, and only 8 stations (4 from Australasia) were south of 18°N latitude. Strachey's analysis of the barograms begins:

Section I.—AIR WAVES

The general features of the remarkable atmospheric disturbance caused by the great explosion on the morning of August 27th, which appears to have been the effect of the final paroxysm of the volcano, and of which alone well-defined indications susceptible of identification and measurement have been preserved by the barometric registers. . . In many cases, *seven* [wave passages] were distinctly observed. For some time before the great catastrophe, minor explosions occurred, of which indications may be found in many of the photographic registers, especially those from the stations least removed from Krakatoa, the trace being, so to speak, *roughened* by many small irregularities, giving it an appearance very different from that of the smooth line which is its usual character.

In the communication on this subject before made to the Royal Society, it was shown that the observed facts clearly established that the successive repetitions of the disturbance at the numerous stations, after varying intervals of time, were caused by the passage over them of an atmospheric wave or oscillation, propagated over the surface of the globe from Krakatoa as a centre, and thence expanding in a circular form, till it became a great circle at a distance of [90°] from its origin; after which it advanced, gradually contracting again, to a node at the antipodes of Krakatoa; whence it was reflected or reproduced, travelling backwards again to Krakatoa, from which it once more returned in its original direction; and in this manner its repetition was observed not fewer than seven times at many of the stations, four passages having been those of the wave travelling from Krakatoa, and three those of the wave travelling from its antipodes, subsequently to which its traces were lost.

The barometric disturbance caused by the great explosion began with a more or less sudden rise, on the summit of which two or three minor oscillations are visible, followed by a deep depression, which was succeeded by a less well marked rise, and by other depressions and rises, the whole disturbance extending over a period of nearly two hours. Such are the characters of the traces of almost all the self-recording instruments on the occurrence of the first two waves, and they are very clearly seen in the photographic barograms obtained at Bombay, Melbourne, Mauritius, and the British Observatories. The traces of these two passages of the wave are, in many instances, remarkably alike, although the second oscillation must have crossed the first at or near the antipodes of Krakatoa. The wave, however, gradually became deformed during its progress from and to the point where it originated, and eventually lost the characters above described. On the third and fourth recurrence the disturbance is commonly indicated by a sudden rise, which has the appearance of replacing the deep central depression of the first and second passages.

From the irregularity of the form of the wave, and its want of persistency, together with the considerable time over which it extended, there has been some unavoidable uncertainty in fixing the exact moment of the passage of the same phase of the disturbance in the several waves over the various stations; but the deep depression which immediately followed the initial rise appears, on the whole, to be the most persistent and easily recognised feature in the first two passages of the wave; and where it can be identified it has been taken as the standard to which reference has been made, especially in fixing the time of the occurrence of the great explosion.

There can, however, be no doubt that the *rise* of the barometer, indicating a sudden increase of pressure, was the first and direct result of the explosion, and that the succeeding fall of the barometer, or decrease of pressure, together with all the subsequent oscillations, were mechanical consequences of the original shock, which in the nature of the case required some considerable time for their development. These remarks have an obvious bearing on the manner in which the exact time of the final explosion may be inferred from the observed times of the atmospheric disturbances, a point to which attention will subsequently be given.

It may here be remarked that the theoretical investigations of Lord Rayleigh indicate that the sudden expansion of an elastic gas, supposed to be confined in a spherical envelope, would cause an oscillation which begins with a wave of compression, followed by one of expansion; a form which appears to correspond with that of the disturbance now under consideration. According to the same authority the amplitude of the wave diminishes as the square root of the distance travelled by it. The data do not admit of any positive opinion being formed as to whether this held good in the present case, but there is at least nothing to suggest any departure from such a law.

[Strachey here presents a lengthy table of passage times at all recording stations analyzed.]

From the times thus recorded may be deduced the probable precise moment of the occurrence of the great explosion, of which there is otherwise no sat-

isfactory or complete evidence, as well as the velocities of the wave's transmission in its course round the earth.

But, as will be more fully shown hereafter, the velocity of transmission was not uniform in all directions, nor did it remain constant as the wave advanced. In order, therefore, to determine the most probable moment of the origin of the wave, it has been considered best to deal only with the data obtained from the stations nearest to, and immediately surrounding, Krakatoa:—viz. Calcutta, Zi-Ka-Wei (Shanghai), Bombay, Melbourne, Mauritius, and Sydney; at all which the records of the first passage of the wave are well defined and satisfactorily comparable, while their distances from Krakatoa are not so great as to make it likely that important variations of the velocity of the wave took place during the time occupied in reaching them.

If T is the time of the origin of the wave, which is to be determined; t, the time of the passage of the wave at any station; d, the distance in degrees from the point of origin; and V, the velocity of the wave's transmission, assumed to be the same in all cases; then

$$V = \frac{d}{t - T}$$

and representing by $d_1, d_2, \ldots d_6$, the several distances of the six stations from Krakatoa; by $t_1, t_2, \ldots t_6$, the several observed times of passage of the wave; and by $\Sigma(d)$ and $\Sigma(t)$ the sums of the distances and times, we shall have for the most probable values of T and V.

$$T = \frac{\Sigma(t).\,\Sigma(d^2) - \Sigma(d.t).\,\Sigma(d)}{6\,\Sigma(d^2) - \Sigma^2(d)}$$
$$= -3.54 \text{ hours}$$
$$= 3 \text{ hrs. } 32 \text{ min. G.M.T.}$$

$$V = \frac{6\,\Sigma(d^2) - \Sigma^2(d)}{6\,\Sigma(dt) - \Sigma(t).\,\Sigma(d)}$$

$= 10.31$ degrees, or 713 English miles per hour.

The residual errors of observation, assuming the above values, are in Table V [not shown] from which it may be concluded that the probable error of the deduced time of origin of the wave is $\pm .04$ hour, or about 2½ min; and that of the velocity of the wave ±.09 degree, or 6 miles per hour.

As was before observed, however, the phase of the oscillation taken as the standard, in reckoning the times of the wave's passage over the several stations, is not the initial extraordinary rise, but the lowest part of the depression following it. It is not easy to define precisely the true commencement of the disturbance which precedes the passage of the standard phase of the oscillation over the several stations, and there may be an error of at least 5 minutes in the determination that has been adopted as most probable. This, however, gives for the mean of five of the last-mentioned stations 36 minutes earlier, and all agree within 4 minutes of that value. Sydney is excluded from this determination, as the trace is too irregular to admit of a satisfactory result being obtained.

Consequently the probable moment of the great explosion was 3 hr 32 min, *minus* 36 min = 2 hr 56 min GMT, or 9 hr 58 min local time.

A corroboration of the conclusion thus arrived at, is afforded by the register of the gasometer indicator at Batavia, which fortunately is available, and which in the absence of a continuous barometric record, supplies a fairly trustworthy indication of the atmospheric pressure at the time in question. Figure 109 is a slightly reduced facsimile of a portion of this register for the first half of August 27th.

[Strachey here presents two tables showing time intervals between successive passages of the wave, traveling in the same direction, past each recording station.]

The velocities of the wave thus obtained will be seen to range from about 9.75° per hour to 10.5° per hour, or from 674 to 726 miles per hour. The velocity of sound in air, of a temperature of 50°F, is 757 miles per hour, and at 80°F it is 781 miles; at a temperature of zero Fahrenheit it is reduced to 723 miles per hour. Thus it appears that the atmospheric disturbance now in question had very nearly the characteristic velocity of sound, and that its mode of propagation by an aërial oscillation, of comparatively short duration, was also closely analogous to that of sound. Moreover, although there is no direct evidence that the great final explosion, which produced this atmospheric disturbance, was accompanied by sounds heard at any considerable distance, it is well established that during the progress of the eruption the sounds of some of the explosions were heard at very great distances; certainly at Ceylon, about 2,000 miles from the volcano, and at many places between 1,000 and 1,500 miles distant;

and probably at Rodriguez, about 3,000 miles distant. Further details on this subject will be found in the subsequent section upon *Sounds*.

[After more discussion of wave velocities, Strachey introduces the summary illustrations.]

In order to illustrate the manner in which the disturbance travelled round the earth, a series of projections, Figure 110, have been prepared, on which the position of the wave is marked for each successive even hour of Greenwich mean time, beginning with 4 hr of August 27th, civil reckoning, till its traces were lost. The projection or development, which is quite conventional, shows Krakatoa and its antipodes in the centres of two circles, representing the two hemispheres of which those points are the poles. The geographical features of the earth are projected on the hypothesis that distances from the centres of the two circles are the distances of the points to be represented, measured over the earth's surface on the arc of a great circle, from Krakatoa or from its antipodes, as the case may be. The diameters of the circles represent great circles passing through Krakatoa, and therefore indicate the paths of the various points of the wave as it advanced.

Section II.—SOUNDS

No sounds were heard before the 26th; and all the reports agree that the most violent detonations occurred on the morning of the 27th. Owing, however, to the great uncertainty which is attached to the times at which it is stated that the sounds were heard—from the somewhat general way in which they are sometimes given, *e.g.*, "at *about* 10 a.m.," or "*between* 9 and 10 a.m.," &c., the unreliability of the clocks, or from other causes—the exact times at which the ex-

Figure 109. Pressure record from Batavia gasworks, August 27 a.m., 1883. Time is local time at Batavia (approximate—see p. 392). Vertical scale is in mm of water (right) and equivalent inches of mercury (left), but these values must be doubled to obtain absolute pressure on the gasometer. The upper limit of the pressure gauge is marked by a dotted line near the top and was exceeded by the largest pulse shortly after 10 a.m. The record was normally changed at noon, but this pencil trace ended at 11:15 a.m. and the next record (reproduced by Verbeek), showed no further perturbations after it was resumed at 4 p.m. A copy of the full record, including the 11 hours preceding the record shown here, is reproduced at a reduced scale on p. 378. This full record shows the change in baseline pressure, as maintained by the gasworks through the day, and the caption to that illustration discusses the changes. The arrows indicate air wave arrival times picked by Latter in his recent reinvestigation and are discussed on p. 389. Strachey's plate IX.

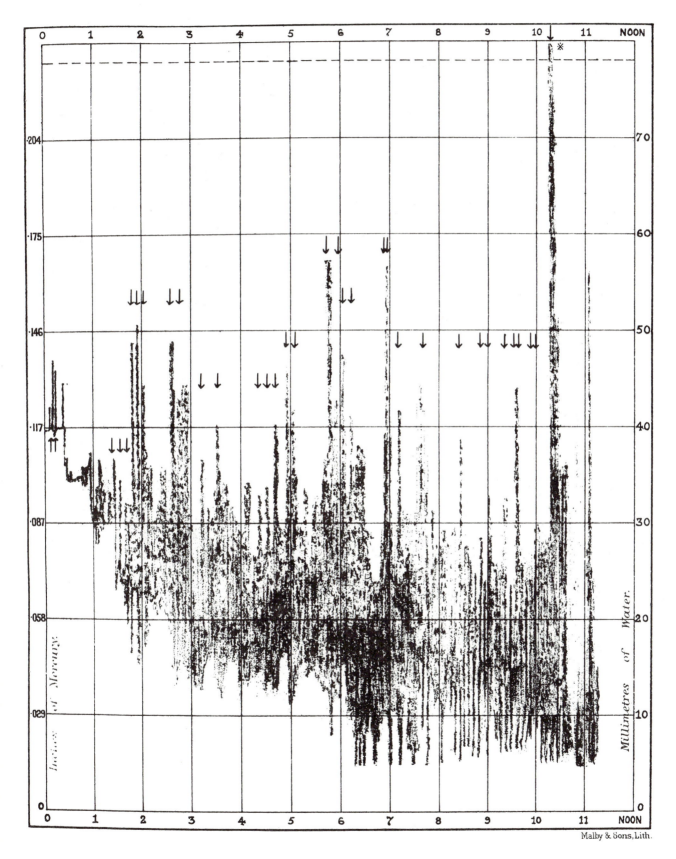

Malby & Sons, Lith.

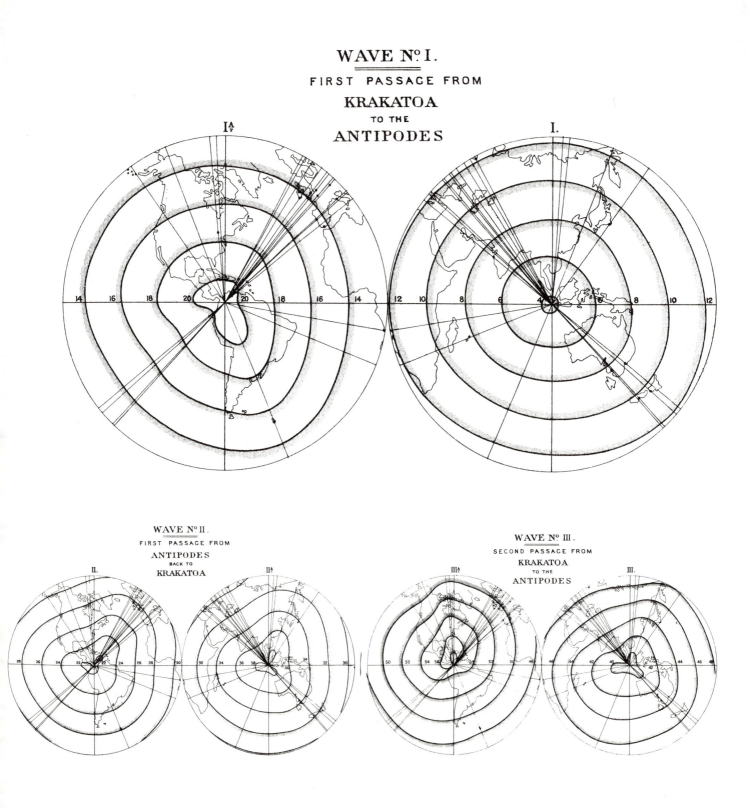

WAVE Nº I.

FIRST PASSAGE FROM

KRAKATOA

TO THE

ANTIPODES

WAVE Nº II.

FIRST PASSAGE FROM

ANTIPODES

BACK TO

KRAKATOA

WAVE Nº III.

SECOND PASSAGE FROM

KRAKATOA

TO THE

ANTIPODES

Figure 110. A series of projections which show the position of the air waves for each successive even hour (GMT) beginning at 4:00 a.m. on 27 August as curved lines. The wave origin is taken by Strachey as 2 hr 56 min (GMT) or 9 hr 58 min local time. The projections have either Krakatau or its antipodes as the center. (Strachey's plates X–XIII.)

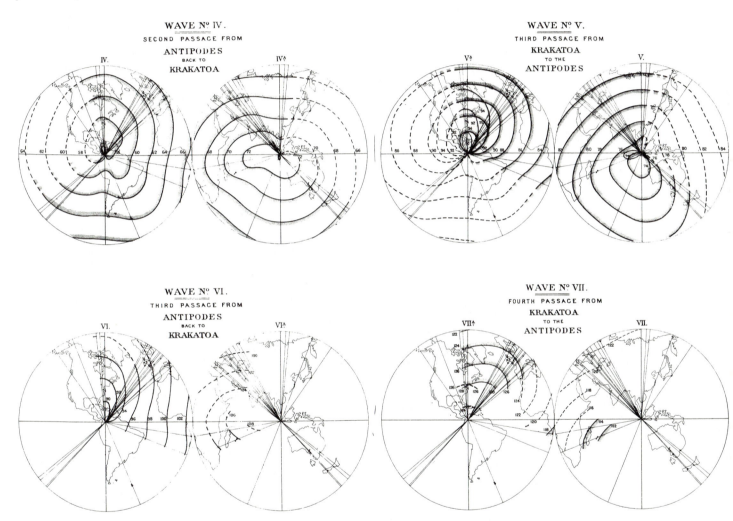

373

plosions occurred cannot safely be deduced from them; although, as far as they bear upon the conclusions already deduced from other sources as to the time of origin of the great air-wave, so far from their being opposed to those conclusions they appear to support them fairly well.

The sounds were heard with great distinctness over the most distant parts of Java and Sumatra throughout the morning of the 27th, but it is very remarkable that at many places in the more immediate neighbourhood of the volcano they ceased to be heard soon after 10 a.m., although it is known that the explosions continued with great intensity for some time longer. Very probably this peculiar phenomenon was caused by the large amount of solid matter which at about that time (10 a.m. local time) was ejected into the atmosphere by the volcano, and which formed in the lower strata of the air a screen of sufficient density to prevent the sound waves from penetrating to those places over which it was more immediately suspended.

[This report ends with an 8-page table, not reproduced here, listing places and times at which explosive sounds were heard.] The principal places mentioned in the Table have been marked upon Figure 111, which is a map constructed upon a projection similar to that used for showing the progress of the air-wave, and having Krakatoa as its centre.

Small circles have been drawn upon this map with radii of 10°, 20°, . . . 50°; and it will be seen that the 30° line is touched, or closely approached, by places almost entirely surrounding Krakatoa; viz., Ceylon to the north-west, Perth and other stations in West and South Australia to the south-east, New Guinea to the east, and Manila to the north-east. Diego Garcia, in the Chagos Group, almost due west of Krakatoa, and Alice Springs, in South Australia, are beyond the 30° line; while Rodriguez, to the south-west of Krakatoa, still more remote, lies beyond the 40° line. The shaded portion of the map represents approximately the area over which the sounds of the explosions were heard, and is roughly equal to rather less than one-thirteeenth of the entire surface of the globe.

A special interest is attached to the report from Rodriguez, owing to the fact that it is not only the most remote place at which the sounds of the explosions were heard, being very nearly 3,000 miles from Krakatoa, but that it is also the only instance on record of sounds having been heard at anything like so great a distance from the place of their origin. It may, therefore, be well to quote here the account given by Mr. James Wallis [reprinted earlier in Narrative section, p. 146].

At Diego Garcia, upwards of 2,250 miles from Krakatoa, the sounds were very distinctly heard, and were supposed to be those of guns fired by a vessel in distress; a belief which likewise prevailed at Port Blair in the Andaman Islands, and at several places less remote from Krakatoa. In Ceylon, and also in Australia, the sounds were heard at many different places far removed from each other; while at Dorey, in New Guinea, they were clearly heard, and their occurrence was recorded at the time, long before it was known to what cause they were due. These circumstances are of value as confirmatory evidence of the sounds having been really heard at those distant places.

That the detonations were heard so much further to the westward than they appear to have been to the eastward of Krakatoa, was most probably due to the westward motion of the lower strata of the atmosphere in the region of the Trades, within which the most distant station, Rodriguez, lies.

It may be noticed also that a communication was made to the "Académie des Sciences," and published in the Comptes Rendus in March, 1885 giving an account of sounds said to have been heard in the Cayman Islands in Lat. 20° N. Long. 80° W. from Greenwich, South of Cuba, on August 26th, 1883, which were attributed to the eruption at Krakatoa. The evidence, however, is of so indefinite a nature that it has not been inserted in the tabular statement annexed.

Sea Waves; The Devastating Tsunami
(Wharton, 1888)

Scientific interest in the sea waves was immediate, and the records of automatic tide gauges were quickly examined. Exactly one month after the August 27 wave origin, Major A.W. Baird, in charge of the tidal survey in India, wrote to the physicist G.H. Darwin (son of Charles Darwin), "The wave caused by the volcanic eruption at Java is distinctly traceable on all the tidal diagrams hitherto received, and I am informed of great tidal disturbance at Aden on August 27; but the daily reports are always meagre in information. Kurrachee and Bombay also show the disturbance, and as far as I have examined the wave reached half way up to Calcutta on the Hooghly." [2] Baird analyzed data from the tide gauges and witnesses throughout the northern Indian Ocean, and in

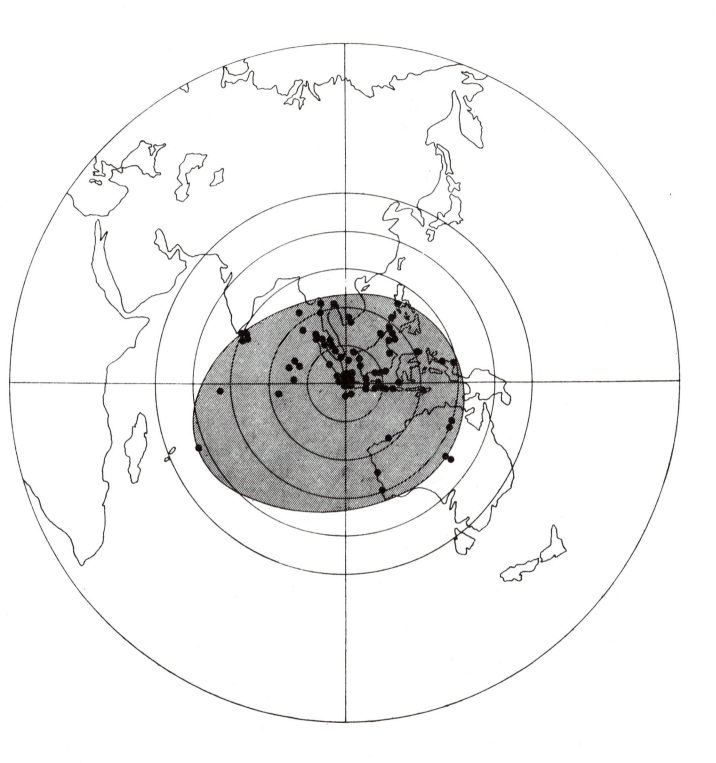

Figure 111. Map showing the places at which the
sounds of the explosions were heard on August 26–
27. The shaded portion indicates approximately the
area over which the sounds were heard. [Strachey's
plate XVI.]

December he presented a 6-page report to the Royal Society.[1] When the Krakatoa Committee was formed, requests for tide gauge records went around the world, and Sir Frederick Evans, a Captain in the Royal Navy, was appointed to investigate the waves. Evans was in poor health, however, and died in 1886. W.J.L. Wharton, also a Navy Captain, was then appointed to the Committee, and given the data and preliminary notes left by Evans. Wharton begins his chapter of the Royal Society Report[3] with a summary of the wave accounts reproduced in earlier sections of this book. We join Wharton on his fourth page, p. 92 of the full Report:

[1] *Baird (1884b).*
[2] *Darwin (1883).*
[3] *Wharton (1888).*

(In this Part Geographical miles [= nautical, or "minute" miles = 1.85 km] alone are used.).

The times of arrival of the waves at different places on the shores of the Strait are but vaguely noted, and this is especially the case with the great wave after 10 o'clock of the 27th. Terror and dismay reigned everywhere, and darkness had settled over the land. At Anjer, also, where this wave must have come, no one was left to see it, the few survivors having fled to the hills.

To some extent the same uncertainty attaches to the height of the waves. All who observed the wave after 10 o'clock, however, agree that it was the largest, and this is supported by all the evidence forthcoming. As this wave alone appears to have travelled to places at great distances, it is the most important. All observations founded on measurements of the marks left by the water are considered as relating to this wave.

The inundated portions of the shores of the Strait of Sunda are indicated on map, [see Figure 66, p. 299] and Mr. Verbeek also mentions, in his account of the disaster, the maximum height in different localities. It is not, however, stated by whom the contours of Mr. Verbeek's maps were obtained, nor is the means of obtaining the limit reached by the water stated in every case.   As far as can be gathered, the following were the altitudes to which the wave attained at places on each shore of the Strait of Sunda, and in the immediate vicinity of the volcano.

Java Shore

At Merak. . . the height of the wave was estimated by Mr. McColl to be 135 feet; by Mr. Nieuwenhuys,

an engineer, 100 feet. It does not appear on what these estimates are based [but see our p. 123 and footnote 65]. The greatest height measured at which buildings were washed away was 47 feet. Mr. Verbeek, on his plan, shows the hillsides to have been washed by the water to a height of 115 feet. The peculiar position of Merak, standing at the head of a funnel-shaped strait formed by the island of Merak, may have caused the wave to be higher there than elsewhere.

At Anjer. . . the height of the wave at 6 hr 30 min is stated to have been over 33 feet. The subsequent and higher waves are not appraised.

At Tyringin. . . 50 feet is mentioned as the measured height of the water at one spot. As people who gained the hills at the back of the plain, stated to be 67 to 100 feet high, were saved, it does not appear that the wave could have been much over 70 feet.

At Princes Island, 25 miles distant, the water is said to have attained a height of 50 feet.

Sumatra Shore

At Katimbang. . . the wave is stated by Mr. Verbeek to have reached a mean height of 80 feet.

At Telok Betong, the water reached within 6 feet of the top of the hill on which the Residence stands at a height of 78 feet, and was consequently 72 feet high. This seems the most accurate measurement of all those given. The man-of-war, *Berouw*, was carried 1.8 miles inland up the valley, and left about 30 feet above the level of the sea.

At the lighthouse on Vlakke Hoek the water rose 50 feet.

From these different measurements I have assumed that the actual height of the wave, before it reached the shore, was about 50 feet.

To ascertain the time of the genesis of the great wave is not, at first sight, easy, nor can it by any means be arrived at with certainty.

How the wave was formed, whether by large pieces of the mass of the island falling into the sea; by a sudden submarine explosion; by the violent movement of the crust of the earth under the water; or by the sudden rush of water into the cavity of the volcano when the side was blown out—must ever remain, to a great extent, uncertain; but more of this hereafter. What precisely took place during this tremendous outburst no one knows. The island was shrouded in smoke and fire, and was never clearly seen; nor did any vessel approach near enough to note any changes in its outline during the eruption. It is, however, evident that the three larger waves were intimately connected with the three great explosions, for, though the testimony of ear-witnesses is not clear on the point of the comparative force of the different detonations, as measured by the sound, happily the pressure gauge at the gasworks at Batavia, before mentioned, gives no uncertain evidence.

This has already been referred to also in [Strachey, p. 370, and Figure 109] whence it will be seen that the three largest movements, viz., those at 5 hr 43 min, 6 hr 57 min, and 10 hr 18 min, were all apparently connected with the highest three waves recorded. As far as that at 10 hr 18 min is concerned, there is reason to believe that the sea and air waves were formed practically synchronously.

[Wharton here discusses the $V = \sqrt{gh}$ relationship (between wave velocity and depth to bottom) treated in more detail below in more recent works.]

The indications of the tide gauge of the harbour of Tanjong Priok at Batavia are most valuable, as giving the nearest and most unmistakable record of the Krakatoa waves. A glance at the diagram [Figure 112] will show the character of the disturbance.

From 20 hr of the 26th, the curve begins to show signs of oscillations of level, which are, however, small until noon of the 27th, not averaging more than 3 inches. Notwithstanding, waves may be traced corresponding to the explosions of 1 hr 42 min, 2 hr 25 min, and 5 hr 30 min of the 27th, of which the best marked is that corresponding to the 5 hr 30 min explosion, which arrived at Batavia at 8 hr 20 min.

At 11 hr 30 min the water began quickly to rise; and at 12 hr 15 min a perpendicular line shows that the final rise was almost a wall of water, as the first great wave arrived and inundated the shore [see p. xx]. This attained a height of 7½ feet above water level at the time, at 12 hr 36 min. It then fell as rapidly to 10 feet below the level. These measurements are those given by Mr. Verbeek, who states that the gauge would not register the full range of the wave. The diagram shows only + 1.60 m, and − 0.23 m, but Mr. Verbeek states that the measurement for high level was taken on the stones of the pier as + 2.35 m.

That for low level he gives as − 3.15 m. The gauge would register − 1.10 m; but Mr. Verbeek gives as his explanation of the lower minimum which he adopts, that the water had already begun to rise under the influence of the second wave, before the level could fall below − 0.23 m. It is not easy to understand, if this was so, how the water could have been noted at − 3.15 m, and the shape of the curve does not give

any justification for the assumption. He does not say how the observations for the minimum were taken, beyond the statement that they were made to fixed points in the port. This figure therefore for the minimum appears doubtful, and I am inclined to think that the range of this first wave cannot be considered as very exact, and is probably under the amount given by Mr. Verbeek, which is 18 feet.

The second wave also was above the highest point the gauge would mark, and may be taken as Mr. Verbeek gives it, 1.95 m. This wave attained its maximum at 14 hr 48 min, or 2 hr 12 min after the first. Its crest was therefore 80 miles distant when the first wave arrived.

It is to be remarked that at Batavia the first phenomenon was a *rise* unpreceded by any fall of level, which appears to indicate that the wave leaving Krakatoa was a positive one.

The first wave is followed by waves of gradually diminishing height, 14 of which are at tolerably regular intervals, and give a mean period of 2 hr 02 min from crest to crest. These are:—

Time	Interval	Height*
1236		6¼ ft
	2 h 12 m	
1448		4½ ft
	1 h 55 m	
1643		1¾ ft
	2 h 15 m	
1858		1½ ft
	1 h 27 m	
2025		⅙ ft
	1 h 55 m	
2220		1½ ft
	2 h 20 m	
0040		1 ft
	2 h 30 m	
0310		9 inches
	2 h 00 m	
0510		11 inches
	2 h 10 m	
0720		9 inches
	1 h 50 m	
0910		4 inches
	1 h 50 m	
1100		4 inches
	2 h 10 m	
1310		2 inches
	1 h 45 m	
1455		3 inches
	2 h 10 m	
1705		3 inches

*These heights are, as all others of waves in this Part, measured from the normal level of the water at the time, as deduced from the tidal diagrams.

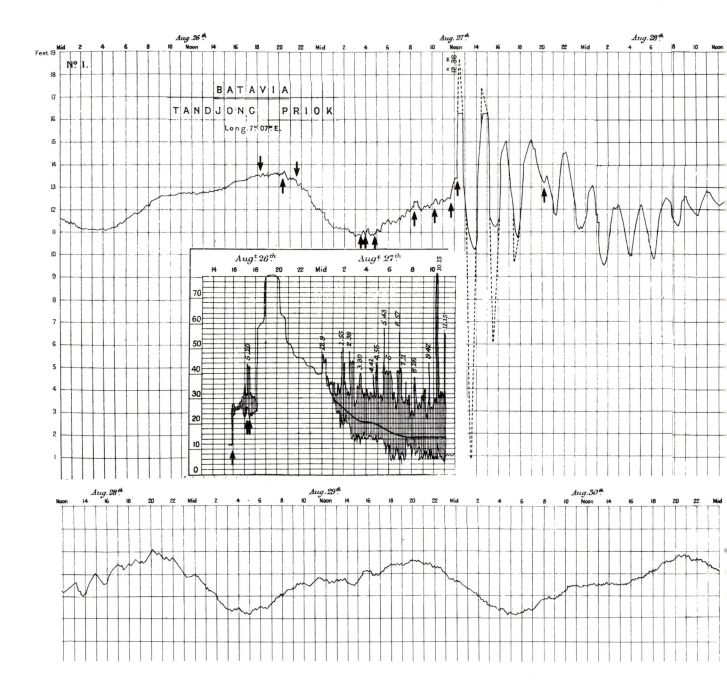

Figure 112. Batavia tide gauge record, August 26–30, 1883. The gauge was located on the harbor at Tandjong Priok, 9 km ENE of Batavia's center. Superimposed on this record, on the same time scale, is the gas pressure record (reproduced from Verbeek, 1885) to illustrate the relationship between air wave and sea wave arrivals at Batavia. Because the water level exceeded the recording range of the gauge, Verbeek used dashed lines to show the actual level as determined by other surveys in Batavia. Wharton reproduced these dashed lines from Verbeek. Time is local (Batavia) time, and vertical scale is in feet. Arrows indicate wave arrivals picked by Latter (see discussion on p. 389) and arrow direction indicates wave onset (positive, or upwards, onset shown by up arrow). Latter (following Yokoyama) interprets the sinusoidal waves following the main arrival as seiches set up in Batavia Bay.

On the inset gasometer trace, the thin continuous line indicates baseline pressure in the gas line, as regularly adjusted throughout the day by the gasworks. Pressure was increased from 4 to 6 p.m. as street lights were turned on; maintained at high levels through 8 p.m.; then lowered in hourly steps until dawn. Fluctuations in atmospheric pressure, caused by the volcanic explosions, were recorded only when gas pressure was low enough for the meter to be affected by them. Therefore the explosions known to have occurred on Sunday evening were not recorded. Verbeek discusses the operation of the gasometer in some detail and cites "King's treatise on the science and practice of the manufacture and distribution of coal gas," vol. 2, London, p. 309 (figure 173) and 325 (figure 189) for further information. The August 27 portion of this record was figured by Strachey and is reproduced at a more detailed scale on Figure 109. Three wave arrivals on August 26, discussed by Latter on p. 393, are indicated here by arrows. (Wharton's plate XVII.)

This period of 2 hr 02 min is very remarkable if the circumstances are considered. If the wave was caused by any sudden displacement of the water, as by the falling of large masses of ejected matter, and huge fragments of the missing portions of Krakatoa, or by the violent rush of steam from a submarine vent through the water, it is hardly to be conceived that two hours would elapse before the following wave, the second of the series, started after it.

If the supposition that the wave was caused by the opening of a great chasm in the earth, by the bursting of the sides of the hollowed Krakatoa, into which the sea rushed, could be maintained, a wave of long period might also be explained; but, though some such inrush must have occurred when the water flowed over the site of the island, to set up a long wave, as is now required, two things appear necessary:

First,—that the chasm was large enough to permit water to flow into it continuously for an hour at a rate sufficiently rapid to cause a great lowering of the water level in the vicinity of the island, in order to set up a wave.

Secondly,—that the first effect reaching the shore was a negative wave.

Now, the first supposition is so improbable that it certainly requires evidence before it can be adopted; and the second is contrary to the record of the Batavia gauge, which shows a distinct positive wave as the earliest phenomenon.

If, however, upheaval of the bottom of the sea, more or less gradual, and lasting for about an hour, took place, we should have a steady long wave flowing away from the upheaved area, which as it approached the shore would be piled up considerably above its normal height. Thus these waves of long period would be set up; and this would also account for the rapid current recorded by the ship *William H. Besse*, which is described as 10 miles an hour, though probably that is an exaggeration. The water would flow back on the motion ceasing.

If we now turn to the condition of the area round Krakatoa and compare it with the previous state of things, we find that upheaval has taken place over a large surface. Two entire islands have appeared where formerly the water was deep. Verlaten Island has been increased by two square miles, and extensive banks have been raised. [Wharton mistakes the deposition of thick pumice and ash deposits around Krakatau for uplift of the sea floor.]

I should have been inclined to consider this as the sole cause of the great waves, more especially as it would entirely explain the somewhat remarkable fact that ships not far from the volcano at the time the wave was travelling from it, felt nothing of the stupendous undulation which rushed so far up the hills.

We find, however, as will be seen when the eye observations at distant places are considered, that, besides the waves of long period, which after travelling thousands of miles were not of sufficient height to attract much notice, waves were observed by eye-witnesses following one another at rapid intervals of from five to fifteen minutes, and of heights of from two to three feet, though, from their short duration, they were not marked upon the gauges.

These seem to demand another cause, and it appears to me that they may be due to the large masses of the island blown away by the force of the explosions and falling into the sea, or possibly, to the sudden displacement of the water over a submarine vent.

The missing mass of Krakatoa may be roughly estimated to be at least two hundred thousand million cubic feet [5.7 km³]. A fiftieth part of this mass dropping suddenly into the water would, by its displacement alone, furnish sufficient liquid to form a wave circle of 100 miles in circumference, 20 feet high, and 350 feet wide. The surrounding islands and shoals would, however, prevent a perfect circle being formed, and the wave might therefore be concentrated on certain parts of the arc, and be at some places higher than at others, varying according to the direction in which the masses fell. It has been remarked that this partiality of the waves was noticed.

I incline then to the opinion that the destructive waves in the Strait of Sunda were mainly due to these masses falling into the sea, or to sudden explosions under the sea after it flowed freely over portions of the former site of the island, possibly to both causes; but that the long wave which was recorded on so many tide gauges had its origin in upheaval of the bottom.

It does not appear unreasonable to assume that at the time of the great explosion of 10 o'clock, waves of both characters would be more or less synchronously formed.

[After a brief discussion of waves formed by an 1886 submarine detonation in SW England, Wharton goes on to discuss the available data in general terms. We extract the following 3 paragraphs:]

The indications of the arrival of the wave on these diagrams are by no means always precise; and the variety in the appearance of the diagrams is very marked. In all cases they show long continued disturbance; but the complication of the waves in some is as remarkable as the regularity of the series is in others. In all cases the more prominent waves are, unlike those registered at Batavia, preceded by minor oscillations, which in some instances merge so insensibly into the higher waves that it is difficult to identify any one wave as the first of what may be called by comparison the greater disturbance.

Seeing that several large waves reached the shores of Sunda Strait before the great one of 10 o'clock, it would not be surprising to find that these earlier waves occur on the diagrams, were it not for the very slight indications of them marked on the Batavia gauge. The path, however, to the westward is so much more open that these possibly shorter waves found their way across the Indian Ocean, while they were killed by the sudden expansion into the Java Sea.

On the east coast of India the arrival of the greater disturbance is unmistakable; which is probably due to the shorter distance and the unimpeded course of the waves in deep water. Here also there appears to be but one series of the larger waves for at least some hours; but at places further removed, several series of long waves can be made out, which much interfere with the regularity of the diagrams.

[Wharton then devotes 41 pages to eyewitness accounts and discussion of the tide gauge records. For each of the 35 records reproduced, he describes the location of the gauge and systematically lists the arrival times extracted. On pages 148–149 of the report he presents the following conclusions:]

1. That the sea disturbance was probably composed of two descriptions of waves, long waves with periods of over an hour, and shorter but higher waves with irregular and much briefer intervals.

2. That the greatest disturbance, probably formed of both descriptions of waves, originated at Krakatoa at about 10 a.m., local time, on the 27th of August, and was, on the shores of the Strait of Sunda, about 50 feet high.

3. That the long waves of this disturbance, of an original period of about two hours, were alone marked by the automatic gauges.

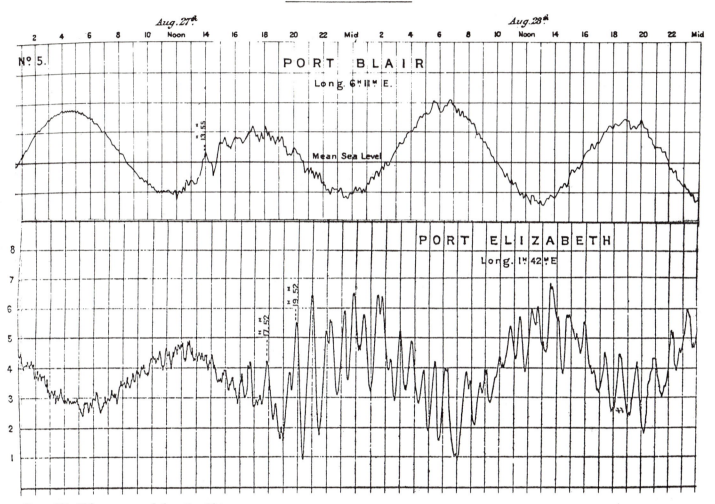

Figure 113. Tide gauge records from Port Blair (2440 km NW of Krakatau) and Port Elizabeth (8685 km WSW of Krakatau). These two records are from the nearest tide gauge to the west of Krakatau (Port Blair, in the Andaman Islands) and from the far side of the Indian Ocean (Port Elizabeth, on the south tip of Africa). Other, more distant, tide gauge records from Wharton's report are reproduced by Press and Harkrider (see p. 384, below). Wharton's plates XIX and XXII.

4. That the speed of the two descriptions of waves was about the same.

5. That the speed of those waves that can be fairly identified, measured by the time of arrival of the first large wave, and counting from the 10 a.m. wave at Krakatoa, was in all cases less than the depth of water would demand according to theory; assuming that the waves taken for comparison were identical with the 10 o'clock wave from Krakatoa.

6. That the first large wave recorded on the gauges was in most cases preceded by smaller undulations, which did not, however, accord with the period of the larger waves.

7. That to the north and east in the Java Sea the long wave can be traced for 450 miles, but it was at this distance reduced to a very small undulation.

8. That to the west the long wave travelled over great distances; reaching Cape Horn and possibly the English Channel.

9. That the shorter waves reached Ceylon and perhaps Mauritius.

10. That to the south and east of Sunda Strait the propagation of the disturbance was limited; probably not extending beyond the west coast of Australia.

11. That the disturbances, noted both by eye observers and by the gauges in New Zealand and in the Pacific, had no connection with Krakatoa, but were the results of other seismic action, and were apparently due to more than one centre of movement.

12. That from the great differences, caused perhaps by local circumstances, in the appearance of the disturbance on the various tidal diagrams, no precise or close comparison between them can be made, and this doubt of the identification of any particular wave at different places, causes much uncertainty in the result, as far as it relates to the speed of the waves.

It may be remarked that, with regard to conclusion No. 5, Professor Milne, in his recent work 'On Earthquakes,' finds the same for such other sea waves as have been traced for long distances across the Pacific; though the point of genesis has never been so certainly known as in this instance.

Air Waves Producing Distant Sea Waves
(Press and Harkrider, 1966)

Krakatau's air and sea waves were not forgotten after the publication of the Royal Society Report in 1888. Among significant contributions were Taylor's 1930 refinement of the air wave data,[1] applying the concept of gravity control, and Pekeris' 1939 recognition of a second mode at higher (ca. 39 km) elevation.[2] Pekeris also calculated the total energy contributed to the atmosphere by the paroxysmal eruption as 8.6×10^{23} ergs. Recognition of the relationship between the air wave and distant sea waves, however, did not come until 1955. Maurice Ewing, the eminent oceanographer and Director of Columbia University's Lamont Geological Observatory, and Frank Press, then an Associate Professor at Lamont and now President of the National Academy of Sciences, published a paper showing that "tide gauge disturbances at distant stations correlate in time with the first aerial wave arriving at the station in the direction from ocean to continent, a result which would be expected from coupling between the barometric disturbance and the ocean surface wave."[3] Heightened interest in large atmospheric explosions helped to gain funding for more research, and the Ewing-Press hypothesis was strengthened by the application of theoretical and numerical techniques. In 1966, Press and Harkrider, both then at California Institute of Technology, published the important paper that we reprint below.[4]

[1] *Taylor (1930).*
[2] *Pekeris (1939, p. 443–447).*
[3] *Ewing and Press (1955, p. 53).*
[4] *Press and Harkrider (1966). For a more detailed discussion of the theoretical aspects, see Harkrider and Press (1967). See also Press (1956) for interesting background on the development of the original hypothesis.*

Abstract. *The distant sea disturbances which followed the explosion of Krakatoa are correlated with recently discovered atmospheric acoustic and gravity modes having the same phase velocity as long waves on the ocean. The atmospheric waves jumped over the land barriers and reexcited the sea waves with amplitudes exceeding the hydrostatic values. An explosion of 100 to 150 megatons would be required to duplicate the Krakatoa atmospheric-pressure pulse.*

The explosion of the volcano Krakatoa in 1883 is remarkable in many respects. In magnitude it was probably the greatest explosion ever recorded. The atmospheric disturbance was detected by barographs at many stations throughout the world on at least three passages around the earth. Sea-level disturbances were observed on tide gages as far away as ports of the English Channel. The various phenomena and original data associated with the explosion have been documented in a report of a committee of the Royal Society.[4]

A selection of tide-gage records redrawn from Symons[4] shows the sea-level disturbance at several distant stations (Figure 114). Although the explosion produced one of the most destructive tidal waves on record, most investigators attributed the distant sea waves to disturbances which had no connection with the Krakatoa tsunami.[1] They were forced to this conclusion because circuitous and highly improbable all-water propagation paths were required to avoid land barriers. In addition, the wave velocities for these paths were much higher than those derived by use of $\sqrt{gH}$ and the known depths of the ocean.

Ewing and Press[1] noted the nearly coincident arrival of the atmospheric pulse (traveling in the direction from continent to ocean) and sea waves, and proposed that the latter were excited by the former. The sea disturbance was much greater than could be accounted for by the hydrostatic effect of the atmospheric pulse, requiring some mechanism of amplification or resonance. Ewing and Press[1] suggested that resonant coupling might be the mechanism if free waves in the atmosphere existed with velocities near 220 m/sec, the velocity of $\sqrt{gH}$ waves in the deep ocean. Their explanation suffered in that such waves were not known theoretically or experimentally.

We have extended the theoretical and numerical techniques developed for the study of internal acoustic-gravity waves generated by explosions in the atmosphere[3] to include the case where the bottom layer is an ocean with a depth of 5 km. The method involves approximating the known temperature variation in the atmosphere by a large number of isothermal layers. The results show that free waves in the atmosphere do exist with phase velocities near the $\sqrt{gH}$ velocity of the ocean. This leads to an efficient transfer of energy from the atmosphere to the ocean, and produces sea waves with amplitudes several times larger than hydrostatic.

Phase-velocity curves for the atmosphere-ocean system are shown in Figure 115. The curve formed by connecting the dots is that of long gravity waves in the ocean (GW_0) in the absence of an atmosphere. At long periods it approaches $\sqrt{gH}$ asymptotically. All the other curves correspond to internal acoustic (S) or gravity (GR) modes in an atmosphere without an ocean. It is seen that the atmospheric modes GR_0, GR_1, GR_2, and GR_3 all have phase velocities which cross the GW_0 mode when the atmosphere and ocean are considered separately. In the combined atmosphere-ocean system, mode crossing does not occur, but the curves turn sharply and join the mode they would have crossed. In the coupled system, the GW_0 mode consists of segments of several modes.

Thus, the purely ocean mode is present in the coupled system and should be excited by an atmospheric source, essentially by the atmospheric modes with the same phase velocity. That this is the case is shown in Figure 116 where the ratio of ocean displacement to atmospheric pressure at sea level is plotted as a function of phase velocity. Resonant peaks are found in all the gravity modes, the ratio being at least ten times greater than the hydrostatic value for the phase-velocity range of 195 to 230 m/sec. Thus amplitude build-up of the sea waves should begin before the arrival of the GW_0.

These results may be combined by Fourier synthesis to form a synthetic time series of sea-level displacement and atmospheric pressure as in Figure 117. The first pressure pulse corresponds to the GR_0 mode and the accompanying sea wave is essentially the hydrostatic response. The main sea waves are in the GW_0 mode and propagate along great-circle paths with phase velocity near $\sqrt{gH}$. These are excited so efficiently by atmospheric waves with the same phase velocity that no corresponding large motion is shown on the pressure record. Intervening land barriers are jumped by the air waves which reexcite the sea wave if a sufficiently long fetch is available.

The theoretical group arrival times for the several modes and tsunami are shown in the tide-gage records of Figure 114. It is seen that the sea waves begin and then reach large amplitudes in the interval between the GR_0 and GW_0 arrival times, as expected from theory. The theoretical tsunami arrival times are too late, and the paths are improbable for San Francisco, Honolulu, and Colon. South Georgia may have received direct tsunami waves. Colon shows large amplitudes beginning just after GR_0 and continuing through GW_0. Its position near the antipodes, where the GR_0 waves are especially reinforced, may account for this. In view of the uncertain response of the in-

Figure 114. Marigrams for San Francisco, Honolulu, South Georgia, and Colon [Panama]. Arrows indicate theoretical arrival times of several modes and the tsunami. Roman superscripts indicate short (I) and long (II) great-circle paths. Abscissa is local civil time beginning 27 August 1883. (The exception is Honolulu which begins 26 August.) [Press and Harkrider's figure 1.]

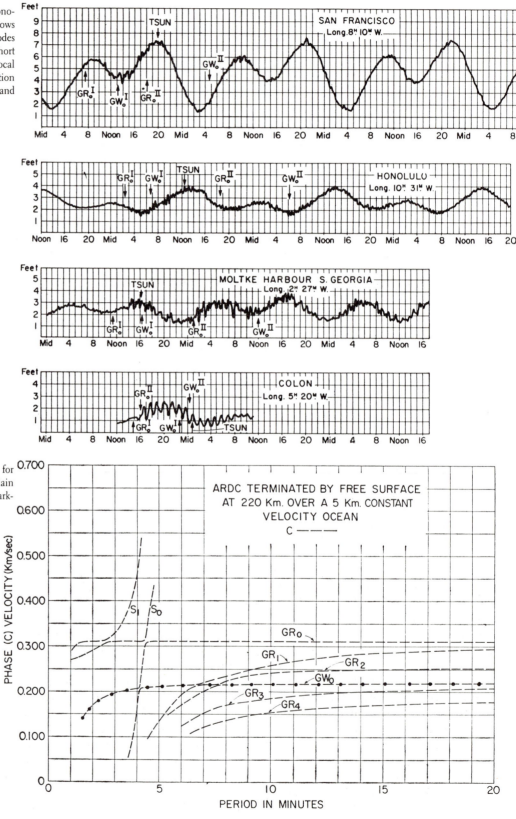

Figure 115. Phase-velocity dispersion curves for modes of a standard ARDC atmosphere underlain by an ocean with a depth of 5 km. [Press and Harkrider's figure 2.]

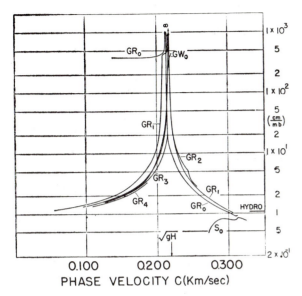

PHASE VELOCITY C(Km/sec)

Figure 116. Dynamic ratio of sea-surface displacement to pressure as a function of phase velocity. [Press and Harkrider's figure 3.]

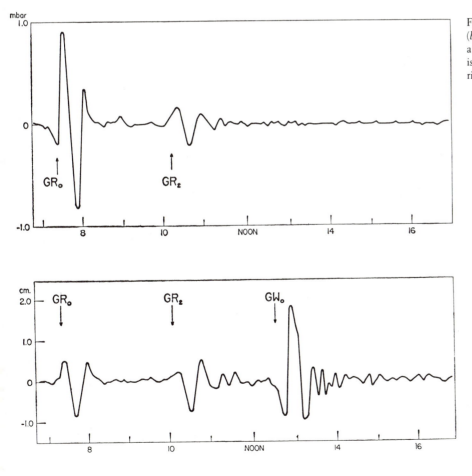

Figure 117. Synthetic barogram (*top*) and marigram (*bottom*) for San Francisco. Source time function is a single-cycle sine wave of a 40-minute period. Time is local civil time, 27 August 1883. [Press and Harkrider's figure 4.]

struments and the possibility of harbor resonances, no attempt was made to account for the absolute height or the spectrum of the sea waves.

Harkrider[2] showed how the properties of the source can be recovered from the pressure record. Using his scaling method, and data from nuclear explosions, we estimate that a surface explosion amounting to about 100 to 150 megatons would produce pressure pulses equivalent to those observed from Krakatoa.

[1]Ewing and Press (1955).
[2]Harkrider (1964).
[3]Press and Harkrider (1964).
[4]Symons (1888).

In 1970, Garrett proposed modification of this explanation of the way in which the air wave caused the tide gauge disturbances, suggesting that it generated free waves at the continental slope. He also looked, unsuccessfully, for tide gauge disturbances resulting from the largest atmospheric nuclear test, the 57 megaton Soviet test of October 31, 1961.

Nearby Sea Wave Travel Patterns
(Yokoyama, 1981)

Principal volcanologic interest, however, is connected with the devastating waves near Krakatau, rather than the distant waves. We return to the Sunda Straits by reprinting below, from a recent discussion of various geophysical aspects of the 1883 eruption, the section dealing with near sea waves. Professor Yokoyama, Director of the Usu Volcano Observatory, Hokkaido University, has conducted gravity and bathymetric studies for many years and his tsunami refraction diagram (below) is particularly useful.

The sea-waves caused by the eruption of Krakatau are classified into two types. One is the near sea-waves which arrived at the shores facing the volcano islands directly. The other is the distant sea-waves which can be interpreted as those coupled to the air-waves caused by volcanic explosions, and propagated to a distance by a mechanism proposed by Harkrider and Press.[1]

Near sea-waves

The sea-waves of this type are so-called tsunami which usually are caused by crustal deformation of the sea-bottom at the time of large earthquakes, or by landslides of volcanic material into the sea at the time of eruption of volcanoes near the sea.

The tidal record at Tandjong Priok near Jakarta [from Wharton,[3] see p. 378] is reproduced. The first arrival of the sea-waves is clearly a rise not preceded by any fall of level but only by small disturbances. The first wave was followed by waves of gradually diminishing height for more than 24 hours, 14 of which were at reasonably regular intervals of about 2 hours.

Periodic disturbances at Tandjong Priok. Considering the sequence of events related to the 1883 eruption, mentioned earlier, it is difficult to attribute the origin of the periodic disturbances of the sea at Tandjong Priok to the explosions of Krakatau. They must be caused by secondary undulation of the Bay of Jakarta [Batavia] excited by the large tsunami from Krakatau. The tidal records at Pangha, Surabaya [Java] and False Point [India] were not sinusoidal and those at Madras, Negapatam [India] and Port Blair [Andaman Islands] have a period of about 1.0 to 1.5 hours, which might depend on the periods of the secondary undulation at each port.

One can calculate the period of the secondary undulation within a bay according to Honda et al.:[2]

$$T = \alpha 4l/\sqrt{gh}$$

where α is a correction for the bay opening and is expressed as:

$$\alpha = \left[1 + \frac{2b}{\pi l} \left(0.9228 - \log_e \frac{\pi b}{4l} \right) \right]^{1/2},$$

and l denotes the length, b the breadth of the bay, h the depth of the water. At the Bay of Jakarta, $l = 20$ km, $b = 30$ km and $h = 20$ m. From this one obtains $T = 125$ minutes, which agrees with the observation. In other words, the large tsunami was produced by the most violent eruption, and the periodic disturbances at Tandjong Priok were the result of secondary undulations in the bay.

First arrivals of the tsunami. The first arrivals of the tsunami at many ports near Krakatau given in the Report[3] are shown in Figure 118, where solid circles

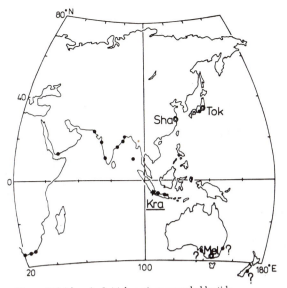

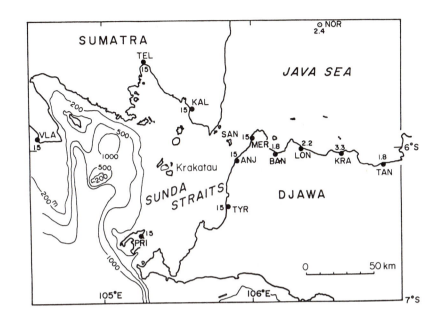

Figure 118 (above). Initial motions recorded by tide gauges of the tsunami caused by the 1883 eruption of Krakatau (after Symons, 1888). Solid circles indicate locations at which the initial motion was upward. The barograms at Melbourne, Shanghai and Tokyo are shown in [Yokoyama's figure 9, not reproduced here. Yokoyama's figure 6.]

Figure 119 (below). Refraction diagram of the tsunami caused by the 1883 Krakatau eruption. Assumed origin of the tsunami is shown by the hatched area which envelops the Krakatau Islands. [Yokoyama's figure 7.]

Figure 120 (right). Distribution of the maximum height of the tsunami in meters (after Symons, 1888). [Yokoyama's figure 8.]

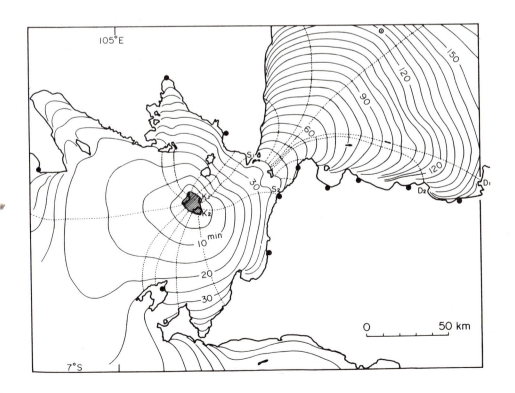

denote rises of sea level. At all ports, except three, the disturbances began with rises of sea level. The three ports in Australia and New Zealand yielded poor records, owing to the small amplitude of the disturbances and to refraction effects.

The first motion, either a rise or fall, is due to upheaval or depression of the sea-bottom, respectively, at the earthquake origin. The Krakatau tsunami may have been caused mainly by either of the following two mechanisms: sudden upward movement of the sea bottom centering on the present deepest region due to a large explosion, or by volcanic material entering the sea, causing sudden upheavals of the sea water around the islands. The latter already was suggested by Verbeek[4] and Symons.[3] The first mechanism however, may be more appropriate, because a large explosion could explain the simultaneous generation of the tsunami and air-waves.

Refraction diagram of the tsunami from Krakatau. It is clear that the origin of the tsunami was on or near Rakata Island, although the details remain unknown. The origin is assumed to be within the area between the Krakatau Islands and the refraction diagram (Figure 119) is drawn using the formula $v = \sqrt{gh}$, where v denotes the propagation velocity of the tsunami, g the acceleration of gravity and h the sea depth. In the figure, the propagation time from Krakatau to Tandjong Priok is about 150 minutes.

The original height of the tsunami can be estimated from the refraction diagram and the observed heights of the tsunami at each port, shown in Figure 120. Heights of tsunami are governed by Green's law describing energy conservation as:

$$H_0 = H_1 \left(\frac{b_1}{b_0}\right)^{1/2} \left(\frac{h_1}{h_0}\right)^{1/4},$$

where H, b, and h denote height of tsunami, distance between two adjacent trajectories, and depth of the sea, respectively, and suffix 0 denotes the origin area and suffix 1 the area concerned. In the present case, h_1 is assumed to be nearly equal to h_0, both being near shore areas. In the following discussion, the loss of amplitude from absorption due to frictional dissipation of the energy of tsunamis will be ignored because of its small magnitude.

Green's law is applied to the tsunami heights observed at Tandjong Priok and Prinsan [Island] to the south of Krakatau. In the refraction diagram shown in Figure 119, the spreading ratio (b_1/b_0) from Krakatau to Tandjong Priok is a product of that from Krakatau to Sangian [Dwars-in-den-Weg] and that from Sangian to Tandjong Priok, and expressed as 8×35, while the spreading ratio from Krakatau to Prinsan is approximately 8. Then the original height of the tsunami is deduced as follows: from the data at Tandjong Priok, $H = 1.8 \times \sqrt{35 \times 8} = 30$ m; from the data at Prinsan, $H = 15 \times \sqrt{8} = 42$ m, where 1.8 m and 15 m are the observed tsunami heights. The sea water was probably elevated to a height of 30–40 m at the area of origin around Krakatau.

[1]Harkrider and Press (1967).
[2]Honda, et al. (1908).
[3]Symons (1888).
[4]Verbeek (1885).

Sea Wave Reinterpretation Based on Explosive Air Wave Record (Latter, 1981)

Our final contribution on waves reached us in this centennial year of Krakatau's 1883 eruption. John Latter, a seismologist with extensive volcanological experience (and based since 1970 with the D.S.I.R. in Wellington, New Zealand), has written a summary paper on tsunami of volcanic origin, including a major restudy of the Krakatau waves. Latter has gathered information on 69 volcanic tsunami, but regards Krakatau as the only eruption sequence with adequate data for a detailed tsunami study. His two primary data sets were the Batavia gasometer and tide gauge records originally figured by Verbeek and reproduced here in the preceding sections by Strachey (p. 371) and Wharton (p. 378) from the Royal Society Report. To avoid duplication, we have added Latter's marks to these illustrations on the earlier pages and refer the reader to them by page number in Latter's valuable reinterpretation below:

Verbeek[5] included in his report reproductions of the continuous record of pressure in the gasometer at the Batavia[11] gas works, and of the tide gauge at Tandjong Priok, 9 km east of Batavia. He read the times of 14 peak deflections on the pressure gauge record, and 18 on the tide gauge record, correlating the former with arrival times of air waves generated by explosions at Krakatoa, and the latter with arrivals of sea waves from the volcano. He assumed the times to be accurate to the minute, converted them to Krakatoa time by subtracting five minutes, and obtained origin times at Krakatoa by subtracting eight minutes for the travel time of the air wave, 151 minutes for that of the largest sea wave, and 173 minutes for the smaller sea waves. He discussed at some length the inertia of the pressure gauge resulting from its complicated design, and pointed out that the tide gauge was established in an unsatisfactory place near the mouth of a navigation canal. At both instruments, therefore, there may have been a delay in recording the arrival of the waves. He deduced an origin time at Krakatoa of 10 h 2 m, Krakatoa time, for the largest air wave, by adopting a velocity which fitted best the arrival times at Batavia and Sydney: for the largest sea wave, he obtained an origin time of 10 h 0 m: this is equivalent to 02 h 58 m G.M.T.

Strachey[4] determined the origin time of the largest air wave as 09 h 58 m, Krakatoa time, by analysing the six closest observatory barographs, at distances ranging from 33° to 51° from Krakatoa: at Batavia, apart from the gasometer pressure gauge, only hourly observations of a barometer were made. He compared this with the largest arrival at the Batavia gasometer, which he read as "some time between 10 h 15 m and 10 h 20 m, local time", corresponding to an origin time at Krakatoa, in Krakatoa time, between 10 h 2 m and 10 h 7 m. He concluded that it agreed "as exactly . . . as could be expected from the somewhat rough character of the trace, the inertia of the recorder, and the possible error of the clock at a nonscientific establishment."

I have read onset times for all deflections on the pressure gauge of ⩾ 6 mm above noise level (in mm of water, as marked on the right hand scale in [the gasometer record on p. 371]): these, amounting to 39, are identified [by vertical dash marks on that record], or, for events on August 26, on the inset [showing the complete gasometer trace on p. 371]. On the tide gauge record, I have read arrival times of all ten waves of amplitude ⩾ 2.7 cm (0.09 ft), zero to peak, up to and including the arrival of the largest wave, together with a single possible wave after this time, during the period when seiches were being recorded. These arrivals are marked in [the figure on p. 371]. Both sets of times are listed, after conversion to origin times at Krakatoa, in Krakatoa time, together with a summary of observations of the air and water waves, in Table 1. Travel times of the tsunamis to the various places mentioned have been estimated from Yokoyama's[10] refraction diagram (Figure 121).

Verbeek's[5] estimate of 151 minutes for the travel time of the largest tsunami to Tanjong Priok has been accepted, a figure with which Yokoyama[10] is in close agreement (Figure 121), and has been deduced from the *onsets* of all the waves recorded at the tide gauge, rather than as Verbeek did, from the *peak* time of the largest wave only. The uncertainties due to bathymetry and the amplitude of the waves in deep water are each thought to amount to 2 or 3% of the travel time,[7] i.e. to between six and ten minutes for the two effects combined.

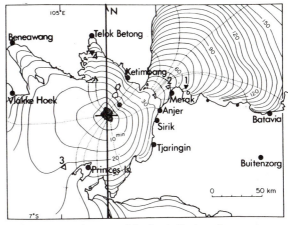

Figure 121. Locality map of the Sunda Straits and refraction diagram, showing travel times in minutes for tsunamis originating at Krakatoa Caldera (hatched area). The vent at which the largest explosion is inferred to have taken place is marked by the intersection of the horizontal dash on the north-south line. Filled triangles represent ships at anchor, and open triangles ships underway; 1 = *W.H. Besse*, 2 = *Charles Bal*, 3 = *Berbice*, 4 = *G.G. Loudon*; "1", "2" and "4" represent the ships' positions at 10 h on 27 August 1883; position "3" is at 15 h on the same day. The point marked with a small "x" in a circle represents the position at which the largest tsunami recorded at Tandjong Priok is thought to have been generated. Note that "Batavia" marks the port of Tandjong Priok and not the city proper. Adapted from Yokoyama (1981). [See p. 387. Latter's figure 4.]

Table 1

REFERENCES (see Verbeek(1886, pp342-359 and notes) for air waves)

Numbered strata after Stehn(1929, plate II) — Lang Is Geological Section Suggested equivalent	AIR WAVES — RECORDED AT BATAVIA — ORIGIN TIME AT KRAKATOA (KRAKATOA TIME) h m	RELATIVE TRACE AMPLITUDE mm	HEARD ELSEWHERE — ORIGIN TIME AT KRAKATOA (KRAKATOA TIME) h m (or h)	GREATEST DISTANCE degrees	WHERE HEARD AND REMARKS	WATER WAVES — RECORDED AT TANDJONG PRIOK — ONSET OF WAVE L.T. UNCORRECTED h m	+ OR −	PERIOD OF WAVE mins	MAX. AMPLITUDE, ZERO TO PEAK cm	APPARENT ORIGIN TIME AT KRAKATOA (KRAKATOA TIME) h m	EXPERIENCED ELSEWHERE — APPARENT ORIGIN TIME AT KRAKATOA (KRAKATOA TIME) h	WHERE WAVE EXPERIENCED AND REMARKS	TIME SEEN (L.T.) h	MAX. AMPLITUDE ZERO TO PEAK m	EFFECTS C = Casualties, D = Damage	REFERENCES
	1883 AUGUST 26				* Timed by Director Batavia Observatory											
22	No record till 11		1253*	3.3	Palembang (Sumatra)						13-13¼	Anjer(telegraphist's account)	13¾-14	1.5		Furneaux(1964, pp56-59)
	15 14		14½	7.7	Siak (Sumatra)											
23	1534	16	15	10.6	Cocos Is.	1810	−	23	3	1537						
			16	12.7	Penang (Malaya)						16¼-17¼	Beneawang(Pajoeng)	17-18		(D)	Verbeek(1886,p59)
24	1654	18	16½	9.9	Bali						17	Anjer	17½	1-2	(D)	" " p43
25	1705	17	17	26.1	Batticaloa (Ceylon)											
			17½	29.2	Daly Waters (Australia)						17½	Ship 'MARIE', Telok Betong	18½		(D)	" " p505
			18	7.2	Pontianak (Borneo)						17½	Telok Betong: wharf flooded	18½		(D)	Metzger(1884)
											17½	Tjanti(N of Ketimbang)	18¼		(D)	Verbeek(1886, pp52-53)
	No record				NB earthquake(s) felt 1950 at First Point Java (SE of Princes Is) (Verbeek (1886) p555)						17¾-18¼	Ketimbang	18½-19		(D)	" "
											18-18¾	Merak : Chinese camp destroyed	19-19½		C	Wharton(1888, pp90,95)
	17 52 till 11					2018	+	31	5	1745	17¼-18½	Tjaringin	18-19		C?	(" " (Verbeek(1886,p46)
26	23 40		20	28.2	Victoria Plains (Australia)	2133	−	22	3	1900	18¼-20¼	Tjaringin : houses set alight	19-21		C?	" " "
			20½	21.8	Port Blair (Andaman Is)						20¼-21¼	Ketimbang : preceeded by recession of sea (Furneaux (1964) p68)	21-22		C?	" " p53, Metzger(1884)
			21		Increased activity seen Anjer (telegraphist's account)											Furneaux(1964,p61)
			21½	6.1	Ship 'AIRLIE' near Lingga											
27			22	24.3	Geraldton (Australia)											
			23	26.1	Batticaloa (Ceylon)											
	2350	7														
	2354	6														
	AUGUST 27															
											0½	Sirik partly submerged (no wave Anjer)	1		D	Metzger(1884)
											0½	Kankoeng, Telok Betong	1½		D	Wharton(1888,p90)
											0½	Vlakke Hoek 'high water'	1			Verbeek(1886, pp56,62)
	0107	6														
	0113	9														Verbeek(1886,p49)
	0121	7														
	0131	21			NB possible earthquake felt(c.0130) at First Point, Java (SE of Princes Is)	0333	+	28	5	0100						
											1-1½	Ketimbang	2		D	" " p53)
28-29	0136	25	1½	7.9	Sinkawang (Borneo)	(0400)	+	(36)	9	(0127)						
	0143	18														
30	0218	25	2	1.1	Sukadana (Sumatra)	0454	+	32	6	0221						
	0226	21			NB 2 earthquakes(?) felt Anjer between 2 and 3h, and possibly a shock at First Point at 3h.											Verbeek(1886, pp43, 49)
	0254	14														
	0312	18	3	5.2	Ambarawa (Cent. Java)											
	0402	12			NB possible earthquake felt at First Point at 4h.											Verbeek(1886,p49)
	0413	12														
	0420	20	4	1.1	Sukadana (Sumatra)											
31	0435	25														
	0443	22														
			5	1.2	Goenoeng Soegi (Sumatra)											
32	0528	40	0525	32.2	Alice Springs (Australia)											

NB no wave at Tjaringin(Verbeek(1886)p409)

TABLE 1 (con'd)

Numbered strata after Stenn(1929, plate II) — Lang Is Geological Section Suggested equivalent	AIR WAVES · RECORDED AT BATAVIA · ORIGIN TIME AT KRAKATOA (KRAKATOA TIME) (h m)	RELATIVE TRACE AMPLITUDE (mm)	HEARD ELSEWHERE · ORIGIN TIME AT KRAKATOA (KRAKATOA TIME) (h m or h)	GREATEST DISTANCE · DISTANCE (degrees)	WHERE HEARD AND REMARKS	WATER WAVES · RECORDED AT TANDJONG PRIOK · ONSET OF WAVE L.T. UNCORRECTED (h m)	+ OR –	PERIOD OF WAVE (mins)	MAX. AMPLITUDE, ZERO TO PEAK (cm)	APPARENT ORIGIN TIME AT KRAKATOA (KRAKATOA TIME) (h m)	(h)	EXPERIENCED ELSEWHERE · WHERE WAVE EXPERIENCED AND REMARKS	TIME SEEN (L.T.) (h)	MAX. AMPLITUDE ZERO TO PEAK (m)	EFFECTS (C = Casualties, D = Damage)	REFERENCES (see Verbeek(1886, pp342–359 and notes) for air waves)
33–34	0534	26									5¼–6	Anjer (Pilot's account)	6–6½	>10	C	Verbeek(1886,pp43,45)
35–36	0543	30				0819	+	?	8	0546*	5½	Telok Betong, Kankoeng: 'BEROUW' and 'MARIE' stranded	6½		C	" " p56
												(*possibly related to 0528 explosion)				
37–38	0553	26	6	25.6	Hambantota (Ceylon)											
	0634	24														
39	0636	41	6½	27.5	Bogawantalawa (Ceylon)						just after 6¼	Beneawang(Pajoeng): Binuangan — * NB Water low c.1h earlier	just after 7*		C	(Metzger(1884) (Verbeek(1886,p59)
	0650	26									6¾	Telok Betong	7¾		?	" " p57
40	0713	28	7?	29.7	Dutch Bay (Ceylon)						6¾	Anjer (not large a short distance N)	7½	>>10	C	" " p44–45
	0807	24	0807*	7.3	Padang (Sumatra)						(7¼)	Tjaringin : 9 villages destroyed (700 dead)	8		C	" " p48
					* Timed by Director Batavia Observatory (Verbeek(1886)pp36,94,342)											
	0831	14									(8¼)	Merak* · * but Verbeek(1886, p42) refers this to the great wave at c. 10h.	9	>>10	?	Metzger(1884,p242)
	0841	18	8½	3.3	Bandar (Sumatra)											
	0859	18	9	3.9	Benkulen (Sumatra)											
	0908	9														
41	0916	29	9½	8.2	Bengkalis (Sumatra)	1139	+	60	24	0906	(9¼)	Possibly wave seen at Vlakke Hoek (where HAMWYK reported 3 waves,– he thought, within the space* of ½h)				Verbeek(1886,p62)
	0927	12														
	0939	15										* Wrongly reported by Wharton(1888,p91) as 3 waves at intervals of c. ½h; however it is very likely that HAMWYK, who was seriously injured, had no clear memory of the time which elapsed between events.				
					* Water wave produced by interaction of air wave at water surface											
42	0958½	>67	10	42.8	Rodriguez Is	(1008	+	35	6	0958*	10	Tjaringin) Soon after 10				Verbeek(1886,pp46–47)
						(1216	+	70	>>161	0943	10	Sangkanila (near Merak))				" " pp412,398)
											(10)	Ship 'CHARLES BAL' near Merak)				(" " pp73: (Watson(1883)
											(10)	Probably Vlakke Hoek HAMWYK's account), see above				Verbeek(1886,p62)
	1044	13														
43–44	1045	41	11	28.8	Mulliyavalei (Ceylon)											
	No record after 10 50										(14)	Telok Betong, ship 'MARIE'	(15)			Verbeek(1886,pp421,506)
											(14¾)	Ship 'BERBICE' near Princes Is : (considered by Verbeek to have been a freak sea wave unconnected with Krakatoa).		6		" " pp74–75, 102
			1625	1.7	Kroe (Sumatra)	correlated by Verbeek(1886,p420) with suppression of expected minimum at 1930, in seiches caused by the great wave at c. 10h.										Verbeek(1886,p64)
						(2014	+	?	11	1741		onset of wave may represent a discrete arrival from Krakatoa, but the record is obscured by the seiches mentioned above).				

As for the air waves, eight minutes, as used by Verbeek, has been adopted as a reasonable estimate for the travel time to the Batavia gasworks, which lie at a distance of between 152 km and 155½ km from the vents which are believed to have been active. With the air heavily contaminated by dust and volcanic gases, and heated by previous eruptions, conditions must have been vastly different to the propagation of sound in still air at constant temperature and humidity. However, there are insufficient data for a more accurate estimate of velocity. At Batavia, the air wave of the largest explosion was probably of very low frequency: it caused some damage, but was not heard. Closer to the volcano, at Tjaringin, Anjer, Ketimbang, Telok Betong, and on board the ships at points 1 and 2 in Figure 121, it was both heard, and, at the last three locations, was accompanied by a violent wind blowing outwards from Krakatoa.[5,6]

All previous investigators have assumed, while admitting the possibility of error, that the clocks at the gasworks and tide gauge were correct. However, there is evidence to suggest otherwise. The Director of the Batavia Observatory, J.P. van der Stok, noted 08 h 20 m as the time of the loudest explosion at Batavia[5] [see p. 202], whereas the arrival is 08 h 26 m on the pressure gauge record ([p. 371]). Others stated that the time was a few minutes later, and a newspaper, evidently quoting J.P. van der Stok, gave the time as 8⅓ h, implying some uncertainty. However, it seems reasonable to accept the Observatory Director's time as accurate, particularly since he also times to the minute the explosion heard in Batavia at 13 h 6 m on August 26, which initiated the climax of the eruptions. Unfortunately, Verbeek[5] did not publish the pressure gauge record covering this earlier period, nor did he list J.P. van der Stok's observations in full. Provisionally, however, a correction of −6 minutes, for the combined inertia and time correction, has been applied to the arrival times, yielding the origin times given in Table 1.

A time correction to the tide gauge records has also been applied. It seems likely that the wave onset at 10 h 8 m on August 27 (Table 1, Column 7) was generated by the arrival of the largest air wave at Tandjong Priok, rather than by a genuine tsunami propagating from Krakatoa. In the latter case, it should have originated at 07 h 32 m, a time which does not correlate well with other observations, the great wave which destroyed Tjaringin "at about 8 h" being more likely to have been the same as that which destroyed Anjer and originated at the volcano at about 6¾ h.

Verbeek[5] ([his] p. 414) thought that the 10 h 24 m wave (his peak time at Tandjong Priok) was a reflection of the wave which arrived at the tide gauge at 08 h 19 m, giving a two hour periodicity similar to that of the two seiches which followed the arrival of the largest wave. This, however, seems unlikely, as the amplitude of the earlier wave was small (Table 1). Interpreted as due to the arrival of an air wave, it would yield an origin time at Krakatoa of 09 h 55 m, Krakatoa time, in close agreement with the figure of 09 h 58½ m deduced from the pressure gauge record, which is itself almost identical to Strachey's[4] estimate. Accordingly, a correction of +3½ minutes has been applied to the arrivals read on the tide gauge, yielding the origin times given in Table 1 (Column 11).

A comparison of origin times in Table 1, estimated as above, shows close agreement between those calculated for the air waves and tsunamis in some cases, but a wide divergence in others. Tsunamis appear to have been generated three minutes after the explosions at 15 h 34 m on August 26, and 02 h 18 m and 05 h 43 m on August 27. This difference is negligible within the limits of error. For three of the waves, however, the origin times are between nine and 15 minutes earlier than the explosions with which they are almost certainly correlated. The largest anomaly corresponds to the largest explosion, with its accompanying tsunami apparently preceding it by 15 minutes. The most reasonable explanation for the anomaly in these three cases, the explosions at 01 h 36 m, 09 h 16 m, and 09 h 58½ m, would seem to be that the tsunamis were not generated at the focus of the eruptions but at distances from the volcano equivalent to the time anomaly observed.

For the largest explosion of all, the tsunami that travelled to Tandjong Priok would then have been produced at the point marked in Figure 121, which, shown on an enlarged scale in Figure 122, is found to coincide with the outer edge of Calmeyer Island, built up by volcanic ejecta during the climactic eruptions in water that was previously 45 to 50 m deep.[1,8,10] This is strong evidence that the tsunami was generated by the violent impact of a huge mass of unwelded ignimbrite, erupted at the instant of the largest explosion, and emplaced at a distance of the order of 10 to 15 km, probably at a low angle trajectory, within a minute or so of the explosion. Following Yokoyama,[10] I have assumed that the eruption took place at what is now the deepest part of the caldera (Figure 122): it is likely that the ignimbrite now forming Calmeyer Bank, and Steers Bank to the northwest, im-

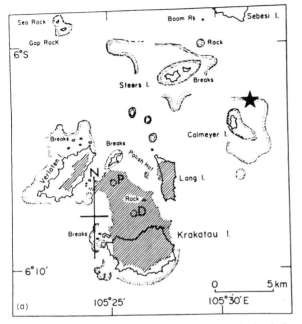

Figure 122. Locality map of the Krakatoa Islands. The hatched areas show the outlines of the islands before the climax of the 1883 eruptions; other outlines show the islands as they were soon after the climax. Steers and Calmeyer Islands were quickly eroded to below sea level. The vent at which the largest explosion is inferred to have taken place, marking the deepest part of the caldera, is the cross on the north-south line: the other two principal vents of the eruption are marked "P" (Perboewatan) and "D" (Danan). The heavy star corresponds to the point marked with an x in a circle on Figure 121, and represents the position at which the largest tsunami recorded at Tandjong Priok is thought to have been generated. Adapted from Yokoyama (1981) [and Judd, 1888. Latter's figure 5].

pacted at some intermediate distance between Lang Island and its final resting place, rolling forward across the sea floor to its present position, and generating the tsunami as it did so.

A suggested correlation is given in Table 1 between the explosion and the products of the eruptions described by Stehn [Figure 71, p. 314][3] from a geological section on northwest Lang Island. The correlation has been made by equating the thickest stratum of the deposit, a lens of up to 11 m thickness of black pumice with a strongly eroded upper surface, with the most powerful explosion at 09 h 58½ m, and two beds lower down in the section, which are described as containing pumice bombs, with the two previous most powerful explosions, at 05 h 28 m and 06 h 36 m. The lower metre, or less, of the deposit, resting on soil and charred vegetation, predates the August 26–27 climactic eruptions. Above this lies white pumice, passing upwards into pale pink pumice. This represents the Plinian stage of the eruption, lasting from 12 h 53 m till about 18 h on August 26, the upper pink part being due probably to eruption of pumice at a higher temperature, from deeper in the magma chamber, as the Plinian phase drew gradually to a climax. Subsidence of part of the island seems to have taken place as early as the explosion at 15 h 34 m, since this was accompanied by a wave with a negative onset at Tandjong Priok. From the beginning of the climactic period of the eruption, small waves were observed at Anjer, due probably to minor pyroclastic flows from Perboewatan (Figure 122) impacting into the sea: activity of this kind was observed by Watson.[6,12]

The tsunami generated with an apparent origin time of 17 h 45 m was the first large one in the series, and is known to have propagated in all directions from north through east towards southeast. Although explosions were heard in Australia, with an origin time of about 17½ h at Krakatoa, no large explosion was recorded at the Batavia gasworks before 17 h 52 m, Krakatoa time, [after which the gasworks pressure increase made the record unreadable as a monitor of atmospheric waves (see p. 371)]. It is therefore likely that the corresponding explosion occurred after this time, and thus at least seven minutes after the apparent origin time of the tsunami. In line with the reasoning above, this tsunami may therefore have been generated by the emplacement of a pyroclastic flow or small ignimbrite, at a distance of the order of five to ten kilometres from the volcano, or, if unconnected with an explosion, may have been due to a large landslide. This eruption probably correlates with Stehn's[3] pumice lapilli bed No. 25, which marks the first of a series of discrete explosions which occurred sporadically until the climax at 09 h 58½ m on August 27.

A marked recesssion of the sea, interpreted as due to subsidence, possibly of the northern part of the island, seems to have begun at Krakatoa at about 19 h 0 m. This was observed both on the tide gauge and at Ketimbang (Table 1). One or more powerful explosions, heard in Australia and the Andaman Islands, took place between 20 h and 20½ h, and it is likely that the largest of these blasted a new vent and deposited the distinctive cinnabar-red pumice lapilli and

393

ash bed, which was described by Stehn[3] as originating in a submarine eruption just west of the islet of Polish Hat (Figure 122). A notable feature of the rocks a little higher in the section is the alternation of pumice lapilli and overlying ash beds; for example, the paired beds correlated with explosions between 01 h 36 m and 05 h 53 m in Table 1. It is likely that all these were erupted from beneath the sea.

A tsunami with apparent origin at about 0½ h seems to have had a different cause to others in the sequence. It was accompanied by no conspicuous explosion, and was, in addition, markedly directional in that it caused damage at Sirik (Figure 121), but was not noticed at neighbouring Anjer [see p. 72], although it also caused damage in the opposite azimuth at Telok Betong and nearby Kankoeng.[13] Possibly its origin is to be sought in a massive rock fall from the slowly subsiding island. Verbeek[5] ([his] p. 411) interpreted the local nature of waves of this kind as due to ejecta falling in different places. Several of the waves which caused damage within the Straits failed to propagate outside. Thus the two great waves, with origins at 05 h 46 m and about 6¾ h, which together destroyed Anjer, were only slightly smaller there than the wave accompanying the largest eruption at 09 h 58½ m, yet both were comparatively insignificant at Tandjong Priok. Indeed, the 6¾ h wave, though read by Verbeek[5] ([his] p. 413), had an amplitude below my chosen threshold, and thus does not appear in the tide gauge readings in Table 1.

Little can be said about the wave which originated at 01 h 0 m: it also failed to correlate with a significant explosion, and may equally have been due to a rockfall. The 02 h 21 m wave accompanied an explosion and was probably due to a localised pyroclastic flow, whereas the 01 h 36 m eruption, like the late 09 h 16 m and 09 h 58½ m eruptions, appears to have emplaced an ignimbrite, and generated a tsunami (destructive at Ketimbang) at a considerable distance, perhaps of the order of ten kilometres from the volcano. There is insufficient information as to whether a tsunami was generated by the final large explosion at 10 h 45 m: all survivors of the earlier waves had by then fled as far as possible from the sea, and once the largest wave had arrived at Tandjong Priok it, and the seiches that followed, effectively masked any later movements that may have taken place. This final eruption, however, is marked by a blocklayer, with overlying pumice, at the top of Stehn's[3] section [see Figure 71, p. 314].

The collapse, rather than explosion, of the greater part of the island, inferred by Verbeek,[5] Stehn,[3] and Williams[9] from the scarcity of old rock in the ejecta, may have taken place gradually. Verbeek[5] ([his] pp. 407, 412) assumed that it was a sudden process, and that it gave rise to the largest tsunami; but the evidence cited above makes it clear that the latter was due to the emplacement of an ignimbrite, erupted radially from a vent, formed probably at the instant of the explosion, at what is now the deepest part of the caldera. Prior to this, from the fact that mud only began to fall in large quantities soon after 10 h, it may be concluded that the principal vents were on land[5] ([Verbeek's] p. 409), although, as mentioned above, some submarine eruptions had occurred, which have left recognisable deposits close to the volcano. The principal eruption at 09 h 58½ m formed a deposit up to 100 m thick[3] [see p. 323] on the southern part of Krakatoa Island and on Verlaten Island, but seems likely to have largely jumped Lang Island, eroding the surface of its basal black pumice before coming to rest in the area of the new banks.

Evidence of the timing of the final large-scale subsidence at Krakatoa comes from the observation, soon after 10 h on August 27, at position 1 in Figure 121, that water was flowing "at about 10 knots" (18 km/h) towards the volcano [see p. 98]. For this negative movement to have propagated the 85 km or so outwards to the entrance of the Straits indicates that it began considerably earlier at the volcano. It did not, however, reach Tandjong Priok, being overtaken, presumably, by the largest tsunami. Within broad limits, it probably originated at Krakatoa between about 02 h 45 m and 07 h 30 m on August 27. As to the cause of the largest explosion, there is no direct evidence. It was probably deep-seated and effectively emptied the magma chamber, because the eruption came to an end soon afterwards. It was clearly exceptionally violent. There was no accompanying earthquake felt on neighbouring coasts. Further geological work is required to decide the extent to which sea water flashing to steam contributed to its violence.[14] The long period nature of the sea waves suggests a large source size (several km³):[7] however, both the pressure gauge and tide gauge records of the climax of the eruption ([p. 371 and 378]) should be interpreted with caution, since both records overloaded, and it is possible that the pens became stuck for a while before commencing to fall back. Verbeek[5] [see p. 217] pointed out that the sea waves were clearly of long period since they were not noticed by ships, with the exception of the vessel close to shore at position 4 in Figure 121, except insofar as they were seen to run up on land. Watson[6] reported that the wave train consisted of at least four major peaks [see p. 103]: these may have been comparatively short period perturbations on a single long period tsunami, as the tide gauge seems to suggest. Later during the day, about 15 h, a ship under way at position 3 in Figure 121 reported a wave 6 m high which struck the ship and stopped the chronometers: Verbeek[5] [see p. 102 and 217], however, thought that this was merely a freak sea wave, unconnected with Krakatoa. [Interference of tsunami and other waves may also produce unusually large individual waves in such circumstances.] Finally it should be noted that a moderate tsunami occurred on 10 October 1883, possibly due to a secondary steam explosion, such as continued for several months in the submarine banks formed of hot ejecta, and in the Krakatoa caldera itself[5] [see p. 219 and 228].

[1]Judd (1888a).
[2]Self and Rampino (1980).
[3]Stehn (1929a).
[4]Strachey (1888).
[5]Verbeek (1886). [Note that Latter's page references are for the 1886 French edition.]
[6]Watson (1883).
[7]Weir, G.J. (1981), personal communication.
[8]Wharton (1888).
[9]Williams (1941).
[10]Yokoyama (1981).
[11]The old name has been deliberately used, instead of the modern Jakarta, in order to facilitate reference to the original accounts. The same applies to other names throughout this paper.
[12]Note that 1 h should be subtracted from Watson's times, in order to bring them into line with his observations of the principal eruption.
[13]A village a short distance from Telok Betong.
[14]Self and Rampino (1980), who appear to have reached similar conclusions to mine, although their evidence is not given, have studied this question.

Atmospheric Effects: Sunsets; Blue/green Suns; Bishop's Rings

Had the fierce ashes of some fiery peak
Been hurl'd so high they ranged about the globe?
For day by day, thro' many a blood-red eve,
· · · · ·
The wrathful sunset glared . . .

St. Telemachus
Alfred, Lord Tennyson, 1892

Of all of the geophysical phenomena related to Krakatau's 1883 eruption, those that affected the atmosphere received the most widespread attention. Surely at least three-quarters of the world's 1883 population of about 1,400 million must have been conscious of the gaudy sunrises and sunsets that decorated the sky in the months following the paroxysmal blasts. Many scholars chronicled their observations, scientific journals and even newspapers were filled with discussion, and fully two thirds of the Royal Society's 1888 report was devoted to description and interpretation of the atmospheric effects. Poets (see quotation above) and artists (see painting by Frederic Church on Plate 14) were inspired by these spectacular transient phenomena. There can be no doubt that the atmospheric effects of Krakatau's 1883 eruption helped to make it one of the most famous eruptions in history.

Several descriptions of sunsets, blue/green suns, and Bishop's ring have been reprinted in the narrative section (see p. 154–159). Of the multitude of published reports interpreting the atmospheric effects of the 1883 eruption, we have selected four that range from early skepticism to modern-day interpretation.

The Extraordinary Sunsets: A Conversion to the Volcanic Hypothesis (Ranyard, 1883–1884)

As accounts of bizarre sunsets and sunrises began to arrive in London soon after the Krakatau eruption, there were initial doubts, at least in some quarters, that these phenomena had anything to do with the eruption of a far-distant volcano. In the discussions below by A.C. Ranyard, published in Knowledge in late 1883 and early 1884, it is interesting to follow the "turnabout" in thinking that led to his acknowledgment of Krakatau's profound influence on much of the world's atmosphere.

The last number of Knowledge contains an extract from a letter received from a resident at Graaff Reinet, in South Africa, mentioning that a brilliant glow in the sky after sunset had for a month past attracted the attention of the inhabitants. Similar letters have been received from places in the northern hemisphere as distant as Ceylon on the one hand and Trinidad on the other; and within the last month sunset and sunrise tints of more than usual splendour have been observed in England and over the continent of Europe.

Dr. J. Arnold, writing to the *Times* of October 9, makes the following quotation from the letter of a friend in the Island of Trinidad:—"Last Sunday (September 2), about five o'clock, the sun looked like a blue globe . . . and after dark we thought that there was a fire in the town, from the bright redness of the heavens." Mr. Arnold adds, "All my correspondents agree as to the blue colour of the sun."

It will hardly be suggested that the volcanic cloud over Krakatoa was carried upwards by the heat of the eruption, and spread outwards over a whole hemisphere, drifting against the prevailing winds to India and South Africa. But the volcanic theory is completely negatived by the observation of the blue sun setting in the fiery heavens as seen from Trinidad (near to the centre of the opposite hemisphere from the Krakatoa eruption) on the 2nd of September, for it cannot be supposed that the volcanic matter was carried half round the earth in the period of seven days which elapsed between Sunday, the 26th of August, when the Java eruption began, and Sunday the 2nd of September, when the blue sun was seen setting at Trinidad.

There remains the not improbable supposition that the earth has encountered a cloud of dust in space. In a paper published in the *Monthly Notices* for January, 1879, I have collected a series of observations which show that meteoric dust is continually being deposited on the earth's surface.

[Four months later, writing in the same journal, Ranyard's views had shifted.]

There can be no doubt that the brilliant sunset colours observed in Europe and other places distant from Krakatoa are due to the ordinary atmospheric absorption, chiefly at the blue end of the spectrum, of the light dispersed by dust floating at a great height in the air in smaller quantities than in the tropical regions where the blue and green sun phenomena of the first few weeks after the eruption were seen.

. . . the facts which have come to light with regard to the Krakatoa dust-cloud have shaken my faith in

the conclusion which I had previously come to . . . .

[A week later, Ranyard wrote:]

There seems to be some evidence to show that brilliant sunset phenomena have been observed on former occasions in connection with volcanic eruptions.

This evidence is not conclusive, but it lends some probability to the assumption that the recent sunset phenomena are connected with the great Krakatoa eruption.

[After another month, on April 18, Ranyard was marshalling more evidence for the Krakatau source. After recounting the optical effects from Mauritius at sunrise on August 29, he wrote:]

About the same time an abnormal appearance of the sun was observed at the Seychelles, over a thousand miles to the north of Mauritius, and three thousand miles due west from Krakatoa. "At the Seychelles, on the morning of the 29th, the sun was more like a full moon than anything, and at sunset on the 28th it looked as it does through a fog or on a frosty day in England." It will be noticed that at the Seychelles only the dimming of the sun's light was observed; the red colour of the sunsets was not noticed, nor is there any mention of the blue or green appearance of the sun's disc, either here, or at Mauritius. Probably the particles floating in the air on the 28th and 29th were too large to give rise to the blue colour of the sun which was seen at a greater distance from Krakatoa, and after an interval of time in the neighbourhood of the eruption.

The "Equatorial Smoke Stream" and Blue/green Sunsets (Bishop, 1884a)

Just over a week after the paroxysmal eruption, Rev. S.E. Bishop (a son of one of Hawaii's original missionary families, but no relation to the Bishop Museum founders), began to observe and document spectacular sunrises and sunsets in Honolulu. Bishop appears to have been the first to document the westward, equatorial motion of high-altitude ejecta from Krakatau, and he is credited with the first description (see p. 156) of the broad opalescent corona that formed around the sun, known to this day as "Bishop's ring." In the article excerpted below, from the May 1884 issue of The Hawaiian Monthly, *Bishop begins with a brief description of the immediate effects of the eruption—"the virulent enormity of Krakatoa's explosion, which has begirt the world with flaming sunsets."*

Gigantic as were these effects, they were surpassed in strangeness and extent, by those conspicuous effects which were left upon the earth's atmosphere, causing the remarkable sunset and sunrise glows which have set the world wondering. These are still the subject of close study by the scientific world, whose substantially unanimous opinion ascribes them to the smoke, or more precisely, the vapor and comminuted dust of lava, blown into the atmospheric heights from Krakatoa, and diffused thence by ordinary atmospheric currents throughout the globe. This peculiar haze with its glows has been conspicuous in all quarters of the globe, from the latter part of November to the end of January, and is still occasionally observed at Honolulu in April, the attendant opalescent corona around the sun being constantly seen.

Residents of Honolulu will not fail to recall the surprising spectacle of Wednesday evening, the 5th of September last, as well as of many nights and mornings following, when on all sides portentous masses of colored light came suddenly pouring out of the pellucid blue, like instant condensations of invisible vapors, and when the whole west outflamed in broad sheets of gold and olive green and blazing crimson, all at last at a late hour settling down into a low deep lurid glow, as of some wide but remote conflagration, which continued visible until ninety minutes after sundown. That evening at setting, the sun was observed to be *green*. On the morning of the same day, passengers on the *Zealandia* steaming hence towards the line [equator], were awakened by *blue* sunshine streaming into their berths.

On the evening of the 4th, a like spectacle with ours of the 5th was observed at Fanning's Island, near the line, and nearly due south of us. On the 3rd, two days earlier than ours, about 2,000 miles ESE, like appearances of wonderful brilliancy were observed from the dismasted bark *C. Southard Hurlburt*. On the second, three days before ours, a green sun filled with wonder the dwellers of Panama, Venezuela and Trinidad along the South Caribbean. On the first of September, four days earlier than Honolulu, the green sun was reported at Maranham near the Amazon, and at Cape Coast Castle on the Gulf of Guinea. Still

four days earlier we hear of the green sun on the same equatorial line in the Indian Ocean, at the Seychelles Islands, only three thousand miles west of Java, and this on the 28th of August, only one day after the great explosion of Krakatoa. Here then we find a vast continuous stream of volcanic vapors, sweeping due west from the ejecting column, to the Seychelles with a velocity of 125 miles an hour, and to Honolulu of nearly 80 miles, or 18,000 miles in ten days.

[Bishop goes on to discuss more northward dispersion of Krakatau ejecta, accounting for the green sun observations in Ceylon 13 days after the eruption and the lurid sunsets still later in North America and Europe.]

This grand phenomenon appeals strongly to the imagination. We marvel at the enormous explosive force at Krakatoa that blew far into the ocean the greater part of an island as high as Lanai, and half as large, and shot to unmeasured heights millions of tons of the fiery entrails of the earth. We think in dismay of that vast pall of volcanic cloud which buried a hundred thousand square miles in darkness that all but stifled, and through which for many hours poured down the ashes and pumice over broad regions of land and sea. But the thought towers to sublimity when we conceive of that strong bright pennon of vapor streaming far and straight in the higher skies away west over the broad Indian Ocean, striking on and on over the Dark Continent and its central lakes, over the upper Nile and middle Congo and lower Niger— flying on across the Atlantic, over the Amazon and the Andes and past the Caribbean, and still on in broadening sweep across the fair Pacific, to far Hawaii and beyond, announcing the great convulsion around the earth, and belting the globe with fiery skies. And meantime the vast cloud mass whence it streamed, having shed its heaviest dust, spreads far abroad, and begins its slow march of months across the continents to cover the whole globe with the same wonderful glares.

The Royal Society Report on Unusual Optical Phenomena (Russell and Archibald, 1888)

Atmospheric optical phenomena resulting from the Krakatau eruption persisted into 1886, and the enormous body of data gathered from around the world took time to assemble and analyze. This work led, however, to significant advances in the understanding of upper atmospheric circulation patterns and the overall geometry of the volcanic veils that spread globally from equatorial regions to higher latitudes. The gathering of both published and unpublished results began at the Royal Meteorological Society in January 1884, but upon learning of the Royal Society's Krakatoa Committee, the former effort was dissolved and its members accepted into the larger committee. Two of these members, F.A. Rollo Russell and E. Douglas Archibald, wrote the various sections of the 1888 report entitled "On the Unusual Optical Phenomena of the Atmosphere, 1883–1886, Including Twilight Effects, Coronal Appearances, Sky Haze, Coloured Suns, Moons, %c." The first section, 112 pages long, describes the various optical phenomena, and this is followed by a 50-page listing of dates of their first appearance. The next subsection discusses the geographical distribution of all the optical phenomena in space and time. The summary of this subsection, written by Russell, follows:

The dates in the general list leave no doubt that, on the whole, the tendency of the matter causing the twilight phenomena was to spread northwards and southwards as well as westwards during the rapid circuit of the blue sun matter from east to west with the tropics. The dates for India and the United States show this most distinctly. Excluding sporadic glows, due probably to small broken-off masses of the great cloud of matter, we find the northern limit near the end of the first circuit to have been about 22°N at Honolulu, or 28° north of Krakatoa, and the southern limit about 33°S at Santiago, or 27° south of Krakatoa. Wellington, New Zealand, at 41°S, cannot be taken as the southern limit; for Australia does not seem to have been affected so early as September 9th. In none of those places which were on the extreme borders of the main stream, or beyond it, were the glows regular and continuous from the date of the first appearance. Nor could they be expected to show continuity, when we have evidence that the cloud causing the rayless sun passed over most places in the tropics within three or four days. Towards the end of the first circuit, that is, in the Pacific, the amount of matter left behind after the passage of the main cloud seems to have been greater than in the Atlantic near the Equator, where

the sky in most parts presented no remarkable appearance after September 5th, until the arrival of the cloud on its second circuit.

At the end of the second circuit, about September 22nd, the glows may be roughly stated to have extended from between 20° and 30°N, to between 30° and 40°S, but their distribution was not regular within these limits.

While the movement westwards may be presumed to have continued after this date, there can be no doubt that a gradual extension northwards and southwards greatly widened the area over which the red twilights were seen during the next fortnight. They were conspicuous at several places between 20° and 36°N, and southwards as far as 27°S, in many different longitudes. Throughout October the Gulf of Mexico and corresponding latitudes were under the full effect of the glows. On October 7th Nashville, about 36°N, and Buenos Ayres, at 34°39′S, had brilliant sunsets; and at Binninag, India, 29°30′N 80°E, there was a fiery after-glow till 7.20 p.m. At the Canary Isles, 28°N, the glows were conspicuous. At Shanghai, or not far south of it, they were observed by pilots.

By October 15th the glows had extended still further north; in the United States they had reached 34°27′N, in Europe partially to 43°42′N, in Arabia to an unknown latitude, and in India to Umballa, 30°N.

By the end of October the glows had spread over the southern, and part of the eastern States of North America, while Australia, Tasmania, New Zealand, South Africa, and Chile, were under their full effect.

Up to about November 23rd glows seen north of about 32° to 36°N were for the most part detached or sporadic.

But about November 23rd, a very remarkable movement took place, in such a manner that the direction in which the main stratum progressed is not clear, in spite of a large collection of dates. Western Canada, British Columbia, California, and north-west Iceland, seem to have been first affected, and then in succession, England, Denmark, France, Italy, Germany, Spain, Algeria, Austria, Turkey, Russia, eastern Siberia, and northern China. To distinguish sporadic from continuous glows is no easy matter. But a general view inclines us to regard this later movement as taking place from west to east. An exact course cannot be determined owing to the inequality in density and irregularity of outline of the great cloud. Excluding occasional displays, the glows were seen in the north-western parts of Europe about a week before they drew attention in the east and south-east. England, as a whole, was affected before Denmark as a whole, Denmark before northern Russia, northern Russia before Kiachta [Kyakhta, S of Lake Baykal]. North Italy and Lisbon, parts of France and Germany, were affected on the 26th [see Plates 10 and 11], southeast Iceland, and a large part of western and central Europe, on the 27th, part of eastern Europe on the 28th, southern Italy and Greece about December 1st.

Over the northern part of North America the direction of movement does not appear, for the glows were seen about November 23rd in both east and west, and we can only infer that they were spreading quickly from the south, where they had long been sporadically noticed. San Francisco, New Westminster [British Columbia], and Oregon and London (Ontario) report them as beginning about the same time. On November 27th they were general in the States.

Perhaps the most probable supposition is that the main cloud both in America and in Europe was moving from nearly west to east; at all events, in the northern parts, with large offshoots extending from S or SW to N or NE. On the assumption of the northern limit having been continuous in the same latitude, it would be difficult to account for the eastern States having had glows at the same time as the western (while in Europe the east was later by about a week), and for England having been the first of European countries to enjoy them in their full splendour.

The movement of the earlier detached clouds, which reached parts of the northern States, England, and Russia, between November 8th and 11th, is equally uncertain. Their structure in England, however, indicated a movement from a point between W and S.

The structure of the main cloud indicated a motion from SSW to NNE, or an initial motion from S to N gaining an eastward drift. Observation showed, if anything, a slow motion from W to E.

A survey of the course of the phenomena of the sunset glows leads us to infer that within the tropics the matter causing them moved at about 73 miles an hour from E to W, and gradually spread southwards and northwards, becoming thinner and more diffused, so that by the end of a period of six weeks, viz., the 8th of October, nearly the whole space included between 30°N and 45°S had been subject to the phenomena; and that the motion from E to W became arrested as the matter travelled northwards and southwards. Further north and south than about 30° or 35°, it seems probable that the motion was from SW and W in the northern hemisphere and from NW and W in the southern hemisphere. The rapidity of propa-

gation to South Africa and Japan was so great that we can hardly doubt the prevalence at the time of a direct upper current in each direction at a level below that of the great current which carried the dust from E to W at the velocity above mentioned. The march of the glows over North America and Europe at the end of November appears to have been part of a movement of the hazy stratum from over the mid-Pacific and mid-Atlantic Oceans respectively, but we have no data for affirming that the glows receded from those vast areas at the corresponding time. From Honolulu, we have a report of an increase in brilliancy on November 25th,[1] and of a prevalence of the glow between Honolulu and New Hanover [New Guinea] continuously during September, October, and November; while the *Papa*, sailing from Apia (Samoan Islands), had nothing of the kind during October and November.

[In his next subsection, Russell illustrates the spreading of the optical phenomena on a global basis. He then goes on to discuss the speed of dispersal and time of origin.]

The series of small maps on Figure 123 show, as far as may be gathered from the scattered observations in our possession, the area affected by unusual phenomena in successive periods from August 26th to the end of November. The dotted lines bounding the shaded portions indicate the approximate northern and southern boundaries of the elevated haze which gave rise to the conspicuous changes in the colour of the sun or sky. A continuous dark line shows a better ascertained limit, and an absence of bounding lines, as in IV. and V., signifies a total failure of available data from which any limit could be drawn.

Isolated observations, such as the two in Ceylon during the week August 27th to September 4th, and the appearances seen at the end of August in a narrow stream from Java to Japan, are omitted in these maps. In No. I. the dotted line enclosing Florida shows the rather extensive area over which red twilights were seen from September 5th to 9th, including probably the West Indian Islands, from which observations are wanting. In No. VI. the front of the cloud is shown, on successive days from August 26th to September 9th, by dotted lines, the only complete blanks occurring during the passage across Central Africa on August 29th, and between 170°E and 135°E on September 8th (Eastern time).

From [tables presented on p. 335–337 of the Royal Society Report] we find that the speed of westward progression of the blue sun phenomena, shown by taking an average of the rates in the above list, was

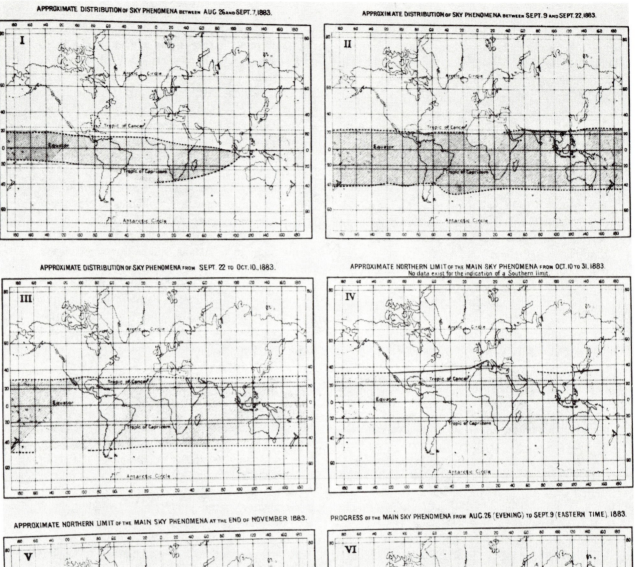

APPROXIMATE DISTRIBUTION OF SKY PHENOMENA BETWEEN AUG. 26 AND SEPT. 7, 1883.

APPROXIMATE DISTRIBUTION OF SKY PHENOMENA BETWEEN SEPT. 9 AND SEPT. 22, 1883.

APPROXIMATE DISTRIBUTION OF SKY PHENOMENA FROM SEPT. 22 TO OCT. 10, 1883.

APPROXIMATE NORTHERN LIMIT OF THE MAIN SKY PHENOMENA FROM OCT. 10 TO 31, 1883.
No data exist for the indication of a Southern limit.

APPROXIMATE NORTHERN LIMIT OF THE MAIN SKY PHENOMENA AT THE END OF NOVEMBER 1883.

PROGRESS OF THE MAIN SKY PHENOMENA FROM AUG. 26 (EVENING) TO SEPT. 9 (EASTERN TIME), 1883.

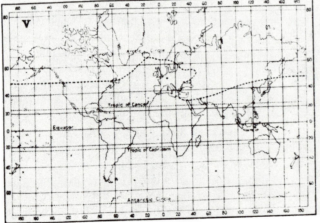

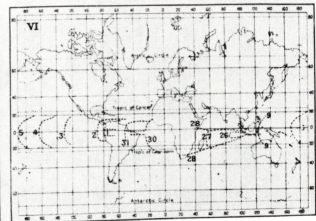

about 70.4 miles an hour for the first circuit of the earth, 76.4 for the second circuit, and 76.3 for the first half of the third circuit, taking Krakatoa as the starting point for each distance; and by taking the intervals of time between intermediate points in the first circuit, 80.1. Seven of the best[2] data in the first circuit give a rate of 76.3 miles from Krakatoa to the various localities.

The speed of progression of the haze in the sky was[3] 70 miles an hour for the first circuit, 77.2 for the second, and 76 between points in the first circuit. Taking two of the best observations—one in 26°30'W, and the other in 161°W (the *Papa*)—the rate between these points appears to have been 80.3 miles an hour, which is probably near the true maximum speed.

The speed of progression of the red fore-glows and after-glows in the first circuit was 76; or excluding Natal, as affected by previous eruptions, 74.8. The mean of eight of the best observations[4] gives 72.2 miles an hour, from Krakatoa to the various localities. For intermediate points the speed was 72 miles an hour by the mean of twelve observations.

The first observation of a blue or rayless sun west of Africa was at Maranham, giving a rate of 83 miles; the first observation of a peculiar hazy or leaden sky was that of a German ship, in 10°N, 26°W, giving a rate of 83.7 miles; and the first unmistakeable appearance of the red glow was at St. Helena, giving a rate of 80 miles an hour. These figures nearly agree with the rate (83 miles) given by the first blue sun observation at Guayaquil, taking Krakatoa as the starting point. The highest calculated rates are obviously the nearest to the true speed, for in many instances the phenomena would not be noted till after the condition had prevailed for some hours; and the atmospheric change producing the red glows would not be noticed during the daylight or night-time. The rate of progression of all three phenomena in a westerly

direction may therefore be taken as between 81 and 84 miles an hour at the maximum; but the main body, causing the most conspicuous appearances, travelled at the rate of only aout 72 miles an hour in the first circuit, if the date of starting is correct. Possibly the speed of the second circuit was somewhat greater, or the matter becoming added to that which remained in the subjacent upper air from the first passage more speedily produced noticeable glow effects. Moreover, observers may have been more ready to note at once unusual appearances. The calculated speed is more reduced in the first than in the second and third circuits by assuming the eruption to have occurred on the 26th, if the phenomena were really due to the eruption of the 27th; so that it is probable that the most conspicuous blue sun phenomena at great distances from Krakatoa were produced by the explosions which occurred early on August 27th, and in that case the propagation must have been considerably more rapid that that shown by the list. For instance, the rate to Panama would be 79 miles an hour instead of 70, supposing the great eruption at 10 a.m. to have been the cause of the blue sun.

Places near the same latitude as Krakatoa and near the Equator were earliest affected by haze and solar obscuration. The difference between the rates resulting from different places of observation would possibly be accounted for by the clouds of matter from the several explosions between 2 p.m. on August 26th and 10 a.m. on August 27th not consisting of a continuous mass but of streams of unequal density and at different altitudes. As the eruptions succeeded each other in a large number of explosions, the intensity of which varied, the height attained by the ejecta would not be the same throughout. The slight haze seen at Seychelles, Rodriguez, Ceylon, and Labuan [E. Malaysia] on August 27th, can hardly be ascribed to the explosions of that day, but were more probably due to the eruptions of the night of August 25th-26th, or of the 26th, or even of the previous week.

A very heavy outburst must have occurred about 11.25 a.m. on August 26th, as the barometer rose and fell about 3/10ths of an inch on board the *Lennox Castle* in 91°E; and the eruption sounds heard at Ceylon at 7 a.m., which must have originated at about 5 a.m. on the 26th, showed that early on this day the volcano was already violently active.

The influence of an incorrect date at the starting-point is so much reduced in the second and third circuits that the rates given by these are probably near the true speed. We have thus for the blue sun, second

Figure 123. I–III show the approximate distribution of sky phenomena for the periods August 26–September 7, 1883, September 9–22, 1883, and September 22–October 10, 1883, respectively. IV and V show the approximate northern limit of the main sky phenomena for the period October 10–31, 1883 and at the end of November 1883, respectively. No data exist for the indication of a southern limit. VI shows the progress of the main sky phenomena from the evening of August 26 to September 9, 1883 (eastern time). [Russell and Archibald's plate XXXVII.]

circuit, 76.4 miles, first half of third circuit, 76.3 miles. These rates thus agreeing with the 76.3 miles obtained from the intervals between Krakatoa and points in the first circuit, where some of the best observations were made.

For the sky haze, we get 77.2 miles an hour for the second circuit, compared with 76 for intermediate points in the first circuit.

For the red glows there is no definite second or third circuit, but the mean of six of the best pairs of observations[5] at intermediate points in the first circuit gives 71 miles an hour.

From these figures we may infer with some force that the eruption which caused most of the blue suns, lofty haze, and red glows at distances beyond two or three thousand miles from Krakatoa on the given dates, occurred not on August 26th, but on August 27th, for in that case the calculated speed of the first circuit approximates very closely to that of the second and third circuits and for distances between intermediate points.

But there seems to be little room for doubt that the earliest effects in the Atlantic and Pacific and at Maranham [now São Luís, Brazil] were in part due to the eruption of the 26th. Therefore, it seems undesirable to calculate from all the data on the assumption of the phenomena being due to the great outburst of the morning of the 27th; and the initial date is accordingly taken as 2 p.m. on August 26th, though doubtless the explosion of that afternoon caused only a part of the effects. The speed of the red glows approaches remarkably near to that of the sky-haze, considering that they were mostly seen only north and south of the main stream of hazy matter, that is, where the haze was less dense and probably slightly less lofty. This close approximation to the speed of the main Equator stream from east to west indicates that the red glow when first seen was caused by the spread northwards or southwards of matter detached from the main stream at no great distance; for, a passage through many degrees would have been subject to appreciable retardation of the east to west movement by the slower motion of the earth in higher latitudes. As there is no reason to suppose that the process of precipitation of particles from the main stream abruptly ceased in the Indian Ocean, the sporadic glows seen far north and south of the blue sun area during the first circuit would, in all probability, be largely caused by the descent of the less finely divided matter into upper currents which would rapidly convey it beyond the tropics, and temporarily add to the brilliancy of sunset skies in regions unaffected, till long after, by the cloud of much lighter particles composing the main body of the haze stratum.

[The next section, by Archibald, is on the twilight glows and the altitude of the stratum that caused them. We reprint Archibald's summary below:]

(1.) That in the brilliant glows which began in the tropics after the eruption of Krakatoa on August 26th and 27th there is distinct evidence of a primary glow caused by the direct rays of the sun, and of a secondary glow succeeding this, and due to reflection of the primary glow by the same stratum. That these primary and secondary glows correspond to the first and second crepuscular spaces of ordinary twilight; and that the main difference between the secondary of the present series and the ordinary second crepuscular space is that the former was coloured, whereas the ordinary second twilight is white, and seen only from high altitudes or in peculiarly favourable circumstances.

(2.) That the glow-causing material appeared suddenly and at about its greatest height, at first in the Indian Ocean, near Krakatoa, and for some degrees north and south of its parallel throughout the tropical zone; that it subsequently spread into the extra-topics, as is fully described in [the list of first appearance dates (not reprinted above)]; and that, partly owing to lapse of time and partly to change of locality, it appeared at a lessened altitude.

(3.) That the height of the upper or middle part of the stratum, as deduced mainly from the particles which were large enough to reflect, progressively diminished from 121,000 feet in August to about 64,000 feet in January, 1884, the inferior limits being more probably those . . . from 104,000 feet in August, to 56,000 feet in January, and the corresponding means, 87,500 feet from the longer durations, and 70,000 feet from the mean durations respectively.

(4.) That by April, 1884, a considerable portion of the larger reflecting particles had sifted out by gravitation, causing a minimum duration and brilliancy of the secondary glow; that, as this occurred coincidentally with a maximum development of the corona, or Bishop's Ring, we are led to conclude that a large portion of the finer material remained in suspension at nearly the same height as at first, and that having become more homogeneous than at first, it was rendered capable of exerting its maximum diffractive power.

(5.) That while the present series of glows, both primary and secondary, reached a decided minimum everywhere about April, 1884, they subsequently exhibited a partial renewal of their former brilliancy and duration in the autumn and winter months of 1884 and 1885, similar to what is found to occur normally at such seasons through the influence of certain meteorological factors in the ordinary twilights—a fact which renders it impossible to arrive at any certain deductions regarding the rate of descent of the stratum as a whole.

(6.) That the brilliancy and duration of the phenomena were closely connected, but how far the duration was dependent on, or independent of, the precise quality or brilliancy of the glow does not exactly appear; of the two glows, the secondary seems to have far exceeded the primary in the amplitude of its variations, and its sensitiveness to general meteorological influences.

(7.) That the rapid decline of the glows both in brilliancy and in duration in the spring of 1884, and their subsequent re-appearances in the latter parts of 1884 and 1885, at a much reduced brilliancy, show that, while they were caused by the presence of an unusual quantity of dust in the upper regions of the atmosphere, this material gradually became eliminated, until, by the commencement of 1886, things had returned to their normal condition.

(8.) That while the duration of twilight was sensibly lengthened, during the prevalence of the glows, the action of the glow-causing material, except in as far as it tended to transmit the blue rather than the red end of the spectrum (partly by diffraction and partly by absorption), and thus produce certain unusual tints and sequences of colour, affected the sun's light in a manner somewhat similar to that produced by the dust and vapour particles ordinarily present in the atmosphere at lower elevations. That the final effects were produced by the prolonged reflection from the lofty stratum of rays (1) partly deprived of their red components by the action of the stratum itself, and (2) to a much larger extent subsequently deprived of their blue components by the ordinary dust and vapour particles of the lower atmosphere. It was, therefore, mainly an intensification of ordinary twilight phenomena, consequent on the presence, at a lofty altitude, of solid particles not usually existent there.

(9.) That similar unusually brilliant and long twilight glows, including the *secondary coloured* glow, which is one of the principal characteristics by which the present series has been distinguishable from ordinary twilight phenomena, have been witnessed at intervals in former years, and generally in association with volcanic phenomena.

[After a discussion of pre-1883 atmospheric phenomena linked to volcanism, and a review of hypotheses suggested for the 1883–1886 phenomena, the Royal Society's long (315 pp) report on optical phenomena ends with a discussion of their connection with the volcanic events. Archibald's summary follows:]

We shall therefore conclude by summarising as briefly as possible the chief reasons for considering all the unusual optical effects (including those seen in extra-tropical latitudes) which made their appearance in September, October, November, and December, 1883, and in part thenceforward up to the end of 1885, to be direct consequences of the eruption of Krakatoa in August, 1883:

(1.) The fact that the entire range of optical effects, including the brilliant and unusually prolonged glows at sunrise and sunset, the blue, green, silvery, and coppery appearance of the sun, the lofty cloud-haze, and the large corona round the sun and moon, made their appearance locally after the minor, and universally after the major, eruptions, in such a manner as to show that they all had a common origin both in space and in time, and that this origin was the neighborhood of the volcano Krakatoa in May and August, 1883.

(2.) That the twilight glows, coloured sun, cloud-haze, and corona (the latter being less frequently observed at first, though not less widely spread than the others) appeared for the most part progressively along and symmetrically with respect to, a line extending west from Java and parallel with the Equator, the motion along this line being evidently real, since in the section where the distribution in space and time is worked out in detail, they are shown to have appeared at places where they had not previously been seen, or to have reappeared where they had temporarily declined, after they had made one complete circuit of the globe, and at substantially the same rate in longitude as at first.

(3.) The unusual character, duration, and universality of the cloud-haze, its effect on astronomical definition, its general similarity to attenuated volcanic smoke or dust, and the general testimony in favour of the fact that this haze was the proximate cause of all the other optical phenomena.

(4.) The unusual character, duration, and large size of the coronal appendage to the sun, showing that the haze which caused it was composed of very small particles, its independence of all ordinary meteorological changes, its survival of the glows, and the gradual disappearance of both haze and corona in the summer of 1886.

(5.) The extraordinary height to which the ejecta of the eruption of Krakatoa on August 26th were observed to ascend, and the fairly close agreement of this and other direct observations with the height of the stratum as calculated from the duration of the twilight glows in the tropics and in the neighbourhood of the volcano. Also the fact that the greatest mean height of the stratum was observed at first in the tropical and Indian area, and that as time went on a gradual subsidence of the material took place everywhere, as would be likely to occur if it were dust ejected from below into the upper regions.

(6.) The evidence given . . . on "Previous Analogous Glow Phenomena" which in many cases are shown to be directly consequent on eruptions of neighboring or distant volcanoes; as also the phenomena observed by Whymper in the Andes, and certain effects noticed in the vicinity during the eruption of Krakatoa, and recorded in Mr. Verbeek's *Krakatau.*

There are many minor considerations which point the same way, and which have been incidentally mentioned or implied in the foregoing sections.

Amongst others, the *continuity* of the propagation of the material and the corresponding optical phenomena, from their first general appearance in the Indian Ocean, after August 26th, including their successive revolutions round the globe from east to west within the tropics, and their subsequent spread from west to east over northern Europe and Asia.

Also the fact that while Bishop's Ring appeared sporadically in a few places after the May eruptions of Krakatoa, it seems never to have been observed by such careful observers as Professor von Bezold, M. Thollon, of Nice, and Mr. T.W. Backhouse, of Sunderland (a halo observer for 25 years), until the general arrival, at their respective localities, of the haze and other optical phenomena which succeeded the August eruptions.

There are one or two minor points which present opportunities for further research; for example, the precise effects of dust, or dust and vapour, upon sunlight. Professor Tyndall's, Professor Kiessling's and Captain Abney's experiments on the dispersion and diffraction of light by small particles, have advanced the question considerably, but much remains to be done.

Amongst others, further information would be desirable on the following points:—

(1.) The inferior limit of the size of ice particles produced from vapour.

(2.) Observations as to the rate of fall of small particles in rarefied air.

(3.) The duration of ordinary coloured twilights under different meteorological conditions.

(4.) The motion of the upper cloud systems near the Equator.

(5.) The meteorological and physical conditions under which ice crystals would produce diffraction coronae and not refraction halos.

[1]Bishop (1884b).

[2]Viz.: *Corona,* Varinas, Guayaquil, *Superb,* Fanning Island, *Papa,* Honolulu.

[3]Excluding the observations on the 27th as probably due to previous eruptions.

[4]Viz.: Mauritius, St. Helena, *Corona, Olbers, British Envoy,* Varinas, *Superb,* Maalaaea.

[5]Namely: St. Helena to 16°5′S 148°45′W; 10°N 26°W to 17°N 125°W; *Corona* to Fanning Island, Rodriguez to St. Helena; Trinidad to Honolulu; and *British Envoy* to C. *Southard-Hurlburt.*

Volcanic Dust in the Atmosphere, A Modern View (Lamb, 1970)

In 1970, the eminent meteorologist H.H. Lamb published his extensive study on volcanic dust in the atmosphere and its meteorological significance. Not surprisingly, the well-known optical phenomena associated with the 1883 eruption of Krakatau figured prominently in Lamb's discussion. At the time of his paper there had been very little direct sampling of high altitude volcanic dust veils, and what was known of their prevailing particle sizes and heights was derived mainly from ground-based observation of optical effects. Lamb's discussion of dust particle sizes, near the start of his paper, provides a modern interpretation of the three main optical phenomena reported after the Krakatau eruption: blue sun or moon, Bishop's ring, and exceptional sunsets.

Particles small in comparison with the wavelength of the incident light, as is the case with most atmospheric dust other than volcanic dust and with smoke haze, scatter the short wavelengths more than the long, so that the Sun and Moon appear red or reddish. There are also many observations of dimmed and reddish Sun after volcanic eruptions, even at points far removed from the origin of the volcanic dust in place and time. [10] Many of the particles concerned are less than half a micrometre [½ μm = ½,₀₀₀ mm = ⅟₅₁,₀₀₀ inch] in cross-section.[7]

On rare occasions the Sun and Moon, seen through a cloud of minute water droplets or solid particles in which some required range of sizes predominates, appear blue or green. These are bigger particles than those discussed in the previous paragraph. At times the colour is merely bluish grey or white, in which hints of a blue tint vary with time. Blue Sun or Moon was reported at various places and times, usually of rather brief duration and occasionally with a notable tendency to red colour in the interim, in association with volcanic dust clouds after eruptions in 1783, 1821, 1822, 1831, 1855, and 1883.[9] Within the first nine months after the great explosive eruption of Krakatau (6°S 105½°E) in August 1883 the Sun, Moon and planet Venus occasionally appeared blue or green when seen from points (mainly) within the tropical zone. Also after the other eruptions mentioned blue Sun or Moon was seen only either near the volcano or within one latitude zone around the world over which the densest dust veil was carried by the upper winds, and where it may reasonably be supposed that there were greater concentrations of rather larger particles than in most of the dust veil. According to Minnaert,[6] from observations of similar phenomena seen through artificial clouds of steam and smoke, the Sun and Moon appear blue when the particle diameters in the cloud are mainly between 1 and 5 μm. Blue Sun and Moon were again observed over Britain and western Europe on 4 or 5 days at the end of September 1950, when shining through a smoke trail in the upper troposphere from exceptionally great forest fires in northern Alberta, Canada.[1] This may be a diffraction phenomenon; though the expected surrounding bright, reddish ring, the radius of which depends on particle size, would be unlikely to be seen unless there were a strong predominance of some quite small range of particle sizes.

After the eruption of Krakatau in 1883 an unusual corona surrounding the Sun was described for the first time by the Reverend S.E. Bishop in Honolulu [see p. 156] and subsequently observed in many places. The sky near the Sun was generally white or bluish white instead of blue and this area of white illumination, sometimes brilliant enough to be described as a white glare, was occasionally seen to be edged with a ring of pink, red, brown or orange-rose colour at an angular distance of about 20° from the Sun. The angle appeared rather less when the Sun's elevation was high and greater when the Sun was low. This phenomenon has ever since been known as 'Bishop's ring'. The coloured ring is apparently never conspicuous and may often have passed unnoticed. It was observed again after the eruptions in the West Indies [and Guatemala] in 1902 and in Alaska in 1912. And after not being seen for 50 years, it was observed again following the eruption in Bali in 1963, at least over central and southern Africa.[2,11] Schuepp reports that it was frequently visible on clear days over the Congo from December 1963 onwards, the sky near the Sun's disk being much brighter than in other years. In December 1964 this anomaly became weaker. In the Krakatau case, although the ring was originally described by Bishop within 10 days of the explosive eruption in August 1883, and possibly first seen near the volcano after the preliminary eruptions in May to July, it was most frequently and widely observed in many parts of the world in 1884 and 1885, reached its maximum brightness almost a year after the eruption and was last seen in the early summer of 1886.

The radius of Bishop's ring should, according to theory, vary inversely with the size of the dust particles or droplets causing it. Moreover, there must be a great predominance of particles within quite a narrow size range, or else the diffraction pattern due to particles of one size would obliterate that of another, rendering the colour invisible. Probably this is the chief reason why the white glare is often seen all about the Sun but the coloured ring at its edge only rarely. De Bary and Bullrich[3] imply that particles of diameter 0.8 to 1 μm would produce a Bishop's ring of 20° radius as observed in 1883–6; smaller particles would produce a bigger ring, radius about 38° for particle diameter 0.5 μm. A faint ring at such a wide angle from the Sun would be very liable to go unobserved, but in fact no ring of radius even approaching 38° has been reported. (Earlier accounts, for instance, by Humphreys[5] have generally followed Pernter[8] in indicating a prevailing particle diameter of about 1.85 um when the ring was observed in the Krakatau dust veil.)

Exceptionally beautiful sunsets and twilight glows have accompanied many volcanic dust veils and attracted much comment. Most prominent in the paintings, photographs and descriptive accounts is simply the brilliant rosy or fiery (also described as 'lurid' or 'flame') red coloured glow which lingers near the horizon unusually long after the Sun has set, when a volcanic dust veil is present. (This colour was much used by J.M.W. Turner in his paintings from about 1807 onwards and especially in the 1830s. Though

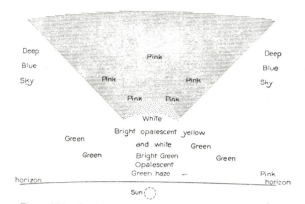

Figure 124. Sketch of 'sunset colours' recorded by F.A.R. Russell at Richmond, Surrey, about 17 h to 17 h 30 min on 9 November 1883. Sunset had been at 16 h 23 min. The pink patch was in view from about 16 h 40 min to 17 h 58 min, descending from about 45° elevation till it disappeared below the horizon. There were two maxima of illumination, about 17 h and 17 h 32 min. The earlier maximum was very bright, the later one was described as 'bright and deep purple coloured'. [Lamb's figure 1a.]

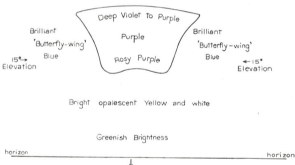

Figure 125. Sky colours observed from Guildford, Surrey at 17 h 05 min to 17 h 10 min GMT on 24 December 1963, as sketched at the time by H.H. Lamb. Sunset was at 15 h 56 min. The purple patch was softly illuminated, but marked off sharply at its edges from the much more brilliantly illuminated parts of the sky on either side and below, though with somewhat less distinction at its upper edge. The patch was in view from about 16 h 30 min for three-quarters of an hour or more, descending towards the horizon. In these earlier stages, before the sketch was made, the sky on either side of the purple patch was brilliant white and below the patch bright, yellowish white with a rose-coloured band along the horizon: the purple patch itself was brighter then and higher in the sky. [Lamb's figure 1b.]

these works did not pretend to accuracy of form, the colour for which his work is famous may well have been suggested by the volcanic dust veils of those years.) Within the dusk and dawn displays a phenomenon fairly often reported is a purplish patch, which may be seen at elevations broadly about 20° when the Sun is between 3 and 7° below the horizon (20 to 50 min after sunset in middle latitudes) but, in the best occurrences, is repeated when the Sun is about twice as far (10 to 13°) below the horizon (60 to 90 min after sunset): the second purple patch may be the more clearly seen against the fainter illumination of the background sky at that time. The optics have been explained by Gruner.[4] The angular distance of the first purple patch from the sun is the same as that of Bishop's ring, and the two may be essentially the same phenomenon[4] ([Gruner's] p. 518). After Krakatau 1883 Bishop's ring was more widely noticed many months later when the twilights were becoming fainter. Purple patch observations from England in 1963–4, 1883, 1855–7, 1818 and 1814–15 suggest dust veils of similar structure in all those years. The same may be deduced from observations in Scandinavia in 1680, 1661, 1636 and 1553. In all these years therefore particle sizes and heights of the dust layer at points far removed from the eruption which produced the veil seem to have been similar to those in the Krakatau case. There is indeed a remarkable similarity between the observations sketched by F.A.R. Russell about an hour after sunset on 9 November 1883 and by the present writer in December 1963, in both cases in Surrey, England, reproduced here as Figures 124 and 125. A similar observation was made at Guildford an hour before sunrise on 17 January 1964.

The brilliant whiteness of the sky, noticeable for much of the day, within about 15 to 20° of the Sun was probably the most frequently observed symptom of the volcanic dust veils in the cases here discussed; though where the dust concentration was particularly dense (as over the equatorial and tropical zones at times in 1883 and 1963 and over northern temperate latitudes in 1783) the sky often had a 'dirty' or 'muddy' look. For some time immediately before sunrise and immediately after sunset the white glare replaced the unusually prolonged red glow. It seems that Bishop's ring must be regarded as a rare phenomenon occurring only when and where the dust particles happen to have been sorted as to size and yielded a strong predominance of the required size: this probably limits it to association with just one of the usually overlapping dust layers in the stratosphere produced probably at one explosive stage of a given volcanic eruption.

With the densest volcanic dust veils the dimming of the Sun, which in southern France in June 1783 was not visible till it reached 17° above the horizon, and the brightness of the dusk lasting well on into the night (also particularly in 1783), have attracted more notice than any ring or colour phenomena. Part of the explanation probably lies in the wider than usual range of particle sizes present in those veils. The dimming of the Sun was also remarked on by observers without instruments in 1601 (in Scandanavia), in 1821 (in France), in 1831 (in Africa), and in 1963 (in Africa and Arabia).

· · · · ·

During the existence of the most persistent volcanic dust veils white glare and prolonged lurid red twilight glows appear to become regular daily occurrences over wide regions of the Earth. Bishop's ring and the bright purple patch were always of more intermittent occurrence, up to ten times a month at any one place, if they occurred at all. Blue Sun and Moon have been still more localized in place and time, chiefly near the erupting volcano or broadly within the same latitude zone. This order of frequency appears to be also the order of size of the particles responsible, the bigger the particles the rarer, more localized and short-lived the occurrence. The biggest particles must tend to fall out before the patch of abundant dust with which they were ejected has time, after being carried round the Earth, to diffuse into a veil of fairly uniform texture covering one or more latitude zones.

It appears from this summary that dust clouds with particles commonly of 1 to 5 μm cross section have remained in existence for several months, but that those dust veils which spread over much of the Earth more characteristically consist of particles of various sizes from ≤ 0.5 to about 2 μm across. Occasionally the denser dust clouds within the veil are size-sorted sufficiently to give Bishop's ring with angular radius corresponding to prevalence of particles of near 1 μm cross-measurement. Confirmatory evidence that the sizes mentioned are most abundant may also be deduced from the lifetimes of several dust veils authenticated over various parts of the globe by visual and actinometric observations. After the Bali 1963 eruption it was confirmed by direct measurement of volcanic dust particles collected at a height of 20 km over Australia between April 1963 and April 1964.[7] Day-to-day variations in the phenomena observed near, or within the same latitude zone as, the volcano are doubtless due to inhomogeneities in the dust cloud attributable to variations in the ejection rate and to subsequent lateral and vertical turbulence of the wind flow in the dust layer. Farther from the volcano, and later in time, day-to-day variations become less and less noticeable: such as do occur may be attributed either to some continued inhomogeneity of dust concentration or, possibly, to condensation effects.

[1]Bull (1951).
[2]Burdecki (1964).
[3]De Bary and Bullrich (1959).
[4]Gruner (1942).
[5]Humphreys (1940, p. 591).
[6]Minnaert (1959).
[7]Mossop (1964).
[8]Pernter (1889).
[9]Symons (1888).
[10]Darkened lunar eclipses were noted in Europe in 1884 and 1964 after the volcanic eruptions in the East Indies more than a year previously: normally in a lunar eclipse the shadowed part of the moon can be clearly seen by naked eye and telescope observation reveals colours, but during the total eclipse observed in Britain on 18 December 1964 this was not so (*New Scientist*, 31 December 1964).
[11]W. Scheup, personal communication, 18 May, 1965.

A.B. and M.P. Meinel include the following illustrations in their book Sunsets, Twilights, and Evening Skies, *soon to be published by Cambridge University Press. The sections through the curving earth's surface illustrate the geometry of color sequences seen after sunset in the presence of a volcanic stratum, and the graph permits the easy determination of that stratum's altitude above the earth.*

Additional Comments on Optical Phenomena (Deirmendjian, 1973)

Shortly after Lamb's report was published, another atmospheric scientist, D. Deirmendjian, undertook an extensive review of the pertinent literature on volcanic turbidity in the atmosphere. This Rand Corporation study assessed not only volcanic influence on climate, but also the expected atmospheric impact of turbidity introduced by future flights of supersonic transport (SST) aircraft. We extract sections of his review that supplement the

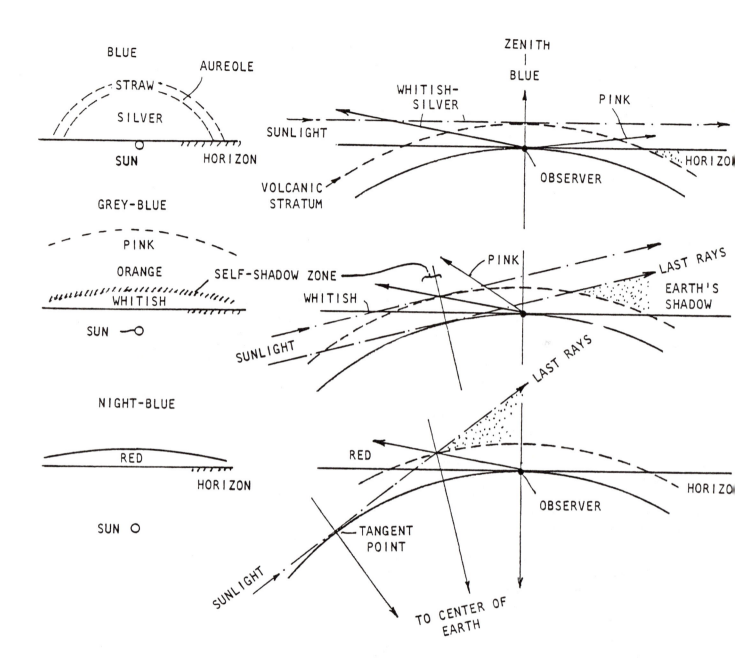

Figure 126. Geometry and view of the western sky at three times after sunset. *Top:* At sunset with afternoon aureole of the sun still showing. Above the sun is a silvery shield with perhaps a touch of yellowish color at the edge of this aureole. All the solar rays shine on the ash layer *from above*, and thus are not colored. *Middle:* About 20 minutes after sunset when the self-shadow zone of the volcanic ash layer is seen 10° above the horizon, with unreddened sunlight shining *down* on the layer below this zone and with light dimmed and reddened by passage through the layer shining *up* on the layer above this zone. In this diagram, the whitish band (see

top diagram) has shrunk toward the horizon, its color being due simply to passage of light from the ash layer through the lower atmosphere to the observer. Where the sunlight passes tangent to the ash layer, center right diagram, the long path of the rays through the ash results in the sunlight being greatly diminished, and the observer will see a shadow band separating the lower whitish band from the orange-pink upper glow. *Bottom:* About 40 minutes after sunset with only the last reddened rays shining upward onto the layer. [Figure and legend from A.B. and M.P. Meinel (1983, figure 6-3). Reprinted with permission of Cambridge University Press.]

Plate 9. Atmospheric effects of the 1883 Krakatau eruption, as shown in pastels by William Ascroft. From late 1883 through 1886, Ascroft's many sketches of evening scenes documented the unusual optical phenomena observed at Chelsea, London. These scenes, selected from 533 in the Science Museum, South Kensington, London (and published with their permission), illustrate some of the more unusual optical effects. Six additional scenes that appeared as the Frontispiece of the 1888 Royal Society Report are included as Plates 10 and 11 (next pages). For more information on Ascroft's sketches, see his own words on p. 158.

A. "Bishop's ring," the broad opalescent corona surrounding the sun. This effect was first described by S.E. Bishop, of Honolulu, Hawaii, and was noticed by many others around the world for as long as three years after the eruption. For additional information, see Bishop's original description (p. 156) and modern interpretations on p. 405 and 417. Ascroft sketch 12B1; 7:35 p.m., May 10, 1884; at sunset.

B. Deep pink and orange afterglow illuminates a largely cloudless western sky. Ascroft sketch 12B4; 8:15 p.m., May 10, 1884; 40 minutes after the sunset shown in Plate 9A.

C. Faint afterglow illuminates the lower western sky. Ascroft sketch 12B6; 9 p.m., May 10, 1884; 1 hour 25 minutes after the sunset shown in Plate 9A.

Plates 10 and 11. Pastels by William Ascroft, sketched at Chelsea on the bank of the Thames, showing successive changes in the evening sky three months after the eruption on November 26. These six scenes were sketched from just after sunset (3:57 p.m.) until just before the dying out of the afterglow at about 5:30 p.m. The atmospheric effects of the Krakatau eruption resulted not only in extraordinarily long and beautiful sunsets, but also in skies that became progressively more brilliant after the cessation of ordinary twilight, as seen in the 4:40 and 5:00 p.m. sketches. From chromolithographs forming the Frontispiece of the 1888 Royal Society Report.

A. About 4:10 p.m. (13 min after sunset), November 26, 1883, London.

B. About 4:20 p.m. (23 min after sunset), November 26, 1883, London.

C. About 4:30 p.m. (33 min after sunset), November 26, 1883, London.

Plate 11. (See Plate 10.)

A. About 4:40 p.m. (43 min after sunset), November 26, 1883, London.

B. About 5:00 p.m. (63 min after sunset), November 26, 1883, London.

C. About 5:15 p.m. (78 min after sunset), November 26, 1883, London.

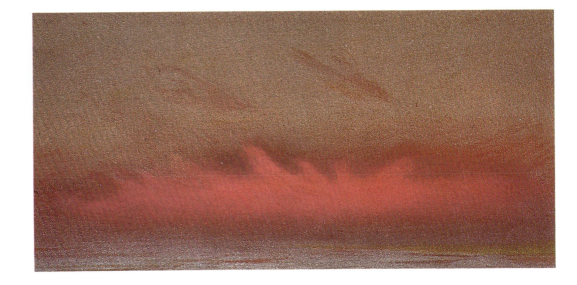

411

Plate 12. Continuation of Ascroft sketches (see introduction to Plate 9).

A. Amber afterglow with radiant spokes of light. These spokes, called crepuscular rays, were the result of shadows cast by clouds far beyond the horizon in the distant west. Ascroft sketch 53A5; 7:10 p.m., September 3, 1885; 28 minutes after 6:42 p.m. sunset.

B. Afterglow, with faint development of crepuscular rays. This is the last of Ascroft's 533 selected sketches and shows that aerosol from Krakatau was still present at high altitudes above England more than three years after the 1883 eruption. Ascroft sketch 72B1; 7:40 p.m., September 13, 1886; about 1 hour 20 minutes after sunset.

C. Brilliant afterglow observed in Wisconsin on October 25, 1963, about 8 months after the powerful explosive eruption of Agung, on the island of Bali, Indonesia. Photograph by A.B. and M.P. Meinel (see caption to Plate 13 opposite). Note the upward progression of color from yellow, orange, red, to mauve—a sequence frequently observed in the anomalous sunsets following the 1883 Krakatau eruption. Compare with Ascroft's sketch shown on Plate 9B.

Plate 13. Recent color photographs of atmospheric phenomena similar to those associated with the 1883 Krakatau eruption. Unless otherwise noted, all photographs by A.B. and M.P. Meinel, and are described in detail in their book (reprinted with permission of Cambridge University Press).

A. Crepuscular rays, formed when clouds in the far-distant west interrupt solar radiation, producing the ray-like shadows. Photograph taken in Taiwan in October 1980, and the afterglow is probably related to the 1980 eruptions of Mount St. Helens, Washington. Compare with the Ascroft sketch shown in Plate 12A.

B. Bishop's ring, a broad opalescent corona surrounding the sun. In this photograph, the sun is hidden behind the giant saguaro cactus, and the corona spreads out over much of the western sky. Photograph taken in Arizona in December 1982, and this unusual optical effect is attributed to the March-April 1982 eruptions of El Chichón, Mexico. Compare with the Ascroft sketch shown in Plate 9A.

C. Deep red and orange afterglow, similar to what Ascroft termed "blood afterglows." Photograph taken in Los Angeles by Don Nicholson of a late 1982 sunset, attributed to the effects of high-altitude material from the March-April 1982 eruption of El Chichón, Mexico.

Plate 14.

A. "Sunset over the Ice on Chaumont Bay, Lake Ontario," a watercolor by the American landscapist Frederic Edwin Church, dated December 28, 1883. Public interest in the "Krakatau sunsets" was at its peak in December (see p. 159) and it is possible that Church, because of his earlier fascination with the volcanoes Cotopaxi and Sangay in Ecuador, purposefully set out to capture the pinks and mauves attributable to the Krakatau eruption. Photograph courtesy of David David Gallery, Philadelphia, Pennsylvania.

B. Now a monument in present-day Teluk Betung, this huge mooring buoy for the steamship Berouw was carried 2 km inland by the great wave of August 27. Its position is shown on the lower map on p. 87. Photograph taken in 1979 by M. and K. Krafft.

C. View, looking eastward toward a light beacon and Sunda Strait Islands in the distance, from the mooring buoy shown in the preceding photograph. The buoy landed nearly 20 m above sea level and the full area shown in this photograph of modern Teluk Betung was flooded. Photograph taken in 1979 by M. and K. Krafft.

Plate 15.

A. *Rakata Island as seen from the north. The southern boundary fault of the Krakatau caldera cut almost precisely through the summit of Rakata Volcano during the collapse of August* 1883. *Compare this photograph with the Verbeek chromolithograph (Plate 8) and the photographs (Figure 39, p. 143) made over 90 years earlier. Photograph by M. and K. Krafft, 1979.*

B. *Close-up view of the steep scarp on the north side of Rakata Island. Note that most of the slope has stabilized, nearly 100 years after its formation, and thick vegetation masks much of the structural detail on this scarp. Photograph taken in 1979 by S. Self.*

C. *Rakata Island as seen from the south. A thick layer of the 1883 tephra blanketed this slope of Rakata and is now exposed only in the sea cliffs; dense tangles of vegetation that have grown during the past hundred years obscure geological relations inland. The tephra blanket was deeply eroded in the months immediately following the 1883 eruption, and the cross-sections of steep-walled gullies can be seen in the sea cliffs. For 1883–1884 views of this same scene, see the Bréon photograph on p. 140 and the Verbeek chromolithograph shown in Plate 7A. Photograph taken in 1979 by S. Self.*

Plate 16. Anak Krakatau (child of Krakatau), the volcano that emerged from the sea in 1928, and built a tephra and lava cone that is still active today. Photographs, unless otherwise noted, by M. and K. Krafft.

A. Aerial view of Anak Krakatau, September 12, 1979. Concentric cones of fragmental debris breached in fore-ground by basalt lava flow. Photo by the Kraffts from SEAN Bulletin, December, 1979.

B. Anak Krakatau as seen from the eastern side of Sertung (Verlaten) Island. The steep north face of Rakata Island, marking the southern boundary of the Krakatau caldera, can be seen in the background. Photograph by S. Self, September, 1979.

C. Strombolian eruption from Anak Krakatau, September, 1979, characterized by the ejection of pasty, incandescent blobs of basaltic lava. Time exposure at night shows paths of many individual projectiles.

above explanations of Krakatau's optical phenomena. On the blue or green Sun and Moon, he notes:

The hoped for discovery of some exotic volcanic gas responsible for the phenomenon did not materialize and it was agreed [by early workers] that the general "cutoff" observed toward the red portion of the spectrum must be attributed to solid particulate material.

The phenomenon was seen mostly in the tropical zone around the equator during the first few weeks immediately following the main eruption, and only rarely and with less reliability outside the tropics. Also the blue coloration was observed mostly when the sun reached an elevation of at least 10° or so above the horizon and even near culmination; whereas, at low elevation near sunset or sunrise, the disk's color tended to be green, "yellowish-green," or "yellowish-white." When the sun set green, the rising moon was also greenish and so were bright stars and planets near the horizon.

Other significant circumstances mentioned are that blue and green suns were observed together with unusually red twilight skies; that a large sunspot was seen by naked eye on the green sun just before sunset; and that the fully eclipsed moon was observed to lack the copper tint usually produced by earthshine.

It is noted that the blue and green sun phenomenon is not uniquely attributable to volcanic dust, since it has been observed also through other aerosol layers such as Sahara dust; conversely, not all volcanic dusts have produced blue and green sun effects.

[Deirmendjian concludes ". . . it is clear that the Krakatoa dust must have depleted the red end of the solar spectrum by an amount greater than the normal atmospheric aerosols" and adds that:]

The "greening" of the blue sun when very near the horizon is not difficult to explain qualititatively in terms of the earth's sphericity and the high level of the volcanic-dust layer (the Chapman effect), as proposed in the Krakatoa Report. However, in the absence of actual measurements of spectral transmission of the setting blue and green suns such a conjecture cannot be substantiated.

[In discussing Bishop's ring, the author points out:]

It was also noted that no change in the overall size of Bishop's ring was observed during the first 12 months of its appearance, but it was most prominent about 8 months after the eruption, and there was an apparent

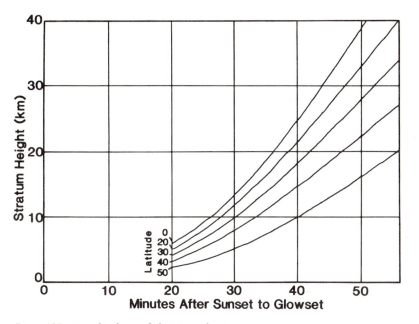

Figure 127. A graphical way of obtaining volcanic ash/aerosol stratum heights from the time after sunset to glowset on the horizon. [For example, an observer at 40°N latitude (e.g., Philadelphia, Madrid, Peking) noting glowset 40 minutes after sunset, could estimate the height of the responsible layer at 15 km. Figure from A.B. and M.P. Meinel (1983, figure 7-3). Reprinted with permission of Cambridge University Press.]

eccentricity of the sun toward the horizon when the ring was observed near sunset. In general, Bishop's ring appears to have been a phenomenon unique in the annals of optical meteorology for size, brilliancy, universality, and protracted duration.

[He goes on to conclude:]

We must therefore assume that the Krakatoa dust in its initial stages conformed to an unusual type of relatively narrow size-distribution law with a modal radius near 0.6 μm, which, when combined with a tropospheric type of aerosol distribution, produced the Bishop's ring phenomenon as reported.

[Under the heading "Unusual Twilights and Crepuscular Phenomena," Deirmendjian adds the following caution and conclusion:]

The descriptions of this aspect of the post-Krakatoa skylight effects, although among the most widespread and noticed, are perforce neither as explicit nor as uniform as those of the blue sun and Bishop's ring. This is owing to the close dependence of twilight features on the optical characteristics of the local and trans-horizon troposphere, and their variation not only along the vertical but along the horizontal direction as well, and to the highly subjective nature of individual impressions of twilight colors, relative brightness, and their changes with time.

The main significance of these unusual twilights lies in their indication of the great height of the responsible dust layer, inferred from their long duration and the presence of secondary glows; in their unusually high brightness, indicating that even if the dust were composed of light-absorbing material, it nevertheless was characterized by a high albedo of single scattering; and in their visibility from locations distributed over a wide latitude zone (where the other optical phenomena were rarely, if ever, observed), indicating the wide spread of the volcanic dust over higher latitudes within both hemispheres.

[Deirmendjian also reviews the atmospheric turbidity introduced by the eruptions of Katmai (Alaska, 1912) and Agung (Bali, 1963). He concludes with some comparative mass calculations for the 3 eruptions and his "worst case" SST evaluation (in parentheses):]

Assuming a substance of unit density for the particles, typical local masses of the volcanic dust content . . . may be estimated as Krakatoa, 1.5×10^{-5}; Katmai, 9.0×10^{-6}; Agung, 2.9×10^{-6}; (500 SSTs, 1.0×10^{-6}) gram per square centimeter column, respectively. Likely values for the total mass of material (of unit density) in each case may be Krakatoa,

3×10^{13} g; Katmai, 1.34×10^{13} g; Agung 9×10^{12} g; (500 SSTs, 1.33×10^{12} g). The most massive injection, that of Krakatoa, could hardly have exceeded 10^{-8} of the mass of the entire atmosphere (5.14×10^{21} g).

As we write these words in Krakatau's centennial year, we are reminded of volcanic turbidity by the continuing atmospheric phenomena resulting from the April 1982 eruption of Mexico's El Chichón. The global spreading of several different cloud layers from this eruption have been extensively monitored by satellites and by laser radar (lidar), and these layers have been analyzed and sampled by balloons and high-flying aircraft. Reports from various groups investigating the El Chichón cloud have been summarized in our SEAN Bulletin over the last 10 months and the January 31 issue[1] contains an estimate of 5.68×10^{12} grams (over 6 million tons) of sulfate injected into the stratosphere by this unusually gas-rich eruption. The major component of the cloud, then, is tiny droplets of sulfuric acid, or aerosol, rather than volcanic ash particles. Archibald, in the 1888 Royal Society report, suggested that the Krakatau "clouds may have been composed of condensed gaseous products of the eruption, besides water, such as sulphurous acid,"[2] and the Meinels[3] expanded this hypothesis in 1967.

The extensive data set being gathered on the El Chichón eruption is relevant to Krakatau because many of the same optical phenomena are now being observed. The current issue of the SEAN Bulletin[1] carries a report from H.H. Lamb describing Bishop's rings observed from England for 3–4 weeks in early January and purple patches (at 22–27, and 52–57 minutes after sunset on January 9) that suggested to him a main layer at 18–20 km altitude and a less dense layer at about 35 km altitude. Many lidar measurements independently showed that the densest layer was centered near 20 km altitude in January,[1] and balloon flights at the end of the month encountered a higher layer at 29–35 km altitude consisting of H_2SO_4 droplets too small (about 0.02 microns in diameter) to be detected by lidar.[1]

[1]*Smithsonian Institution, SEAN Bulletin, Vol. 8 (1), p. 9–12.*
[2]*Russell and Archibald (1888, p. 445).*
[3]*Meinel and Meinel (1967).*

Climatic Effects: Cooling under Filter of Airborne Ejecta

August 27, 1883, was cold in Batavia— Neale mentions a record low of 65°F (see p. 106)—and the Princes Wilhelmina (see p. 113) recorded only 75°F in the darkness of that noon. Afternoon temperatures recorded at the Batavia Observatory (Figure 58) were 13°F below normal, and they resulted from the inability of solar radiation to penetrate the heavy filter of airborne volcanic ash. Analysis of much more detailed data below the May 18, 1980 dust plume from Mount St. Helens showed that the temperature was locally suppressed by as much as 8°C that afternoon.[1] The preceding section has detailed: the global spread of volcanic aerosol from Krakatau in 1883; the great altitude of that cloud; and the extremely small size of its constituent particles. Particles 1 μm in diameter, whether they be aerosol droplets or solid volcanic fragments, require weeks to fall through only 1 km of stratosphere and ½ μm particles require months.[2] From the initial cloud heights variously estimated[3] at 37 to well over 50 km, there was clearly sufficient time for Krakatau particles to fall to the base of the stratosphere (probably about 16 km altitude[4]) where atmospheric rains and storms soon flush small particles to earth. The nearly 3-year duration of optical phenomena after Krakatau is thus easily explained, and it is natural to ask if this long-lived filter to solar radiation had a measurable effect on global temperatures at the earth's surface. We reprint below three discussions of the fascinating relationship between volcanoes and climate.

[1] *Robock and Mass (1982).*
[2] *Lamb (1970, p. 441).*
[3] *Archibald (see p. 402) estimates 121,000 feet (37 km) and Lamb (op. cit.) 50 km.*
[4] *Reid and Gage (1981).*

Figure 128. Portrait of Benjamin Franklin by Pierre H. Alix after Charles A.P. van Loo. National Portrait Gallery, Smithsonian Institution, Washington, D.C.

Volcanic Influences on Climate: An Early View (Franklin, 1784)

Nearly one hundred years before the Krakatau eruption, while serving as U.S. Ambassador to France, Benjamin Franklin linked abnormally cool temperatures to a major eruption in Iceland. The colossal 1783 eruption of Lakagígar Volcano produced 12.3 km³ of basalt in history's largest lava flow eruption.[1] Franklin experienced unusually cool weather during the following year in Europe and wrote, in May of 1784, a short paper entitled "Meteorological imaginations and conjectures." The paper was read before the Literary and Philosophical Society of Manchester on December 22, 1784, and we reprint an excerpt below. It is interesting to note in passing that two of the world's most important historic eruptions, Lakagí-

419

gar in 1783 and Krakatau in 1883 share their bicentennial and centennial, respectively, in 1983.

[1]*Thorarinsson (1969). Another contributor to climate impact in 1783 was the large eruption of Japan's Asama on July 26 of that year. The Icelandic eruption, however, started on June 8 and was in a better location to influence atmospheric conditions in Europe.*

During several of the summer months of the year 1783, when the effect of the sun's rays to heat the earth in these northern regions should have been greatest, there existed a constant fog over all Europe, and great part of North America. This fog was of a permanent nature; it was dry, and the rays of the sun seemed to have little effect towards dissipating it, as they easily do a moist fog, arising from water. They were indeed rendered so faint in passing through it, that when collected in the focus of a burning glass, they would scarce kindle brown paper. Of course, their summer effect in heating the earth was exceedingly diminished.

Hence the surface was early frozen.

Hence the first snows remained on it unmelted, and received continual additions.

Hence the air was more chilled, and the winds more severely cold.

Hence perhaps the winter of 1783–4, was more severe, than any that had happened for many years.

The cause of this universal fog is not yet ascertained. Whether it was adventitious to this earth, and merely a smoke, proceeding from the consumption by fire of some of those great burning balls or globes which we happen to meet with in our rapid course round the sun, and which are sometimes seen to kindle and be destroyed in passing our atmosphere, and whose smoke might be attracted and retained by our earth; or whether it was the vast quantity of smoke, long continuing to issue during the summer from Hecla in Iceland, and that other volcano which arose out of the sea near that island, which smoke might be spread by various winds, over the northern part of the world, is yet uncertain.

Krakatau's Effect on Climate (Abbot and Fowle, 1913)

In 1913, C.G. Abbot, then the Director of the Smithsonian's Astrophysical Observatory and later Secretary of the entire Smithsonian Institution,

collaborated with F.E. Fowle in investigating relationships between volcanism and climate. This work was stimulated by the June 1912 eruption of Katmai, on the Alaskan peninsula. Although this major eruption produced more ejecta than Krakatau in 1883, its remote location prevented it from receiving widespread attention. Its far-traveled products, however, soon attracted the notice of Abbot and Fowle, who were then making measurements of solar radiation in, respectively, Algeria and California. In the brief excerpts presented here, we see that they were able to correlate, in a general way, the effects of volcanoes with the intensity of incoming solar radiation.

It is only since just before the Krakatoa eruption of 1883 that we have had measurements of the intensity of solar radiation comparable to those that were available in 1912. From a paper of Prof. H.H. Kimball[1] we copy the data for the top line of the accompanying Figure 129, which shows the departures of the annual solar radiation received at the earth's surface, as measured at Montpelier and other stations. The smoothed curve (A) of the figure is formed from the combination of these results by adding to twice the value for the year in question the value for the year next preceding and the value for the year next following, and dividing the sum by 4. It is apparent that very great departures from the usual intensity of solar radiation occurred from 1883 to 1887, from 1888 to 1893, and from 1902 to 1904 respectively. The departure which followed the Krakatoa eruption is only what we should have expected, but it is interesting to find, if we can, the causes of the diminished solar radiation having minima in 1891 and 1903 respectively.

[The authors go on to discuss the major 1888 eruption of Bandai-San, in Japan, and several lesser eruptions of other volcanoes in following years (but they do not mention a major 1889 eruption in the Ryukyu Islands that probably also contributed to the low temperatures in 1888–1893). The famous and devastating 1902 eruptions of Mont Pelée (Martinique), La Soufriere (St. Vincent), and Santa Maria (Guatemala) are discussed as probable sources of the 1902–1904 effects, many of which were measured by Dr. Abbot at his Washington Observatory.]

Volcanoes and Terrestrial Temperatures

We have made some preliminary study to determine if the haziness produced by volcanoes causes a

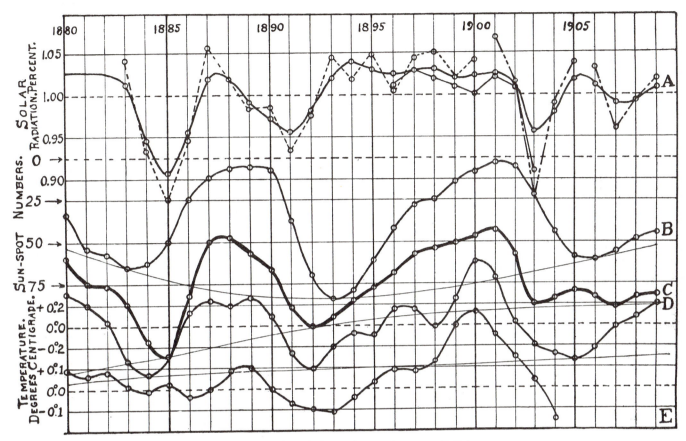

Figure 129. Solar radiation, sun-spots and temperatures.

A. Observed and smoothed mean, annual, noon, solar radiation. (Kimball, 1910.) Volcanic effects, 1885, 1891, 1903.

B. Wolfeis smoothed sun-spot numbers.

C. Combined solar radiation and sun-spot numbers.

D. Smoothed annual mean departures, United States maximum temperatures (15 stations).

E. Smoothed annual mean departures, world temperatures (47 stations). [Abbot and Fowle's figure 3.]

decreased temperature at the earth's surface.

· · · · ·

In order to see if . . . [an] effect was caused by the dust cloud emanating from Krakatoa in 1883 we have studied the temperature departures for Pic du Midi, Puy de Dôme and Schneekoppe for the years 1882 to 1884 inclusive, but there does not appear to have been at that time any such marked decrease of temperature following the eruption of Krakatoa, August 27, 1883, as occurred in July, 1912. Nevertheless at Pic du Midi there was a very well marked decrease in the daily temperature range beginning with September, 1883.

We have found for some other stations a similar decrease of the daily temperature range following the volcano of Krakatoa.

· · · · ·

Referring to Figure 129, the curve A is a smoothed representation of the average intensity of the direct solar radiation. The method of smoothing the curve is as follows, taking for example the year 1895: Add to the value for 1894 twice that for 1895 and that for 1896, and divide by 4. Curve B is the smoothed sun-spot curve as given by Wolfer. The sun-spot numbers run from 0 to about 80. Curve C is a combination of A and B. They are taken in the following proportions: Multiply the percentage departure of radiation shown in A by 6 and subtract from it the sun-spot number for the given year.[2] Curve D represents the departures of mean maximum temperature for 15 stations of the United States distributed all over the country. It is smoothed in the same manner as curve A. Curve E represents the departures of temperature for the whole world, also smoothed in the same manner as curves A and D.[3]

Although there is a considerable degree of correspondence between curve B and curve D yet it is not hard to see that there is also much discordance. For example, the sun-spot maximum of 1893 was greater than that of 1883 or 1906, yet the temperature curve D indicates a gradual increase of temperature for the three periods. Also the temperature had begun to fall in 1890, although sun-spots were still at the minimum; and the temperature had begun to rise in 1892, although sun-spots had not yet reached their maximum. Similar discrepancies occur in other parts of the curves.

When, however, we compare the curves C and D, that is to say, the combination of the effects of sun-spots and volcanic haze with the mean maximum temperature for the United States, the correspondence of the curve is most striking. It seems to us in consideration of this, that there can be little question that the volcanic haze has very appreciably influenced the march of temperature in the United States. When we take the march of temperature for the whole world the correspondence, though traceable, is not so striking; but in this case there are so many conflicting influences at work that it is perhaps too much to expect so good an agreement.

In view of this slight preliminary study of temperatures, it seems to us that the question of the effect of volcanic haze on terrestrial temperature is well worth serious consideration. Although a large group of stations may by their contrary local influences mask the influence of the haze, we believe it may be found eventually that temperatures are influenced, perhaps as much as several degrees, by great periods of haziness such as those produced by the volcanoes of 1883, 1888 and 1912.

[1]Kimball (1910).
[2]Perhaps a better result would have come if 5 instead of 6 had been used.
[3]The data for the curves D and E are taken from Annals, Astrophysical Observatory, Vol. 2, p. 192, and from the *Monthly Weather Review*.

Krakatau Compared with More Recent Eruptions (Mitchell, 1982)

The 1963 eruption of Agung, on the island of Bali, came at a time of greatly increasing interest in atmospheric science, and the eruption's substantial effects drew a new generation of meteorologists' attention to volcanism. In 1974, Guatemala's Fuego produced another atmospherically significant eruption and its source was conveniently close to increasingly sophisticated atmospheric monitoring instruments in North America. Studies of these and other eruptions led to the conclusion that major eruptions decrease global temperatures, but only by 0.2°–0.4°C on an annual average.[1] The 1980 eruption of Mount St. Helens is the best studied in history, and its carefully monitored atmospheric effect (beyond the short-term cooling mentioned above) has been slight.[2] The 1982 El Chichón eruption, however, has produced an unusually large aerosol cloud (despite an ejecta volume smaller than that of Mount St. Helens). Its detailed study (see p. 418) is providing valuable new information on volcanic turbidity. J. Murray Mitchell, a distinguished senior research climatologist with the National Oceanic and Atmospheric Administration, has written a popular article entitled "El Chichón — Weather-maker of the Century?" from which we reprint the following excerpt. He places Krakatau in the context of other major eruptions of recent centuries and provides a seasoned perspective on the imperfectly understood relationship between volcanism and climate.

[1]*See, for example, Mass and Schneider (1977), Robock (1981), Rampino and Self (1982).*
[2]*IAFORS symposium study; see Newell and Deepak (1982).*

We know that volcanic veils like El Chichón's take something away from the warmth of the sun's rays and tend to cool the lower atmosphere. We can see in our weather records that this happened after such mammoth eruptions as Krakatoa's in 1883, Agung's in 1963, and several others that occurred back around the turn of the century. We can also draw on theory that tells us to expect such effects when unusually

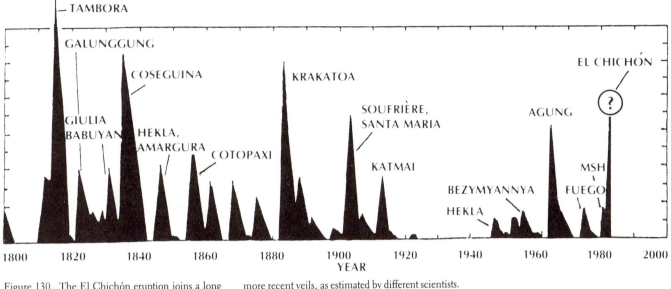

Figure 130. The El Chichón eruption joins a long and infamous parade of important volcanic events around the world. Those since A.D. 1800 are shown here as the chronology of ash veils they are estimated to have created in the upper atmosphere. There are large uncertainties in the relative importance of the more recent veils, as estimated by different scientists. Even greater uncertainties apply to earlier veils for which reliable information is lacking. (Based primarily on studies by H.H. Lamb, English climate historian, and adapted with permission from Alan Robock, University of Maryland.)

large numbers of very small particles of any origin, of any kind, are present in the upper atmosphere. Because each volcanic veil survives only a year or two in the atmosphere, the cooling effect tends to be concentrated in the first year or two following the eruption that produced it. But some slight cooling may persist several years after that because the oceans are slow to respond to the cooling effect and equally slow to recover from it.

A cooler atmosphere could well go on to have other weather effects too. It could slow the cycling of moisture between the oceans and the atmosphere, resulting for a time in slightly less rainfall over the world as a whole. It could also slow the global-scale atmospheric winds, thereby shifting the paths of weather systems and the distribution of weather, including rain or snow, associated with them. The greater the atmospheric cooling, and the more long-lasting the cooling, the greater such effects might be. But here we should pause to realize that the cooling apparently caused by even the largest eruptions of the past has been just a degree or so Celsius—more typically a fraction of that. The further effects on rainfall, atmospheric wind currents, and local weather conditions should have been similarly modest in relation to the ever-present vari-

ability of the atmosphere. No wonder, then, that the famous "year without a summer," back in 1816, is still disputed today as proof positive of the weather-making potential of eruptions even those on the epic scale of Tambora's.

All this notwithstanding, it is conceivable that the El Chichón cloud now overhead has already brought a slight chill to our weather since last summer and fall. Whatever the climate effect to date, it is likely that the greater effect will be in 1983 and 1984. By then, not only will the cloud have become a truly global veil, but the slow-to-respond surface layers of the oceans will have had an opportunity to share in the cooling, as necessary for the atmosphere to respond more fully. That is by no means to imply, however, that El Chichón will bring us an uninterrupted run of cold winters and cool summers. As experienced long-range forecasters are well aware, the weather of a season is shaped by many factors having little to do with volcanoes, sunspots, or any other single phenomenon that has sometimes been touted in the newspapers as the magic key to long-range weather forecasting. What it does mean is that for the next few years El Chichón will probably be tilting the odds slightly in favor of cooler weather than we would otherwise have in store. These days, with recent cold winters still fresh in our memory, probably that is chilling enough.

Biology: The Return of Life to Biologically "New" Islands

After the culminating explosion on August 27, significant ashfall continued for 3 days, successive passages of the airwave were recognized around the world for 5 days, and atmospheric effects were witnessed for nearly 3 years. However, the return of life to these devastated islands did not begin until the eruption ended, and early biologic colonizers found only the inhospitable surfaces of tens of meters of new ash and pumice, still retaining enough heat that walking was difficult two months after the eruption. But life did return, and biologists recognized the opportunity to learn from this natural experiment in colonization. By the early part of this century vegetation had become so thick that it impeded exploration of the islands. We reprint here summaries of plant and animal population growth through the first 46 years and then conclude with some references to more detailed and more recent biological studies.

Plants
(Docters van Leeuwen, 1929)

At the time of the Fourth Pacific Science Conference in Batavia, Dr. W.M. Docters van Leeuwen was Director of the Botanical Gardens at Buitenzorg and Professor of Botany at the Medical Faculty of Batavia. He had been studying the flora of Krakatau for 10 years and reviewed "Krakatau's new flora" for the 1929 conference.

Viewed from on board ship today the island of Krakatau is seen to be entirely clothed with vegetation from the coast to the summit of the Rakata mountain; only the scarred face where part of the island fell away and areas adjacent show bare or little-clothed patches. But in 1919 when I first visited the island this continuous forest was not yet there and one saw on every side small groups of trees against the grass-covered

slopes (*Saccharum spontaneum* L. and *Imperata arundinacea* Cyr.) These islands of forest in the grassy expanse have grown and spread, and becoming merged together, have killed off the grass with their shadow. It is only on the driest slopes of Mt. Rakata (above 700 metres), that one finds the grasses surviving in small patches, and here and there at lower elevations also. Verlaten Island and Lang Island are almost entirely tree-covered but one can still find grasses everywhere, though they are dying out under the vigorous extension of the flora in recent years especially.

A comparison of Figure 131 taken in 1886 with Figure 132 of 1924 shows how rapid the process has been and how great the difference in 38 years. The former was taken during the visit of Prof. Treub,[10] the first botanist to visit Krakatau after the eruption. But before Treub was a Belgian explorer, Cotteau,[2] who was there only a few months after the event and found not a single plant on the island.

After Treub's visit in 1886 Krakatau has been visited by Penzig[8] in 1897, Ernst[6] in 1906, Backer[1] in 1908 and from 1919 every two years by me.[3,4,5] Not but what there have been other explorers too at the same time, but these have left no description of the plants they found.

There are a few problems of general significance which emerge from the researches into Krakatau's flora viz.

1. In what manner is an island that has been robbed of its vegetation furnished with a new flora?

2. How does the vegetation develop and in what consecutive order do the plant communities grow?

All the explorers who have visited Krakatau and left an account of their researches assume that the eruption destroyed all plant life on the island and that all the plants now found on it are therefore imported plants. Backer[1] is the most positive. He says: "the result of all researches have so far absolutely confirmed

Figure 131 (above opposite). Photograph taken by Woodberry and Page in 1886. Bare slopes. In sitting posture Prof. M. Treub. [The author reprints this photograph in his 1936 monograph with the following caption "W side of Zwarte Hoek, June 20th, 1886. Tuff-covering with sparse vegetation." He also identifies the standing figure as J.W. de Bruyn Kops and the photographer as H. Busenbender. Docters van Leeuwen's photo 1.]

Figure 132 (below opposite). South-East of the island Rakata in 1924. [Docters van Leeuwen's photo 2.]

the supposition that the old flora was completely destroyed, so that the new one must comprise imported elements only". I should not like to be so positive myself. We shall never be able to prove that not a single seed or rhizome survived; several persons, e.g. Lloyd Praeger[7] and Scarff,[9] have expressed doubt and are unable to believe that all life was destroyed by the catastrophe. We have therefore the choice between two opinions: the first which is shared by all students who have visited Krakatau, that all life was destroyed and that all the present elements are derived from imported plants, spores or seeds; the second, that part of it was latent, in the form of seeds or otherwise, under the layer of ashes and later grew up and formed new plants. I consider the former the more probable for the following reasons:

1. Verbeek[11] on his first visit in October 1883 a few months after the eruption found not a single plant; a year later he found only a few shoots of grass. Treub[10] found in 1886 26 species embracing 11 Cryptogams, 5 Moncotyls and 10 Dicotyls; Penzig[8] found in 1897 61 species viz. 12 Cryptogams, 16 Monocotyls and 33 Dicotyls; Ernst[6] collected 108 species in 1906 viz. 16 Cryptogams, 1 Gymnosperm, 19 Monocotyls and 72 Dicotyls; I myself have found from 1908–1928 276 species, embracing 62 Cryptogams, 2 Gymnosperms, 66 Monocotyls and 146 Dicotyls. The increase has thus been very gradual, going hand in hand with the gradually increasing suitability of the environment. True forest plants could not at first get a footing on the sunny island and it was not till after the first trees had formed denser groups that they could get a firm hold. That is best shown by the epiphytes. Treub and Penzig found no epiphytes, not even attached on stones on the ground. Ernst found an epiphytic fern, but not a single epiphytic orchid. I found 23 epiphytes, including 13 epiphytic orchids. It is difficult to believe that the spores and seeds of all these plants were latent in the layer of ashes for over 30 years and were then conveyed to the stems and branches of tree and shrub to germinate afresh.

2. All the plants found by Treub have seeds that can be spread by winds or ocean currents. Penzig was the first to find species whose seeds are spread by animals. That, too, is easily understood for fruit-eating birds and bats would have found at first, on the little-clothed island, no trees with edible fruits and seeds, and, if they alighted there, would soon have had to wing their way onward.

3. If among the new plants there were species that originated from forms that survived the eruption, we should expect to find plants having thick-shelled, hard seeds or root stocks. But that is not the case with the species growing inland. Trees like *Terminalia catappa* L. and *Calophyllum inophyllum* L. and other shore-plants, have hard fruit or seed but their distribution by ocean-currents is a matter of such common knowledge that there is no need to doubt it in the present instance.

4. A striking fact, noticed by Treub, is that plants growing on the shore differed from those growing inland on the mountain slopes. I consider Scarff mistaken where he says that if the new plants came by sea they would have established themselves in the vicinity of the shore first and slowly spread inland. But, besides ocean currents, winds too would have carried over a number of plants to deposit them both on the coast and farther inland, and Treub's observations harmonize fully with that fact.

5. We observe a gradual succession of plants when circumstances are favourable to their growth. When the whole shore and the volcanic cone were bare, only those plants could grow which can survive on such exposed places, and it is such plants that we can find in Treub's list. Then follow plants whose seeds and fruit are distributed by the agency of animals and in the first place such sorts as are the first to come up on open secondary terrain, such as *Macaranga Tanarius* L. (whose seeds were found in the digestive organs of birds on Krakatau and came up after being sown), *Pipturus incanus* Wedd., *Ficus variegata* Bl., *F. hispida* L. and *F. fistulosa* Reinw. Plants with edible seeds, found especially in the shade such as *Ficus quercifolia* Roxb., *Villebrunea rubescens* Bl., etc., were not found until the latest expeditions.

6. One must take it, of course, that the seeds of all these plants were not brought in only when circumstances were favourable but, rather, that they were being constantly carried in but could only strike root when the environment was favourable for survival.

7. On the island of Sebesie, 20 km from Krakatau, which was also covered during the eruption by a (thin) layer of ashes and on which, too, all the visible trees and plants were destroyed, there are a number of rhizome bearing plants, e.g. *Zingiberaceae*, *Araceae* and *Musaceae*. Moreover, it was observed (by Cotteau[2]) that shortly after the eruption several plants had come up from the buried rhizomes through the layer of ashes, which was not the case on Krakatau. Again, the flora of Sebesie is much richer in species than that of Krakatau and in the higher regions of the island especially it makes a more normal impression.

8. So long as we are not able, therefore, to say which species survived the eruption and could have come up afterwards nor to state the reasons for such a view as the above, I think we must hold to the opinion that the entire flora of the Krakatau group has been imported from outside. And even if there had been a few survivors, they would form only an extremely small part of the number of species now present, especially when one considers not only the higher plants but also the lower ones and the epiphytic species in particular.

When Treub[10] visited the island there was only a very small beginning of the formation of plant communities to be seen. There were, indeed, a few shore plants but inland there were ferns especially and among them, here and there, a few Phanerogams. But on every hand the bare soil was visible between the more isolated plants, as Figure 131 plainly shows. In 1897, on Penzig's[8] visit, it was found that continuous vegetation had formed on several areas and that plant communities had come into existence. The *Pescaprae* community especially, consisting of various shore-plants was greatly in evidence. Farther inland the country was largely covered with a sort of grass steppe, forming thick jungle here and there. In the midst were numerous ferns and also Phanerogams (though much less numerous). Shrubs were poorly represented and trees were very rare.

On Ernst's[6] visit it was seen that the increase in the number of species was contributed chiefly by the Phanerogams. The number of ferns was not much larger. Some plants were very numerous. The soil was covered everywhere with *Saccharum spontaneum* L. and *Imperata arundinacea* Cyr.; the ground-orchid *Spathoglottis plicata* Bl. clothed the steep walls of ravines, in some cases right up to their margin. Besides the *Pescaprae* community, the *Barringtonia* was also well represented. In the former the well-known shore-grasses, *Spinifex littoreus* Merr. and *Ischaemum muticum* L. were common. The *Barringtonia* community consisted principally of *Casuarina equisetifolia* Forst., *Barringtonia asiatica* Merr., *Hibiscus tiliaceus* L. and *Terminalia Catappa* L. This community was succeeded by a narrow strip of mixed forest, and that again by the impenetrable grasses. In the ravines of the mountains a few trees grew e. g. *Ficus fistulosa* Reinw., and on their walls a grass (*Pogonatherum paniceum* Hack). The zone of ferns that Treub saw had been pushed up to a higher elevation, as the topographical expedition to the top of Mt. Rakata found in 1908.

On my first visit important changes in the flora seemed to have already taken place. The number of communities was larger and many plants which had been common at first had for the most part disappeared. The grass-steppes still covered large areas but there were islands of forest to be seen on every side which we found, on making the ascent, to consist of a few different species. At the present time the steppes have practically disappeared and with them the plants which accompany the grasses in such communities, viz. a few ferns and the orchids *Spathoglottis plicata* Bl. and *Arundina speciosa* Bl. The zone of ferns, too, has practically vanished; here and there near the summit there are ridges thickly overgrown with ferns, and in the lower regions, *Nephrolepis hirsutula* Pr. forms a dense carpet but this is partly secondary and a fresh growth on areas where the trees have grown taller and more light is admitted.

In 1919 there was from 400 m up to nearly the summit a remarkable community consisting almost entirely of one plant namely *Cyrtandra sulcata* Bl. While in its natural habitat this plant forms in the shade a little shrub, here on these exposed slopes and in the ravines it had grown into a many-branched bush with straight erect stems as thick as a man's wrist. In this *Cyrtandra* community were scattered all sorts of herbs and trees, among them various species of *Ficus* and *Villebrunea rubescens* Bl., and these have slowly gained the mastery, bringing the *Cyrtandra* back to its proper role of a little forest shrub. In 1928 the *Cyrtandra* community was to be found only above 700 m, and dead shrubs on every side showed that here too survival is menaced in the struggle for existence. There are at the present time even on the summit a few species of trees, chiefly *Ficus lepicarpa* Bl. and *Nauclea purpurascens* Korth. The *Cyrtandra* forest was apparently an excellent home for all sorts of epiphytes, a number of epiphytic mosses, ferns and higher plants including many orchids. The destruction of the *Cyrtandra* entailed the destruction of the epiphytes, so that in a few years the number of epiphytes will probably decline once more or other species will have to be brought in. The thick garlands of the moss *Floribundaria floribunda* Flsch. are now to be found only on or near the summit.

The following plant-communities are to be distinguished on the island of Krakatau at the present time:

1. The *Pescaprae community*, which is very richly grown on Zwarte Hoek beach, on the north coast, especially. On the other side it occurs only locally in a narrow strip, because the waves constantly lash the

shore and this group is the first to be destroyed. It comprises the familiar species and exhibits no special peculiarity.

2. *The Barringtonia community.* This is pushing inland here and there but it is chiefly limited to a narrow strip close to the shore. It comprises several species, such as *Barringtonia asiatica* Merr., *Calophyllum inophyllum* L., *Hernandia peltata* Meissn., *Erythrina indica* L., *Hibiscus tiliaceus* L., *Thespezia populneus* Soland., *Terminalia Catappa* L. and *Guettarda speciosa* L. In a few places one finds in this community large specimens of *Cerbera Manghas* L., which is really one of the mangrove group, entirely unrepresented on Krakatau otherwise, having no opportunity to get a footing anywhere.

3. *The Casuarina community.* The *Casuarina* is generally grouped in the previous category but that is incorrect, in my opinion, because it is only when it grows alone that it forms true communities. This tree grows best on open sandy places, especially where these sandy areas are extending, as is the case towards the northern point of Verlaten Island, so that it can continually renew itself on the spreading sands. When other species (and these are largely plants from the *Barringtonia* community but include *Macaranga Tanarius* L. and *Pipturus incanus* Wedd.), come up among the *Casuarinas*, the latter gradually die off. A few climbinig plants also assist in the process, bringing the old *Casuarinas* down. It is chiefly *Vitis trifolia* L. and *Ipomoea denticulata* Chois., which choke and kill them. See Figure 133. *Casuarinas* are found also on the steep tuff walls, but not in close groups.

4. *The Macaranga community.* This is to be found on every side in the ravines and on open areas occupied by the grass steppes before. This group contains chiefly *Macaranga Tanarius* L., *Pipturus incanus* Wedd., a few species of *Ficus* and, as undergrowth, a large number of ferns, chiefly *Nephrolepis hirsutula* Pr. It is limited mainly to the lower part of the island.

5. *Mixed Forest.* This occurs both in the lower and the higher regions, although differently composed in the one and the other. At the lower elevations are found everywhere the trees of the previous formation, which has developed out of these; there are, besides, all sorts of shrubs, bushes and climbing-plants e.g. *Bridelia tomentosa* Bl. and *stipularis* Bl., *Ficus ampelas* Burm., *Mucuna acuminata* Gr., *Homolanthus populneus* O. K., *Leea aequata* L. and *indica* Merr., *Melochia umbellata* Stapf., *Carica Papaya* L., *Lantana camara* L. and *Aristolochia Tagala* Cham. At higher elevations we find some of the above species

but more especially *Villebrunea rubescens* Bl., *Pericampylus glaucus* Merr., *Polyscias nodosa* Seem., *Merremia nymphaeifolia* Hall. f., *Radermacher glandulosa* Miq., *Nauclea purpurascens* Korth., *Muisaenda frondosa* L. and *Vernonia arborea* Ham. At the very highest elevation *Ficus pubinervis* Bl. and *Ficus subulata* Bl. especially. In a few areas, especially about 400 m up, the forest consists of tall trees, *Radermachera*, *Nauchea* and some *Ficuses*. This forest is comparatively poor in epiphytes; the ravine walls are overgrown with many ferns.

6. *The Grass Steppes*, with the plants appertaining to them, have completely disappeared except on a few small areas. *Spathoglottis plicata* Bl. has become very scarce.

7. *The Cyrtandra community* has almost entirely disappeared except from 700 m to the summit (Figure 134): The plant occurs in lower elevations only as a forest plant in the ravines. Well-developed specimens, wherever such are still to be found, have branches and trunk covered with a number of epiphytic mosses and higher plants. (Figure 135). Of the Pteridophytes may be mentioned the following: *Trichomanes bipunctatum* Poir. and *humile* Forst., *Lycopodium squarrrosum* Forst., *Ohioglossum pendulum* L., *Antrophyum reticulatum* Kaulf., *Asplenium Belangeri* Kze., *Cyclophorus adnascens* Desv., *Humata heterophylla* Desv., *Hymenolepis brachystachys* J. Sm., *Pleopetis accedens* Moore and *heraclea* v. A. v. R. and *Vittaria zosterifolia* Willd. Very many orchids: *Acriopsis javanica* Reinw., *Dendrobium crumentatum* Sw., *mutabile* Lindl. and *secundum* Lindl., *Liparis parviflora* Lindl. and *viridiflora* Lindl., *Oberonia monstruosa* Lindl. and *Thrixspermum comans* J.J.S. and a few Gesneriaceae: *Aeschynanthus pulchra* Don. and *volubilis* Jack. and the Melastomatacea: *Medinilla pterocaula* Bl. are also general.

Of the above plant-communities the *Pescaprae* and the *Barringtonia* are permanent, belonging as they do to the groups generally found in the tropics. All other communities are subject to constant change and will in the long run be absorbed into the true virgin forest, which may differ more or less in composition from lower to higher elevation but forms a type by itself.

The vegetation on Verlaten and Lang is poorer than that on Krakatau; both islands are much lower but they otherwise present the same aspects as Krakatau. They require separate treatment, however, for which there is no place in the present work.

Subjoined [in the original paper is a 13-page] list of the plants found by me on Krakatau and Verlaten

Figure 133. Ancient, nearly destroyed Casuarina-community. [The author reprints this photograph in his 1936 monograph with the following caption: "Krakatau, SE side, June, 1928. *Casuarinas*, covered and choked by *Ipomoea gracilis*. In the front *Hibiscus tiliaceus, Macaranga Tanarius*, and *Desmodium umbellatum*, and in front of this a narrow strip of *Ischaemum muticum*." Docters van Leeuwen's photo 3.]

Figure 134. Cyrtandra-forest on the summit, 813 m. 1928. [The author reprints this photograph in his 1936 monograph with the following caption: "Krakatau, S side, July, 1924. *Cyrtandra* association, alt. about 700 m above sea level. On the ground, *Selaginella plana*; to the right *Nephrolepis exaltata*." Docters van Leeuwen's photo 5.]

Figure 135. Cyrtandra-forest, 500 m. 1921. [The author reprints this photograph in his 1936 monograph with the following caption: "Krakatau, S. side, May, 1928. *Cyrtandra* asssociation, alt. about 800 m. Branches densely festooned with pendulant *Floribundaria floribunda*." Docters van Leeuwen's photo 4.]

Island. The *Hepaticeae* and many *Fungi* are still being studied.

[1]Backer (1909).
[2]Cotteau (1885).
[3]Docters van Leeuwen (1921).
[4]Docters van Leeuwen (1922).
[5]Docters van Leeuwen (1923).
[6]Ernst (1907).
[7]Lloyd Praeger (1911).
[8]Penzig (1902).
[9]Scarff (1925).
[10]Treub (1888).
[11]Verbeek (1885).

Animals
(Dammerman, 1929)

The zoological counterpart of Docters van Leeuwen was Dr. K.W. Dammerman, Director of the Zoological Museum at Buitenzorg. He reviewed "Krakatau's new fauna" for the same 1929 conference. As with Docters van Leeuwen's paper, we reprint the full text but not the detailed species list at the end.

Researches into Krakatau's new fauna have brought us up against the following problems and theories, which are briefly summarised below and further discussed in the pages following.

1. There is every reason to believe that the fauna of Krakatau was totally destroyed in the eruption of 1883.

2. The sequence in which the different species have since populated the island is very probably as follows: first, detritus forms, next plant-eating species, and, finally, carnivorous and parasitic forms. This only means that the animals have established themselves in such consecutive order and not that they reached the island in that sequence, for there are indications that right from the beginning all kinds of animals were arriving, including even parasitic and predaceous ones, but they could only get a footing in the order indicated as the island reverted more and more to normal conditions.

3. The conditions on the island today, in respect of the fauna, are still not yet normal. Some animal groups, for example winged forms like birds and insects, have probably reached 50 to 60% of what may be regarded as the norm; the same is true of the soil fauna. Other groups, like the moss fauna, may be

regarded as fairly normal already.

Newly arrived species usually multiplied with extraordinary rapidity at first and only in the long run more normal proportions are established, while a species which was at one time abundant can even disappear altogether in the course of years.

4. In the first place creatures reached the islands by air, either actively flying or passively transported by the wind; in the second place by sea, either swimming or carried along with driftwood or other flotsam; in the third place, by the agency of other animals or man. The last-named agency has played a very insignificant part in the case of Krakatau, while arrivals by air may be put down at about 90% of the island's fauna today.

5. Whether it is animals from Java or Sumatra that have found a home on this island cannot generally be known, except in the few cases of subspecies or species that are confined to one or other of these neighbouring islands.

The great majority of the species now found on Krakatau are extremely common and very widely distributed.

6. Since on the islands of the Krakatau group a few subspecies of one and the same species occur together, or species exist here under conditions that vary from the normal, it is not impossible that we shall be able to observe here the origin of peculiar subspecies or the varying of species.

In addition to the above problems, Verlaten Island presents us with a separate problem in the brackish-water lake that formed there in 1908. This is inhabited by a large number of brackish-water forms but already there are also a few fresh-water forms, while the water will very probably become less and less saline in the course of time.

1. Was Krakatau's Fauna Totally Destroyed in the Eruption of 1883?

All those who have taken an active part in the study of Krakatau have expressed the opinion that the fauna at least must have been totally destroyed in the eruption of 1883; only a few scientists take the view, on theoretical grounds, that a larger or smaller number of animals could very well have survived the catastrophe.

We can now urge the following arguments for our view that this last was not the case.

Let us first examine the conditions shortly after eruption, as they have been excellently described for us by Verbeek. Not only did eruption follow eruption for months while in the last and most severe explosion that took place in August 1883 two-thirds of the former Krakatau was blown away, but all the islands were covered with a layer of hot ashes and pumice-stone thirty to sixty metres thick.

Mr. Verbeek, in a personal letter written to us shortly before his death, expressed the opinion that all life was destroyed on Krakatau after the eruption. He said: "the old basalt surface was covered with a layer of pumice-stone and ashes; the ejected matter was so hot that the coolies danced on their bare feet, while a very hot steam issued out of several fissures in the rock and out of the loose pumice-sand, where it had already begun to be washed out". That was two months after the disaster!

It is not probable that any animal could have continued to live under such circumstances, even if it had survived the eruption concealed in a fissure of rock or buried underground. Moreover a year later Verbeek could not find a single plant, save only a few blades of grass. It is obvious that all animals which live on plants or vegetable matter could not then exist on the island, much less other animals depending in their turn on these. A still stronger argument is provided by Cotteau, who visited Krakatau at the end of May 1884, which was nine months after the eruption. "Notwithstanding all my searches, I was not able", he says, "to observe any symptoms of animal life. I only discovered one microscopic spider — only one; this strange pioneer of the renovation was busy spinning its web".

All this notwithstanding, Scharff thinks that the larvae of many insects, as well as earthworms, could very well have survived the eruption deep down in the earth or that many adult insects even, as well as spiders and snails, perhaps even lizards, could have found a hiding-place in deep rock fissures.

Michaelsen, too, thinks that earthworms could have survived the catastrophe buried deep down in the earth. Arguing especially from the *Pheretima* of Krakatau that has been described as a new species, found in fairly large numbers in different places, he considers it probable that this is an endemic species and not one that has been brought in from abroad.

I do not consider that a sufficient reason because numerous new *Pheretima*'s and other earthworms are still recorded from the East Indian Archipelago, so that it is not impossible that a species hitherto undescribed has reached Krakatau.

There is, however, a much more conclusive argument against Michaelsen's view which is that in 1908 when Jacobson visited Krakatau there were as yet not earthworms there and they are still not to be found on Verlaten Island today. He says (on p. 203): "Evidence of the total destruction of the fauna on Krakatau is supplied also by the absence of earthworms. I did not find, at any rate, the species that live in the soil, although I looked for them in various places". He did find one species though, in a decayed tree-trunk, and he thinks that earthworms, too, could have been brought over in that way.

One cannot believe that a species that survived the eruption could have been still so rare, 25 years later, as to remain undiscovered and then suddenly emerge in large numbers. That applies not only to earthworms but also to a number of other species that were found for the first time after 1908.

The history of the molluscs found on Krakatau is further evidence for the theory that all animal life was destroyed. By a very lucky chance we know something about the mollusc fauna of Krakatau before 1883. In 1867 von Martens described four species from this island, namely two *Hemiplecta*, one *Chloritis* and *Amphidromus inversus*. Although these are all fairly large species — the *Hemiplecta*, are very large and striking forms — yet none of them were found after the eruption. There is yet another indication that these species did actually perish and that the present forms are new arrivals. Six years after the catastrophe, in 1889, Strubell visited the island and found only one *Neritina*, five *Littorina* species and one *Acmaea*, all marine or sub-marine forms. It is out of the question that a naturalist, who visited the island especially in order to collect molluscs, could have overlooked all the land-forms that are found on Krakatau to-day, among which are species like those belonging to the genus *Pythia*, which are common along the coast under dry leaves, or again such striking forms as *Amphidromus porcellanus*.

Let us now consider what insect-larvae could have survived the eruption by burrowing deep into the soil. We shall observe the remarkable fact that it is just the very insects whose larvae have best adapted themselves to a sub-surface existence, moving about actively in the soil, that are still lacking. Such are the tiger beetles (*Cicindelidae*) of which no less than six species are found on the neighbouring Sebesy Island. Cockchafers (*Melolonthidae*) are also not yet to be found, while Sebesy has one species. The cicada, *Dundubia rufivena*, whose larvae most probably live on roots of plants, and which are now very numerous on both

Krakatau and Verlaten Island, was not found by Jacobson in 1908. There are yet other insects, which pass a certain stage of their existence underground; for several moths, for instance, pupate in the soil. But here the question arises — Where could the emerged moths lay their eggs and on what could the young caterpillars feed?— if a year after eruption not a single plant was to found on the island, a few blades of grass excepted.

Now, as regards the reptiles, which, Scharff says, can quite well date from before the eruption, we must remark in the first place that Jacobson found only two species in 1908, namely *Varanus salvator* and a *Hemidactylus*, both species of very wide and facile distribution. *Varanus salvator* has been found swimming in the sea and *Hemidactylus* is easily carried over it unintentionally by human agency or by driftwood in the egg-stage. We ourselves found recently on Krakatau a totally decayed tree trunk, in which lay buried deep the eggs of a *Hemidactylus*. The lizard (*Lygosoma atrocostatum*) now so numerous on Verlaten Island was certainly not there in 1908. Moreover, we were so to speak the eye-witnesses of the arrival of a second species of lizard on Krakatau, the *Mabuia multifasciata*. In 1924 this species suddenly appeared on the island in large numbers, although we can say with a fair amount of certainty that it was not to be found there before that date. This is good illustration of how casual is the process of repopulation, for we should rather have expected that the species already known from Verlaten Island would have been the first to reach Krakatau.

2. The Sequence in Which the Different Species Have Populated the Island.

It is unfortunate that zoologists have not given the problem of Krakatau the attention it deserved. In consequence it is not possible to give a satisfactory answer to the question of the sequence in which the animals populated the island. We can only make a comparison between our own researches in 1920 and 1921 and those of Jacobson in 1908.

We may state with a fair degree of certainty that it was not till after 1908 that the following animals arrived on Krakatau:— in the first place, all the mammals now present; secondly, a number of birds, the lizards and snakes; among insects, the water-beetles and water-bugs, numerous scale-insects, the carnivorous Coccinellids, the cicada *Dundubia*, and the praying mantises; of invertebrate animals, a number of molluscs and the earthworms.

In support of the proposition that the sequence in which the animals established themselves is: first chiefly scavengers, then plant-feeding animals, and lastly predaceous and parasitic forms, there is now little evidence to adduce, because unfortunately the zoological researches were begun too late, viz., 25 years after the eruption. But in regard to the comparatively late settlement of carnivorous and parasitic species a comparison between 1908 and 1921 is fruitful of results. As regards the parasites we must eliminate those species which could have reached the island together with their hosts (external or internal). We see, in the first place, that while in 1921 there were already numerous fruit-eating bats (*Cynopterus*), the first insectivorous species (*Hipposideros*), was only recently discovered. Against one ground beetle observed in 1908 stand 10 species found in 1921. While in 1908 only one insect-eating ladybird had been discovered on Lang Island and none on Krakatau, there are now 5 species known from the Krakatau group. Before 1908 there was not a single raptorial bug (*Reduviidae*) listed; in 1921 there were two species known on Krakatau. The carnivorous mantids were not represented on the island before 1908, nor those Neuroptera which are raptorial in their larval stage. The number of dragonflies, of which there were two species mentioned before 1908 (one on Krakatau itself), has since increased to 12.

Parasitic forms have increased to a much smaller degree; the number of Hymenoptera parasitica on Krakatau in 1921 was double that in 1908, although in the former year the total of insects was three times the number found in 1908.

3. Conditions in Respect of the Fauna Are Not Yet Normal.

Normal conditions in regard to the fauna will certainly not be established on Krakatau until the flora has been completely restored and, as the researches of Prof. Docters van Leeuwen have shown, a further enrichment of the flora and supersession of some species by others is certainly yet to be expected.

We could not describe the new fauna as really normal until it is composed of the same elements as before the eruption. But since we unfortunately know practically nothing of Krakatau's fauna before 1883, we can only make some sort of a guess at what may be taken to be the norm by means of a comparison with other islands. An examination of the fauna of the neighbouring Sebesy Island, which also suffered severely in the eruption of 1883, has shown that a number of animals or animal groups occur there which are still lacking on Krakatau and which have possibly survived the catastrophe on Sebesy. Of these we may mention two species of snakes, the Cicindelids, of which Sebesy has not less than 6 species, a large number of Lepidoptera, especially a couple of striking butterflies such as a few species of *Papilio* and *Hestia*, and a number of remarkable bugs, such as *Derepteryx feana*, *Leptoglossus membranaceus*, and *Sycanus annulicornis*. Further, Sebesy is richer especially in Orthoptera, among which are stick-insects (*Phasmidae*) which are still lacking on Krakatau. Among the insects our attention is drawn further to the larger number of gall-producing flies and Thysanoptera on Sebesy, while among the invertebrates the greater abundance of Myriopods and molluscs among then a few slugs (*Helicarion*, *Collingea*, and *Vaginula*) is particularly striking.

The majority of the species enumerated above we may certainly expect to find on Krakatau at some time in the future.

Since Sebesy, however, suffered considerably by the eruption of 1883 and its original fauna perished to a degree that was little less complete than was the case on Krakatau, we have drawn into our inquiry, for the purposes of comparison, yet another island, namely Durian in the Rhio Archipelago [S of Singapore]. Although this island too, has not satisfied our expectations in all respects, for its fauna must be regarded as rather poor on the whole, yet our inquiry has taught us something. For we have reached the conclusion that in regard to the winged forms, like birds and insects, Krakatau has probabaly recovered 50 to 60% of its original fauna already. A comparative study of the soil and surface fauna in different regions has likewise shown that here again Krakatau has reached 50 to 60% of the normal. Although this remarkable result has been attained in less than 40 years, we may not expect that a normal level will be reached in about 80 years from the time of the eruption, because the increase in the number of animal species is not in direct proportion to the passage of time. The curve is undoubtedly a parabolic one, as the increase is more rapid at first than later.

There is yet another respect in which the fauna of Krakatau displays an abnormal character. Some species occur in strikingly large numbers probably on account of the fact that, having settled on the island

and found conditions favourable, they were able to multiply rapidly in the absence both of competition from allied species and of enemies or parasites. For example, we were struck by the fact that the lizard *Mabuia multifasciata* was suddenly found in large numbers on Krakatau in 1924, while a few years before the creature had not yet arrived. Noteworthy also is the great abundance of field rats (*Mus rattus jalorensis*) on Lang Island, where in a single night 49 were caught in 5 traps only. The only woodlice on Verlaten Island was found there in enormous numbers, up to 258 to the square metre, while on Krakatau where there were already three species in 1908, they numbered at the utmost 48 to the same area.

The proportions become more normal with time and the number of individuals can decline greatly. There are a few animals and animal groups, which were very numerous in 1908 according to Jacobson's statement, but have now greatly decreased, such as the large Scolopendras and *Spirostreptus*, while at that time ants and spiders also were infinitely more abundant than at the present day. The latter fact, of course, is connected with the gradual disappearance of open grass-land and the covering of the whole island with forest.

4. How Have the Animals Reached the Island?

Our first study of the fauna of Krakatau has taught us that the number of winged creatures on this island is very high, being more than 80%. From which we conclude that the majority of the new fauna reached the island on the wing. There are other indications pointing the same way. Among the ants known on Krakatau and Verlaten Island there are no species of which the females are apterous, while there is one (*Dorylus laevigatus*) on Sebesy. Likewise, wingless forms are lacking among the numerous Tenebrionids, a family in which otherwise wingless species are not so rare.

Again, the difference is very small between the number of butterflies on Krakatau and Durian, while moths, which apparently are less easily spread by air, are three times as numerous on the latter island as on Krakatau.

Jacobson found not a single wingless creature on Verlaten Island in 1908, while we now know 58 species there which cannot fly.

Besides very young caterpillars which can easily be carried by air-currents, there are among the wingless forms on Krakatau several which can be spread by the wind, such as young spiders, smaller mites like Ori-

batids, and probably all the species belonging to the moss fauna.

Altogether about 90% of the animals could have reached Krakatau by the air.

It is probably only the large monitor, the python and crocodile that swam over independently. Carried on driftwood or other flotsam were presumably the smaller reptiles, a number of wingless insects such as the scale-insects and Aptera, the Myriapods, a few Arachnids, including the scorpions, Pedipalpi and some mites, the terrestrial Crustaceans and Molluscs and the earthworms. Most probably these creatures were brought over in the egg-stage, for the eggs of these species are found in the soil, or attached to portions of plants, or concealed in cracks and holes of half-decayed tree-trunks.

The agency of man or other animals has certainly contributed the smallest percentage. The house-rats on Krakatau have certainly been introduced by man, as these creatures first appeared on the island shortly after the sojourn there of a certain Mr. Händl in 1917. That is less probable in the case of the field rats on Lang Island, which were met with in enormous numbers by the Staff of the Vulcanological Survey, who camped on the island at the beginning of 1928. Before that date the island had neither been inhabited nor even visited for any length of time.

The possibility that some of the smaller reptiles were unintentionally transported in native fishing-boats is not exluded, but it is more probable that the eggs of these animals came in with driftwood.

The mites found on Krakatau that are free-living as adults are all actual or semi-parasites in the larval stage and can be brought over in that form by their hosts (birds or insects). Again, the minute moss-dwelling creatures can be spread by birds, either adhering to their feathers or in particles of earth on their feet, although in this instance, too, the agency of the wind is more likely.

5. Did the Animals Come from Java or Sumatra?

In most cases it is impossible to answer this question because most of the species now found on Krakatau are extremely common and of wide distribution and are found both in Java and in Sumatra. It is only in those few cases, where well distinguished subspecies occur in the two latter islands, that their origin can be traced with any greater degree of certainty. We can, however, say that, in those cases also where a species is known from both Sumatra and Java, the probability is that its origin is Sumatra, because between Sumatra and the Krakatau group there is a chain of islands, of which Sebesy is only 15 km distant from Verlaten Island, while the island-group is separated from Java by a strait at least 41 km wide.

A more detailed study of this problem cannot be carried out, until the material has been further investigated and the distribution of each species has been ascertained.

6. The Possibility of New Subspecies Arising.

The possibility that new forms or subspecies will arise in the islands of the Krakatau group is indicated by the three cases following. In the first place, a species brought here by chance can meet different conditions from what it is accustomed to and those new conditions can cause a permanent variation. Secondly, a few aberrant specimens of a species or the eggs of such can reach one of these islands and, if they continue to be isolated, they can in the end exhibit constant features, distinguishing them from the original species or subspecies from which they sprang. A third possibility is that two nearly related forms reach the islands at about the same time and a new form originates by hybridisation.

An example of the first nature is presented by the house-rats that were introduced into Krakatau. As this island has been made a nature reserve and will therefore continue to be uninhabited, these animals that have adapted themselves to an existence in or near human dwellings, find here utterly different conditions from what they are used to. If the view is correct that the Malay house-rat (*Mus rattus diardi*) is descended from the field rat found wild here (*M. r. jalorensis*), it is not impossible that the house-rats on Krakatau will in the end begin to exhibit characteristics that belong rather to the field rats, since they have to live a life that is in all respects similar to that of the latter. But since it is probable that a number of generations have passed before the house-rat acquired the characteristics that distinguish it from the field rat, the reversion to the original type can take a long time, too. It is to be hoped that the house-rats will remain isolated and that it will prove possible to pursue this question further.

There is no example of the second case yet known but the third possibility is provided for, since there are found now on a few islands two subspecies of one and the same species. Thus there now occur side by side on Krakatau the *antiphus* and *adamus* forms of

Papilio aristolochiae and the subspecies *melanippus* and *insularis* of *Danais melanippus*; and on Verlaten Island *intacta* and *lara* of *Asota* (*Hypsa*) *heliconia*. On Sebesy island there are found together the *sumatrana* and *intensa* forms of *Danaid plexippus*. *P. aristolochia antiphus* is peculiar to Sumatra and Borneo, while *adamus* belongs to Java; again the *sumatrana* form of *Danais plexippus* comes from Sumatra, the *intensa* from Java. As regards the *insularis* form of *D. melanippus*, which is described as a new Krakatau subspecies, it is only slightly divergent from the typical *melanippus* of Java; the same is true of the subspecies *krakatauae* of *D. juventa*, which is scarcely distinguishable from the typical Java form (*D. j. juventa*). It is not impossible, however, that these new forms have arisen for the first time on Krakatau.

Here again it will be interesting to see what will happen to these subspecies in their mutual relationship in the future. The case is probabaly different with the two *Asota* forms, which are not geographically distinct forms, for they are found together elsewhere also.

7. The Fauna of the Brackish-Water Lake on Verlaten Island.

This brackish-water lake, which was only recently shut off from the open sea, presents us with two interesting problems. There are indications that it will slowly lose its salinity and the question is now, in the first place, how brackish-water forms now found in it will behave in the long run, as the water becomes more and more fresh; and, in the second place, how the lake becomes populated with typical fresh-water forms, whose appearance on the Krakatau islands had hitherto been precluded. In 1908 it was still open to the ocean (see Figure 136) and it is only after that year that it was cut off. The first researches into the fauna[2] were made in 1920–1921; the percentage of salinity was liable to seasonal variation fluctuating between 20.6 and 29.0‰.

The species found in the lake are for the most part species which are found also in the open sea or in brackish water, while most of them can stand considerable differences in the salt-content of the water.

The question has not been studied long enough to allow differences in the components of this fauna to be definitely established.

In my previous publication on Krakatau[1] I took it that the actual marine fauna of this lake had existed there before it was cut off from the sea and could not

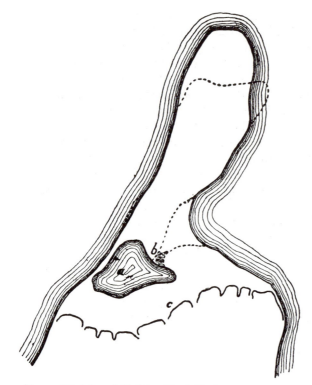

Figure 136. Map of Verlaten Island North. *a*, brackish-water lake; *b*, brackish pool. The dotted lines indicate the coast-line of 1908; at *c* begins the hilly land; hereabouts was the coast-line shortly after the eruption. [Dammerman's p. 95.]

have been washed in subsequently in stormy weather. On our visit in February 1928, however, we found at the most northerly point of Verlaten Island a number of fresh-water pools (Figures 137 and 138) with a very slight percentage of salinity (2.49‰) which had probably resulted from inundations of lower-lying areas, to which the dead tree-trunks left in the water bear plain witness. I saw in these pools numerous fishes and some crabs, that must have been washed in on a high tide either in a young stage or as eggs. It is possible, therefore, that the same thing happened in the case of the brackish-water lake.

As regards the fresh-water forms inhabiting the lake, these now consist exclusively of insects and are all forms that are winged in the adult stage and could very well have reached the lake flying.

[1]Dammerman (1922).
[2][Dammerman's paper includes a 20 page list of animals known from the Krakatau Islands, and a 1½ page list of animals found in Verlaten's brackish-water lake.]

The two review papers reprinted above were written for the Fourth Pacific Science Congress, held in Batavia and Bandung during the month of May 1929. At that meeting a joint session of physical and biological scientists discussed thoughtfully the question of whether all plant and animal life had been annihilated by the 1883 eruption.[1] The consensus of opinion was that if life was not totally destroyed it was close enough to total destruction that the island could nevertheless be considered biologically sterile in 1883.

Shortly after that international meeting, however, an academic bombshell burst in the form of a book by a man who had taken no part in the meeting. His name was C.A. Backer, a botanist who had worked with Docters van Leeuwen at the Buitenzorg Botanical Garden and had visited Krakatau in 1906 and 1908. Although his own paper after that visit[2] favored extinction of Krakatau life in 1883, and the reviews that we have reprinted above were far from dogmatic in favoring that view, Backer's book was an unremittingly virulent attack on that position. The book, published at the author's expense, emphasized the difficulty of field investigations on an island that "is ploughed in all directions by innumerable deep (down to 40 m) and very precipitous ravines which at every moment hinder or arrest the penetration of the island; the investigation is made still more difficult by the locally often very dense, almost impenetrable vegetation, by the humid heat, and by hosts of most aggressive ants and mosquitoes. There is, at the surface at least, no water, there is no living man, hence neither food nor coolies are available. Without coolies an extensive botanical investigation in very accidented localities in the tropics cannot possibly be carried out."[3] After offering these views, Backer goes on to excoriate all previous botanical field workers for insufficiently thorough examination. His book contains, however, some interesting information not available in earlier Krakatau literature and some quoted correspondence with Verbeek before his death in 1926. Backer describes, for example, the stay of Johann Händl on the island from 1915 to 1917. In addition to introducing both livestock and plants, Händl dug many wells and "found in many places un-burnt tree-trunks and other parts of plants"[4] beneath the thick pumice layer of 1883.

Probably the most important result of Backer's book, though, was that it drove the two men most directly attacked, Docters van Leeuwen and Dammerman, back to their studies to produce landmark monographs on the flora (1939, 506 pp) and fauna (1947, 574 pp), respectively. Figure 139, from Docters van Leeuwen's monograph, shows the growth in species numbers during the first 50 years after the eruption, and emphasizes vividly that little, if any, island life survived the 1883 eruption. Subsequent field investigations in 1951 (see Hoogewerf, 1953, and Borssum-Waalkes, 1960) and more recent work by Hull University[5] and others have continued monitoring biological changes, and some useful biological work has been done on the effects of the Anak Krakatau eruptions as well.

Although the repopulation of Krakatau is a continuing study, with important lessons for science, it is not the only biologic aspect of the 1883 eruption. Eyewitness accounts (p. 128) have described dramatic changes in local insect populations—proliferation of flies with the many unburied bodies, and decreased numbers of mosquitoes, presumably from seawater scouring of coastal swamp breeding areas—and Dr. Gelpke has written an interesting account (p. 117) of the eruption's effects on distant crops and other plants. The effects on the marine ecosystem have not been described, but must have been at least as dramatic. We know that blocks of coral reef weighing 600 tons were ripped from the sea floor and thrown ashore, that large areas of the ocean bottom were covered with tens of meters of hot ash, and that large bays were so thoroughly choked with floating pumice that ships were unable to enter for 3 months.

The floating pumice provides, for us, the most intriguing biological aspect of the eruption. Huge masses of pumice floated westward across the Indian Ocean, carrying the bones of eruption victims 6170 km to Zanzibar in 10 months (p. 153), while currents stranded other pumice rafts in motionless masses likened to the Sargasso Sea (p. 152). Easterly currents carried other masses through the Java Sea and into the Pacific, bringing unfamiliar trees (and no doubt seeds) to the Caroline Islands (p. 153). These floating masses— locally thick enough, and coherent enough, to support heavy iron bars, men, and trees—must be biologically important Noah's Arks, carrying seeds and eggs over thousands of kilometers of ocean to unfamiliar shores. Eruptions like Krakatau's probably occur, on the average, more than once a

Figure 137. Submerged land on Verlaten Island North. Photo Dr. Stehn, 1928. [Dammerman's figure 1.]

Figure 138. View of brackish-water lake, Verlaten Island. Photo Prof. Docters v. Leeuwen, 1920. [Docters van Leeuwen reprints this photograph in his 1936 monograph with the following caption: "Verlaten Island, S side of the lake, April, 1920. Dying *Casuarina* forest with *Terminalia Catappa*, *Hibiscus tiliaceus*, and *Cocos nucifera*." Dammerman's figure 2.]

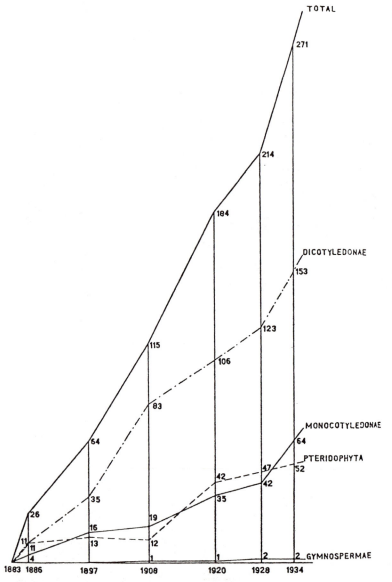

Figure 139. Increase in number of plant species found on the three islands of Krakatau from 1883 to 1934. Figure 4 of Docters van Leeuwen (1936, p. 210).

century, and the vastly larger eruptions of the recent past (p. 23) must have been even more effective agents of biological distribution. At Krakatau, the great waves and winds of August 27 were clearly able to mix biological materals with pumice at the time of eruption, but there were also abundant opportunities for organisms to board pumice rafts in the following months (as, for example, in the pumice-choked Lampong Bay) before being swept off to sea. And "boarding" pumice rafts is not the only way that organisms are distributed by floating masses. The pumice provides protection for shore fish and other marine organisms that form a floating ecosystem moving large distances over the open ocean (see the description by Captain Reeves on p. 152). The suggestion that pumice is important in biological dispersal is not new,[6] but the Krakatau eruption provides a particularly strong illustration of its efficacy.

[1]*Pacific Science Congress (1929).*
[2]*Backer (1908).*
[3]*Backer (1929, p. 5).*
[4]*Backer (1929, p. 197).*
[5]*Flenley and Richards (1982), Whittaker et al. (in press).*
[6]*Wood-Jones (1910, p. 291) referred to floating pumice as "a mighty fleet of passenger vehicles for the use of Nature's colonists." Sachet (1955) has discussed the biological significance of pumice on ocean islands, and geologic aspects of floating pumice have been summarized by Fiske (1969) and Bryan (1971).*

V. Bibliography

This bibliography carries full citations for the various sources referenced in this book (including, therefore, some references only peripherally related to Krakatau). We have attempted to annotate those citations in which the title did not reflect the contents or those that we had difficulty locating with the citation information at hand. We have also included some references not mentioned in the text when we thought that they might be helpful to the reader. We have not generally included derivative references such as popular articles or the many Krakatau accounts in geology textbooks.

This bibliography does not pretend to be comprehensive. The reader seriously interested in Krakatau should consult the 1982 selected bibliography by Brodie, Kusumadinata, and Brodie (1,013 citations arranged under 6 disciplinary headings), or the thorough bibliography being prepared by the Volcanological Survey of Indonesia for the August 1983 Krakatau Commemoration (over 7,500 titles). Only 12% of the publications in this last bibliography are in English.

Abbot, C.G., and E.E. Fowle
    1913.   Volcanoes and Climate. *Smithsonian Miscellaneous Collections*, 60(29): 24 pages.

Abbot, H.L.
    1881.   Report upon Experiments and Investigations to Develop a System of Submarine Mines for Defending the Harbors of the United States. *Professional Papers of the Corps of Engineers of the United States Army*, No. 23.

Aitken, J.
    1884.   The Remarkable Sunsets. *Proceedings of the Royal Society of Edinburgh*, 12:448–450.

Allard, P., C. Jehanno, and J. Sabroux
    1981.   Composition Chimique et Isotopique des Produits Gazeux et Solides de l'Activité Eruptive du Krakatau (Indonésie) Pendant la Periode 1978–1980. *Comptes Rendus Hebdomadaires des Seances de l'Academie des Sciences*, series 2, 293:1095–1098.

Alluard
    1883.   Lueurs Crépusculaires du 27 Décembre, Observée au Sommet du Puy de Dôme. *Comptes Rendus Hebdomadaires des Seances de l'Acadamie des Sciences*, 98:161–163.

Alvarez, L.W., W. Alvarez, F. Asaro, and H.V. Michel
1980.   Extraterrestrial Cause for the Cretaceous-Tertiary Extinction, Experimental Results and Theoretical Interpretation. *Science*, 208(4448):1095–1108.

Anderson, T.
1914.   The Volcanoes Bromo and Krakatau. A Brief Account of a Visit to Them. *Alpine Journal*, 28(204):178–182.

Anonymous [See also titles of newspapers, journals and organizations, plus "Film," and "HMS" (shipname)].
1883a.   Great Sea-Wave. [Letter to the editor.] *Knowledge*, 4:365.
1883b.   Phénoménes Volcaniques du Détroit de la Sonde (26 et 27 Août 1883); Examen Minéralogique des Cendres. *Comptes Rendus Hebdomadaires des Seances de l'Academie des Sciences*, 97:1100–1105 and 98:1303. [Erroneously attributed to Daubrée in some references.]
1884.   *Les Premiéres Nouvelles concernant l'Éruption du Krakatau en 1883 dans les journaux de l'Insulinde.* 23 pages. Paris: Imprimerie Ch. Maréchal and J. Montorier. [Newspaper articles about the eruption, collected by M. Dietrich and translated into French, with map of Bantam coast.]
1889.   The Krakatoa Eruption and Java Chronicles. *Trübner's American and Oriental Literary Record*, series 3, 1:85. [See Judd, 1889, and our p. 308.]
1973.   Film letusan G. Krakatau dan. G. Semeru Selesia. *Berita Direktorat Geologi* (Geosurvey Newsletter), 5(5):2.
1978.   Tsunami, and Other Waves. *The New Pacific*. Jul-Aug, pages 17–20. [Excerpted from *100A1*, the magazine of Lloyd's Register of Shipping; and from NOAA, the magazine of the National Oceanic and Atmospheric Administration, and other material provided by the International Tsunami Information Center in Honolulu.]

Archibald, E.D.
1883.   Sunset Glow. [Letter to the editor.] *Nature*, 29:176–177.
1887.   Upper Wind Currents Near the Equator and the Diffusion of Krakatoa Dust. *Nature*, 36:152–153.
1888.   [Archibald wrote several sections of the joint report (see Russell and Archibald, 1888) in the Royal Society monograph (Symons, 1888).]

Ascroft, W. (See: South Kensington Museum, London.)
Ashdown, E.
1883.   A Floating Lava Bed. [Letter to the editor, reprinted from the *London Times*.] *Nature*, 28:532-533. [Also in *Nature*, 29:55, reprinted from the *Sind Gazette Bulletin*, 12 Oct.]

Avallone, M.
1969.   *Krakatoa, East of Java.* 142 pages. New York: Signet (New American Library).

Backer, C.A.
1909.   De Flora van het Eiland Krakatau. De opneming van de Krakatau-Groep in Mei 1908. *Jaarverslag van den Topogr. Dienst in Nederlandisch-Indie over 1908* (Batavia), page 40.
1929.   *The Problem of Krakatoa As Seen by a Botanist.* 286 pages. Batavia: published by author.

Baird, A.W.
1884a.   Report on the Volcanic Eruptions at Java in August, 1883. Dehra Dun (India), sm. folio.
1884b.   Report on the Tidal Disturbances Caused by the Volcanic Eruption at Java August 26–27, 1883, and the Propagation of the 'Supertidal' Waves. *Proceedings of the Royal Society of London*, 36:248–253.

Ball, R.
1902.   Eruption of Krakatoa. *National Geographic Magazine*, 13:200–204.

Baron, J. van
1931.   Properties and Constitution of a Volcanic Soil Built in 50 Years in the East-Indian Archipelago. *Mededeelingen van de Landbouw hooge school te Wageningen*, 35(6):3.

Bary, E. de, and K. Bullrich
1959.   Zur Theorie des Bishopringes. *Meteorologische Rundschau*, Berlin, 12:89–92.

Bealby, J.T.
1883.   The Java Eruption and Earthquake Waves. *Nature*, 29:30–32.

Bemmelen, W. van
1908.   Oplooding van het Krakatau-Bekken. In De Opneming van de Krakatau-Groep in Mei 1908. *Jaarverslag van den Topogr. Dienst in Nederlandisch-Indie over 1908* (Batavia).
1909.   Over Krakatau in 1908. *Natuurkundig Tijdschrift voor Nederlandsch-Indie*, 68:242–244.

Bemmelen, R.W. van
1941.   Krakatau no. 18. *Bulletin of the East Indian Volcanological Survey*, Bandoeng, no. 95–98:53–60.
1949a.   Report on the Volcanic Activity and Volcanological Research in Indonesia During the Period 1936-1948. *Bulletin Volcanologique*, series 2, 9:3–30.

1949b. The Geology of Indonesia, IA. General Geology of Indonesia and Adjacent Archipelagos. 732 pages. The Hague: Govt. Printing Office.

1953. Relations entre le Volcanisme et la Tectongenese en Indonesie. Bulletin Volcanologique, 13:57–62.

1963. Volcanology and Geology of Ignimbrites in Indonesia, North Italy and the U.S.A. Bulletin Volcanologique, 25:151–174.

Berg, N.P van den
1884. Vroegere Berichten Omtrent Krakatau. De uitbarsting van 1680. Tijdschrift voor Indische Taal-, Land-, en Volkenkunde, (Batavia), 29:208–228.

Bertelli, I.
1890–1. Studi Comperativi fra alcune Vibrazioni Meccaniche Artificiali ele Vibrazioni Sismiche. Annali dell' Ufficio Centrale Meteorologico e Geodinamico Italiano, series IIa, vols. 10 (1890) and 11 (1891).

Bezemer, T.J.
1904. Volksdichtung aus Indonesia [Legend of Dajang Sambi and Sangkuriang]. 429 pages. The Hague: Martinus Nijhoff.

Bibliotheca Bogoriensis
1968. Bibliografi Mengenai Krakatau [Biological bibliography of Krakatau]. Bibliotheca Bogoriensis, Seri Bibliografi, 9: 19 pages.

Bishop, S.E.
1883. [Afterglows.] Saturday Press, Honolulu, 22 Sep.
1884a. The Equatorial Smoke-Stream from Krakatoa. Hawaiian Monthly, May 1884: 106–110.
1884b. The Remarkable Sunsets. [Letter to the editor.] Nature, 29:259–260.
1884c. The Remarkable Sunsets. [Letter to the editor.] Nature, 29:549.
1884d. September Stream of Krakatoa Smoke at Strong's Island. Nature, 30:357 and 31:288.
1885. Krakatoa. [Letter to the editor.] Nature, 31:288–289.
1886. Origin of the Red Glows. American Meteorological Journal, July and August 1886. [Printed also in History and Work of the Warner Observatory, 1887, 1:63–70.]

Blanke, W.
1933. Langs Welke Wegen Kwamen Flora en Fauna naar het Eiland Krakatau? In Java Bode (1933a), page 56.

Blong, R.J.
1982. The Time of Darkness: Local Legends and Volcanic Reality in Papua New Guinea. 257 pages. Canberra: Australian National UnivPress, and Seattle: Univ. of Washington Press.

Bolt, B.A.
1976. Nuclear Explosions and Earthquakes. 309 pages. San Francisco: W.H. Freeman and Co. [Krakatau page 41.]

Bonney, T.G.
1912. Volcanoes, Their Structure and Significance. 379 pages. London: J. Murray. 3rd edition.

Borssum Waalkes, J. van
1960. Botanical Observations on the Krakatau Islands in 1951 and 1952. Annales Bogorienses, 4(1):5–64.

Bosch, C.A. van den
1929. De wordingsgeschiedenis van het Tenggergebergte. Nat. Tijdschr. v. Ned.-Indië, 89:1–48.
1930. De calderavorming. Nat. Tijdschr. v. Ned.-Indië, 90:27–84.
1931. Nog eens de calderavorming. Nat. Tijdschr. v. Ned.-Indë, 91:118–134.

Boutelle, C.
1884. Water Waves from Krakatoa. Science, 3:777.

Bréon, R., and W. C. Korthals
1884. Sur l'état Actuel du Krakatau. Comptes Rendus Hebdomadaires des Seances de l'Academie des Sciences, 99:395–397.
1885. Rapport sur une Mission Scientifique dans le Détroit de la Sonde. Archives des Missions Scientifique et Litteraire, 12:433–437.

Brodie, A., K. Kusumadinata, and J.W. Brodie
1982. Krakatoa. A Selected Natural History Bibliography. Miscellaneous Publication, 96. 87 pages. New Zealand Oceanographic Institute, Wellington.

Brouwer, H.A.
1928. Bibliographie Volcanologique des Indes Nederlandaises Orientales. Bulletin Volcanologique, 18:293–304.

Brown, W.H., E.D. Merrill, and H.S. Yates
1917. The Revegetation of Volcano Island, Luzon, Philippine Islands, Since the Eruption of Taal Volcano in 1911. The Phillippine Journal of Science, C. Botany, 12(4):177–243. [p. 204–205 compares Krakatau's revegetation to Taal's.]

Brun, A.
1911. Recherches sur l'Exhalaison Volcanique. Paris and Geneva. 277 pages. [Krakatau: pages 45 and 231.]

Bryan, W.B.
1971. Coral Sea Drift Pumice Stranded on Eua Island, Tonga, in 1969. Bulletin of the Geological Society of America, 82:2799–2812.

Bull, G.A.
1951. Blue Sun and Moon. Meteorological Magazine, London, 80:1–4.

Burdecki, F.
1964.   Meteorological Phenomena After Volcanic
            Eruptions. *Weather*, London, 19:113–114.
Campbell, D.H.
1909.   The New Flora of Krakatoa. *American Nat-
            uralist*, 43:449–460.
Ceylon Observer
1883a.   The Receding of the Sea. 28 Aug 1883: page
            unknown.
1883b.   The Volcanic Eruption in Sunda Straits. 6 Sep
            1883: page unknown.
1883c.   Details of the Destruction of Anjer by the Re-
            cent Volcanic Eruption in Sunda Strait. 2 Oct
            1883: page unknown. [Translated from *Ba-
            taviaasch Handlesblad*, 9 Sep 1883.]
1883d.   Further Particulars of the Volcanic Outbursts
            in Sunda Straits. 5 Oct 1883: page unknown.
1883e.   The Volcanic Outburst in Sunda Straits. 17
            Oct 1883: page unknown.
Clark, J.E.
1887.   The Recent Sky Glows. *History and Work of
            the Warner Observatory*, 1:39–51.
Coffin, H.G.
1983.   Erect floating stumps in Spirit Lake, Wash-
            ington. *Geology*, 11:298–299.
Cool, H.
1908.   De Opneming van de Krakatau-Groep in Mei
            1908. *Jaarverslag van den Topogr. Dienst in
            Nederlandsch-Indie over 1908* (Batavia), pages
            22–?.
1909a.   Mededeeling Omtrent de Geologie van de
            Krakatau-Groep. *Jaarboek van het Mijnwezen
            in Nederlandsch Oost-Indie* (Batavia), 37.
1909b.   Over Krakatau in 1908. *Natuurkundig
            Tijdschrift voor Nederlandsch-Indie*, 68:244–
            247.
Cotteau, E.
1884.   Krakatau et le Détroit de la Sonde. *Le Tour
            du Monde*, 51:113–128.
1885.   A Week At Krakatoa. *Royal Geographic Society
            of Australasia, S. Australia Branch, Proceed-
            ings*, 2:103–106. [Or *Proceedings of the Geo-
            graphical Society of Australasia, N.S.W. and
            Victorian Branches*, 2.] [Reprinted in German
            ("Eine Woche aus Krakatau") in *Das Ausland*,
            1885, 58:47–51.]
1888.   [Krakatau.] Page 35 in *Océnie Voyage autour
            du Monde en 365 jours, 1884–1885*. Paris.
Cotteau, E., and W.C. Korthals
1884.   Mission Française au Krakatau. *Comptes Ren-
            dus des Seances de la Societe de Geographie*
            (Paris), 15. [See also *Nature*, 1884d.]
Dalby, R.J.
1937.   The Krakatoa Eruption in 1883. *The Listener*,
            17 March, pages 496–498.

Dammerman, K.W.
1922.   The Fauna of Krakatau, Verlaten Island and
            Sebesy. *Treubia*, 3:61.
1929.   Krakatau's New Fauna. In *Proceedings of the
            Fourth Pacific Science Congress* (Batavia), pages
            83–118.
1948.   The Fauna of Krakatau 1883-1933. *K. Aka-
            demie van Wetenschappen, Afdeeling Natu-
            urkunde, Verhandelingen*, section 2, 44:1–594.
Dana, J.D.
1890.   *Characteristics of Volcanoes, With Contribu-
            tions of Facts and Principles from the Ha-
            waiian Islands*. 399 pages. New York: Dodd,
            Mead and Co. [Krakatau: pages 249–250.]
Darwin, G.H.
1883.   The Great Tidal Wave. [Letter to the editor,
            with extract of a letter from A.W. Baird.] *Na-
            ture*, 28:626.
de (See under family name; e.g., for C. de Groot, see Groot,
     C. de.)
Decker, R.
1959.   Renewed Activity of Anak Krakatoa. *Contri-
            butions of the Department of Geology, Institute
            of Technology* (Bandung), 34:1–5.
Decker, R., and B. Decker
1982.   *Volcanoes*. 244 pages. San Francisco: W.H.
            Freeman and Co. [Krakatau pages 43–55, 84,
            179–181, 183–184.]
Decker, R.W., and D. Hadikusumo
1961.   Results of the 1960 Expedition to Krakatoa.
            Journal of Geophysical Research, 66:3497–3511.
Deirmendjian, D.
1973.   On Volcanic and Other Particulate Turbidity
            Anomalies. *Advances in Geophysics*, 16:267–
            297.
Delisle
1883.   Les Secousses de Tremblement de Terre a la
            Reunion et a Maurice Comme Consequence
            de l'Eruption Volcanique du Detroit de la
            Sonde. *Bulletin de la Society de Geogographie*
            (Paris), pages 524–526.
Delsman, H.C.
1933.   Het Wetenschappelijk Onderzoek van den
            Karkatau Sedert 1883. In *Java Bode* (1933a),
            page 54.
Descroix, L.
1883.   L'Oscillation Atmospherique Produite par
            l'Eruption de Krakatoa. *L'Astronomie*, 3:183–
            184.
Diamond, J.M.
1977.   Colonisation of a Volcano Inside a Volcano.
            Nature, 270:13–14. [Comparison with reco-
            lonization of Long Island, Papua New Guinea.]
Dinas Hidrografi Angkatan Laut Republik Indonesia
1972.   Selat Sunda, 1:200,000. Chart 71.

Divers, E.
1884.   The Remarkable Sunsets. [Letter to the editor.] *Nature*, 29:283–284.

Docters van Leeuwen, W.M.
1921.   The Flora and Fauna of the Islands of the Krakatau-Group in 1919. *Annales du Jardin Botanique de Buitenzorg*, 31:103–139.
1922.   The Vegetation of the Island of Sebesy, Situated in the Sunda Strait, near the Islands of the Krakatau-Group. *Annales du Jardin Botanique de Buitenzorg*, 32:135–192.
1923.   On the Present State of the Vegetation of the Islands of the Krakatau Group and of the Island of Sebesy. In *Proceedings of the Pan-Pacific Science Congress* (Australia), 1:313.
1925.   Nature's Clean Slate on Krakatau. *The Illustrated London News*, 167:564–566.
1929.   Krakatau's New Flora. In *Proceedings of the Fourth Pacific Science Congress* (Batavia), part 2:56–79.
1936.   Krakatau 1883–1933. *Annales du Jardin Botanique de Buitenzorg*, 46–47: 506 pages.

Doorn, M.C. van
1884.   The Eruption of Krakatoa. *Nature*, 29:268–269. Translated and partially abridged by E. Metzger. [From *Eigen Haard*, 1883, no. 51, dated Batavia, 23 October.]

Dorn, W.G. van
1965.   Tsunamis. *Advances in Hydroscience*, 2:1–48.

Dufour, C.
1884.   Les Lueurs Crépusculaires de l'Hiver 1883–1884. *Biblioteque Université*, 15 Feb. [See also *Comptes Rendus Hebdomadaires des Seances de l'Academie des Sciences*, 98:617–620.]

Dutton, C.E.
1884.   Hawaiian Volcanoes. Fourth Annual Report of the U.S. Geological Survey, pages 75–250. ["Caldera" introduced on p. 105.]

Easton, N.W.
1926.   Ter Gedachtenis van Dr. R.D.M. Verbeek. Bijlage van het *Jaarboek van het Geologische Mijnbouwkundig Genootschap voor Nederland en Koloniën*, voor 1926: pages 1–31. [Also, "Verbeek als Musicus," by D.R.J. van Lynden, pages 31–34.]

Eichelberger. J.C.
1978.   Andesitic Volcanism and Crustal Evolution. *Nature*, 275:21–27.

Ernst, A.
1907.   Die Neue Flora der Vulkaninsel Krakatau. *Vierteljahrschrift der Naturwissforschende Gesellschaft* (Zürich), 52.
1908.   *The New Flora of the Volcanic Islands of Krakatoa*. Translated by A. C. Seward. 74 pages. Cambridge: Cambridge University Press.

1934.   Das Biologische Krakatau-problem. *Naturforschende Geselleschaft, Vierteljahrsschrift*, Zurich, 79:1–187.

Escher, B.G.
1919a.   *Excursie-gids voor Krakatau, Samengesteld voor de Excursie*. 7 pages, 5 illustrations. Weltevreden: Albrecht and Co. Samengesteld voor de Excursie, te houden door het Eerste Nederlandsch-Indisch Natuurwetenschappelijk Congres, Oct 1919.
1919b.   De Krakatau Groep als Vulkaan. In *Handelingen van het Eerste Nederlandsch-Indisch Natuurwetenschappelijk Congres* (Weltevreden), pages 28–35.
1919c.   Veranderingen in de Krakatau Groep na 1908. In *Handelingen Eerste Nederlandsch-Indisch Natuurwetenschappelijk Congres* (Weltevreden), pages 198–219.
1928.   Krakatau in 1883 en in 1928. *Tijdschrift van het Koninklijk Nederlandsch Aardrijkskundig Genootschap*, series 2, 45:715–743.
1937.   Rapport sur les Phenomenes Volcanologique dans l'Archipel Indien pendant les Annees 1933, 1934 et 1935 et sur les Ouvrages de Volcanologie Publies durant ces Annes, Concernant les Volcans des Indies Neerlandaises. *Bulletin Volcanologique*, 1:127–178.
1948.   *Grondslagen der Algemene Geologie*. 442 pages. Amsterdam-Antwerp: Wereldbibliotheek N.V. [Krakatau pages 19–20, 309–312, 316–319.]

Ewing M., and F. Press
1955.   Tide-Gage Disturbances from the Great Eruption of Krakatoa. *Transactions of the American Geophysical Union*, 36:53–60.

Faber, F.J.
1964.   Modderkogels, Mergelconcreties of Askogels van Krakatau [Mud Balls from Krakatoa]. *Geologie en Mijnbouw*, 43:467–475. [Abstract in English.]

Film
1933.   *Krakatau*. Teaching Film Custodians. 26 min sd [sound], 16 mm b. and w. [black and white] motion picture. [A teaching film made for the Library of Congress.]
1955.   *Man vs Nature*. Twentieth Century-Fox Film Corp. 9 min. sd, 35 mm b. and w. motion picture. [Includes Krakatau eruption.]
1966.   *Krakatau*. Joe Rock Productions. 28 min. sd, 16 mm b. and w. motion picture; also in 35 mm. [A revised version of the 1933 film. Made for Library of Congress.]

Filson, J., T. Simkin, and L. Leu
1973.   Seismicity of a Caldera Collapse: Galapagos Islands 1968. *Journal of Geophysical Research*, 78:8591–8622.

Fisher, R.V.
1979.   Models for Pyroclastic Surges and Pyroclastic Flows. *Journal of Volcanology and Geothermal Research*, 6:305-318.

Fisher, R.V., A.L. Smith, and M.J. Roobol
1981.   Destruction of St. Pierre, Martinique, by Ash-cloud Surges, May 8 and 20, 1902. *Geology*, 8:472-476.

Fiske, R.S.
1969.   Recognition and Significance of Pumice in Marine Pyroclastic Rocks. *Bulletin of the Geological Society of America*, 80:1-8.

Fitch, T.J.
1970.   Earthquake Mechanisms and Island Arc Tectonics in the Indonesian-Philippine Region. *Bulletin of the Seismologic Society of America*, 60:565-591.

Fitch, T.J., and P. Molnar
1970.   Focal Mechanisms Along Inclined Earthquake Zones in the Indonesian-Philippine Region. *Journal of Geophysical Research*, 75:1431-1444.

Flammarion, C.
1884.   Les Illuminations Crepusculaires. *L'Astronomie*, 3:19-27, 65-68.
1902.   *Les Eruptions Volcan et les Tremblements de Terre*. 534 pages. Paris. [Krakatau is discussed in pages 1-95. This part is reprinted in *La Météorologie*, series 16, 1979.]

Flenley, J.R., and K. Richards, editors
1982.   The Krakatoa Centennary Expedition: Final Report. *Hull University Geography Department Miscellaneous Series*, 25: 196 pages.

Forbes, H.O.
1883.   Floating Pumice [Letter to the editor.] *Nature*, 28:539.
1884.   The Volcanic Eruption of Krakatau. *Proceedings of the Royal Geographic Society*, 7:142-152. [Attributed by several later authors to H.O. Forbes, but no author listed in the original.]

Fouqué, F.A.
1879.   *Santorin et ses Eruptions*. 440 pages. Paris: G. Mason.

Franklin, B.
1784.   Meteorological Imaginations and Conjectures. *Manchester Literary and Philosophical Society Memoirs and Proceedings*, 2:122 or 375. [Read before the Society on December 22, 1784.]

Franssen, H.A.
1908.   De Opneming van de Krakatau Groep in Mei 1908. *Jaarsverlag van den Topograph. Dienst in Nederlandisch-Indie* (Batavia), 4:150-170

Fridriksson, S.
1975.   *Surtsey*. 198 pages. New York: Halsted Press. [Comparison with colonization after new Island of Surtsey built 1963-1967.]

Furneaux, R.
1964.   *Krakatoa*. 224 pages. New Jersey: Prentice-Hall.

Garrett, C.J.R.
1976.   A Theory of the Krakatoa Tide Gauge Disturbances. *Tellus*, 22(1):43-52.

Gestel, J.T. van
1895.   The Krakatoa Eruption: Described for the First Time by an Eye-Witness of its Horrors. *The Cosmopolitan*, 18(6):719-727.

Gredilla Y Guana
1887.   Pumita del Krakatoa. *Annales de la Real Sociedad Espanola de Historia Natural*, 16:201-208.

Griggs, R.F.
1922.   *The Valley of Ten Thousand Smokes (Alaska)*. 344 pages. Washington, D.C.: National Geographic Society.

Groot, C. de
1883.   Mededeelingen naar Aanleiding van de uitbarsting van den Vulkaan Rakata in Straat Soenda. *Tijdschrift Koninklijk Nederlandsch Instituut van Ingenieurs*. [Reports concerning the Eruption of Krakatau.]

Gruner, P.
1942.   Dämmerungserscheinungen. In *Handbuch der Geophysik* (ed. F. Linke), Bd. 8, ch. 8, pages 432-526.

Guppy, H.B.
1889.   The Cocos-Keeling Islands, Pt. I, II, III. *Scottish Geographical Magazine*, 5:281-297, 457-474, 569-588. [Concerning pumice which floated onto these islands; Krakatau pages 284-287.]

Haan, F. de
1919.   Dagh - Register gehouden int Casteel Batavia for 1681. *Bataviaasch Genootschap voor Kunsten en Wetenschappen*, Batavia.

Hadikusumo, D.
1964.   Report on the Volcanological Research and Volcanic Activity in Indonesia for the Period 1950-1957. *Bulletin of the Volcanologic Survey of Indonesia*, 100:122.

Hadikusumo, D., L. Pardyanto, and M. Alzwar
1976.   Possible Energy Sources in Indonesian Volcanic Areas. *In* Halbouty, Maher, and Lian, editors, *American Association of Petroleum Geologists Memoirs*, 25:135-139.

Hague, A., and J.P. Iddings
1883.   Notes on the Volcanoes of Northern Califonia, Oregon, and Washington Territory. *American Journal of Science*, Sept. 1883.

Hall, M.
1883.   The Java Earthquake Wave. *Monthly Weather Report for Jamaica*, Nov 1883 and Jan 1884.

Hamilton, W.
1981.   Tectonic Map of the Indonesian Region. *United States Geologic Survey Map*, I-875D.

Hansen, J.E., W.-C. Wang, and A.A. Lacis
1978.   Mount Agung Eruption Provides Test of a Global Climatic Perturbation. *Science*, 199:1065–1068.

Harkrider, D.
1964.   Theoretical and Observed Acoustic-Gravity Waves from Explosive Sources in the Atmosphere. *Journal of Geophysical Research*, 69:5295–5395.

Harkrider, D., and F. Press
1967.   The Krakatoa Air-Sea Waves: An Example of Pulse Propagation in Coupled Systems. *Geophysical Journal*, 13:149–159.

Harloff, C.E.A.
1929.   Cordierite in the Krakatau Pumice. Pages 48–49 in Stehn (1929a).

Harrington, P.F.
1883.   [Letter describing the Straits of Sunda following the eruption of 26–27 Aug, 1883, as a report to Hydrographic Office, 15 Sep 1883.] U.S. National Archives, Hydrographic Office, sec XI, box 2, index 1478.

Hatherton, T., and W.R. Dickinson
1969.   The Relationship Between Andesitic Volcanism and Seismicity in Indonesia, the Lesser Antilles, and Other Island Arcs. *Journal of Geophysical Research*, 74:5301–5310.

Haughton, S.
1884.   Remarks on the Unusual Sunrises and Sunsets Which Characterised the Close of the Year 1883. *Proceedings of the Royal Dublin Society*, 4:203–205.

Hazen, H.A.
1884.   The Sun Glows. *American Journal of Science*, 27:201–212.

Hedervari, P.
1979.   The Relationship between Tectonic Earthquakes and Volcanic Eruptions with Particular Reference to Santorini (Aegean Sea) and Indonesia. *Geologie en Mijnbouw*, 58(2):213–224.

Heerdt, P.T. van
1884?   [Report of Captain Visman of the *Prinses Wilhelmina*. Letter to Symons at the Royal Society of London.]

Hehuwat, F., S. Nishimura, J. Hishida, and M.T. Zen
1981.   Preliminary Survey around Krakatau, Indonesia. [Abstract.] In *IAVCEI Tokyo Meeting Abstracts*, page 125.

Hesse, E.D.
1690.   *Ost Indianische Reise-Beschreibung oder Diarium.* . . .. Pages 151–152. Leipzig.
1694.   *Drie Seer Aanmerkelyke Reysen na en door Velerley Gewesten in Oost-Indien; gedaan door Christophorus Frikius, Chirugyn, Elias Hesse, Berghschryver, Christophorus Schweitzer, Boekhouder; Yeder Bysonder; van 't Jaer 1675 tot 1686.* Translated from German to Dutch by Simon de Vries. Utrecht.

Hill, A.W.
1937.   The Flora of Krakatau. *Nature*, 139:135–138. [Review of Docters Van Leeuwen (1936).]

Hinloopen Labberton, D. van
1921.   Oud Javaansche Gegevens Omtrent de Vulkanologie van Java. *Natuurkundig Tijdschrift voor Nederlandsch-Indie*, 81:124–158.

HMS *Magpie*
1883?   Log Book of HMS *Magpie*. Log adm. 53/12002, Public Record Office, London.

HMS *Merlin*
1883?   Log book of HMS *Merlin*. Log adm. 53/14540, Public Record Office, London.

Holmes, A.
1965.   *The Principles of Physical Geology.* 1288 pages. New York: The Ronald Press Co. [Krakatau pages 336–338.]

Honda, K, T. Terada, Y. Yoshida, and D. Isitania
1908.   An Investigation of the Secondary Undulations of Oceanic Tides. *Journal of the College of Arts and Sciences*, Imperial University, Tokyo, 24:1–113.

Hoogewerf, A.
1953.   Notes on the Vertebrate Fauna of the Krakatau Islands, with Special Reference to the Birds. *Treubia*, 22(2):319–348, 6 plates.

Hopkins, G.
1884.   The Remarkable Sunsets. *Nature*, 29:222–223.

Hull, E.
1892.   *Volcanoes: Past and Present.* 270 pages. London: Walter Scott, Ltd. [Krakatau pages 201–216.]

Humphreys, W.J.
1940.   *Physics of the Air.* 676 pages. New York and London: McGraw-Hill (3rd edition).

Hunt, B.G.
1977.   A Simulation of the Possible Consequences of a Volcanic Eruption on the General Circulation of the Atmosphere. *Monthly Weather Review*, 105:247–260.

Hunt, J.N., R. Palmer, and W. Penny
1960.   Atmospheric Waves Caused by Large Explosions. *Philosphical Transactions of the Royal Society of London*, series A, 252:275–315.

Hurlbut, G.C.
1887.   Krakatau from the Study by R.D.M. Verbeek. *Bulletin of the American Geographical Society*, 19:233–255.

Hutchison, C.S.
1976.   Indonesian Active Volcanic Arc: K, Sr and Rb Variation with Depth to the Benioff Zone. *Geology*, 4:407–424.
1982.   Southeast Asia. Pages 451–512 *in* Nairn, A.E.M., and F.G. Stehli, editors, *The Ocean Basins and Margins*. New York and London: Plenum Press. 776 pages.

Huxley, T.H.
1885.   [Address to Royal Society, delivered 30 Nov, 1885.] *Nature*, 33:112–119. [Krakatau Committee discussed on page 115.]

Iddings, J.P.
1884.   Pumice from Krakatoa. [Letter to the editor.] *Science*, 3:144.

Illustrated London News
1883.   The Straits of Sunda: Terrible Volcanic Eruption. 8 Sep 1883:228–230, 8 illustrations.

Jaggar, T.A.
1929.   Engulfment at Krakatoa 1883. *Volcano Letter* (of the Hawaiian Volcanological Research Association), 234:1.

Java Bode
1933a.   "Herdenking Krakatau Uitbarsting van 1883." *Java Bode*, Batavia. [Issued for the 50th anniversary of the Krakatau eruption. Original edition lacks pagination; page numbers here refer to consecutive numbering from the beginning.]
1933b.   De Flora en Fauna van Krakatau. In *Java Bode*, (1933a), page 55.
1933c.   Krakatau ligt op een Gevaarlijk punt, waar de Vulkaanhaarden van Sumatra, Straat-Soenda en Java Samenkomen. In *Java Bode* (1933a), pages 57–58.
1933d.   Persberichten. In *Java Bode* (1933a), pages 29–34.
1933e.   Pseudo-Erupties van den Krakatau. In *Java Bode* (1933a), page 61.
1933f.   De Reis van de "Bijlandt." In *Java Bode* (1933a), page 27.
1933g.   Verbeek: Krakatau voor Mei 1883. In *Java Bode* (1933a), pages 13–26.
1933h.   10 Dagen na de Uitbarsting door Straat-Soenda. In *Java Bode* (1933a), page 28.

Joly, J.
1885.   Notes on the Microscopical Character of the Volcanic Ash from Krakatoa. *Proceedings of the Royal Dublin Society*, 4:291–299.

Jongh, A.C. de
1918.   Puimsteen op de Krakatau-Eilanden. *Jaarboek van het Mijnewezen in Nederlandsch Oost-Indie* (Batavia), 45 (part 2).

Judd, J.W.
1881.   *Volcanoes: What They Are and What They Teach*. 381 pages. New York: D. Appleton and Co.
1884a.   Krakatoa. *Proceedings of the Royal Society of London*, May 1884.
1884b.   The Dust of Krakatoa. *Nature*, 29:595.
1888a.   On the Volcanic Phenomena of the Eruption, and on the Nature and Distribution of the Ejected Materials. *In* Symons, 1888, pages 1–56.
1888b.   The Natural History of Lavas As Illustrated by the Materials Ejected from Krakatoa. *Geological Magazine*, 5:1–11.
1889.   The Earlier Eruptions of Krakatoa. [Letter to the editor.] *Nature*, 40:365–366.

Karsten, G., and J.H.L. Flogel,
1884.   Feste Ruckstande im Regenwasser. *Schriften des Naturwissenschaftlicher Vereins für Schleswig-Holstein*, 5:137–141.

Katili, J.A.
1973.   Geochronology of West Indonesia and Its Implications on Plate Tectonics. *Tectonophysics*, 19:195–212.
1975.   Volcanism and Plate Tectonics in the Indonesian Island Arcs. *Tectonophysics*, 26:165–188.

Kemmerling, G.L.L.
1926.   L'Archipel Indien Centre Important de Volcanisme. *Bulletin Volcanologique*, 7–8:87–98, one colored map.

Kennedy, H.G.
1884.   Notes of the Report from H.M. Consul, Batavia, Including Extract from Log Book of Steam-ship G.G. *Loudon*. *Proceedings of the Royal Society of London*, 36:203–205.

Kent, D.V.
1981.   Asteroid Extinction Hypothesis. *Science*, 211:648–650.

Kiessling, K.I.
1884.   Die Diffractionsfarben in Künstlichen Nebeln und die Dämmerungs-Erscheinungen. In *Tageblatt der 57 Versammlung Deutscher Naturforscher und Aerzte zu Magdeburg*, p. 293. Also in *Die Naturforscher*, No. 43.
1887.   On the Cause of the Remarkable Optical Atmospheric Effects in 1883 and 1884. *History*

and Work of the Warner Observatory, 1:31–37.

Kimball, H.H.
1910   Solar Radiation, Atmospheric Absorption, and Sky Polarization at Washington, D.C. *Bulletin of the Mount Weather Observatory*, 3(2):69–126.

Kloos, J.H.
1884.   Die Vulcanische Eruption. *Badische Landeszeitung*, 16 Feb.

Krafft, K., and M. Chaigneau
1976.   Sur les Rapports entre Chlore et Brome dans les Gaz Volcaniques de douze Volcans Indonésien. *Comptes Rendus Hebdomadaires des Seances de l'Academie des Sciences*, series D, 282:341–343.

1977.   Composition des Gaz Volcaniques émis par des Volcans d'Indonésie. *Comptes Rendus Hebdomadaires des Seances de l'Acadamie des Sciences*, series D, 284:429–431.

Kuenen, P.H.
1935.   Contributions to the Geology of the East Indies from the Snellius Expedition, Part 1, Volcanoes. *Leidsche Geologische Mededeelingen*, 7(2):273–330 [Krakatau chemical analyses included on variation diagrams, pages 327–329.]

Kusumadinata, K., editor
1973.   Energi Letusan Terakhir Gunung Krakatau. *Berita Direktorat Geologi (Geosurvey Newsletter)*, 5(34):4.

1979.   *Catalog of References on Indonesian Volcanoes with Eruptions in Historical Time*. 820 pages. Republic of Indonesia: Direktonal Vulk. [In Indonesian.]

Lamb, H.H.
1970.   Volcanic Dust in the Atmosphere; with a Chronology and Assessment of its Meteorological Significance. *Philosophical Transaction of the Royal Society of London*, series A, 266:425–533.

Latter, J.H.
1981.   Tsunamis of Volcanic Origin: Summary of Causes, with Particular Reference to Krakatau, 1883. *Bulletin Volcanologique*, 44:467–490. [Published in late 1982.]

LeConte, J.
1884.   Atmospheric Waves from Krakatoa. *Science*, 3:701–702.

Lewis, H.C.
1884.   A Near View of Krakatoa in Eruption. *Science*, 3:702–703.

Lindemann, T.H.
1884.   Report from H.B.M. Consul at Batavia, Inclosing Extracts Relating to the Volcanic Outburst in the Sunda Strait, from the Log-book of the Steam-ship *Governor-General Loudon*. *Proceedings of the Royal Society of London*, 36:199–203. [Author's name misspelled as "Linderman." See also Kennedy, 1884.]

Lipman, P.W., and D.R. Mullineaux, editors
1981.   The 1980 Eruptions of Mount St. Helens, Washington. *U.S. Geological Survey Professional Paper*, 1250:844 pages.

Lloyd Praeger, R.
1911.   Clare Island Survey, Part 10. *Proceedings of the Royal Irish Acadamy*, 31, section 68, 15 pages.

London and China Telegraph
1883a.   13 Sep 1883: page unknown.
1883b.   The Volcanic Eruption in the Sunda Straits. 13 Oct 1883: page unknown.
1883c.   The Volcanic Eruption in the Sunda Straits. 9 Nov 1883: page unknown.
1884.   The Eruption in the Sunda Straits. 28 Feb 1884: page unknown.

London *Times*
1883a.   Volcanic Eruption. 3 Jul 1883:10, column f.
1883b.   The Volcanic Eruption in Java. 30 Aug 1883:3, column e.
1883c.   The Volcanic Eruption in Java. 31 Aug 1883:3, column e.
1883d.   The Volcanic Eruption in Java. 4 Oct 1883:10, column c.
1883e.   The Java Eruption. 9 Oct 1883:7, column f.

Luce, J.V.
1969.   *The End of Atlantis*. 187 pages. Great Britain: Paladin Paperback. [Krakatau pages 61-71.]

Macdonald, G.A.
1968.   Krakatoa. In *Encyclopedia Britannica*, 13:485–486. Chicago: Willaim Benton.

1972.   *Volcanoes*. 510 pages. New Jersey: Prentice-Hall, Inc.

McLeod, N.
1884.   De Uitbarsting van de Krakatau. *Tijdschrift van het Koninklijk Nederlandsch Aardrijkskundig Genootschap*, series 2, 1:184–191.

Maine, H.C.
1887.   The Red Light. *History and Work of the Warner Observatory*, 1:53–62.

Manley, W.R.
1883.   A Green Sun in India. [Letter to the editor.] *Nature*, 28:576–577.

Marie-Davy, E.H.
1884.   Sur Les Oscillations Barométriques du 27 Auôt. *Comptes Rendus Hebdomadaires des Seances de l'Academie des Sciences*, 98:246–248.

Mass, C., and S.H. Schnieder
1977.   Statistical Evidence of the Influence of Sunspots and Volcanic Dust on Long Term Temperature Records. *Journal of Atmospheric Science*, 34:1995–2004.

Meijboom-Italiaander, J.
1924.   *Javaansche Sagen, Mythen en Legenden*. 325 pages. Zutphen.

Meinel, A.B., and M.P. Meinel
1967.   Volcanic Sunset-Glow Stratum: Origin. *Science*, 155:189.

1983.   *Sunsets, Twilights and Evening Skies*. Cambridge: Cambridge University Press.

Meldrum, C.
1885.   A Tabular Statement of the Dates at Which, and the Localities Where, Pumice or Volcanic Dust Was Seen in the Indian Ocean in 1883–4. *Report of the British Association Association for the Advancement of Science*, 55th meeting, pages 773–779. [Reproduced *in* Symons, 1888: pages 48–56.]

Metzger, E.
1883.   Die Umwälzungen und Zerftörungen in der Sundastrake. [The Wave and Disturbance in Sunda Strait.] *Globus*, 14(15):232–237.

1884.   Gleanings from Reports Concerning the Eruption of Krakatoa. *Nature*, 29:240–244.

1886.   Der Ausbruch von Krakatau in Jahre 1883. *Petermann's Geographische Mittheilungen*, 32:10–24.

Miles
1933.   Wat ik 50 Jaar Geleden bij de Uitbarsting van den Krakatau Beleefde. In *Java Bode* (1933a), pages 46–49.

Milne, J.
1911.   Catalogue of Destructive Earthquakes. *British Association for the Advancement of Science Report*, 81st meeting, 1911:649–740.

Minnaert, M.
1959.   *Light and Colour in the Open Air*. 362 pages. London: G. Bell and Sons, Ltd.

Mitchell, J.M.
1961.   Recent Secular Changes in Global Temperature. *Annals of the New York Academy of Sciences*, 95:235–250. [Includes the effects of eruptions such as Krakatau.]

1982.   El Chichón. Weather-maker of the Century? *Weatherwise*, 35:252–259.

Mohr, E.C.J.
1938.   The Relation between Soil and Population Density in the Netherlands East Indies. In *Comptes Rendus du Congrés Internationale de Géographie Amsterdam 1938*, 2 sect. IIIc, pages 478–493. Leiden: Brill.

1944.   *The Soils of Equatorial Regions with Special Reference to the Netherlands East Indies*, pages 146–151, trans., Robert L. Pendleton. Ann Arbor: J.W. Edwards.

1945.   Climate and Soil in the Netherlands Indies. *In* P. Honig and F. Verdoorn, editors, *Science and Scientists in the Netherlands Indies*, pages 250–254. New York: Board of Netherlands Indies.

Mossop, S.C.
1964.   Volcanic Dust Collected at an Altitude of 20 km. *Nature*, 203:824–827.

Multatuli
1933.   Feuilleton de Banjir. In *Java Bode* (1933a), pages 37–38.

Murray, J., and M.A. Renard
1884.   Volcanic Ashes and Cosmic Dust. *Nature*, 29:585–590.

Murray-Aaron, E.
1900.   The Greatest Explosion of Historic Times. *St. Nicholas*, 27:889–891.

Nairn, I.A., and S. Self
1978.   Explosive Eruptions and Pyroclastic Avalanches from Ngauruhoe in February 1975. *Journal of Volcanology and Geothermal Research*, 3:39–60.

Nakamura, S.
1982.   1883 Krakatoa Tsunami in a Scope of Numerical Experiment. *La Mer (Bulletin de la Société Franco-Japonaise d'Oceanographie)*, 20:29–36.

Nash, J.M.W.
1929.   Twee Vliegtochten naar den Krakatau. *Tijdschrift van het Koninklijk Nederlandsch Aardrijkskundig Genootschap* (Leiden), 46(4):498–505.

Nature
1883a.   [On the 20-21 May 1883 volcanic eruption of Krakatau.] 28:329.

1883b.   [Letter from Lloyd's agent in Batavia, 1 Sep.] 28:577.

1883c.   [From a communication by C. Meldrum to the Mauritius *Mercantile Record*.] 29:32–33.

1883d.   [Notes on a communication from Rénard.] 29:134.

1884a.   [Excerpts of a letter from E.L. Layard.] 29:461.

1884b.   Krakatoa. 30:279–280. [Report on communications from Meteorological Society of Mauritius.]

1884c.   [Notes on the French Mission to Krakatau by Cotteau and Korthals.] 30:372.

1885a.   [Notes on Krakatau; Subterranean Sounds.] 32:161.

1885b.   Krakatoa. 32:601–604.

1886.   Deposits of Volcanic Dust. 35:174–175.

Neale, P.
1885.   The Krakatoa Eruption. *Leisure Hour*, 34:348–351, 379–388, 544–557, 635–638. [Printed also in *Living Age*, 166:693, 753, 819; 167:174.]

Neeb, G.A.
1943.   The Composition and Distribution of the

Samples. In *The Snelling Expedition*, volume 5, part 3. Leyden.

Neumann Van Padang, M.

1933a.   De Krakatau voorheen en thans. *De Tropische Natuur*, 22(8):137–150.

1933b.   *Verslag van het Onderzoek van Anak Krakatau van 5–9 Januari 1933*. Volcanological Survey of Indonesia, unpublished report. 12 pages.

1934.   Die Eruptionsregenfrage im Bezug auf den Groszen Krakatau Ausbruch vom 26–27 August 1883. *Tijdschrift Koninklijk Nederlandsch Akademie van Wetenschappen* (Amsterdam), 37:3–8.

1935.   *Verslag van de Krakatau uitbarsting van 6 tot 13 Juli 1935 en het bezoek aan Krakatau op 7–10 Aug. 1935*. Volcanological Survey of Indonesia, unpublished report. 17 pages.

1936a.   *Bezoek aan Krakatau van 11–14 Dec.* Volcanological Survey of Indonesia, unpublished report. 3 pages.

1936b.   Der Krater Des Anak Krakatau. *De Ingenieur Ned. Ind.* (Batavia), 3:101–107.

1951.   Indonesia. In *Catalog of Active Volcanoes of the World*, 1. 271 pages. Rome: IAVCEI. [Krakatau pages 51-64.]

1955.   A Swedish Sketch of the Island of Krakatau in 1748. *Bulletin Volcanologique*, 17:135–140.

1963.   The Temperatures in the Crater Region of some Indonesian Volcanoes Before The Eruption. *Bulletin Volcanologique*, 26:319–336.

1971.   Two Catastrophic Eruptions in Indonesia, Comparable with the Plinian Outbursts of the Volcano of Thera (Santorini) in Minoan Time. *In* A. Kaloyeropoyloy, editor, *1969 Thera Symposium*, pages 51–63.

Nève, G.A. de

1953.   Le Group des Îles de Krakatau. Pages 4–7 *in* Rapport Concernant l'Activité Volcanique en Indonésie Pendant le Premier Trimestre de l'Année 1953. *Berita Gunung Berapi* (*Commun. Volc. Surv. Indonesia*), 1(3–4):3–16.

1956a.   Krakatoa and Anak Krakatoa, with a Communication on the Latest Investigation in October 1953. [Abstract.] In *Proceedings of the Eighth Pacific Science Congress*, 2:178–179.

1956b.   The New Seismological Equipment for the Permanent Observation Posts of the Volcanological Survey of Indonesia. [Abstract.] In *Proceedings of the Eighth Pacific Science Congress*, 2:?.

1981.   Anak Krakatau (1930–1980). *Proceedings PIT X Ikatan Ahli Geologi Indonesia*, Bandung, 8–10 December, pages 7–40.

1982.   The Krakatau-Group and Anak Krakatau's Eruptivity: Snapshot of 1981. *Berita Geologi* (Geosurvey Newsletter), Bandung, 14:195–211.

1983.   Krakatau's Earliest Known Activity: Was It Prehistoric. *Berita Geologi* (Geosurvey Newsletter), Bandung, 15:39–44.

Newell, R.E., and A. Deepak, editors

1982.   *Mount St. Helens Eruptions of 1980. Atmospheric Effects and Potential Climatic Impact. A Workshop Report*. 119 Pages. Washington, D.C.: NASA SP-458.

Newhall, C.G. and S. Self

1982.   The Volcanic Explosivity Index (VEI)—An Estimate of Explosive Magnitude for Historical Volcanism. *Journal of Geophysical Research*, 87:1231–1238.

New York Times

1883a.   The Sun Instead of a Fire. 28 Nov 1883:2.

1883b.   The Red Light in the Sky. [Letter to the Editor.] 7 Dec 1883:4.

1883c.   Two Sunsets on the Same Evening. 8 Dec 1883:3. [From *Virginia* (Nevada) *Enterprise*, 29 Nov 1883.]

1883d.   The Recent Sunsets, 25 Dec 1883:4.

1884.   The True Explanation, 23 Jan 1884.

Niel, R. van

1963.   The Course of Indonesian History. *In* R.T. McVey, editor, *Indonesia*, pages 272–308. New Haven: HRAF Press.

Ninkovich, D.

1976.   Late Cenozoic Clockwise Rotation of Sumatra. *Earth and Planetary Science Letters*, 29:269–275.

1979.   Distribution, Age and Chemical Composition of Tephra Layers in Deep-Sea Sediments off Western Indonesia. *Journal of Volcanology and Geothermal Research*, 5:67–86.

Ninkovich, D., and W.L. Donn

1976.   Explosive Cenozoic Volcanism and Climatic Implications. *Science*, 194:899–906.

Ninkovich, D., R.S.J. Sparks, and M.T. Ledbetter

1978.   The Exceptional Magnitude and Intensity of the Toba Eruption, Sumatra: An Example of the Use of Deep-Sea Tephra Layers as a Geological Tool. *Bulletin Volcanologique*, 41:286–298.

Oebbeke, K.

1884.   Ueber die -Asche. *Neues Jahrbuch für Mineralogie*, 2:32–33.

Pacific Science Congress, Fourth

1929.   The Case of Krakatau. *In Report of the Fourth Pacific Science Congress for Natural Sciences, Joint Div. Meeting, May 20 1929. Proceedings of the Fourth Pacific Science Congress*, Java, 1:214–219. [Discussion by 15 participants of question whether all life was sterilized on Krakatau in 1883.]

Paul, H.M.
1884.   Krakatoa. *Science*, 4:135–136.
Pekeris, C.L.
1939.   The Propagation of a Pulse in the Atmosphere. *Proceedings of the Royal Society of London*, series A, 171:434–449.
Pelagaud, E.
1883.   Sur une Illumination Aurorale et Crépusculare du Ceil Observée dans l'Océan Indien. *Comptes Rendus Hebdomadaires des Seances de l'Academie des Sciences*, 98:250–253.
1884.   Nouvelles Observations d'Illuminations Crépusculaires a l'Ile Bourbon. *Comptes Rendus Hebdomadaires des Seances de l'Academie des Sciences*, 98:1301–1302.
Pelzer, K.J.
1963.   Physical and Human Resource Patterns. *In* R.T. McVey, editor, *Indonesia*, pages 1–23. New Haven: HRAF Press.
Penang Gazette and Straits Chronicle
1883.   [Report of Survivors in Lampong Bay.] Sep 3: page 3.
Penzig, O.
1902.   Die Fortschritte der Flora des Krakatau. *Annales du Jardin Botanique de Buitenzorg*, 18:92.
Pernter, J.M.
1889.   Aur Theorie des Bishopringes. *Meteorologisch Zeitschrift*, Vienna, 6:401–409.
Perry, S.J.
1884a.   Extraordinary Darkness at Midday. [Letter to the editor.] *Nature*, 30:6.
1884b.   Black Rain. [Letter to the editor.] *Nature*, 30:32.
Petroeschevsky, W.A.
1947.   Brief Review of the Status of Published Information on the Volcanic Activity of the Dutch East Indies. *In* Vulkanologische Berichten. *Bulletin of the Bureau of Mines and the Geological Survey of Indonesia*, 1(1):12–13.
1949.   Een Eerste na-oorlogse Verkenning van Lang Eiland en Anak Krakatau op 5 Juni 1949. *Chronica Naturai* (Batavia), 105:247–249.
Petroeschevsky, W.A., and T.H.F. Klompe
1951.   Vulcanological Investigations in Indonesia. *Organization of Scientific Research of Indonesia*, 23:187–204.
Popular Science Monthly
1884.   The Volcanic Eruption of Krakatau. 25:365–376.
Press, F.
1956.   Volcanoes, Ice and Destructive Waves. *Engineering and Science Monthly*, November, pages 26–30.
Press, F., and D. Harkrider
1962.   Propagation of Accoustic-Gravity Waves in the Atmosphere. *Journal of Geophysical Research*,
67:3889–3908.
1966.   Air-Sea Waves from the Explosion of Krakatoa. *Science*, 154:1325–1327.
Rampino, M.R., and S. Self
1982.   Historic Eruptions of Tambora (1815), Krakatau (1883), and Agung (1963), Their Stratospheric Aerosols and Climate Impact. *Quaternary Research*, 18:127–143.
Ranyard, A.C.
1883–4.   The Extraordinary Sunsets. *Knowledge*, 4:341–342; 5:155–156, 177–178, 261–263.
1884.   The Collection of Dust from the Snow. [Letter to the Editor.] *Knowledge*, 5:15.
Reck, H.
1926.   Mitteilungen über Trombenbilding während der Ausbrüche des Santorin-Vulkans. *Central Blatt für Mineralogie, Geologie und Paleontologie*. Jahrg. Apt. B:542–549.
1932.   Ein Ruckblick auf den Ausbruch des Krakatau von 1928-1930. *Zeitschrift für Vulkanologie*, 14:118–134.
Reck, H., et al.
1936.   *Santorin, der Werdegang eines Inselvulkans und sein Ausbruch 1925–1928*. 3 vols. Berlin.
Reeves, C.
1884.   Concerning Pumice Sightings in Indian Ocean by Barque *Umvoti*. [Letter to G.J. Symons, 25 Jun 1884, at the Royal Society of London, including a handwritten copy of a letter to *Madras Mail*, Feb., 1884.]
Reid, G.C., and K.S. Gage
1981.   On the Annual Variation in Height of the Tropical Tropopause. *Journal of Atmospheric Science*, 38:1928–1938.
Reitsma, A., and W.H. Hoogland
1921.   *Gids voor Bandoeng en Omstreken*. [Guidebook for Bandoeng and Vicinity.] Bandoeng.
Rénard, A.
1883.   Les Cendres Volcanologiques de l'Éruption du Krakatau Tombées á Batavia, le 27 Août 1883. *Bulletins de l'Acadamie Royale de Belgique*, 6:1–14.
Rendall, S.M.
1884.   Krakatoa. *Nature*, 30:287–288. [On floating pumice.]
Renou, A.
1884.   Sur Les Oscillations Barometriques Produites par l'Eruption du Krakatoa. *Comptes Rendus Hebdomadaires des Seances de l'Academie des Science*, 98:160–161, 245–246.
Retgers, J.W.
1885.   Onderzoek van de Vulkanisch Asch van Krakatau Gevallen te Buitenzorg den 27 Augustus 1883. *In* Verbeek (1885), pages 217–285 (pages 227–298 in the French edition).

1886. Die Mineralien de Krakatau asch Gefallen zu Buitenzorg. *Zeitschrift für Kristallographie und Mineralogie*, 11:415–419.

Rice, A.
1981. Convective Fractionation: A Mechanism to Provide Cryptic Zoning (Macrosegregation), Layering, Crescumulates, Banded Tuffs, and Explosive Volcanism in Igneous Processes. *Journal of Geophysical Research*, 86:405–417.

Ringwood, A.
1884. Red Sunsets. *Nature*, 30:301–304.

Rittmann, A.
1953. Magmatic Character and Tectonic Position of the Indonesian Volcanoes. *Bulletin Volcanologique*, series 2, 14:45–58.

Robock, A.
1981. A Latitudinally Dependent Volcanic Dust Veil Index, and its Effect on Climate Simulations. *Journal of Volcanology and Geothermal Research*, 11:67–80.

Robock, A., and C. Mass
1982. The Mount St. Helens Volcanic Eruption of 18 May 1980: Large Short-Term Surface Temperature Effects. *Science*, 216:628–630.

Royal Society of London
1888. *The Eruption of Krakatoa, and Subsequent Phenomena*. Report of the Krakatoa Committee. [See Symons (1888), Judd (1888a), Russell and Archibald (1888), Strachey (1888), and Wharton (1888).]

Rudolph, E.
1887. Ueber Submarine Erdbeben und Eruptionen.
[1898] *Berlands Beiträge zur Geophysik*, a.I(1887) pages 133–365, B.III(1898).

Russell, D.A.
1982. The Mass Extinctions of the Late Mesozoic. *Scientific American*, 246(1):58–65.

Russell, F.A.R.
1884. The Sunsets and Sunrises of November 1883 to January 1884. *Quarterly Journal of the Royal Meteorological Society*, 10:139–152.

Russell, F.A.R., and E.D. Archibald
1888. On the Unusual Optical Phenomena of the Atmosphere, 1883–1886, Including Twilight Effects, Coronal Appearances, Sky Haze, Colored Suns, Moons. *In* Symons, 1888:151–463. [Different sections of this report written separately, and jointly, by both authors.]

Russell, I.C.
1897. *Volcanoes of North America*. 346 pages. New York and London: McMillian Co.

Rykatchev, M.A.
1884. Note sur les Ondes Atmospheriques Produites par l'Eruption de Krakatoa. *Bulletin Acadamie Imperiale Sciences St. Petersburg*, 29:389–404.

Sachet, M.H.
1955. Pumice and Other Extraneous Volcanic Materials on Coral Atolls. *Atoll Research Bulletin*, 37:1–27.

Sandick, R.A. van
1884a. Le Désastre de Krakatau. *Bulletin Mensuel de la Société Scientifique*, 2:4–28.
1884b. Eruption du Krakatau. *Cosmos-Les Mondes*, 8:677–678.
1884c. De Ramp van Krakatau. *Tijdschrift van het Koninklijk Nederlandsch Aardrijkskundig Genootschap*, 7:146–153.
1885. Sky Effects Due to Ice Crystals. *Année Scientifique et Industrial*, 1885:50–52.
1890. *In het rijk van vulkaan: die Uitbarsting van de Krakatau en hare Gevolgen*. Zutphen.

Scarff, R.F.
1925. Sur le problème de l'Ile de Krakatau. In *Comptes Rendu au Congrés de Grenoble*. Association Française pour l'avancement des Sciences, page 1.

Schmincke, H.-U.
1977. Phreatomagmatic Phases in Quaternary Volcanoes of the East Eifel. *Geologische Jahrbuch*, series A, 39:1–45.

Science
1884. The Geologic Relatives of Krakatoa and its Late Eruption. 3:762–765.

Scientific Event Alert Network (SEAN) Bulletin, Smithsonian Institution
1981. Krakatau Volcano. 6(10):4.
1983. El Chichón Volcano. 8(1):9–12.

Scott, R.H.
1884. Note on a Series of Barometrical Disturbances Which Passed over Europe Between the 27th and the 31st of August, 1883. *Proceedings of the Royal Society of London*, 36:139–143.

Self, S.
1976. The Recent Volcanology of Terceira, Azores. *Journal of the Geological Society*, 132:645–666.

Self, S., and M.R. Rampino
1980. Krakatau, West of Java: a Reappraisal of the 1883 Eruption. *EOS*, 61(46):1141. [Abstract.]
1981. The 1883 Eruption of Krakatau. *Nature*, 292:699–704.
1982. Comments on "A Geophysical Interpretation of the 1883 Krakatau Eruption" by I. Yokoyama. *Journal of Volcanology and Geothermal Research*, 13:379–383.

Self, S., and R.S.J. Sparks
1978. Characteristics of Widespread Pyroclastic Deposits Formed by the Interaction of Silicic Magma and Water. *Bulletin Volcanologique*, 41–3:196–212.

Self, S., L. Wilson, and I.A. Nairn
1979.   Vulcanian Eruption Mechanisms. *Nature*, 277:440–443.

Shaler, N.S.
1884.   The Red Sunsets. *Atlantic Monthly*, April 1884, pages 475–482.

Sieberg, A.
1923.   *Erdbebenkunde*. Jena. [Pages 93–94.]

Simkin, T., and K.A. Howard
1970.   Caldera Collapse in the Galápagos Islands, 1968. *Science*, 169:429–437.

Simkin, T., and L. Siebert
1983.   Explosive Eruptions in Space and Time: Durations, Intervals, and a Comparison of the World's Active Volcanic Belts. In *Explosive Volcanism: Inception, Evolution, and Hazard*. Geophysics Study Committee, National Research Council, National Academy of Sciences Press, Washington, D.C.

Simkin, T., L. Siebert, L. McClelland, D. Bridge, C. Newhall, and J.H. Latter
1981.   *Volcanoes of the World. A Regional Directory, Gazetteer, and Chronology of Volcanism during the Last 10,000 Years*. 240 pages. Stroudsburg, Pennsylvania: Hutchinson Ross Publishing Co.

Smith, C.M.
1887.   Observations on a Green Sun and Associated Phenomena. [Read 7 July, 1884.] *Transactions of the Royal Society of Edinburgh*, 32:389–405.

Smith, C.P.
1883.   The Remarkable Sunsets. *Nature*, 29:149–150.

Smith, R.L.
1979.   Ash-flow Magmatism. *Geological Society of America, Special Paper*, 180:5–24.

Smith, R.L. and R.G. Luedke
1983.   Potentially Active Volcanic Lineaments and Loci in the Western Conterminous United States. In *Explosive Volcanism: Inception, Evolution, and Hazard*. Geophysics Study Committee, National Research Council, National Academy of Sciences Press. Washington, D.C.

Smithson, J.
1813.   On a Saline Substance from Mount Vesuvius. *Philosophical Transactions of the Royal Society of London*, 103:256. [Read July 8, 1813.]

Smyth, P.
1883.   The Green Sun in India. [Letter to the editor.] *Nature*, 28:575–576.

South Kensington Museum, London
1888.   "Catalogue of Sky Sketches by William Ascroft—Illustrating Optical Phenomena Attributed to the Eruption of Krakatoa in the Java Straits, August 27, 1883. Lent for exhibition in the South Kensington Museum, London." 18 pages.

Sparks, R.S.J., and T.C. Huang
1980.   The Volcanological Significance of Deep-Sea Ash Layers Associated with Ignimbrites. *Geological Magazine*, 117:425–436.

Sparks, R.S.J., S. Self, and G.P.L. Walker
1973.   Products of Ignimbrite Eruptions. *Geology*, 1:115–118.

Sparks, R.S.J., H. Sigurdsson, and L. Wilson
1977.   Magma Mixing: A Mechanism for Triggering Acid Explosive Eruptions. *Nature*, 267:315–318.

Sparks, R.S.J., and G.P.L. Walker
1977.   The Significance of Vitric-enriched Air-fall Ash Associated with Crystal-enriched Ignimbrites. *Journal of Volcanology and Geothermal Research*, 2:329–341.

Sparks, R.S.J., and J.V. Wright
1979.   Welded Air-fall Tuffs. *Geological Society of America, Special Paper 180*, pages 155–166.

Sparks, R.S.J., L. Wilson, and G. Hulme
1978.   Theoretical Modeling of the Generation, Movement and Emplacement of Pyroclastic Flows by Column Collapse. *Journal of Geophysical Research*, 83:1727–1739.

Spitta, E.J.
1885.   Observations of the Moon During the Eclipse of October 4, 1884. *Monthly Notices, Royal Astronomical Society*, 7 Jan, 1885.

Stanley, W.F.
1884.   On Certain Effects Which May Have Been Produced in the Atmosphere by Floating Particles of Volcanic Matter from the Eruptions of Krakatoa and Mount St. Augustin. *Quarterly Journal of the Royal Meteorological Society*, 10:187–194.

Stehn, Ch.E.
1928a   Krakatau. *Bulletin of the Netherlands East Indian Volcanological Survey* (Bandoeng), 1–3: multiple pages.

1928b.   De Krakatau en Zijn Jongste Eruptie. *De Ingenieur*, 43e Jaargang no. 43, 27 Oct 1928:57–77. Voordracht Gehouden voor de Afdeeling voor Mijnbouw, Tak Nederlandsch Indie van het Kon. Instituut van Ingenieurs.

1929a.   The Geology and Volcanism of the Krakatau Group. Proceedings of the Fourth Pacific Science Congress (Batavia), pages 1–55.

1929b.   Einige Mitteilungen uber den Vulkanologischen Dienst in Niederlandischindien und Seine Arbeiten. *Bulletin Volcanologique*, 19:13.

1933a.   *Een Kort Overzicht over de Werking van den Krakatau in de laatste 50 Jaren*. In *Java Bode* (1933a), pages 9–12.

1933b.   Funfzig Jahre Krakatau. *Umschau*, 37(34):659–663.

1933c.   Krakatau. *Bulletin of the Netherlands East Indian Volcanological Survey*, Bandoeng, 61-65:7–10, 16–18, 25–32, 41–43, 55-57, 69–70.

1939.   Krakatau. *Bulletin of the Netherlands East Indian Volcanological Survey* (Bandung), p. 22.

1940.   Vulkanische Verschijnselen in het jaar 1938. *Natuurkundig Tijdschrift voor Nederlandsch-Indie*, 100:29–31.

Stephenson, D., and H.G. Reading
1979.   Discussion on Magmatism and Tectonics in SE Asia. *Journal of the Geological Society*, 136:587–588.

Stoddard, O.N.
1884.   The Remarkable Sunsets. *Nature*, 29:355–356.

Story-Maskelyne, T.
1884.   The Remarkable Sunsets. [Letter to the editor.] *Nature*, 29:285–286.

Strachey, R.
1883.   The Krakatoa Airwave. [Abstract.] *Nature*, 29:181–183.

1884.   Notes on R.H. Scott's Paper on Barometrical Disturbances of August, 1883. *Proceedings of the Royal Society of London*, 36:143–151.

1888.   On the Air Waves and Sounds Caused by the Eruption of Krakatoa in August, 1883. *In* Symons, 1888:57–88.

Sturdy, E.W.
1884.   The Volcanic Eruption of Krakatau. *Atlantic Monthly*, 54:385–391.

Sudradjat (Sumartadipura), A.
1982.   The Morphological Development of Anak Krakatau Volcano, Sunda Strait. *Geologi Indonesia*, 9(1):1–11.

Sullivan, W.
1974.   *Continents in Motion, the New Earth Debate.* 399 pages. New York: McGraw-Hill Book Co.

Suryo, I.
1961.   Report on the Volcanic Activity in Indonesia for the Years 1958, and 1959. *Bulletin of the Volcanological Survey of Indonesia*, 101: 27 pages, and 102: 31 pages.

1978.   Volcanic Phenomena During the Year 1960. *Bulletin of the Volcanological Survey of Indonesia*, 103: 42 pages [Krakatau pages 1–2, 14–18.]

Sutadi
1965.   Seismicity Maps of Indonesia. *Geophysical Notes*, 4. Djakarta: Direktorat Meteorologi Geofisika.

Svalnov, V.N., I.O. Murdmaa, M.A. Repechka, and Demidenko
1976.   Volcanoclastic Material in Quaternary Sediments of the Eastern Indian Ocean. *Okean-*

ologiya, 16:479–487.

Symons, G.J., editor
1888.   *The Eruption of Krakatoa, and Subsequent Phenomena.* Report of the Krakatoa Committee of the Royal Society. 494 pages. London: Trübner and Co.

Tacchini, P.
1884.   Sur les Oscillations Barometriques Produites Par l'Eruption du Krakatoa. *Comptes Rendus Hebdomadaires des Seances de l'Academie des Sciences*, 98:616–617.

Taverne, N.J.M.
1922.   Krakatau. Report of the Month of February 1922 Volcanologic Survey, unpublished, in Archives of Geological Survey of Netherlands Indies.

1926.   Vulkaanstudiën op Java. *Vulkanologische Mededeelingen* no. 7.'s Gravanhage.

Taylor, G.I.
1930.   The Air Wave from the Great Explosion of Krakatau. In *Proceedings of the Fourth Pacific Science Congress*, IIB:1–11.

Tenison-Woods, J.E.
1884.   The Earthquake in the Straits of Sunda. *Sydney Morning Herald*, 16–18 Jan, 1884: pages unknown.

Thomas, I.L., R.C. Child, S.R.L. Richards, and J.W. Brodie
1978.   Waterline Mapping of the Krakatau Islets Using LANDSAT Imagery. *New Zealand Cartographic Journal*, 8(1):14–19.

Thorarinsson, S.
1963.   *Askja on Fire.* 48 pages. Reykjavik: Almenna Bokafelagid.

1969.   The Lakagígar Eruption of 1783. *Bulletin Volcanologique*, 33:910–929.

Times of Ceylon
1883a.   The Effect at Bombay of the Recent Volcanic Disturbance, 18 Sep 1883: page unknown.

1883b.   Effects of the Recent Eruption at Mauritius. 28 Sep 1883: page unknown.

1883c.   The Volcanic Outburst in Sunda Straits. 1 Oct 1883: page unknown.

1883d.   Relief Works in Java. 3 Oct 1883: page unknown.

1883e.   The Tidal Wave in New Zealand. 31 Oct 1883: page unknown.

1883f.   Netherlands India. 14 Nov 1883: page unknown.

Times (London), *see* London *Times*

Tjia, H.D.
1967.   Volcanic Lineaments in the Indonesian Island Arcs. *Bulletin Volcanologique*, 31:85–96.

1968.   Volcanic Lineaments of the Indonesian Island Arcs. *Pacific Geology*, 1:175–182.

1977.   Active Faults in Indonesia. [Abstract]. In *Tenth*

INQUA Congress Abstracts, page 467.

Topographic Bureau of Batavia

1883.   Map of the West coast of the Residency of Bantam from St. Nicholas Pt. to Tjaringin, indicating the topographic condition of that strip of terrain before and after the eruption of Krakatau on 26 and 27 August, 1883. Scale 1:100,000.

Toxopeus, L.J.

1950.   Over de Pionier-fauna van Anak Krakatau, met Enige Beschouwingen over het Onstaan van de Krakatau Fauna. *Chronica Naturae*, 106(1):27–34.

Treub, M.

1888.   Notice sur la Nouvelle Flore de Krakatau. *Annales du Jardin Botanique de Buitenzorg*, 7:213–223.

Truby, J.D.

1971.   Krakatoa—The Killer Wave. *Sea Frontiers*, 17:130–139.

Umbgrove, J.H.F.

1928.   The First Days of the New Submarine Volcano near Krakatoa. *Leidsche Geologische Mededeelingen*, 2:325–329.

1930.   The End of Sluiter's Coral Reef at Krakatau. *Leidsche Geologische Mededeelingen*, 3(5):261–264.

USGS

1974.   Bathymetric Map of the Indonesian Region. *United States Geological Survey Map*, I-875A.

Usher, J.E.

1888.   Personal Reminiscences of the Great Eruption of Krakatoa (Java). *Transactions and Proceedings of the Royal Geographical Society of Australasia (Victorian Branch)*, Part I, 6:28–37. [Usher was in Batavia on August 27.]

van (See family name; e.g., for R.W. van Bemmelen, see Bemmelen, R.W. van.)

Verbeek, R.D.M.

1881.   Topographische en Geologische Beschrijving van Zuid-Sumatra. *Jaarboek van het Mijnwezen in Nederlandsch Oost-Indie*, 1881, part 1. [Verbeek (1885, Note 8) adds "Krakatau is discussed on pages 154–156, 179–181, and 213–215. A sketch of the island group can also be found there on profile 7."]

1883a.   *Topographische en Geologische Beschrijving van een Gedeelte van Sumatra's Westkust.* 674 pages. Batavia.

1883b.   Over het Voorkomen van Gesteenten der Krijtformatie in de Residentie Westeren afdeeling van Borneo. *Verslagen en Mededeeling der Koninklijke Akademie van Wetenschappen, Afdeeling Natuurkunde*, 19:39–43.

1884.   The Krakatoa Eruption. *Nature*, 30:10–15.

1885.   *Krakatau.* 495 pages. Batavia. [A French edition was published in two parts, shortly after the Dutch version. Part One (pages 1–104) is dated 1885 and Part Two (pages 105–567) is dated 1886, although they appear together in one bound volume. Many authors cite the 1886 French edition and its pagination which varies from that of the Dutch.]

1886.   Mr. Verbeek on Krakatāo. *Nature*, 33:560–561. [Translation and condensation of Foreword in 1885 monograph. Translation apparently by a Mrs. Leucky.]

1908.   Photographieen van den Steilen wand van Krakatau. *Tijdschrift van het Koninklijke Nederlandsch Aardrijkskundig Genootschap*, series 2, 25:1194–1195.

Verbeek, R.D.M., and R. Fennema

1881.   Nieuwe Geol. Ontdekkingen op Java. *Verhandelingen der Koninklijke Akademie van Wetenschappen, Afdeeling Natuurkunde*, 21.

1882.   Perliet and Sphaeleriet Gesteente van Java's Eerste Punt. Pages 22–17 in Niewe Geologische Ontdekkingen op Java. *Natuurkundig Tijdschrift voor Nederlandsch-Indie*, 1–48, map.

Vereker, F.C.P.

1884.   Extracts from Log of HMS *Magpie*. *Proceedings of the Royal Society of London*, 36:198–199.

Veth, P.J.

1884.   De Uitbarsting van den Vulkaan Krakatau in 1680. *Tijdschrift van thet Koninklijk Nederlandsch Aardrijkundig Genootschap*, series 2, 1(1):24–27.

Vogel, J.W.

1690.   *Journal einer Reise aus Holland nach Ost-Indien.* Frankfurt and Leipzig.

Volcanological Survey of Indonesia

1957.   Report of the Volcanic Activity in Indonesia. *Bulletin of the Volcanological Survey of Indonesia*, pages 100–102.

Walker, G.P.L.

1972.   Crystal Concentration in Ignimbrites. *Contributions to Mineralogy and Petrology*, 136:135–146.

1973.   Explosive Volcanic eruptions—A New Classification Scheme. *Geologische Rundshau*, 62:431–446.

1979.   Volcanic Ash Generated by Explosions Where Ignimbrite Entered the Sea. *Nature*, 281:642–646.

1980.   The Taupo Pumice: Product of the Most Powerful Known (Ultraplinian) Eruption? *Journal of Volcanology and Geothermal Research*, 8:69-94.

Walker, J.T.
1884a.   [Dust falls from Krakatoa 20 May 1883.] *Mercantile Record (Mauritius)*, 16 June 1883.
1884b.   Earthquake Disturbances of the Tides on the Coasts of India. *Nature*, 29:358–360.

Watson, W.J.
1883.   The Java Disaster. *Nature*, 29:140–141. [Passage of the *Charles Bal* through the Straits of Sunda during the 26–27 August 1883 Eruption.]

Westerveld, J.
1951.   Vergeten Berichten over Krakatau. *Tijdschrift van het Koninklijk Nederlandsch Aardrijkskundig Genootschap*, 68:129–131.
1952.   Quaternary Volcanism on Sumatra. *Bulletin of the Geological Society of America*, 63:561–594.

Weston, E.R.
1884.   Atmospheric Waves from Krakatoa. *Science*, 3:531–532.

Wexler, H.
1951.   Spread of the Krakatoa Volcanic Dust Cloud As Related to the High-Level Circulation. *Bulletin of the American Meteorological Society*, 33:48–51.
1952.   Volcanoes and World Climate. *Scientific American*, 186:74–80.

Wharton, W.J.L.
1888.   On the Seismic Sea Waves Caused by the Eruption of Krakatoa August 26th and 27th, 1883. *In* Symons, 1888:89–151.

Whipple, G.M.
1888.   Report on the Magnetical and Electrical Phenomena Accompanying the Krakatoa Explosion. *In* Symons, 1888:465–491.

Whittaker, R.J., K. Richards, H. Wiriadinata, and J.R. Flenley
In press   Krakatau 1883–1983: A Biogeographic Assessment, *Progress in Physical Geography*.

Williams, H.
1941.   Calderas and Their Origin. *University of California Publications in Geological Sciences*, 25:239–346. [Krakatau pages 253–265.]

Williams, H., and A.R. McBirney
1968.   *An Investigation of Volcanic Depressions: Part I—Geologic and Geophysical Features of Calderas*. A Progress Report of Work Carried Out under NASA Research Grant NGR-38-033-012, pages 1–87. [Krakatau pages 9–10.]
1979.   *Volcanology*. 397 pages. San Francisco: Freeman Cooper and Co.

Williams, N.
1975.   *Chronology of the Modern World*. 1020 pages. Harmondsworth: Penguin Books.

Wilson, L.
1980.   Relationships Between Pressure, Volatile Content and Ejecta Velocity in Three Types of Volcanic Explosions. *Journal of Volcanology and Geothermal Research*, 8:297–313.

Wilson, J.T., editor
1976.   *Continents Adrift and Continents Aground*. Readings from *Scientific American*. 230 pages. San Francisco: W.H. Freeman and Company.

Wood-Jones, F.
1910.   *Coral and Atolls*. 392 pages, London.

Woods, J.E. Tenison- (see Tenison-Woods, J.E.)

Worsfold, W.B.
1893.   *A Visit To Java*. 283 pages. London: R. Bentley and Son.

Yokoyama, I.
1971.   Comparative Studies of Subsurface Structure between Thera and Krakatau. *In* A. Kaloyeropoyloy, editor, *ACTA of the First International Science Congress (1969) on the Volcano Thera*. Athens: Archeological Services of Greece.
1981.   A Geophysical Interpretation of the 1883 Krakatau Eruption. *Journal of Volcanology and Geothermal Research*, 9:359–378.
1982.   Author's Reply to the Comments by S. Self and M.R. Rampino. *Journal of Volcanology and Geothermal Research*, 13:384–386.

Yokoyama, I., and D. Hadikusumo
1969.   Volcanological Survey of Indonesian Volcanoes, Part 3: A Gravity Survey on the Krakatau Islands, Indonesia. *Bulletin of the Earthquake Research Institute*, University of Tokyo, 47:991–1001.

Zen, M.T.
1969.   Structure and Evolution of the Krakatau Complex. *IAVCEI Symposium*, Oxford, page 71. [Abstract.]
1970.   Growth and State of Anak Krakatau Volcano. *Bulletin Volcanologique*, series 2, 34:205–215.

Zen, M.T., and D. Hadikusumo
1964.   Recent Changes in the Anak-Krakatau Volcano. *Bulletin Volcanologique*, series 2, 27:259–268.

Zen, M.T., and V.T. Radja
1970.   Result of the Preliminary Geological Investigation of Natural Steam Fields in Indonesia. *Geothermics*, Special Issue 2. Produced for the United Nations Symposium on the Development and Use of Geothermal Resources, 2:130–135.